UNDERSTANDING ETHIOPIA'S TIGRAY WAR

MARTIN PLAUT
AND
SARAH VAUGHAN

Understanding Ethiopia's Tigray War

HURST & COMPANY, LONDON

First published in the United Kingdom in 2023 by
C. Hurst & Co. (Publishers) Ltd.,
New Wing, Somerset House, Strand, London, WC2R 1LA

Distributed in the United States, Canada and Latin America by
Oxford University Press, 198 Madison Avenue, New York, NY 10016,
United States of America.

A Cataloguing-in-Publication data record for this book
is available from the British Library.

ISBN: 9781787388116

www.hurstpublishers.com

We would like to thank the very many people from all over the world who have helped us write this book and who, for obvious reasons, are not named. You know who you are—and we are very grateful.

For Daniel. And for Ermias.

CONTENTS

CONTENTS

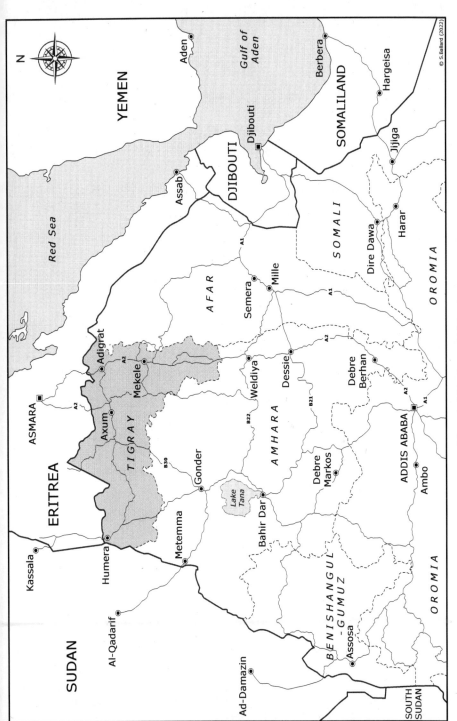

Map 1: Northern Ethiopia

Map 2: Tigray Region and Adjacent Areas

Hatched areas to the south of Tigray indicates extent of Tigrayan advance towards Addis Ababa, November 2021. Areas under Eritrean control in northern Tigray are highlighted as well as areas in western Tigray under Ethiopian, Amhara and Eritrean forces.

LIST OF ABBREVIATIONS

Aben	National Movement of Amhara (NAMA)
ADFM	Amhara Democratic Forces Movement
AGOA	African Growth and Opportunity Act
ALA	Agaw Liberation Army
ANDM	Amhara National Democratic Movement
AU	African Union
CUD	Coalition for Unity and Democracy
EDORM	Ethiopian Democratic Officers' Revolutionary Movement
EDU	Ethiopian Democratic Union
EFFORT	Endowment Fund for the Rehabilitation of Tigray
EHRC	Ethiopian Human Rights Commission
ELF	Eritrean Liberation Front
ENDF	Ethiopian National Defence Force
EPDM	Ethiopian People's Democratic Movement
EPLF	Eritrean People's Liberation Front
EPRDF	Ethiopian Peoples' Revolutionary Democratic Front
EPRP	Ethiopian People's Revolutionary Party
EU	European Union
Ezema	Movement of Ethiopians for Social Justice

LIST OF ABBREVIATIONS

FDRE	Federal Democratic Republic of Ethiopia
GHI	Global Hunger Index
IDP	internally displaced person
IGAD	Intergovernmental Authority on Development
INSA	Information Network Security Agency
IOM	International Organization for Migration
ISEN	Institute for the Study of Ethiopian Nationalities
LPP	Liberal Progressive Party
MSF	Médecins Sans Frontières
NAMA	National Movement of Amhara (Aben, in Amharic)
NISS	National Intelligence and Security Service
OCHA	UN Office for the Coordination of Humanitarian Affairs
OFC	Oromo Federalist Congress
OLA	Oromo Liberation Army
OLF	Oromo Liberation Front
OMN	Oromo Media Network
ONLF	Ogaden National Liberation Front
OPDO	Oromo People's Democratic Organisation
PFDJ	Popular Front for Democracy and Justice
SEPDM	Southern Ethiopian People's Democratic Movement
SNNPRS	Southern Nations, Nationalities and Peoples' Regional State
TDF	Tigray Defence Forces
TLF	Tigray Liberation Front
TPLF	Tigray People's Liberation Front
UNFPA	UN Population Fund
UNHCR	UN High Commissioner for Refugees
VOA	Voice of America
WPE	Workers' Party of Ethiopia

INTRODUCTION
LAND, POWER AND EMPIRE

Sarah Vaughan and Martin Plaut

During the night of 3/4 November 2020, the first shots were fired in a brutal war between the government of the regional state of Tigray and the government of the Federal Democratic Republic of Ethiopia. On this single fact most accounts agree, but on little or nothing else. The dominant narrative of the war, pushed strongly by government spokespersons in Addis Ababa, is that it was a limited 'law and order' operation by the federal government and its allies to arrest a small group or 'junta' of rogue Tigrayans (soon labelled 'terrorists') in the northern regional state: the leaders of its ruling Tigray People's Liberation Front (TPLF).

The war was—in the Ethiopian federal government's view—the fault of this 'traitorous gang', an 'illegal clique' who had 'treasonously' attacked units of the Ethiopian national army stationed on their northern border with Eritrea. Seeing 'a red line crossed', the federal government then moved to 'save the country and the region from spiralling into instability'. The narrative of prime minister Abiy Ahmed's government has been simple, clear, pervasive and persuasive. From the first hours of the war, it was repeated endlessly and, on the face of it, seemed to be widely believed by many Ethiopians and international observers: but, like the claim that the 'operation' would be completed within three weeks, the narrative was false. It disguised more than it illuminated.

The Ethiopian government and its allies' occupation and devastation of Tigray in November and December 2020 had been long in the preparation and gestation. What the government portrayed as a treasonous plot by a faction in Tigray can also be seen as the result of the long-held ambition of their opponents to eliminate the Tigrayans as a political force. This plan, conceived at least partly in Eritrea, was further developed after 2018 together with Ethiopia's newly appointed prime minister, Abiy, and others from Ethiopia, and also involved the government of Somalia. From the first, the conflict was more than just an Ethiopian civil war: Eritrean and Somali troops participated in the fighting. Their preparations were low-key, and some aspects of military planning were carefully concealed, although the rhetoric was not. What the Ethiopian premier insisted was a 'domestic matter' would soon be seen for what it was: a war involving international combatants from two neighbouring states, which at times threatened to embroil other Horn neighbours, including Sudan, Kenya and Djibouti.

Close observers knew that war was coming—and just how devastating it would be. Six months before it erupted, veteran Tigrayan exile and former military strategist Siye Abraha warned from the US that, if fighting were to start,

> it will be a full-fledged war. No one will have any idea where it will end. We can already see the interference of foreign forces in our country and the war of words being waged on social media. We are seeing it daily, are we not? If we once allow real bullets to be added on top of this verbal violence, our entire country will degenerate into a cheap bar for the amusement of all our most meddling and insolent neighbours. We will be inflicting harm on one another not just with words on social media but with kalashnikovs. Anyone who thinks it is safe to play with this kind of fire, counting on their tanks and heavy weaponry to be able to come out on top, will themselves get burned. These aren't idle words: my warning is based on my personal experience of war, and what I know of the current situation in our region.[1]

Siye was right. The outbreak of hostilities came as a surprise to few close observers, but the ferocity of the onslaught was unexpected and appalled many. The war had been carefully prepared over several years, but its causes drew on wellsprings of bitterness and resentment deep in collective memories of the history and politics of the region. Many accounts would have it that the TPLF were simply 'bad losers': piqued to see their star waning after they had been displaced from power at the centre in 2018, and jealous of the neo-liberal 'reforms' and 'peace-making' of the new prime minister, Abiy, a popular national leader and soon also a Nobel laureate. But the drivers of the war reach back far beyond the immediate period. In the minds of its protagonists they were entangled in long-standing patterns of power, land and empire across—and beyond—the Ethiopian state.

This book explores these historical memories and resources and their continuing relevance and remobilisation during the Tigray war. These apparently deep and intertwined roots make this a particularly intractable conflict. The war has brought a complex— and shifting—constellation of allies into play on either side. Running centrally through the motivation for war is a profound dispute over the nature of the Ethiopian state and the balance of power across it: should Ethiopia be centralised at the national level, or decentralised and devolved to its constituent peoples, and how? Where should the balance of power lie? This argument itself has a long history—and it mobilised interpretations of the history of a much longer period.

Complicating this central power struggle are a number of other dynamics: contemporary land hunger and the creation of opportunities—and 'historical' excuses—for its forcible annexation; the desire for revenge and score-settling for past injustices, real or perceived; perceptions of the betrayal of promises of 'reform' or 'inclusion' under a new government established in 2018; and deeply entrenched historical stereotyping and socio-cultural prejudice. The sustainable resolution of the war depends on the emergence of a new equilibrium in the constellation of power, in the control of land, and in the shape of the Ethiopian empire state. Given the degree of controversy and polarisation that had become associated with each of these issues, this kind of outcome was increasingly hard to envisage in 2022. The weight of Ethiopian history suggests that settlement of such disputes could be (and usually was) 'enforced' by military means (at least for a cycle of thirty to fifty years). As a result, a negotiated consensus remained vanishingly unlikely throughout 2021 and into early 2022.

* * *

This book is about a current war and a long history. It situates the Tigray war in the context of an oscillating pattern of political power in Ethiopia and the Horn of Africa: a pendulum swinging between centralising and decentralising influences over many decades— arguably in flux over millennia. One factor that distinguishes several of these areas of the Horn from much of the rest of sub-Saharan Africa is their close ties across the Red Sea. Several of the region's cultures and languages are tied to the Arabian Peninsula and the wider Middle East. Parts of what are now northern Ethiopia and Eritrea were relatively unusual in having developed written languages and records over time. These allowed its elites and historians to trace (or reinvent) the roots of power back through the centuries in a way few other sub-Saharan African societies have been able to. It meant that rights and lineages could be traced and disputed down the generations, with apparently long-held divisions smouldering for years before being reinvented, reignited and fought over.

History is never over in Ethiopia, and the brutality of its contestation is a remarkably persistent pattern across enduring 'frontiers of violence'.[2] Richard Reid has explored 'how force of arms was an extension of polity and economy, and a very practical instrument for construction as well as destruction; and how war was understood and interpreted, how military culture came to be imbued in society, and how the past was remembered in military terms'.[3] Like Reid, the analysis of this book is 'interested in both war as fact and war as image, war as policy alongside war as constructed truth'.[4]

The argument is not that Ethiopia's violent history led inexorably to the Tigray war: it did not. It is rather that their different interpretations of Ethiopia's history tended to lock the antagonists of the war into particular patterns of relations with one another. The point is not that one needs to understand Ethiopia's history in order to understand Ethiopia's Tigray war. Rather, one needs an understanding of the multiple ways in which different aspects of Ethiopia's history have been differently understood by the contemporary parties to the war; and of how and why these different understandings made them antagonists. In a country as large, populous and diverse as Ethiopia, with such plural understanding of the significance of its history, generating this understanding is a complex business. This book is structured into five distinct parts designed to increase the accessibility of this intricate story.

Part One, 'History', recounts controversies over the essentials of Ethiopia's long history which are centrally implicated in Ethiopians' various understandings of the war in which the whole country is—to one degree or another—now embroiled. Part Two, 'Living Memory', examines the most recent cycle of political history, the evolution of the Ethiopian Peoples' Revolutionary Democratic Front (EPRDF) federal period from 1991 to 2018, during which the protagonists emerged. Part Three, 'Path to War', discusses the whirlwind drama of frenetic domestic change and regional political upheaval as tension mounted during the first two and a half years of Abiy Ahmed's premiership, from April 2018 to November 2020. Part Four, 'War', gives a detailed account of the outbreak of the conflict, and of the 14 months of military activity during 2020 and 2021. Finally, Part Five, 'Impact of War', looks at the devastating damage to society and economy primarily (but not only) in Tigray, at the humanitarian crisis caused by the way the war was waged, and at its diplomatic fallout internationally.

* * *

Tigray was a focus of empire during the early Axumite period (roughly 100–940 CE) when a growing trading power was centred on the towns of Yeha and Axum at the heart of the region. This apparently more centralised pattern of power dissipated, fractured and re-coalesced over the centuries. One focus of this fissiparous pattern shifted to Gonder, with Tigray again at the margins. In the nineteenth century a series of gradually centralising emperors again began an incremental process of consolidation away from the highly decentralised constellation of power of the so-called Era of Princes (1769–1855). Tigray was intimately involved in the processes by which the modern Ethiopian empire state was formed and its current borders established. After Emperor Tewodros's suicide

(r. 1855–68), Tigrayan emperor Yohannes IV (r. 1869–89) then consolidated Abyssinia's western flank, defeating the Mahdist forces of Sudan in 1885.[5]

After his death, power shifted south to the province of Shewa from where Emperor Menelik II (r. 1889–1913) transformed the empire, producing approximately the borders of Ethiopia familiar today. Menelik had observed the imperial ambitions of European powers, and in a decade of military campaigning (1879–89) he expanded his direct and indirect rule over vast swathes of territory to the west, south and east of the highlands. Menelik's Amhara and Oromo forces moved south-east and south-west to conquer the southern plateau and lowland peripheries, incorporating myriad Oromo, Southern and pastoral communities within Ethiopia's borders. In so doing he incorporated dozens of new peoples, with very different traditions. Many of his new subjects were Muslim, with cultures far removed from those of the predominantly Christian Orthodox highlands. Some had traditionally been enslaved by highland Ethiopians and were treated with the racism that slavery brings with it. The empire thus forcefully established 'sowed the seeds of future conflicts'.[6]

Meanwhile, in the north, in March 1896, Ethiopian forces inflicted on Italy one of the few defeats by an African power on a European state at the famous battle at Adwa, blocking further Italian encroachment. Nevertheless, on 2 May 1889 Menelik II signed the treaty of Wuchale which recognised Italian rule over the coastal region of Eritrea. This saw the Tigrigna-speaking population of the northern highlands bifurcated along the Mereb River. The northern half remained—as Eritrea—under Italian occupation. The southern half, Tigray, became a new periphery broadly external to Ethiopia's centre of power for the next century.

After the Second World War, Haile Selassie I (r. 1930–74) pushed through a second process of modernisation and centralisation which further curbed the power of the regional aristocracy and landowning classes that the nineteenth-century expansion had established. Under his rule Ethiopia also experienced a second Italian attempt to conquer Ethiopia (1935–41), which was eventually defeated with British help during the Second World War. In both Italian attempts to invade Ethiopia, Eritrean troops—known as 'askaris'—fought alongside the Italians. They were conscripts, but their role in these wars was not forgotten.

A second chapter on history (Chapter 2) looks at the emergence of twentieth-century challenges to the empire. Emperor Haile Selassie moved incrementally in the middle decades of the twentieth century to undermine a compromise Ethio-Eritrean federation that had been cobbled together in the post-war period, and resentment began to coalesce as Eritrea was re-annexed. In 1961 the first shots were fired in Eritrea's 30-year struggle for independence. During the feverish period of Marxist politics in the late 1960s and 1970s, emancipation and self-determination slogans swept like a contagion through Ethiopia's growing student movements. A new and radical generation of activists agreed on the need for reform of a 'feudal' socio-economic order, which would return land rights 'to the tiller'. They disagreed violently over the prominence and power to be given to the different 'national' or 'ethnic' identities which made up the population. This visceral divide has riven Ethiopian politics ever since.

Rigid centralisation under the ageing emperor saw politics stagnate in the late imperial period, but the 'creeping coup' of 1974 brought a very different centralist government to power. The Derg (r. 1974–91), a military committee, espoused Marxism as a vehicle for mobilisation—domestically, but also in its post-1977 alliance with the Soviet Union. Radical land reform did much to diffuse popular opposition in rural areas, especially in the Oromo areas and the south of the country. Meanwhile an intensification of the Derg's 'Ethiopia first' (*Etyopia tikdem*) rhetoric of pan-Ethiopian unitary nationalism and centralised control exacerbated a series of subnational conflicts. Nationalist and ethno-nationalist movements gradually gained momentum in different parts of the empire state: in Eritrea (annexed by Ethiopia in 1962 after a decade of federation), but now also in the Somali and Afar areas of the lowland east, in parts of Oromia, and along the far western borders with Sudan, in Sidama, and in Tigray.

The present Ethiopian state is a peculiar combination of African and European norms. On its northern Abyssinian plateau it evolved over the *longue durée* from a series of indigenous and long-standing political communities at its centre, very much along the lines of European states. At the peripheries, meanwhile, its borders look just as much the arbitrary result of nineteenth-century imperial expansion as elsewhere in Africa: in this case, competition between Emperor Menelik II and his Italian, British, French or Anglo-Egyptian neighbours.[7] Communities living on Ethiopia's peripheries straddled these arbitrarily drawn borders. In the context of Cold War competition, many drew on support from the neighbouring states of the Horn, breathing new life into a well-entrenched mantra according to which 'my enemy's enemy is my friend'. Compared with the rest of the African continent, the Horn of Africa is home to a particularly high concentration of secessionist and irredentist claims. Many of these were fed by the unique history of modern Ethiopian state formation.[8] Cold War competition made matters worse as the US and the Soviet Union juggled allies, and Eritrean anti-colonialism was infectious.

During the late 1970s and 1980s the remote mountainous areas of rural Tigray were home to a number of different kinds of movements all fighting the Derg government: remnants of the aristocracy seeking a return to the imperial order; a pan-Ethiopianist leftist opposition grouping; and the ethno-nationalist TPLF. Tigray and other parts of the north of Ethiopia experienced a devastating famine, greatly exacerbated—if not caused—by the manner of the Derg's counterinsurgency strategy against the rebels. By the end of the 1980s the TPLF had forged an alliance with other groupings under the banner of the EPRDF. As support for the Derg from the Soviet bloc now began to fail, and the army was left reeling from an attempted coup in 1989, the military pendulum swung away from the centre. The EPRDF fought its way south in a tactical alliance with the Oromo Liberation Front (OLF) and the Eritrean People's Liberation Front (EPLF) of Isaias Afwerki. In coordinated EPRDF and Eritrean offensives, Asmara fell to the Eritreans on 24 May 1991; four days later Ethiopian rebel troops, supported by Eritrean artillery, captured Addis Ababa.

With Eritrea seceding *de facto* in 1991 (*de jure* after a referendum in 1993), the new EPRDF-led government in Addis Ababa now adopted a system of federalism based on the 'self-determination of nations, nationalities and peoples' in the Leninist phrase. PartTwo of this book looks in closer detail at this most recent cycle of Ethiopia's political history: the period well within living memory, from 1991 to 2018, during which the contemporary protagonists of the Tigray war began to evolve and their grievances deepened. Chapter 3 looks at the period from 1991 to 2012. Ethiopia's system of multinational or 'ethnic' federalism drew together representatives of many of the various language groups across Ethiopia which had—to one degree or another—opposed the Derg government. However, it excluded members of the Derg's Workers' Party of Ethiopia (WPE), along with key pan-Ethiopian nationalist organisations that had opposed them. These groups joined the new Eritrean government in condemning the federal arrangement as a system of 'divide and rule' that would weaken the Ethiopian state, along the lines of the former Yugoslavia, which in the early 1990s was disintegrating in violent fashion. The Derg's imperial opponents and its victims had fled abroad during the 1970s; Derg officials now fled the EPRDF's new federation, consolidating a vociferous and sustained diaspora opposition chorus.

Two blocs of domestic opposition to EPRDF and to federalism gradually emerged through the 1990s. Pan-Ethiopianist nationalists loathed the imposition of the federal arrangement, deriding it as intrinsically divisive and as undermining the narrative power of Ethiopia's ancient history. Meanwhile, several of the other ethno-nationalist groups which had also fought the Derg and also supported the federation were manoeuvred out of power by the ruling party in the 1990s. They complained that federal practice fell far short of constitutional principle; that it was in effect 'fake', serving as a cover for continued control by the centre, now under an EPRDF apparatus dominated by Tigrayan politicians. Important ethno-nationalist groups representing the Oromo, the Somali and the Sidama left government and returned to armed opposition.

By the early 2000s, the pan-Ethiopianist bloc launched a concerted process of political mobilisation in an attempt to unseat the ruling EPRDF. In highly contested elections in 2005, its parties won an overwhelming majority of seats in Addis Ababa and a number of other multi-ethnic cities, and a large number of seats also in Amhara and in the Gurage zone of the Southern region. Believing that the ruling EPRDF had stolen what it claimed was an overall national victory, pan-Ethiopianist opponents boycotted parliament, and the standoff ended in violence, mass arrests and prosecutions. Key nationalist leaders finally went abroad and joined their militant ethno-nationalist colleagues in 'armed struggle', in many cases based in Eritrea.

Barely five years after Eritrean independence, relations between the new government in Asmara and the EPRDF Ethiopian government had soured and erupted into another brutal round of bloodletting along the northern border (1998–2000). In the cold-war standoff that followed the Ethio-Eritrean war, EPRDF's political adversaries won military training and logistical support from an Eritrean government hostile to Addis Ababa and Mekele. Asmara had been stung by its military defeat in 2000; it seethed over Ethiopia's refusal to cede the contested border town of Badme under the Algiers accords; and it resented the imposition of UN sanctions in 2009, in which it saw the hand of the TPLF-led Ethiopian government. Eritrea emerged as a third vehement opponent of federalism and of the TPLF, working consistently to undermine both.

Chapter 4 examines the period after the unexpected death of the Tigrayan EPRDF leader and prime minister, Meles Zenawi, in 2012. Between 2012 and 2018 the cohesion of the EPRDF began to dissolve and, under weaker leadership, differences between the four constituent fronts began to emerge. Mutual recrimination and jockeying between Amhara and Tigrayan politicians became particularly vicious—even if kept mostly away from the public eye. Claims about land and border disputes between the two regions were remobilised, and exacerbated tensions between the two blocs. Arguably the most significant of the policy problems of federalism began to become pressing: its static allocation of land between ethnically defined federated units. As Ethiopia's economy and its population grew, pressure on arable land intensified, and nowhere more visibly than in and around the land-poor and densely populated regions of the old Abyssinian north. This included commercially valuable fertile land in the western peripheries (Gambella and Benishangul-Gumuz), but also—and explosively—in the border areas of western and southern Tigray. As demography and economy shifted, the federal dispensation did not. Ruling politicians in Amhara began to see this as a potential focus for shoring up their popular support in the region, which the 2005 elections had exposed as shaky.

Political mobilisation in several of the EPRDF-administered regions had been relatively cautiously managed during the 1990s and 2000s. It now began to take on an overtly and competitively ethnicised tone, as regional politicians sought shortcuts to bolster their constituencies as power at the centre began to fracture. Amhara's EPRDF ruling politicians faced new challenges from ethno-nationalist competitors, eventually including a new National Movement of Amhara (NAMA). A newly ethnicised vision of Amhara interests emerged, at variance with an older generation of nationalists who had elided their interests with the Ethiopian empire state. Meanwhile, after 2014, Oromo street protests began to spread, driven by a combination of savvy diaspora social media agitation and tacit facilitation from Oromo ruling party politicians. Like their Amhara peers, they were newly keen to flex their muscles and leverage their large constituency at the centre of the country, no longer constrained by a powerful Tigrayan premier. By early 2018 a moribund, weakened centre and a fragmenting ruling EPRDF had no answers to the groundswell for change.

Part Three of the book ('Path to War') looks at the extraordinary convulsion of the politics of Ethiopia and the Horn after the appointment of Abiy Ahmed as prime minister in April 2018. Chapter 5 describes the dramatic series of revolutions in domestic politics; and Chapter 6 examines the new international military alliances which paved the road to war just over two and a half years later. By the time Ethiopia's prime minister Hailemariam Desalegn (2012–18) resigned in February 2018, the rise of Oromo nationalism meant that his successor could only be an Oromo, and Abiy rode to power on this carefully cultivated wave. In a remarkable irony, however, the appointment of the new prime minister served also to elevate the interests of pan-Ethiopian nationalists, who quickly returned from exile. They brought with them highly effective satellite TV and radio broadcast outlets, which now began to transmit a long-standing diaspora barrage of anti-TPLF and anti-federal narratives into the homes of millions of Ethiopians. These entrenched division and whipped up prejudice and hostility.

The new prime minister's facility with language meant that he was able to win over different constituencies with different narratives. Ambiguity became confusion as his rhetoric became more unitary and nationalist. Ethno-nationalist competitors and supporters of federalism who had also returned were gradually marginalised, jailed or manoeuvred out in a series of dramatic shifts through 2019 and 2020—especially but not only in Oromia. When a new unitary national ruling Prosperity Party was formed in late 2019, 'pro-Federalist' opposition began to coalesce around the TPLF, which refused to join it. The TPLF had increasingly drawn in its horns after 2018, members returning to its home region as its influence at the centre decreased and its record and leaders were attacked. From the start of the new government a sustained campaign of scapegoating the TPLF leadership for the collective sins of the EPRDF period embittered relations. When the federal government and Tigray government fell out over the legality of postponing elections beyond the constitutionally defined term, Addis Ababa cut funding flows.

Meanwhile, there had also been a seismic shift in the geopolitics of the Horn. The new prime minister upturned a regional political constellation which had persisted since the 1990s, forging alliances with Asmara and Mogadishu and, in the process, releasing the Eritrean regime from a decade of international sanctions. The new constellation united three heads of government known to favour strong centralisation over the more devolved arrangements which had persisted in Somalia and Ethiopia—three antagonists of the TPLF and the system of federalism they had instituted. In February 2018 Eritrean president Isaias Afwerki declared 'game over!' for the TPLF, which he loathed, and the new tripartite alliance set about bolstering its military and security cooperation. The stage was set for a showdown.

Ethiopia's war in Tigray is the latest in a long series of rounds of competition for control of the Ethiopian state, and between centralising and decentralising forces. Tracing the roots of these conflicts in what has gone before, however, does not mean that the war that erupted in November 2020 was unavoidable or somehow dictated by history. Nor was this return to violence inherent in a system of federalism which recognised the self-determination of 'ethnic' or linguistic groups. As the discussion of history in Part One of the book illuminates, the thoroughgoing politicisation of Ethiopia's multiple identities had long been a feature of the country's political evolution, since before the modern empire state was established in the nineteenth century. Rather, the war that erupted at the beginning of November 2020 was the result of active choices by contemporary politicians in Ethiopia and its neighbours in the Horn. The new upsurge in the manufacture and mobilisation of 'ethnic hatreds' may draw on perceptions of deep historical division, but it was set in train by the contemporary calculations of political elites. Things could have been otherwise.

Part Four of the book gives the first detailed account of the fighting itself: the military trajectories of the war from the beginning of November 2020 until the end of the following year. A pair of chapters look at the two major phases of the ebb and flow of the military conflict. Chapter 7 describes the Ethiopian federal government and its allies' rapid defeat and subjugation of Tigray in the last two months of 2020, and a gradual fightback from the Tigrayan forces which saw federal forces ousted from much of eastern and central Tigray by the end of June 2021. A second military phase (Chapter 8) saw an equally dramatic ebb and flow of military fortunes, as forces loyal to the Tigray government gradually pushed south into Afar and Amhara in the second half of the year, occasionally linking up with federalist allies. They came within a hundred miles of the capital Addis Ababa, before abruptly pulling their forces north again in late November 2021, in the face of overwhelming airpower, particularly from Addis Ababa's newly purchased armed drones.

If the war was widely expected for many months before it began, its consequences have been extraordinarily devastating, particularly (but not only) for the civilian population of Tigray. The exceptionally damaging civilian impact of the war seems to have been, at least in part, a function of the way in which it was waged: with extremist calls to erase even the memory of the TPLF and 'those who resemble them' beyond the recovery of later researchers. Part Five of the book explores three aspects of the concrete impact of the war in Tigray: its socio-economic devastation (Chapter 9); the deliberate starvation of its population by means of a strategy of siege warfare (Chapter 10); and the fallout in terms of diplomacy and advocacy (Chapter 11). At the beginning of 2020, an anonymous author had commented:

> Victory is virtually impossible in the likely Ethiopian scenario of multi-dimensional infighting among relatively symmetrical forces. We would be fighting each other, brother against brother, neighbour against neighbour. The costs would be astronomical in human and material terms. And, the bigger risk is not just the collapse of Ethiopia as a federation, but a perpetual state of war where no faction can win. We are seeing that in Libya and Yemen, we see it in Syria, in Afghanistan, and in other places.[9]

Hugo Slim has recently observed that 'most people experience war as poverty rather than as battle … It is the civilian, not the wounded soldier, who stands at the centre of the moral frame we put around war.'[10] In Tigray, civilians have experienced both violence and impoverishment in quick succession: a devastatingly brutal period of military occupation, characterised by extrajudicial executions of civilians, systematic rape, ethnic cleansing, and the wholesale destruction and looting of the means of survival; followed by a year (at the time of writing in mid-2022) not just of poverty but of starvation, as the Ethiopian government subjected the region to what the United Nations called a '*de facto* blockade'. But these desperate civilians have not been at the centre of the moral frame placed around the war by the international community. Their experiences have been silenced and 'invisibilised'—rendered 'ungrievable'[11]— by Ethiopia's systematic media, telecommunications and internet blackout. If nothing else, this book is an attempt to understand something of the disaster that has befallen them.

PART ONE

HISTORY

1

THE LONG ARC OF HISTORY
SHIFTING EMPIRES

Sarah Vaughan

Nationalisms everywhere are forged from the resources and memories of shared histories. The longer those collective histories are perceived to be, the more complex the nationalist projects become. As the maverick intellectual Gedamu Abraha once noted, 'gaps between illusion and reality are endemic to old nations'.[1] The war which broke out in November 2020 pitted Ethiopian state nationalism and Tigrayan nationalism against each other. Like all nationalisms, both are contingent projects, meaning that they might always have been constructed differently. This is one of the reasons why propagandist struggles over the narration of history form such a vital 'second front' in this war, complementing the violence on the ground.

To set out the historical background to Ethiopia's war in Tigray in this and subsequent chapters is to tread a fine line: avoiding the temptation to essentialise the challenges Ethiopians face by suggesting they are dictated by its history, on the one hand; yet documenting the multiple historical resources and preferences that inform protagonists' contesting calculations, on the other. Two wars erupted in November 2020: a brutal military campaign and an almost equally vicious propaganda front. Both were the product of decisions by contemporary political and social elites about strategies they had chosen—then and daily—to perpetuate. Understanding the ways in which these politicians selected among different historical resources and narratives in order to serve their contemporary political purposes can shed light on their motivation. The Tigray war is fundamentally a political dispute which should never have been allowed to escalate into violence.

But this is not how Ethiopia's elites tend to deploy history. Most believe that the historical justifications with which they defend their actions are conclusive: the causation—and the historical causes— binding, natural and right. History is the weapon with which political narratives are justified. Politicians and activists often feel not only that they have history and truth on their side, but even that they have God there too. A more political analysis, meanwhile, suggests that they could always have chosen—and could still choose—to do otherwise. The legacy of the past undoubtedly 'weighs heavily on Ethiopia's modern political life and is frequently manifested in crises that topple regimes and threaten the state's survival'.[2] History may or may not inform the present in any particular case, but it doesn't dictate it.

Ancient empire: The memory of Axum and the 'survival' of the polity

The central highlands of modern Tigray formed the heart of what was the ancient Axumite Empire, a trading power that flourished in the first seven centuries CE from a centre around Axum and Yeha. The Tigray region is thus inextricably entwined in the notion of Ethiopia as an ancient polity. 'Tigray is seen by many as the cradle of Ethiopian civilization. It is the site of the ancient Aksum kingdom, the predecessor state of what would become modern Ethiopia. Tigray thus has always been at the core of the evolving Ethiopian polity.'[3] The historical reality is, of course, more complex and episodic. There is little or no historical evidence of a continuity of polity, or of royal lineage, between the period of the Axumite Empire, which seems to have ended in the seventh century CE, and the emergence of the modern Ethiopian empire state after the mid-1850s.

From the third century CE Axum emerged as a major power, controlling land to the Red Sea and trade beyond. David Phillipson situates the elusive kingdom in socio-economic developments across the northern Horn of Africa between 3,000 and 700 years ago, preceding (possibly by a gap of several centuries) two later Ethiopian dynasties:[4] the Agaw Zagwe dynasty at Roha (later Lalibela, in what is now the north-east of Amhara region) from sometime after 900 CE; and a series of kings from further south, later associated with the region of Shewa (also now part of Amhara), who superseded the Zagwe in 1270 CE. The 'Axumite civilisation' evolved several centuries earlier, and over a much wider geographical area, than its period of 'political hegemony', but relatively little is known of the earlier and later phases. Much historical and archaeological work remains to be done, particularly on the later period as the empire declined. These uncertainties have made the Axumite Empire the perfect cipher onto which later nationalist histories have been projected. The conflation of the Axumite Empire with the romantic narrative of the mythical 'Queen of Sheba', and her legendary visit to King Solomon's Jerusalem, further embellished later cycles of myth making.[5]

Axum's lucrative trade in local elephant ivory (from the lowlands north and south of the Tekeze River) helped it emerge as a significant socio-economic power during the early Roman Empire. By the second half of the third century CE, Axum had grown into a wealthy power holding sway over a growing area—although the evidence of archaeological sites, oral tradition and stone inscriptions is remarkably inconclusive. Archaeological references to the Beja (now in Sudan east of the Nile), to the Hamassien plateau around the Eritrean capital Asmara, to Adulis on the Eritrean coast, and to Simien and Welkaiyt to the south-west are plausible but not definitive.[6] Fourth-century inscriptions indicate that neighbouring rulers were gradually brought under the control of the kings of Axum and obliged to pay tribute. The imperial power began to mint coinage, and to establish a series of royal palaces and regalia and systems of lower-level administration.

Tradition has it that Christianity came to Axum in the fourth century CE. Archaeological and numismatic evidence suggests that Axum flourished between the mid-fourth and early seventh centuries CE under Christian rule.[7] The Church at Axum seems to have maintained relations with Alexandria through the period. There is evidence of diplomatic relations with Constantinople, and indications of links as far as Syria and with areas south-west of Lake Tana, as well as with the Arabian Peninsula across the Red Sea.[8] The emergence of Christianity in the Axumite context has been central to the subsequent narration of the continuity of Ethiopian history and Tigray's role in this. Thus, for instance, 'Tigray formed not only a durable component of the Ethiopian nation but was also part of the backbone of the Ethiopian state … Christian Aksum must be said to have comprehensively defined and anchored the Ethiopian state since it came into formal existence.'[9]

By the early sixth century, Axum and its allies had apparently consolidated their control of the Red Sea waterway, and this formed the basis for prosperous trading relations over several hundred years.[10] The reasons for the demise of the commercial and political power of Axum are unclear, but decline of trade and control of the waterway from 570 CE seems to have been among them. Gradually 'the factors that had led to the establishment of Aksum as the capital of a major kingdom no longer operated'.[11]

The decline of Axum was followed by 'a period of fluidity' before the rise of a new dynasty, the Zagwe kings of Agaw, based further to the south at Roha (now Lalibela in Lasta, in the east of Amhara regional state).[12] From 1270 power shifted further south again, with the emergence of Yekuno Amlak, first of a series of kings that later became known as the 'Solomonic dynasty' (a term 'coined by modern historians'[13]), who reigned through the fourteenth and fifteenth centuries. The power of this dynasty declined in 1528 when Emperor Lebna Dengel was defeated by Ahmed ibn Ibrahim al-Ghazi (derogatorily nicknamed 'Gragn' or 'the left-handed' in the Christian tradition) of the Muslim Adal Emirate around Harar. To the north, during the sixteenth century, regional rulers in Tigray lost control of the Red Sea coast to the Ottoman Empire, further entrenching the marginalisation of the northern areas.

In the wake of the Muslim victories, a series of Oromo movements from the south shrank the imperial territories into relatively small areas of the north (Eritrea, Tigray, Gojjam and Gonder), and only from the mid-seventeenth century did a new Abyssinian centre emerge at Gonder (now in north-west Amhara region).[14] After a cultural flowering during the reigns of Fasilides, Yohannes, Iyasu and Mentewab, the series of kingdoms centred on Gonder also succumbed to regional, ethnic and religious factionalism. These divisions ushered in the so-called Era of Princes (or *Zemana Mesafent*, 1769–1855),[15] who warred with one another for most of this period, as their armies fought backwards and forwards across a patchwork of territories, and power shifted to local courts. The period provided an archetype in which 'decentralisation' was seen as synonymous with chaos and violence—a trope which continued to resonate for those political actors who opposed the introduction of a 'decentralised' federal system at the end of the twentieth century.[16]

From the perspective of Tigray, meanwhile, the standard narrative of Ethiopian history looks somewhat different. During the *Zemana Mesafent* 'Tigray became "virtually independent", its rulers "wielding power comparable to that exercised by the emperors of former time".'[17] The powerful Tigrayan *Ras* Mikhael Sehul, as regent to a series of relatively less powerful Gonderine emperors to the south, was governor of Tigray from 1748 to 1771 and from 1772 to 1784, up to his death. With close ties by marriage to the Gonderine empress Mentewab, *Ras* Mikhael was able to move on Gonder, and played a role in the disintegration of the succession (he was briefly imprisoned at Gonder in 1771–2).[18]

To the north, meanwhile, he was able to consolidate his authority over areas across the Mereb River (in what is now Eritrea), and defeated the ruler of Hamassien at Tseazega, installing its Hazega rivals. Mikhael Sehul, however, 'failed to establish a Tigray dynasty'.[19] His successors Wolde Selassie (from Enderta around Mekele) and Subagadis (from Agame in the north-east) were less able to wield authority over the whole Tigrigna-speaking region. The Tigrayan *Ras* Wolde Selassie achieved the relative consolidation of rule north and south of the Mereb River, between 1790 and 1816. This still constituted a period of significant Tigrayan influence over the *Medri Bahri* (or *Mereb Melash*), the coastal domain, some form of which had emerged as early as 1137 in areas now part of Eritrea. Meanwhile, in 1879—a year before the Italians began to move in—Tigrayan emperor Yohannes IV formally annexed the area north of the Mereb, installing *Ras* Alula Aba Nega as his governor from 1877 for the next decade. This now formed part of the new process of centralisation which saw the construction of the modern Ethiopian empire state.

Modern empire: Menelik, Adwa and imperial expansion

In a remarkable forty-year period between 1855 and 1898, under the successive rule of the three emperors (Tewodros II of Gonder, the Tigrayan Yohannes IV and Menelik II of Amhara Shewa), the heirs of a shifting pattern of Abyssinian kingdoms were unified into something approaching a single polity. In the words of Sylvia Pankhurst, 'modern Ethiopia dates from the reign of Emperor Menelik II'.[20] From 1887, Menelik pursued a dramatic policy of expansionary conquest east, west and south from his base in Shewa. Within two years of the Battle of Adwa, which put an end to Italian encroachments from Eritrea in the north in 1896, the 'process of territorial expansion and the creation of the modern empire state had been completed'.[21] The empire had swollen exponentially, expanding its territory many times over, and growing to a point approaching the boundaries of the modern Ethiopian state as they apply today.[22] By 1908 these had been delimited (but not always demarcated) in a series of international agreements.[23]

The empire also now encompassed dozens of new groups of subjects. At the outset of this short and dramatic decade of change, the overwhelming majority of the polity's populations had been, like their rulers, Orthodox Christian speakers of the two major languages, Amharic and Tigrigna, descended from a common Semitic linguistic ancestor.[24] A little over forty years later, the old Abyssinian populations of Orthodox believers (while still providing the majority of its rulers, and the cultural type to which those rulers almost uniformly conformed) constituted only a minority of the new Ethiopian Empire's subjects. After the expansion, modern imperial Ethiopia was a 'mosaic' of multi-ethnicity, no more a 'nation state' than any of the other products of colonial conquest which pressed around it to fill the African continent. The diversity of the new state's populations encompassed culture, economy and language, with 'about a dozen Semitic languages, 22 Cushitic, 18 Omotic, and 18 Nilo-Saharan'.[25] It extended to religion, with animism/paganism, Judaism, Islam and Christianity all represented in this 'region of religious confusion'.[26]

Following the rule of Tewodros II (which brought to an end the fragmented Era of Princes while perpetuating many of its social, political and administrative practices),[27] Tigrayan Yohannes IV took a more strategic approach to centralisation. He now envisaged a 'loosely united Ethiopia, with autonomous regional rulers under an emperor exercising benevolent political suzerainty'.[28] Competition between two of these rulers, Menelik of Shewa and Tekle Haimanot of Gojjam, particularly over the control of lucrative long-distance trade routes to the south, was an important factor precipitating subsequent southward expansion and conquest. The Battle of Embabo in mid-1882, at which Menelik defeated his rival,[29] opened up the south-west to his troops, at the same time securing his eventual succession. Menelik's victory at Chalenquo in early 1887, a year before Yohannes IV's death in 1889, had the same effect in the east, paving the way for his conquest of Harar and the Hararghe highlands.[30] His defeat of the Italians at Adwa in 1896, which forestalled the colonial counter-threat from the north, completed the triangle of military victories that 'were crucial in establishing Shewan hegemony over the Abyssinian north and in conquering the south'.[31]

Coming to power in Shewa, Menelik inherited a prosperous region with traditions of autocratic leadership,[32] which had already expanded to control neighbouring Shewan Oromo populations under his grandfather Sahle Selassie (r. 1813–47).[33] Menelik's suzerainty had already extended to encompass Gurage areas. Between 1882 and 1886 his forces moved west to conquer Nekemte, Qellam, Jimma and the other Gibe River states, and Illubabor, as well as south-east into Arsi (all now in Oromia), where they met greater resistance but eventually prevailed. After the conquest of Harar in 1887, the kingdom of Welaiyta finally also fell to Menelik in 1894 after much bloodshed. Welaiyta provided foot soldiers for further brutal pushes west into Kaffa, Konso, Benishangul and Assosa, and east into Bale and the Ogaden. Maji in the south-west, Borana in the far south, and the Afar sultanate in the north-east were added over the course of the subsequent decade.

This extraordinary process had two consequences of long-term significance for subsequent patterns of ethnicity and power in Ethiopia. First, the new empire's rulers were, whether by assimilation or inheritance, Abyssinians (*habesha*), and specifically Amharic-speaking Christians. They forged a system under which, in many newly conquered territories to the south, class and ethnic divisions coincided, establishing a nexus of potential conflict dynamics. Second, power shifted south, reflecting the new economic interests of Ethiopia's Shewan rulers now based in Addis Ababa. Up to this point Tigrigna-speakers (across what is now modern-day Tigray and the highland areas of Eritrea) had regularly wielded power over large areas of the Abyssinian core, dominating them as recently as Yohannes IV's reign a few years earlier. The bifurcation of the northern highlands with the cession of *Mereb Melash* (the territory 'beyond the Mereb River'—now Eritrea) to the Italians, a deal initially forged at Wuchale, and sealed in the wake of the Battle of Adwa,[34] seemed to render Tigrayan loss of power to the Shewan Amhara dynasties irreversible.

'Identity jilted': The peripheralisation of the empire in the north

Ethiopians have long speculated about why Menelik failed to capitalise upon his victory over the Italians at Adwa to drive the Italians out of *Mereb Melash*, and to reunite the Tigrigna-speaking part of the Abyssinian core.[35] They posit three explanations: firstly, the fear that his absence during a potentially extended campaign in the north would encourage rebellion in the (much more lucrative) south; secondly, his dim view of the prospects of success;[36] and, finally, the Machiavellian determination often attributed to him permanently to weaken his northern rivals in Tigray.[37] In the north, Menelik's decision has long been a thorn in the side of Tigrayan nationalists—the seminal instance of 'Shewan perfidy', which only served to entrench the resentment that had already developed at his ouster of Yohannes's son Mengesha from the imperial succession.[38]

Another key figure in shaping northern Ethiopian perspectives of this period was the Tigrayan *Ras* Alula Aba Nega, who engaged in a 'struggle to maintain Tigrean hegemony under Yohannes IV and then to preserve its autonomy under Shoan dominance'.[39] The key features of Alula's career continue to resonate in northern Ethiopia and Eritrea: his rise to become Yohannes IV's governor in Eritrea (1877–87), his failure to preserve Tigrayan hegemony, or create a common Eritrean–Tigrayan alliance against Menelik on Yohannes's death (1889–92), and, finally, his acceptance of Shewan hegemony under Menelik (1894–7). Of course, these histories have subsequently been viewed differently on either side of the Mereb River. Diametrically opposed views of *Ras* Alula in Tigray and in Eritrea, for instance, returned in the 1980s to colour relations between the EPLF and TPLF (see Chapter 3).

Although the 'restless militarism' of Menelik's imperial project subdued a vast new territory,

> he had created deepening pools of hostility for the longer term. Menelik would have been only too aware of this, as his army was continually attacked by Tigrayan, Azebo, and Oromo peasants alike on its march back from Adwa ... Tigray was subordinate but simmered with bitterness at the imposition of the 'southern Abyssinians' who had impoverished vast districts in the run-up to the battle of Adwa, and at the apparent greed of Menelik who kept the compensation paid by the Italians for himself, even though Tigrayan leaders were the 'chief sufferers of the war and bore the brunt of the fighting'.[40]

Whatever Menelik II's intentions in the period after Adwa, the bifurcation of the Tigrigna-speaking highlands had a profound and immediate impact. It converted 'a region which might (once in a while, anyhow) provide an emperor, into one in which local notables squabbled for local prizes, and in the process rendered themselves increasingly dependent on either the colonial authorities in Asmara, or the Shoan emperor in Addis Ababa.'[41]

As if to add insult to imperial injury, much of Tigray was devastated between 1888 and 1892 by an exceptionally severe rinderpest epidemic and famine that affected a large part of Sudan and East Africa.[42] Its impact may have strengthened Menelik's southward impetus (healthy cattle from newly incorporated Harar and Bale

25

were distributed to those affected), and curbed his resolve to pursue Ethiopian interests in Eritrea post-Adwa (food supplies in the north were at a premium).[43] In Tigray the much-remembered dark days of that famine have become conjoined in the popular imagination with the advent of modern Ethiopian rule from Shewa.[44]

There is debate about the historicity of an 'ethnic' interpretation of these events in Tigrayan and Amhara areas at the end of the nineteenth century. Some commentators assert that 'Amhara' and 'Tigrayan' were political rather than ethnic categories at the time;[45] others bring evidence from the next two decades that suggests they did have an 'ethnic' flavour, as 'the political power of the Amhara was accompanied by their cultural hegemony'.[46] This is likely an instance where the set of conventions attaching to what are now thought of as ethnonyms was either shifting or multiple. Modern-day usage of the terms 'Amhara' and 'Tigrayan' continues to indicate the strength of each as political (as well as ethnic) signifiers.

Whatever the conventions that were attached to the two terms, the work of prominent intellectuals in the early twentieth century suggests they were well established in common usage—not surprising given the clear juxtaposition of the two distinct written language blocs. The writings of the Tigrayan author Gebre Hewet Baykedagne (1912) and the Amhara author Afewerk Gebre Yesus (1901) also indicate that they involved a high degree of animosity or competition. In the words of the historian Bahru Zewde, the 'virulently anti-Tegréan sentiments' and 'unjustified vituperation' with which Afewerk wrote elicited a 'sober criticism' from Gebre Hewet, commenting on the 'impoverishment of [Tigray], the migration of its people, and the rampancy of banditry, largely a result of the political disarray that had ensued in Tegray after the death of Yohannes at Mätämma'.[47]

The division between the two writers has often resonated powerfully in the period since they wrote. Gebre Hewet's correlation of the impoverishment of Tigray region with the advent of Amhara rule became a central precept of the nationalist movement in Tigray, which emerged along with the TPLF in the late 1970s and 1980s. Meanwhile, the title of the first Amharic novel, *Tobia*, written by Afewerk, became better known during the 1990s and 2000s as the name of a leading anti-EPRDF–TPLF private newspaper. The complicated period between the Battle of Adwa and Mussolini's occupation of Ethiopia in the run-up to the Second World War provided numerous instances of what was later construed as 'patriotism' or 'treachery' on the part of Amharas and Tigrayans. Elites from either side of the border switched sides, often more than once. This history has provided an abundance of accusatory material more than sufficient for propagandists to show that important members of each group were more—or less—loyal to the Ethiopian state than the other.[48]

After the Battle of Adwa, the Amharic language became entrenched as the language of administration of the Ethiopian empire state, under its new Shewan rulers.[49] The main impact of the cession to Italy of *Mereb Melash* was politically to divide and to weaken the Tigrigna-speaking highlanders vis-à-vis their Amharic-speaking neighbours to the south, removing them from the centre to the edge of the polity, while the centre of power had shifted far to the south. For the time being, little otherwise changed in what was now a relatively peripheral and impoverished part of the empire: Tigrayan elites retained local powers under Menelik II, and traditional arrangements governing land and taxation were barely modified.

Expropriation and militarism: The empire in the south

Menelik's movements south, meanwhile, were often brutal and widely overturned existing land and property arrangements. Tedla Haile, writing in 1930, set out three alternative imperial approaches to the southern peoples: enslavement and expropriation, assimilation, and indirect rule.[50] Areas that succumbed to Menelik's forces regained a degree of autonomy based on a form of indirect rule by existing elites and annual fixed tribute. Those which had put up a fight against incorporation saw the imposition of so-called *gabbar-malkagna*[51] relations transferred from the north. The heavily extractive Abyssinian system of multiple appropriation of labour and 'surpluses' was extended south, but divested of the complex arrangement of hereditary land tenure 'safeguards' which had underpinned (and moderated) it in the north. The conquered lands now 'came under the jurisdiction of Menelik's generals,

27

providing them with the source for both their wealth and their military strength ... Officials and retainers of the governors were then assigned a number of gabbar commensurate with their rank ... rang[ing] from 5 to 100.'[52]

Not content with the expropriation of labour, surplus produce, and (gradually) land from the newly created southern *gabbars*, the new ruling class also took labour in the form of slaves. A long-standing endemic slave trade was given new impetus by the extension of Ethiopia's borders: 'in the absence of effective and responsible administration, Menelik II's incorporation of new areas only tended to accentuate the predatory tendencies of the ruling class and the soldiery'.[53]

Each of these strategies had implications for the constellation of subjugated language and ethnic groups in relation to the state and state power. Some newly incorporated groups were targeted for slave-raiding,[54] while others were reduced to tenant-farmer or serf-like status, the full implications of which emerged only later in the twentieth century, when land began to be appropriated in large volume. The practical effects of the abrupt changes in the system of land rights were obscured and (initially) mitigated because those who took land needed peasant labour, so that the process did not immediately result in widespread alienation. The elites of some incorporated groups, meanwhile, emerged as minorities whose status, livelihood and culture became increasingly entwined with the emergent cultural, religious, military and political dominance of the Shewan Amhara Christian aristocracy.[55]

Those who wished to join the ranks of the powerful were required to demonstrate their loyalty to the empire by means of a specific set of cultural credentials. Although many members of the new ruling class were not from Shewa, they were increasingly required to behave as if they were, conforming closely to a set of stereotypical cultural features and markers. These included fluency in the Amharic language, adherence to Orthodox Christianity (often involving the change of Muslim or other personal names to Amharic ones with a Christian meaning), and the general adoption of a set of norms of Abyssinian codes and styles.[56] Assimilation was not a matter of choice. It was sanctioned in ways which made it essential: 'public office, the economic benefits of the state, land and property rights [were] all denied to non-believers'.[57] Whereas in the north, religion had proved a 'unifying ideology, [it] now became a divisive factor in the multicultural state.'[58]

Woven around this hegemonic cultural core, a reinvigorated series of myths of origin and legitimacy of the state was now fashioned from the 'ancient' fabric of the conquering polity's long ancestral lines on the highlands. Where its resources proved threadbare, traditional warp was supplemented with elaborately manufactured new strands of weft. It was around this time, for instance, that the narrative of the Solomonic origins of the imperial dynasty in the fourteenth-century epic *Kebra Negast* (Glory of Kings) was revived and reworked to stress the primacy of Shewa. All manner of imperial paraphernalia was introduced in the period in question, including much now commonly regarded as ancient in origin.[59] Such refashioning and fabrication have, of course, complicated contemporary perceptions of Ethiopia's own historical continuity. Throughout, the consolidation of the new political project was underpinned by state violence. Richard Reid concludes that during the imperial period culminating with Menelik, 'a dangerously potent militarism had been created which would not easily be undone. It seems possible to suggest that the region has hardly demobilized since the early nineteenth century.'[60]

Why does this matter now?

The dynamics and interpretation of imperial expansion remain controversial. There are two central controversies. Did Menelik's conquests reunite territories which had previously (and, by implication, properly) formed a part of, or at least rendered tribute to, historical Abyssinia, or should they be considered as acts of colonial aggression no more justified than the adjacent projects of aggrandisement undertaken by Europeans? Secondly, and relatedly, should these conquests be lauded as key to the survival and consolidation of an independent African giant, a beacon for nationalist aspiration across the continent? Or should they be decried as evidence of African complicity in an extractive form of 'dependent colonialism',[61] whose iniquities have yet to be reversed, leaving us today with the few disgraceful remnants of unfinished, albeit 'internal', colonial business?

These questions—less queries of historical fact than calls for normative judgements about legitimacy, justice and the 'proper' reparation of damage—have been debated for several generations in Ethiopia. Answers to them often serve as shorthand means of marking out the respondents' positions on a host of political issues, including their views of the TPLF, and of the system of ethnic or multinational federalism they introduced in 1991: they are still at the centre of debate about the war in Tigray. They rely on the accumulation of 'confirmatory' historical evidence either way, in support of competing nationalisms. Given the complexity of the historical processes involved, there is, of course, no shortage of material to bolster any number of interpretations associated with the two views. The current account is less concerned with assessing the validity of each claim than with tracing the processes by which the questions, and the views which prompt them, emerged.

If those fighting for or against 'self-determination' vis-à-vis the Ethiopian empire state in the recent period had an important external audience, so too did Tewodros II, Yohannes IV and Menelik II before them, surrounded by European colonial ambitions. 'Performative' statements about Ethiopia's antiquity and extent—that is, claims which attempt to bring into being what they assert—have a long history in the region. Performative success was—as ever—greatly enhanced by the perceptible exaggeration of the right and proper 'natural' truth of what was claimed. Fuelled by Menelik II's rhetoric and the enthusiasm of the Church, the tradition took root that imperial expansion sought only the rightful return to highland populations of areas from which they had been expelled during the period of Ahmed 'Gragn' (r. c.1526–42) and the subsequent Oromo incursions (usually dated from movements into Bale beginning in the 1520s). It seems clear that Menelik pushed the frontiers of the Ethiopian state to areas beyond the reach even of the renowned medieval empire-builder Amda Tseyon (r. 1314–44) or the maximal limits ruled by Zera Yacob (r. 1434–68), but this fact did nothing to shake the belief in 'rightful reunification'.

Polemical emphasis on modern Ethiopia's continuity with the ancient polity correlates with what is often a 'perennialist' focus on the continuity of Abyssinian cultural norms and socio-economic circumstances—one which sees them as natural, enduring, axiomatic. Not surprisingly, therefore, it also draws on academic assertion of such continuities, particularly where these assertions are incautious enough to lend themselves to the interpretation that both the particular set of continuities selected for analysis and their cultural contents are in some sense 'right' in virtue of their 'truth'— 'valid' in its widest sense.[62]

Donald Levine's later work rejects the 'erroneous view that before the conquests of Menelik II in the late nineteenth century the other peoples of Ethiopia had lived independent and self-sufficient lives', apparently not least on the circular grounds that this view 'fails to provide any leverage for getting at the properties of the larger Ethiopian system directly'.[63] Thus, by positing 'Greater Ethiopia' as a 'single societal system'[64] and documenting pan-Ethiopian traits common to its groups of citizens, Levine is able to prove it to be such. The work is something of an exemplar of the performativity of categorisation. Yet, these narratives were used to critique federalism in the 1990s (Chapter 3), were revived in the 2016–18 period (Chapter 4), and were fostered again under the new government from 2018 (Chapter 5).

There is nothing inevitable about the evolution of conventions, whatever the weight of 'logic' of the circumstances in which they evolve. Even those few slices of the history of the populations of an area as large as modern-day Ethiopia that have been researched and documented are rich enough to resource any number of interpretations. The interpretations which have survived and dominated have done so primarily because they have had influential patrons. This remains true at the time of writing in 2022, as history is again energetically rewritten. In the next part of the imperial period, a rapidly centralising and bureaucratising state under Haile Selassie I was the most influential of these patrons. Equally energetic new processes in the early twentieth century further served to inflame resentment of some members of Ethiopia's populations at the perceived 'ethnocratic' rule to which they were subject.[65]

Centralising empire: Solomonic nationalism, occupation and post-war consolidation

In the period from the 1890s to the early 1930s, successive Ethiopian governments under Menelik II (r. 1889–1913), Iyasu (r. 1913–16), Zewditu (r. 1916–30) and Haile Selassie I (r. 1930–74) worked to establish the legitimacy and integrity of the situation in which the multi-ethnic empire was ruled and 'unified' under an Abyssinian state. Commentators have speculated as to whether the brief period of *Lij* Iyasu (designated emperor but uncrowned between 1913 and 1916) might have set the country in another direction. His reign, 'one of the most enigmatic in Ethiopian history', seemed to indicate the potential for a different approach—particularly to the empire's relations with its many Muslim subjects.[66] The moment rapidly passed. The five-year period of Mussolini's occupation of Ethiopia from 1936 to 1941, and British involvement in the disposal of Italy's colonial possessions during and after the Second World War, now also set new precedents. Both powers mooted a range of alternative administrative and sovereign arrangements. Italian occupation had a powerful impact on the subsequent relationships between ethnic groups and the state.

The disruptions of Italian Imperial East Africa

First of all, the Italian conquest undermined the 'divine' Solomonic credentials of two generations of Abyssinian rule, by demolishing its inevitability. The ignominious circumstances of Emperor Haile Selassie's flight into exile in the UK in 1936 compounded this. Secondly, the Italian occupation presented many of Ethiopia's subject peoples with an alternative experience of imperial rule, from which a number drew comparisons unfavourable to the emperor's return. A third factor exacerbated the trend: an Italian policy of divide and rule 'to facilitate the conquest' deliberately sought 'to foment internal discord and warfare', pitting Ethiopia's subject races against the Amhara regime. Italy actively offered a range of inducements from the 1936 Maichew campaign onwards.[67] Italian hopes rested on Ethiopia's non-Amhara and Muslim populations: thus 'Oromo oppression under Amhara domination became the central theme of Italian propaganda and of de-Amharization campaigns. Amharic was displaced as the legal language; and Arabic, Oromonya [sic] and Kaffinya were taught in schools.'[68]

Italy's efforts had mixed results. Oromo 'nobles and ordinary people were perplexed and disoriented' by the conquest and remained 'mistrustful'.[69] Apparently more reliable was the response from Ethiopia's Muslims when Mussolini sought to present himself as a regional champion of Islam. Poor relations with the Ethiopian Orthodox Church were guaranteed, but this was also partly a function of Italian attempts to curry favour with Ethiopian nationalist sentiment by removing the Church from the orbit of Alexandria.[70] Meanwhile, Muslims 'gave the Italians unconditional help in return for the Italian government's support of their religion and institutions'. Occupation saw an intensive programme of mosque construction and schemes for the establishment of centres of Islamic study and propaganda.[71] As a result, Ethiopia's Muslim and non-Abyssinian populations occasionally recount with nostalgia the relatively favourable conditions they or their antecedents enjoyed during the Italian period. New Italian infrastructure drove roads into previously inaccessible areas, and drilled wells among pastoralist groups, particularly to the benefit of Somalis in the Ogaden. It impressed many.

Some communities were unenthusiastic about the return of Abyssinian imperial rule, but there were also doubts and new ideas among those who resisted Italian rule. A republican patriot movement, for instance, 'argued for the unity of all patriots … [and] advocated a federalist approach to accommodate the diversity of Ethiopia's constituent regions'.[72] Encouraging such views was a fourth significant factor: Italian imperial administrative arrangements drew a strong correlation between sovereign units and language areas. When the territorial governorships of Italian Imperial East Africa were established, 'ethnic principles were applied in dividing the territory'.[73] 'The main Italian concern was the elimination of the Amhara's claim to superiority over other populations. [They] framed the division of Ethiopia into Governorships in such a way that [this] hegemony was eliminated. Employing Amhara in government offices and using the Amharic language in non-Amhara territories

33

was prohibited'.[74] Rather, the occupation administration sought to take account of 'traditional laws, customs, religion, and language' following ethnicity when possible, although 'the principle of political opportunism prevailed, rather than the ethnic one'.[75]

The echoes in 1990s federalism of the Italian occupation of the 1930s have (perhaps unsurprisingly) drawn little or no comment.[76] Parallels with occupying fascism were hardly likely to enhance the legitimacy of the incoming transitional government. Nevertheless it is hard to escape the conclusion that the Italian period (itself within living memory in 1991) provided important and widely experienced precedents. This must have had a bearing on the continuing evolution of the politicisation of ethnicity during the post-war period. Centralised Abyssinian rule was no longer the only option, the single 'prominent solution', but had to be explicitly fostered and bolstered to exclude the alternative political constellation, which the Italians had elaborated all too clearly. The possibility of alternatives to centralised Shewan Amhara rule did not neatly disappear with the defeat of the Italians—simultaneously proving and exacerbating the impact of these precedents.

A fifth factor which drove nationalist investigation of alternatives to the restitution of Shewan imperial rule was a thread of ambivalence in Italian and British policy-making, alternating so-called 'Shewan' with 'Tigrayan' policies. The Italians, in the run-up to the invasion, had pursued a twin-track policy, attempting to sow disaffection among the Tigrigna-speaking populations, while adopting a conciliatory approach to the Ethiopian government. The post-Italian British involvement (military administration in Eritrea and ambiguous dealings in Ethiopia)[77] saw continued administration of Tigray from Asmara rather than Addis Ababa, thereby perpetuating this ambivalence.[78] Divergence between the British Foreign Office and War Office meant that British policy wavered between the restitution of centralised rule from Addis Ababa and the amalgamation of Tigray with Eritrea, thereby establishing a so-called Greater Tigray.[79]

Meanwhile, Eritrean politics in the decade from 1941 up to its federation with Ethiopia in 1952 saw intense and fragmented political activity and lobbying in support of a multiplicity of potential fates for the various parts of Eritrea.[80] This left a legacy of Eritrean suspicion of dismemberment. The next two chapters explore aspects of the continuing relevance of these complexities in the relations between Ethiopia and Eritrea and between Tigray and Eritrea.

Tremors from the occasionally violent post-war uncertainties continued to affect Ethiopia long after the Italian period. Already in 1936 western Oromo leaders (perhaps with British connivance) had forwarded a petition to the League of Nations for a separate protectorate pending independence. A revolt then shook eastern Tigray in 1943 (see the next chapter). The British continued to administer the rich Haud pastureland inside the Ethiopian border, exacerbating violent conflict over grazing access between the Ogaden and other Somali clans, until as late as 1954. It took what Richard Greenfield has called 'two decades of intrigue' for Haile Selassie to attain anything like the autonomous, stable, centralised arrangement he sought.[81] Many of the fault lines exposed during the period of the Second World War and its aftermath remained problematic long after his fall.

Curbing the old regional elite: Imperial centralisation ...

The underlying strategy of Haile Selassie was a centralising one,[82] continuing the tradition of the great centralising emperors from 1855 onwards.[83] He finally succeeded 'in realizing the unitary state of which Tewodros had dreamt'.[84] In his role as regent during the reign of Zewditu, when he was known as *Ras* Teferi, he had already accumulated a range of powers, embarking on a power struggle with the traditional elites. In the period up to 1930 he met and faced down early challenges to his increasing powers from the regional aristocracy—including in Tigray. Days after the coronation of Zewditu in February 1909, for instance, *Ras* Welde Giorgis was crowned king of Gonder and 'for the sake of his kingship, authority over the [imperial] Tigre province was added for his enhancement'.[85] The point still rankles.[86]

A year after his coronation as *negusa negast* (king of kings), in 1931 Emperor Haile Selassie declared a new constitution which 'set up the juridical framework of emergent absolutism'.[87] It gave him power to appoint and dismiss the nobility, to administer justice, and to grant land and other honours. The nobility lost their authority

35

in foreign relations, the acquisition of arms and warfare.[88] Curbs on the power of the regional elites continued in the post-war period, as Haile Selassie negotiated the complicated fallout from the pattern of Ethiopian aristocratic collaboration, betrayal and resistance of the Italian period.[89] Haile Selassie 'continued where the Italians left off' in reducing the power of the regional aristocracy to 'dependence on the centre'.[90] Although he used the aristocracy to 'maintain connections between the central government and the more traditional sectors of the state',[91] the emperor conferred few titles, and allocated positions of greatest influence to those he had himself raised to high office.

A new regional administration established after 1941 provided for 14 new provinces, around 100 counties (*awraja*), and 600 districts (*wereda*). During this process of reorganisation, a number of geographical territories were reallocated, especially those that had been associated with Tigrayan regional elites seen as 'traitorous' after collaborating with the Italians. The most noted traitor was Haile Selassie Gugsa, later tried for his fascist collaboration. A few years later, other areas of Tigray were also brought under the control of neighbouring provinces. The areas of Welkaiyt and Tsegedé, which, according to his son, had been administered by *Ras* Seyoum Mengesha of Tigray, were brought under Gonder province in 1948. They remained part of this formal dispensation until the federal arrangement was introduced in 1991 (see Chapter 3).[92] Similarly, Kobo, which had also been under the administration of *Ras* Seyoum Mengesha, was given to the heir to the throne, Asfaw Wossen, and formed part of Wollo from 1949.[93]

For the first time in Ethiopia's history, Haile Selassie had succeeded in curtailing the power of Ethiopia's regional elites and, with it, the autonomy of its regions. A professionalised national bureaucracy and army performed the functions traditionally carried out under shifting alliances of decentralised fiefdoms nominally subservient to the 'king of kings'. In an era of modernisation, Haile Selassie needed educated administrators to fill these structures. His reign now saw the dramatic expansion of education in Ethiopia, in what was perhaps the single most important socio-political transformation of the period. 'The Emperor is certainly the hub of the government, but he is far from being the whole of it; for to further his policy of centralisation, and to carry out the new and complex tasks involved by modernisation and administrative expansion, he has had to recruit a ruling class of administrators and politicians—aptly termed "the new nobility"'.[94]

... and bureaucratisation: Educating a new elite

After the Battle of Adwa, Ethiopians had begun to go abroad for education or to mission schools in neighbouring Sudan and Eritrea. The first modern school in Ethiopia was opened in Addis Ababa in 1908, followed in 1912 by Alliance Française schools in Dire Dawa and the capital. In 1925 the Teferi Mekonnen School in Addis Ababa was established, and more schools now opened in different parts of the country. Growing numbers of Ethiopians were sent abroad during the 1920s, later becoming an educated class prominent in the expanding state administration. The development of education also 'disseminat[ed] ideas of change'.[95]

The intellectual 'exuberance and vibrancy of the 1920s' initially saw collaboration between emperor and intellectuals in 'a fascinating experiment in social and political reform'.[96] This was an experiment to which the Italian invasion and occupation put a stop. While many of the older generation of intellectuals went into exile, a majority of its younger members were executed by the Italians, creating 'a generation gap in the intellectual and political history of the country' and contributing to 'the drab intellectual climate' of the post-war period, in which 'the educated elite saw its mission as one of loyal and dedicated service rather than engagement in social and political critique'.[97]

Meanwhile, the old power structure of the regional aristocracy was still in place. As a result, 'the first fifteen years after the Liberation were dominated by divisions between largely traditional forces, notably the nobility, and the personal *protégés* of the Emperor'.[98] This situation gradually shifted as educated politicians worked their way through the ranks of government, and by the early 1960s 'most of the important ministers [were] men with advanced education'.[99] The emerging bureaucracy, including the Ministry of Land Reform and Administration and the Ministry of Finance, worked with the emperor to provide 'the major forces representing the centralisation of the political system'.[100] The educated elite, however, had not 'scaled the "commanding heights" of the political system, which are still held by a man who, whatever his claims to be a moderniser, is very far from them in outlook; and they have not so far provided that driving force which is what the government most obviously lacks.'[101]

The middle decades of the twentieth century, after the liberation from Italian occupation, saw a series of regional or local rebellions in different parts of Ethiopia: the *weyane* or rebellion in eastern Tigray in 1943; the eruption of Bale (south-east Oromia) between 1963 and 1970; the uprising in Gojjam (western Amhara) in 1968; disturbances in Yejju in Wollo in 1948 and 1970; and the uprising in Gedeo (in the south) in 1960. While these disturbances are often bracketed together, in fact they have little in common in respect of origin, cause, duration, form or participants. Few drew, at the time, on an explicit or widely shared ethnic rationale,[102] but the precedent of local resistance to central rule offered resonant resources to subsequent generations of ethno-nationalists. The *weyane* in Tigray (further discussed in Chapter 2) seems to have arisen when administrative corruption and greed ignited a situation of existing instability and insecurity, and one awash with weaponry in the wake of the Italian defeat.

Gradually a new class of young people had the education and experience to begin to understand the iniquitous basis on which the imperial state was established. When these individuals also happened to be assimilated members of the ethnic groups most disadvantaged by the arrangement (as they increasingly were), they began not only to understand it, but to resent it. Two factors seem to have operated as triggers for a shift in the nature of their opposition to the imperial regime. These were the attempted coup of 1960, and the annexation of federated Eritrea, effectively completed with the imposition of Ethiopian law the previous year. While the coup attempt of Mengistu and Germame Neway was relatively easily suppressed at the time, and Haile Selassie succeeded in having the Asmara parliament vote away its own autonomy, the notion of traitorous perfidy in the north persisted through the post-war period. Seeds of a different level of dissatisfaction had been sown in each case. Of the various groups among whom these seeds took root, the growing body of students at Haile Selassie I (later, Addis Ababa) University was the most important.

If the period from the mid-1850s marked the rise of a series of centralising emperors, which brought the decentralised pattern of the Era of Princes to an end, the late 1960s saw the emergence of modern political forces demanding the reconstitution of the imperial state along more decentralised lines that recognised sub-state identities. These critics saw that the imperial state was founded on an 'explosive ... correlation of ethnic, cultural and class differences that made it inherently unstable',[103] and Haile Selassie's attempts at centralisation, bureaucratisation and militarisation ultimately failed to satisfy them.

The forceful criticism of these new political groupings has had a long legacy:

> the era of Haile Selassie continues to evoke contradictory attitudes. For some it was a period of peace and national unity, a golden age by contrast with the upheavals and violence that followed, when Ethiopian was governed skilfully and with a light hand, and its inherent conflict and contradiction were kept at least relatively under control. For others, it was a period of repressive feudalism, built on injustice and inequality, when government was dedicated to the service and glorification of a single man, and opportunities to secure peaceful reform were spurned.[104]

The ongoing polarisation between these two different views has, if anything, become as important as their validity: they have become badges of political identity to be defended rather than perspectives to be debated. The emergence of new political forces, their opposition to the ageing emperor in the late 1960s and 1970s, and their defeat of the authoritarian centralised state led by the military regime at the beginning of the 1990s, form the focus of the next chapter.

2

CHALLENGING THE EMPIRE
TWO VISIONS OF ETHIOPIA

Sarah Vaughan

The previous chapter examined the imperial expansion of Ethiopia, which forcibly incorporated a mosaic of different peoples, and the struggles to centralise the polity during the nineteenth and twentieth centuries, before and after that expansion. This chapter explores the emergence of what is commonly referred to as the 'national question' in Ethiopia's politics: how best to represent the needs and interests of modern Ethiopia's many different ethnic and language groups. It traces the fractious politics and ideological debates of the so-called Ethiopian student movement over the final years of Haile Selassie I's reign (1960–74). It looks at how their divisions influenced the pattern and style of political and armed mobilisation against the government; this finally saw the emperor deposed and replaced by the military Marxist regime known as the Derg (1974–91), and continued to fight the new government after 1974. By the outbreak of the Tigray war in 2020, this was history still just about within living memory of the oldest generation of Ethiopian and Eritrean politicians and analysts who remained influential.

Opposition to the centrist Derg regime was itself riven into two broad groups by the issues of the 'national question': those who favoured a unified national mobilisation against its predations, and those who organised on the basis of specific language or ethnic groups, seeking 'self-determination' and greater autonomy. Prominent among the first group were the leftist Ethiopian People's Revolutionary Party (EPRP) and the All-Ethiopia Socialist Movement (known as Me'ison), as well as the more conservative Ethiopian Democratic Union (EDU) led by the old imperial aristocratic elites. In the second category, a wide range of groups emerged through the 1970s and 1980s to oppose the Derg government. A series of 'liberation fronts' representing the Afar, Berta/Benishangul, Gambella, Western Somali (later Ogaden) and Sidama all took to the field. The most significant in terms of their emergent military muscle and popular support were the EDU and EPRP (at least initially), the Oromo Liberation Front (OLF), and the Tigray People's Liberation Front (TPLF). The last part of this chapter focuses on the emergence of the TPLF and the resources with which it mobilised Tigrayan nationalism.

Meanwhile, the sharp ideological division between the unitarist political movements (the Derg, EPRP, Me'ison and the EDU) and the plethora of ethno-nationalist liberation fronts was complicated by events in the north: the long and bitter thirty-year Eritrean struggle for independence from Ethiopia. The first shots of the Eritrean war of 'decolonisation' had been fired in 1961, within a couple of years of the imperial government dissolving the federal compromise adopted after the Second World War and annexing Eritrea. The movements which emerged in Eritrea, particularly Isaias Afwerki's Eritrean People's Liberation Front (EPLF), rejected both the ethno-national organisation of the Ethiopian liberation movements and the unitarist approach of the pan-Ethiopianist nationalists. Rather, they set out an alternative 'united, national and anti-colonial' strategy focused on the separately 'unified' political identity of the former Italian colonial territory of Eritrea. The next chapter (Chapter 3) returns to this part of the story and its implications for relations between Ethiopia (including Tigray) and post-independence Eritrea in the 1990s.

The Ethiopian student movement and the 'national question'

The rise of the 'Ethiopian student movement' constitutes a watershed in modern Ethiopian political history. It was arguably as transformative of the political culture and ideas of Ethiopia's elite as Menelik II's expansion had been of its political space. Many of the events that followed in its wake proved equally bloody. In the absence of political parties and strong associational life, students emerged at the end of the imperial period as 'the most outspoken and visibly the only consolidated opposition group', constituting 'a disproportionately large section of what could be called the bearers of public opinion'.[1]

The dynamics of these radical student politics are still deeply contested in Ethiopian political circles and analysis.[2] Few of the students' preoccupations are more vigorously contested than that referred to by its Marxist label as the 'national question': the call for the 'self-determination' of the 'nations, nationalities and peoples' of the empire state.[3] Until relatively recently (arguably until the emergence of the new prime minister in 2018), almost all the political organisations and movements which had fought over the Ethiopian body politic since the 1970s traced their roots back to the student movement or could identify its strong influence upon them. The central political fissures that drove the war in Tigray can still be traced back to student debates in the final years of the imperial period— to divisions between generations, cliques, or diaspora groups of activists; and to disputes over ideology, analysis, and their application to different aspects of the Ethiopian situation, then as now.

The student movement's political significance is responsible for the popular mythology which has surrounded it.[4] For half a century it has been credited or damned with responsibility for just about everything that has happened in Ethiopia since the early 1970s. On the other hand, neither the students nor the various political organisations descended from them came to power after 1974. Instead, the military seized power, establishing a regime, the Derg, which rapidly turned on and consumed many of the major successors to the Ethiopian student movement during the Red Terror of the late 1970s.

If anything, this has further deepened the romanticism, sometimes uncritical and idealised, with which the heady student period (a sort of 'age of innocence') has often been viewed, particularly among Ethiopian diaspora communities.[5] What had always been internecine struggles among the more committed student factions became, after the rise of the Derg, literally deadly. The deaths of so many further constrained the ability (or willingness) of survivors to analyse the experiences of their 'generation'.[6] Those who had an interest in formulating a critique of the student movement in order to learn from its mistakes and further their struggle in opposition often did not survive to tell their stories.[7] Those who escaped were often silenced by the bitterness or guilt of longevity; those who remained in Ethiopia, by the ongoing imperatives of survival. All learned that struggling for their beliefs could involve a fight to the death.

With several notable exceptions, analysis of the student movement remained relatively muted for most of the Derg period.[8] Political enthusiasm after the fall of the Derg in 1991 suggests that its emotional, ideological and strategic pull had remained strong. The change of government in 1991 provoked new consideration of the student movement's legacy, not least by a new regime keen to lay claim to it. The TPLF and EPRDF later repeatedly emphasised their debts to those elements of the Ethiopian student movement that first elucidated notions of the 'self-determination of nationalities' within the Ethiopian empire state and laid the ideological basis for political mobilisation on the basis of 'nationality'. In 1991 other members of the Transitional Government joined them in averring that it was only then—twenty years later—that the student movement was finally 'coming to power'.[9] By contrast, since 2018 a new premier has (rhetorically at least) explicitly sought to distance himself from the ideologies of this period, while also actively seeking out and embracing others of its protagonists.

In the post-1991 reconsideration, Walleligne Mekonen, author of an explosive November 1969 article 'On the Question of Nationalities in Ethiopia', emerged as a focus for singular veneration.[10] A well-established narrative held that it was in his terse analysis that the 'national question' burst onto the political scene, fully formed and endorsing self-determination up to and including secession, transforming Ethiopian politics forever and at a stroke. Like most oft-repeated political mythologies, this one is an oversimplification. Although the contribution of Walleligne's paper was fundamental, it emerged from a collective accumulation of experiences, discussion and thinking over a period. Overall radicalisation of the student movement grew slowly, and a concern with 'regionalism' only gradually emerged, culminating in explicit disputes over the 'national question'. Divisions about modernism and traditionalism, about leftist ideological influences, and about the Eritrean nationalist struggle were also hugely important.

Radicalisation of the student movement

Five phases have been traced in the steady radicalisation of the Ethiopian student movement:[11] challenges to authority from 1958 to 1962; demands for participation from 1962 to 1966; a period of confrontation between 1967 and 1968; the 'revolution that failed' in 1969; and the prelude to the subsequent change of government from 1970 to 1973. Radicalisation was extremely rapid, as reflected by the evolution of student publications. By January 1968 'an editorial in *Struggle* stated: "the basic role of the university students in our country is to make the masses conscious of the suffering they are enduring resignedly"'.[12]

Several factors drove the changes. The impact of modern Western education combined with the visibility of 'the anti-colonial, nationalist emancipation process in Africa'.[13] Ethiopian students were radicalised by the presence of several hundred scholarship students from other parts of Africa from the end of the 1950s; and were shocked by the revelation at the Addis Ababa UNESCO conference on education in 1961 of Ethiopia's poor record relative to other African countries. Student political activism along lines that were 'anti-imperialist, anti-American, anti-authoritarian, and inspired by Marxist theory'[14] meant that left-wing publications, radical Peace Corps volunteers, and an extremely active diaspora were all important. Foreign members of the university teaching staff also played a role. Although some were 'authoritarian and paternalistic',[15] others were 'sympathetic to the trends within the student movement'.[16]

The repressive response of the government 'did more to gather the students behind the protests than any ideological or factual arguing could ever have done'.[17] Popularity born of repression increased as the regime vacillated between beating student demonstrators and 'encourag[ing] them to petition the Emperor'. The tactic of closing the schools 'invariably backfired, since the government was obliged to seek ways to lure the students back [and] accept embarrassing compromises which served to embolden its youthful opponents'.[18] Finally, the mid-1960s saw the beginning of the 'really militant phase of the student movement' with 'the emergence in 1964 of a radical [undercover] core known as the "Crocodiles"': both 'uncompromising opposition to the regime' and 'acceptance of Marxist ideas [were] traceable to this period'.[19] 'The emperor had too late heeded *Ras* Kassa's advice: "Teferi, don't teach these children of the poor or else they will sit on your head"'.[20]

Evolution of concern with 'regionalism'

Discussion about the 'national question' was slower to emerge on the students' rapidly radicalising agenda than a range of other less controversial issues. This reflects a policy climate in which 'the nationality issue was a taboo subject, and even after years of fighting in Eritrea and elsewhere, was not part of public discourse'.[21] As a result of the imperial government's adoption and dissemination of the Amharic language, the assimilation of non-Amhara populations to Amhara culture and religion throughout the twentieth century, and university admissions policy, all students were fluent in Amharic. By 1961 it was illegal to ask a person's ethnic origin.[22] Most students started out hostile to the political assertion of ethnicity: 'Student writing extolled Ethiopian nationalism, a sentiment perceived to transcend all other identities and loyalties ... The Abyssinian nature of Ethiopian nationalism and identity was taken for granted. No mention was made, for example, about the neglect of all other languages in favour of Amharigna, or the identification of Ethiopia with Christianity'.[23]

In the early 1960s student support for Ethiopian unity could be taken for granted. Students wrote in support of reuniting Eritrea with 'the motherland' and supported the war against Somalia in

1964. For several years, student publications continued to provide 'abundant evidence of enthusiastic pride in and loyalty to Ethiopia, even if toward the end of the 1960s there was a clear tendency to turn against the government's one-sided, pretentious propaganda about the country's past and present'.[24] Even at the end of the decade, a comparative study found Ethiopian students less likely to refer to tribal and regional identities than their African peers.[25]

The first indication that the position of nationalities within Ethiopia was seen as complex and problematic came with a series of reflections on what it meant to be an Ethiopian. The best known is Ibsa Gutema's *Ityopyawi Man New?* (Who is an Ethiopian?), which won a poetry prize in 1966. In the same year, the university paper carried an article by Haile Mariam Goshu reflecting on 'Ethiopianism' as 'transcend[ing] personal, tribal, and regional loyalties'.[26] By the end of 1968, however, the student paper *Struggle* had adopted a more controversial and nuanced—if still tentative—editorial line, 'that although there was a feeling of nationalism in Ethiopia, it had not yet in the country as a whole or in the student body become stronger than the regional and tribal impulses'.[27]

Around 1967 the 'nationalities issue' began to be discussed in closed study circles of the more theoretically conscious students;[28] it was also on the agenda at the 1967 meeting of the national student union. Four factors had encouraged this: increasing criticism of the neglect of Ethiopian culture in the educational curriculum; burgeoning interest in Marxism-Leninism; diaspora discussion of the 'national question'; and the activities of Eritrean nationalists after 1960.[29]

Also significant were ethnic sentiments and divisions within the university which students 'acknowledged and deplored'.[30] The closure of the university boarding system meant that 'students from the same school background and language group tended to find accommodations together'. As a result, 'at the end of the 1960s almost half the dormitory rooms were occupied by students on the basis of ethnic connections'.[31] This situation at once reflected and fostered the prominence of ethnic affiliation, and Afaan Oromo, Gurage and Tigrigna languages began to be spoken on and around the campus as well as Amharic.

Tension had been developing between the three major student language groups: Afaan Oromo, Amharic and Tigrigna. In one instance at the Laboratory School of the Faculty of Education in 1967 it resulted in a 'serious fight involving two groups of students [Tigrayan/Eritrean and Amhara, that] went on for several days, reportedly on a "tribal basis"'.[32] Oromo consciousness was rising around this time, in the wake of the banning of the Oromo Metcha-Tulama development organisation in 1966, and was fanned in the capital by the trial of its leaders in June 1968. On campus, 'radical Oromo groups were forming' and 'a Tigray students' association ... existed unofficially in the university'.[33]

The student union presidential elections in November 1968 triggered more public and bitter divisions among student leaders. Tigrayan 'radical' Tilahun Gizaw was defeated by Amhara 'moderate' or 'conservative' Mekonnen Bishaw after a sour and bad-tempered campaign. Hustings involved 'ethnic politicking', during which, the radical camp alleged, a whispering campaign had linked Tilahun with secessionist Eritrean nationalism.[34] The stakes were raised dramatically when, a month after his election as student union president the following year, Tilahun was assassinated. The violent precedent continued to reverberate half a century later, for many who witnessed it remained influential, as did the bitterness that divided them.[35]

Explicit discussion of the 'national question'

Walleligne Mekonen was an arts undergraduate from Amhara Sayint in Wollo. His paper 'On the Question of Nationalities in Ethiopia' reads decades later like a blueprint of the ideological position advocated by the TPLF–EPRDF. He contrasts the 'true picture' of Ethiopia he describes with the 'fake nationalism' of the ruling class, based on Amhara/Amhara–Tigray supremacy, which, since 'culture is nothing more than the super-structure of an economic basis', reflected the economic exploitation of the south by the Amhara/Amhara–Tigray imperial system. Neither the impoverishment of Amhara and Tigrayan peasants nor, he argued, the elevation of individual assimilated southerners to positions of influence did anything to undermine the facts of this situation, albeit the result of 'historical accident'.

Ethiopia is not really one nation. It is made up of a dozen nationalities, with their own languages, ways of dressing, history, social organisation and territorial entity. And what else is a nation? Is it not made of a people with a particular tongue, particular ways of dressing, particular history, particular social and economic organisations? Then may I conclude that in Ethiopia there is the Oromo Nation, the Tigrai Nation, the Amhara Nation, the Gurage Nation, the Sidama Nation, the Wellamo Nation, the Adere Nation, and however much you may not like it the Somali Nation.[36]

To change this, he says, 'we must build a genuine national state' in which 'all nationalities participate equally in state affairs, ... where every nationality is given equal opportunity to preserve and develop its language, its music, its history ... a state where no nation dominates another nation be it economically or culturally'.[37] This was to be done not by military coup, and not by armed movements such as those in Bale or Eritrea, since 'they do not attempt to make a broad-based assault on the foundations of the existing regime'. Most controversially of all (and of great relevance to the Ethiopian federal constitution adopted in 1995), Walleligne went on to say, that '[he did] not oppose these movements just because they are secessionists. There is nothing wrong with secessionism as such: as long as secession is led by the peasants and workers and believes in its internationalist obligation, it is not only to be supported but also militarily assisted.'[38]

In putting a distillation of radical student discussion of this issue on paper, Walleligne's article shattered taboos on the discussion of nationalities within the empire state, and brought about a profound shift in the frame of reference of the domestic student movement, which had, in public, essentially advocated Ethiopian unity. In positing an independent Bale, the paper undoubtedly sounded absurd or naive to many. Its power lay in forcing its readers to think the unthinkable: the issues raised by peripheral nationalists in Eritrea and the Ogaden were now brought straight to the heartland of the empire state. Walleligne's article also played a significant role in the transformation of student politics into the seedbed for the later series

49

of radical political organisations. The paper defined the purpose such an organisation might fight for and a possible organising principle: the equality and autonomy of nationalities. The paper is couched not so much in theoretical terms as in the practical political terms of 'what we must do' and 'how we must do it'. As such it marked a crucial turning point for the domestic student movement from activism to action.

Drivers of the 'national question'

The 'correct balance' between modernism and 'traditionalism'— how to combine 'Ethiopian values' with new and internationally informed ideologies and education—was much discussed by the student movement as it wrestled with questions of nationalism. This is an issue that came back into contemporary political debates in 2018, with the current prime minister's nationalist advocacy of a 'return' to 'indigenous Ethiopian values'. In the 1960s and 1970s activists worried about the ways education alienated students from their backgrounds. Many felt ambivalent about modernisation, bringing an attitude that was at once imitative and hostile, proud of Ethiopian identity and embarrassed by Ethiopia's 'backwardness' and poverty.[39]

Already in the 1960s the dissonance was acute: 'modern education imbues [the student] with admiration and longing for such secular values as enlightenment, progress, equality, efficiency, and prosperity which he finds manifestly lacking in his world. The realization that Ethiopia lags behind most other African countries in the drive for development comes as a painful shock.'[40] Students were concerned that 'the schools had failed to transmit *culture* and *heritage* and to imbue the student with an *identity*. Opposition was voiced to foreign educational advisers who were incapable of devising solutions to Ethiopian problems and seemed to have created a system designed to destroy Ethiopian culture.'[41] These are all anxieties that persist.

The so-called miniskirt riot of March 1968, where (male) students disrupted a campus fashion show they claimed exemplified 'cultural alienation, moral degradation, [and] western imperialism',[42] illustrated the tension. Frustration was regularly directed at the Ethiopian Orthodox Church, whether from a Marxist rejection of religion or from those who had joined the Haimanote Abew (Faith of Our Fathers) student association to denounce neo-colonialist influences and the failure of the official Church to engage with populations in the south. On the one hand, 'the fact that many activists felt Ethiopian identity was somehow connected to the tradition of the Orthodox Church means that this view had not yet become controversial'. On the other hand, 'the clandestine circulation of Oromo proverbs and songs shows that there were definite signs of a search for identity on the part of Ethiopia's subject peoples'.[43] The intertwining of the Orthodox Church with this debate about identity has continued to characterise present-day polemic about Ethiopianism.

From 1963, students spent a compulsory year of National University Service in rural areas. The university establishment saw the programme as a means of dispersing and minimising ethnic sentiment—a deliberate policy of sending students to areas other than their home regions was adopted.[44] In the event it backfired. The programme increased student knowledge of the situation of peasant farmers in different parts of the empire; and it helped them establish an effective network of links with the high school student body throughout the country. The radicalising impact on both groups soon became apparent, and from 1969 the programme was reduced.[45] Widespread disruption of schools in 1969 suggests the move came too late.

International ideology also had a huge impact. Although the University Service programme helped the student radicals to understand Ethiopian realities better, the movement was also 'swept off the ground ... by European ideologies and organizational models'[46] in 'an uncritical, hasty, and impetuous emulation of [ideological] currents then in vogue'.[47] 'Marxism was presumed to be an unchallengeable truth ... It generated a mass hysterical loyalty. Many did not read it ... they were obsessed by it'.[48]

The large Leninist corpus on the 'national question' formed an essential component of students' unofficial ideological 'curriculum'. Stalin's 1913 treatise on 'Marxism and the National Question' provided an approach designed to resolve the 'national question' within a multi-ethnic empire such as the Soviet Union. Lenin's writings, meanwhile, provided a broader theoretical approach to the questions of self-determination and nationalities in an era of imperialism, which found particular resonance in anti-colonial situations. Both strands were studied and argued over by student factions, and many of the divisions which emerged reflected disagreements about the process by which the Ethiopian empire state had been established. Central to Marxist-Leninist approaches was the commitment to the right of secession for 'appropriate units' in the context of socialist emancipation.[49]

The question for the Ethiopian student radicals was whether the empire state incorporated colonies or fully fledged nations, and, if so, whether those advocating their secession were 'socialist' forces deserving of support or negative forces to be opposed. Eritrean, Ogadeni Somali and (increasingly) Oromo nationalists favoured the categorisation of their secessionist claims as 'colonial questions', deserving, in Lenin's terms, rights of self-determination. Those with a stronger commitment to the authenticity of empire were drawn to the Stalinist preference, while accepting self-determination over 'national cultural autonomy'. For all its fire and vigour, Walleligne's seminal paper stopped unhelpfully far short of clarity on the immediate practical problem: whether the Eritrean Liberation Front (ELF) should receive support from the students.

Meanwhile, diaspora Ethiopians began to be intellectually influential, and the movement developed a distinctive external wing.[50] Diaspora students operated with greater freedom and stronger organisation outside the constraints imposed by the imperial regime. Controversial issues like the 'national question' were first discussed outside Ethiopia. The diaspora groups developed more coherent and sophisticated theoretical analyses than those at home and indulged the luxury of acrimonious in-fighting. Major divisions over the 'national question' were also played out in the international arena. Two months before the publication of Walleligne's paper, a congress in North America had debated a series of presentations by leaders who represented a generation of activists slightly older than the radicals in Addis Ababa.[51] The congress adopted resolutions that condemned regionalism and opposed separatism.[52]

Any chance that the differences could be bridged was abruptly terminated with the publication of a 'venomous' paper by 'Tilahun Takele' (a pseudonym).[53] A combination of abusive personal vitriol and insistence on 'one true' understanding of the 'national question' set the tone for future intransigence—and violence—between the heirs of the factions. The paper advocated the recognition of the Leninist right of self-determination, including secession, for nations and nationalities within Ethiopia. Tilahun Takele split the students, opened the door to support for the Eritrean nationalist movements, and 'chart[ed] an ideological trajectory whose full impact is being felt only today'.[54] Profound polarisation continues to resonate in contemporary politics, exemplified, for instance, by the strength of the current determination to do away with (or retain) the constitutional right of secession (the famous Article 39 of the 1995 federal constitution). The poison which seeped into Ethiopian political discourse, and the venom directed across the lines of this debate, re-emerged after 2018 to motivate and entrench the 2020 war in Tigray.

The Eritrean question

The final, and arguably most important, factor that influenced the student movement of the 1960s—which is also of great contemporary relevance—was the precedent set by self-determination (or 'traitorous secessionism', depending on one's point of view) in Eritrea. 'Struggle in Eritrea has given prominence to the manifold nationality problem in [Ethiopia] … Eventually, after a long and agonising consideration, the radicals came to accept the Eritrean movement on its own merits and, consequently, they explicitly upheld the unconditional right of self-determination for all nationalities in Ethiopia'.[55] In sum, the situation in Eritrea forced the issue.[56] The relationship between the Ethiopian student movement and the Eritrean nationalist movement, particularly in its second incarnation following the establishment of the EPLF in 1971, was a recursive one.

Following the emperor's annexation of Eritrea and annulment of the federal arrangement between 1959 and 1962, there were close links between the student bodies in both Addis Ababa and the diaspora and radicalisation in Eritrea. The rise of nationalist sentiment and expression in Eritrea tallied closely with the period of radicalisation of the Ethiopian student movement, with many Eritrean nationalist leaders being part of the Addis Ababa student body. A high point of radicalisation—the massive Addis Ababa demonstrations in 1965 calling for 'land to the tiller'—coincided with a three-day strike of secondary school students in Asmara demanding a referendum on the future of Eritrea and the return of its jurisdiction over social and economic institutions.[57]

Many of those who split from the ELF to form the EPLF in 1971, including Isaias Afwerki himself, had been members of the student movement in Ethiopia, where they acquired much of the radical perspective they brought to the younger organisation, and had been closely involved in Ethiopian politics.[58] The Eritrean question was an integral part and key catalyst of the discussion of the 'national question', but the emergence of the issue was not merely the result of manipulation by Eritrean nationalists. The fact that many EPLF nationalists emerged from the Addis Ababa student movement demonstrates the complex of mutual influences between the two. Tigrigna-speakers (both Eritrean and Tigrayan) had become prominent in all student factions.

In 1966, an international student union resolution of support for the ELF was something which Ethiopian students had to respond to. Most were strongly opposed to it, precipitating a resolution the following year affirming that Eritrea was an indivisible part of Ethiopia.[59] Ethiopian student opposition to Eritrean secessionism was sustained until 1968–9.[60] Meanwhile, most Eritrean students favoured secession, and conditional support grew.[61] The fact of an armed struggle in Eritrea forced the student movement to confront the practical implications of principled support for self-determination, and to consider concrete resolutions for or against support to the Eritrean nationalist leadership.

Ethiopian student support finally shifted when the nature of Eritrean nationalist leadership shifted: from the more conservative Muslim-dominated ELF, to the more radical, better-educated and more politically networked EPLF. Active Eritrean nationalism now set a clear precedent for leftist armed struggle against the imperial regime. When factions of students themselves later considered the future of their struggle, Eritrea provided an exemplar of the organisation of a liberation movement: a cradle for practical education, including military training, and a useful conduit to contacts and support in the internationalist movement.

As the imperial regime drew to a faltering close, 'a traditional ethnic hierarchy was promoting national integration through a process of assimilation utilizing traditional spiritual and ethnocentric criteria', infuriating educated radicals and promoting 'centrifugal forces'.[62] For the first time, famine in the north was politicised, as terrible pictures of starving peasants in Wollo and Tigray began to emerge, to the anger of new generations of students and their teachers.[63] All appointments and decision-making continued to centre upon the person of the emperor, so that with his removal in 1974, the only group with sufficient organisational capacity to replace his rule was the army.

The Derg: 'Ethiopia first'

The military finally ousted the ageing emperor in September 1974, ushering him unceremoniously into a small Volkswagen at the end of the period of the so-called creeping coup, and executing him soon after. His fate was sealed when, on the day he was deposed, excruciating scenes from British journalist Jonathan Dimbleby's film of the 1973 Wollo famine were screened on TV, intercut with lavish footage from an imperial wedding.[64] So abrupt and shocking was the disjuncture that it seemed '1974 was the year when Ethiopia was suddenly thrown into the modern world'.[65] The Provisional Military Administrative Committee, or Derg, constituted a group of 120 relatively young soldiers, ranging in rank from private to major.[66] 'Innocent of ideology and bereft of political programme',[67] they looked to the noisy urban influence of the students and intelligentsia, and rapidly adopted their radical Marxist rhetoric and revolutionary terminology.

In response, the various political organisations, which had split as they emerged from the student movement, divided again over whether to co-operate with the Derg. Me'ison (the All-Ethiopia

Socialist Movement) agreed that it would, and the larger Ethiopian People's Revolutionary Party (EPRP) opted to continue 'the struggle'. Accurately or not (and in the mid-1970s it was probably not), the division gradually came to be perceived in terms of ethnic categorisations: 'in the popular perception, Me'isone also came to be identified as a predominantly Oromo organisation, and EPRP as predominantly Amhara—perceptions that became self-fulfilling'.[68]

The immediate consequence of the new Marxist colouring of the military's approach was its move to nationalise the economy, including rural and urban land—a radical change already proclaimed and pretty much implemented by the end of 1975.[69] Nationalisation of land 'destroyed the economic foundation of the imperial system and ruled out a return to the *status quo ante*'. Cultivators were given usufruct rights over plots divided roughly equally between them. 'Those who benefited most were the people in *yeqign ager* [conquered land, the south] who were freed from the exactions and services due to alien landlords. Most of the latter ... congregated in the towns or returned to the region of their origin.'[70]

Accompanying and facilitating the implementation of land reform was the Derg's other dramatic (and enduring) innovation in local government, the introduction of the *kebele* (literally 'neighbourhood') system.[71] In 1976, *kebele* powers were extended to encompass the registration of houses and residents, births, death and marriages, local tax collection, and 'public safety'. The widespread implication of urban *kebeles* in the horrifying bloodshed of the Red Terror of the late 1970s earned them a feared notoriety,[72] the scars of which are still perceptible in local government relations. By the end of the 1970s, and now with Soviet advice,[73] the Derg established an elaborate hierarchy of government premised on 'democratic centralism'. The *kebele* system formed the outermost level of this centralised hierarchy, by means of which 'safeguarding the revolution' was bloodily implemented. The powerful commitment to national centralisation did not change with the introduction of the constitution of 1987, which institutionalised the single-party system of the Workers' Party of Ethiopia (WPE). The Derg retained the pre-existing imperial regional administration system, subdividing a number of provinces and shifting a number of boundaries. Regional first secretaries of the party had some degree of autonomy over local matters, including resettlement, but the goal of the regime remained the 'centrally commanded and organised state—which it [had] inherited and sought to extend'.[74]

Attitudes to 'nationalities'

The incoming military regime was quick to denounce the 'Abyssinian chauvinism' of its predecessors and proclaim the equality of all nationalities and cultures in Ethiopia. Given the presence of Teferi Banti, an Oromo, as second-in-command of the Derg up to his death in 1977, and of significant numbers of Oromo in the ranks of Me'ison and heading the land reform (particularly popular in Oromo areas), 'the regime was often regarded as an Oromo one' in its early years.[75] The Derg promised the abolition of traditional customs which 'hamper the unity and progress of Ethiopia' and removed the official status (and much of the property) of the Orthodox Church while recognising Islam. It tolerated an upsurge in the printing, broadcasting and teaching of languages other than Amharic,[76] and an enthusiasm for cultural diversity. At the political level, however, there was little room for manoeuvre. In 'the soldiers' perception "national contradictions" [were] limited to the realm of culture. The overthrow of the feudal regime, [they] claimed, had ended national and class oppression, and guaranteed the equality of all peoples and cultures in Ethiopia. Consequently, national contradictions no longer existed, only the legacy of cultural oppression remained'.[77]

The commitment of the new regime to the 'indivisibility of Ethiopian unity'[78] was never in question. The clearest demonstration of this came with the Derg's abrupt confrontation with the nationalist campaign in Eritrea. When the ELF and EPLF rejected the attempts of General Aman Andom to persuade them to give up their goal of independence and join the socialist revolution, the parties went swiftly back to war.[79] Given its socialist credentials, the Derg had to be seen to recognise rights of self-determination, and respect for them was duly enshrined in its 1976 Programme for the National Democratic Revolution.

Derg pronouncements were careful to refer only to nationalities, never to nations, so that potential rights of secession and independence were never in view. Derg policy-making and propaganda made much of the cultural emancipation of nationalities, while determinedly ignoring calls for corresponding political autonomy. Although in substance there was remarkably little change, the ideological basis of Derg policy on nationalities did mark a shift from that of Haile Selassie, in that the government appointed chief administrators who originated from the regions in question, in an unsuccessful attempt to assuage regional disaffection.[80] These appointees found themselves simply 'caught between the centralisation of the regime, and the intensification of local opposition'.[81]

As the centralising policy came under strain, in 1983 the Derg established an Institute for the Study of Ethiopian Nationalities (ISEN), on Soviet advice, to investigate the potential for a political structure along the lines of the Soviet model. To obtain a demographic baseline, the regime carried out a population census in 1984 that incorporated enquiries about mother tongue and religious affiliation. There were two shortcomings in the ISEN data. First it was incomplete, since it did not cover 'insecure areas' in Tigray, Eritrea and the Ogaden. Second, census-takers and researchers encountered confusion about the ethnonyms by which groups identified and classified themselves: some used names different from those used by outsiders or the government; others used clan or religious descriptions instead of ethnonyms.[82]

Nevertheless, the census provided a major source for ISEN's researchers who, taking language as the criterion of identity, produced a list of 89 ethnic groups. ISEN members supplemented the census data with a number of visits to study different parts of the country at first hand, and considered the available ethnographic and socio-linguistic data. Much effort was invested in the elaboration of possible constitutional arrangements based on Ethiopia's ethnic groups, but ISEN's researchers were under no illusions that ethnicity or the language criterion would guide the final arrangement: 'the latitude open to it was slight'.[83] On the contrary, it was the Derg chairman President Mengistu Haile Mariam's declared view that 'what is to be done, should be done from the viewpoint of unity'.[84] Conveniently, the results of research demonstrated that only 30 of Ethiopia's 580 weredas could be considered monolingual,[85] and language-cum-ethnicity was happily abandoned in favour of more acceptable criteria associated with economic development. Although the new constitution included provisions guaranteeing rights to cultural and linguistic expression, the government was simultaneously engaged in resettling and villagising rural populations, in what amounted to processes of ethnic integration.

Finally, in 1987, nominal autonomy was offered in a few cases. The military government was particularly interested in making concessions (to the Afar, Kunama and Beni Amer) that might undermine support to the EPLF by subdividing Eritrea. Most of the proposed 'autonomous areas' were those where conflict was by now most intense, and where (in practice) there was little prospect of much being implemented. The proposals, which provided 'only the most formal and symbolic expression of local self-government',[86] were too little and too late. They fell far short of stemming growing centrifugal momentum, particularly in Eritrea, Tigray and Oromia, and were greeted with scorn by the opposition movements. The Derg did not make use of the ISEN research it had commissioned, but after 1991 its successors did. Among these opposition successors, the TPLF, with its calls for the full autonomy of nationalities within a democratised Ethiopia, was emerging by this time as one of the most powerful.

The 'national question' in the north: The emergence of the TPLF and EPRDF

Tigrayan histories, identities, and ethnic or national sentiments were mobilised and shaped—both as resource and product—as the nationalist movement emerged in Tigray in the period up to 1991. Several of the older historical memories and resources have been explored in the previous chapter, and many of them created important political precedents. 'Yohannes IV's rise to power and the first and second Woyane rebellions were all empowered by the resilient belief that Tigray did not receive appropriate recognition as the cultural and political co-founder of Ethiopia. There were thus forceful reactions to exclusions from the center'.[87]

Chapter 1 has also pointed to the complex and ambivalent relationship between Tigray and Ethiopia (at once central and peripheral) as political entities evolved over many years. In the 1920s, Gebre Hewet Baykedagne wrote that 'Tigray is the foundation of Ethiopia' and added that 'it is Tigray, above all, which should most call for the longevity of the kingdom of Ethiopia'.[88] By the 1970s things looked rather different. An astute Eritrean observer commented that 'nostalgia nourishes self-esteem and compensates for what is no longer enjoyed. It suffused the collective memory in Tigray and was easily domesticated by the TPLF ... Treated as history-less by the absolutist Amhara state, Tigrayans reacted by summoning the past'.[89]

The origins and resources of Tigray's 'perennial disaffection'[90]

TPLF interlocutors interviewed in the late 1990s were adamant that strong feelings against the Ethiopian state, including anti-Amhara sentiment, were already widespread in Tigray during the imperial period, and that this was not restricted to the ruling or educated elite. Many of those interviewed singled out two historical factors.

> Firstly, Tigray, like other parts of the empire-state, was made part of the new Ethiopia by force, and this took place against the background of rivalry between different parts of Abyssinia. The second historical factor was the hatred and suspicion which had arisen between Tigrayans and Amharas, due to the repeated battles between different centres of power. This history had been repeated and inculcated by the ruling class, so that it spread hatred and suspicion even amongst the common people, feelings were not just restricted to the ruling class. However, these views were particularly strongly disseminated amongst the youth, students and intellectual classes. [They] cannot be dismissed as a minority issue in Tigray: they were widespread.[91]

Quite how far these beliefs in their political interpretation extended throughout Tigrayan society in the late 1970s is debated.[92] There is evidence of a range of ideas which, at least from the mid-twentieth century, seem to have contributed to a well-established Tigrayan sense of self and of the Amhara 'other'. '[Tigray] provincialism thrives on the conviction that it represents purity and continuity in Ethiopian culture', wrote one academic authority at the end of the imperial period.[93] Notions of continuity and purity focused on the proximity of Tigrigna to the liturgical language Ge'ez, and on the centrality of the Orthodox Church in Tigrayan life. Tigrayans (including members of the TPLF) reiterated the argument that it was the Christian Church and its doctrine and institutional apparatus that were the key links between ancient Axum and the modern state of Ethiopia, rather than the imperial throne.[94]

If continuity was provided by the Ethiopian Church, the site of that continuity (legendary fourth-century scene of Ezana's conversion and Frumentius's ministry) was Axum in the heart of Tigray.[95] The sense of competition between Tigray and Amhara was mirrored (and perhaps driven) by competition within the Church between the two important centres at Axum and the monastery at Debre Libanos in Shewa, established by Tekle Haimanot in the thirteenth century. Debre Libanos sprang back into prominence when the area was reincorporated with the southward expansion under Menelik II. Christian competition was closely bound up with the introduction of the mythology of the Solomonic dynasty (see Chapter 1), which 'also marked the beginning of a competition for dominance between Amhara and Tigrayan elites'.[96]

> Menilek tried metaphorically to move Aksum to Shäwa. He planned a magnificent new church, the center of a new capital, at a place he called Addis Alam, 'new world' ... He richly endowed the church, called it [like the church in Axum] St Mary of Zion, and gave its head a title, neburä'ed, hitherto the monopoly of the head of the Aksum church.[97]

These developments came at a time when Tigrayan politics were reasonably cohesive, and its elites could be expected to resent and resist them. The reign of Yohannes IV was significant partly because he had

> unified all the local dynastic houses and his reign witnessed an expansion of the Tigray political elite. To that extent, it can be said that Yohannes forged Tigray into a protonation ... [However,] this protonation expressed itself in historical-political rather than ethnic terms. The focal points were Aksum and Ethiopia rather than the Amhara and the Tigray. The linguistic division

between these two groups was still irrelevant, in contrast to some arcane doctrinal differences between them which proved politically contentious.[98]

Meanwhile, according to Walter Plowden's much-quoted observation of 1848, 'Teegray is now almost universally acquainted with the Amharic language, and their customs, food and dress have become so assimilated to those of the Amharas as not to require separate description, though their hatred of that people is undiminished'.[99]

The events that followed Yohannes IV's death and defeat at Metemma are discussed in the previous chapter. After the Battle of Adwa, the loss of Eritrea, and the severe famine of the 1890s, 'Tigray found itself politically orphaned, militarily battered, economically shattered and psychologically disoriented'. It was during the period between 1889 and 1935 that 'ethnicity appeared on the political scene in Tigray, along with dynastic claims and individual political ambitions'.[100] This was also a period during which there was little change in Tigray, and when the stagnation and underdevelopment, much resented by later generations of nationalists, took root. 'During modern times, socio-political changes were much slower in Tigre than in other regions in Ethiopia'.[101] By the time Haile Selassie was well established, only Tigray was ruled by hereditary leaders, and there were many of them.[102] Tigrayans were more divided than populations in other parts of the country, as a result of the longer history, better establishment and greater segmentation of the elites in question.[103] Fragmentation provided numerous opportunities for collaboration, primarily with the Italians across the Mereb, which, Haggai Erlich stresses, 'did not stem from a separatist instinct or a modern sense of Tigrean nationalism'. Rather, 'the ultimate goal of the Tigrean chiefs co-operating with the foreigners was to eliminate local rivals in order to be recognized as Tigre's negus by Ethiopia's emperors. The Shoans for their part, unable to force an Ethiopian centralist government on Tigre, chose to promote local jealousies and rivalries, thus helping to preserve the status quo'.[104]

A precedent rediscovered: The first 'weyane'

In 1943 the British air force helped Haile Selassie's government to put down the so-called *weyane* or rebellion. This had brought together the 'divergent interests' of agro-pastoralists of the lowlands, highland cultivators, and a 'sectarian nobility' against the government in eastern and southern Tigray.[105] The rebellion developed in three phases, spreading from Raya and Wajirat in May, to capture the provincial capital, Mekele, in September, before defeat and collapse in October 1943.[106] The 'ideology of protest drew upon a combination of ideas and symbols: ethnic pride and particularism, memories of a "golden past", the symbols of Tigrean royalty and the greatness of Yohannes IV, xenophobia, and religious conservatism'.[107] As a result 'there is no doubt that [the *weyane*] tapped a deep source of discontent. It stemmed from peasant dissatisfaction—it was primarily a peasant revolt—coupled with overtones of Tigrean desire to be independent of Shoa'.[108]

The 1943 *weyane* has acquired a retrospective status arguably in excess of the significance of the events at the time. Even at the time, it was the suppression of the revolt, rather than the uprising itself, that had a lasting impact as 'a main watershed in Tigre's history. Following this, the emperor finally managed to demilitarise Tigre and thus deprive the leading families of the province of their source of independent power'.[109] More than thirty-five years after the event, the revolt itself regained prominence when the youthful leaders of the TPLF explicitly reinvented it as a popular nationalist precedent, and widely recognisable indigenous advertisement, for the movement's own struggle. Four years after its foundation, at its first congress in 1979 the TPLF changed its name in Tigrigna from the original *tegadelo harnet hezbi Tigrai* ('Tigray people's liberation struggle', adapted from the ELF's *tegadelo harnet Ertra*) to *hezbawi weyane harnet Tigrai* ('Popular revolution/rebellion for the liberation of Tigray'). As one of those present put it, 'we wanted to take something from our own history'.[110]

The reincarnation of the *weyane* as a precedent for revolutionary nationalist struggle involved a measure of creative thinking.[111] The original *weyane* did not show evidence of a widespread 'class consciousness' and lacked a coherent set of goals; the 'diversity of interests compromised ideological clarity', and what resulted was a rebellion rather than a revolution. It was unclear that its 'leaders were committed to the peasant cause [being] primarily interested not in destroying or even in reforming the *status quo* but in finding a comfortable place within it'.[112] Secondly, the *weyane* was not Tigray-wide. 'The aggrieved parties united, temporarily, around a sense of "provincialism". Yet the notion of provincialism cannot be stretched too far ... Only Enderta, Kilte Awlaalo, Tembien, and Maichew were fully involved. [Others] remained on the fence until the outcome of the conflict was known'.[113]

Despite its various *historical* shortcomings as a prototype for the revolutionary ethno-nationalist project with which it has come to be associated, in the late 1970s the original *weyane* offered precisely the kind of minimal but broadly familiar framework suited to re-envisioning in TPLF hands. Memories concentrated half-a-dozen features useful to later mythologising. First, the first *weyane* involved a 'fairly high level of spontaneity and peasant initiative';[114] it demonstrated popular participation and reflected widely shared grievances. Secondly, the uprising was unequivocally and specifically directed against the central Amhara regime of Haile Selassie I rather than the Tigrayan imperial elite. It therefore 'manipulated traditional symbols of identity and ethnic homogeneity'.[115] This point seems to have been of particular importance.

> The areas which were actively involved were [not the whole of Tigray] and this is perhaps why it is dismissed as not being a nationalist issue. However, it was a popular movement [and] called for justice, self-administration, lower taxation and the expulsion of corrupt officials [and] blamed the central Amhara government for these problems ... It was national in character because it was specifically aimed at the central government and its apparatus in Tigray.[116]

Thirdly, the involvement of British bombers in subduing the *weyane* in 1943 cemented the popularly perceived alignment of external 'foreign' aggressors against Tigray, which became relevant in the late 1970s when the Derg government won Soviet support.[117] Fourth, the *weyane* briefly controlled the Tigrayan provincial capital, Mekele; this was an important precedent the TPLF sought to emulate in the 1980s. In a fifth parallel, an immediate trigger of the rebellion in 1943, the brutality of imperial militia particularly around Quiha, resonated strongly as the Red Terror spread to the same area in the late 1970s and 1980s. Finally, although the *weyane* had happened within the living memory of older members of the community at the time when the TPLF began to talk about and draw parallels with it at the end of the 1970s, it had been concentrated in a relatively small geographical area, with the consequence that many remembered it happening rather than remembered experiencing it. *Weyane* was a highly recognisable and popular but malleable cipher, eminently suited to bear whatever conventional meaning later interaction and propaganda would invest it with. In the late 1970s, the invocation of the *weyane* of nearly forty years previously 'did not contradict the remembered landscape. And herein lies the potency of history as political ammunition'.[118]

Triggers for nationalist organisation: Well-told tales

History and symbolism may have shaped the form of the TPLF's 'second *weyane*', but many other more concrete factors and drivers were also at work.[119] 'During the later period of Haile Selassie the region faced open discrimination in terms of education, allocation of employment opportunities, etc., and these measures offended the emerging intellectual class. Gradually the sense of discrimination touched every sector of society and was thus becoming a national issue'.[120]

A series of individually minor incidents triggered emerging nationalist sentiment, in the few years before the establishment of the TPLF. In 1969 the meteoric career of the Tigrayan football team was eclipsed when it was promoted to the premier league, where it was no longer victorious. In 1973 it was returned to the second division, but in October (angering many) the team was controversially disqualified after protesting against a derogatory spelling of the name 'Tigray' as 'Tigre' (widely seen as a veiled slight).[121] In 1969–70 a folk troupe toured the region. 'Folk poems and music were collected and shown on stages all over Tigray ... Many wept ... Cultural revival created fertile ground for the upcoming war of liberation. Indeed *Bahli Tigrai* [the troupe] was designed as a vehicle for political ends'.[122] Thirdly, a funeral cortège returning the body of a Tigrayan teacher to Mekele became a 'major show of Tigrayan feeling'.[123] The person of 'Sehul', an early member of the TPLF who had organised the repatriation of the corpse, emerged as a key convenor and instigator of nationalist sentiment during this period.[124] Older than those in student circles, as a delegate to the imperial parliament from western Tigray he enjoyed increasing status among the radicals, particularly as his exploits began to challenge the more conservative nationalist activities of *Ras* Mengesha Seyoum and his Tigray Development Organisation.[125]

A series of radicalising experiences were also common to those emerging from high school into university over the period—the cohort which went on to form and lead the TPLF. By 1973 the collaborative efforts of school and university students had closed high schools in Tigray for two months; in 1974 they remained shut all year. Meanwhile, Addis Ababa University had a Tigrayan student association, dedicated to the study of the problems of the people of Tigray, and the need to regenerate its economy, culture and language. Increasingly, the relegation of the Tigrigna language in favour of Amharic became a focus of frustration, with bitterness developing over the common jibe that labelled Tigrigna pejoratively as 'a language of birds'.

The eventual formation of the TPLF in February 1975 was a function of the juxtaposition of the aspirations and experiences of educated Tigrayans as high school and university students, with their awareness of life in an impoverished, underdeveloped and stagnant Tigray—problems increasingly perceived as the result of a deliberate and ethnically motivated government policy of discrimination against the northern region. If these experiences generated a non-specific disgruntlement, what marked a much more specific boundary was the requirement in Haile Selassie I's modernising and centralising empire state to speak and write the language of the imperial regime, Amharic. Language had come to mark a boundary to an extent that shaped their decisions, as the student radicals moved to armed activities.

There was a discussion about what form of struggle: armed, yes, but organised how? If people come from the same nationality, then even radicals and non-radicals can talk to each other with confidence, where radicals of different nationalities might not. Armed struggle was going to be a serious matter. If secrets were to be kept from betrayal, then this dynamic would be most important.[126]

There were important political and historical fault lines among Tigrayans, which nationalism had to overcome. The early period of TPLF history was marked by competition with three other organisations: the conservative Tigrayan nationalist EDU of *Ras* Mengesha Seyoum and others of the imperial elite; the Tigray Liberation Front (TLF), a radical proponent of 'greater' Tigray–Tigrigne nationalism (see Chapter 3), wiped out early on in a reportedly bloody purge; and, most importantly, the EPRP, the Tigrayan-led pan-Ethiopianist movement which had emerged from the student movement. EPRP had established bases in north-eastern Tigray and suggested the TPLF form military units under its political leadership—an overture the TPLF (itself also a committed Marxist organisation) rejected. The competitive challenges of each of these three organisations had been effectively pushed outside Tigray by the end of the 1970s,[127] leaving the TPLF with a strong sense of the urgent practical imperative of uniting Tigrayans around the nationalist project.

One of the early periods of division within the organisation during its first years, the *hanfishfish*, or confusion, is often cited as evidence of the struggle to establish a pan-Tigrayan identity, above and to the exclusion of localist attachments or *awrajawinet* ('districtism'). Disquiet at the existence of an east–west division within TPLF, and its domination by cadres from the western Axum–Adwa–Shire axis (to the disadvantage of Tembien, Enderta, and Kilte Awlaalo), proved a resilient—if usually quiescent—thread over several decades of official insistence on Tigrayan unity. The notion of an undercutting east–west political division in Tigray was also one of the legacies of the invocation of the first *weyane*.

Mobilising and manufacturing ethno-nationalism and the ethnic nation

Memories, motifs and themes were now woven into the fabric of the Tigrayan 'imagined community', and a wide range of techniques of teaching and dissemination was employed by the TPLF to render this imagining a broadly collective one.[128] A competition to design an emblem for the new Front selected one incorporating the ancient obelisks at Axum. For TPLF leaders who cut their teeth on student movement debates, 'nationality was the primary contradiction in the sense of being in the forefront of people's minds in Tigray … It is in people's minds and you have to focus on it … It was easily felt as a slogan amongst ordinary people, much more than the class issue'.[129] Tigrigna-language poetry and song, and the cadres, cultural troupes, radio broadcasts and cassettes that spread the slogans, were central.

The TPLF evolved highly sophisticated mobilisation mechanisms, based around a core network of *kifle hezbi*, or lead cadres.[130] These relatively senior political cadres were resident over extended periods within particular communities, to learn from, mobilise and teach populations with whom they had lengthy interaction and got to know well. The priority accorded to continuity of contact with rural populations was a key means by which the Front learned about rural life. Initiatives couched in the language, proverbs and histories of the people were effective, and long immersion in rural culture equipped TPLF propagandists to recognise this conventional knowledge. 'In 1974 I came to realise my national identity through the songs. They stirred emotions in me'.[131]

The nationalist movement made a significant investment in Tigrigna language and curriculum development. Tigrigna had been used as a literary language for the publication of newspapers, books and articles, so this undertaking was one of reclaiming and re-establishing a heritage widely felt to have been undermined by the imperial and Derg regimes. The fight against poverty provided another strand of nationalist rhetoric, which stressed the responsibility of successive Amhara governments in impoverishing Tigray. Towards the end of the Derg, government rhetoric about Tigray chimed with these arguments, referring to the impoverished province contemptuously as a 'liability', having 'nothing but stones'.[132] Nothing deterred, the nationalists celebrated Tigray's famously stony ground with massive programmes of terracing that transformed the look of farming hillsides in an attempt to improve their productivity.

Surviving famine, encirclement and neglect in the 1980s

The brutal military and socio-economic strategies of the Derg as the war dragged on into the 1980s did even more to turn the population in Tigray (and indeed in Eritrea) towards support for the nationalist cause. 'One consequence of the government's military policies, particularly during the 1980s, was the creation of famine'.[133] Estimates for those who died across northern Ethiopia range between 300,000 and 1.2 million, with most credible estimates for famine deaths being in the region of 400,000.[134] In Tigray, 'the government preferred to withhold aid from the province, thus starving the people'.[135] A particularly brutal 1985 military offensive was aimed at disrupting aid supplies to Tigray across the border from Sudan, and 'relief convoys, feeding centers and refugees were all attacked from the air'.

In an ominous prefiguring of recent events, described in Chapters 9 and 10, 'the government's counter-insurgency methods tore at the very sinews which kept the rural economy together, turning a period of hardship into one of outright famine'.[136] Much has been written about the slowness of international responses, slowness which continued long after the story of the famine finally broke in the international media in October 1984.[137] In a famous British parliamentary exchange a month later, the head of the Save the Children Fund confirmed that the organisation had reported to the British government about the famine, 'which in our reckoning started two years ago'. When asked about the British official response, he replied (in a response censored in the Hansard record), 'They did fuck all, sir'.[138]

The overwhelming majority of emergency support was delivered through government channels, and when Tigrayan farmers trekked to emergency food distribution centres in government-held towns, they risked being taken forcibly for resettlement in other parts of the country. 'One settler likened them to rat-traps with relief food acting as bait.'[139] The Derg government's answer to drought was a massive programme of resettlement out of the highlands, which between 1984 and 1986 moved just under 600,000 people from Shewa, Wollo and Tigray.[140] In Tigray the programme was widely seen as part of its counterinsurgency strategy of 'draining the sea to catch the fish'—the Maoist phrase attributed to Ethiopian president Mengistu Haile Mariam by none other than his relief and rehabilitation commissioner.[141] As Peter Gill notes,

> the Derg did not always make much of an effort to deny the purpose of its tactics against the rebels ... When US Chargé d'affaires, David Korn, called on the acting foreign minister, Tibebu Bekele, in December 1984, he was told 'probably with more candour than he intended that "food is a major element in our strategy against the secessionists."'[142]

Amidst such suffering as the civil war in the north ground on, Tigray nationalism (like Eritrean nationalism) evolved in opposition to the Addis Ababa narrative of the centralised unified polity, under the slogan *Etyopia tikdem* (Ethiopia first), which did so much to 'other' these Tigrigna-speaking opponents.

If the brutality of the Derg did plenty of mobilisation work for them, the TPLF kept a determined focus on the 'mass popular base' that was to underpin national struggle.[143] Central to the securing of that base was an early understanding that 'men do not in general become nationalists through sentiment or sentimentality, atavistic or not, well-based or myth founded',[144] and that national sentiment alone would not nourish the attempt to remove the Derg. From an early stage, nationalist rhetoric was underpinned by the commitment to deliver socio-economic advantage to an overwhelmingly rural peasant population. After the dislocation of the mid-1980s famine, which saw a predicted 300,000 Tigrayans trek to become refugees in Sudan between 1984 and 1985, later in the decade a strong cross-border relief pipeline into the region from eastern Sudan was set up to protect and support their return.[145] The terminology used in songs and poems to describe these benefits had emotive collective overtones. Terms like *shewit*, meaning a new green ear of grain, were used interchangeably of the vehicles bringing relief grain from the Sudan and of the youthful fighters, the new green shoots of a people.[146]

From 'narrow nationalism' to fraternal ethnicities-in-arms?

From around 1980, the TPLF actively cooperated with the Ethiopian People's Democratic Movement (EPDM), a multi-ethnic grouping with which it later established the EPRDF.[147] EPDM had been established by the so-called Belessa group which split from the EPRP around 1978, and left Gonder and Gojjam to work with the TPLF in Tigray. There it grew steadily into a multinational ally of the Tigrayan Front. Their collaboration saw an increasing formalisation of Marxist-Leninist organisational structures, with both organisations establishing embryonic Marxist-Leninist structures from 1983 and full Marxist-Leninist Leagues from mid-1985.[148] It also saw a shift in the TPLF approach to the mobilisation of Tigrayan nationalism.

Having actively fostered Tigrayan nationalist sentiment in its mobilisation strategy, the TPLF in the late 1980s reversed the thrust of its propaganda in a bid to convince the population of Tigray to endorse an extension of the armed struggle to other parts of Ethiopia. It had to persuade its people to take the struggle beyond Tigray, to Addis Ababa. The TPLF encountered difficulties in explaining to its farming constituencies its new role as a founder member of the EPRDF, now stressing its dual commitment to Tigray and to Ethiopia. Little is documented about the period when the TPLF tried to persuade its fighters and their families in the peasantry to move beyond the borders of Tigray, but it is known to have been fraught.

> A[n] immediate obstacle to the EPRDF's advance was caused by TPLF fighters, and Tigrayans generally, questioning the need to carry the war south into Oromo and the Amhara populated lands. Fighters in Gondar and Wollo reportedly 'thought they were at the end of the world' … Some 10,000 fighters virtually spontaneously withdrew and returned to Tigray. One TPLF cadre attributed this problem to the Front's emphasis on the national problem and the legacy of feudalism which fostered parochialism.[149]

Two factors helped the TPLF leadership overcome popular opposition to an Ethiopia-wide campaign, over the course of two years of debates across Tigray. One was the continuation of the Derg's aerial bombardment of Tigray. Although the battle for Shire Enda Selassie, concluded in early February 1989, was certainly a 'turning point',[150] marking the end of Derg forces on the ground in Tigray, it did not prevent aerial attack from bases to the south. Secondly, the Tigrayan clergy 'argued forcefully that Tigrayans were part of the Ethiopian Orthodox Church and they should not be separated from it'.[151] The discussions which took place in Tigray during 1988 and 1989 were protracted and laced with ethnic imagery.

> No, we should free Tigray and think of ourselves, our future, the development of our land and lives: isn't that what you have taught us to value, to struggle for? How can we send our children to fight in those other areas—let alone for the Amhara: isn't it their oppression of us we have been fighting? Remember what our Tigrayan king [Emperor Yohannes IV] did when Tekle Giorgis [Waagshum Gobezie] sent him a bowl of teff as a peace offering! He burned it and sent it back. That is what we must do now if the Amharas ask us for help![152]

National sentiment, which had been actively encouraged for more than a decade in most of rural Tigray, now in the late 1980s proved complex to reverse. Many months were spent in securing popular acceptance of the strategy of moving south into other parts of Ethiopia; political work between 1988 and early 1991 was intensive. But when the military move south came, it was relatively rapid, with fighting moving from Dessie to Addis Ababa in a matter of weeks. When EPRDF fighters entered Addis Ababa in May 1991, they did so formally under the joint military command of the four organisations which then constituted the front: the TPLF, the EPDM, the Oromo People's Democratic Organisation (OPDO)[153] and the Ethiopian Democratic Officers' Revolutionary Movement (EDORM).[154] The EPRDF had been established in 1989 by the TPLF and the EPDM. The 1989 agreement formalised an eight-year *de facto* alliance between the two movements.[155]

By 1991, the ambition of Tigray nationalism was relatively comfortably couched within the context of a reformed Ethiopia. The unifying impetus of the Orthodox Church was key: it had persisted in the face of polarisation and politicisation. This is worth reflecting on in the context of the 2020 war, which has sharpened the interest of a new generation (including the Church in Tigray) to look for a more fundamental political autonomy—including full separation—from Ethiopia. In the 1990s, meanwhile, 'the invention of history and the selective summoning of the past had limited impact in remapping popular consciousness ... Peace was what [Tigrayan civilians] yearned for, not political independence, flag, national anthem, etc.'[156]

The last part of this chapter has examined processes of collective social construction of a common understanding of Tigray and Tigrayan interests, to make sense of the political project the TPLF represented when it came to power in 1991. The mobilisation and formation of Tigrayan identity, including political identity, during the 1970s and 1980s were vigorous, cohesive and built on foundations buried in long historical memory. It is precisely their collective mobilisation and daily construction or reinvention which render ethno-nationalist projects real, effective—and of great sociological and political import. Like all social identities, nations operate not directly because of the truth or validity of the resources on which they draw, but because of the vitality of the shared view about that validity. This is a continuously contested and evolving story, and Tigray's relationships with Ethiopia (and with Eritrea) evolved again after 1991, as the battle-hardened TPLF and EPRDF leaders now established a new federal dispensation.

PART TWO

LIVING MEMORY

3

REWORKING THE EMPIRE
FEDERALISM AND SELF-DETERMINATION, 1991–2012

Sarah Vaughan

In the early hours of 21 May 1991, the head of the Derg, Lt Colonel Mengistu Haile Mariam, took off from Addis Ababa with his normal security entourage to visit a military camp in the south-west of the country. En route, the light plane was diverted to Nairobi, from where he went into exile in Zimbabwe, bringing 17 years of military Marxist rule to a close. Within days Derg officials had left for London for US-brokered talks with the EPRDF, with their Eritrean counterparts (the EPLF), and with the Oromo Liberation Front (OLF). The talks were scheduled for 27 May. By then the movements' forces had captured the Eritrean capital, Asmara, and stood encircling Addis Ababa's airports. No conference took place. Instead, on 28 May 1991 EPRDF troops and tanks rolled virtually unopposed into the city, with the support of several Eritrean armoured and artillery units—up from the plains in the south and west, and down the twin tracks over Mount Entoto from the north, converging on the old palace of Menelik, where they met some limited resistance.

Six weeks later, observed by envoys from 15 countries and a range of international bodies, representatives of 27 Ethiopian political organisations and groupings gathered at the Organisation of African

Unity's iconic Africa Hall. The July 1991 Charter conference, which Eritrea's new leaders agreed to attend only as observers, resigned itself to the *de facto* separation of Eritrea. It then agreed upon a 'Transitional Charter': a compact for government, which, given the *de facto* separation of Eritrea, they hoped would guide the remainder of Ethiopia through three major sets of dramatic transformations over the forthcoming period.[1] Their aspirations were for democratisation of politics, under a multi-party electoral system; for liberalisation of the economy, in a neo-liberal international climate; and for decentralisation of the state, with the introduction of a system of 'ethnic' or multinational federalism. Democratisation, socio-economic advancement and federal decentralisation were all seen as mechanisms for the resolution of conflict and removal of its deeply rooted causes.

The motivation for a new and apparently more liberal approach to Ethiopia's political and economic transformation seemed clear. Given Ethiopia's catastrophic recent past, all were aware of the one-party state as the spectre at the feast. Ethiopia's economy had flatlined under a regime that had nationalised the means of production (land, housing, farming and industry) and sacrificed growth to war. In view of the early 1990s climate of political conditionality on aid, the demise of the Soviet donor bloc, and the parlous state of incomes in the wake of the Derg, some form of liberalisation—economic opening and political competition—was apparently the only option for consideration. In the event, the form of government approved by the conference calmed the fears of the international community. All were conscious that its approval and support were requisites according to which the new government might stand or fall. The question then remained not so much why a strategy that on the face of it *looked* liberal democratic was adopted, but quite how it would be implemented in practice.

This chapter examines the first half of the EPRDF period, from 1991 up to 2012, when the remarkably astute and dominant EPRDF–TPLF chairperson and head of government, prime minister Meles Zenawi, a Tigrayan, died unexpectedly. By 2012, just over two decades after the federal period began, much had changed. Ethiopia's economy was by then booming and (some) sections of it had been opened up. Federalism and district-level decentralisation under nine new regional states had had a profound impact on the architecture of the state and the services it provided, particularly to the poor and to many in the rural majority; and the country had taken exemplary strides to reach Millennium Development Goals. Four rounds of federal, regional and local elections had shaped the trajectory of the country's politics—but in ways which were often highly problematic.

The continuities were strong. The state continued to dominate, even monopolise, strategic sectors of an economy in which many in the private sector felt marginalised. Political control of the levers of the economy remained strong. The promise of radical devolution offered by the federal constitution (at least on paper) still seemed a long way off. Most important of all, EPRDF had continued to administer the overwhelming majority of the population in the four large central regions throughout the period, and its allies or affiliates governed in the peripheries almost as consistently. A succession of challenges from opponents had done nothing to dent this arrangement. In practice, social, political and economic development continued to be planned from on high, by a single ruling political coalition.

This is not what liberal democratic observers in 1991 expected or hoped for. Over the second decade of its rule from 2001, the EPRDF under prime minister Meles evolved an alternative, explicitly non-liberal narrative to conceptualise its single dominant party approach. Under the paradigm of the Ethiopian 'developmental state' processes of economic liberalisation, decentralisation and even democratisation began to be presented by the government not just as centrally managed, but as desirably so. For members of the ruling party, EPRDF's 'vanguard leadership' of this state-driven process was essential to achieving socio-economic growth that was broadly inclusive, sustainable, and not open to capture by wealthy elites or 'rent-seekers'. For its critics, this arrangement preserved intact the fundamental problem of twenty years previously: the extreme concentration of state power in the hands of a leadership the legitimacy of whose rule they questioned. This chapter explores these contradictions.[2]

The chapter is organised in three sections covering the 1990s, the Ethio-Eritrean war of 1998–2000, and the post-war period. Each also looks at the emergence of one of three categories of vehement opponents of the ruling EPRDF–TPLF and of the type of federalism it ushered in during this period. These three sets of antagonists returned to the Ethiopian domestic political scene, being invited back after 2018; and each was centrally involved in following, even planning, the path to the 2020 war. In this chapter, a first section looks at the design and implementation of the new federal arrangement, and the anger and resistance that EPRDF's approach drew from ethno-nationalist competitors, who were gradually squeezed out of the political arena. The second section looks at the relationship with the Eritrean government of President Isaias Afwerki, with which the Ethiopian government under EPRDF was again at war from 1998 to 2000. Finally, the chapter looks at political evolution from 2001 to 2012 when state structures were re-centralised, and the ruling party faced a new level of challenge at the ballot box in May 2005, especially (but not only) from a resurgent pan-Ethiopian nationalist opposition political bloc. After the crisis, the ruling party responded with an intensive process of reconstruction as a mass-based political party, which by 2012 was closely fused with the structures of government at each level of the federation. Opposition seemed quiescent, but resentments, particularly towards the TPLF, continued to fester.

Many of the political opponents of the EPRDF were unhappy with the way federalism was implemented in practice and gradually withdrew from the transitional government in the mid-1990s. However, the Eritrean regime and the pan-Ethiopianist nationalists shared profound reservations *in principle* about the form of federalism EPRDF introduced in 1991. In both cases their opposition, meeting with strong intransigence, degenerated during the period discussed in this chapter into violent confrontation: war with Eritrea between 1998 and 2000; and the bloody fallout in June and November 2005 from the vigorously contested elections in May of that year.

The 2005 elections resulted in the jailing and prosecution of opposition political leaders of the Coalition for Unity and Democracy (CUD), before key groups moved into armed insurgency later in the decade. Both the Eritrean government leaders and the Ethiopian nationalists (members successively of the Derg-era EPRP, the 2004–5 period CUD [or Kinijit], and the contemporary Movement of Ethiopians for Social Justice [Ezema]) have their roots in the period of student politics discussed in the previous chapter. By the end of the period discussed here, and the death of Meles in 2012, they had joined forces in an evolving attempt to bring down the EPRDF–TPLF and its federal project. Beginning with the federal project and ending with the tightly controlled constellation of power under EPRDF, the chapter discusses the two critical factors to which these two opponent forces took strong exception. This fundamental schism persisted at the heart of Ethiopia's politics and had a key role in motivating the outbreak of war in Tigray in November 2020.

Building the federation: Power decentralised?

If reformist proposals to democratise politics and liberalise the economy provoked relatively little disagreement in 1991, the third thread of reform, radical federal reconstruction of the state, was controversial from the outset. Recognising the separation of Eritrea, federal reform then involved redrawing administrative and political boundaries to carve up the rump empire state into a series of federated units. Each was drawn up along the lines of the major language—or ethnic—groups constitutionally referred to in Ethiopia as 'nations, nationalities and peoples'.[3] As discussed in Chapter 1, modern Ethiopia since its nineteenth-century expansion encompassed more than 70 recognised language groups of vastly different population sizes, with heterogeneity being particularly strong in the south-west of the country. The 1991 Charter ascribed broad rights of 'self-determination' to all these groups: to preserve, promote, use and develop their own culture, history and language; to administer their own affairs in their own territory, and participate equitably in central government; and to secede from the arrangement if they felt their rights had been denied or abrogated.

Federal principles of self-determination underpinned both a transitional period of government (1991–5), and the establishment of the Federal Democratic Republic (FDRE) under the new constitution in 1995. The FDRE constitution formalised the division of the country into nine federated National Regional States (or *kilil*), 'delimited on the basis of settlement patterns, identity, language and the consent of the people concerned' (Articles 46 and 47). The groups in question were those 'who have or share a large measure of a common culture, or similar customs, mutual intelligibility of language, belief in a common or related identities, and who predominantly inhabit an identifiable contiguous territory' (Article 39). It is noteworthy that history was not mentioned in either article.

Ethiopia's new federated regional states (Afar, Amhara, Benishangul-Gumuz, Gambella, Harar, Oromia, Somali, the Southern Nations, Nationalities and Peoples' Regional State (SNNPRS) and Tigray)[4] were asymmetrical on every social indicator, with vast differences in population size, demographic distribution and profile, and levels of development and resources. The Southern regional state (five separate *kilils* in the initial 1992 configuration) constituted a kind of 'federation within a federation', made up of a series of ethnic administrative units encompassing 56 recognised groups.[5] Gambella, Benishangul-Gumuz and Harar also retained administrative mechanisms to accommodate ethnic diversity at the subregional level.[6] Two large municipalities (the federal capital, Addis Ababa, and Dire Dawa in eastern Ethiopia) remained separately administered under the federal government.

Vehement—and ethnicised—opposition

While the government pressed ahead with its federal plans, the arguments were fierce. The EPRDF architects of the new arrangement and their allies saw federalism as a means of conflict resolution, a new departure designed to bring an end to the country's impoverishment after decades of civil war; and it was taken up by many in the international community unwilling to contemplate the collapse of a lynchpin state in the Horn.[7]

> From a purely legal point of view, what we were trying to do was to stop the war and start the process of peaceful competition ... The key cause of the war all over the country was the issue of nationalities. Any solution that did not address them did not address the issue of peace and war ... People were fighting for

the right to use their language, to use their culture, to administer themselves. So without guaranteeing these rights it was not possible to stop the war, or prevent another one ... People were already expressing themselves even at that early stage before the conference in terms of nationalities: that is manifested in the way they organised themselves.[8]

The new government's most powerful critics—then and since—claimed that it was creating a problem where there had been none—that it was 'ethnicising' Ethiopian politics where previously this had not been an issue. This has been a resilient claim. The government, pointing to the nature of opposition against the Derg as evidence of the vehement sense of ethnic oppression in many parts of the country, counter-claimed that the only way of 'lancing the pain' was to address its roots directly, and meet demands for local emancipation by means of a robust form of self-determination. Whatever the merits of ethnic federalism, there is little doubt that ethnicity had by 1991 long become a significant factor in shaping many (if not most) of the various power struggles waged by armed movements in different parts of Ethiopia, and that it was understood as such, at least by their active and elite participants.

Chapters 1 and 2 have already indicated the depth of division about the interpretation of Ethiopia's ancient and modern histories, and about whether this kind of ethnic or 'nationality-based' mobilisation was a reasonable or just response to it. A howl of protest now greeted the introduction of federalism from those keen to pursue the unity and centralisation of Ethiopia—albeit one muted domestically by the comprehensive military victory over the Derg that the Tigrayans, Eritreans and Oromos had just achieved. Internationally and in the diaspora, the introduction of federalism was decried as an eristic initiative, which set its face squarely against the integrationist nation-building currents then reaching a peak in other parts of Africa—most notably in Eritrea and South Africa, both of whose governments publicly expressed concern about the Ethiopian experiment.

Its most radical critics saw the new federal arrangement as a 'minority Tigrayan plot' to 'divide and rule' Ethiopia—a strand of political opposition which now began to elide legitimate political critique with an established ethnic slur rooted in historical tropes. The Derg's propaganda had vilified Tigrayans as secessionists for a decade and a half. An element of anti-Tigrayan prejudice now crept into complaints across the spectrum of opponents, particularly (but not only) among those who were opposed to federalism on principle. Many argued that there had been nothing 'ethnocratic' about the old arrangement and that a centralised system was, in principle, much to be preferred: better for 'unity'. Ethiopian (and international) intellectuals who subscribed to this view often also shared 'the belief that talking about ethnicity creates or reinforces ethnic divisions even when the talk is directed at how to prevent such divisions from overwhelming a future democratic state'.[9] These were (and remain) views shared by opponents and critics of the EPRDF–TPLF government.

Critics also mounted a range of attacks on ethnic federal policy and its implementation. Ethnicity was denounced as a 'red herring'—some alleged that there was no such thing as Amhara ethnicity, let alone a tradition of Amhara 'ethnocracy'. Others suggested that the introduction of ethnicity into political life could only result in disaster, along the lines experienced in the former Yugoslavia.[10] Given the ongoing disintegration of the former Yugoslavia, and the collapse and fragmentation but persisting irredentism of neighbouring Somalia, in the early 1990s, the act of giving explicit recognition to ethnicity in the politics of Ethiopia appeared to offer an open target. Another set of commentators questioned the viability of federalism additionally on grounds of expense.[11]

As the transition evolved, the ranks of critics grew. Many, including ethno-nationalist enthusiasts of the new federal principles, now began to agree that the new arrangement was not in practice as egalitarian and inclusive as alleged, but that it effectively institutionalised a new but still highly discriminatory constellation, this time favouring a new EPRDF elite. In practice they blamed what they saw as a primarily Tigrayan elite—they blamed '*weyane*'. Across the spectrum, whether the EPRDF's political opponents supported the introduction of multinational federal principles or saw it as 'ethnicising' Ethiopia's politics, few of them proved to be above ethnicising their critique.

The transition: A new map

Seats allocated in a new legislature reflected the political balance of power at the time, along with an attempt at comprehensive ethnic representation. EPRDF parties retained a substantial majority, alongside representatives of other ethnically based liberation movements which had opposed the previous regime, a raft of newly established parties representing the smaller ethnic groups, and a number of new and older pan-Ethiopianist groups.[12] The parliament elected the EPRDF–TPLF chairman as head of government and ratified a selection of ministers reflecting the hierarchy of influence among the political organisations represented. While EPRDF retained key portfolios, the OLF were offered significant positions, and remaining cabinet jobs were distributed among representatives of other groups.

The government appointed a Boundary Commission to draw up an 'ethnic map' of the proposed new political units. The visible involvement of non-EPRDF organisations in the project was a particularly important coup, since both the project itself and the content of the decisions reached were highly controversial. The Boundary Commission, which began work in August 1991, had ten members, and represented seven political groups: three from EPRDF, two from OLF, one Gurage, one Hadiya, one Harari, one Somali and one Afar. Whatever the subsequent complaints of the opposition, key players were implicated in the mapping. The mixed group helped force compromise and speed decisions, reining in the more ambitious claims of powerful players, and deflecting and diffusing conflict within the group. The balance also lent a degree of transparency and legitimacy to the outcome, which the government could claim was 'thrashed out around the table'. Plural and enthusiastic involvement veiled both the extent to which the process was managed and the irony of 'granting self-determination' to groups in parts of the country that had neither demanded nor fought for it.[13]

All expected that the OLF would forward strong claims that a large, disputed area be incorporated into Oromia. It was politically important that these were countered not only by EPRDF, but also by a range of representatives from other ethnic or political blocs. When the OLF representatives claimed much of Amharic-speaking Wollo as 'really' (i.e. historically) Oromoland, the Hadiya commission member is reported to have countered that much of Arsi and Bale should then be regarded as 'really Hadiya or Sidama'.[14] Both suggestions were dropped.

The commission drew only the outlines of the regions and left it to new regional state governments to sort out their own internal boundaries. Problems arising along the borders between regions were to be settled at some future date by canvassing the relevant *kebeles* (local councils) and registering the preference of the majority in each. A draft map of 14 regions appeared in the Boundary Commission bulletin (issues 1, 2 and 3) towards the end of the year, but was rapidly withdrawn and replaced with a list of the numbered regions and the names of the nationalities included in each. Difficult issues were postponed (e.g. Dire Dawa), sidestepped (e.g. North Omo in the Southern region), or siphoned off for separate negotiation by interested parties (e.g. Harar). Other boundary issues (most notably between Amhara and Tigray regional states) emerged only much later—only after the 1991 generation of political elites had retired, died or been pushed aside by younger politicians. Chapter 4 returns to these issues, which greatly complicated the dynamics of the war in Tigray in 2020.

While the federated states were constitutionally 'delimited on the basis of settlement patterns, identity, language and the consent of the people concerned', current language use became the single effective criterion applied, being considered a more visible and conclusive marker than history (for instance). The commission was dismissive of claims based on history. In fact the commission (and later the FDRE constitution) explicitly excluded them, fearing their open-ended potential for dispute,[15] and preferring to deal in 'currently verifiable demographics'.[16] Even this relatively tangible criterion was not straightforward. The commission drew heavily on the work of the Derg's Institute for the Study of Ethiopian Nationalities (ISEN), even including among its number one of its former research members. ISEN, in a much more leisurely study of the ethnic profiles of the country during the 1980s, had (as noted in the last chapter) established that of 580 districts 'only around 30-odd were actually monolingual'.[17]

In 1991, however, there was not much discussion in the commission about adopting this policy based on language use: only about certain of the boundaries, notably between Oromia and its Gurage, Sidama, Kefficho and Somali neighbours. The commission did some preparatory work to clear up these disagreements, and other issues were reported back to the transitional parliament. Meanwhile, M.L. Bender's 1976 language map was there for reference, ISEN's copious research was used to double-check its accuracy, and the work was finished within a few months. There was a clear political rationale for such haste. All parties sought stability, the reduction of controversy, and the rapid and peaceful demarcation of the local government jurisdictions, which each could then seek to colonise. By contrast, the later periods of dispute, debate, violent conflict and adjustment associated with these boundaries were protracted and painful. As will be discussed in Chapter 5, they became all the more painful after 2018.

A Constitution Commission was appointed to draft a range of constitutional proposals and questions for popular discussion, and for debate and ratification by a Constituent Assembly elected in 1994. Two issues were controversial: the inclusion of a right of secession of nations, nationalities and peoples (Article 39); and the retention of land in state ownership. Both were challenged then and since by the political opposition. When the FDRE constitution was finally adopted, it was premised on strong residual sovereignty at the regional government level. But in practice this power was tempered in two ways: by formal requirements to follow a framework of federally sanctioned policy directions (FDRE Constitutional Chapter X), and by the dependence of states in practice on the flow of subsidies from the federal centre.

Exclusionary politics

At the beginning of the transitional period, observers were pleased with the surprisingly inclusive manner of their engagement with the coalition government. Those middle-class and intellectual members of ethnic groups, particularly from the south, whom EPRDF had encouraged to form their own parties and join the government in senior positions, spoke of the 'magnanimity of the EPRDF', who, despite their decisive military victory, seemed to have committed themselves to sharing power. Many took the coalition at face value. They assumed that they were being offered a permanent place at the table, representing rural constituents among whom they had done little to mobilise political support or establish party political organisational infrastructure. They thought of EPRDF as a northern party (operating in Amhara and Tigray, and some parts of Oromia only) and saw themselves as taking over a complementary role in the south and on the peripheries.[18]

It was only in the run-up to the first elections in mid-1992 that it became clear that the EPRDF did not intend to leave the rest of the country to their opposition peers. Despite the objections of the OLF, it had been agreed that the EPRDF's forces would operate as a national army for the duration of the transition. EPRDF had made careful preparation for the organisation's swift move into the south: a caucus from southern groups had been separately organised, mobilised and trained well before the fall of the Derg. Many had been taken prisoner in Tigray and Wollo as Derg soldiers, joined the movement, and moved quickly into their home areas as the Derg collapsed. During the summer months of 1991 the EPRDF fanned out across the south of the country, establishing so-called peace and stability committees from among local people.

From the beginning, EPRDF's strategy of political mobilisation began a process of elision of party and state, simultaneously selecting proto-administrators while promoting the party's ideology and seeking to recruit members. The seamless consolidation of party and administration continued unconstrained and at breakneck speed throughout the south. Thousands of young recruits went through EPRDF's Tatek political training centre in 1991 and 1992, mostly drawn from Oromia and the south, but also from the pastoralist peripheries.[19] Meanwhile, those who had been members of the workers' party of the Derg were excluded from government office, and a campaign tracked down and arrested senior cadres suspected of involvement in Red Terror and war crimes.

As these activities began to run up against rival campaigns, tension mounted. In Oromia, where the Oromo nationalists constituted seasoned and determined competitors, the OLF nursed bitter memories of attempts at military and political collaboration with the TPLF in the early 1980s. They had been infuriated by the EPRDF's establishment of its own Oromo organisation, the Oromo People's Democratic Organisation (OPDO), in 1989–90. Violent clashes escalated as a first round of elections approached. On the eve of the polls in 1992 the OLF withdrew from government, announcing its inability to work with the EPRDF and its decision to return to armed opposition. The brief threat of renewed civil war receded as the government neutralised the immediate military threat, and 30,000 OLF fighters were taken prisoner in re-education camps. The ensuing political impasse in Oromia was described in a 2005 report from Human Rights Watch:

> the OPDO has used the specter of an ongoing OLF 'armed struggle' to justify widespread repression. Regional government and security officials routinely accuse dissidents, critics and students of being OLF 'terrorists' or insurgents. Thousands of Oromo from all walks of life have been targeted for arbitrary detention, torture and other abuses even when there has been no evidence linking them to the OLF. Even some apolitical civil society organizations have been treated as subversive threats to the regime, hampering their ability to operate effectively. Thus, the OLF and the OPDO are engaged in a tragic charade: The OLF pretends to be waging the kind of armed struggle that Meles Zenawi and the TPLF fought to bring down the Derg. The OPDO and the TPLF/EPRDF use the OLF's quixotic guerrilla campaign to justify political repression. And the people of Oromia suffer from both sides' pretensions.[20]

Meanwhile, in perhaps the most free elections of Ethiopia's history, the Ogaden National Liberation Front (ONLF) won control of the Somali regional state in 1992, and quickly pushed for an independence referendum—a move which Addis Ababa promptly blocked, triggering a second long-running thread of conflict.[21] Nationalists in Oromia and Somali found their legal avenues for political participation blocked, and cycles of insurgencies resumed—too low-level to threaten the centre, but devastating for lives and livelihoods in both areas. In both cases a repressive and exclusionary approach to popular ethno-nationalist elements deemed too radical by the centre saw thousands detained in brutal circumstances by a security apparatus still visibly dominated by former TPLF fighters. This brought strong Oromo and Somali criticism—again couched in anti-minority and anti-Tigrayan language.

By the mid-1990s, EPRDF took control of local government across the four core regional states of Amhara, Oromia, SNNPRS and Tigray. Realising that, with federal elections looming, their influence and positions in government would vanish, other non-EPRDF members of the transitional government began to protest against the non-level playing field, and several others withdrew, including the Sidama Liberation Movement. Some joined forces with diaspora-based opposition blocs, which had been excluded from the beginning. They began calling for a process of 'national reconciliation' which would start the process of state constitution-making anew, incorporating those increasing numbers of actors who now operated outside the legal framework. Positions polarised. For the next decade, the opposition parties that remained in the country were torn between risking all by withdrawing from the elections (1994 and 1995; 2000–1) or lending a veneer of multi-party legitimacy to a process they now saw as vitiated.

As pluralism dissolved, observers questioned the ability of EPRDF to work in coalition with other political parties. By the end of the transitional period, the government no longer looked like the magnanimous mechanism for power-sharing some had envisaged. Rather, the transition had secured the initial support and buy-in of representatives from communities all over the country, including all the major armed liberation movements, for the controversial new state structure of ethnic federalism. It won EPRDF a brief period of grace during which the new arrangement could be viewed by almost all sides (and especially the international community) as marking a distinct ideological break with the past, nominally introducing pluralism, multi-partyism, inclusivity, and apparently 'liberal' democracy. It gave the ruling party essential breathing space to establish and activate an infrastructure for political mobilisation in those core areas of the south of the country where it had not previously operated.

The transitional period, with the involvement and even, initially, approval of many outside the party, achieved the formula which became entrenched over the subsequent decade: a highland core administered by EPRDF parties, and a lowland periphery administered by EPRDF affiliates or associates.

Reining in an ethnic 'free-for-all'?

From 1995, there was an observable and orchestrated move by the centre to claw back control over what some described as an ethnic free-for-all in the establishment of the federation. During the early 1990s, groups of all sizes, claims and credibility had been encouraged to organise and mobilise for self-determination.[22] Now, however, the federal government started to push for the 'efficient' reconsolidation of some zones, regions and political parties, particularly in the Southern region. In 1997, the EPRDF's parties were amalgamated, and a number of separate small zones proclaimed 'non-viable'—Kaffa and Sheka, Bench and Maji in the south-west— were unceremoniously stuck back together, much to the disgust of those in towns that lost jobs, construction, and budget control to ethnic neighbours and competitors.

Separatist claims were either rejected or deferred through the 1990s, including notably recalcitrant campaigns by the Silte and the Welaiyta. The ruling party seems to have been taken aback at the enthusiasm with which its own cadres were involved in spearheading local drives for autonomy, responding to new and often conflictual local incentive structures. Opponents who had always feared that ethnic federalism would lead to the balkanisation of the Ethiopian empire state warned that the government was trying to re-pack Pandora's box.[23] A clear integrating impetus characterised federal policy, which now refused to countenance 'fragmentation'. The integrative dynamic strengthened when war broke out with Eritrea in 1998.

Also of concern as the war erupted was the poor quality of governance under federalism, and corresponding instability, especially in the pastoralist periphery. Four regional states were struggling with federal self-government: the Muslim pastoral Afar and Somali areas to the east, and the mixed areas of Benishangul-

Gumuz and Gambella on the western border with Sudan. These territories had been governed for a century by imperial envoys and civil servants from the centre. Corruption, embezzlement and instability thrived as the new political status of under-educated and inexperienced officials shifted the local balance of power. Central interference to curtail the activities of more independent-minded politicians at any sign of incipient secessionism (as in Somali *kilil* and Berta zone) regularly complicated matters. In 1997, teams of federal advisers were dispatched by the federal prime minister's office, to provide the so-called emergent states with professional and technical 'support'. When it emerged that this encompassed the investigation of funds given the *kilils* in federal budget subsidies, and the control of political matters, tensions rose. Central meddling was again interpreted in ethnic terms, as most of those who were sent to the lowland regions were highlanders, often including Tigrayan security officials.

The new federal and regional governments were regarded with resentment by the political opposition that had been comprehensively outmanoeuvred during the transitional period. Officers of a number of parties were harassed or imprisoned, including notably the chairman of the All-Amhara People's Organisation, who died soon after his release from lengthy detention. The OLF continued sporadic guerrilla attacks, alongside a series of Islamist bombings in 1996 coordinated from southern Somalia. Ongoing Western diplomatic efforts to reconcile the OLF and the EPRDF ran into the sand in 1998 when a new generation of OLF leaders rejected federalism in favour of the struggle for an independent Oromo state. When the Ethio-Eritrean war broke out, many allied with Asmara. The evolution of the war with Eritrea from 1998 to 2000 saw the grip of the federal government and National Defence Force tighten on the peripheries as governance issues gave way to concern for the security of state borders.

Eritrea: The independence struggle, a new dawn—and a return to war

On 23 May 1993, after thirty years of war, and two years of *de facto* autonomy, 'the Ethiopian province of Eritrea officially became an independent state. For the international community this outcome, which put an end to over half a century of legal ambiguities and embarrassing diplomatic contradictions, brought a general feeling of relief'.[24] The relief was short-lived. Within five years, the two countries were again at war in a sudden outbreak of hostilities most observers found inexplicable and senseless: 'two bald men fighting over a comb'.[25] Observers were mystified. So soon after the EPLF and TPLF–EPRDF had collaborated to topple the Derg regime, were they not 'brothers in arms'?[26] Wasn't it the TPLF-led EPRDF which had insisted on supporting, recognising and facilitating the process of Eritrea gaining its independence from Ethiopia, often risking (and multiplying) the wrath of their Ethiopian nationalist political opponents?

The relationships between the two fronts had long been more complicated. In his 1993 speech in Asmara, on the occasion of Eritrea's independence celebrations, Ethiopian president Meles Zenawi expressed the hope that the 'wounds of the past would be healed'[27]—for they were many. The grievances which fed the 1998–2000 Ethio-Eritrean war, as well as the renewed bitterness of its legacies, remained relevant to the 2020 war in Tigray, in which the government of Eritrea, still led by the EPLF's founding chairman, President Isaias Afwerki, emerged as a key protagonist (see Chapter 6).

Eritrean nationalist sensitivities

The historical, social and political relations between what are now highland Eritrea and Tigray are long and complex. The first 'semi centralised political structure' in the region, the Axumite Empire, encompassed parts of both areas over many centuries, but 'was neither "Ethiopian" nor "Eritrean" even if it embodied elements of both'.[28] Much later, as already discussed in Chapter 1, single patterns of taxation or administration across the two areas also emerged during the periods of Yohannes IV and *Ras* Mikhael Sehul, before the advent of a more consolidated Italian presence to the north of the Mereb River. In social terms, interrelations between Tigrigna-speakers north and south of the Mereb remained close and multiple, and inter-marriage into the adjacent areas of Seraye and

Akele Guzai (now in Eritrea) was particularly frequent. In political terms, discussion of the relations between the TPLF and the EPLF usually begins with the TPLF's early 'secessionist' manifesto, drafted in 1976.

A conference of 120 members held on the TPLF's first anniversary in February 1976 adopted organisational by-laws and elected its leadership for the first time. These leaders were tasked with drafting a political manifesto; it was printed and circulated several months later as a 'white paper'. The draft stressed the lack of democracy and foreseeable change within Ethiopia and suggested establishing an independent state of Tigray as 'a likely preferred option under the circumstances';[29] but it emphasised that if Ethiopia could be democratised, it would struggle for autonomy within Ethiopia. When the organisation's central committee met to review the document, it was rejected and 'condemned' as a 'narrow nationalist deviation'.[30] Commentators have discussed whether the draft was a 'mistake' or 'deliberate sabotage' by a conspiratorial clique.[31] The order of priority of the two objectives was reversed, and the TPLF's objectives were redrawn in terms that remained in effect throughout its subsequent history: the emphasis on establishing self-determination within a democratised context for any nation or nationality group, but with the option of secession should the population so decide.

As may be imagined, the allegation that the TPLF had for some time advocated independence for Tigray (as a priority objective above mere self-determination) long provided ammunition for the TPLF's critics, starting with the Derg, whose propaganda exploited the early manifesto to portray the group as secessionist. It is not difficult to see that Eritrea's primary nationalist Front, the EPLF, was also not enthusiastic about the Tigrayan nationalist declaration of a struggle for independence when it emerged in the mid-1970s. Commentators agree that the EPLF was not pleased.[32] One needs to go further back into the 'Eritrean question' to understand EPLF sensitivity to anything which might complicate its nationalist quest or render it less clear by muddying the waters with considerations of Ethiopian domestic politics (see Chapter 2).

When the EPLF emerged as one of three splinter groups of the earlier Eritrean Liberation Front (ELF) in 1970, it defined its objective of establishing an independent Eritrea as the right of any colonised population—albeit, in this instance, seen as colonised by a neighbouring African rather than a European power. In promoting this nationalist agenda, couched as a 'colonial question', the Eritrean movement faced a number of potential obstacles or risks. All had to do with the challenges of building a consolidated single Eritrean 'nation', with a single nationalist voice. A cohesive position was not beyond doubt in the 1970s; rather, the historically fragmented nature of Eritrea's politics had repeatedly undermined the success of earlier nationalist moves.

The EPLF criticised and split from its forerunner, the ELF. Not only, they said, was it dominated by the primarily Muslim lowlanders, to the exclusion of the highland Christian Tigrigna-speaking populations, but it had also allowed its organisational structure to degenerate into a series of fiefdoms based on local affiliation; this only encouraged differentiation among Eritrea's nine separate ethnic or language groups. Both dynamics were to be opposed as counter to the development of popular attachment to the idea of an Eritrean national entity. The reasons for sensitivity on the point were clear. Overcoming differences between Eritrea's peoples (its Christians and Muslims, its highlanders and lowlanders, its agriculturists and pastoralists, and its different language groups) was not only a theoretical nicety. During the period after the Second World War, overt social and political differences had impinged directly on the disposal of Italy's former colonial possession. Some had suggested the partition of Eritrea between Sudan and Ethiopia, for instance, on the basis of the socio-economic and cultural affinities of different parts of the territory.

Eritrean political debate and activity in the post-Second World War period were energetic, fractious and shifting, with distinct communities perceiving and pursuing their interests in different ways at different times, not least in relation to the question of desirable relations with Ethiopia. As the Four Power Commission and, later, the UN discovered, there was little or no consensus. Different groups lobbied for unity, federation or confederation with Ethiopia, for the independence of the so-called Western Region of Eritrea, for a union of Massawa with Ethiopia, or the cession

95

to it of Assab–Dankalia, for separate statehood or protectorate status for the whole of Eritrean territory, and—of most enduring controversy—for the establishment of a 'Greater Tigray' from the union of highland Tigrigna-speaking populations on either side of the border. The diversity of debate culminated by 1950 in clashes and political violence: 'disorder spread rapidly throughout the most vital areas of Eritrea. The most combustible material caught fire first. The structure of Eritrean political unity, erected during the Italian regime, had concealed the fundamental conflicts of culture and interest among the Eritrea communities. The Italian regime had had the effect of anaesthetizing the passions dividing them.'[33]

If Tigrayan nationalists had work to do to consolidate the relatively homogeneous 'nation' of Tigray, so too did the Eritrean nationalist movement. The degree of post-Second World War political fragmentation in Eritrea belies the nationalist thesis later put forward by the EPLF, of a united Eritrean nation forged by its shared Italian colonial experience. It also complicates the narrative of straightforward colonial expropriation of Eritrea by Ethiopia when Haile Selassie dissolved the federation. On the contrary, it seems clear that before federation with Ethiopia there was support in Asmara for the Unionist Party advocating a return to the links with Ethiopia (which for the Christian highland population, at least, had strong historical and cultural roots).

These events are controversial, of course, and much contested. For some, Eritrean support for unionism was spontaneous and indigenous.[34] For the nationalists it was the result of imperial Ethiopian manipulation. None of this is to suggest that the overwhelming majority of Eritreans did not over the subsequent decades come to support the nationalist project in the strongest terms, and come to identify their interests and sense of themselves as lying with an independent state. Unequivocally they did, and the 1993 referendum result corroborated this. But in the 1970s, the Eritrean post-colonial 'nation' had to be consolidated from among disparate ethnic, linguistic and religious elements, divergent economic interests, and on the basis of a claim to shared colonial status.[35] The unifying, centralising 'nation-building' approach which the EPLF adopted is familiar from other anti-colonial contexts.

Differences between the EPLF and TPLF in the 1980s

While the Eritrean project was premised on the struggle to forge one nation from the country's different nationalities, the Tigrayan campaign of the 1970s was to extract Tigray, and subsequently others of Ethiopia's multiple ethnic groups, from the 'ethnocratic' stranglehold of the centralised Ethiopian state, and to foster their diverse development in a radically transformed context. There is irony in the fact that these two political projects, which had fundamentally diametrically opposite dynamics, were jointly dismissed for decades with the single label 'secessionist'. During the ideologically intense days of the 1970s and early 1980s, differences between the TPLF and the EPLF about the 'national question' rapidly brought the two movements into conflict. There were also other issues at stake, including questions of military strategy and an appropriate approach to the Derg's international patron, the Soviet Union; but the theoretical dispute also had practical (including military) implications given that Saho, Kunama and Irob minorities straddled the border.

Eritrean and Tigrayan sources agree that the breakdown of relations began with differences of military approach. The TPLF wanted to withdraw troops they had stationed in Eritrea around the time of the Red Star or Sixth Offensive in 1982, bringing an angry response from the EPLF. The TPLF was critical of the EPLF strategy of operating from behind front lines in a cohesive territory in the remote north-east, rather than working actively in and among the most densely populated highland communities of central Eritrea. They criticised the approach not only from a military perspective (that it did little to wear down the enemy) but also from a political perspective, since it limited contact with and mobilisation of the wider population, reducing the scope for social transformation or recruitment.[36]

Kjetil Tronvoll's 1998 account of a highland village in Akele Guzai indicates that EPLF mobilisation and recruitment in this area were often coercive and carried out by units sweeping through the area. Without a system of permanently stationed cadres, the EPLF (unlike the TPLF in the areas they controlled) 'neither nationalised

97

nor sought to distribute land equally',[37] but focused on technical capabilities and the prosecution of the war.[38] Rightly or wrongly, Tigrayan nationalist sources contrasted the Eritrean approach with the system of intensive popular mobilisation and social administration through their own system of *kifli hizbi*, by means of which the TPLF was closely woven into the fabric of Tigrayan rural society.[39]

As practical tensions accumulated, the ideological underpinnings of their differences over self-determination also began to cause friction. The EPLF broke off all cooperation between the two organisations in June 1985 (at the height of the famine), ostensibly because it was angered by the TPLF's analysis of their relationship. A year later, the TPLF wrote that 'if the future of Eritrea is to be truly democratic it will have to respect the right of nations and nationalities up to and including secession',[40] and that to 'rule out the possibility of secession would amount to contradicting its own democratic principles'.[41] The EPLF did not comment on the situation of Eritrean nationalities or language groups, but stated that Ethiopian nationalities had the right to self-determination though not to independence. This last was conditional (the EPLF argued) on having been previously independent or separately colonised, and on a minimum level of economic cohesion.[42] Observers have seen three reasons for the EPLF's limited interpretation of this right: to deny Tigrayan and other Ethiopian nationalities the basis for a right to independence which might have complicated the Eritrean claim; to reaffirm the distinctive character of the Eritrean *colonial* right to independence; and, finally, to rule out of question any such right for individual minorities within Eritrea by restricting the definition of anti-colonial self-determination struggles to 'multinational peoples'.[43]

The position infuriated the TPLF, which had long claimed precisely the opposite: that the degree of oppression of non-Amhara ethnic groups by the Ethiopian state had reached a level at which it coloured the thinking of this vast majority in a fundamental way, with the consequence that they could *only* be effectively mobilised within their own nationality group, by their peers. This issue was more than an article of faith within the TPLF; it had operated as a key basis for survival in the period of the 1970s when it fought off better-known forces, notably the multinational EPRP (see Chapter 2). The TPLF concluded that its relationship with the EPLF could only be 'tactical', based on nothing more than a shared commitment to the overthrow of the Derg. In doing so it called into question the relationship of the EPLF with the Eritrean population. If that relationship was not 'democratic', as the TPLF understood the term, the organisation retained the right to enter into other alliances, tactical or strategic, with the EPLF's competitors.[44]

A particularly bitter resonance of the 1985 row has relevance at the time of writing in 2022, as Tigray continues to face a long blockade of the delivery of food and medicines as part of the war which began in 2020. Many Tigrayans believe that the EPLF's move to cut their relations in the mid-1980s was precisely timed to cause maximum distress at the height of the 1984–5 famine. From October 1984, starving Tigrayans had trekked west in large numbers, with around 200,000 of a projected 300,000 reaching refugee camps in eastern Sudan. Death rates in the camps were some of the highest ever recorded. An immediate corollary of the rupture in June 1985 was the simultaneous and unannounced refusal of the EPLF to allow either relief vehicles or refugees from Tigray to make use of the most direct route to sustenance in Sudan which passed through its territory.

It took months for the Tigrayans to establish an alternative southerly route into Sudan at Anghereb. Some believe that the EPLF alerted the Derg forces in Mekele to its decision to close the Barentu road, leaving precious relief vehicles pinned against the Eritrean border, with little possibility of escape from government forces forty kilometres away. For three years, from 1985 to 1988, the two movements refused to cooperate, only shifting their stance for pragmatic reasons as the pendulum of the war finally swung decisively away from the Derg. In 1988, the EPLF took Afabet, and the TPLF won a major tank battle at Axum, following up in February 1989 with defeat of the garrison at Shire.[45]

Eritrea and Ethiopia diverge: Tensions from 1993 to 1998

Although the two fronts fought a coordinated campaign to defeat the Derg in 1991, nevertheless after independence the EPLF (soon renamed the Popular Front for Democracy and Justice (PFDJ) in government) continued to express public concern and strong criticism of the federal system being built in Ethiopia, particularly of the inclusion of the constitutional right of self-determination up to secession. By contrast, in 1995 new local administrative boundaries in Eritrea were designed explicitly to cut across traditional units of local administration. Eritrean government rhetoric continued to be surprisingly undiplomatic, such as this statement from an official 1995 publication.

> There was a time when people thought in terms of 'we' and 'they' using religion and regional boundaries as bases ... A person should be judged not by his place of origin ... Those who think otherwise are mentally sick and we should not allow them to impose their will on us. The government will not restrain itself from taking appropriate measures regarding those who misinterpret and misconstrue administrative or developmental policies in order to create religious and regional conflicts.[46]

Tensions over their different systems notwithstanding, the two new governments established a series of joint committees designed to discuss and manage aspects of their evolving relationships as two separate sovereign states. Ethiopia took over Derg-era Soviet debt responsibilities, and there were debates over the disposal of materiel and cargos between the territories. But multiple issues brewed tension. On the economic front, national interests and self-conceptions quickly diverged.

> Eritrea had been designed by its Italian godfather as an industrial nucleus which should have been the core of a wider agricultural development area ... As a result the small Eritrea economy found itself painfully dependent on an Ethiopian hinterland which had always been seen as a 'natural outlet' for northern industrial production. But after 1993, the limited but real economic development of Ethiopia in general and of Tigray in particular started to interfere with that 'pre-ordained' pattern.[47]

New industrial import substitution capability was being established across Ethiopia, including Tigray, by the TPLF in a series of industrial companies (under a party-associated endowment fund). This seemed to the Eritreans to be a provocative attempt to undermine the competitive manufacturing and exporting edge which they now expected to leverage, exploiting Ethiopia's raw materials.[48] Eritrea's continued use of the Ethiopian national currency, the birr, and the circumstances of its eventual establishment of a new currency—the nakfa—also provoked much controversy.[49] For Ethiopia, Eritrea's use of the birr, including its sustained use of a parallel market, represented a backdoor drain on the Ethiopian economy. Ethiopian sources insisted Ethiopia pushed Eritrea to establish its own currency, but Asmara dragged its feet. Eritrean sources claimed that the Ethiopians were taken aback when they did so. Ethiopia's not unreasonable insistence that the two currencies should now float against the dollar rather than trade at parity did much to exacerbate tensions: the new nakfa rapidly depreciated against the birr, in an all too visible demonstration of economic realities. Other tensions revolved around 'illicit' Eritrean re-exports of Ethiopian products (allegedly coffee, but more importantly gold); around re-import of construction materials from elsewhere, exploiting a duty-free agreement between the two countries; and over proper levels of port use fees to be charged at Assab.

Economic disputes and friction seem to have been exacerbated by a 'basic political and cultural disconnect'. While many Eritreans had been skilled workers and soldiers during the Italian colonial period, Tigrayans 'had supplied much of Eritrea's casual labour to the point where "Agame" [the district in Tigray's north-east] acquired a pejorative connotation among highland Eritreans'.[50] Mutual accusations of superiority or inferiority proliferated, and this began to affect relations at the highest levels of government. 'Issayas was constitutionally incapable of working with the TPLF on an equal basis and still looked down on his [migrant labourer] cousins as a subordinate kind. It was hard for him to realize that once the TPLF was in control of Ethiopia, its priorities would become national rather than parochial'.[51]

Amidst all the other priorities of newly initiated state formation processes, outstanding issues of the demarcation of the international boundary between Ethiopia and Eritrea were persistently shelved, and this eventually triggered fighting. The border at Badme in the north-west of Ethiopia had been particularly unclear. A fertile plain accessed by seasonal herders and migrant labourers from both sides of the border, the area had been under the ELF during the 1970s, before the TPLF defeated them and pushed them out. The Eritreans complained that the Tigray regional government retained administration of Eritrean territory, and made allegations that the government in Mekele had an expansionist agenda. Finally, in March 1998 the Eritreans sent troops, and a number of Tigrayan militia were killed. It seems likely that Asmara may have miscalculated the way in which this 'invasion' could escalate into full-scale war, as quickly happened when the issue was brought not just to local decision-makers but to the decision-making body of the full EPRDF. A number of EPRDF Amhara and Oromo leaders reacted with great anger. It is possible that this was a miscalculation.

Once the conflict escalated, Eritrean sources were persistent in their assertion that the Ethiopian government led by the TPLF deliberately 'tricked' the Eritreans into invading (something the Tigrayans deny): that they had in fact gone to great lengths deliberately to lure Eritrean forces into Ethiopia-administered territory precisely in order to have an excuse to re-annex Eritrean territory.[52] The reason? In pursuit of the establishment of that post-Second World War historical model, the 'Greater Tigray', which would take in all Tigrigna-speakers, unifying the highlands on both sides of the Mereb River. In this Eritrean analysis, the famous 'Tigray–Tigrigne' project of a 'Greater Tigray with the Eritrean port of Assab as a capital city' was always the secret 'ultimate aim' of the TPLF: a 'long-held dream' and 'centrepiece of the TPLF's political programme' allegedly outlined in the 1976 secessionist manifesto.[53] Except that it was not. Eritrean claims about the 1976 manifesto were untrue, however often they were repeated; neither was evidence produced to support Asmara's whispered claims of an Ethiopian–Tigrayan conspiracy for war. On the contrary, the evidence suggests that Addis Ababa was caught entirely unprepared by the Eritrean incursion.[54]

Although it is possible to see that the notion of a 'Greater Tigray' had important antecedents in historical narrative, the explicit political project to bring Tigrigna-speaking areas of what are now

Tigray and Eritrea (historically, Tigray Mekonnen and Bahr Negash) into a political union—the so-called Tigray–Tigrigne project—originates in the modern era during the Italian period. During the Italian occupation of Ethiopia, one of the administrative units into which Italian Imperial East Africa was divided was the whole of this area. The possible relocation of its capital from Asmara to Adwa—site of the famous Italian defeat—was talked of as Mussolini's final act of revenge on Ethiopian nineteenth century resistance under Menelik II. Much has been written about the political idea of Tigray–Tigrigne, but there are three actors with whom the promotion of the project was particularly associated. They were the Italian colonial administration in Eritrea; elements of the British military administration of Eritrea after the Second World War; and the Liberal Progressive Party (LPP), led by *Ras* Tessema Asmerom and Woldeab Wolde Mariam, that emerged in Asmara during the British military administration.

In each of these three cases the project was promoted from north (not south) of the Mereb River and was perceived (with various political motivations) as a means of adding a part of Ethiopia onto Eritrea: aggrandising the latter rather than the other way round. The two British ministries involved in Eritrea after the war—the Foreign Office and the War Office—split down the line regarding the desirability of carving up Ethiopia in this way.[55] Eritrea's nationalist LPP became perhaps the most significant proponent of this division as a viable alternative to the union or federation, and most assumed they had the support of the British.[56] With the exception of a brief period of flirtation with the so-called Italian *politica Tigrigna* by elements in Tigray during the Italian occupation, who saw it as a means of countering Shewan influence in the empire, there is almost no evidence that the idea of Tigray–Tigrigne as a political project for unification of the two areas has ever gained much currency within Tigray itself.[57]

The 1998–2000 Ethio-Eritrean war and its aftermath

The deep drivers of the Ethio-Eritrean war of 1998–2000 extended well beyond its territorial triggers. They included economic competition, tensions over regional hegemony, deep ideological differences, and a history of bitterness between neighbours. 'No single issue caused this war. It was the outcome of years of suspicion and hostility that finally exploded into open conflict'.[58] If this was true in 1998, it was even more clearly the case when the war in Tigray erupted in 2020. The brutal devastation of the 1998–2000 war, and its aftermath, added greatly to the store of Eritrean grievance. Two years of attritional trench warfare had a high cost in human lives.[59] 'Estimates of war dead vary, but most accounts place the total killed on both sides at between 70,000 and 100,000. Large numbers of civilians were caught up in the fighting, leading to large-scale displacement'.[60] Bouts of large-scale fighting were interrupted by periods of relative calm. In February 1999 Ethiopia re-took the town of Badme on the western border where things had begun, but in May 2000 it launched a more decisive campaign. Ethiopia 'broke through Eritrean defences in the west of the country forcing a mass Eritrean retreat into the highland plateau'.[61] Peace talks began in June, and six months later the two heads of government signed up to the terms of the Algiers Agreement, according to which they would abide by the results of an independent Boundary Commission.

When the commission reported in April 2002, although it awarded substantial territories to Ethiopia, it also awarded Badme to Eritrea, and Addis Ababa refused point-blank to accept it findings. Christopher Clapham suggested that in failing to adopt a 'positive law' approach to the settlement broadly in line with the balance of power on the ground, the commission had in effect decreased, not increased, the chance for peace.[62] Relations froze and the period of active fighting was followed by a long 'cold war' standoff with periodic clashes, particularly after the withdrawal of UN peacekeepers in 2008. 'Ethiopia refused to accept the boundary ruling and wanted to reopen negotiations on the question; and Eritrea accepted the boundary commission findings and refused to entertain further discussion, accusing Ethiopia of illegal occupation of its territory.'[63]

The war had dramatically different effects on Ethiopia and Eritrea. In the short to medium term, defeat was a disaster for Eritrea and a driver of extreme antipathy. 'Isayas Afewerki in Eritrea was forced back into the struggle mentality that became the all-encompassing leitmotiv of state and regime survival. The euphoria of the post-liberation period was abruptly extinguished, along with any plausible agenda for development, and displaced by an overwhelming concern for security, at whatever level'.[64]

The profound securitisation of the state in Eritrea saw the emergence of one of the most repressive and secretive regimes in the world, commonly dubbed the 'North Korea of Africa'.[65] Opponents were rounded up and military conscription extended indefinitely. Asmara had been stung by its military defeat in 2000; it seethed over Ethiopia's refusal to cede the border town of Badme under the Algiers accords; and it resented the imposition of UN sanctions in 2009, in which it saw the hand of the TPLF-led Ethiopian government. Commentators have speculated that the isolation of Eritrea as a pariah state must have been a particular irritation given Isaias's self-conception as a regional elder statesman. In response, Eritrea developed its role as 'safe haven' for opponents of the Ethiopian government. In the 'cold war' standoff that followed the Ethio-Eritrean war, EPRDF's political adversaries won military training and logistical support from an Eritrean government hostile to Addis Ababa and Mekele.

Already by 2006, the Eritrean government was backing the Islamic Courts Union in Somalia, encouraging them to move on Kismayo, and precipitating an Ethiopian military intervention. The polarisation also stirred nationalist frustration in Ethiopia's own Somali region. The ONLF, now with support from Asmara and Mogadishu, including training camps in Eritrea, grew in scale, launching a spectacular lethal attack on an oil exploration facility at Abole in April 2007. Ethiopia's counterinsurgency in the region from 2008 to 2010 was swift and brutal. In 2009, Eritrea gave refuge to members of the defence forces who fled Ethiopia after an unsuccessful coup attempt in Bahir Dar. At the end of the year, it was sanctioned for its breaches of international arms embargoes on Somalia. In mid-2011, the UN monitoring group on Somalia and Eritrea confirmed Ethiopian reports that Addis Ababa had thwarted a 'massive bomb attack on the African Union summit', affirming that 'the plot was genuine and represented a qualitative shift in Eritrean tactics in the Horn of Africa'.[66] Eritrea denied all claims.

There were also reasons for the two sides not to return to all-out war after 2000. The Ethiopians may have feared 'potential blowback … while Somalia remains engulfed in violence', and they had 'consistently outmanoeuvred Eritrea diplomatically, politically, and economically'. The Eritrean government may have feared military and diplomatic losses 'given the government's conviction that it abided by the Algiers Agreement while Ethiopia [did] not'.[67] Eritrea suffered bitterly during almost a decade of UN sanctions. Tigray in important ways also continued to be badly damaged by the 18-year standoff from 2000 to 2018. If, during the imperial period, its relatively close proximity to routes to the outside world and the sea had advantaged Tigray (for instance, during the nineteenth-century scramble for firearms), the region now found itself in a cul-de-sac—up against a hard and heavily militarised border. Families continued to be divided, and patterns of trade and labour migration were disrupted to the disadvantage of Tigray, as Ethiopia reconfigured its trade and port use towards Djibouti.

The Eritrean regime continued to drip poison against its Tigrayan antagonists, whispering well-established narratives that the EPRDF had sacrificed Ethiopia's other nationalities on the battlefield, while keeping Tigrayans in reserve.[68]

One of the least documented aspects of the politics of the Horn over the last quarter-century has been the extent to which sources linked to the regime in Asmara have fostered anti-TPLF and anti-Tigrayan sentiment, with the determination of a fixation. As Richard Reid encapsulated it, in an Eritrea still effectively at war throughout the cold war period of 2000–18, 'it doesn't matter what the question is, the answer is *Woyane*'.[69] (The next chapter returns to this issue.) A growing cast of Asmara-backed antagonists was to play an increasingly influential role in Ethiopia's domestic politics, particularly after the death of prime minister Meles Zenawi (Chapters 4 and 5). These new dynamics underscored the sense that 'ultimately Eritrea was never big enough for Isaias'.[70] It was only finally in 2018 (see Chapter 6) that a new Ethiopian prime minister was to offer him the run of the much larger Ethiopian canvas—a return to influence in the larger polity in which he had grown up and come of age politically in the 1960s and 1970s.

Meanwhile, commentators traced Isaias's misadventures in 1998 to his certainty that a federal Ethiopia, with its multiple political leadership, was weak, and that it would crack apart when placed under pressure; that is, to confirmation bias on the part of a fierce critic of federalism and self-determination of nationalities. In the short term, the opposite proved to be true, as (in another ironic twist) Ethiopia's EPRDF-led government drew on the resurrection of pan-Ethiopian nationalist tropes to mobilise against the Eritrean 'invader'. After the end of the period of brutal military confrontation, however, with Ethiopia dominant and refusing to give ground diplomatically, a dramatic political split did emerge. In March 2001, the differences within the TPLF central committee (exacerbated but not caused by the Ethio-Eritrean war) reverberated through the organisation. Tensions over the middle months of 2001 saw the expulsion of a so-called dissident group and the subsequent 'renewal' of organisational thinking and culture. This marked an important moment of change which saw the introduction of strategies and leadership arrangements—including growing autocracy—that broadly shaped the Ethiopian government's development strategy up to 2012.

EPRDF and its challengers after 2001: Power recentralised?

A second federal government was elected in May 2000 amidst high drama on the battlefields along the northern border with Eritrea. The major shake-up within the leadership of the ruling party in 2001 in the wake of the Ethio-Eritrean war ushered in a second round of decentralisation under federalism, shifting its focus from the (usually ethnically defined) states or zones to the (usually demographically defined) district. The devolution of budgeting, expenditure and accounting to district level had been a stated objective of government decentralisation for a decade, and was introduced abruptly in 2002. The scope for decentralisation in practice was initially greeted with much scepticism but was pushed through remarkably quickly in the four large EPRDF regions, with strong investments of political capital and international support. Nationally devised development 'packages' and a uniform national approach to district-level service delivery furthered the perception of this second phase of the federal consolidation as one of 'centralised decentralisation'. Influential factors militated against real devolution: policy and political uniformity were forged at the centre. The potential of Ethiopia's multi-level governance arrangements for accommodating divergent political and policy interests was little tested in practice.[71]

Capacity-building became the watchword from 2002, when a new federal super-ministry was established to spearhead it, and the number of civil servants assigned at *wereda* level grew from around 150,000 in 2002 to more than 400,000 by the end of the decade. But capital expenditures had been hit hard by the war, and the financial balance of power remained decisively tipped towards the centre.[72] Most revenues were generated at federal level, not least because of the economic dominance of the capital, but most spending on service delivery was the responsibility of the states. The so-called vertical fiscal imbalance was regulated by federal subsidies and transfers, which accounted throughout the EPRDF period for the overwhelming majority of local spending. Some ethnic constituencies finally won recognition for the separate zones for which they had lobbied (Silte split from Gurage; Welaiyta and others from North Omo); others saw abrupt repression, with civilians killed by state security actors in Sheka, Gambella and Sidama. Later in the decade, brutal counterinsurgency in the Somali region entrenched the use of state violence.

The 2005 elections

In the run-up to a third round of federal and regional elections in May 2005, a confident ruling party opened up the electoral campaign to include a series of televised multi-party debates. Several opposition groupings, particularly the Coalition for Unity and Democracy (CUD) with its swiftly and covertly communicable two-finger 'victory' symbol, began to capture the mood, particularly in urban and middle-class areas. The EPRDF, assuming public support after renewal, seems to have miscalculated. Much to their surprise, CUD (and, to a lesser extent, the ethno-national opposition) not only swept the polls in Addis Ababa and a number of other ethnically mixed towns, but also made strong inroads among significant rural farming constituencies, normally notoriously reluctant to vote against an incumbent government.

Various reasons for this have been advanced. The period of the Ethiopian-Eritrean war (1998–2000) had been marked by an upsurge in pan-Ethiopian nationalist rhetoric[73] and a return of official legitimacy to views not considered politically correct since the demise of the Derg. The EPRDF was seen as weakened by the airing of internal grievances and by the high-level expulsions that resulted from the 2001 TPLF split.[74] That crisis saw the independent capacity of the EPRDF party organs substantially curtailed, with power consolidated in state structures in the period leading up to the 2005 elections.[75] In some rural areas of the north, the very fact of 'sitting down with its enemies' to conduct televised debates was seen as a sign of terminal weakness, which boosted the opposition vote.[76]

Rural Amhara and Gurage communities in particular responded with recognition to pan-Ethiopian nationalist suggestions that ethnic federalism threatened their economic and political interests in mobility and urban linkages. These anxieties were shared by educated elites. An explicit EPRDF change of policy in 2002 to reverse its previous disregard of urban professionals came too late to address their grievances and merely gave them oxygen. The demolition of a series of prominent Addis Ababa neighbourhoods at the time of the poll in preparation for road construction was a physical manifestation of 'too little too late'. The CUD benefited from a strong protest vote against the incumbent government's record and from middle-class distaste for what the opposition derided as 'ethnic politics'. In many urban areas, this was conceptualised in terms of a preference for CUD 'civic' over EPRDF 'ethnic' nationalism.[77] The challenge was an existential one: not only to EPRDF rule, but also to the very nature of the multinational federal state. The 2005 polls left the notion of a national consensus in tatters.

Violent dispute erupted over doubtful opposition claims to have won a victory nationally. The CUD clearly won full control of the capital, but its new opposition MPs refused to take up their seats. Long debates saw CUD leaders come under threatening pressure for a boycott from their hardline supporters, especially in the diaspora. As the mood radicalised, the government cracked down. Tens of thousands, mostly young urban men, were arrested. Protests in Addis Ababa in June and November 2005 dissolved into violence and several hundred people were killed by the security services, amidst mutual recrimination.[78] The government accused the opposition of fomenting revolution.

The leadership of the CUD was arrested alongside two NGO officials (including Daniel Bekele, Ethiopia's post-2018 human rights commissioner) and several journalists (including Eskinder Nega, later to head the opposition Balderas). All were charged and eventually found guilty of a series of 'crimes against the constitution'. Most were released and left the country after petitioning for pardon several years later. They included Berhanu Nega and Andargachew Tsigé (charged in absentia), who went on to lead the armed struggle of Patriotic Genbot 7 from Asmara, returning to Ethiopia only in 2018.[79] Also included in the group was Judge Birtukan Mideksa, who, as leader of a new opposition organisation, was re-arrested a second time, before eventually also going into exile. In 2018, she too returned under the new prime minister's amnesty, and headed Ethiopia's post-2018 Election Board.

A particularly controversial aspect of the 2005 election campaign was the eruption of ethnicised hate speech. The government abruptly switched off the new mobile SMS facility when texts calling for lethal attacks on Tigrayans 'standing next to you' suddenly began to circulate. Eskinder Nega's *Asqual* newspaper called for the 'ruling group to go back to where they came from and be knocked out'.[80] In a febrile atmosphere, a week before the election, prime minister Meles made a dramatic intervention, accusing the opposition of trying to foment ethnic hatred, and drew a parallel with Rwanda.

'I call on the people of Ethiopia to punish opposition parties who are promoting an ideology of hatred and divisiveness by denying them their votes at election on May 15,' he told an interviewer during a four-hour question and answer session aired by state television late on Thursday. 'Their policies are geared toward creating hatred and rifts between ethnic groups similar to the policies of the Interahamwe when Hutu militia massacred Tutsis in Rwanda,' he said. 'It is a dangerous policy that leads the nation to violence and bloodshed.'[81]

The strength of the reference to Rwanda, a connection initially made by the senior Amhara EPRDF politician Addisu Legesse, shocked many observers. Few observers treated the remarks with much seriousness. Most interpreted them as playing politics, even as an attempt to

> mobilise Tigrayans ... and stay in power. So the TPLF sought to rally the people of Tigray by instilling a collective fear of losing ground if another party came to power: if you do not vote for us, you are doomed. The rhetoric painting the opposition as the Interahamwe of Ethiopia served to substantiate this logic: the Tigrayans, like the Tutsi of Rwanda, would be eradicated if the opposition came to power.[82]

Read again from the perspective of mid-2022, Meles's comments strike a new chill; so does the international analytical consensus of the late 2000s, which tended to dismiss them.[83] Meanwhile, a defensive EPRDF leadership felt that journalists and civil society had conspired with the political opposition against them. Three pieces of legislation—curbing the activities of media and civil society, and outlawing 'terrorist' activities—soon constrained the activities of all opponents and 'closed political space' after 2005.[84] As important, but much less analysed, were the intensive activities of the reconstructed party in uniformly reoccupying that political landscape. In the run-up to the 2010 election, EPRDF piloted a comprehensive approach to the mobilisation of the population for party political as well as for developmental ends. The melding of the twin objectives marked a new phase in the dominance of EPRDF under Meles.

EPRDF 2.0: Melding party and developmental state

Immediately after its poor showing at the polls, EPRDF moved to reconstruct and reinvigorate the party on a massive scale. Within weeks senior members of the organisation were reassigned from state to party political roles. Over the next three years, intensive campaigns in rural and urban areas boosted membership from around 700,000 to an alleged 6 million—and more.[85] The ruling Front became strongly institutionalised, especially in rural areas across the country, and increasingly closely intertwined with local state structures. Recognising the weakness of its support among wealthier and more highly educated groups, the party began to campaign in urban areas and on university campuses.

In 2001 the EPRDF finally abandoned its commitment to socialism (long in abeyance, but never until then formally renounced), in favour of a managed transition to 'developmental capitalism'. The new framework of state-led development saw new goals fused with existing commitments to the 'revolutionary democratic' vanguard role of the ruling party. Economic growth rates rose to double digits as investment boomed. The developmental state was premised on the belief that a government could be both developmentally activist and avoid the 'socially wasteful rent-seeking activities' associated with a dominant public sector.[86] It explicitly rejected the notion that markets represented the ideal tool for boosting production and allocating surplus in a transformatory developmental context. EPRDF saw the developmental state system as achieving its legitimacy and hegemony from the single-minded pursuit of broad-based, long-horizon development, based on a 'strong national consensus' broadly shared across the mass of the population. Critics, including the international financial institutions, were not enthusiastic.

Believing this to be in the interests of accelerated socio-economic change for the majority of smallholder agriculturists (rather than the wealthy elite), the government was keen to preserve what Dani Rodrik had called the 'autonomy' of the developmental state from private sector influence.[87] It emphasised the importance of government having the will and the capacity to discipline market and private sector forces, both domestic and international. The private sector was seen as likely to threaten the integrity and pro-poor orientation of policy-making and the bureaucracy. On the leadership side, the influential role of the TPLF chairperson of EPRDF obscured an underlying shift towards an organisational decision-making practice that better balanced the roles of the four member fronts. Paradoxically, an EPRDF-wide national leadership that replaced disproportionately powerful veteran bosses was engineered and emerged under the influence of its visibly more dominant (TPLF) chairman.

Attempts to build a new national consensus began with the Ethiopian millennium celebrated in September 2007, which ushered in a new government narrative of renaissance and the achievement of middle-income status. For the first time, the prime minister surprised (and pleased) many in his audience by speaking of the longer history of the Ethiopian polity, over several thousand years back to Axum. A wave of popular economic nationalism culminated in the sale of national bonds to finance the Millennium Dam on the Nile towards the western border, the construction of which began in 2011. Urban enthusiasm had also been tempered by high levels of inflation since 2008, driven both by global price hikes and rapid growth in domestic money supply to finance expansion of the state's investment programme and by insecurities about legislation to tighten state control of urban land leasing.

Dramatic new levels of investment in regional hydropower projects and road infrastructure were often concentrated in the lowland peripheries or the edge of the escarpment. In combination with the federal granting of large-scale land leases to those investing in commercial agriculture in relatively sparsely populated lowland areas, and attempts at the widespread resettlement of pastoral or transhumant farming populations, these massive infrastructure projects drew criticism for their likely impact on marginal populations and environments. The government reacted angrily, accusing international critics of double standards, and redoubling its efforts to expand the combined envelope of domestic investment by the state, foreign direct investment, and the subsidy for local service delivery under an ambitious five-year programme for Growth and Transformation (GTP), 2010–15. Despite disputes over growth figures, all agreed that rates were impressive for at least a decade from the early 2000s.

Critics questioned the extent to which the capacity and will needed to make a success of state-led development existed in practice at federal level, let alone at lower levels of government. The technocratic integrity of the civil service was open to question both in terms of the extent of corruption and in terms of its willingness to 'speak truth unto power'—the latter consistently underdeveloped in Ethiopian political culture.[88] The problem was compounded by limitations on the scope of the national consensus, which placed the talents and energies of key educated groups outside the national development project. Political opponents and private sector actors were increasingly alienated and marginalised, and the government now had three sets of armed—and militantly 'anti-*weyane*'— opponents: the ethno-national OLF and ONLF; the Ethiopianist national opposition CUD–Genbot 7; and the Asmara regime, which hosted both.

By 2012 Ethiopia's leaders enjoyed unprecedented economic leverage over the developmental process. A large (and, in some cases, profitable) array of public enterprises dominated strategic service and manufacturing sectors, cross-subsidising unusually high levels of public sector investment, and strengthening the policy leverage of the executive. State actors could also rely on a spectrum of politically and developmentally aligned non-governmental regional development associations and some private business conglomerates. State control of land facilitated both economic investment and social engineering. It allowed efficient sequestration but also opened new challenges for policy-makers around rent-seeking and compensation.

Massive investment in energy generation from clean sources (including the massive—and now renamed—Grand Ethiopian Renaissance hydropower dam on the Nile, launched in 2011) was being channelled through state-owned enterprises to boost government access to natural resource rents, while having a dramatic impact on regional integration and the balance of power. For advocates, this was far-sighted, long-horizon, pro-poor developmental investment. For critics, it placed vast national resources and extraordinary levels of spending under the control of an unaccountable cartel of exceptionally powerful politicians. When the EPRDF chairman, the brilliant and dominant architect of Ethiopia's unorthodox economic and political revolution, died unexpectedly in August 2012, the stakes could not have been higher.

4

THINGS FALL APART
THE LOST YEARS OF HAILEMARIAM AND
THE RISE OF THE REGIONS

Sarah Vaughan

During the five and a half years of Hailemariam Desalegn's premiership, the quality of political leadership and the nature of political activity in Ethiopia changed significantly in ways that prepared the ground for later shifts but that were, at the time, largely hidden from external view. When Hailemariam, the deputy prime minister, took over after the unexpected death of his predecessor in August 2012, observers were impressed by what was misleadingly described as Ethiopia's first 'peaceful transfer of power'. In fact it was no such thing: rather the ruling party, which its advocates had seen as the 'motor' of the developmental state, remained in position but began to atrophy and fragment under a less decisive or powerful leader. A prominent Ethiopian news editor, asked about the prospects for Ethiopia under a post-Meles EPRDF, commented wryly that 'a stone can continue to roll downhill under the weight of momentum, gravity and inertia, for quite a while until it begins to hit bumps in the road'.[1] Naturally those bumps were not long in coming. As one well-placed commentator observed less than three years into the new premiership:

since the death of Meles Zenawi, the top part of the power structure has exploded into a multiplicity of competing centres. All of them affect total loyalty towards the dead man's memory and political line because all are afraid that deviating from that line would open them to attacks from a coalition of competing enemies ... Ethiopia at present is like a ship without a skipper, with a respectful but passive crew and a faltering engine.[2]

A series of profound and closely interrelated economic, political and social trajectories now played out simultaneously, derailing the potential of Ethiopia's socio-economic transformation. Firstly, the government and its Western allies were distracted by the potential for religious conflict, particularly Muslim–Christian tensions, and this arguably shifted their focus from other political dynamics within the ruling party. Secondly, Ethiopia's economic 'Great Run'[3] of consistently high 'double-digit growth' began to falter as the government's determined focus on export performance waned and long-horizon policy discipline declined. Thirdly, EPRDF's party-led regional governments, unconstrained by a strong centre, began to evolve in different and more autonomous directions, many of them increasingly inert, corrupt and instrumental. The ruling party, without a strong united leadership began to flounder and fragment while competition for positions exacerbated and drove internal clientelism and cronyism.

As a result, ethnic mobilisation, which EPRDF ideologues had long condemned as 'narrow nationalism', began to flourish within the party. This was weaponised by local ruling politicians themselves as an effective shortcut to popular legitimacy as the delivery of socio-economic benefits on which the party had earlier relied began to falter. Domestic political opportunism was also fed by a series of vigorously anti-EPRDF and increasingly vicious anti-Tigrayan diaspora-based activist media campaigns, in which ethnicised hate speech gradually became more overt. Both inside and outside the ruling party and the country, political identities began to be deliberately ethnicised, as a remarkable new coincidence of interests began to emerge: between EPRDF members vying to outmanoeuvre the previously dominant TPLF and opposition and diaspora activists intent on discrediting the ethnic federal system itself.

Most critically, Ethiopia's federated states began quietly to boost their potential for independent security activity—a dynamic which exploded after Hailemariam's resignation in March 2018, when the implications of the federal centre's incremental loss of control over the monopoly of violence abruptly emerged.

The Muslim protests as a template for new anti-government action

In the months after Meles's death, concern focused on the potential for religious division and radicalisation, rather than the internal dynamics of the ruling party or divisions associated with ethnicity. Religious identity had begun to take on increased importance as processes of urbanisation, unemployment and the youth boom began to be felt as 'dislocation'. The contested formal political arena had also had a spillover effect over the preceding decade. A series of church burnings and Muslim–Christian clashes (in Jimma and Kemise) had followed the post-2005 electoral debacle. Meanwhile Ethiopia's dispatch of its (predominantly highland Christian) troops into southern Somalia in pursuit of the Somali Islamic Courts Union and its Eritrean allies in late 2006 had brought hostile coverage, notably from Al Jazeera. The government's brutal counterinsurgency activities in the Somali region during 2008–9 (after a fatal Ogaden National Liberation Front (ONLF) attack on a Chinese oil installation in April 2007) also exacerbated the sense of a Muslim–Christian divide. The federal government under EPRDF (and its Western 'war on terror' partners) became increasingly preoccupied with the risks of fragmentation or division along religious lines, and a new directorate was set up in the Ministry of Federal Affairs to try to 'deal with' this risk.

In mid-2011, the government was accused of meddling in Muslim institutional politics, encouraging (or imposing) a 'moderate Sufi' al-Ahbash sect in the teeth of local opposition.[4] For several months, the government's inept handling of Muslim protests had worsened a tense situation. Protest peaked in April 2012 after the death of an imam in Arsi region of Oromia, and arrests of what the government called 'a few Muslim extremists' followed. The period of Ramadan fasting over the summer was tense, but protests were muted in August and September by the period of national mourning

117

that followed the death of Meles. By the end of October 2012, a new Meijlis had been elected, but with prime minister Hailemariam only weeks into office, Eid al-Adha celebrations had morphed into widespread protests, and in November 2012 a twitchy new administration stepped up the arrests.

For the first time in Ethiopia, new technologies had driven the organisation of anti-government protests: religious networks and activists on Facebook helped with the organisation and coordination of Muslim protest.[5] New voices had begun to emerge to challenge the narrative of the government. *Addis Standard* magazine, established in February 2011, provided a newly independent-minded journalism, closely analysing the real dynamics of the Muslim protests under its ground-breaking woman editor, Tsedale Lemma. Meanwhile a previously unknown Ethiopian analyst, then studying at Columbia University in the United States, disputed the government's narrative of theological or ideological radicalism, claiming it was rather an extension of 'the regime's war against dissenting voices'.[6] A Muslim Oromo from Arsi, he was soon to emerge as one of the most prominent and effective social media activists against the EPRDF government: Jawar Mohammed.

Muslim protests ground on through 2013, as the trials of Muslim activists and journalists also ground through the courts. The issues underlying the protests were not resolved, and the situation in Arsi in particular continued to be tense and violent over the next year, only gradually subsiding. As a well-placed observer noted in early 2014, 'though the Muslim–Christian and Muslim–EPRDF situation has been relatively quiet in recent months, the problem has not gone away and it is not clear to me where it is headed'.[7] A few months later, however, an answer began to emerge from another part of Oromia, where protest was now organised in terms of Oromo identity.[8] Meanwhile, a faltering economy provided the seedbed within which youth protest flourished.

Ethiopia's economic 'Great Run' begins to run its course

Accelerated economic growth began from 1992 and this momentum was renewed in 2001 with a focus on agricultural development as a driver of industrialisation. From the early 2000s Ethiopia's economy really began to take off. Between 2004 and 2014 its real GDP grew at a 'remarkably rapid and stable' average of 10.9 per cent, the highest rate the country had ever achieved.[9] Even a highly critical World Bank agreed that 'the growth acceleration was part of a broader and very successful development experience' which saw poverty rates drop from 55 per cent to 33 per cent between 2000 and 2011 and the country achieve most of its Millennium Development Goals.[10]

Although Ethiopia's economy continued to grow over the period from 2015, the rates began to falter, and from 2011/12 flatlining or declining exports (particularly its 'non-traditional exports' in manufactured goods, clothing, textiles, leather) gave an early indication of trouble ahead. Ethiopia's overall exports declined from 9 per cent of GDP in 2010/11 to less than 3 per cent of GDP in 2018/19. But for a sudden dramatic change of banking regulation that allowed for an increase in Ethiopia's sale of gold to Switzerland during 2019/20, the value of exports would have dropped still further.[11] With the death of Meles in 2012, the federal government lost its laser-like focus and coordinated action on export progress. This is palpable in the figures and suggests the emergence of a more profound vulnerability than the decline in the growth figures alone might indicate. The loss of the long-horizon focus on the development of an export-oriented economy which could keep pace with population growth and service delivery gradually left Ethiopia vulnerable. By 2014 *The Economist* concluded that 'Ethiopia is stuck'. As private transfers dropped off in 2015/16, and levels of foreign direct investment, which had been growing steadily, faltered the following year, instability and corruption as well as division and inertia were by this time also driving economic uncertainty.

A frenetic series of government initiatives during 2014 and 2015 began to focus on the urgent need for new institutionalisation in order to improve 'good governance'. In January 2015, the federal parliament passed three pieces of anti-corruption-related legislation designed to increase the powers of federal investigators and the anti-corruption commission. In August a government think tank was involved in an urgent study of sectors identified as a priority for tackling corruption: land administration and management; investment; revenue development; business and market development; justice; and infrastructure development. The work was rushed through between the May election and a September party congress. The congress talked up the need for change, but little seemed to result. In October, the think tank reported, and the discussion of its highly critical conclusions among senior government officials was televised. In November 2015 a national good governance campaign was launched, and in the first four to six months of 2016 thousands of officials were dismissed at all levels of government and across the states. In May 2016 Hailemariam took the controversial step of pushing through legislation to bring the attorney general under the office of the prime minister. Prosecution capacity was boosted, but again little seemed to change in practice—except that an important institutional precedent boosting the centralisation of power around the prime minister had been set.

A number of areas of economic policy divergence had also begun to emerge, and without the leadership which had retained strategic oversight, the contradictions looked ever more problematic. As one observer noted, 'Business as usual is taken care of but nobody dares to confront the major contradiction of the economic situation: the constant proclamation that the market economy is the only way towards development and the consistent refusal to play by its rules'.[12] The party's focus had been on the transformation of agriculture at the micro-level of the peasant farmer economy as a motor of industrialisation. Attention now shifted to the macro-level, in favour of the Bretton Woods preference for 'islands of success', with more and more emphasis placed on industrial parks. Rumours of splits and tensions around economic policy-making began to emerge, and gridlock set in. The late Meles Zenawi had postulated that economic development was contingent on the emergence of a dedicated, disciplined, collective political leadership, with the capacity and will to use rents for developmental ends. The gradual loss of coordination and cohesion in Ethiopia's ruling party now began to have a profound impact. So how did this evolve?

The slow disintegration of the ruling EPRDF

In 2012–13, after the post-2005 changes discussed in the last chapter, EPRDF comprised four ruling fronts, and had around 6.3 million members. The highly distinctive internal dynamics and characteristics of each of the four fronts belied the general external impression of a ruling 'monolith'. In fact the character of each of the fronts varied significantly, as did its social relations in—and within—each of the states it governed. In Tigray, for instance, formal adult party membership reached between 16 and 18 per cent of the overall population (remarkably high given the youthful profile of Ethiopia's demography—almost half the population was under the membership age limit of 18); in Amhara, by contrast, it hovered between 7 and 8 per cent of the population, and it was lower still in the two federal chartered cities, Addis Ababa and Dire Dawa. A widespread popular perception that all civil servants were party members became in fact markedly less true at higher levels of the federal civil service in Addis Ababa, where member numbers were relatively modest beyond a small cadre of influential 'political appointees' in leadership positions. Disincentives to party membership operated particularly strongly in urban areas, and among the most educated and productive, where they included onerous meeting hours and membership dues (rising sharply among salaried civil servants) as well as a hierarchical political culture. As the 2005 election had demonstrated, the urban middle class was generally not supportive of the party.

By contrast, at the level of the local state beyond the cities, party and state structures had been effectively fused after the reforms that expanded membership in 2006. The political 'basic organisation' (*meseretawi dirigit*) structures were by 2011 precisely mapped onto the administrative systems of the *kebele* and *wereda* levels of government. With the exception of periods of the electoral cycle, these structures were occupied with socio-economic 'developmental' rather than with political activities, drawing on a *zemecha* or 'campaign-style' approach to improving systems for farm productivity, sanitation or educational enrolment. Some of these campaigns were effective in transforming productivity, and this process of intensive mobilisation

121

was key to Ethiopia's Millennium Development Goals success. But it was also the case that they were generally top-down, centralised and uniform—ill-suited to the specific needs of individual rural communities, particularly as these began to evolve in more complex ways, as socio-economic trajectories at the micro-level became more diverse and plural, and both mobility and aspiration increased.[13] In many cases, the temptation was that party cadres were loyal up the hierarchy to their bosses, rather than focused on the interests of their communities and peers.

This meant that the health of the relations between party and society at the micro-level (and of Ethiopia's development processes) precisely reflected the quality of the leadership provided by the political structures of the fronts in each region, the specific patterns of sociology and social interaction that characterised their relationships with local communities in each local area, and the extent to which these micro-level relationships were able to broker and combine the demands of the higher levels of the state apparatus with the needs and desires of the population. There were important gender differences too between the fronts.[14] Where interaction was relatively dense, trusting and well established, robust debate and active social engagement could negotiate effective solutions that satisfied all sides. In the frequently less successful instances, however, many who joined the ruling party when its membership expanded dramatically between 2006 and 2010 did so to maximise their own benefits and connectivity with the resources of the state—not in service to their communities. This was a recipe for authoritarianism, ill-discipline and abuse of power.[15]

From 2011–12 tens of thousands of high- and mid-level party leaders had gone through extensive rounds of training, in an attempt to reinforce a genuinely 'national' cohort of political elites who would lead state and development processes in each region, though at the lower levels these training processes were also devolved. Developments over the next six to seven years indicated that these attempts at a process of political integration were broadly unsuccessful, as deeper local socio-political dynamics gained traction. Where communities felt that the EPRDF political constellation had benefited them, and saw (for instance) members of their community promoted at senior level, they took opportunities to become supportive and involved. Thus, for instance, Silte zone's population had been strongly supportive of the ruling party while also vociferously critical of its failings and demanding of better delivery. In many parts of Tigray the debate between party and population (especially in rural areas) was similarly robust and responsive, although also often criticised. Elsewhere (to put it mildly), things were often markedly less successful. Farmers in Amhara in particular reported resentment at being 'forced' to engage in development initiatives they didn't value, and processes were formalistic and sometimes antagonistic. Meanwhile, in Oromia and other parts of the south, complaints about corruption and the attempt to control lucrative cash crops or land-leasing systems became increasingly vociferous.[16]

Meanwhile, at the macro-level, relations were becoming fractious and more difficult to manage, and this also had the tendency to reinforce upward-facing personalised networks and patronage systems within each of the fronts. In an early indication of the tensions that emerged in 2013, Hailemariam attempted to broker a new style of decision-making by 'consensus', appointing a series of three deputy prime ministers—one from each of the other fronts, and with a specific area of expertise—allegedly to formalise a more 'collective leadership' and stronger accountability within EPRDF. Although the organisation continued to express a general desire to move towards a single national party, the depth of differences among the elites of each of the four EPRDF member fronts—of history, culture and style as well as of capacity and commitment, both between and within the four fronts—indicated that this was unlikely to happen soon. Meanwhile, tensions were becoming gradually more overt—and were increasingly framed in terms of ethnicity.

Controversies about the balance of representation within and beyond EPRDF had been suppressed while Meles was alive, either in a reflection of better organisational cohesion and discipline, or because of the swiftly effective suppression of dissent in the wake of the split in the TPLF in 2001 (see the previous chapter). Either way, the hierarchy was clear, and few chose to destabilise it. After Meles's death, three sets of organisational controversies emerged. The first was a failure to include the groups from the 'developing' regional states of Afar, Benishangul-Gumuz, Gambella and Somali. This rankled with many politicians from the lowlands and seemed less and less legitimate as lowland political elites rose to positions of prominence. It fostered the impression of a 'two-tier' federal system, which did much to undermine the legitimacy of the system in these areas—particularly (but by no means only) in the Somali region, where the government's brutal counterinsurgency activities had by this time reduced the threat presented by the ONLF at the cost of shattered lives, gross abuses of human rights, and deep bitterness.

The second was the relative hierarchy of 'real power' between members of the four different fronts within the EPRDF. TPLF, as the 'elder' front, was widely seen as still dominant, with the Amhara organisation, rooted in the Ethiopian People's Democratic Movement (which had partnered in establishing the EPRDF in 1989), also seen as powerful. The Oromo People's Democratic Organisation (OPDO), established around the same time, was seen as more of a protégé of the others, particularly of the TPLF; and the Southern Ethiopian People's Democratic Movement (SEPDM), which was not finally formally established until after 1991, more junior still (this perception did not shift with the elevation of a southerner to the position of chairperson). As one trenchant critic put it in 2016, 'Both ANDM [Amhara National Democratic Movement] and OPDO were created by the TPLF. They have never broken free of its oversight, at least to the extent of being considered legitimate representatives by the Amhara and the Oromo.'[17] Finally, the organisational structure of the party—which gave an equal quarter share of executive and central committee votes to each front regardless of the size of its membership or the population it claimed to represent—was also seen as consolidating the TPLF's disproportionate organisational influence.

Over the next few years, factional in-fighting and what the ruling party leadership itself acknowledged was an explosive growth of corruption made cohesion impossible, and the developmental state's 'motor of development' soon began to stutter. At the ninth EPRDF congress in Bahir Dar, which was finally held in March 2013, Hailemariam was reconfirmed in his position, but he launched strong attacks on corruption and sabotage, describing the Ethiopian Electric Power Corporation, for instance, as a 'wounded hyena' resisting reform.[18] After a year of new protests in Oromia in 2014, the TPLF celebrated in early 2015 the fortieth anniversary of its founding in Mekele, and a barrage of historical TV documentaries reminded Ethiopians of the leading role it had played and the sacrifices it had made. Ethiopia's leaders were pictured ceremoniously visiting the caves at Hagere Selam in central Tigray, from where the struggle against the Derg had been led. TPLF's leaders clearly felt that their EPRDF peers needed to be reminded of the critical historical role of the TPLF in the achievement of federalism. Whether the reminder served to do anything other than entrench the resentments towards TPLF that were emerging is less evident.

Three months later, the 2015 elections passed in a surreal, almost trance-like performance, 'an exercise in controlled political participation',[19] with no international observers and an overwhelming win for the ruling party. The scope for social control inherent in the EPRDF's intensely interwoven party–state system and mass membership was neatly demonstrated: no one was in any doubt as to whom to vote for. Overt conflict was confined to the political elites, as the government pressured the opposition Blue Party, banning opposition rallies and preventing diaspora mobilisation. TPLF was engaged in an intense internal discussion, as veteran 'old guard' members, some of whom had been sidelined post-2001, joined young Tigrayans in criticising the decline and degeneracy of the current leadership at its twelfth congress in August–September 2015. Soon afterwards, in the autumn of 2015, anti-government protests began again, continuing and escalating through 2016. By now, discussion of the evils of poor governance, corruption and lack of accountability was public,[20] and in November the federal government launched a new campaign of 'tehadso' or renewal.

The following year things declined further, and internal political tensions escalated as external conflict grew—extending from Oromia also to Amhara, and with an increasingly anti-Tigrayan or anti-weyane tone. In October 2016 the OPDO removed two leaders associated with Meles,[21] replacing them with the more popular figures of Lemma Megersa and Workneh Gebeyehu. The federal government declared a State of Emergency in a new attempt to quell anti-government protests and the violence overtaking the country.

Kjetil Tronvoll notes that devolved or federal systems can often exacerbate political party cohesion, enhancing local dynamics, and projecting local conflicts onto national politics. There seems to be little doubt that this was allowed to happen in Ethiopia during this period.[22] Underpinning this—both driving and being driven by elite political in-fighting—were increasingly violent ethnic rhetoric and conflict newly framed in ethnic terms. The full ethnicisation of politics was pursued most vigorously among EPRDF's own cadres. Already in mid-2015, René Lefort recorded the views of Tigrayan and Amhara political commentators—first from Tigray Online:

> 'the fight in Ethiopian politics ... is between those who fabricate lies to bring the old system and stay on top of the majority of Ethiopians' – in other words: the 'chauvinists' or more broadly the Amhara—'and those who want to build a just and equitable society'. In clear terms, this quote asserts that Ethiopian politics continue to be dominated by the age-old conflict between Amhara and Tigreans. For its part, the ANDM, or at least its mid-level cadres, often express a symmetrical resentment. They are no longer ready to tolerate bearing their Amhara identity like a cross, in other words being pilloried because they are descendants of the ethnic group whose leaders dominated Ethiopia for a century. They frequently employ the same language as used by the Tigrean militants during their armed struggle, claiming to have become 'second class citizens'.[23]

Festering through 2015 and 2016, things did not improve in 2017, as violence between Oromo and Somali regional state 'special forces' along the inter-state border was widely seen as fomented by the politicians of the two regions, to increase their leverage. It displaced 700,000 civilians during the year.[24] In March, a controversial paper by veteran politicians Abbaye Tsehaye (TPLF) and Bereket Simon (ANDM) set out for discussion the challenges to the federal order, including the rise of intolerant ethnic politicking within the party. By October 2017 ethnic grievance in senior cadres' speeches was public and overt. The EPRDF and its member fronts should have held congresses in the autumn of 2017, but in a marker of the extent of the internal breakdown, they were postponed to the following year amidst wrangling and tension. Veteran Oromo politician Abadula Gemeda resigned as speaker from the House of People's Representatives,[25] citing 'disrespect' and attack on the 'dignity of the Oromo people', according to media sources.[26] By November 2017, in a previously unheard-of bilateral move, the Oromo and Amhara ruling fronts convened a joint conference in Bahir Dar, where issues of internal party representation were explicitly discussed, and a joint strategy evolved to limit the influence of the TPLF.

The growth of regional special forces

As Ethiopia's regional states became more autonomous of the federal centre over the period between 2012 and 2018, they were increasingly able to back their assertiveness with force. The implications of this became starkly clear after 2018, as the country descended into violence and the proliferation of security sector actors exploded, with further fragmentation and informalisation after the outbreak of war in 2020. All of Ethiopia's states had by 2018 begun to maintain so-called special forces, some members being reportedly attracted away from the national army by better remuneration. The process was some time in the gestation: the gradual loss of the monopoly of violence of the central state and its security institutions is a trajectory that had evolved gradually over the period from 2012.

It was the initial decision to devolve responsibility for regional state security and counterinsurgency to the Ethiopian Somali regional government in 2008–9 that had set a major new precedent in the country's security arrangements. Federal Ethiopia first experimented with establishing small 'rapid response' (*fetno derash*) forces under the regional state governments during the 1990s, but these units were soon dismantled or brought back under federal control in the early 2000s. In 2008, following the ONLF attack on the Chinese oil exploration facility at Abole, in a highly significant departure from earlier practice, the Somali region was authorised to establish a regional Somali 'special police' (*liyu polis*) to lead counterinsurgency in the region.

After its controversial campaign against the Islamic Courts Union in southern Somalia in 2006, the Ethiopian federal government saw this shift in its counterinsurgency strategy in the Somali region as key to changing the dynamics and optics of a conflict which had placed a (highland, predominantly Christian) federal military against a (lowland, Muslim, Somali) Ogaden National Liberation Front (ONLF) insurgency. There is some evidence that the prime minister had planned to reverse the decision at the time of his death in 2012, but that his successor found this impossible to effect in practice. The Somali force was armed and trained by the Eastern Command of the national army. It was recruited by the regional government and was regularly accused of grave human rights abuses. During the period of Somali regional state president Abdi Mohammed Omar (2010–8), its leadership and rank and file were increasingly drawn from subclans closely connected with him.[27]

During Hailemariam's premiership, there were a number of incidents in which regional 'special forces' fought against the national military.[28] While Article 52.7 of the FDRE constitution in principle allowed state governments to 'establish and maintain a state police force, and to maintain public order and peace within the state', the constitutionality of wider 'paramilitary' forces, and the security dilemmas they posed, had been questioned (after 2018) by the new federal minister of peace, among others.[29] She began to push for reformist legislation to standardise the nature of the training and armaments of legitimate regional police forces, as well as set limits on their number and mandate. Few credible force figures were available. In late 2020, the state-owned *Addis Zemen* newspaper estimated the number of special forces between ten thousand and hundreds of thousands.[30] By then, there was a common consensus that special forces were loyal to their regional state governments rather than to the centre.[31]

Breaking the EPRDF covenant: The deliberate ethnicisation of Ethiopia's politics

During the 1990s the EPRDF had been taken aback by the strength of what it called 'narrow nationalism' among many of its members.

It took steps to try to reduce the potential and actual conflicts which emerged when the benefits of the new federal arrangements—jobs and budgets—began to be allocated to ethnically defined units. As noted in the previous chapter, ethno-national rhetoric was on occasion intentionally muted in favour of a more integrationist approach. However, until 2005, the ruling party's leaders considered chauvinism to be a largely insignificant force within Ethiopian politics. The issues raised in the 2005 election campaign changed its mind, and in the wake of the election the balance tipped again in favour of ethno-nationalism, with Oromia in particular gaining momentum vis-à-vis Addis Ababa. The Oromia regional state relocated its capital (and fleets of regionally plated taxis) from Adama back to 'Finfinne' (the Oromo name for the capital, Addis Ababa) under a more robustly nationalist regional president from 2005 to 2010— the same Abadula Gemeda who resigned amidst the high drama of disintegration in 2017.

In moments of stress successive Ethiopian governments have used the 'Oromo threat' to cow critics in urban areas,[32] and the EPRDF's reaction to the 2005 poll was one of these moments. In retrospect this period laid the groundwork for much that came later, most notably the 'Oromo protests' of 2014–18. Oromo politicians arguably learned the value of leveraging momentum in their large and centrally located regional state.

Oromo protests

Oromo protests were initially triggered in early 2014 by publicity given to ruling OPDO claims that the federal administration of Addis Ababa intended to appropriate land in the surrounding areas of Oromia. OPDO members in Adama discussed a proposed master plan for the coordinated development of infrastructure between Addis Ababa and the surrounding Oromia Special Economic Zone.[33] News of what was reported as a planned federal appropriation of Oromo land, seen in effect as 'Addis Ababa expansionism', was leaked from the meeting, and broadcast on the Oromo language service of the government's Ethiopian TV. Demonstrations quickly erupted on university campuses across Oromia, spreading like wildfire from Haromaya to Jimma, Ambo, Nekemte, Bale Robe,

Adama and elsewhere. Clashes erupted sporadically over several weeks, many targeting non-Oromo students, with many injured. University campuses emerged as a particular focus of anti-government resistance, and nationalist rhetoric. The evolution of radical student ethno-national politics seems to have been a striking blind spot in government thinking, which is surprising given the student movement history (discussed in Chapter 2).[34]

In an atmosphere of ethno-nationalist tension in May 2014, student protests culminated in riots in Ambo (West Shewa) where a number of non-Oromo businesses and property were targeted and destroyed. Clashes occurred amidst heightened rhetoric and multiple accusations and counter-accusations. An inter-regional state football tournament in Bahir Dar turned sour when Oromo officials were jeered with abusive language; meanwhile, OPDO was widely criticised for a 'provocative' monument to the Oromo killed or dispossessed during imperial incorporation.[35] Senior OPDO politician Abadula Gemeda promised to address Ambo grievances and a lid was kept on things until after the 2015 elections. By the autumn, rumours that the master plan was going ahead brought more tension, and in a context of heightened ethnic sensitivity, the ill-advised comments of a senior TPLF politician (that corruption and bad governance within Oromia were the real causes of anti-government anger) merely fanned the flames of the ethnic antipathy which was by now conflated with anti-government antagonism.[36]

Protests were fuelled by social media activism and a complex EPRDF–OPDO tussle over 'good governance' and corrupt land administration, as lease values escalated in the development corridors around Addis Ababa. On 14 November 2015, in Ginchi town of Dandi *wereda*, West Shewa, demonstrations by elementary and high school students and young unemployed people focused on two local issues of land and resources. *Wereda* authorities had issued a commercial contract to cut trees in Chilimo Forest around Ginchi, allegedly (though this was disputed) to 'reafforest it to regenerate the forest'; secondly, they had reportedly reallocated a large plot next to the elementary school (then used as a football field) to build themselves houses. Rumours and resentment spiralled into suspicion and demonstrations, and young people and school students clashed with the police. The next day, violence spread to Ambo and Gindaberet towns, and the issue of farmers' displacement from Addis Ababa's surroundings also became part of the agenda. On the third day influential blogger Jawar Mohammed organised an online discussion of intellectuals relating to the causes of the conflicts, bringing a range of different Oromo grievances and setting light to the issue. Conflict then spread to Wellega and continued through November and December 2015. The issue of farmers' displacement from Addis Ababa's surroundings also returned to the fore.

Local government systems began to disintegrate, and, when federal police were killed, the military were deployed in a crackdown.[37] Bekele Gerba of the moderate opposition Oromo Federalist Congress (OFC) was arrested in December, accused of fomenting conflict, one of 22 opposition politicians arrested. In January 2016, the OPDO abandoned the 'Addis Ababa master plan', but after the Ethiopian Christmas a new round of violence was triggered by clashes following a wedding celebration in West Arsi: wedding guests on a bus singing a patriotic song in Afaan Oromo clashed with the police and the groom was injured. Conflict immediately spread to all six *weredas* of the zone, and sixteen churches were burned in the course of the violence. In Shashamane a number of local police were killed. By now, senior federal officials had begun to point fingers at Eritrean complicity in fomenting protest, though few took these claims seriously.[38]

Internal ruling party recrimination through 2015 and early 2016 noted that the ruling OPDO had been slow to respond and had seemed ambivalent about dealing with protest. From the top at the federal level, they tended in the beginning to see the 'problem' of the protests as OPDO, and there was a persistent notion that OPDO officials heavily involved in corruption (especially in relation to land accumulation and speculation) invoked narrow nationalism and violence to 'cover their tracks'. By the time the prime minister apologised to the Oromo people in April 2016, the internal evaluation had further shifted and held that it wasn't just OPDO that suffered from corruption and venality. Hailemariam said publicly that the same issue of poor governance had spread across the board from Tigray to the south, and that it was not just a problem of one part of the organisation. Meanwhile, in June 2016, 800 Oromo regional officials were sacked for land-related corruption: administrators in Sebeta, Burayu and Dukem were brought to court, and prosecutions reached as high as a regional state vice president and the mayor of Sululta (these prosecutions were dropped post-2018).

In August 2016, protests extended to Amhara national regional state, amidst growing Amhara ruling party discontent at the balance of power within the EPRDF, and in September Lemma Megersa and Abiy Ahmed replaced an Oromia president and vice president seen as pro-EPRDF–TPLF. By now, anti-TPLF sentiment was overt. At the traditional Oromo *Irreechaa* annual thanksgiving festival in Bishoftu in early October 2016, shouts of 'Down down *weyane!*' echoed around the crowd. Brutal policing and a stampede triggered the deaths of a large number of celebrants who had gathered from across Oromia. An explosion of anger engulfed the region during the subsequent 'week of rage'.[39] The federal government declared a State of Emergency, and a violent crackdown ensued. Oromo nationalist sentiment mobilised further in the context of clashes on the Oromo–Somali border from the end of the year, as accusations and counter-accusations were traded between the two regional governments. The State of Emergency was lifted in August 2017, but protesters were again killed by government forces in Ambo in October 2017. By this stage, Oromia had become ungovernable, and the federal government had proven itself incapable of responding other than with force.

There has been much debate about the real nature of the *qeerroo* networks of young Oromos who led the protests between 2014 and 2018 and, indeed, their relations with political and local government actors.[40] On the face of it, they evolved as straightforwardly anti-government. But it seems likely that many members of the Oromia ruling party were deeply implicated in their evolution—and that in the end they served its purposes, leveraging its relative power within EPRDF. *Qeerroo* organisational structures seem to have been amorphous and spontaneous on the ground, and sometimes chaotic, fragmented or competitive locally. Nevertheless, the role of social media, and of the diaspora activist Jawar Mohammed in particular, seems to have been critical to their coordination, such as it was.[41] The romantic notion of a spontaneous 'Oromo street', however, took a knock after 2019–20 when, now without the supportive facilitation of the Oromo ruling party and the coordinating social media presence of Jawar, *qeerroo* activity was rather quickly snuffed out, driven instead into the underground of more militant opposition.

Protests and conflict in Amhara: Tsegedé, Qemant, Welkaiyt

If there was friction in the relations between the ruling OPDO in Oromia and the TPLF, the relationship between the TPLF and the Amhara ruling front became downright hostile during the Hailemariam period. This was exacerbated by the re-mobilisation of a series of localised identity and land-related conflicts (some new, some dormant, some newly furbished) which emerged to become drivers of further violence in this period. As discipline and unity eroded within the EPRDF ruling fronts, each of these issues was used for political mobilisation.

The first was a small-scale boundary dispute between the two regions of Amhara and Tigray over land at Gicho-Tsegedé. Tsegedé *wereda* includes the strategic crossroads at Dansha,[42] which had been the scene of an ambush and heavy fighting between the Derg's military and the TPLF during the critical military campaign of 1988.[43] Tsegedé lay along the route of the TPLF's cross-border road from Sudan, constructed in the early to mid-1980s, after the EPLF denied them access through Kassala via Barentu in western Eritrea. To the south, Tsegedé is bounded by the Amhara region, and a precise boundary between Tigray and Amhara at Gicho-Tsegedé had remained undefined, though this had little or no impact locally through the 1990s and 2000s.

For twenty years, the areas north and south of the border were relatively lightly populated. This changed after the mid-2000s, following 'internal resettlement' of highland populations into areas adjacent to the border by both regions. According to official censuses Tsegedé *wereda*'s population increased from less than 60,000 in 1994[44] to over 103,000 in 2007, and the preponderance of Tigrigna-speakers increased. Resettlement into Tsegedé (and neighbouring Kafta Humera) *wereda* on the Tigray side was mirrored by resettlement into neighbouring Kwara, Lay Armachiho and Dangila *weredas* on the

Amhara side. The combination of new population pressure and new investment in infrastructure in these border areas drove demarcation up the political agenda. Other factors included the digitisation of land certification in these areas during the period, with new satellite image-based mapping of holdings.

A second issue had been brewing over decades, further south in Gonder zone. The Amhara regional state government had been confronted by a long-standing unresolved identity claim raised by the Qemant minority. The Qemant live along an axis stretching from Chilga *wereda*, north to Lake Tana in Lay Armachiho, Qwara, Dembia, Metemma and Wogera *weredas*. They were recorded as a separate group in the 1984 (Derg era) and 1994 censuses, numbering 172,000 by 1994. The Qemant minority had lobbied since the 1990s for a separate administrative district uniting their disparate villages and giving them a voice at Amhara regional level. In 2007, however, it emerged that the Qemant category 'code' had been deleted from the latest census, and this triggered a new round of demands. In August 2009, a self-appointed Qemant Committee delivered a petition for self-administration to the federal House of Federation, which referred it back to the region for review. The Amhara regional government finally investigated the issue in January 2011, and in March 2020 reported back that since the Qemant lacked a distinctive language, contiguous territory or much evidence of interaction, their identity claim should be rejected. In 2013, the Amhara state parliament formally turned down the Qemant request, reporting their decision to the House of Federation in July.

In September 2013 the Qemant Committee appealed against the Amhara regional state decision to the House of Federation, claiming 126 distinctive *kebeles* and a separate psychological make-up and history. The House sent an investigation team to the region, but it returned after arrests and tension. A new Amhara state committee recommended that the 42 adjacent Qemant *kebeles* be recognised, and the regional state parliament passed proclamation 229/2007EC for 'up to 42 kebeles'. This did not resolve the issue, and, still feeling that its participation was inadequate, the Qemant Committee applied to hold a demonstration at Aykel town in June 2015. The request was denied, and a number of Qemant were killed and wounded, as demonstrations for and against began across Chilga *wereda*. In early November clashes spread to Mawra *wereda*, in Armachiho, and the killing of regional special forces commanders triggered a '3-day shootout' which the federal human rights commission later said had led to the deaths of 22 unarmed civilians.[45]

Mobilisation was now ratcheted up (both against the Qemant claim and on a third issue of Welkaiyt), and in November several thousand people demonstrated in Aykel. By December 'some 60,000–70,000 people of which 15,000–20,000 were armed; from Wogera, Gondar town area, Chilga, Quara, Lay Armachiho, all kebeles of Metema wereda, Genda Wuha and from Metema Yohannis towns, had taken part in the demonstration [in Metemma town]. Evidence indicates that the preparation to organize such a demonstration was known to some officials'.[46] The issue now degenerated into a toxic marker of tension between the Amhara and Tigray ruling parties, with the former accusing the latter of fomenting the Qemant issue behind the scenes. When the federal human rights commission's report was presented to parliament in June 2016, the Amhara parliamentarians abstained. Demonstrations erupted in Gonder in July 2016, with violent pogroms targeting Tigrayans. Many from the Tigrayan community fled Gonder in mid-2016, and the issue provoked bitter EPRDF–ANDM recrimination throughout the summer. After further pressure from the federal government, a referendum was held in September 2017. One out of eight *kebeles*—Quaber Lomye—voted to join the Qemant self-administrative zone. This did not resolve the issue. By now, many Amhara regarded the Qemant as 'TPLF fifth columnists', and violence continued through 2018 and beyond. As it intensified under cover of the Tigray war from late 2020, thousands of Qemant fled to Sudan.

A third issue formed the basis for the evolution of a much-wider irredentist claim, which has been a major driver of the war in Tigray, building both on the relatively minor boundary dispute at Gicho-Tsegedé and suspicion about the Qemant issue—both of which also had their roots in competition for newly valuable farmland. 'Irredentism is one of the ways Amhara nationalists seek redress against what they describe as their marginalisation. The claim for the annexation of Wolqayt, Tsegedé and Raya to the Amhara region was, from 2016 onwards, the cement bringing together Amhara nationalists.'[47]

Activists involved in Qemant, Welkaiyt and Amhara nationalism began to mobilise in earnest during the last two years of the Hailemariam period. The massive demonstrations of mid-2016 provided an indicator of how the issues had caught alight. The political salience of this mobilisation became more visible later on, with the emergence in 2018 of a new Amhara ethnic political competitor to the ruling party, the National Movement of Amhara or Aben (see the next chapter). 'The speed at which a new trend of Amhara nationalism emerged and became ubiquitous over the period 2016–2018 took many by surprise.'[48]

In the 1990s, an early attempt to mobilise Amhara ethnic nationalism, under the banner of the All-Amhara People's Organisation (AAPO) of the medical doctor Asrat Woldeyes, had been relatively unsuccessful, beyond urban elites. Rather, it was pan-Ethiopian nationalist opposition that confronted the EPRDF in Amhara. This led to some soul-searching in Amhara ruling party circles after the 2005 elections, when the vigour of opposition support in the region surprised them.[49] As the Amhara ruling party's relations with its EPRDF peers—and particularly with the TPLF—began to fray, mobilising a disgruntled domestic constituency with land claims against Tigray became an irresistible temptation. Activists began to dust off copies of the imperial maps of 'Tigray' province, purporting to show that the federal regional state of Tigray had 'stolen' land beyond the Tekeze River.[50] As discussed in Chapter 3, the federal dispensation drew on the language distribution of the population, not on historical precedent. The fact that the Welkaiyt area (like the rest of Ethiopia) has historically been administered in different ways, by different peoples, over different periods of history was clear— but irrelevant, in the view of the architects of the federation.[51] They were interested only in contemporary demography and language use, and this placed Welkaiyt (like Raya) unequivocally under Tigray, albeit with important Amharic-speaking minorities.[52]

The 1994 census indicated that more than 95 per cent of the population of Welkaiyt was Tigrayan. By 2007, as in Tsegedé, the population had risen because of resettlement and the in-migration of casual labour from 90,000 to just under 140,000. Welkaiyt saw settlement from other parts of Tigray earlier than elsewhere, as demobilised TPLF veterans were given commercial farmland in the lowland sesame plains from the 1990s. Many were integrated into an export value chain under Guna, the commercial trading arm of the regional Endowment Fund for the Rehabilitation of Tigray, known as EFFORT. Along with the growth in the overall population, the two rounds of census figures indicated that ethnic Amharas had grown from 3 to 6 per cent of the population, still a relatively small minority.[53]

This last point suggested a complicating factor which seems to have been exploited in both the Welkaiyt and the Raya cases.[54] In both areas, some argued that a highly evolved, highly local sense of distinctive identity had emerged. On this basis, it was argued, under some circumstances and for some purposes, some members of the local population distinguished themselves both from Amharas and from Tigrayans. These identity categories—albeit not based on distinct language usage—now offered an enticing possibility for political actors to mobilise to their own advantage. The stage was set for influential but disgruntled individuals and politicians to seek to 'flip' their identity in each case, arguing that their own identities (and the identity of farmers who happened to occupy particularly lucrative and fertile agricultural areas) 'really' belonged in one state rather than another. This is precisely what has been attempted, emerging by 2020 also as an important driver of war.[55]

In 2014–15 a number of civil servants and farmers from the Welkaiyt area fell out with the Tigray regional state government over the implementation of its recently revised investment laws and lost out on the claims for additional 'investment' land they had been advancing.[56] The Welkaiyt area had become a relatively lucrative commercial farming centre, producing sesame for commercial export. Among this group was a TPLF veteran from the area, Colonel Demeke Zewdu, one of many veterans who retired from the defence force and sought to move into agriculture. He was among those who fell out with the Tigray regional government authorities, feeling that he had been ill-treated, when new investment laws and new land certification processes came into effect. He and others then took their grievances to Gonder where, during the post-Second World War period of Haile Selassie, a number of relatively wealthy families of Welkaiyt origin had moved. Gonder was one of a number of towns which, although important historically and during the imperial era and Italian period, had not flourished under federalism: it emerged in the 1990s as a centre of antipathy to the federal project.[57] Although something of a backwater during the 1990s, with recalcitrant water supply issues, Gonder began to draw in new wealth, from the Ethiopian diaspora as well, in the following decade.

This relatively wealthy Gonder-based Welkaiyt 'diaspora' now supported these claims, and the Welkaiyt Committee for the Restoration of the Welkaiyt Identity to Amhara was formed. It was launched publicly in September 2015, just as the Qemant issue was beginning to reach fever pitch. Welkaiyt ignited an already tense situation. The reaction in Mekele was not enthusiastic, and the Tigray regional state government dismissed the Welkaiyt Committee as a vehicle for 'wealthy Amhara elites' to pursue an anti-government agenda. Colonel Demeke was jailed in July 2016 and later charged with multiple murders. His arrest helped provoke the huge demonstrations already noted and the violence against Tigrayans in Gonder.[58] No formal irredentist claim had been submitted, the Tigray government argued; and in the view of Mekele, the ill-treatment of Tigrayans in Gonder, many thousands of whom fled the city in July 2016, illuminated the real dynamics of the issue.

'Jostling between the Amhara and Tigrayan wings of EPRDF' was cited as a cause at the time. 'Among activists from Amhara, disavowal of the ethnicity-based system is at the crux of disagreements over how to oppose the EPRDF'.[59] Meanwhile, in an echo of the Oromo *qeerroo* networks, Amhara militia and youth groups which had mobilised during the violence in mid-2016 began to refer to themselves as *fano* (roughly 'a free fighter' or Christian peasant fighting for the 'motherland'), consciously drawing on a well-known category with strong—and strongly positive—nationalist connotations across the Amhara region.[60] In naming themselves in this way, the *fano* groups were drawing on the nationalist historical connotations of a complex term which sometimes equated with 'patriot', someone who historically fought in the service of the empire.[61] Here things stuck until 2018, while the collapse of tourism income that followed the October 2016 State of Emergency in Gonder only compounded local resentments.

Anti-'*weyane*' sentiment, the Oromara 'coup' and the rise of Abiy Ahmed

There was little that was spontaneous about the anti-government protests which developed from 2014, and the increasingly anti-Tigrayan edge of the anti-government protest rhetoric was also not a matter of chance. Diplomats and aid officials appointed to Ethiopia in or since 2018 have found it hard to understand the depths of anti-TPLF (and often also anti-Tigrayan) venom which they have encountered in Ethiopia. Some have concluded that 'the Tigrayans' must have 'done something' to have engendered such hatred, and that their actions must have meant that they 'deserved' such public disapprobation.[62] Few non-Amharic speakers have understood or imagined the extent of the deliberate mobilisation of a highly ethnicised form of anti-TPLF and anti-Tigrayan sentiment, particularly over the period from 2016. The antipathy developed threads in both Oromo and Amhara nationalist sentiment. With critics and activists repressed and arrested within country, important sources of amplification now flourished outside.

The social media mobilisation of Jawar Mohammed and the Oromo Media Network drew on the anti-TPLF sentiment which had emerged after the repression of Oromo Liberation Front (OLF) supporters in the 1990s. OLF rhetoric in the 1990s had labelled the ruling OPDO in Oromia as 'condoms'—a thinly disguised Oromo covering for Tigrayan power. Jawar's rhetoric now began to use the Tigrayan name 'Hagos' as a shorthand slur to identify those he claimed were profiteering from EPRDF rule as ethnic Tigrayans.[63] Meanwhile, in the US the group of political exiles associated with Genbot 7 established the Ethiopian satellite TV station ESAT in April 2010, soon setting up production facilities in Washington DC, Amsterdam and London. The station amplified the views of anti-government critics, particularly (as noted) during the violence in and around Gonder in mid-2016. By mid-2017 it had been dubbed the 'Voice of Genocide' by a Tigray activist.[64] Its broadcasts were blocked in Ethiopia.

A year after the violent events of 2016 (in and around Gonder in the summer, and at the *Irreechaa* festival in Bishoftu in October), the Oromo and Amhara EPRDF fronts brought things to a new head, convening a 'bilateral' conference without the involvement of their Southern and Tigrayan peers. By now protests in Amhara paralleled the protests in Oromia. The activities of the youthful Oromo *qeerroo* activists across Oromia were mirrored by the emergence of the *fano* youth groups in north-western Amhara. Explicit parallels were now being drawn between the struggles of the Amhara and the Oromo 'street', and EPRDF leaders at local level in each of these two regions sought to ride and steer rather than counter these movements, continuing to fan them as each became more explicitly anti-TPLF and anti-Tigrayan. The November 2017 conference in Bahir Dar discussed the issue of 'proportionate' internal representation within the EPRDF and the need for a rebalancing of the constellation of power.

In a remarkable statement at the closing of the meeting, the Oromia regional president, Lemma Megersa, made a statement which (in the context) reverberated through the body politic, and which is worth quoting at length.

> What Ethiopianism truly is has been revealed to me today [by this conference]. Though its name isn't pretty (and nor have I tried it) Ethiopianism is like hashish; Ethiopianism is an addiction. If it were possible to open and see into the hearts and minds of every one of us, we would find what we saw here [at this conference]. When the people freely express their feelings, Ethiopianism has penetrated into their hearts above all else. This is something that sparks hope. Our Ethiopian [identity] is not darkening: it exists. It is not something that ceases to exist easily. Since it is an identity and a symbol that has kept on being built, one layer over another, over the ages, it is not something that easily breaks or loses its light.
>
> So this has taught us a great [lesson]. When we were preparing this conference [in collaboration] with the officials of the Amhara region, we had planned to quietly discuss what we are to discuss

and return to our abode without talking much about it on our media. However, the news of it went beyond the entirety of Ethiopia and became the talk of the world. These are what we are seeing and hearing during the past 2 or 3 days. This shows that when it comes to the issue of one's country, one's Ethiopianness, one's unity, every Ethiopian, wherever they may be, has a thirst and a hunger. Thus the journey [and] the solution is one thing and one thing only: to strengthen this. It is the responsibility of all of us to do our part to bring it to fruition.[65]

In principle, the sentiment is perfectly compatible with the federalist EPRDF line consistent since the beginning of the federal period: that one could be Tigrayan Ethiopian, Somali Ethiopian, Oromo Ethiopian, and so on.[66] In the fractious, violent and polarised context of late 2017, however, the statement was electric. It suggested an affinity and enthusiasm for a nationalist sentiment that suddenly seemed to map two of EPRDF's own fronts onto an alliance with anti-government sentiment and protest; and—much more of a challenge to the architects of federalism—it now also opened up the potential for the re-emergence of, and an alliance with, older Ethiopianist forces whose approach was less tolerant of multiple identities.

Immediately after the 'Oromara alliance' conference, in November–December 2017 the TPLF leadership began a grim 35-day internal evaluation meeting. It concluded by electing Debretsion Gebremichael to replace the older president, Abbay Woldu, in the process removing Meles's widow Azeb Mesfin and several others from the leadership. It was a leadership purge which was broadly welcomed in Tigray, albeit one which came too little and too late for their critics in Tigray. Many were asking why Tigrayans were being attacked all over the country but the TPLF was able to do nothing to protect them. Debretsion made a public acknowledgement of a comprehensive 'leadership failure', and accepted responsibility for the fact that EPRDF had lost its focus on poverty and socio-economic transformation, and that even federalism itself was now being questioned.[67] Such honesty may have further damaged the standing of the organisation. If the TPLF finally undertook what they considered to be a substantive evaluation, renewal and purge of their leaders, it is less clear that any of their peers across the EPRDF had any intention of adopting a similar approach. Little happened. When the TPLF finished their internal deliberations, the debate returned to the federal level and ran again into the sand.

When prime minister Hailemariam resigned in February 2018, the federal government again reimposed a State of Emergency, but by this time it looked abundantly clear that only an Oromo replacement for the outgoing prime minister could hope to quell the violence. In a final act of brinkmanship, the TPLF leaders at the March 2018 party meetings which finally elected Abiy Ahmed leader vigorously opposed his candidacy. A number of veteran politicians, in particular, insulted him to his face as lightweight, ignorant, arrogant and incompetent. They seem to have been influenced, among other factors, by the personal antipathy of Tigrayan veteran Tekleberhan Woldearegay, who had clashed with Abiy during his time at the Information Network Security Agency.

In one notable exchange witnessed by those at the meeting, Abiy is reported to have said to a senior TPLF veteran with remarkable chutzpah, 'If Meles were alive I would have been his preferred candidate,' to which the terse retort came, 'You are no Meles.'[68] The TPLF, meanwhile, advocated the candidacy of another southerner, a senior politician whose career was by then mired in corruption-related controversies. This was hardly the basis for the kind of fundamental transformation everyone knew the country needed; rather, it was a move that confirmed that the creativity of their political vision had atrophied, and that their leadership had run out of road. They were outmanoeuvred by their peers when the Amhara party elite pulled their candidate at the last minute. Abiy won 108 out of 180 votes and was sworn in as prime minister in April 2018.

Conclusion

At the time of writing, much more remains to be researched and written about the key period of political disintegration during Hailemariam Desalegn's premiership from 2012 to 2018. When he took over in 2012, Hailemariam was seen as the 'decent' choice. A civil engineer and water management academic scientist from

Welaiyta in the south, he was thought likely to be able to balance between the larger blocs of Amhara, Oromia and Tigray. An apparently principled and committed man, publicly committed to his Protestant faith, and with a stronger intellectual understanding of the EPRDF political and developmental project than many of his peers, he was expected to be able to keep a steadying—and clean—hand on the tiller. As a leftist Ethiopian intellectual commented when he became prime minister, 'I like everything about him apart from his faith.'[69] By the time of his resignation on 15 February 2018, however, the prime minister was seen by many Ethiopians as weak—eventually unable to break the logjams and in-fighting which had brought an increasingly dysfunctional, fractious, distracted and competitive central government to a standstill, trapped while waging its internal power struggles through cycles of violent protest, repression and states of emergency.

There was no doubt more to Hailemariam than this narrative would indicate. He had, after all, presided over a remarkably tough crackdown on Sidama protesters in Hawassa during his period as Southern regional state president in the early 2000s. In apparently struggling against corruption within the ruling party, Hailemariam took the fateful step of increasing the power of the premier, controversially bringing the institution of attorney general under his direct control, at the beginning of 2016.[70] But if there was ever any possibility that he might re-emerge onto the national political stage after resigning, his successor adroitly neutralised this threat, sending him to meet the exiled Derg-era Ethiopian president Mengistu Haile Mariam when he led an African Union election observation mission in Zimbabwe in mid-2018. The extraordinary smiling photographs of this encounter ensured that his career was at an end among the generation of older EPRDF veteran influencers who might later have wanted to reconsider their decision to accept (or precipitate) Hailemariam's resignation.[71]

The most damaging legacy of his period in office was the violent ethnicisation of ruling party politics—the determination with which regional elites began to mobilise ethnic discord in order to manoeuvre against their peers in the ruling party. In 2004, this author suggested that 'the most serious threat to the stability of the government might be expected to come not from external pressure, or from a weak opposition, but from any further fracturing of its leadership'.[72] The analysis proved correct. The next chapter examines these dynamics as the new prime minister, and a remarkable constellation of disparate new allies, drove wedges into the schisms they inherited, and the stage was set for war.

PART THREE

PATH TO WAR

5

THE REVIVAL OF IMPERIAL POLITICS AND THE PATH TO WAR

Sarah Vaughan

'Move fast and break things':[1] *The new dawn of Abiy Ahmed*

Chapters 2 and 3 explored the divisions between the political groups which emerged towards the end of the imperial period, and whose violent conflicts shaped the period after the Derg's creeping coup. These post-imperial political groups and their heirs were still active in 2020 as the protagonists of the war in Tigray. However, the longer arc of history discussed in Chapter 1 also continued in play, and the new prime minister who emerged onto the Ethiopian stage in April 2018 was self-conscious in his invocation of these older threads. Dr Abiy Ahmed drew on a well-established conservative tradition in which the fall of the imperial regime in 1974 marked the moment of a national 'fall from grace'.

> For many lovers of Ethiopian culture, 1974 was the year of doom, of de-sacralisation, of impiety. The country-as-myth which they had long cherished had come to a bad end. King Solomon had died a second death and Ethiopia had landed in the modern world with a painful thud. Then came the new narrative: communism, mass starvation, civil war, dictatorship, population

displacements. After having long been the embodiment of a timeless biblically rooted myth, Ethiopia had now been thrown into a pit of unmitigated evil that was in itself a new (counter) myth.[2]

In 1991, the incoming EPRDF government had been able to distance itself from the Derg's 'pit of evil', not least because it had defeated it military. It launched a new period, initially of great optimism, with a revolutionary broadening of access to state resources and provision under federalism. As discussed in Chapter 3, this delivered an extraordinary expansion of the state and of service delivery to the rural population and remarkable economic growth. But continuities of top-down political culture and authoritarianism persisted. They were exacerbated by the fallout from the Ethio-Eritrean war of 1998–2000 and the 2005 election, and by the violent opposition of armed groups now hosted by a hostile Eritrea. By 2014, as discussed in Chapter 4, things were beginning to come unstuck. By 2018, after four years of violent anti-government protests, to which the state seemed to have no response other than violence and increasingly draconian States of Emergency, the reputation of EPRDF had unravelled as its cohesion frayed. Many now saw continuities with the outright totalitarianism of the past. A younger generation that had little or no recollection of the period before 1991 (of the Red Terror, the civil war and military conscription, or the famine and economic collapse) began to label the EPRDF government as 'just as bad as' or 'worse than' the Derg. This narrative did not stand up to historical scrutiny, but it was vigorously fanned by diaspora-based satellite and social media.

Once sworn in, Abiy Ahmed quickly demonstrated a gift for telling different audiences what they wanted to hear, often in a smattering of their own language—a gift that impressed those who did not share his facility. The genius of the silver-tongued new prime minister in his early months from April 2018 was to re-categorise the EPRDF period and the ruling party system of which he was an internally selected and promoted product. It was now bracketed together with the Derg era as part of a 50-year period of national 'aberration' in which Ethiopia had lost its way, under the malign sway of foreign—

Marxist—ideologies. In this breath-takingly audacious narrative flip, the developmentally successful EPRDF government (from whose ranks the new prime minister had emerged as an increasingly senior member) had presided over a 27-year 'period of darkness'.[3] Ethiopia, now led by an evangelical Christian whose rhetoric was highly coloured with the language of the lay preacher, was only now fulfilling the biblical prophecy—emerging into the light, and once again 'stretching out her hands unto God'.[4] Finally after 50 years, the new prime minister suggested, Ethiopia was turning away from the influences of alien secularism and returning to what he described as its indigenous sensibility.[5] This from a leader who 'has repeatedly drawn parallel between his task as Prime Minister and a mission for Ethiopia's salvation'.[6] 'An ancient Christian imperialism [was] resurging under Prime Minister Abiy Ahmed'.[7]

Prime minister Abiy's populist new framing of Ethiopia's return to its roots, and to the true path of righteousness under its charismatic new leader, drew on the appealing but vacuous notion of *medemer* or 'synergy'. This proposed an (apparently depoliticised) new enthusiasm for shared Ethiopian values and togetherness, hinting at unity but without explicitly invoking the more divisive concept of *andinet* (unity as oneness, uniformity, singularity; a historically freighted *Ethiopiawinet* without the pluralism to include and respect other identities). In the words of an enthusiast, '*medemer* is a concept of unity for diversity. However, to be united does not mean to be one; it is about bringing together our collective forces for collective security, prosperity, cherishing diversity and power'.[8] The mantra of *medemer* suggested that the new government, like its Panglossian new leader, could be all things to all people. To accompany it, prime minister Abiy declared a blanket amnesty, inviting back into the domestic political arena all of those who had been excluded from it.[9]

This reframing initially proved hugely popular, especially but not only among Ethiopia's growing urban and evangelical communities and among Oromos who initially saw in Abiy an Oromo nationalist and spiritual leader finally on the throne. Abiymania spread like wildfire through the summer months of 2018, with the delirium of a contagion. By the end of the honeymoon summer, however, an astute commentator had already identified what he called 'three mammoth strategic errors'.

> First, [Abiy] believed that—or at least acted as if—he could carry out his agenda by relying on his charisma, his immense popularity, and a handful of stalwarts ... Second, the salvo of reforms he fired off created the positive shock of which whole swathes of public opinion were dreaming. But without any adequate preparation, without anticipating their effects, and therefore without being able to control their consequences. The most obvious overhastiness concerned the thorniest questions, like the return of formerly outlawed armed opposition groups and the 'normalisation' with Eritrea ... Third, in order to capitalise on the movement [for the end of domination by the Tigrayan elite] Abiy has continued to reinforce it. He has gone so far as to flirt with the political and historical rhetoric of the fiercest enemies of federalism, and therefore of the TPLF.[10]

This chapter considers the political implications of these sets of decisions and looks at two simultaneous processes, both aspects of the shifts in the domestic constellation of power which developed in parallel between 2018 and 2020. The first was the rebalancing and rebranding of the EPRDF, initially by scapegoating only the TPLF for the problems of the past, and then by establishing at the end of 2019 a new governing vehicle, the Prosperity Party, which was by then bound to exclude them. The second was a gradual increase in the toxicity of inter-ethnic relations, and the inflammatory (and violent) impact of the return of the full spectrum of political groups on the politics of Amhara and Oromia and at national level. Each of these two dynamics, which ran in parallel, also contributed to laying the grounds for war in 2020. The changes coincided as well with a gradual erosion of stability and the rule of law, as security actors proliferated. The chapter ends with a brief discussion of the constitutional wrangling over the postponement of elections during the Covid-19 pandemic, which operated as a proxy trigger for war.

With the perspective of hindsight, one wonders whether René Lefort's three 'errors' were not in fact elements of a deliberately crafted strategy designed to crack apart a well-entrenched federal system of government; one that deployed a carefully targeted, energetic and personalised campaign against its primary architects. After more than a quarter-century, Ethiopia's multinational federalism was relatively well institutionalised; the majority of Ethiopia's youthful population knew no other system and took many of its arrangements for granted. On the face of it, it was unclear how this political system and the constellation of power that supported it could be overturned, without active disruption by the incoming government—and Abiy quickly proved himself a consummate 'disruptor'.

In this he was greatly assisted by the multiplier effect of 'reliable external support' from the Trump administration in the US. 'Crucially Washington's tight embrace of Abiy—quickly followed by the EU and UAE—strongly incentivized the incoming elite to plot a more uncompromising course of action than would otherwise have been plausible'. It encouraged 'more aggressive and destabilizing strategies of power consolidation'.[11] Their unquestioning enthusiasm for Abiy's 'reforms' 'led Western actors to unwittingly underwrite the swift personalization of power in the Prime Minister's hands, with devastating consequences'.[12] Meanwhile, in two parallel security dramas—at domestic and Horn regional levels—other dynamics were also moving towards war. Inside Ethiopia, security sector actors proliferated and fragmented as the rule of law continued to erode. Violent conflict escalated in many parts of the country as the military was reformed and the constitutional order challenged. Meanwhile, the geopolitics of the Horn of Africa were also being abruptly reconfigured, in a remarkable rapprochement with neighbouring Eritrea and Somalia. The involvement of these two neighbouring states in the events that led to the outbreak of war in November 2020, and the wider regional dynamics of the encirclement of Tigray, are discussed in Chapter 6.

'Kana Government': Detoxifying and relaunching the brand

In April 2018, the new incumbent and the government he established were still EPRDF. 'In the best traditions of democratic centralism, the TPLF accepted the vote [for Abiy], if with little enthusiasm.'[13]

But the prime minister elected to move swiftly and energetically to dissociate himself from his predecessors, so as to be seen to deliver the 'change' craved equally by the Ethiopian popular mood and by Ethiopia's frustrated Western partners. EPRDF at its peak had proved a recalcitrant and independent-minded partner for Western donors, determined to tread a development path separate from the Washington Consensus, to develop strong ties to China, and to learn from the Asian state-led developmental models. Prime minister Abiy's reform project seemed to offer a 'once-in-a-generation opportunity' to change what had been a deeply 'fraught strategic partnership' with EPRDF. He offered an 'ideal vehicle for rebalancing US–Ethiopia relations and a broader new approach to regional and global competition'. The US 'spearheaded the embrace of the new leader', and the international financial institutions and new Gulf creditors were quick to buy in.[14]

For all the talk of a new beginning, there was still a need to ring-fence responsibility for the problems of the past, and detoxify and relaunch the government brand, in order to co-opt, compete with or outflank the political competitors who were also shortly to return to the country. There was a risk that restive youth movements in Oromia and Amhara would now mobilise behind returning opposition idols rather than their existing 'new' ruling elites. A scapegoat was required, and the ascendant 'Oromara' groupings at the head of government already had their ethnically and politically isolated candidate: the TPLF. As Harry Verhoeven and Mike Woldemariam explain, Western members of the international community also willingly colluded, lapping up this part of the new narrative.

> Key western officials stressed the lengths to which Abiy went to present himself as 'the most pro-American leader Ethiopia has ever had'. Having campaigned hard against the TPLF to become Prime Minister, Abiy lost no time in reinforcing suspicions about the TPLF–CCP relationship and sharing half-truths about those ties with his Western interlocutors: 'We liked this of course. We wanted China to play a quieter, less ideological role.'[15]

Riding a wave of domestic euphoria and 'gushing' enthusiasm from Western diplomats, the new prime minister decreed an avalanche of changes—breath-taking in their speed, dramatic, and hard for anyone to keep up with. They ranged from the ideological to the aesthetic, introducing into government both the socio-economic fantasies of speedy privatisation and liberalisation, and the interior designs of a 'slick corporate capitalism'.[16] Both were designed to soothe and stroke the aspirations of global capital and of an expanding urban middle class newly in thrall to the wildly popular Turkish soap operas of Kana satellite TV.[17] After a redrawing of communication codes across government under newly recruited spin doctors, 'statements [were] now made under bright white lights and posted on the PM's Twitter and Facebook pages'.[18] Ethiopia's 'new' nationalism looked fabulously seductive.

Isolating and scapegoating the TPLF

As the new prime minister set about establishing the new narrative for his 'reformist' government, the temptation to identify enemies of the reform was always close to the surface.

> Whether intended or not, the phrase 'daytime hyenas' used once to describe opponents of his reform agenda, was interpreted by many as an ethnic dog whistle. For some, it has become a rallying cry—a slogan used in protests and rallies to stir up anger against Tigrayans and the TPLF—which is worrying. Dangerous, too, is his language of 'saboteurs' and 'forces' against the reform process, which recalls some of the worst rhetorical devices of his predecessors.[19]

Already in his first speech to parliament, the new prime minister outlined reforms that gave the TPLF much about which to be concerned. As a well-placed observer noted, his proposed changes 'appeared to be largely aimed at limiting what he saw as the TPLF's underlying control of governance, the economy and security, in its influence and command of the deep state. Abiy's ideas also appeared to threaten the "developmental state" as established by the TPLF/ EPRDF, and even threaten the operation of the federal constitution.'[20]

Prime minister Abiy's first visits outside the capital in April 2018 were to Mekele and Bahir Dar, and observers noted the contrast in his reception in the two capitals. The popular reception in Tigray was positive, even 'rapturous'[21] (not least when he commented that the Amhara claim on Welkaiyt in western Tigray was a diaspora social media invention);[22] meanwhile, the regional TPLF political leadership were wary. The opposite was true in Bahir Dar: enthusiastic Amhara ruling politicians welcomed him with apparent delight while popular reaction to the newcomer was muted and suspicious.[23] Nevertheless, the new prime minister's restructuring quickly focused on the reform of the security institutions; and the removal and discrediting of the TPLF leaders and veterans began in earnest soon after.

Between 1991 and 2018 Ethiopia's national security and military institutions had each been led by only two people, all four of them former TPLF combatants during the Derg period. The Tigrayan general Samora Yunis replaced the long-standing chief of staff General Tsadkan Gebretensae in 2001. At national security, after his predecessor, Kinfe Gebremedhin, was killed in the same year,[24] the more controversial deputy, Getachew Assefa, headed the service (National Intelligence and Security Service [NISS]) from 2001 to 2018. Getachew led intelligence operations internationally (including against the Eritrean government after the 1998–2000 war), domestically (against Ethiopian opposition groups after the contested 2005 elections), and against a range of regional armed opponents, many backed by Asmara. Many of those he had worked against were now back in favour and about to return to the country. Barely two months after his inauguration, at the beginning of June 2018 the incoming prime minister removed Getachew and General Samora.

Two weeks after their dismissal, a grenade went off at a Meskal Square rally in what the authorities quickly said was an assassination attempt on Abiy's life. The prime minister blamed the security services, and 'despite the fact that little to no evidence was offered, the US embassy in Addis strongly backed the narrative of a beleaguered reformer assailed by reactionaries'.[25] Other 'discordant' events were either dismissed or blamed on TPLF saboteurs, including the unexplained death in July of the Grand Renaissance Dam director, found shot dead in his car in a Meskal Square rush hour.[26] At the end of July prime minister Abiy spoke to diaspora gatherings in

Washington DC, Minnesota and Los Angeles, and on each occasion Tigrayans felt his remarks to be anti-Tigrayan.[27]

In early August a group of 40 heavily armed federal forces who had flown in by Antonov were detained at Mekele airport, where the regional government said they did not know who they were and why they had been sent.[28] Also in August, in a broadly popular but violent and unconstitutional move, the prime minister sent the federal military into Jijiga in a 'bold but reckless ... operation to dethrone' the regional state president—'a showdown that was months in the making' between the new prime minister and politicians seen as allies of the old guard of the TPLF.[29] In October a 'video-recorded incursion of special forces into palace grounds'[30] provided an excuse for the establishment of a new Republican Guard reporting directly to prime minister Abiy. In November sweeping changes were made in the security and prisons administrations and 36 officials were arrested. Investigations also saw a broad crackdown on the government's military industrial conglomerate METEC, with another 27 people arrested, including the Tigrayan head, Major General Kinfe Dagnew, who had resigned a few months earlier.

The day after the arrests, pro-government media aired a powerful documentary alleging embezzlement, corruption and incompetence at METEC and presuming the guilt of those arrested. Tigrayan commentators took exception to the trial by media and what they saw as the singling out of Tigrayan suspects for prosecution.[31] More was to come. A second documentary on the abuse of human rights by the security institutions was aired in December 2018, provoking domestic revulsion at the grim story it detailed, and international concern about the 'court of public opinion'.[32] A warrant for Getachew Assefa's arrest had been issued in November 2018, and human rights charges were added in early 2019. The Tigray regional state government did not give him up, and he apparently remained a member of its leadership. His whereabouts were unknown.

By now, offers of amnesty and overtures were being made to many of those who had fallen out with the TPLF leadership. Its veteran dissidents Aregawi Berhe and Ghidey Zeratsion returned to the country in July 2018; and by the beginning of 2019, Aregawi had been nominated to join a newly established Boundary and Identity

Commission. The TPLF quickly condemned the establishment of this new body, labelling it an unconstitutional attack on the rules of federalism. The concentration of a range of their political enemies among its members only added to their anger. Aregawi (a TPLF founder removed and exiled in the late 1980s, now heading an opposition party) was joined by Andargachew Tsigé (a British citizen whom the EPRDF had extradited from Yemen and jailed for terrorism offences for his Eritrea-based armed opposition to the government while he led Genbot 7) and Dr Negasso Gidada (a former president of Ethiopia who had been unceremoniously ousted and stripped of his privileges after the TPLF split in 2001, when he supported the dissident faction).

Also returning from the diaspora to positions of influence were several of those whom the TPLF–EPRDF government had prosecuted for crimes against the constitution in the wake of the 2005 elections. They included Judge Birtukan Mideksa, a former CUD leader who became the new head of the National Election Board, and Dr Daniel Bekele, now appointed to head the government's Human Rights Commission.

> For Abiy, the TPLF were always going to be a potential threat to his ambitions, both personal and governmental, once these became clear. Even after the TPLF members of the EPRDF council had all voted for him as Chair of the front [in October 2018] Abiy remained highly suspicious of any Tigrayan presence in government and in the upper ranks of the military and security services.[33]

As the capital gradually became a more hostile political environment, TPLF members began to move north to Tigray. The withdrawal to which many veterans had looked forward as a blessed retirement back 'home' to Mekele was recast in the narrative of the new media in Addis Ababa as one of embittered (and dangerous) truculence in defeat. In the region the initial popular enthusiasm for the new prime minister quickly evaporated.[34] By October 2018, ordinary Tigrayans in Mekele were already feeling under siege—a prefiguring of the grotesqueries to come.

The first open Amhara moves against Tigray came in mid-2018, when the Amhara administration started closing off roads from Amhara into Tigray. By the end of the year it was almost impossible for Tigrayans to get to Addis Ababa through the Amhara region. They were being forced to take a long detour through the Afar regional state into Oromia and then to Addis Ababa. Federal police refused to take action when Tigrayan merchants buying grain in the Amhara region were robbed by local youths. Over 130,000 Tigrayans felt obliged to withdraw from other regions and move back to Tigray.[35]

Unsurprisingly, in the region popular support for the TPLF under the acting president Debretsion, now seen as a Tigrayan hero, had already reconsolidated by the last quarter of 2018. By December, popular anger towards Addis Ababa and its energetic rewriting of history was palpable and widely shared: 'if they say they were in darkness for 27 years their minds are not working'.[36] Even those who swallowed the federal government's narrative that it faced resistance to reform from the TPLF cautioned that 'the Prime Minister needs to be careful not to allow his targeting of anti-reform elements within the TPLF [sic] to become an attack on the people of Tigray'.[37]

A new party: From 'revolutionary democracy' to 'prosperity'

In 2017, the EPRDF had agreed to establish a team to explore the potential for a merger of the four member fronts into a single party. Each recommended a number of members, and (in one of many ironies later thrown up by the war, along with its horrors) the TPLF put forward Dr Mulu Nega Kahsay, then a former parliamentarian and academic who specialised in education quality assurance, to participate in the study. Dr Mulu seems to have got on better with prime minister Abiy than with those who nominated him, and in 2020 he was made federal minister of science and higher education. Days after the war broke out, on 7 November 2020 Dr Mulu was appointed by the House of Federation to head its short-lived puppet 'Transitional Government' in Tigray, and when Mekele was taken, he was dispatched to the region.[38]

The committee of which Dr Mulu was a member in 2018 undertook its study, initially intended for presentation to the EPRDF congress held in Hawassa in October. It was not discussed, amidst procedural and substantive objections from the TPLF and mutual recrimination.[39] By the time of the congress, the Oromo and Amhara parties of EPRDF had already undergone rebranding exercises, in a further move to distance themselves from the old EPRDF and from the TPLF. Meanwhile, Abiy was almost unanimously re-elected as EPRDF chairman in Hawassa (with the support of the TPLF leadership), but again differentiated his position on federalism in provocative terms, stating: 'if we are able to form regional administrations without confusing it with ethnic identities, then there is no question that federalism is the best option for Ethiopia's situation'.[40] Once again his position was an overt challenge to the core project of EPRDF–TPLF and to its architects.

Plans for a unified party, which would also include the peripheral regional ruling parties, had been facilitated by the removal during 2018 of recalcitrant regional state presidents in Somali (in August), Gambella (in October) and Afar (in December) and reshuffles in Benishangul-Gumuz. With the Tigrayan old guard increasingly marginalised in Tigray, two veteran Amhara–Agaw founder architects of the EPRDF, Bereket Simon and Tadesse Kassa, were also now removed, arrested on corruption allegations in January 2019 and detained at a facility near Bahir Dar. The party merger plans continued to advance through 2019, and at a meeting in November that year three of the EPRDF member fronts (Southern, Amhara and Oromo but not TPLF) voted to disband the EPRDF and merge to form the new single national Prosperity Party, also joining the ruling parties in Ethiopia's other regions: Somali, Afar, Harar, Benishangul-Gumuz and Gambella. At the time, the TPLF objected that the three other member fronts didn't have the legal authority to disband the EPRDF, but after deliberation it announced the end of the coalition at the beginning of January 2020, stating that EPRDF had been 'demolished with betrayal'.[41]

The TPLF was not alone in its objections. The Oromo and Southern fronts had also been divided, and a number of key allies of the prime minister (including notably Oromia president Lemma

Megersa and minister of peace Muferiat Kemal) abstained from voting. Many others, including intellectuals who had nominated Abiy for the Nobel Peace Prize, later stated that they had 'begged him not to do it in such a rush'.[42] The creation of the Prosperity Party at the end of November 2019 was a key turning point at which many of his most vocal Oromo supporters—journalists, academics, and ruling and opposition politicians—broke with the prime minister. Many felt later that the award of the Nobel Peace Prize the month before had given him an unrealistic sense of the possibilities for peaceful political transformation,[43] and concurred with the suggestion that the prize 'was being awarded [to him] too early'.[44] 'It all seemed too good to be true and it was'.[45]

Meanwhile, little seemed to have been done to institutionalise new systems in the new unitary ruling party, no congress was held, and the significance of the national merger in terms of day-to-day political practice was not clarified. Rather, power continued to be invested in the person of the prime minister, 'and the growing chasm between the promise of liberalization and the reality of concentrating power became even more painful'.[46] Regional state Prosperity Party chapters continued to operate as had the fronts before them, and the process of balancing between these blocs—particularly between the party's Oromo and Amhara wings—increasingly consumed the energy of those around the seat of power. Rather than institutional development, commentary centred on the personality of the prime minister; many saw the new organisation as a mere vehicle through which his persona was 'writ large' on Ethiopia's constellation of power. 'His own certainties, coupled with impatience and refusal to listen to criticism or even questions have too often negated any possibility of dialogue over his proposed policies, despite the supposed centrality of dialogue and unity to his philosophy of Medemer'.[47]

As Lefort noted two months after the establishment of the Prosperity Party, prime minister Abiy was 'preaching unity but flying solo':

> Regardless of the fate of his leadership, Abiy should have focused
> on trying to lead the country to a peaceful and orderly transition
> in order to give it its best chance of success. Instead, he seems to

have deprioritized the transition's success in favour of becoming the next in a long line of Ethiopian 'Big Man' rulers ... One example of his personalised approach has been the way Abiy bypasses institutions. If these operated according to the constitution, they would be powerful enough to exert control over his activities ... Abiy has allowed the demonization of the TPLF and threatened to strangle the Tigray region it represents, riding a wave of wide criticism, even hatred, and aligning with Amhara and Oromo elites. This has exacerbated ethnic division, exactly the opposite of his motto of medemer.[48]

In 2019–20 the TPLF began once again to emphasise the importance of the federal system, in an attempt to mobilise an alternative new coalition of federalist forces, as part of which it would fight national elections scheduled for May 2020. With the unravelling of the political consensus in Oromia there was by now some interest in this project, especially among Oromo federalists, and in July 2019 opposition leader Bekele Gerba visited Mekele to attend a conference.[49] The attempt at coalition-building was an uphill struggle, however, with 'real reluctance to offer support to the TPLF because of the perception that it had for quarter of a century operated a repressive and latterly highly corrupt regime'.[50] The strong and emotive narratives of the government and a range of its media outlets and allies had proved effective. The chorus of diaspora media vilification of alleged TPLF and Tigrayan perfidy grew steadily as journalists, bloggers and vehement opponents returned from exile, and social media sources proliferated. The role of Eritrean anti-TPLF rhetoric and mobilisation during this period was remarkable.

Immediately after the war in Tigray had begun, 'as part of his demonization of the TPLF and Tigrayans' prime minister Abiy ascribed the upsurge of conflict during the 2018–20 period to 'the machinations of the TPLF, arguing that this was all part of a policy aimed at inciting violence to discredit his government and derail his reforms, and ultimately [aimed at] restoration of TPLF control'.[51] He told parliament in November 2020 that there had been 113 outbreaks of ethno-nationalist violence that 'could be ascribed to the TPLF activity' since he had become prime minister.[52] The fact that, almost alone of all of the regional states of Ethiopia, Tigray under the TPLF had continued to be peaceful and unaffected by ethnic conflict over the period seems (ironically) to have been used to substantiate the allegations. As Anthony Shaw noted, 'nothing has been produced in support of such accusations and they seem highly implausible'.[53] The unsubstantiated narrative that the TPLF had sought to destabilise Ethiopia's 'reform process' after Abiy came to power continued to have strong traction with audiences internationally and domestically long after the war began. By 2022 there was still no evidence to support it, but the view had become both an article of faith and a signifier of government loyalty, endlessly repeated by pro-government media sources and by the wide range of returning political actors who had been welcomed back into Ethiopia. Increasingly inflammatory behaviour and speech, by government officials and private individuals, were now encouraged and fostered with what later came to look like wilful determination.

Benzine on the fire: Managing—or inflaming—combustible nationalisms?

From April 2018, under a sweeping amnesty as part of the 'national reform agenda', multiple government opponents were brought back into the domestic political arena, either from jail or from exile in the diaspora. Three sets of political opponents of the EPRDF were invited to return to Ethiopia in 2018, and each included groups which had been based in Eritrea. They were the pan-Ethiopian nationalists who were opposed to multinational federalism; a series of new nationalist Amhara movements and individuals who felt it had discriminated against them; and, thirdly, Oromo (and other groups of) ethno-nationalists pleased to see an Oromo finally in power. All were pleased by the displacement of the TPLF from the centre of power, and actively colluded in demonising them. But they agreed on little else. If the 2016–18 period had seen division within EPRDF over the constellation and implementation of federalism, the post-2018 amnesty brought a far more combustible set of wholly incompatible political perspectives into the mix.

After four years of Oromo protests, the emotional outpouring that greeted the return of the Oromo Liberation Front (OLF) to Ethiopia in 2018 caused anxious ripples in Addis Ababa, which Oromo nationalists claimed as the capital—Finfinne—of Oromia. Rival Oromo and Ethiopianist gangs faced off, clashing and painting areas of the city in the colours of rival flags. If the return of Dawd Ibssa's OLF was emotional, social media activist Jawar Mohammed was given a rock star welcome by euphoric young *qeerroo* supporters whom he had mobilised from overseas to join the Oromo protest movement since 2014. Meanwhile, a whole series of politicians with links to and roots in the Amhara region also returned to the country or were released from jail, many espousing a much more radical overhaul of the federal constitution, which they had viscerally opposed for decades. They included Genbot 7's Berhanu Nega and Andargachew Tsigé, as well as Eskinder Nega, who, as editor of a series of critical nationalist newspapers *Ethiopis*, *Askual*, *Satenaw* and *Menelik*, had been repeatedly detained by the EPRDF government, and would later be detained again.

In strikingly parallel processes in both Amhara and Oromia, radical militants associated with a spectrum of these groups returned from their training camps and bases in Eritrea and began to operate in their home rural areas. In both regions, while some were co-opted into government, others bowed out of the formal demobilisation, disarmament, and reintegration processes, preferring to continue their military activities, either illicitly or with the tacit approval of local authorities.

The return of the Ethiopian Nationalists: Genbot 7, ESAT and Ezema

The overall effect of the presence of multiple opposition actors was to sharpen the nationalism of prime minister Abiy's ruling party, discouraging a softening of the ruling party's line which might have resolved emerging problems of federalism or of inter-state competition for land. This was especially true in the Amhara regional state where these issues played out most strongly, and the ruling party had begun to embrace the diaspora narratives of Amhara oppression—even genocide. The new presence of strong opposition nationalist voices radicalised the position of the ruling cadres as their members were co-opted. A central conundrum of the period from April 2018 (both before the outbreak of war in Tigray in November 2020 and since) was the extent of federal influence of the nationalist Movement of Ethiopians for Social Justice, or Ezema. Ezema emerged in 2019 as the contemporary heir of the nationalist tradition embodied by the EPRP (of the student movement period), the CUD (of the 2005 elections) and Genbot 7 (the armed opposition movement which had been based in Asmara from 2008 to 2012).

A number of the returning nationalist or Amhara-affiliated opposition groupings had complex and opaque links with one another, with the ruling party, with the Genbot 7–Ezema opposition, and of course with the Eritrean government. Key Amhara opposition political and security actors had been hosted by Asmara, and these links with the government of Eritrea continued to be influential. At the international level, there are indications that members of Ezema– Genbot 7 were important brokers in the thawing of Ethio-Eritrean relations after prime minister Abiy came to power. Andargachew Tsigé, for instance, claimed in 2018 that he had played a pivotal role in mediating between Abiy and Isaias prior to the peace accord. He was able (he reported) to draw on the trusting relationship he retained with President Isaias and his advisers, and on his conversations with the prime minister, who had apparently broached such mediation with him immediately after he was released from prison in Ethiopia in May 2018.[54] But the influence of this network of nationalist politicians may have been broader and more concrete than this. In a curious incident a year later (to which most online references were later deleted), Andargachew announced at a meeting in Atlanta in late July 2019 that Genbot 7 had effectively coached the new prime minister on the dynamics of the transition, providing him with a 60-page 'roadmap' towards 'unity and democracy' (something he claimed the ruling party lacked). He indicated that he was only making this secret cooperation known because of concern that Abiy had derogated from their agreement—essentially by flirting too long with (Oromo) ethno-nationalism.[55]

In May–June 2019, Genbot 7 merged with a series of other political oppositions groupings to establish Ezema as a domestic political organisation.[56] The founding congress of Ezema elected a 21-member executive committee made up from members of the founding parties. From the known Genbot 7 leaders, only Berhanu Nega joined the executive committee (with an Ethiopian passport he was allowed to stand and campaign from the district level for the Ezema leadership election and later for parliament). After the congress, Ezema embarked on expanding its organisational presence throughout the country, establishing branch offices in all regions and trying to organise officers in all electoral constituencies. It held talks in Ethiopia's Somali state with the Ogaden National Liberation Front (ONLF) on cooperation but decided to organise there on its own. Ezema was an early advocate for a delay to the election schedule (if peace could not be achieved) and for a two-year all-party unity transitional government, an arrangement the prime minister was also privately said to favour. In some constituencies such as Addis Ababa, Ezema was assumed to have strong support, and it seemed likely to try to coordinate an outcome with other opposition parties. In the event, when elections were finally held in mid-2021, they were astutely outmanoeuvred in the capital as the government released from jail rival Balderas politicians just before the poll, and split the opposition vote.[57]

Arguably the most significant aspect of the return of Genbot 7– Ezema was the unbanning of its diaspora-based Ethiopian satellite TV station and radio service ESAT, which was among more than 200 websites and TV stations unbanned by the new prime minister in 2018. ESAT, along with the Oromo Media Network (OMN), had been charged in absentia for inciting violence and acts of terror in February 2017.[58] After Abiy came to power in 2018, the charges were dropped. When Genbot 7 was dissolved in May 2019 it was finally formally acknowledged that the movement had indeed set up and financed ESAT TV broadcasts from Amsterdam from 2012 (and Amharic Radio services from Washington DC after disturbances in Gonder in mid-2016). In June 2019, senior journalists and editorial staff of ESAT returned to Addis Ababa, and the channel now opened studios in the capital.

Now unblocked, ESAT's broadcasts rapidly became a powerful presence in middle-class households across Ethiopia, particularly in urban areas. The diet of anti-federalist and anti-TPLF propaganda began to have a galvanising effect. ESAT aired and amplified the allegations of other pro-government broadcasters, and went beyond them with a line-up of trenchant commentators who were consistent and strident in their condemnation of TPLF 'sabotage'. In the final four to five months before the war began, a number of ESAT broadcasts included more specific calls, prefiguring with remarkable accuracy the strategies of the war. As the country boiled in the grip of a crisis in Oromo politics in the first days of July 2020, ESAT reiterated its allegations of a link to the TPLF (see below). Its discussants called for 'fraternal' joint military activity by Ethiopia and Eritrea against the TPLF. A few days later, the government-aligned Walta TV station also broadcast remarkable comments from a retired Derg general who had reportedly returned to the country to become a close associate of prime minister Abiy:

> The military and security officers [should order] those that hold sticks or arms in villages [in Tigray] to put them down. If they refuse, they should shoot them. That's it! It is state of emergency. There is nothing [more important] beyond Ethiopia. The main snake got hit around its middle: it then fled and got under a rock in Mekelle [capital of Tigray]. I will not give out the details here, but the government … it is possible! A good plan has to be prepared and they have to be hit [destroyed].[59]

In October 2020 ESAT commentators called for the disruption of services (banking, electricity, and telecoms) and livelihoods in Tigray. In due course, all of the returning nationalist parties expressed strong and sustained support for the Tigray war and for the federal government to pursue the toughest course of action. Their radical calls ran like a thread throughout the mobilisation of collective antipathy towards the TPLF and its politics.

Violent élite instability in Amhara

Not surprisingly, the return of these various nationalist and Amhara-supported opponents of the EPRDF regime in 2018 had a destabilising impact in an already tense Amhara region, and between the Amhara regional and federal governments. A number of key individuals in these networks were former military officers who had fled or been detained and charged after an attempted coup against the government of Meles Zenawi in Bahir Dar in 2009. Another faction, the Amhara Democratic Forces Movement (ADFM), was formed in Eritrea by three or four officers who fled Ethiopia at that time. In Eritrea, they joined Genbot 7 but rapidly split away again—gaining an independent budget from the government of Eritrea in the process. Founders included Alehubel Amare, previously appointed by Genbot 7 leaders Berhanu Nega and Andargachew Tsigé to lead the Genbot 7 army in Eritrea.[60] Alehubel returned to Ethiopia from Sweden in 2018 and was appointed to lead Amhara regional state intelligence from early to mid-2019 after the ruling party integrated ADFM fighters with the regional security apparatus. Alehubel squabbled with another 2009 coup plotter, General Aseminew Tsigé, who was appointed head of Amhara regional state security in 2018, the two reportedly jockeying over control of matters of regional security.

Meanwhile, only a proportion of these various groups of fighters in Eritrea agreed to sign up to the peace deal with the Amhara state government that preceded their return, while others remained outside the formal process.[61] Clandestine training camps were established in North Gonder, South Gonder, Welkaiyt, Raya, Jawi and North Shewa, with continuing networks. Given unsuccessful attempts at disarmament, demobilisation and reconciliation, fighters returned from Eritrea and were not otherwise integrated. Other members of the group prosecuted as coup plotters in 2009 became influential. General Aseminew Tsigé was released from prison and was rapidly appointed by the regional state government as head of security and administration until his death in July 2019. Brigadier General Tefera Mamo also later became head of the Amhara regional special forces, and was detained for some time in mid-2022, as part of a later crackdown, when the federal and Amhara governments finally moved against radicals in the region. During the period 2018–20, leading members of this group were able to operate inside and outside the purview of the regional state government.

The return of these and other groups encouraged co-option and competition between the ruling party and some of these new forces at regional as well as national level. Three other factors also destabilised the federal balance of power between Amhara and non-Amhara politicians: differences over the future of federalism, with many Amharas thought to favour a return to a more unitary or non-ethnic arrangement; the rights to land of Amharas living beyond the regional state borders (and the prospect of land annexation by Amhara regional state, particularly but not only in Tigray); and, thirdly, the position of Amharas in the overall political constellation, with many wanting to see the restoration of a historically dominant position. As noted above, the anti-Tigrayan rhetoric which had characterised the 2016–18 period continued under prime minister Abiy, and there were roadblocks and attacks on Tigrayans in the region during the first year of the new government. A series of high-level political assassinations in Bahir Dar and Addis Ababa in June 2019 brought abruptly to the fore the seriousness of the political division and power struggles in the region.

The government quickly described the killings in Bahir Dar in June 2019 as a 'regional coup' attempt. On the face of it, a moderate pro-federal Amhara president, Ambachew Mekonnen, was murdered by his more militant Amhara nationalist head of security and administration, General Aseminew Tsigé (released from jail a year earlier). Superficially this looked like a bid to strengthen the autonomous assertion and cohesion of Amhara regional politics vis-à-vis central government. However, General Aseminew was himself shot the following day, precluding any prospect of further investigation of his political motivation and objectives or of the wider network of his political allies. Conspiracy theorists adduced the odd circumstance that he had failed to flee Bahir Dar in the wake of the killings, to suggest wider official complicity in his actions: that Aseminew anticipated official support. Others speculated that, after a series of public discussions across Amhara, Ambachew may have become an inconvenience to those pushing for war, convinced of a lack of popular support for military moves against Tigray.[62]

The shock wave of the Bahir Dar killings was amplified by the murder the same evening of the highly respected Tigrayan chief of staff of the Ethiopian National Defence Force (ENDF), General Se'are Mekonnen, in the Bole district of Addis Ababa. There is much which remains unexplained. There were witness reports of a protracted shootout in the Tor Hailoch area of Addis Ababa the same night.[63] It may be that the simultaneous killings in Addis Ababa were coincidentally organised by other actors, but this is difficult to assess in the absence of a public investigation and published findings or a public record from the judicial process. General Se'are's bodyguard was charged and jailed. The assassination of two highly respected Tigrayan military veterans added further salt to the wounds—and fear—felt by the TPLF. It also removed an ENDF chief of staff who would most likely have been inimical to the development of plans for the war with Tigray launched less than 18 months later.

It is possible that the grievances of multiple overlapping interest groups over the direction and momentum of political change in the Amhara regional state may have driven the Amhara assassinations. The plot may also have been the result of frictions within the Amhara ruling system between rivalrous power bases in South Gonder and South Wollo seeking to secure economic interests, which developed into a power struggle in the leadership of the regional state's ruling party. In the run-up to the removal of long-standing Amhara president Gedu Andargachew in March 2019 and the assassinations in July, South Wollo zonal networks had coalesced around vice president Laké (South Gonder) and regional head of security and administration General Aseminew Tsigé (North Wollo). Networks affiliated with two regional opposition parties, the National Movement of Amhara (NAMA) and the Amhara Democratic Forces Movement (ADFM), as well as some former fighters of Genbot 7 (including Tefera Mamo), were among those arrested after the killings. Other 'firebrands' were later reassigned to Addis Ababa.

Attempts by Addis Ababa to harness and also to control more radical forces in Amhara coloured the period from 2018 and have continued since the outbreak of war. In 2019 prime minister Abiy installed as Amhara regional state president Temesgen Tiruneh, one of his close national security advisers and a loyalist former colleague at the Information Network Security Agency (INSA). The appointment of Temesgen signalled an effort to consolidate power within the fragmented Amhara administration, tangled as it was in the contest between South Wollo and South Gonder zonal networks. For many observers it also demonstrated the ability of the prime minister to impose his choice of candidate on the Amhara ruling party and government. After the alleged coup attempt and assassinations, deputy prime minister Demeke Mekonnen also tried to encourage rival groups to agree on an agenda to settle insecurity, knocking heads together over personal disputes in the security apparatus, struggles over budgets, power and money, and the Muslim–Christian violence that was also now unfolding in parts of Amhara.

There was a broader reshuffle in September 2019, apparently geared at instilling loyalty and coherence at various levels across the regional government. Well-placed observers indicated that following the 'coup attempt' of June 2019, rivalry between the Gonder and Wollo camps may have been overtaken by rivalry between Gonder and Gojjam. When the war began in November 2020, Temesgen was brought to head the federal National Intelligence and Security Service. He and deputy prime minister Demeke Mekonnen were both from Gojjam, while the next Amhara president, Agegnehu, was a Gonderi, in common with a number of those involved in the later annexation of western Tigray. Gonder and Gojjam elites were seen as having linked (but separate) interests in the fate of land claimed in western Tigray and in the Metekel zone of Benishangul-Gumuz. The regional centrality of the Gojjam–Gonder balance of power seemed likely to make the Amhara land claims in both areas all the more intractable.

The emergence of 'ethnic' Amhara nationalism

What also drove this febrile political competition and jostling was the sudden emergence of a new 'ethnic' form of Amhara nationalism between 2016 and 2018, which took many observers by surprise.[64] In 2018 it quickly took on an organised political form, with the abrupt rise to prominence of the new political party, the National Movement of Amhara (NAMA), also known by its Amharic acronym, Aben. This new organisation appealed primarily to a young generation of Amhara nationalists who had grown up under federalism. Amhara nationalism had long been associated with the pan-Ethiopianism of the Derg-era EPRP, with the 2005 Coalition for Unity and Democracy (CUD), with Genbot 7 and (most recently) with Ezema. Formally established in 2018, NAMA employed a rhetoric that had a tougher and more ethnic edge, and advanced specific concrete demands for federal reform. It gained ascendancy during the early phases of the transition, arguing that the TPLF had extended structural inequalities against Amhara in the constitution promulgated by the EPRDF in 1995. These provisions (the new party argued) had limited political representation of Amhara interests to the Amhara regional state, undermining minority rights in other states where ethnic Amhara were also present because of a first-past-the-post electoral system.

With elections expected in February 2020, Aben restructured its leadership and agreed to work together with Eskinder Nega's new Balderas grouping in Addis Ababa and the region, in one Amhara-affiliated camp. The party offered formal political support to the multiple Amhara land claims and grievances discussed in the previous chapter. It was rumoured that the party had privately drawn up plans for territorial restructuring to include areas demarcated as within Tigray, Benishangul-Gumuz and Oromia, which it sought to see 'rightfully returned' to Amhara. It lobbied for the introduction of a presidential system and planned to seek the imprisonment and prosecution of EPRDF Amhara officials whom it deemed to have failed to protect 'real' Amhara interests under the TPLF-led EPRDF system. An unspecified number of underground fighters formerly affiliated with Genbot 7 defected to the more radical appeal of Aben, and were joined by many of the *fano* militiamen who had emerged in 2016. Aben in this period emerged as strong competitors to Ezema, competing for hearts and minds in Amhara state (while trying to maintain credibility nationally and internationally). Conflict had almost occurred in 2019, when chairman Berhanu Nega cancelled a visit to Bahir Dahr. In the event Aben did well in the Amhara region in the 2021 elections and was offered a seat in the cabinet of the new federal government in October 2021, an honour it shared with Ezema's Dr Berhanu. By the outbreak of war in November 2020, a radicalised Amhara regional government, working with a range of radical Amhara (and other) nationalist allies, was ready to move against Tigray in pursuit of its land claims in Raya and Welkaiyt. Many in the region and beyond were ready to support it.

Dismantling Oromo nationalism: Divide and rule

If the new prime minister consolidated his influence only incrementally in Amhara, he moved quickly in Oromia to assert himself in 2018, initially working extremely closely with other members of the closely knit 'team Lemma' which had led Oromia and the Oromo ruling party from 2016. Between 2014 and 2018, a strongly ethno-nationalist 'pan-Oromo' narrative drove the Oromo protests which leveraged Oromo influence within the EPRDF and across most Oromo areas. Ruling politicians in the region rode the wave, holding out for the election of an Oromo chairperson and prime minister in 2018. Over the following 18-month period, however, prime minister Abiy and allied Oromo ruling elites shifted in favour of a more centralist narrative, which by late 2019 and early 2020 had become divisive and controversial among Oromo politicians and people.

The popular Lemma Megersa remained president of Oromia until early 2019, when the prime minister moved him to the federal Ministry of Defence, replacing him with a more pliable loyalist as he (and others) grew more critical of the increasing concentration of power, unitarist rhetoric, and antipathy towards Tigray. As the post-2018 period evolved, prime minister Abiy became gradually more dominant in Oromo (and national) ruling party politics, increasingly able to exclude those who had hoped for a more robust Oromo nationalist line, and to co-opt, reward and promote loyalty. Critical flashpoints included his controversial rehabilitation and re-opening of Emperor Menelik II's national palace in October 2019 (complete with new statues of former emperors), and the determined move, in November, to bring the Oromo front into the new single unitary Prosperity Party, in the teeth of opposition from half of its executive committee members, including Lemma.

The remarkably rapid shift from the energy of robust Oromo ethno-nationalism to a more centrist unitary line was eased by constructive ambiguity about the specific impact on Oromia's autonomy or pre-existing party-political decision-making practices at regional, zone and local levels. It was underpinned by 'divide and rule' tactics. During 2019 and 2020 the growing number of Oromo critics of the new prime minister pointed to the devastating ability of an 'Oromo insider' to dismantle a pan-Oromo movement carefully crafted during the protest period of 2014–18. This was achieved, in part, by mobilising strongly resonant sub-regional differences (called *genduma*, or 'regionalism', similar to the Amharic *awrajawinet*).[65] The marginalisation of key pan-Oromo mobilisers (including the nationalist singer Hachalu Hundessa, the social media activist turned politician Jawar Mohammed, and a younger generation of activists, journalists and academics) was critical to the success of the project to subdue and tame the wave of Oromo nationalist aspiration on which the new prime minister rode to power. From the beginning of 2019 the government had also launched a brutal military counterinsurgency to try to quell fierce resistance in the Wellega zones of western Oromia.

Attitudes to Oromo nationalism and nationalist politics tended to divide along the lines of attitudes to the establishment of the modern Ethiopian state in the nineteenth century—the two visions of Ethiopia discussed in Chapter 2. For ethno-nationalists, Oromo territories were conquered by the Shewan Abyssinian emperor Menelik II, in his 'colonial' move south. Oromo farmers were divested of their land and their labour under northern settlers (historically referred to as *neftegna*,[66] or 'rifle carriers'), who were the primary instruments of imperial expansion. For pan-Ethiopian nationalists, meanwhile, the modern Ethiopian state merely consolidated the unity of a long-standing natural 'culture area' under a process in which Oromos were also protagonists.[67]

Attitudes towards this complex history were not uniform across all areas of the large and diverse region of Oromia. Oromos in many parts of Shewa (broadly the areas of Amhara and Oromia around the capital) often had a different historical experience of engagement with the Ethiopian state. Many were more closely implicated in, and sympathetic to, the historical process of state expansion or consolidation than, for instance, Oromos in Wellega, Jimma, Arsi, Bale and Borena, who more often saw themselves as oppressed or exploited by it. There were historical exceptions of course: General Tadesse Birru, who became an important leader of 1960s anti-imperial Oromo sentiment, was from Selale in Shewa (although the

Metcha-Tulama Self-Help Association movement he led was more closely associated with Bale); and contemporary perspectives on the incorporation and status of the Jimma area (from where the new prime minister's father originated) were in some ways complicated by the nineteenth-century agreement reached between Sultan Abajifar and Emperor Menelik at the time of the expansion of the empire.

Central to the post-2018 shift in Oromo politics under prime minister Abiy was the elevation of a cohort of Shewan Oromo ruling politicians willing to accept a more 'pan-Ethiopianist' approach, which saw Oromos as integral to (even rightfully leading) the long evolution of the Ethiopian state rather than being colonised or co-opted by it. These elite politicians tended to be more tolerant of a politics of national unity and willing to dilute the provisions of the multinational federal constitution, seeing themselves as leading and controlling even a unitary national government. Meanwhile, ruling and opposition political elites from other parts of Oromia, many of whom felt greater concern to preserve the gains won under federalism, were gradually marginalised, excluded or neutralised. By 2020 they included the architect of the Oromo movement within the ruling party, Lemma Megersa, its diaspora social media mobiliser Jawar Mohammed, and its nationalist icons in the OLF, including Dawd Ibssa, and the Oromo Federalist Congress (OFC), including Bekele Gerba—all from Wellega or Arsi.

The division between Shewa and the rest of Oromia has never been a hard and fast one. In particular, the West Shewa areas around Ambo played a key role in launching nationalist protests in 2014 and 2015. West Shewa also had a well-established recent history of supporting opposition parties, including those led by prominent OFC politician Merera Gudina from that area. It was unclear, too, how much the support of elite politicians from Shewa for Abiy's ruling party was shared more broadly across populations in Shewa, and evidence was mixed. Nevertheless, it was broadly the case that, at the elite level, prime minister Abiy's most vocal supporters among Oromo ruling politicians included a disproportionate number from Shewa. As with the politics of other parts of Ethiopia, Oromo politics have long been an emotive matter, connected as they have been with divergent perceptions about what some see as deep-seated social prejudices, discrimination and racist stereotypes. For the critics of Oromo nationalism, nationalist positions were unreasonable and divisive. For some Oromos, unacknowledged prejudice and contempt continued to undermine their pride in a culture that remained subaltern, even under a nominally Oromo prime minister.

Silencing the Oromo ethno-national political opposition

On 23 October 2019 protests erupted in Ethiopia's capital, after the OFC's Jawar Mohammed made a series of social media posts accusing the authorities of threatening his security, a claim police denied. Government reported that 86 people died as violence spread across Oromia, especially in Dodola and Ambo, and to Dire Dawa and Harar. Human Rights Watch put the violence down to amplified ethno-nationalist sentiment, dissatisfaction over the pace of reforms, a weakened administrative and security apparatus, and delayed response or inaction by government.[68] They complained about the lack of credible investigation or prosecutions. Others saw a more overtly political hand at work, engineering an opportunity for government forces to begin to dismantle Jawar's *qeerroo* networks and the threat which the Oromo opposition posed to the government. In February 2020, a Burayu police chief who had opposed federal and regional state moves to block Jawar's OFC rallies in the town was killed.[69]

Nine months later, tensions had grown as the government postponed planned elections, drawing criticism from opposition parties. The unexplained murder of popular Oromo singer Hachalu Hundessa on 29 June 2020 saw an eruption of violent protests and killings across Oromia over the next three days. Analysis of these events proved extremely divisive: 'The party line is that officials who were negligent, disloyal, or complicit in the violence were removed. The counter-narrative is that the unrest was stoked and then used to purge opponents and ruling figures who sided with Lemma, or with the opposition, by falsely blaming them for orchestrating the violence.'[70]

Violence was concentrated particularly (but not only) in Bale and Arsi, often following religious lines, as for instance in Shashamane, where the demographic balance of the town had recently been changing, with more Muslim traders resident. Around 9,000 people were arrested and 4,000 prosecuted, including Jawar Mohammed and Bekele Gerba. The OLF leadership were also detained and chairman Dawd Ibssa was put under effective house arrest. The government immediately closed the Oromo Media and Oromia News Network.

Six months later, the Ethiopian Human Rights Commission (EHRC) reported that 123 people had been killed and at least 500 injured over three days of violence in which 'the attacks meet the elements of a crime against humanity with large numbers of people, organised in groups, having selected their victims on the basis of their ethnicity or religion'. EHRC also criticised the response of Oromia and federal security officers:

> where the security forces had minimal preparedness, such as in Batu (Ziway), Shashemene, Chiro, Haromaya, Woliso, Adama, Goba, Arsi Negelle and Arsi Robe in particular ... The damage was extensive ... Local authorities and security did not respond to victims' repeated calls for help ... police stood watching. [Meanwhile, elsewhere] the proportionality of the force employed in some contexts is highly questionable ... [with] people killed with bullet wounds to the head, shots to the chest area or the back.[71]

Oromo interlocutors complained that the EHRC report was itself biased, part of a campaign to discredit Oromos and Oromo authorities and feed a convenient narrative of ethno-nationalist pogroms.

Clearly 'viewpoints on contentious incidents align[ed] neatly with political outlooks'.[72] An unpublished report on West Arsi concluded that 'the political situation in the area played a major role, and religion and ethnicity were used as covers (instruments) to mobilize the people. This political situation was the result of activities by government, opposition parties, activists and other politically driven actors'.[73] While the death of Hachalu was universally seen as the trigger of the violence, other causal factors included leadership failure, unhealthy political competition, differences related to the interpretation of Ethiopian history, youth unemployment, and religious intolerance. In sum, inter-communal hostility had been fanned in the area for some time and was easily ignited.

The effect was to close off Oromo nationalist political opposition across Oromia.[74] It was also to preclude criticism of the war in Tigray from an influential federalist opposition bloc which might have protested when the 'law and order operation' was launched in November 2020. Nationalist politicians of the OLF and OFC were discredited by the government media and removed from the public sphere, either jailed or placed under house arrest. With their silencing, pan-Ethiopian nationalist opponents of multinational federalism were now able to call—largely unchallenged—for military action against the TPLF. On 1 July 2020, in the immediate wake of the killing of Hachalu Hundessa, ESAT broadcast its first call for joint Ethiopian and Eritrean military action against the TPLF.[75] The call was re-posted the following day by Eritrean Press[76] and is worth quoting in full, as it marked the crossing of a new line.

> We are witnessing that the current situation is well under the control of the Government. After the killing of Hachalu and after they thought that they could set Ethiopia on fire through demonstrations, the Ethiopian security forces are controlling the situation. However Ethiopia's problems are beyond that. Ethiopia's problem is not a problem only for Ethiopia: beyond Ethiopia they are also setting a blaze in Eritrea. There is a force that has been igniting fires in both countries. So if Ethiopia and Eritrea are to have peace I believe that there has to be all necessary cooperation with the Eritrean Government. They are our brothers and the cause of all of the problems both of us face is the TPLF. As long as the TPLF exists in the Horn of Africa there will not be peace in Ethiopia or in Eritrea. Thus in the process of making this force history there shouldn't be [consideration of any] such thing as sovereignty. I don't understand the difference between TPLF and EPLF [from that point of view]. The EPLF fought for 30 years and then left to be a nation. TPLF fought for 17 years and took control of Ethiopia and has been working from Ethiopia. So I don't see a difference between them. Therefore, in order to save Ethiopia and help Eritrea I believe that we have to think that far.[77]

Proliferation and reorientation of security actors

The level of killings of civilians, notably ethnically defined 'others', had escalated particularly in Amhara, Oromia and Benishangul-Gumuz. A federal crackdown on powerful opposition political challengers began to take shape in the autumn of 2019. In Oromia, the opposition OLF and OFC (by then including Jawar Mohammed and Bekele Gerba) reported increasing repression as they began to conduct pre-election activities towards the end of the year. Federal repression escalated after controversial constitutional moves to postpone elections in the spring of 2020 (and the murky assassination of Oromo nationalist singer Hachalu Hundessa in June). July 2020 saw a return to a full-blown campaign of securitisation and authoritarian control, including state-perpetrated human rights violations and mass arrests, under States of Emergency *de facto* or (later in the year) *de jure*, accompanied by internet and telecoms blockages. Beyond Tigray, conflict continued elsewhere, especially (but not only) in Benishangul-Gumuz (Metekel) and Oromia (Wellega), where it drew in the national military as well as regional state forces.

Reforming the military?

The historical lesson of the risk of an independently powerful military at a moment of political disarray was also not lost on the incoming prime minister in 2018—and his moves to replace the chief of staff and head of security were noted above. Military reforms did not stop here, however, and around 500 senior military officers were retired from active service in 2018. Although, by 2016, the majority of those in senior military positions were no longer Tigrayans, nevertheless many Tigrayans were removed in 2018. Key figures in the senior military leadership of METEC, many also Tigrayan, had been arrested within months on corruption charges, and court cases are ongoing. METEC companies were relieved of major national contracts and broken up, and reforms were drafted. Elite special forces and bodyguard units were rapidly reorganised. Prime minister Abiy as commander-in-chief took a number of opportunities to project a martial persona (he was filmed in October 2018 performing press-ups with protesting soldiers). A new and well-resourced Republican Guard was established to protect the persons of the heads of state and government in the week before the June 2018 grenade explosion.[78]

The role and function of the national military was allowed to continue to shift after 2018, in two strongly linked respects, which seemed to have little to do with deliberate reform strategies. Firstly, the role of the national military progressively evolved from its 'outwardly focused' role in the protection of Ethiopia's borders, notably in the north, and in the Somali arena in the east, towards a more 'internally focused' role in stabilisation and law and order within the country. This gradual shift had begun as States of Emergency were declared in response to Oromo protests in late 2016 and 2017. Secondly, the States of Emergency system of establishing command posts, under joint military and civilian administration in different parts of the country, brought the military closer into what would normally be considered policing, local government or political decision-making processes. Once again, this had the potential to erode the difference between civilian and military functions and to affect the national civilian–military balance of power.

Special forces running out of control?

Regional instability touched the military at the highest level in June 2019, when the newly appointed (Tigrayan) chief of staff Se'are Mekonnen was gunned down in Addis Ababa with a fellow Tigrayan general. As noted, the killings were blamed on the radical Amhara regional state head of security, General Aseminew Tsigé, but suspicion of a government 'inside job' on the ENDF leader in Addis Ababa has lingered.[79] Little had been done during 2018 and the first half of 2019 to rein in 'provocative behaviour' and violence on the part of Amhara and Oromo special forces (then under the command of a controversial ex-military man, General Kemal Gelchu, considered to be an ethno-national 'radical'). Localised violence was associated with tension between groups who were 'pro-federalism' and others who (may have) favoured a change to a more unitary political system.

The apparently sharp expansion and re-training of paramilitary-style special forces in Oromia[80] and Amhara between 2018 and 2020 was associated in each case with controversial former generals, later regional state heads of administration and security, both considered 'radical' ethno-nationalists: Amhara Aseminew Tsigé, who was killed in June 2019, and the former army general, then Eritrea-based OLF member Oromo Kemal Gelchu who had been removed in April of that year.[81] The loyalty and scale of the Amhara special forces became a matter of heightened concern in early June 2019, when at a special forces graduation ceremony, General Aseminew claimed that Amhara special forces (by then thought to number around 35,000) were facing greater threats than at any time in the previous five hundred years.[82] Since November 2020, Amhara special forces have been heavily involved in fighting in western Tigray, south of Tekeze, and in Metekel zone of Benishangul-Gumuz.

In Tigray, heavily militarised regional government special forces were also scaled up from 2018, with large but unknown numbers under arms, including a large village-level militia force. Estimates made in 2020 were later queried.[83] In the run-up to war, former generals, of Tigrayan origin, who had been retired from the military, were remobilised and deployed to the region for the training and organisation of the regional state's forces, and to lead their operations. As is discussed in later chapters, the special forces of several regional states were involved in the theatre of conflict in Tigray, alongside regular Ethiopian, Eritrean and Somali troops, with Amhara special forces being particularly prominent.

Counterinsurgency in Oromia

As in Amhara, when the OLF returned with its fighters from Eritrea to Ethiopia in September 2018, at least one faction did not participate in the demobilisation and reintegration programme but continued to operate under the new banner of the Oromo Liberation Army (OLA).[84] A group or individual referred to as 'Abba Torbee' was alleged to have assassinated government agents in and around Dembi Dolo from 2017, and the government also claimed that what it called 'OLF Shanee'[85] was assassinating and kidnapping civilians, amidst tension with the Gumuz. In January 2019, an Oromo traditional elders' council intervened, and a committee of political leaders was established to 'oversee the OLA's integration into regional forces'. The maverick OLA western region commander, Kumsa Diriba (nicknamed Jaal Marroo), was not among them.[86] Many who had initially entered demobilisation camps complained they were being mistreated, disrespected, even poisoned—and returned to armed activity.

In January 2019, in an escalation that shocked observers, the federal government conducted air strikes against the OLA in Kellem Wellega, as the federal army moved into these western zones in force, undertaking a sustained military operation in the area.[87] As the pressure mounted, the OLF announced it no longer controlled significant elements of the armed OLA. On 1 April 2019 OLA formally established a command separate from OLF leaders in Addis Ababa to continue the armed struggle without compromising those leaders.[88] OLA started to operate independently of the OLF, primarily in the Wellega zones, and in Bale and Guji areas further south and east. Although initially thought to be acting as a series of disparate groups, OLA seems to have consolidated over the period under the authority of the most influential of these groups, that of Jaal Marroo, operating in western Oromia. On 3 January 2020 mobile and landline phone and internet services to the four Wellega zones were cut off and remained so more than two years later.[89]

Oromo rights organisations accused the government of 'adding fuel to the fire'.[90] A few weeks later *The Economist* reported that the crackdown in western Oromia was 'bloody and lawless':

> by December 2019 the Oromia Support Group had documented 64 extra-judicial killings and at least 1,400 cases of arbitrary detention over the previous six months. Since then many more abuses have been reported, including the burning of homes. In January activists claimed the army had massacred 59 civilians in Wollega. The OLF alleged another 21 had been killed nearby. The government has denied all allegations. This is unconvincing, but it is possible atrocities reflect a breakdown in the chain of command rather than orders from the top ... Senior federal officials may not know the full extent or nature of the military's operations in Wollega.[91]

In the same March 2020 article, *The Economist* concluded that the years of unrest in Oromo areas since 2014 had weakened local government and left a security vacuum.

In Wollega (to the west) and Guji (in the south) returning rebels stepped into the breach, sometimes working with the police to enforce order. But they soon began accusing the government of betraying the Oromo cause and reneging on promises to give them jobs in the police. The government, in turn, accused the OLA of keeping its weapons.

Attacks in western Oromia continued, with large numbers of civilian casualties and allegations of ethnic profiling. On 1 November 2020, the BBC reported at least 32 people killed in Gawa Qanqa, Guliso *wereda*, Wellega; Amnesty International put the figure as high as at least 54 and quoted witnesses identifying them as Amhara and blaming the OLA. The killings took place 'just a day after ENDF troops withdrew from the area unexpectedly and without explanation'.[92] The federal government blamed the massacre on the TPLF and OLA, but social media activist critics suspected a 'false flag' operation, designed to create a trigger for the Tigray war.[93] These killings did not stop with the outbreak of the Tigray war. On 9 March 2021, 29 people were reported killed in a church in Jarte *wereda*.[94] On 18 June 2022, more than 200 were killed near Gimbi.[95] OLA sources vigorously denied responsibility for all of these killings.[96] In each of these cases, sources alleged that government security forces left the area ahead of the killings, fuelling complicated suspicions of collusion.

Unravelling the constitution: Fights over a state of emergency and the slide towards war

Following the dramatic establishment of the Prosperity Party at the end of 2019, tensions with the TPLF and with a series of other ethno-nationalist opponents were running high. They were about to get higher still.

> Appealing for TPLF's 'experience', Prime Minister Abiy made a clumsy and painful attempt at reconciliation, through the mediation of the group of around fifty Tigrayan businessmen in Addis Ababa. It produced deeper tension. Abiy offered no political arguments but proposed three options. The first was that the TPLF should merge with Prosperity Party or secondly that it

should join Prosperity Party with the same status that the 'agar' affiliated parties previously had with EPRDF. A third option was for the TPLF to send, say, ten high-level figures to Addis to work with him. He also proposed that Debretsion could be appointed as Deputy Prime Minister ... The TPLF categorically refused. It said it could not compromise over the Prosperity Party program but it was ready to negotiate on national issues, particularly security and the holding of peaceful elections.[97]

The December 2019 mediation process brought new indications of what was to come, in terms of federal government planning. There were 'reports that the prime minister may have told [the] meeting of Tigrayan businessmen in December 2019 that the region could face economic sanctions absent greater cooperation with the federal government'.[98]

The Prime Minister reacted by threatening a full blockade of Tigray, the cutting of federal funds (around 70 percent of Tigray's budget), the firing of all Tigrayans in the federal institutions, cutting off all communications between Tigray and the rest of the country and even changing the banknotes. Such 'a blockade would be tantamount to a declaration of war', said a TPLF military figure.[99]

It took less than ten months for this warning to be implemented. Things degenerated rapidly when the government announced its decision to postpone federal and regional elections scheduled initially for May, and then for August 2020, arguing that the Covid-19 pandemic made it impossible to hold them safely.[100] Some international observers suggested that the delay could provide an opportunity for a 're-set' for a transition which by now was widely regarded as going off the rails. On the other hand, with the situation unravelling in Amhara and Oromia, opposition parties were increasingly uncomfortable with any prospect of a delay, sensing a stitch-up. Delay beyond September 2020 was widely regarded as unconstitutional—other than in the extreme circumstances covered by a sustained State of Emergency, which was not the strategy the government adopted. One member of the Election Board resigned when the federal government insisted on the delay. The TPLF was adamant that the delay was unconstitutional.

However, the federal government's determined direction of travel was also becoming clearer. At the beginning of August 2020, a month after ESAT commentators had called for military action against Tigray, the president of the Supreme Court posted remarkably incautious (and historically questionable) remarks online. In response to a question about the situation in Tigray from Dr Aregawi Berhe, she suggested that the US federal government under President Eisenhower had responded with military force when states failed to respect a Supreme Court ruling during the civil rights movement.[101]

Political actors took decisions which brought the crisis to a head. The Tigray regional state government ignored the ruling of the federal authorities to postpone the regional state poll, because it considered this decision breached the constitutional limits placed on governmental terms. Two different conceptions of 'rule of law' were by now in play: the Tigray regional government adopted an approach based on underlying (constitutional) principles of self-determination and residual sovereignty, while flouting the alternative 'positive law' framing according to which it should indeed have gone along with the prescriptions of the centre. The regional parliament determined that the Tigray regional state election would proceed within September. It argued that the federal and regional parliaments' terms of office had expired and that to extend their mandates was unconstitutional.

Even as the election was announced, the TPLF accused Eritrea of attempting to interfere in the election. The TPLF chairman and deputy president of the Tigray region, Debretsion Gebremichael, said: 'armed men are roaming in border areas and trying to mobilize the public to boycott the election'. After months of deteriorating relations, the situation had become extremely tense. Holding the ballot was a highly controversial decision. If the federal government's decision to postpone elections was unconstitutional, the right of a regional state government to proceed without the remit of the National Election Board was also constitutionally questionable. But by now the issue was beyond legal nicety:

The feud between Ethiopian Prime Minister Abiy Ahmed and the ruling party in the strategically important Tigray region is escalating, raising fears of military confrontation and the break-up of Africa's second most-populous nation. The tensions revolve around the regional government's decision to press ahead with organising its own election for the Tigray parliament on Wednesday, in an unprecedented act of defiance against the federal government.[102]

The federal government warned that Tigray elections were illegal, saying that only the National Electoral Board had the power to organise polls, and there was no mandate for the initiative to be taken at regional state level. The 9 September 2020 election had been declared unconstitutional by the Ethiopian federal parliament four days before it took place.[103] It went ahead regardless. The result was overwhelmingly in favour of the ruling TPLF, which took all the elected seats.[104] The outcome came as little surprise. As an exercise in democracy the votes indicated that the Tigrayan ruling party retained widespread support—hardly surprising in a context where even those Tigrayans who had doubts and reservations about the TPLF decided that now was not the time to voice them. But it did nothing to resolve Tigray's dispute with Addis Ababa. The stage was set for full confrontation.

With the backing of parliament, the federal government didn't just condemn the elections as illegitimate, but it now moved to treat the newly elected government as illegal. The federal House of People's Representatives abruptly decreed that all federal budget transfers and all inter-governmental relations with Tigray be cut.[105] As Herman Cohen noted on 8 October 2020, 'this very likely indicates that the Abiy regime in Addis is planning to use force against Tigray. It could mean all out civil war'.[106] By 11 October, the federal Ministry of Education had halted the delivery of Covid-19 supplies to the regional state Bureau of Education.[107] By 22 October, the provision of safety net support to the poor in Tigray had been suspended.[108] On 30 October, Eritrean Press reported a source saying that 'the Ethiopian government has now begun military and legal proceedings against the TPLF-led *de facto* Tigray region government'.[109] As a controversy over the reorganisation of the Northern Command leadership escalated, a press release from the Ethiopian army warned the regional state in terms described by a prominent Oromo journalist as a 'harbinger of war'.[110]

Conclusion

Underlying talk of reform and transition, the key themes of Ethiopia's domestic politics during the 2018–2020 period were deepening violence and displacement; and deepening polarisation between the country's politicians over the future of the federal project and the balance of power across the federation. Each of these dynamics was coloured by the concentration of power in the person of the prime minister and by his co-option of new allies and marginalisation of old ones (especially ethno-nationalists and federalists). Meanwhile, as Ethiopia's social fabric began to fray, ethnicised rhetoric and the cult and threat of violent polarisation all grew. This chapter has reviewed several of the patterns of mobilisation and tension in Tigray, Amhara and Oromia, and the deepening suspicion between the principal political players at the centre and between the states. This was a far cry from the wild enthusiasm of the Abiymania of 2018.

Many in Amhara and Addis Ababa heard the new prime minister's enthusiasm for 'synergy' and Ethiopianism as offering the prospect of a move away from the ethnic federal project of the EPRDF. A disproportionate number of educated and middle-class Ethiopians supported this trajectory, and welcomed both the criticism of the past and the scapegoating of the TPLF. Many of the most vocal urban elites were supportive of the pan-Ethiopianism of Ezema and ESAT. These elite voices continued to influence the embassies and missions of the international community in support of moves against what they saw as the (inherent) dangers of ethnic politics and the 'extremism' of ethno-nationalist politicians, whether Oromo or Tigrayan. Broadly oblivious of the violent extremism now creeping into pan-Ethiopianist nationalist rhetoric, Ethiopia's diplomatic and development partners were slow to recognise the poisoning of Ethiopia's political practice beneath the attractive veneer of speedy reforms. This was greatly exacerbated as travel declined as a result of insecurity and the pandemic, and Addis Ababa became ever more of an echo chamber.

Critics of the TPLF over this period argued that it should have been more conciliatory towards Abiy and the new federal government; that it should have recognised that no central power could be expected to tolerate the level of disdain and distance it adopted. From a TPLF perspective, two factors combined to preclude this in practice. One was the collective shock at the extraordinary barrage of negative propaganda—led by government media sources, but ably assisted by ESAT—against the TPLF–EPRDF's record in government and against individuals who had led the movement. Many Tigrayans saw these campaigns as having increasing overtones (at the least) of ethnic discrimination. The second factor—as Lefort astutely noted in 2018—was the government's provocative alliance with political groups who were enemies not just of the TPLF but of federalism itself. These alliances, in combination with Abiy's evident personal enthusiasm for quasi-imperial ideas, histories and aesthetics, made it unthinkable that the ideological authors of multinational federalism could countenance joining the new Prosperity Party. Such a move would have required many Tigrayans (and not just TPLF members) to abandon self-determination tenets forged and held dear over more than half a century.

As the period of the 'transition to democracy' ground on, new grievances deepened bitterness. Targeted killings of civilians continued under cover of the media blackout. The damage to lives and livelihoods has been immense. The killings of Amhara civilians in Oromia radicalised opinion among Amhara politicians and diasporas. Concern about an 'Amhara genocide' gradually reinforced opposition to the federal status quo. Meanwhile, Oromos who had greeted the new prime minister in April 2018 with hopes of an 'Oromo revolution' that would effect a transition away from the repression and marginalisation of the past, saw their optimism evaporate. Tigrayan elites, too, felt increasingly threatened, fearful and hemmed in. When elections were finally held after three years of Abiy, Tigray was under occupation, Amhara extensively radicalised, and in large areas of Oromia youngsters had been driven into armed opposition, while space for competitive polls had closed off.

Although a detailed discussion of the war in Oromia (or conflicts elsewhere) lies beyond the scope of this book, it is important to remember that the war that broke out in Tigray in November 2020 was only one of the powerful and complex threads of violence that now dogged Ethiopia; and that when it erupted, the Ethiopian government had already been waging a counterinsurgency campaign against the OLA in Oromia for almost two years. Three years after the government's counterinsurgency in Oromia began, it was clear that it was not working. In February 2022, an Oromo MP stated in parliament that the OLA administered 398 small towns and villages in Oromia, even 'collecting taxes'.[111] Since the end of 2018, the scope and extent of the activities of the OLA had clearly grown very considerably, although documenting this growth and understanding its potential political implications were difficult in the context of an ongoing media blackout.

Many saw an increase in 'ethnic conflict' as an unavoidable consequence of actions to 'open up' political space in 2018. This assessment does not bear scrutiny. Rather, much of the conflict in and around Oromia and Amhara can be traced back to elite political struggles for the control and direction of national politics before and since 2018. Richard Reid reminds us that atrocity is nothing new in Ethiopian history. 'Ethiopian chronicles are replete with references to massacres and deadly destruction.'[112] In 2015, an experienced commentator had remarked that 'the Derg's orgy of violence has had a kind of immunizing effect on the social body. Violence is not anymore a simple acceptable fact as it had been for centuries.'[113] Only a year later, in 2016, Tigrayan civilians had begun to move out of Amhara in large numbers, fearing for their lives. From 2018, civilian displacements were triggered at record levels in other areas too under the new prime minister. As the rule of law continued to unravel in Ethiopia between 2018 and 2020, it began to be clear that the Ethiopian body politic was no longer inoculated against outbreaks of extreme violence—if it ever had been.

Meanwhile, in parallel, another set of critical dynamics emerged during the 2018–20 period: the reconfiguration of the politics of the Horn of Africa, premised on the remarkable rapprochement between the three leaders of the governments of Ethiopia, Eritrea and Somalia. The involvement of these two neighbouring states in the events that led to the outbreak of war in November 2020, and the wider regional dynamics of the encirclement of Tigray, form the focus of the next chapter. The new involvement of international forces—Eritrean and Somali—would only further darken the polarising domestic political picture.

6

ERITREA, THE HORN AND THE PATH TO WAR

Martin Plaut

The period from the appointment of Abiy Ahmed as prime minister in April 2018 to the outbreak of war at the beginning of November 2020 was an intense one. As discussed in the previous chapter, a series of complex shifts in the domestic politics of Ethiopia brought war closer. The ruling party which had elevated the new prime minister now turned on its founding member, the TPLF, and was reconstituted on a unitary basis to exclude it. With Tigray's political leadership on the defensive, the new government pandered to its antagonists, facilitating the return and amplifying the narratives of pan-Ethiopianist nationalists, many of whom sought to reverse the federal system. Meanwhile, the wave of Oromo ethno-nationalism on which the new prime minister rode to power was broken and driven underground. Each of these processes resulted in increased violence and ethnic hostility in and around Ethiopia's two most populous regional states, Amhara and Oromia, where armed militants, who had returned under amnesty from bases in Eritrea, refused to demobilise. An already unstable security situation degenerated as the rule of law eroded and security sector actors proliferated. A dispute over whether to postpone the elections merely escalated events.

These dramatic domestic changes tell only a part of the story of the path to war, however. Of equal—maybe greater—importance was the simultaneous evolution of international events in the Horn of Africa. These changes now saw Eritrean president Isaias Afwerki gain a remarkable level of influence over the Ethiopian domestic political sphere. It was an influence that the EPRDF had previously done so much to prevent him from exercising. This chapter discusses the Ethiopian–Eritrean peace deal of 2018 and explains how it triggered a new tripartite constellation in the Horn, uniting the interests of three national leaders with a shared antipathy towards federalism and the TPLF.

The Eritrea peace deal and the new Horn constellation

With Abiy Ahmed installed as prime minister, immediate steps were taken to end the 'cold peace' with Eritrea that had prevailed for nearly two decades, following the 1998–2000 border war. President Isaias moved swiftly to win the new Ethiopian leader's confidence and to gain Abiy's support for a scheme to destroy his Tigrayan enemies once and for all. None of this was undertaken in public. Eritrea is the most secretive place on the African continent—among the most secretive in the world.[1] Obtaining information about the country is notoriously difficult and is frequently dependent on private, informal channels. The relationship between the Eritrean and Ethiopian leaders was the result of complex, backdoor negotiations. In a move that took the public completely by surprise (and even surprised the Ethiopian Foreign Ministry, although the foreign minister was told in advance), Abiy flew to Asmara on 9 July 2018. The Ethiopian leader was given an ecstatic welcome by the Eritrean public and government, just three months after he had assumed the Ethiopian premiership.[2] As Reuters reported:

> In his boldest move, Abiy offered last month to make peace with Eritrea, 20 years after the neighbours started a border war that killed an estimated 80,000 people … On Sunday, he flew to neighbouring Eritrea and embraced Isaias on the airport runway. Thousands of Eritreans came onto the streets to cheer them and

the two men danced side by side to traditional music from both countries at a dinner that evening.[3]

It was a breakthrough, which was followed in less than a week by a visit to Addis Ababa by President Isaias—his first time in the city for 22 years. He received an equally rapturous reception.[4] For this achievement Abiy (but not Isaias) was awarded the Nobel Peace Prize. The evidence suggests that the Eritrean leader was at least as much responsible for the change in policy as his neighbour: indeed, it formed part of his long-term plans to reshape the region.

A historic peace?

The first indication that these historic events might be possible came on 4 June 2018. Abiy declared that he would accept the outcome of an international commission's ruling over where Ethiopia and Eritrea's disputed border lay: a controversy that had led the countries into a bitter border conflict (6 May 1998–9 July 2018).[5] The commission had been part of the peace brokered in Algeria that ended the war. However, when the commission ruled against Ethiopia over the town of Badme, the Ethiopians refused to accept the border that was legally designated by the Boundary Commission in 2007.[6] The result was that tens of thousands of heavily armed troops from both nations confronted each other along their thousand-kilometre-long border. It was this stalemate that was resolved by Abiy's ground-breaking trip to Asmara in July 2018. The neighbours were, finally, genuinely at peace.

Some of the first moves toward this breakthrough were quietly taken by religious groups, which worked hard to end the Ethiopia–Eritrea rift. In September 2017 the World Council of Churches sent a team to see what common ground they could find.[7] Donald Yamamoto, US assistant secretary of state for Africa, and one of America's most experienced Africa hands, also played a major role in ending the confrontation. Diplomatic sources suggest he held talks in Washington at which Eritrean minister of foreign affairs Osman Saleh was said to have been present, accompanied by Yemane Gebreab, President Isaias's long-standing adviser. They met former Ethiopian prime minister Hailemariam Desalegn, laying the groundwork for the deal. Yamamoto visited both Eritrea and Ethiopia in April 2018.[8] Although nothing of substance was announced following the visits, they are said to have been important in firming up the dialogue.

Achieving reconciliation took more than American diplomatic muscle: Arab nations also played an important role. In May 2018, a month after his inauguration, Abiy visited Saudi Arabia. While there, he encouraged the Saudi crown prince to get the Eritrean president to pick up the phone and talk to him. President Isaias declined, but—as Abiy later explained—he was 'hopeful with Saudi and U.S. help the issue will be resolved soon'.[9] In June 2018, shortly after the Yamamoto visit to Eritrea and Ethiopia, Isaias also paid a visit to the Saudis.[10] Another actor that played an important role was the UAE, and during his tour President Isaias also visited the Emirates. There are suggestions that substantial investments were offered to help Eritrea develop its economy and infrastructure. Finally, behind the scenes, the United Nations (UN) and the African Union (AU) had encouraged both sides to resolve their differences. This culminated in UN secretary general Antonio Guterres flying to Addis Ababa just hours after Abiy's first visit to Asmara on 9 July.[11] Guterres told reporters that in his view the sanctions against Eritrea that the UN had imposed because of Eritrea's threats to security in the Horn could soon be lifted since they were likely to become 'obsolete'.[12]

The peace deal between the two former bitter rivals was therefore far from the miracle it first appeared to be. It had been long in the making and involved careful diplomacy—an impressive combined effort by the international community to resolve a regional issue that had festered for years. Yet the end of one problem proved to be the beginning of another. No sooner had Abiy and Isaias settled their differences than they began planning how to remove a mutual enemy, the Tigrayans.

The two men began a series of bilateral visits as they planned what to do next. 'Mr. Abiy and Mr. Isaias met at least 14 times from the time they signed the peace deal until war broke out, public records and news reports show,' the *New York Times* reported.[13] 'Unusually, the meetings were mostly one-on-one, without aides or note-takers, two former Ethiopian officials said.' The relationship was cemented by discussions at ministerial level. In July 2018 both Isaias and Abiy made a joint visit to the UAE, which their hosts lauded as 'bold and historic'.[14] The official statement—like almost all press releases issued in the region—gave no insight into what had really taken place. It did, however, mention enhanced security in the Horn of Africa and the wider region. With the benefit of hindsight, knowing as we now do of the UAE's role as a springboard for military supplies for both Eritrea and Ethiopia during their war with Tigray after November 2020, this may have been more significant than it at first appeared.

The next meeting was—at least on the surface—of greater importance. It was certainly held with great pomp and circumstance. On 16 September 2018 Abiy and Isaias signed a formal peace agreement at a summit in Jeddah, witnessed by the Saudi king and the UN secretary general.[15] Guterres declared: 'There is a wind of hope blowing in the Horn of Africa.' These events were a prelude to a rapid deepening of relations between Eritrea and Ethiopia, with repeated reciprocal visits.[16] 'They also met in secret,' reported the *New York Times*. 'On at least three other occasions in 2019 and 2020, Mr. Isaias flew into Addis Ababa unannounced, one former official said. Aviation authorities were instructed to keep quiet, and an unmarked car was sent to take him to Mr. Abiy's compound.'

A moment of optimism

The events preceding the conflict did not all point in a single direction: there were brief moments when it seemed possible that war might be avoided. The public joy that greeted the re-opening of the Ethiopian–Eritrean border was a case in point. In September 2018, to great jubilation, the border restrictions at Zalambessa were lifted. 'Hundreds of people from the two countries hugged each other and some wept as their leaders led celebrations to mark the reopening.'[17] Soon trade between the two nations was booming, to the obvious benefit of both Eritreans and Tigrayans. Merchants in the Tigrayan border town of Adigrat were delighted. The BBC captured the atmosphere.

> The sun had just risen but the market in Adigrat was already coming alive when I went to visit. Dozens of makeshift stalls lined the street where a group of women traders were sifting

chickpeas. In another place an elderly man was removing chickens from cages and placing them outside his shop. You can buy almost anything at the market: spices, building materials, fridges and washing machines. The market in this Ethiopian town, just 38 km (24 miles) south of the border, has been transformed since the border opened four months ago after a peace deal ended the 'state of war' between the two nations. Many Eritreans now cross over to see what they can buy.

Mebrhit Gebrehans, a middle-aged woman with a big smile, is one of the traders whose business is booming. She was busy opening a sack full of fresh spices and was calling over potential customers when I met her. 'What we fear is war. We love peace. When the Eritreans come to this market, I welcome them with a smiling face. They buy spices, honey, grains and even biscuits. And we buy different clothes from them,' she said. 'When the border reopened, we were worried there would be shortages of some things, but there hasn't been. Everything is normal,' she added.[18]

Eritreans returned home with lorries piled high with goods to sell in their towns and villages. Products that had been in short supply for years were suddenly plentiful and affordably priced. The euphoria did not last. In December 2018, without warning or explanation, Eritrea closed the border once more. The Tigray regional administration said Ethiopian citizens and Ethiopia-licensed vehicles travelling to Eritrea from the town of Rama were asked for 'permits'. A day later those using a crossing in Zalambessa were required to show the same thing.[19] 'The restrictions have only been imposed on the Eritrean side. We did not receive any prior notice'.

Eritrea gave no explanation for its action. It is only possible to guess at what lay behind President Isaias's decision to reimpose restrictions. One reason may have been the exodus of Eritreans, who poured across the border into Tigray while the opportunity existed.[20] Many left to escape Eritrea's indefinite conscription, which can continue for 20 years and more. Others left in search of a better life, but flood out of Eritrea they did. 'Since the border opening, buses have reportedly been sweeping in to the small Ethiopian border town of Zalambessa, just beyond the Eritrean checkpoint, to collect hundreds of Eritrean asylum seekers who muster there over the course of a few days', reported the New Humanitarian in November 2018.[21] They joined the flight of Eritreans, many of whom were living in four refugee camps in Tigray, while others were scattered across the rest of Ethiopia, including Addis Ababa.

The United Nations refugee agency reported at the outbreak of the war in November 2020 that they had registered 96,223 Eritrean refugees in four refugee camps in western Tigray: Mai Aini (21,682), Adi Harush (32,168), Shimelba (8,702) and Hitsats (25,248).[22] An additional 8,424 Eritrean were refugees living in Tigrayan communities, benefiting from the government's 'Out of Camp' policy. Others were in the Afar region (approximately 51,800) and in the capital Addis Ababa (approximately 30,722). In total, Ethiopia was home to nearly 180,000 Eritreans. President Isaias loathed the fact that so many had fled the country, fearing that in time the refugee camps might become recruiting grounds for opposition movements bent on overthrowing his regime.

There may be another reason for Isaias's action. Eritreans crossing the border witnessed at first hand the relative prosperity of Tigray and compared it with their own, poorly performing economy. Eritreans traditionally saw themselves as more developed than their southern neighbours; coming face to face with modern factories across the border must have been something of a surprise. For Isaias the idea that young Eritreans were choosing to escape his underdeveloped nation to go to Tigray, which he had derided for years, must have been galling.

Despite the closure of the border crossing in the central sector, another was opened in January 2019—this time in the far west, at Humera–Omhajer, the point at which Eritrea, Ethiopia and Sudan meet.[23] It provided a rare opportunity for a meeting between President Isaias, Prime Minister Abiy and the Tigrayan leader Debretsion Gebremichael. Isaias gave this account of his tense discussion with Debretsion in the interview with Eritrean TV on 17 February 2021.

We met Debretsion in Zelambessa on 11 September 2018. I was not in a mood to talk to him. This was followed by another meeting in Omhajer. I only agreed to do so late the previous night having said I would not meet him up to that point. I had only one message/question and repeatedly asked myself if I should say it or not. In the end, I thought better to say it. I asked Debretsion, why are you preparing for war? Why? He replied, 'it won't happen'. I asked what do you mean? This is the reason why I agreed to meet you and we cannot discuss any other business. This was a message of warning PM Abiy was trying to convey i.e., that war preparation was unnecessary. I therefore passed his message to Debretsion on his behalf. Hearing his reply, I concluded by saying in that case let's wait and see. The TPLF seemed concerned about potential attacks from the South and from Eritrea in the North. We started to carefully study the situation and to make our own preparations.[24]

In this statement President Isaias was acknowledging that as early as January 2019 he believed war was on the cards, and had begun to prepare for this eventuality.

Underlying motivation and a trilateral alliance

If optimism about the 'peace deal' between Ethiopia and Eritrea was misplaced, it is worth pausing to understand what drove the leaders, and to assess what was really taking place between them. One—Isaias—had effectively led his party and then his nation through wars and regional conflicts since the mid-1970s. A ruthless, canny leader who trusted no one but his closest associates, he had a reputation as a man who schemed and plotted across the region, while peering down the years. By comparison, Abiy was a novice when they first met in 2018. Isaias was thirty years Abiy's senior, with a wealth of experience behind him. Abiy's reasons for loathing the leadership of the TPLF have been discussed in previous chapters; here we will consider what drove President Isaias.

Isaias's dislike of the TPLF and concern over its policies go back a long way. This animosity can be traced to the earliest years of the relationship between the Eritrean and Tigrayan movements in the 1970s. What had begun as differences of strategy and tactics had evolved, particularly following the Ethio-Eritrean border war, into a burning hatred. Isaias was determined to rid himself of his Tigrayan adversaries. The war of 2020 was the logical outcome of his grievances, combining as they did with Abiy's own resentment towards the Tigrayans. However, Isaias was not simply driven by a desire to remove the Tigrayan leadership. He saw himself as more than the president of a small nation on the Red Sea; rather, as a senior Africa leader who could extend his influence across the Horn of Africa and beyond.

Isaias had interfered in the affairs of his neighbours ever since he came to rule Eritrea after its independence in 1993. In fighting from 15 to 17 December 1995, Eritrean naval forces clashed with Yemen over the Hanish islands in the Red Sea.[25] The dispute went to law and was finally amicably resolved. Then, in October 1996, Isaias sent troops across the continent, to fight in the Democratic Republic of Congo, alongside Rwanda.[26] By May the following year Eritreans had helped oust Congo's President Mobutu Sese Seko. Less than a year later Eritrean arms were being used to support Sudanese rebels against the Sudanese government.[27] Had it not been for the outbreak of the 1998 border war with Ethiopia, it is suggested his involvement in Sudan could have led to the fall of Khartoum.

This intervention was followed by backing for Somali Islamists of al-Shabaab.[28] Isaias, despite having no truck with militant Islam, provided training and arms for al-Shabaab. As UN experts reported to the Security Council in 2011:

> Asmara's continuing relationship with Al-Shabaab, for example, appears designed to legitimize and embolden the group rather than to curb its extremist orientation or encourage its participation in a political process. Moreover, Eritrean involvement in Somalia reflects a broader pattern of intelligence and special operations activity, including training, financial and logistical support to armed opposition groups in Djibouti, Ethiopia, the Sudan and possibly Uganda in violation of Security Council resolution 1907 (2009).[29]

Finally, Eritrea clashed with neighbouring Djibouti in a border dispute that has spluttered on since 2008.[30] These conflicts were in addition to the border war with Ethiopia from 1998 to 2000.

Sometimes Isaias extends his influence by force of arms. More often it is via a network of agents who carry out his instructions. This not only stretches across the Horn of Africa, including Sudan and Kenya, but extends across the world to Europe and North America.

Eliminating the Tigrayans, whom both Isaias and Abiy regarded as an obstacle to their objectives, was a priority—the cement in their relationship. As Nizar Manek and Mohamed Kheri Omer argued in *Foreign Affairs*:

> Both Abiy and Isaias ... have a bloodlust for the TPLF. This shared hostility toward Ethiopia's former regime, rather than any brotherly love, was the principal motivation for their commencement of diplomatic relations two years ago, for which Abiy was feted with last year's ill-judged Nobel Peace Prize; the Norwegian Nobel Committee failed to see that the prize rewarded a peace process that really intended to end one war while laying the groundwork for another, as it has today.[31]

To understand how this was pursued we need to examine the intense series of meetings they held prior to the outbreak of the war. These did not simply involve Eritrea and Ethiopia: from January 2020—nearly a year before the fighting erupted—their relationship included Somalia. What was being formed was a tripartite alliance that would send troops to invade Tigray in November 2020. It was built on a reconciliation deal between Eritrea and Somalia, which restored diplomatic ties between the countries after 15 years, signed in July 2018, the same month that Abiy and Isaias mended fences.[32]

The Eritrea–Ethiopia–Somali relationship was sealed at a summit meeting in Asmara between the leaders on 27 January 2020.[33] Somali president Mohamed Abdullahi Farmaajo joined Abiy at a tripartite meeting hosted by Isaias. The formal declaration, although bland, revealed a plan to cooperate across a wide range of sectors, including security.

> The three leaders adopted a Joint Plan of Action for 2020 and beyond focusing on the two main and intertwined objectives of consolidating peace, stability, and security as well as promoting economic and social development. They also agreed to bolster their joint efforts to foster effective regional cooperation.
>
> On the security front, the three leaders formulated a comprehensive plan to combat and neutralize the common

threats they face, including terrorism, arms and human trafficking and drug smuggling.[34]

The plans of the new tripartite alliance extended beyond the conflict that lay ahead. It envisaged a framework that would replace the existing regional organisation, the Intergovernmental Authority on Development (IGAD), which President Isaias had long held in contempt. In 2007 Eritrea suspended its participation in IGAD, accusing the organisation of supporting Ethiopia's invasion of Somalia.[35] In 2011 Eritrea attempted to resume its role in IGAD, only to find its re-entry blocked by Ethiopia. In January 2020 Eritrea, Ethiopia and Somalia proposed a new regional bloc: the Horn of Africa Cooperation Council.[36] This was designed to work alongside Saudi plans to increase its influence by establishing a nine-nation 'Red Sea, Gulf of Aden Council'.

What was being outlined was a novel reorganisation of the Horn of Africa, with the Somali leader being offered a junior partnership in reshaping the region. Western diplomats now accept that they badly misunderstood the implications of the trilateral relationship, which was a prelude to war. This was acknowledged by an unnamed European official: 'I was as wrong as everyone on Eritrea and Abiy's rapprochement. We failed to think regionally: that what looked like peace could actually increase insecurity for everyone.'[37]

The path to war

In the months running up to the Tigray war in November 2020, the plans were refined and developed. The Eritrean leader made a series of visits to Ethiopia's regions as well as the capital, something few foreign leaders had previously undertaken. His motivation for making these trips was never fully clarified.[38] As the war drew closer, Abiy and Isaias's links deepened, and they visited each other's key military facilities. These were unprecedented events and highly unusual. In July 2020 Abiy went to Eritrea's training facility at Sawa.[39] It is here that young Eritreans are taken as conscripts for their national service. It is a tough, sometimes brutal environment and not open to public scrutiny. That Abiy was taken there at all was remarkable: the

Eritrean Foreign Ministry described Abiy as the 'first ever [foreign] leader to visit Sawa'.[40] This was followed by President Isaias going to the Ethiopian air force base at Bishoftu in October 2020, less than a month before the outbreak of war.[41] It seems that both leaders were sizing up the military preparations that had been made, the state of readiness of their allies' forces.

With tensions rising in the region, there was one final, critical meeting of which the author is aware. Just prior to the conflict erupting in Tigray, Isaias brought his closest political and military advisers together for an intense discussion on how to proceed.[42] The president told them that the country had to accept that it had a small and not very viable economy and a lengthy Red Sea coast, which Eritrea could not patrol on its own. He is reported to have suggested that some sort of 'union' with Ethiopia might be possible, at least in terms of economic cooperation and maritime security. In so doing Isaias appeared to be echoing Abiy's grandiose dream of re-establishing the old empire state of Ethiopia.

This is not as far-fetched as it would appear, despite Isaias's leadership of Eritrea's 30-year war of independence from Ethiopia. Isaias seems to have believed that he could control and manipulate the younger, more inexperienced Ethiopian leader. His vision was aptly summed up by this assessment, made eight months *before* the outbreak of the war: 'Eritrean observers believe that Isaias has a grand vision of uniting the region, envisioning himself at the Horn's helm. And he also believes that the biggest obstacle to the realisation of this vision is TPLF. Hence, the irreconcilable enmity.'[43]

A series of developments ratcheted up the tension, culminating in the Tigray war of November 2020. Sorting fact from fiction has been, and remains, difficult. The Eritrean authorities allow no independent journalists to be based in the country. Over many years reporters have only been allowed to visit on the odd occasion for carefully staged tours, under close supervision. Ethiopia also has a poor record of press freedom: visas were not granted to visiting media teams and local journalists were repressed. When Abiy took over the premiership he lifted many of these restrictions. However, over time this was reversed. 'Unfortunately, Ethiopia has rejoined the list of worst jailers of journalists in sub-Saharan

Africa,' commented Muthoki Mumo, of the Committee to Protect Journalists.[44] When the Tigray war erupted, it appeared that Abiy, perhaps adopting Isaias's strategy, imposed a ring of steel around the region. No independent journalists were given permission to provide first-hand accounts of what was taking place. The media had to rely on government information, supplemented by reports from UN agencies and aid groups and news from carefully cultivated sources inside Tigray.

This information blockade was associated with official dissembling. One example will suffice. From the outbreak of the war in November 2020 until March 2021 there was no acknowledgement from either Addis Ababa or Asmara that Eritrean forces were involved in the war. The information did leak out, however, as a result of satellite analysis and following a number of slip-ups by Ethiopian broadcasters. In December 2020, for instance, an Ethiopian major general 'inadvertently disclosed that the troops who took Sheraro were actually coming from Tokombiya, a village deep into Eritrean territory, thus confirming the Eritrean involvement the government kept on denying'.[45] On 26 March 2021, long after the Eritrean presence was an open secret, Abiy finally acknowledged their participation in the fighting.[46] 'Eritrea has agreed to withdraw its forces out of the Ethiopian border', the prime minister said on Twitter during a trip to Asmara for talks with President Isaias. Eritrean state-controlled media had nothing to add. Yet even this acknowledgement proved wide of the mark: Eritrean forces remained in northern and western Tigray while Eritrean security forces were embedded in Addis Ababa, helping control entry to and exit from Bole International airport.

A study by the Harvard Kennedy School found that both sides have engaged in intense efforts to spread propaganda and false information.[47] The study indicated that there have been 'two broad campaigns seeking to shape international policy around an active military conflict. It is a complex case that interacts with the geopolitics of the Horn of Africa, historical trauma, activism, hate speech, misinformation, platform manipulation, and propaganda, all in the midst of an ongoing civil conflict.'

Tigrayans respond and a purge begins

As the Eritreans and Ethiopians prepared for war, the Tigrayans were also aware of the approaching danger. Tom Gardner, the *Economist* correspondent in Ethiopia, wrote:

> by the end of 2018, Debretsion was already speaking in public about Tigray's willingness to defend itself militarily against Abiy's overreach, and by the end of the following year, he had accused Abiy's government of working 'to destroy the people of Tigray'. Ethnic tensions rose and Tigrayans living in other parts of Ethiopia began to feel insecure. Almost all senior TPLF officials and many TPLF-connected businessmen left Addis Ababa for the ostensible security of Mekelle in the intervening months.[48]

Soon after Abiy came to power in April 2018, the federal government began purging the Ethiopian military and the security forces of Tigrayans, who had been the backbone of both organisations for many years. In June Abiy appointed a new army chief of staff, the first such change in 17 years.[49] The new chief of staff, Se'are Mekonnen, was a Tigrayan, but the restructuring left Tigrayans wondering about the policies Abiy was adopting. They did not have long to wait. In December 2018 Reuters carried a report on the removal of Tigrayans from key positions: 'Now many leading Tigrayans are being detained or sidelined as reformist prime minister, Abiy Ahmed attempts to draw a line under past abuses. One adviser to Abiy told Reuters that the prime minister has sacked 160 army generals for actions he said amount to "state terrorism"'.[50]

In the run-up to the war Tigrayans were not only replaced, but changes were made to the location, strength and structure of the army's commands. In December 2018 troops were to be moved away from the Eritrea border, and the Shire HQ in Tigray disbanded.[51] Although personnel moved, much of the hardware seems to have remained *in situ*. The Tigray government took steps to ensure they could protect themselves as the mood in the region darkened. The weapons had been stationed close to the Eritrean border to repulse any potential attack following the 1998–2000 border war.[52] In January 2019 ordinary Tigrayans took to the streets of towns along the border with Eritrea to prevent the removal of heavy artillery and military vehicles. The protests were held despite reports that the authorities in Mekele had asked them not to go ahead, as they 'could lead to conflict'.[53] Whether the Tigrayan authorities really attempted to halt the demonstrations is a moot point.

Military personnel were relocated to a new command established to the south, headquartered at Hawassa and coordinating Ethiopian Defence Force activities in parts of Oromia. Two other new commands were announced in the run-up to war: West/Central Command (headquartered in Bahir Dar in Amhara) after the existing Western Command was relocated from Bahir Dar to Nekemte; and a further new command (HQ Addis Ababa) was also added. An intelligence source in February 2021 described the attempted appointment of a new Northern Command leadership (see below) as the 'final act' in a 'meticulously implemented' plan for the Tigray operation, under way since April 2018, 'notably through a deep-rooted reform of the Ethiopian army high command'.[54]

What began as a purge of the armed forces and the security services gradually extended to Tigrayans across government services and industries. Staff working for Ethiopian airlines were ethnically profiled and removed from their positions.[55] A number of airline staff spoke up, saying that they had been targeted because they were Tigrayan; some found themselves stripped of their jobs and left isolated around the world. Others were refused permission to fly on the airline. The *New York Times* reported in December 2020:

> even the CEO of the national carrier, Ethiopian Airlines, who is an ethnic Tigrayan, was barred from leaving the country earlier this month, according to a pilot at the airline and a foreign diplomat who spoke on the condition of anonymity because of the sensitivity of the matter. The pilot said that the CEO, Tewolde GebreMariam, was prevented from boarding a flight to Paris on 8 November 2020 because of his strong links to senior members of the TPLF.[56]

Ethiopian Airlines contested these reports,[57] but the airline's chief executive, Tewolde GebreMariam, subsequently resigned, apparently on grounds of ill health.[58]

Purges intensified after the fighting erupted. Ethiopian cabinet ministers were instructed to fire staff simply because of their ethnicity. In an interview with the *Washington Post*, former minister of women and children Filsan Abdi (herself an ethnic Somali) said that while still a member of the cabinet, she had been told by an official 'that all Tigrayans on her staff—and at other ministries, too—were to be placed on leave immediately. I said, "I won't do it unless the prime minister calls me himself, or you put it in writing," she said, adding that subordinates of hers enforced the order anyway.'[59]

By 2021 the situation had deteriorated further. Vigilantes were scouring the cities, searching for Tigrayans. Some were arrested; all were interrogated, abused and intimidated. It was a clear example of ethnic profiling and was denounced by Human Rights Watch.[60] 'Ethiopian security forces in recent weeks have carried out rampant arbitrary arrests and enforced disappearances of Tigrayans in Addis Ababa,' said Laetitia Bader, Horn of Africa director at Human Rights Watch.

Arms and troops moved to the front

During 2020 there were repeated rumours of Ethiopian troops and military equipment being transferred to Eritrea in preparation for a possible conflict with Tigray. Flights allegedly took place at night, with planes landing in Asmara and the soldiers being ferried to military camps outside the capital. These reports were shared by the Eritrean community. Some came from the Freedom Friday underground network inside Eritrea.[61] The information was impossible to verify but plausible.

The Ethiopians were not the only foreign soldiers arriving in Eritrea. Several thousand Somali youths were sent to Eritrea for training by President Farmaajo. Although he originally denied it, the president finally conceded that the reports were indeed accurate.[62] The Somalis were subsequently sent to fight in Tigray. The initial reports, published in January 2021, said that dozens of soldiers had been killed after being 'used as cannon fodder' following their deployment to the region.[63] The *Daily Telegraph* reported that the Somali government had recruited the young men to work in Qatar, only for the paper to later find out they had been sent to Eritrea.[64]

Families of soldiers who were killed were offered up to $10,000 in compensation.[65] The Qatari government reacted angrily to the apparent deception, calling for an official investigation.

In 2022 Voice of America carried a detailed report on the role of the Somali troops in Tigray.

> Several sources with direct knowledge of the program—three Somali officials and a foreign diplomat—confirmed to VOA that Somali troops have been training in neighboring Eritrea since 2019 ... The training program in Eritrea came to light in January after unverified social media reports suggested that Somali troops had been killed in Ethiopia's Tigray region. The reports indicated those soldiers were allied with Eritrean and Ethiopian federal forces confronting Tigray fighters in the regional conflict.[66]

The independent journalist Lucy Kassa later wrote that as many as 10,000 Somalis had been sent to Eritrea.[67] This figure was supported by a former Somali intelligence officer, who told the BBC that he had confirmed the 10,000 figure with Eritrean and Ethiopian officers.[68] He said they had been 'illegally deployed' to Eritrea and fought alongside Eritrean forces, wearing Eritrean uniforms.

In January 2021 Somali mothers, frantic about the fate of their sons, protested in the capital Mogadishu, demanding to know their fate.[69] 'I heard that our children who were sent to Eritrea for military training have been taken and their responsibility was turned over to Abiy Ahmed to fight for him,' Fatuma Moallim Abdulle, the mother of a 20-year-old soldier, told Associated Press. 'According to the information I gathered, our children were taken straight to Mekele city', the capital of the Tigray. Other stories appeared. One conscript escaped from Eritrea and appeared on Somali television when he managed to make his way back to Mogadishu, only to be killed after describing what he had experienced.[70]

The balance of forces

As the clouds of war gathered, the Tigrayans faced a range of forces including the Ethiopian and Eritrean defence forces. Both were substantial and—unlike many African armies—had seen combat in several foreign wars. The US Central Intelligence Agency estimated that Ethiopia had 150,000 active-duty troops,[71] and assessed their army as 'one of the region's largest and most capable'. The International Institute for Strategic Studies put the figure somewhat lower. Its *Military Balance, 2021* gave the Ethiopian strength as 135,000, organised in four regional commands, of which the Northern Command (based in Tigray) consisted of one mechanised division and four infantry divisions.[72] They were supported by an air force 3,000 strong. In addition, there were the troops of two foreign powers. Eritrea had an estimated 150,000–200,000 personnel.[73] There were also perhaps as many as 10,000 Somalis who been pre-positioned in Eritrea, as well as tens of thousands of militia from Ethiopia's regions, of which the Amhara special forces were the most immediately involved.

Confronting these diverse forces were the Tigrayan military and their special forces, which had been scaled up after 2018. The CIA estimated that there were up to 250,000 Tigrayan troops at the start of the conflict,[74] and the International Crisis Group gave the same estimate, including a large village-level militia force. These estimates were later queried, with some sources giving a much lower figure.[75] The International Institute for Strategic Studies suggested that in November 2020 the Tigrayan forces were outnumbered about three to one by the combined troops arrayed against them.[76]

These stark figures say nothing about their training, armaments and state of readiness. The Tigrayans had held senior positions in all of Ethiopia's security services for nearly three decades. In the run-up to war, a number former Ethiopian generals, of Tigrayan origin, who had been retired from the military, were remobilised to the region for the training and organisation of Tigray's forces, and now led its operations. They had an intimate understanding of the Ethiopian military and may have continued to receive intelligence from inside government—at least at the start of the conflict. At the same time, they did not have the resources of the state or access to the outside world once the fighting commenced. Their only significant source of munitions and armaments would come from supplies they had retained or captured from their opponents.

November 2020 and the outbreak of war

In the run-up to the outbreak of the war on the night of 3/4 November, the situation deteriorated gravely. The Tigrayans believed they were surrounded and imperilled. Kjetil Tronvoll, who has studied the region for thirty years, argued in May 2020:

> Tigrayans felt 'encircled by enemies' with their back against the wall with a vengeful and gloating Eritrean Commander in Chief threatening them on their northern border, as Amhara political entrepreneurs on their southern border also turned against Tigray and advocated to forcefully reclaim what they perceived to be their lost territories of Welkeit and Raya, simultaneously as they blocked the main thoroughfares in and out of Tigray regional state to rest-Ethiopia and the capital Addis Ababa. As a consequence of these events, a siege mentality started to fester, influencing Tigrayan interpretations and perceptions of political dynamics in Ethiopia and beyond.[77]

It was a situation that was plain for all to see—not a judgement made with the benefit of hindsight. On 21 June 2020 this author posed a question: 'Is Isaias looking for a final confrontation with his Tigrayan enemies?'

> If there is one issue that unites Isaias and Abiy it is Tigray's TPLF, about which they are both almost pathologically obsessive, making little or no effort to hold any serious discussions or dialogue. The TPLF, which is concerned over the future of federalism in Ethiopia in the face of the Prime Minister's drive to centralise the Ethiopian state, is a thorn in Abiy's side. Isaias has long regarded the Tigrayans as his predominant enemies.[78]

Following the disputed elections in Tigray in September 2020, it appeared clear that Tigray was heading for a conflict with its neighbours. Social media were full of warnings. On 26 October Tronvoll declared there had 'seldom been a clearer case of a coming conflict'.[79] With the smell of gunpowder in the air, the final moves in this disastrous course of events unfolded.

On 29 October 2020 the Tigrayan authorities refused to accept a new commander of the Ethiopian army's largest division, the

Northern Command, headquartered in Mekele. General Jamal Muhammad was detained on his arrival at Mekele airport and put on a plane back to Addis.[80] As the Africa Intelligence newsletter reported a day after the war erupted:

> For the past week, the Northern Command's base has been the focus of a power struggle between regional and federal authorities. At the end of October, Abiy appointed three new military officers to head the command: Brig. Gen. Belay Seyoum Akele and two of his deputies, Brigadier General Jamal Mohammed and Seid Tekuye. On 29 October, as Jamal Mohammed arrived at Mekele airport to take up his post, he was turned away by the local authorities and asked to return to Addis Ababa. Belay Seyoum Akele and Seid Tekuye never managed to arrive in Mekele.[81]

This was a challenge to Abiy's authority that no premier could have tolerated.

With the situation spiralling towards war, Debretsion, president of the Tigray administration, issued an appeal to the international community. On 27 October he wrote to seventy world leaders, calling for them to head off the coming conflict.[82] It received little public acknowledgement, although the European Union was clearly aware of the dangers. The EU's vice president and high representative, Josep Borrell, on 2 November warned against what he called 'provocative military deployments', declaring that 'coercion or the threat of force can never be an alternative'.[83] On 3 November 2020 Debretsion took the ultimate step, warning the Tigrayan people to prepare for war.[84] He said Tigrayans wanted peace, but if war came, they were prepared to fight and to win. The speech had a grim inevitability about it. By this time few analysts in the Horn of Africa thought a conflict could be avoided.

The events of 3/4 November

What took place on the night of 3/4 November 2020 remains deeply controversial. There are diametrically opposed views about the events, and their interpretation colours how this tragic conflict is perceived. For this reason, they are examined here in some detail.

Prime minister Abiy argued that the Tigrayans launched an unprovoked attack against units of the Northern Command.

> While I was preaching peace and prosperity for my country and people, and working day and night to realize it, a violent attack was launched against my government and people. On the night of 03 November 2020, the TPLF leadership launched, under cover of darkness, what they later described, on public television, as a 'lightning pre-emptive attack' against the Northern Command of the Ethiopian National Defence Force (ENDF), which had been stationed in the Region since the outbreak of war with Eritrea over two decades ago. Using traitors recruited from within the army along ethnic lines, not only did the TPLF leadership cause the massacre of unarmed soldiers in their pyjamas in the dead of night, they also took possession, illegally, of the entire military arsenal of the Northern Command. I was thus left with a decision only of how, not whether, to fight to defend the integrity of my country and restore the constitutional order.[85]

Abiy's account changed several times, with one version suggesting that soldiers had fled naked into Eritrea—something that the Ministry of Defence did not corroborate.

What is certain is that fighting did occur at the Northern Command's main base in Mekele and that its capture provided the Tigrayans with heavy weaponry as well as some missiles. The Tigray government has yet to provide an authoritative account of what took place, but its supporters suggested that their forces were responding to attacks by commandos flown in from Addis Ababa.

> Close to midnight on November 3, 2020, armed members of the Tigray region defense forces demanded to see the commander of the Northern Command camp located there. An argument broke out and the first shots were fired. The finer details of that confrontation, such as who shot first, are not on the public record. Fighting would then ensue at Northern Command camps across the Tigray region, as well as a civilian airport in the Tigray region capital. Fighting at the airport can be linked to reports of an aircraft carrying commandos that took off from Addis Ababa the previous evening.[86]

One independent report was provided by the UN Office for the Coordination of Humanitarian Affairs (OCHA).[87] 'In the early hours of 4 November, the Ethiopian Defence forces and the security forces of the ruling Tigray People's Liberation Front (TPLF) clashed near Mekele airport. Military confrontation was also reported near Dansha in Western Tigray.'

It is significant that the UN placed the confrontation near the airport rather than at the Northern Command camp. This is closer to the Tigrayan account, but because the government has so severely restricted access to Tigray, it has been difficult to corroborate the competing narratives. Professor Mirjam van Reisen, Klara Smits and Kibrom Berhe of the University of Tilburg in the Netherlands have attempted to do this.[88] They were part of an ongoing research project working with the University of Mekele and were in a unique position to assess information they received from their contacts over this critical period. The report they published was drawn from contemporaneous notes they took at the time. Given the importance of this evidence and their unique character, the Tilburg University assessment is quoted here verbatim and in detail.

On the evening of November 3rd 2020, we received a call from our colleague at Mekelle University—in the regional capital of Tigray. We were working on an educational project and we were regularly in touch with them to set up our joint work. We have checked the phone log and the notes made that evening.

The Mekelle University professor phoned late in the evening of November the 3rd. Shooting had erupted at Mekelle Airport and later in the surrounding area of the city. Students also contacted us to share their concern about the fighting that broke out on the evening of November 3rd.

In subsequent briefings the university Professor said that two planes belonging to Ethiopian Airlines had landed at Mekelle airport. They had sought permission to land to bring new bank notes to the banks in a currency exchange. Instead, the planes brought in special forces.

The planes have subsequently been identified as ET3102, which flew the ADD-MQX-ADD route, AC B789 and tail ETAUR. This was a cargo plane. This flight departed from Addis

Ababa on the 3rd of November 2020 at 17:31 and arrived in Mekelle at 18:34 and waited there until 04:20 before departing for Addis Ababa at 04:21 on 4th of November. The second flight was ET3100 on ADD-MQX-ADD route, AC A350 (Airbus) and tail ETATY. It was also a cargo plane. This flight departed from Addis Ababa on the 3rd of November, 2020 at 21:05 and arrived at Mekelle at 22:25. It waited until 04:06 and departed for Addis Ababa at 04:07 on 4th November.

The true purpose of sending these planes to Mekelle and what transpired while they were in the city, has never been explained. The gunfire that was heard by many citizens of Mekelle on the night of the 3rd of November has also never been explained. Tigray government insiders have told us that special forces from the Ethiopia National Defense Forces were sent on these planes to capture and arrest (and kill) leadership of the regional government of Tigray.

The regional government of Tigray had been warned in advance by its intelligence network about this plan. As a result, when the planes landed the forces of the regional government were ready. They met the special forces arriving from Addis Ababa and shooting between the two sides erupted. The commandos from Addis Ababa failed in their aim to arrest the regional Tigray government. In the days that followed the Tigrayan authorities withdrew to the mountains and regrouped.[89]

The fighting in Mekele was one aspect of the story. The Northern Command had bases elsewhere in Tigray, located to face Ethiopia's old enemy, Eritrea. The BBC interviewed two soldiers about what had taken place at a base at Adigrat close to the Eritrean border.[90] They described events just before midnight on 3 November, explaining how Tigrayan special forces surrounded their base. One—Sergeant Bulcha—described the battle that erupted after they managed to get hold of weapons that had been stored under lock and key by their Tigrayan officers.

We took up our positions, inside and outside the camp, using rocks, barrels, walls as shields. It was around 01:00 when the battle started. There was a distance of no more than 50 m (164 ft) between us and them. We killed more than 100 of them. They killed 32 of us. In my unit, one died and nine were wounded.

Most of our deaths were caused by the Tigrayan soldiers who had defected to the other side. The battle lasted for about 11 hours until noon when our senior commanders ordered us to stop fighting, return our weapons to the storeroom, and to go back to our rooms. We obeyed.

Shortly thereafter the priests and elders of the town came. They negotiated a surrender. At around 16:00, we were ordered to hand over all our army belongings to the TPLF forces. Again, we obeyed.[91]

Corporal Ibrahim Hassan was in another camp in Adigrat, but he and his comrades capitulated to the Tigrayan forces. 'They ordered the soldiers, including myself, to surrender. We refused, saying federal troops could not surrender to regional troops. But in the end we agreed on the orders of our seniors, who were Tigrayans.'[92] Sergeant Bulcha and Corporal Ibrahim explained how they were transported from Adigrat. 'Then more than three weeks later, we were given three options—if we were married with children in Tigray, we could live as civilians, or we could join the TPLF or we could leave. Most of us chose the third option.' Corporal Ibrahim described the difficult journey they made, but finally they were freed and put across the Tekeze River into the neighbouring Amhara state. 'My guess is that we left 3,000 to 4,000 behind, and close to 9,000 of us managed to leave.'

Other soldiers said the Tigrayans had launched similar attacks on their bases at Dansha[93] and Sero.[94] The fighting was described to Reuters.

Shots were fired at the Sero base, where 250–300 government troops were stationed, at around 5 a.m. on the morning of Nov. 4. Initially, the attackers retreated when government soldiers returned fire, they said. Within days, food and water were running low, forcing those inside to ration supplies, they said.

They said the siege reached a climax on day 10 when TPLF reinforcements arrived with tanks, anti-aircraft guns and mortars to try to seize the base. They described a six-hour barrage in which some soldiers tried to escape from the back of the compound but were captured.

'Even after we surrendered, they stabbed one of our members for no reason,' one of the soldiers, Takele Ambaye, said. He said he saw the bodies of 15 comrades, some with slash wounds, others who had been shot.

Important as these clashes at bases were, the most important fighting took place at Northern Command headquarters in Mekele. In December 2021 Reuters published an interpretation of events based on information from 16 Ethiopian troops, provided by the Ethiopian government.

> They describe a sneak attack in different locations on the Ethiopian army by Tigrayan forces that night. Reuters did not speak to the soldiers and could not independently verify their accounts ...
>
> Ethiopian prosecutors said they have collected 20,000 pages of documents and interviewed 510 witnesses as part of their investigation into the Nov. 3 assault. They said the investigation has found that Tigrayan forces simultaneously attacked or seized over 174 locations, including army bases, police stations, banks, petrol stations, airports and communication offices.[95]

Reuters said the Ethiopian authorities had presented them with Tigrayan documents, apparently seized in Mekele, which suggested that the TPLF-led regional government had built up its forces before the attack, training up to 50,000 fighters and preparing for a war they expected to win within three months. 'The government points to all of this as evidence that the TPLF began the conflict and is responsible for what followed,' Reuters explained. 'The TPLF attacked without warning, the government alleges, and in some instances gave federal soldiers no opportunity to surrender. It accuses the TPLF of committing murder and other war crimes.'

The suggestion that the Tigrayans 'attacked without warning' and that the Ethiopians were caught off guard is the narrative also offered by Eritrea's President Isaias. As he put it in his interview with Eritrean state media on 17 February 2021: 'In the end and unexpectedly, on 3 November 2020, we witnessed a mad and out of control attack on Ethiopian troops based in Tigray. It was a miraculous scenario and if you look back, it is truly surprising. The Northern Command had between 30,000 and 32,000 troops of which approximately one third were Tigrayans.'[96]

The idea that the fighting came like a bolt from the blue is simply implausible. Given the many meetings between the Eritrean, Ethiopian and Somali leaders, together with the pre-positioning of troops along Tigray's borders and the repeated warnings cited above, this version of events is hard to credit. Perhaps the events were best summed up by Tom Gardner of *The Economist*, one of the few foreign correspondents to remain in Ethiopia throughout this period. His article was published by *Foreign Policy* on 5 November 2020, just after these events.

> It was not immediately clear who really fired the first gunshots ... It is plausible, as Abiy claims, that the TPLF tried to seize assets belonging to the command. But it is not certain whether this took place before or after federal troops were deployed ... But it is also apparent that there were significant movements of federal troops in the days preceding Nov. 4. According to a United Nations diplomat, units had been withdrawn from several parts of southern Ethiopia, including the areas of Hararghe and Somali in the southeast, and from the Welega zone in western Oromia region. '[The federal government] will have difficulty convincing anyone worth their salt that this wasn't pre-planned,' the source said.[97]

PART FOUR

WAR

INTERLUDE

NAYNA'S STORY—A TIGRAYAN LONDONER AT THE START OF THE WAR

'The noise grew louder and louder. I could feel it deep inside my chest. At first, I saw nothing, but then I could see a jet flying low, so low, over the city.'

Nayna[1] is 27 and, like so many Tigrayans, has family scattered across the globe. Her father, who grew up in Mekele, works in local government in London. Her mother—from Irob, the most northern area of Tigray—is employed by a development agency in the Middle East.

It wasn't what Nayna had been expecting. Returning to Tigray should have been a time of joy and celebration. Instead, she had stumbled into a war.

Nayna arrived in Tigray's capital, Mekele, just before the critical days of 3 and 4 November 2020, when fighting erupted that has torn northern Ethiopia apart.

She makes a point of returning to Tigray just about every year to keep in contact with her roots. This, she says, is central to her identity. 'I feel much better in Tigray. People talk and look like me. I was sizing it up as a possible place to live. And having a good time!'

After a couple of days quarantining in her hotel, Nayna was out on the streets of Mekele, meeting friends and family. 'Listening to the Tigrinya spoken all around me is so lovely. It's very beautiful, so sweet and melodic on the busy streets.'

Before leaving Addis, Nayna had been warned that the situation in Tigray was tense. 'I laughed. Even if there was trouble, they wouldn't dare stop the flights. "We can always get out," I said! How naive I was.'

'On 3 November I was out with a friend for dinner at a hotel. I got a call from my uncle in the USA pleading with me to leave. I thought: this is an exaggeration. I told my friend: "They are beyond themselves!"' Her friend was also sceptical. 'There's no shooting! It could just be people getting drunk, letting off their guns,' he said.

'After dinner I went back my hotel room. Just then my phone rang. It was a friend from abroad: "War has started - they have entered Mekele!"' Nayna laughed. 'But I'm in Mekele. There's nothing here!'

Then she started to hear shooting. A local friend called: the situation is dangerous; she must sleep on the floor and not go anywhere near the windows. '"Do you understand?" my friend insisted. I just say whaaaat?'

'My father tried to contact me on Viber. But it shut down immediately. The only power in the hotel was from a generator. By this time all phone lines had been cut. There's speculation soldiers are in the city, but no one knows.'

The next day—4 November—Nayna walked to her aunt's house. Her aunt had heard bombs and shooting, but her uncle slept through it all. Nayna's flight back to Addis was due that day, but at the airline desk she's told: 'There are no flights. As of now, no flights out.'

The city was in limbo. All banks were closed, and nothing seemed to be working. Yet the streets were bustling and life continued as normal.

On Friday 5 Nayna went for a traditional Ethiopian coffee ceremony with her aunt. 'Suddenly I heard a noise. My aunt has trouble walking, but she ran to the window and called to her girls on the street: "Get inside! Get inside!" The noise gets louder and louder. My aunt's face was very red—she'd heard this noise in previous wars.' She was in Mekele when the city was attacked during the Ethiopia–Eritrea border war of 1998–2000.

The plane thundered overhead—then it was gone. Days passed and there were more Ethiopian flights over the city. Sometimes bombs were dropped. Nayna, like everyone else, was frightened.

In the coffee house there were leaflets which had been dropped over the city: 'Hand over the TPLF and you will be OK'. Prime minister Abiy Ahmed made a broadcast telling the people of Tigray's cities not to gather at major landmarks.

The electricity came back on intermittently. People gathered round their televisions. Al Jazeera broadcast a warning that people should leave if they can.

'We were told to go to the UNICEF office,' Nayna explains, and she did, only to be told to return at six the following morning. She was reluctant to go. But her aunt and uncle insisted. 'My uncle said: "If you stay you will die!"'

She packed her belongings and headed for the UNICEF office in the early morning and got into one of the buses and vans assembled there. They were told the destination was Addis, but no one was sure.

Minutes after the convoy moved off, the bus came to a halt. A woman, an Eritrean, was told to get off. That was followed by a painstaking search of luggage and under seats. 'What are you looking for? A bomb?' Nayna asked. 'Yes,' replied an Australian. 'The Eritreans have been planning this war.' Nayna was shocked. She had no idea the Eritreans were involved.

After many hours' travel the buses arrived at the Afar border, but the Tigrayan drivers were not allowed to cross. Everyone was told to walk to where another convoy was waiting. There was a mad panic. Everyone ran. 'It felt like an avalanche—as if we are falling off a cliff.'

UN staff were on the bus. One, an American, shouted for them to keep quiet. He threatened to leave behind anyone who didn't behave. Finally, the convoy arrived at the Afar town of Semera. It's one of the most desolate parts of Ethiopia and unbearably hot. The passengers were told to leave the buses and were then held for hours while police searched their luggage.

One of the policemen opened her case. He picked up her underwear, waving it in her face, before dropping it in the sand. In her purse were her credit cards and receipts. 'This is too much!' he said, and tossed them away.

'They asked why I had a UK passport but an American driving licence. "Why? You are lying!" they shouted at me. I said it's British not American—look at the flag on the licence.' The policeman eventually accepted that it was. But he took her box of tampons and threw them away. All her clothes were covered in sand.

They were taken to a hotel and allowed to eat for the first time in a day. The passengers scraped together enough money to pay for the food. An hour later a UN officer told them to be in the lobby at 6 am sharp.

Nayna got there early, but it was midday before the UN officer called them together for a briefing. '"There is good news and bad news. Good news: some of you can fly." We were overjoyed. "Bad news: Some will not be allowed to leave Semera." Panic.'

'At the airport we were told to queue by nationality.' Indians, Somalis, Sri Lankans, all in a long queue, lining up at the foot of the plane. First the foreigners were allowed to board. Then they called for Eritreans. Then UK-born Eritreans. Finally, just Tigrayans remained. Some of the women were sobbing.

'We were at the end of a long line and there was only one plane. We saw the plane door close.' The plane taxied and took off. 'We felt so hopeless—we thought we would be left behind permanently.' But the following day they told there was another flight and were taken back to the airport. It was unbearably hot, with no ventilation.

There were two exits onto the runway. 'A man said to me: "When the door opens—just run for it!' I was so tired—but he said: "Just do it!"'

When the plane finally arrived and the door opened, there was chaos. 'Children were pushed out of the way. Some fell; someone punched me. A girl kindly helped me. I was sobbing and out of breath. I was in disbelief.'

Nayna scrambled on board and by that evening was in Addis. The police there spoke in Amharic. They insisted that the Tigrayans had to check in with the authorities every two days. Nayna was shocked. Surely, she was an Ethiopian like anyone else! Why were they being discriminated against? 'If you don't sign in, we will come and arrest you. If you are not there, we will harass your families,' the officer told her.

The passengers were taken to a UN compound where they met representatives from their countries. Nayna spoke to a woman from the British embassy, who kept apologising for the way they were being treated, but said there was nothing they could do. They were all advised to leave the country as soon as possible; it was not safe in Addis.

On Saturday, 28 November, Nayna was back at the airport. After many further security checks, during which some passengers were accused of being Tigrayan fighters, she made it on to a British Airways plane and was on her way back to London.

'I had so many emotions. I felt I should not have left Tigray. I felt guilty. When will I be back again? I don't know. But I hated Addis.'

Since then, it's been very hard for Nayna, as for so many in the diaspora. 'I experienced sadness previously, but never like this. I wanted to sit on the sofa and listen to old Tigrinya songs. Sometimes I just cried.'

Gradually Nayna has come to terms with the war. 'After a while you get desensitised,' she told me. Being active in the Tigray Youth Network has helped, but the terrible stories of the suffering back home keep coming.

'I get very sad. It's heart-breaking … How will it end?'

7

TIGRAY FROM DEFEAT TO RECOVERY

Martin Plaut and Ermias Teka

Introduction

It is perhaps worth pointing out that the Tigray war is unlike the vast majority of conflicts across Africa.[1] Most of the continent's wars are skirmishes or attacks by small rebel forces, often against civilians, with few major battles. They can be vicious and cost many lives, but they are seldom conventional wars. The Congo, for example, has been involved in fighting of one kind or another across its vast territory ever since its independence in 1960. Somalia has been a violent, dysfunctional state since the fall of President Siad Barre in 1991. By contrast, the Tigray war involved hundreds of thousands of troops, some well-trained, others poorly armed militia, fighting across complex, often mountainous terrain. They fought with everything from medium-range missiles and the latest drones to machetes, hoes and the ever-reliable AK-47. Casualties in some offensives ran into thousands, if not tens of thousands. It was the bloodiest conflict in the world at this time.[2] Most fighting took place away from the international media, who were forbidden by Ethiopia and Eritrea to report from the front lines.[3]

The war erupted with attacks by the Ethiopian military supported by Amhara special forces. A report of the UN Office for the Coordination of Humanitarian Affairs outlined the Ethiopian response to the outbreak of the war. 'An official statement by Prime Minister Abiy Ahmed on 4 November announced that the EDF [Ethiopian Defence Force] were given orders to start military offensive against TPLF in Tigray. According to an official statement by the Prime Minister, "operations by federal defense forces underway in northern Ethiopia have clear, limited and achievable objectives—to restore the rule of law and the constitutional order, and to safeguard the rights of Ethiopians to lead a peaceful life wherever they are in the country"'.[4] The claim that this would be a short-lived conflict that would soon be over convinced the Trump administration. 'We completely bought into the myth of the short war. That the conflict in Tigray would be over in no time, that the troops would be home before Christmas'.[5]

The multi-pronged invasion of Tigray soon overwhelmed the Tigrayan defences. Two weeks after the initial clashes, Ethiopia and its allies were on the doorstep of Mekele. Abiy declared that the military operation was entering its 'final phase'. On 18 November he said that a three-day deadline for Tigray's forces to surrender had expired.[6] On 28 November Ethiopian troops began an assault on Mekele. Ambulances rushed through the streets collecting the dead and wounded, following what the *New York Times* described as 'indiscriminate artillery barrages on civilian areas'.[7] The next day Abiy declared that the battle for Mekele was over: government forces were now 'fully in control'.[8] After briefing elders of the city, and with a minimum of publicity, the Tigrayan forces had left their capital. They said they had withdrawn to avoid the destruction of the city and would continue to fight from the surrounding rural areas.[9]

This was a period of intense suffering for Tigrayans. Prime minister Abiy put in place a transitional administration which ran the region, although it is not clear if it had any influence over the subsequent fighting. With the Tigrayan leadership on the run, terrible atrocities were committed against civilians. A *Financial Times* headline said it all: 'Ethiopia "will be digging up mass graves for a decade": inside Tigray's dirty war'.[10] The Ethiopian military, backed by Amhara special forces and Amhara militia, in alliance with Eritrean and Somali troops, rampaged across Tigray. Men were hauled out of their homes and shot at will. Monasteries dating back to the dawn of Christianity and mosques built at the time of the Prophet were shelled and destroyed. Priests and monks were killed or forced to abandon their sanctuaries and their congregations. But the most terrible fate awaited the women of Tigray, who were systematically sexually abused. Some were raped while their families looked on. Some, no more than children, were successively violated by men for days. One incident, reported by Reuters, exemplified the suffering inflicted on women and girls: 'It was the beginning of an 11-day ordeal in February, during which she says she was repeatedly raped by 23 soldiers who forced nails, a rock and other items into her vagina, and threatened her with a knife. Doctors showed Reuters the bloodstained stone and two 3-inch nails they said they had removed from her body.'[11]

These atrocities were so widespread that they appear to have formed an organised campaign of sexual abuse. At the same time, Tigrayan troops were also involved in similar abuses once they regained the initiative. They too engaged in atrocious killings and sexual abuse.[12] Appalling as these were, they do not appear to have been on a comparable scale. However, this will only become clear if an independent, international investigation of all these abuses is undertaken and made public.

While enemy troops were advancing across Tigray, the Tigrayan leadership and their commanders attempted to reorganise their forces and their administration after being forced to flee Mekele. Despite being defeated and scattered, they were not without resources. For Abiy the fall of Mekele presaged the end of the war; for Debretsion and his colleagues it was just beginning.

Eritrean and Somali troops join the war

Within days the Ethiopians were joined by Eritrean and Somali troops, who attacked across Tigray's northern border as well as launched an offensive to cut off western Tigray from Sudan. The military planners in Ethiopia and Eritrea understood only too well how important Sudan had been in supplying Eritrean and Tigrayan rebels. Isaias knew the pain he could inflict on the Tigrayans, having closed their access to aid via Sudan in 1985 at the height of famine. The TPLF was consequently forced to march tens of thousands of people into Sudan for their survival, many of whom died along the way. 'I do not hesitate to call it a savage act,' a Tigrayan leader later recalled.[13] Depriving Tigrayans of access to Sudan in November 2020 was vital to breaking their resistance. Seizing western Tigray, which linked the region to Sudan, would disrupt Tigray's supply lines to the outside world. For this reason western Tigray was the site of much of the early fighting. Taking this area was also an important motivation for the Amhara, who had long claimed western Tigray as their own. Amhara militia joined the Ethiopian, Eritrean and Somali troops in the attack on Tigray. As the war developed, other Ethiopian militia would be mobilised to support the war effort.

Little has been written about the role of the Eritrean forces in the fighting, because Eritrea is among the most closed societies in the world. Our understanding of its role is limited but not negligible. Mesfin Hagos, Eritrea's former minister of defence, lives in exile in Germany.[14] He is still revered by many Eritreans for his leadership during their war of independence from Ethiopia (1961–91). Early in the Tigray war Mesfin appealed to the Eritrean people, calling for them not to become involved in the conflict.[15] Mesfin's argument was that the war had been 'in the making by President Isaias and Prime Minister Abiy for the last two years. It was a planned conflict.' He confirmed that Ethiopian troops had been flown into Eritrea in the weeks leading up to the outbreak of fighting, and that further Ethiopians had entered Eritrea once the conflict began. Mesfin pleaded with the Eritrean nation and its armed forces to refuse to fight in what he regarded as other people's war.[16]

Mesfin's appeal was broadcast on 20 November on Erisat, an opposition satellite television station, which has a significant audience inside Eritrea, but it had no apparent effect on the Eritrean troops invading Tigray. After the fall of Mekele, the Eritrean army annexed parts of northern Tigray—some of which had been awarded to Eritrea by the Boundary Commission. Military administrations were instituted around Zalambessa, Rama, Irob, Gerhu Sirnay and Sheraro. Eritrean identity cards and currency were issued to the local populations. Several Eritrean army units, including the infamous 525 commando division, were deployed alongside Ethiopian troops in campaigns to crush Tigrayan forces.[17] Residents reported that few, if any, areas of central and northern Tigray were not attacked by Eritrean troops. As early as December, there was a permanent Eritrean presence in Tigrayan towns including Wukro, Adigrat, Adwa, Shire and Nebelet.[18] The Eritreans proved to be a terrible occupation force.

In December 2020, Abiy was still attempting to deny reports that Eritrean troops were participating in the war.[19] Despite the denials, the participation of Eritrean forces in the invasion of Tigray soon leaked out, first from the Tigrayans, then in off-the-record briefings by aid agencies. Eritrea's foreign minister Osman Saleh dismissed the claims as 'propaganda'.[20] Finally, a month after the war began, Washington described reports of Eritrean involvement in the conflict as 'credible'.[21]

It was against this background that Mesfin wrote a second assessment of Eritrea's role, based on his personal contacts inside Eritrea and neighbouring Sudan.[22] He described fighting deep inside Tigray, citing reports of the deaths and injuries of large numbers of Eritrean troops, including officers.

> Through Zalambessa alone, the Eritrean president sent in the 42nd and 49th mechanized divisions and the 11th, 17th, 19th and 27th infantry divisions. On reaching Edaga-Hamus, south of Adigrat and north of Mekelle, these divisions were reinforced with addition of five Eritrean divisions, including the 2nd brigade of the 525th commando division. He also unleashed the 26th, 28th, and 53rd infantry and 46th and 48th mechanized divisions on the Adwa front along with only one division of the Ethiopian federal army. In addition, the TPLF claims that Eritrean technical and combat units also took active part in the Alamata front, southeast of Mekelle.

It was not until March 2021 that Abiy finally, and reluctantly, acknowledged that Eritrean forces had participated in the war, while at the same time declaring that they were about to withdraw.[23] More than a year later the withdrawal had still not been concluded.

The Somali role in the war was as poorly understood as the Eritrean involvement. When the Tigray war began, the immediate impact on Somalia was the withdrawal of 3,000 Ethiopian troops who had been fighting al-Shabaab as part of the African Union force.[24] This redeployment caused immense problems for the Tigrayan contingent. Between 200 and 300 Ethiopian troops were ethnic Tigrayans and were instructed to hand in their weapons.[25] Reuters was sent an explanation by the Ethiopian authorities: 'The peacekeepers are not being disarmed due to ethnicity but due to infiltration of TPLF elements in various entities which is part of an ongoing investigation.'[26]

By January 2021 the focus had changed to the Somalis who had been conscripted and sent to Eritrea to be trained to fight in Tigray.[27] The UN's human rights rapporteur for Eritrea, Mohamed Abdelsalam Babiker, summarised their role.

> In addition to reports of the involvement of Eritrean troops in the Tigray conflict, the Special Rapporteur also received information and reports that Somali soldiers were moved from military training camps in Eritrea to the front line in Tigray, where they accompanied Eritrean troops as they crossed the Ethiopian border. It is also reported that Somali fighters were present around Aksum. The Government of Somalia denied the participation of Somali soldiers in the Tigray conflict.[28]

In January 2022 detailed reports of the Somali role in Tigray were published by the journalist Lucy Kassa. She put the number of Somalis in Tigray as high as 10,000 and outlined appalling acts they had committed.

> Survivors told The Globe that the Somali troops had massacred hundreds of civilians in villages controlled by the Eritrean military, often beheading them. No Ethiopian troops were present in the villages, they said. 'They showed no mercy,' said Berket, a 32-year-old farmer in the Tigrayan village of Mai Harmaz. 'The Eritreans interrogate you before they kill you. But the Somali troops were full of contempt for that.' One of his neighbours, a 76-year-old priest, was among those killed by the Somali troops, he said. Kibrom, a 37-year-old man who fled the village of Hamlo in January, said the beheadings by Somali troops became an 'everyday reality' in his village.[29]

In May 2022 Somalia's new president, Hassan Sheikh Mohamud, was handed a dossier by his predecessor, President Farmaajo, with the names of over 5,000 Somali troops in Eritrea.[30] President Mohamud promised he would work for their repatriation 'as soon as possible'. Some, however, would never return, having died in Tigray. The Somali presence had a purpose: it strengthened Isaias's hold over the region. As Michelle Gavin of the US Council on Foreign Relations remarked: 'It's difficult to see how sending thousands of soldiers to Eritrea indefinitely could ever have been in the best interest of Somalia's security. But it's easy to see how this exercise gave Eritrea leverage'.[31]

A history to draw upon

For the Tigrayans the atrocities inflicted by the invading forces were an excruciating experience. There was little they could do to resist in the initial phases of the war, while attempting to reorganise their forces and their administration after being forced to flee Mekele at the end of November 2020. But even though they were apparently defeated and scattered, they were able to reorganise before going on the offensive.

The Tigrayan leadership retreated into the rural areas, falling back on strategies the TPLF had perfected during their long years of war, ending with the capture of Addis Ababa in 1991. Their ideology was summed up in these slogans:

> The mountains of the land are our fortresses.
> Revolutionary zeal is our sustenance.
> Our weapons are from the enemy.
> Our resolve is our cause.
> Our strength is in the people's army.
> Our pillar is the revolutionary people.[32]

The Tigrayans also drew on a sophisticated strategy of guerrilla warfare that the TPLF had developed over many years. Their tactics had been developed following a painful defeat in 1976, just after the birth of the organisation. Their over-eager fighters had attacked a well-fortified army unit, only to be routed at considerable cost. The

229

survivors retreated into Sudan, where they could re-evaluate their tactics. 'The TPLF wisely changed its tactics to guerrilla warfare, striking in bands of as many as fifty. The switch was effective.'[33] The Tigrayans adopted the Maoist strategy of avoiding the enemy when strong, harassing them when they rested, and attacking when their forces were tired or in retreat. Working in small, highly mobile groups, they wore down the Ethiopian army. 'Light portable weapons were key. The guerrillas fought a war without frontiers, moving in small groups of thirty to forty at a speed twice that of the regular troops, forty to sixty kilometres a day, mostly at night.'[34] The leaders of the TPLF were far too old to engage in such activities by 2020, but they inspired the young men and women who joined the movement to adopt these tactics.

The Tigray military could also draw on leaders who had an intimate knowledge of the strengths and weaknesses, strategy and tactics of the Ethiopian military. Men like General Tsadkan Gebretensae had led the reconstruction of the Ethiopian army after 1991.[35] At the end of the 1998–2000 Eritrea–Ethiopia border war, General Tsadkan argued that the victorious Ethiopian military should push on towards Asmara and overthrow President Isaias's government. The general was overruled by prime minister Meles Zenawi, leading to a deep split inside the Tigrayan leadership.[36] As Alex de Waal argues: 'After the war, the TPLF split rancorously over both the war aims and the party's political direction. Mr Meles fired Gen. Tsadkan as chief of staff.'[37] After 2018, the general attempted to mediate between the newly installed government of Abiy and his former colleagues in Tigray, but failed. As the threat of war mounted, and sensing the danger Tigray faced, General Tsadkan returned to Mekele and joined the resistance. He brought a wealth of expertise and a deep knowledge of the Ethiopian military, which he put to good effect.

This war had the opposite effect on the Ethiopian army, which faced a significant decline in its operational capability. Most of the powerful Northern Command joined the Tigrayan forces. The remainder fled into Eritrea, or were killed or captured. From Addis Ababa's point of view, its most powerful command had ceased to exist. The Tigrayans struck back with what they had captured: medium-range missiles, which they briefly used to attack the Eritrean capital, Asmara, as well as some targets inside Ethiopia.[38] Eritrea said its towns were hit by a total of 22 Tigrayan missiles.[39] The United States strongly condemned Tigray's 'unjustifiable attacks against Eritrea ... and its efforts to internationalize the conflict.'[40] Targets inside Ethiopia's Amhara state were also attacked. The airport at Gonder was hit, while a rocket aimed at Bahir Dar airport apparently missed the target.[41] But by the end of November 2020 the missile attacks were over—the supplies having been exhausted or destroyed by Ethiopian counter-attacks. At the same time thousands of Tigrayan members of Ethiopian armed services were removed from their posts or imprisoned by the Ethiopian government. Since they were the most experienced members of the military, their removal reduced Ethiopia's ability to wage war. Moreover, the swift capture of Mekele resulted in heavy Ethiopian casualties and substantial losses of equipment.[42] Abiy might optimistically announce that his 'law and order' operation was over by the end of the month, but Tigrayan forces refused to concede defeat.

The scale of the atrocities which the Eritrean and Ethiopian forces inflicted on Tigrayan civilians had an immediate effect: they were the Tigrayans' most effective recruiting sergeant. Tigrayan youths rapidly understood that they had only two options: fight or flee. To remain in their homes would lead to abuse or death. Some 60,000 Tigrayans crossed into Sudan, but soon the border was no longer in Tigrayan hands. In early December 2020 Ethiopian and Eritrean troops were deployed to prevent Tigrayans reaching Sudan.[43] Tens of thousands went into the hills and joined guerrilla operations.

Return to the hills

With little effective communication equipment, the TPLF leadership remained disconnected from those of their troops that had lost touch with the main forces in various parts of Tigray.[44] Confused and isolated, some chose to surrender. But many Tigrayan fighters remained defiant and continued mounting isolated resistance in small units throughout the occupied territories. Local militia in Wajirat, Atsbi, Ahsea, Bora Selewa, Neksege, Mai Maedo and

Tselemti carried out small-scale ambushes of Ethiopian, Eritrean and Amhara forces.[45]

The leadership had one major advantage: the main corps of the Tigray special forces remained intact. The assault and retreat strategy was designed to reduce their casualties, while inflicting maximum damage on their enemies. But the hasty withdrawal meant they faced severe shortages of arms and military equipment.[46] During December 2020 Ethiopian and Eritrean sweeps forced the Tigrayan troops to constantly shift their positions. Tigrayan officers prioritised mobility over size and were rumoured to have temporarily halted military recruitment.[47] The Tigray government spokesman Getachew Reda recalled that at this time their units were repeatedly at risk of being encircled, but had managed to break out of these entrapments, preventing their forces from being annihilated. This required ferocious fighting around Tigrayan strongholds throughout December and the following January. These consisted of most of the districts of south-central Tigray: Medebay Zana, Naeder Adet, Abergele and Kola Tembien as well as parts of Asgede Tsimbla and Degua Tembien.

Tigrayans attacked their enemies whenever they ventured off the main highways. They used guerrilla tactics: swift attacks by small, agile units. Vital supply lines along the B30 and A2 highways were repeatedly ambushed. The result was predictable: the erosion of government morale and the loss of weapons and ammunition, which the Tigrayans seized to rearm themselves. By the end of December 2020 the leadership had recovered sufficiently to re-establish a more reliable command structure. At this time the exiled government of Tigray issued its first statement since retreating into the hills, calling on the youth of Tigray to come and fight for their people. These appeals were repeated on 9 and 15 January. The Tigrayan military was ready to expand its forces.

There was, however, a secondary but equally predictable outcome of these hit-and-run tactics. Ethiopian, Eritrean and Somali troops, responding to the losses they were sustaining and their apparent inability to respond, took out their frustration on the civilian population.

Massacres and atrocities

As the weeks turned to months, the war saw repeated accusations of massacres. The first major incident occurred in the far west, around Humera, as Ethiopian and Eritrean forces attempted to seal off Tigray from Sudan. There were several atrocities, but the best documented was around Mai Kadra on the night of 9 November 2020. Amnesty International produced a rapid report on Mai Kadra, which it published within three days.

> Amnesty International has not yet been able to confirm who was responsible for the killings, but has spoken to witnesses who said forces loyal to the Tigray People's Liberation Front (TPLF) were responsible for the mass killings, apparently after they suffered defeat from the federal EDF forces. Three people told Amnesty International that survivors of the massacre told them that they were attacked by members of Tigray Special Police Force and other TPLF members.[48]

Accusing the Tigrayans, even indirectly, of responsibility so early on in the conflict, with so little time to gather and consider the evidence, was controversial. A later report by Human Rights Watch was more even-handed.

> Witnesses said that some of the victims were suspected TPLF members, fighters, or supporters and retired soldiers … In the town of Mai-Kadra, a number of refugees reported seeing hundreds of dead bodies which had been shot, stabbed, or hacked with knives, machetes, and axes, including those of ethnic Amharas but also of Tigrayans … People who remained in their homes or went back to their towns after the heavy fighting had subsided said they saw Amhara 'special forces' and Fanos,[49] as well as unidentified gunmen, detain those who remained, and loot abandoned and inhabited homes, shops, and hospitals.[50]

Investigators and journalists found it almost impossible to access the site to obtain an accurate picture of what had happened. However, Reuters reported that after the initial attacks by Tigrayans there were revenge attacks by Amhara.[51] The clashes were followed by systematic attempts to force Tigrayans from their homes. In January 2021 Reuters reported: 'Tens of thousands of Tigrayans fled western Tigray into central and eastern Tigray, saying they were being driven out by Amhara forces. Many spoke of looting and killing.'[52]

The Mai Kadra atrocities became central to Ethiopian and Amhara propaganda. The Tigrayan authorities, while attempting to respond, were at a considerable disadvantage. As Nic Cheeseman and Yohannes Woldemariam pointed out, the Ethiopian government could get its version of events widely circulated, but the Tigrayans found this much more difficult.[53] 'Abiy achieved his near-total news blackout in Tigray through a mix of old and new strategies for controlling information. He blocked mobile phones, landlines, and the Internet, choking off most communication from the region from the earliest days of the conflict. "Overnight," the journalist Simon Allison reported, "the region went silent and has remained so."' This has been largely true throughout the war.

Soon the atrocities at Mai Kadra would be eclipsed by even more horrific events. As the invasion unfolded, a series of killings were committed that changed the nature of the war. As 2020 drew to a close and 2021 dawned, it became increasingly evident to Tigrayans that this had become an existential crisis and that resistance was the only means of survival. This was underlined by the cold-blooded murder of several Tigrayan veterans, including Ethiopia's widely respected former minister of foreign affairs Seyoum Mesfin.[54]

The most notorious events took place in the sacred city of Axum between 19 and 29 November 2021. Ethiopian forces had captured Axum and were, therefore, responsible for the city, but it was Eritrean troops who carried out most of the abuses. It appears that after the city fell to the Eritrean and Ethiopian forces, a small contingent of Tigrayan militia attempted to mount a counter-attack.[55] Infuriated that they were being resisted, the Eritreans first fought off the militia and then went door to door, looting what they could, raping women, and killing any men or boys they came across.

Because Tigray was sealed off from the outside world, little hard information was available until December, with a full picture emerging by March 2022. Human Rights Watch provided this summary of events.

On November 19, Ethiopian and Eritrean forces indiscriminately shelled Axum, killing and wounding civilians. For a week after taking control of the town, the forces shot civilians and pillaged and destroyed property, including healthcare facilities. After Tigray militia and Axum residents attacked Eritrean forces on November 28, Eritrean forces, in apparent retaliation, fatally shot and summarily executed several hundred residents, mostly men and boys, over a 24-hour period.[56]

Amnesty International interviewed refugees who had managed to reach Sudan, who told much the same story.[57] There were several other eyewitness reports,[58] but perhaps the most telling testimony was given to the Associated Press by a deacon of Axum's church of St Mary of Zion.

> 'The deacon, who spoke on condition of anonymity because he remains in Axum, said he helped count the bodies—or what was left after hyenas fed. He gathered victims' identity cards and assisted with burials in mass graves. He believes some 800 people were killed that weekend at the church and around the city, and that thousands in Axum have died in all.[59]

The Axum massacre was so shocking that when details finally leaked out, they caused international revulsion. The events were condemned by the European Union and in the British Parliament.[60]

The Axum massacre was by no means a lone event. Similar, less publicised attacks were a routine part of attempts to crush Tigrayan resistance.[61] Researchers have been chronicling these atrocities, while stressing that their figures were an underestimate, because so many bodies were dumped in unknown locations, while all along the Eritrean border there has been little access to sites and 'very little is known'. Nonetheless, they concluded that they had been able to document 3,240 deaths by 16 November 2021 in 283 massacres.[62] The oldest victims were in their nineties and the youngest were still infants.

Widespread rape, killing and abuse fuelled a determination to fight. Several pro-TPLF radio stations were opened, allowing the leadership to broadcast their message and provide links with people in remote rural areas. The Tigrayan public rallied to the support of their leadership. Young men and women flocked to the military training sites. Within weeks the leadership no longer had to rely solely on the hard core of the remaining special forces: they had a sizeable and growing volunteer army. The young people needed training and equipping, but they were highly motivated and ready to lay down their lives for the cause.

From guerrilla attacks to conventional warfare

When the war began, Ethiopia's Abiy Ahmed claimed it would not continue for long. 'Our rule of law operation ... will wrap up soon,' he claimed just five days after fighting commenced.[63] By 4 April 2021 the prime minister was forced to accept that the fighting was still under way across a wide area.[64] 'Currently, the national defense forces and the federal forces are in a major fight on eight fronts in the north and the west against enemies which are anti-farmers, anti-civilians and causing strife among Ethiopians,' Abiy admitted.

After the fall of Mekele, the Ethiopian and Eritrean forces advanced deeper into Tigray to try to extinguish the resistance. Towns and villages were shelled and bombed from the air. Yet the advance proved more difficult than they had thought. In several towns they found it impossible to make headway. Tigrayans were reportedly able to repulse an Ethiopian offensive around Adi Achelai.[65] It remained a Tigrayan stronghold from which they mounted subsequent attacks. Fighting was also reported around Asgede Tsimbla, Edaga Hamus, Saesi Tsadaimba and Dengelat, with apparently inconclusive outcomes.[66]

The beginning of January saw new fronts being opened and a deeper penetration of Eritrean and Ethiopian forces into previously unconquered areas of central and northern Tigray. However, the allied forces discovered that holding towns far from the highway was much more difficult than capturing them. The Tigrayans attacked their supply routes regularly, as well as mounted surprise attacks on the towns themselves, only to withdraw before reinforcements could arrive from nearby garrisons. The Tigrayan troops attacked towns of northern and central Tigray in mid-January, including Daero Hafash, Edaga Arbi, Mai Kinetal, Nebelet and Hawzen. Some were so successful that the Tigrayans were able to overrun several of them, even if only temporarily. The fighting around Daero Hafash, near Axum, was lengthy and intense. Tigrayan sources claimed to have inflicted some 4,000 casualties on their enemies.[67]

Fighting intensified throughout February. Ethiopian and Eritrean forces continued to mount attacks on the mountainous areas of central Tigray, while the Tigrayans responded with ambushes and lightning strikes against vulnerable targets. With the approach of Tigray's annual 'Lekatit 11' celebration (18 February 2021), commemorating the start of the Tigrayan armed struggle, the leadership planned a series of high-profile attacks as a show of strength. After a number of battles in the surrounding area, the Tigray forces claimed to have defeated a battalion-sized contingent of enemy troops.[68]

By mid-February even more significant battles were fought in Mai Kinetal, Gijet and Samre, lasting several days. Tigrayan forces temporarily recaptured the towns, allegedly inflicting heavy losses on Eritrean and Ethiopian troops before withdrawing to the mountains.[69] In Mai Kinetal alone, Tigrayan troops claimed to have killed or captured more than 2,000 Eritrean soldiers. This was the first time since November that the Tigrayans had faced such a sizeable force. In the aftermath they claimed that 'the defeat showed that the Eritrean army is not as formidable as it is claimed to be'.[70]

On 20 February 2021 the government of Tigray issued a statement listing its terms for peace negotiations. These included the unconditional withdrawal of Eritrean and Amhara forces from Tigray; an independent investigation into alleged atrocities committed in Tigray; and a vehement denunciation of the Tigray interim administration appointed by the Ethiopian government.[71] More than anything, the statement revealed the Tigrayans' belief in the ability of their military to maintain such a sustained resistance that they would eventually force negotiation to be held on their own terms. Meanwhile, the Ethiopian army was by this time moving into a defensive posture, digging trenches around Mekele, and thereby apparently confirming a gradual shift in the military strength between the antagonists.[72]

March 2021 saw an enhanced military capability on the part of the Tigrayan troops. They began engaging in semi-conventional battles between brigades from both sides, with correspondingly high levels of casualties. During the first week of March there were offensives around Samre, Bora and Ofla by the combined armies of Ethiopia and Eritrea, supported by Amhara regional forces, in an attempt to overwhelm southern Tigray and weaken the Tigrayan presence.[73] This was evidence that the Eritreans had moved troops from northern to southern Tigray. It coincided with reports of Ethiopian forces being redeployed to central and southern Ethiopia, to head off an increased threat from the Oromo Liberation Front. The Ethiopians were gradually yielding Tigray to Eritrea, while transferring their forces to Oromia, which was—at least at this point—an entirely separate conflict.

After several days of fighting, Tigray's units carried out successive ambushes as well as engagements in the area. They wore down their enemies, killing, wounding and capturing large numbers of soldiers. March also saw a strengthening of the Tigrayan forces in southern Tigray, which laid the foundations for attacks into neighbouring Amhara territory. Towards the middle of March two offensives were carried out by Tigrayan forces deep into Amhara territory. On 18 March Tsata town, an administrative centre in the Wag Himra zone of the Amhara region, was attacked by Tigrayan infiltration units.[74] Besides aiming to acquire much-needed military equipment and supplies, while weakening Amhara forces in the area, the Tigray leadership were indicating that they could strike beyond Tigray.

As March drew to a close, Abiy announced that the Eritrean forces (whose presence inside Ethiopia he had denied) were about to withdraw.[75] 'Eritrea has agreed to withdraw its forces out of the Ethiopian border,' he said in a statement on Twitter during a trip to Asmara for talks with Eritrean president Isaias Afwerki.[76] The acknowledgement came as no surprise to the diplomatic community, which had been reporting that Eritrean forces had been involved in the war for some months.[77] The announcement came soon after US secretary of state Antony Blinken said he wanted Eritrean forces replaced in Tigray by forces that would respect human rights. Yet it soon became clear that neither Abiy's declared aim nor Blinken's wishes carried much weight in Asmara. President Isaias had planned the war, and he was set on seeing it to its conclusion.

In early April, determined to break Tigrayan resistance, Ethiopia and Eritrea launched fresh offensives described as 'once and for all' attacks.[78] Several divisions were mobilised across central and southern Tigray. A Tigrayan website reported extended fighting around Endabaguna, Seleh Leha, Zana, Hawzen, Mai Kinetal, Edaga Arbi and Wajirat.[79] On several fronts the battles involved mechanised divisions with aerial support. They continued until the middle of April, with both sides claiming major victories, though these were difficult to verify. However, the offensive clearly failed to eradicate the Tigrayans. Several videos were uploaded showing large Tigrayan units celebrating victories, as well as mobilising for further operations.[80] On 26 April Tigrayan units attacked Nirak, inside the Amhara region. They were reported to have destroyed Amhara special forces encamped in the area.[81]

During the first week of May 2021, Tigrayan troops carried out a limited offensive against Eritrean positions near Gerhu Sirnay town, bordering on Eritrea.[82] Tigray's activities in April and May suggested that they were moving beyond attacks on supply lines and attempting to confront their enemies where they seemed weak. At the same time, the Tigrayan forces did not appear strong enough to face Ethiopian and Eritrean forces head-on. Seven months after the start of the Tigray war, and despite repeated attacks from the numerically superior allied forces, Tigrayan troops had managed to hold their own, guard key strongholds, and even take the initiative in some areas.

Young men and women, faced with the atrocities committed against their communities, had signed up to join the forces loyal to the administration ousted from Mekele, which had emerged as a truly national resistance movement, not tied to any particular political party. Its ranks were no longer just drawn from the TPLF. Rather, it attracted members of the opposition as well as TPLF supporters, who joined the military.[83] Their numbers were bolstered by large numbers of raw recruits, although the Tigrayan leadership later admitted that some had been forced to enlist.[84] The Tigrayan diaspora became a highly vocal support group, which did all it could to aid their people.[85] The resistance had been transformed into an inclusive people's war, even if some recruits were forcibly conscripted into the ranks.

As the Tigrayans grew in strength their enemies were weakening. Ambitious but ill-conceived campaigns in central Tigray, coupled with the Tigrayans' adept utilisation of guerrilla warfare, resulted in Ethiopia losing some of its most experienced troops.[86] Since most Ethiopian divisions were tied up in Tigray, this period also saw the rise of other insurgency movements, like the Oromo Liberation Army[87] and Gumuz Liberation Front,[88] in other regions of Ethiopia. By the beginning of February, Tigrayans were repeatedly insisting that two-thirds of the Ethiopian national army had been 'neutralised' and that most of the fighting in northern and central Tigray was against Eritrean units.[89] This is impossible to prove and seems to be an exaggeration. It was also claimed that should the Eritreans withdraw, the Ethiopian military would be unable to contain the Tigrayans.[90] With mounting international pressure on the Eritrean army to leave Tigray, reports started to emerge that the Eritrean army had begun to wear Ethiopian Defence Force uniforms. A CNN team in central Tigray said they had 'witnessed Eritrean soldiers, some disguising themselves in old Ethiopian military uniforms, manning checkpoints, obstructing and occupying critical aid routes, roaming the halls of one of the region's few operating hospitals and threatening medical staff'.[91]

Recapturing Mekele

It is against this background that the Tigrayans launched their first major offensive, Operation Alula Abanega.[92] It was on a scale that no one outside the leadership had anticipated, taking Ethiopia and Eritrea by surprise as well as astonishing external observers. Recruitment had increased Tigrayan numbers considerably, reportedly to the size of a force organised at corps and army levels. Sources close to the Tigrayans indicated that they had as many as four separate armies at their disposal, allowing the leadership to transform the war from a guerrilla campaign to a conventional conflict.

Ethiopia and its allies had little inkling of what was about to take place; their intelligence was limited and largely inaccurate. By contrast, Tigrayan generals appeared to be well aware of Ethiopian deployments and strength. Ethiopian forces apparently assumed that Tigray had no more than 13 inexperienced and unmotivated battalions and had thus adopted lofty plans to complete their defeat in a couple of weeks. Underestimating their enemy's capability had been an Ethiopian blind spot, but that was not the only one. The Ethiopian forces also assumed that the bulk of the Tigrayan army was concentrated in central Tigray, around Adet and Naeder. According to a senior Tigrayan commander, they encouraged the Ethiopians' misapprehensions by deploying a handful of units in these areas as decoys, while the majority of Tigrayan forces were quietly withdrawn from central and southern Tigray to areas around Guroro and Guya, in Kola Tembien.

According to General Tadesse Worede, commander-in-chief of Tigrayan forces, the majority of his troops were brought together in one location to implement a series of major reforms. These were designed to transform them from a disjointed aggregate of semi-militia units into a uniform and structured army, one that would be capable of launching a conventional war.[93] Intense military training and indoctrination were carried out at all levels for about a month. The structure of the army was also changed from 'fronts', which operated in distinct zones, to 'armies' that could conduct synchronised operations together. Tigray's military command believed their army was ready for a bigger challenge.

The central command proceeded to deploy the newly reformed Tigrayan forces from lowland areas to the highland areas of east and southern Tigray. It was in the lowlands that the Tigrayans had evaded pursuing Ethiopian and Eritrean units, but now they had grown strong enough to face their opponents head-on. Tigrayans moved to the highlands where heavily fortified larger towns, occupied by their enemies, were located. However, the route into eastern and southern Tigray was blocked by the Ethiopian army's 11th division. This presented the Tigrayans with a challenge, but also the opportunity for a major offensive that might destroy the entire 11th division. On 18 June 2021, Tigrayan forces launched offensives against the 11th division, from Yechila to Shewate Higum, without warning. This was the start of Operation Alula.

Nearly all Tigrayan forces participated in coordinated, simultaneous attacks from all directions. Additional detachments were placed at key locations to prevent Ethiopian reinforcements coming to the rescue of the 11th division. Ethiopian troops from the 11th division, captured during the operation, described a series of intense, rapid battles, during which their units were broken up by the Tigrayans and destroyed. The Ethiopian 21st division was sent from Mekele to try to provide support for the 11th division, but was ambushed around Addi Eshir, about ten kilometres from Yechila. Similarly, the 31st division, also sent to the rescue, was intercepted by Tigrayans around Agbe. The Ethiopian units disintegrated under intense, multi-pronged Tigrayan attacks. Eyewitnesses described chaotic scenes, with the Ethiopian chain of command collapsing, leaving soldiers to fend for themselves.

Tigrayan forces, which had previously lacked mechanised units, were now in possession of heavy artillery as well as captured transport. These were rapidly serviced and put back into operation by captured Ethiopian troops, who had been protected by Tigray's leadership for precisely this purpose. The Ethiopians attempted to respond with overwhelming force, deploying the 20th, 23rd, 24th and 25th divisions, accompanied by large convoys from Abiy Addi towards Shewate Higum and Yechila. However, the Tigrayan forces had fortified the area, bringing in reinforcements and deploying their newly acquired weapons and ammunition. The incoming Ethiopian detachments were allowed to march forward without resistance until they moved past Shewate Higum towards Dawsira where they faced a blocking force with converging support from either flank. The Ethiopians walked into near-certain defeat: over three days of fierce fighting ensued during which the ENDF units endured the Tigrayan onslaught yet managed to penetrate beyond a sequence of Tigrayan bottlenecks. However, the Ethiopian side yielded just before it reached Yechila town. In the midst of the battle, the Tigrayan anti-aircraft unit shot down an Ethiopian Air Force Lockheed C-130 Hercules, further boosting the spirits of their fighters. During the ten-day battle Tigrayan sources claimed around 30,000 Ethiopian forces were neutralised, of whom around 6,000 were taken prisoner.

Tigrayan forces swiftly regained control of several towns in central and south-western Tigray while the Ethiopians fell back on Mekele. A Tigrayan detachment cut the A2 highway and captured

Wukro, which left a brigade-sized Ethiopian force isolated and surrounded near Negash.

The reaction of the Eritrean army to the Ethiopian losses was unexpected. Eritrean units situated around Shire were included in the Ethiopian plans and were supposed to complete the encirclement of Tigray between Zana and Adet, as well as carry out offensives towards central Tigray. But, to the astonishment of many in Addis, their allies failed to come to their rescue when they faced devastating losses around Yechila. Some Tigrayan sources have claimed that a few Eritrean brigades did attempt to assist their allies but were intercepted by Tigrayan troops at key junctions, forcing them to abandon their plans. Others saw the failure differently. Fearing defeat, Eritreans decided that discretion was the better part of valour.

The Eritrean army withdrew its forces without serious fighting from most of central Tigray and established defensive fortifications along the Ethiopian border.[94] However, it retained several areas in the north-east, including towns such as Rama and Zalambessa as well as Badme. Amhara forces, which had established a presence in central Tigray around Debre Abay and Adi Gebru, retreated across the Tekeze River, their traditional boundary with Tigray, but not before they destroyed the Tekeze bridge connecting Amba Madre with Adi Gebru, to prevent Tigrayan forces advancing. However, all territory to the west and south of the Tekeze, the disputed area of western Tigray, remained firmly under the control of Ethiopian and Amhara forces. What the Ethiopians and Eritreans were doing was to withdraw from most of the areas that they accepted were part of Tigray, while retaining hold of areas of northern, western and southern Tigray to which the Eritreans and the Amhara had laid claim.

Most of the A2 highway, leading north and south of Mekele, had fallen into the hands of Tigrayan forces, and some Ethiopian units were forced to flee eastwards towards the Afar region through the border town of Ab'Ala. Tigrayan troops claimed to have caught up with them near Amentila and apparently inflicted further losses on the retreating forces. Ethiopians and Eritreans withdrew from much of the central and southern parts of Tigray that they had captured. The Ethiopian government said the withdrawal was effected because it had decided to declare an immediate and unilateral ceasefire. This was said to have been in response to a request from the Tigrayan interim administration which it had installed, to allow the delivery of aid and for the planting season to get under way. Ethiopia's main planting season lasts from May to September. 'This unilateral ceasefire declaration starts from today June 28, 2021 and will stay until the farming season ends,' the federal government said in a statement.[95] 'Until all our enemies leave Tigray, we will fight,' responded Liya Kassa, a TPLF spokesperson.

Eight months after Abiy ordered his army to remove Tigray's governing party from power, federal troops and Eritrean forces had abandoned almost all the territory they had taken. Thousands of soldiers had been forced to flee. On 28 June, advancing from several directions, Tigrayan troops marched into their capital, Mekele, to a rapturous reception.[96] Men and women flooded onto the streets, riding every vehicle and hugging the fighters, who proudly waved their weapons and Tigray's flag of yellow and red. Abiy reacted to the defeat by declaring a ceasefire, but the Tigrayan leaders were not having any of it and rejected his offer.[97] The withdrawal marked an extraordinary success for the people of Tigray, even though the toll on the population had been huge. The World Bank found that the number of Tigrayan households unable to purchase the staple, teff, had risen from just 5 per cent to almost a quarter.[98] By comparison, households in neighbouring Amhara and Oromia had been largely unaffected. The rout of November 2020 had been followed by a complete transformation of Tigrayan forces and the recapture of Mekele. The first phase of the war was over.

8

THE PENDULUM OF WAR SWINGS—
AND SWINGS AGAIN

Martin Plaut and Ermias Teka

Introduction

It is worth pausing to reflect on the significance of the re-emergence of the Tigrayan military following the defeat of November 2020. The Tigrayan forces had been transformed from a local militia—or special force—and adapted to guerrilla warfare. They then developed their fighting capability so that they could confront two of Africa's largest militaries, Ethiopia and Eritrea. Between them they had a total of some 335,000 troops plus substantial reserves.[1] They had been augmented by Somali troops, Amhara special forces, and other militia. Many African armies are largely paper organisations, but this is not the case with either Ethiopia or Eritrea. They had fought each other in the vicious border war of 1998–2000 using everything from aerial attacks to heavy artillery and tanks. Ethiopia had a deservedly strong reputation as a contributor to UN and African peacekeeping forces, with troops stationed in Somalia, South Sudan and several other complex and difficult locations. The Eritreans had limited experience of recent warfare but had trained almost their entire younger generation by means of their system of mandatory and indefinite conscription. Confronting these combined forces was an extraordinary achievement for Mekele, even if the Ethiopian government was correct when it alleged that the Tigrayans had been developing their special forces prior to the conflict.

By the end of June 2021 the Tigrayans had recaptured their capital and driven the invading forces from large parts of Tigray. They rapidly re-established their administrative structures. Key political figures returned to their offices, with Debretsion Gebremichael resuming his role as president of Tigray. The regional House of Representatives resumed its sessions.

At the same time all communications with Tigray remained severed, and Abiy and Isaias established what amounted to a siege of the region. A senior UN official conceded that starvation was being used as a weapon while the UN Office for the Coordination of Humanitarian Affairs described the situation in Tigray as a 'de facto aid blockade'.[2] Banking, telecommunications and electricity were discontinued after the Ethiopian forces withdrew. The International Crisis Group reported: 'Retreating federal soldiers looted UN satellite internet equipment and reportedly emptied banks before fleeing Mekele. Addis Ababa has closed Tigray's airspace and Ethiopian soldiers and Amhara forces have been blocking World Food Programme trucks from reaching Mekelle'.[3] Some humanitarian flights into Mekele were permitted, but most aid convoys by road were slowed to a trickle, restricted or halted altogether. In a public statement Abiy said that the government was determined not to repeat the mistakes made by the Derg during its long confrontation with the TPLF in the 1980s.

> The main reason why Woyane [the Tigrayans] defeated the Derg during the war of 'Ethiopia first' was by using the Derg's weapon and food. So, given the current situation, if we stay there for long, we are going to provide them with many weapons. When it comes to food [aid], if one family has five children, they register that they have 7, 8, or 10 children. Then they receive the rations of ten. They use five of it themselves and give the remaining five to the Junta … So, we discussed this issue for a week and decided not to accept this any longer.[4]

It was not only aid, finance and communications that ceased. All access to Tigray was denied to journalists, both national and international. The Ethiopian government halted the flow of independent news. The only remaining sources of information about the region and its people came from the radio and television broadcasts by the Tigrayan authorities, supplemented by the occasional interviews Voice of America, BBC, CNN and Al Jazeera managed to establish with Tigrayan leaders by satellite.

Although the Tigrayans had re-established control over much of Tigray, the region remained surrounded by enemies and under intolerable humanitarian pressure. It was an untenable situation. Without access to essential supplies and services the region and its people were having the life drained out of them. For the Tigrayan leadership there was really only one alternative: to attempt to break the siege.

Breaking the siege?

If the siege was to be broken, the question for the leadership in Mekele was in which direction they should launch an attack. An offensive eastward might cut Ethiopia's critical road links with Djibouti. It might even provide Tigrayans with their own access to the sea. The second option was to drive northwards, into Eritrea and its capital, Asmara. The Tigrayans believed President Isaias had persuaded Abiy to launch the war, and their invasion would provide retribution for the deaths and the sexual abuse their women had suffered at the hands of Eritrean troops. However, the Eritreans were reported to be heavily dug in along the Tigray border, occupying defensive positions that would be difficult to capture. An assault on Eritrea might trigger Eritrean nationalism in support of Isaias as well as attract international criticism. Perhaps the most obvious choice was to strike westward, towards Sudan. This would provide Tigray with a corridor to the outside world, something it had enjoyed during its war against the Ethiopian state that ended in victory in 1991. It would also have the advantage of recovering the large area of western Tigray currently occupied by the Amhara. But the lands between the Tigrayan highlands and Sudan are flat

247

and open, providing easy targets for the Ethiopian and Eritrean air forces and artillery. Moreover, much of the Eritrean army was based in western Tigray, as were Amhara militia and the Ethiopian army. The route was, perhaps, too heavily defended. In the end the Tigrayan leadership opted for what may have seemed the least attractive option: a drive south and south-westward. It was an offensive that would see Tigray directly confront its Amhara enemies, and might even allow an assault on Addis Ababa. Best of all, it would allow the Tigrayans to link up with the Oromo Liberation Army. In the end it was the southern offensive that was chosen.

Preparations were relatively rapid for an operation of such magnitude. It seems that the Tigrayan military was keen not to lose momentum. It had acquired quantities of heavy artillery during its successes in central Tigray and had formed a number of mechanised units that could support conventional offensives, though fuel remained a concern. On 12 July 2021 a fresh offensive, dubbed Operation Tigray Mothers, began on the southern and south-western fronts.

On the southern front the immediate objective was to capture the towns of Korem and Alamata. The Ethiopian and Amhara defensive line lay on and around a strategic mountain range near Korem, which made a direct southward offensive along the A2 highway all but impossible. Tigrayan units, instead of attacking Korem, sent their troops to the east, against the towns of Bala and Ger Jala, before arcing round to attack Korem from the rear. Fighting in the vicinity of Korem was very intense, lasting an entire day, with both sides suffering heavy losses. Faced with the unexpected assault, and fearing that they would be surrounded and cut off, the Ethiopian forces withdrew from Korem and established new fortifications near the more defensible town of Kobo. By seizing the mountains around Korem, the Tigrayans gained artillery control over Alamata and surrounding areas, forcing the Ethiopians to abandon the city without a fight. Tigrayan soldiers entered Alamata on 13 July 2021, then rapidly advanced as far as Waja. After several months under the occupation of Amhara forces, the contested territories of southern Tigray were back under Tigrayan control.

On the southwestern front, the initial intention was to capture the towns of Amba Madre and Mai Tsebri. Even prior to the start of Operation Tigray Mothers, Amhara sources claimed that a small-scale Tigrayan attack was repulsed around Amba Madre. This meant Tigrayan reconnaissance units had already crossed the Tekeze River and secured safe zones on the southern bank. On 13 July Tigrayan infantry units swam across the Tekeze River at several points. To the east the offensive focused on driving Amhara forces from Fiyelwiha and the surrounding Dima district. A well-coordinated attack from several directions succeeded in breaking through Amhara and Ethiopian lines. The next day Amba Madre, Mai Tsebri and Fiyelwiha were captured. Tigray's south-western territories were once more under Tigrayan control.

Defeat in these first conventional battles sent shock waves through the Ethiopian, Eritrean and Amhara leadership. A day after Tigrayan forces captured Alamata and Mai Tsebri, Abiy released a statement revoking the unilateral ceasefire and calling on all Ethiopians to support the national army.[5] Regional administrations responded with ceremonies mobilising their special forces and sending them to the battlefront. Footage was carried on national television, emphasising support for the federal government from all of Ethiopia's regional states as well as the general public. The war was portrayed as a national, patriotic endeavour. Tigray's leadership, on the other hand, made it clear that they had no intention of halting their offensives as long as the siege of the region remained in effect and while western Tigray remained under occupation.

After initially being forced to retreat from Mai Tsebri by determined resistance from Amhara forces, Tigray launched a successful counter-offensive, enabling it to penetrate the North Gonder zone of the Amhara region and capture Adi Arkay on 23 July. General Tadesse Worede, commander of the Tigray Defence Force, claimed that the terrain had made their advance very challenging. Indeed, the presence of several easily defensible commanding heights in one of the most mountainous areas of northern Ethiopia meant the defenders were at a distinct advantage. However, rugged terrain also prevented large-scale battles, reducing the effectiveness of the Ethiopia's superior firepower and its control of the skies. The

Tigrayan strategy of using smaller units and launching coordinated attacks from several fronts enabled them to isolate and overcome pockets of Amhara resistance. Soon their forces were advancing rapidly into northern Gonder. In three days they captured the towns of Beremariam, Chew Ber and Zarima.

Pushing east: The Afar front

Towards the end of July 2021 Tigray opened another front: this time their attack was eastwards, into the Afar region. At about the same time as Tigrayan forces were locked in fighting to capture Kobo, another army-sized Tigrayan detachment crossed into Yalo *wereda* of Afar region. It was the start of another major offensive against Ethiopian and Afar forces. The leadership believed their enemies had concentrated forces in the Afar region, in preparation for a renewed invasion of Tigray. Given the flat landscape of the Afar region, the Tigrayans had to deploy a sizeable percentage of their infantry against Ethiopian defensive positions. Attacking over open ground was extremely hazardous, in view of their opponent's superior firepower and numbers. The Ethiopians had heavy artillery which could decimate the Tigrayan troops, who had to confront well-entrenched Ethiopian troops in full-frontal battles. The normal tactics of small-scale operations from a variety of directions could not be employed. Ethiopia also used its air force to good effect in supporting their defences, while the intense heat made any attack extremely arduous.

Despite these odds, the Tigrayans are reported to have launched a massive frontal assault on the right flank. The attack was successful. By 23 July they had captured Yalo, Golina and Awra *weredas* of Zone 4 and penetrated further south, to within a few kilometres of the strategic town of Chifra. In the course of their advance Tigrayan forces claimed to have completely destroyed the 23rd division of the Ethiopian army and seized large quantities of weaponry. The successes in Afar were deemed so significant by the Tigrayan leadership that the next day General Tsadkan Gebretensae, a member of the central command, commented: 'The TDF can move swiftly to control the Addis Ababa–Djibouti road and will be in a position to accept humanitarian assistance directly.'[6] The Tigrayan spokesman Getachew Reda went further: 'Abiy Ahmed's war machine is, essentially, destroyed.'[7] The offensives had inflicted a series of tremendous defeats on the Ethiopians, but—as later events revealed—the Tigrayan assessment was over-optimistic.

On 26 July the Tigrayan commander General Tadesse Worede announced the successful conclusion of Operation Tigray Mothers.[8] Although fighting was continuing, the Tigray military leadership believed it had inflicted sufficient damage on its adversary to achieve the primary objective of the operation—containing the Ethiopian threat of re-invasion. Ethiopian preparations for offensives in Gonder, Wollo and Afar had been prevented. The official statement claimed to have 'neutralised' over 30,000 Ethiopian troops.[9] Analysts who followed the war agreed that the Ethiopians had suffered major losses, especially in Tembien and Kobo. At the same time the Tigrayans had captured sufficient weapons to turn their forces into a well-equipped army, capable of conventional warfare. The spoils of war, combined with a highly experienced military leadership, had transformed the Tigrayans into a formidable force that was now a real threat to both Addis Ababa and Asmara. The response from the Ethiopian side reflected just how seriously the army had been affected. Agegnehu Teshager, vice president of Amhara regional state, made the unprecedented call on civilians to join the military with any weapons they had. He called on 'all young people, militia, non-militia in the region, armed with any government or personal weapons, to join the war against the TPLF'.[10] Photographs appeared on social media showing lorryloads of Amhara civilians being taken to the front line armed with nothing more than machetes and hoes.

Tigray's Operation Sunrise

Although the Tigrayans had fought off the invasion and expelled Eritrean and Ethiopian forces from large parts of Tigray, they had achieved only a partial victory. The whole of western Tigray was in enemy hands, while Eritrean forces held swathes of the north. Tigray remained cut off from the outside world and isolated from the external supplies and communications necessary for survival.

Military operations had to continue. Operation Sunrise took the Tigrayan advance southwards down the A2 highway.

The Tigrayans were relatively unchallenged until they reached the gates of Weldiya. Much to the indignation of the town's residents, Ethiopian detachments were ordered to withdraw from Weldiya without a fight, choosing to retreat to better defensive positions in the hills to the south, between Weldiya and Sirinka. There they would attempt to halt the advance. But Weldiyans were not willing to concede defeat without a fight. Led by the town's mayor, who called on every able-bodied person to take up arms, locals volunteered to resist. Tigrayan forces encountered determined resistance from locals and Amhara *fano* militia.

Weldiya's stand was celebrated as heroic by the Amhara government, which lauded it as a model of urban resistance, to be replicated by other towns of Amhara region facing the threat of occupation.[11] The residents of Debre Tabor and Debark organised similar urban resistance, which played no small part in staving off a Tigrayan advance. The battle of Weldiya–Sirinka was the largest battle along the A2 highway since the fighting for Kobo. According to Tigrayan sources, it involved two Ethiopian divisions, more than 11,000 Oromo special forces, Amhara *fano*, Ethiopian special commando battalions, and mechanised divisions. After a fierce encounter Tigrayan forces emerged victorious, again capturing large quantities of heavy and medium weapons. Video footage of the aftermath, on Tigray TV, showed scores of Ethiopian vehicles and weapons destroyed or captured. By the end of August, after facing sporadic resistance around Mersa, Tigrayan forces had advanced as far as the rural areas around Hayq, a town 28 kilometres from Dessie.

While the fighting was important, another development took place in August 2021 which had long-term implications. An alliance between the Tigrayans and the Oromo Liberation Army (OLA) was made public.[12] 'The only solution now is overthrowing this government militarily, speaking the language they want to be spoken to', OLA leader Kumsa Diriba (also known as Jaal Marroo) told the Associated Press. He said the agreement was reached at the suggestion of the Tigrayans. 'We have agreed on a level of understanding to cooperate against the same enemy, especially in military cooperation', he said. 'It is under way'. They shared battlefield information and fought in parallel, he said, and while they were not fighting side by side, 'there is a possibility it might happen'. Talks were also said to be under way on a political alliance as well, and Kumsa Diriba said that other groups in Ethiopia were involved in similar discussions: 'There's going to be a grand coalition against [Abiy Ahmed's] regime'.

A new front

Operation Sunrise had, until this point, involved a push southwards. Towards the end of July another front had been opened, to the west of Kobo. Several Tigrayan divisions advanced, encountering only Amhara forces along the way. By the beginning of August, Tigrayans had control of the towns of Muja and Kulmesk. From there they rapidly advanced north-west and, after sporadic fighting with Amhara forces, took control of the historic town of Lalibela. Capturing Lalibela was significant. It was not just symbolically important— well known outside Ethiopia—but it also denied the Ethiopian air force access to Lalibela's strategic airport. It was a base from which air support had been provided to Ethiopian forces' ground assaults around North Wollo and Wag Himra.

Part of the Tigrayan offensive then moved from Muja south-east to Dilb, where it sought to sever the Weldiya–Woreta road. After sweeping away the Ethiopian force entrenched around Dilb, they advanced in the direction of Weldiya, as far as Sanka. To the east of Dilb, Tigrayan forces made a rapid advance along the B22 highway and captured the strategic towns of Gashena and Geregera, as well as all the towns in-between. It appears that at least part of the detachment that captured Lalibela was re-routed via Dubko, a small town along a secondary road connecting the Lalibela–Muja route with the B22 highway, to take part in the assault on the strategic town of Gashena. By mid-August, Tigray had taken control of most areas of North Wollo and was advancing along the B22 towards neighbouring Lay Gayint *wereda* of South Gonder zone.

By this time, it was apparent that the objective of Tigrayan operations along the B22 highway was to sever the Bahir Dar–Gonder road at the strategic town of Woreta. If this was successful, it would cut the supply line to the north-west, putting the entire Ethiopian Western Command in jeopardy. Determined not to let this happen, the Ethiopian coalition deployed a huge force, including several army divisions and Amhara special forces, in the rugged mountainous area between Nefas Mewcha and Kimir Dingay. A brutal two-day battle started on 15 August 2021. It culminated in a major defeat for the Ethiopian side and enabled the Tigrayans to establish control of territory all the way to Kimir Dingay. Moreover, Mount Guna, the strategic high ground a few kilometres from Kimir Dingay, came under Tigrayan control. This crippled Ethiopian chances of mounting a meaningful resistance as far as Debre Tabor. It may have been a defeat for the Ethiopians, but it did not allow Mekele to achieve its aim of getting to or capturing Debre Tabor.

Meanwhile, a new front opened up to the north-west, as Tigrayan forces, in alliance with a few battalions of the newly formed Agaw Liberation Army (ALA) (which drew its support from ethnic Agaw population[13] in Wag Himra and Agew Awi zones of Amhara region) attempted to wrest control of Sekota from the hands of Amhara special forces. The Tigrayan–ALA offensive reportedly took place around mid-August as a force advancing from Korem was joined by another Tigrayan detachment from Lalibela. By 17 August, Sekota, the capital of Wag Himra zone, was under the control of Tigrayan and Agaw troops.

The coalition retaliates

However, it wasn't long before the coalition of Ethiopian forces and their allies struck back in attacks which continued until the end of 2021. In mid-August, they launched well-planned, massive counter-offensives on several fronts in an attempt to reverse Tigrayan gains.

On 19 August, as Tigray was preparing to take Debre Tabor, the Ethiopian coalition launched a major offensive in an attempt to slice through and surround the bulk of Tigrayan troops in Lay Gayint and South Wollo. One attack, involving a sizeable detachment of Ethiopian and Amhara forces, advanced from Wegeltena in an attempt to capture Gashena. The aim was to cut the supply line of the huge Tigrayan detachment that was heading for Woreta. Another Ethiopian counter-offensive sought to break through at Sirinka, to destroy the troops around Mersa. Tigrayan sources claimed that on the Gashena front alone, as many as five Ethiopian divisions and more than 10,000 Amhara troops took part. The encirclement of the Tigrayan detachment encamped around Mersa involved several brigades of Abiy's elite Republican Guard, special commando, federal police forces and the militia of South Wollo. The plan was for specialised assault units to surround and neutralise the enemy.

It appears that the Ethiopian plan was initially successful. Gashena was captured and the B22 highway was severed, leaving the bulk of Tigrayan forces in Gayint and Debre Tabor with no way out. Similarly, the Weldiya–Mersa road was cut at Sirinka, leaving Tigray's southern detachment stranded. However, Tigrayan forces soon converged from three sides on the Ethiopians occupying Gashena. After at least two days of intense and brutal fighting, in which both sides suffered immense losses, the Ethiopians retreated towards Kon. Similarly, Tigrayan forces were also able to repel the Ethiopian forces from Sirinka and re-establish links with their units in Mersa.

Towards the end of August, Ethiopian and Amhara troops began a series of counter-offensives on the south-western front that intensified during early September. By this time the Tigrayans had reached Dib Bahir, near the great escarpment of Limalimo. Moreover, reconnaissance units had penetrated the rural areas of North Gonder as far as Dabat. A series of large-scale 'human wave' attacks by Ethiopian troops, involving units of local militia and barely armed farmers, posed a serious challenge to the Tigrayans' advance. At least one counter-offensive on Tabla, between Dib Bahir and Zarima, involving several brigades of Ethiopian troops, attempted, but apparently failed, to cut off Tigrayan forces deployed south of Dib Bahir. The Chenna massacre, in which more than a hundred civilians were allegedly killed by Tigrayan units, in retaliation for guerrilla attacks, was reported at this time.[14] 'Tigrayan forces showed brutal disregard for human life and the laws of war by executing people in their custody,' said Human Rights Watch.[15] It was apparent that Tigray was finding it increasingly difficult to sustain its advance into Gonder.

All in all, from the beginning of September, even though Tigray's high command was able to save most of their forces, which had become stranded and faced annihilation, they were nevertheless forced to relinquish significant, hard-fought territorial gains on the Woreta–Weldiya and Gonder fronts. Subsequently, Tigrayan forces came under sustained attacks from local militia and Ethiopian units, and also withdrew from Debre Tabor and Lay Gayint. They retreated all the way to the edge of North Wollo, concentrating their forces around Filakit and Gashena. Eventually, the Tigrayan operation to take Woreta and sever the Bahir Dar–Gonder highway was also abandoned. Similar rapid advances towards Gonder came to a grinding halt around Dib Bahir, and Tigrayan troops were eventually forced to retreat to Zarima.

There is no authoritative assessment of the number of troops in the war. The accompanying table, by Ermias Teka, provides a 'best estimate' of the rival alliances in early September 2021.[16]

Balances of forces in the Tigray war, September 2021

Opposition alliance		Ethiopian, Eritrean and other forces	
Tigray Defence Forces (TDF)	300,000	Ethiopian National Defence Force (ENDF)	50,000
Oromo Liberation Army	20,000	Eritrean Defence Forces	300,000
Agaw Liberation Army	5,000	Amhara Special Forces	50,000
Afar	3,000	*Fano* plus Amhara militia	200,000
Gumuz Liberation Front	10,000	Oromo Special Forces	30,000
Gambella Liberation Army	5,000	Afar Special Forces	10,000
Qemant Liberation Movement	5,000	Somali Special Forces	5,000
Sidama National Liberation Front	5,000	Republican Guard	3,000
		Air force commando	3,000

It must also be borne in mind that the Ethiopian and Eritrean forces had planes and drones to draw upon. The small size of the Ethiopian military is explained by the setbacks the army and its associated militia had experienced in the previous months. The army—once among the most powerful in Africa—had been much reduced in size and combat ability. Its numbers were overtaken by the militia and special forces that had replaced it. The Ethiopian military launched a major recruitment drive in mid-2021, and is believed to have expanded by nearly 200,000 in the second half of the year, creating a number of new divisional commands. Some estimates put the total military strength of the ENDF at 350,000 by March 2022, though it seems that many, perhaps most, of the new recruits had no more than six months' basic training.

The Tigrayan's 'territorial adjustment' and 'recalibration'

On 9 September 2021, the leadership in Mekele released a statement announcing that they had decided to make what was described as a 'temporary territorial adjustment' of the areas they controlled.[17] The retreat was in reality a major reversal. The Tigrayans were finding it increasingly difficult to hold the less defensible areas of Amhara, and decided on a complete withdrawal from Afar. The leadership said the decision was based on two main factors. One was the Amhara region's mass mobilisation of barely trained civilians 'in hundreds of thousands', who were then used in human wave attacks. The government's call on patriotism and nationalism had been very effective. The second factor was what was described as the deployment of Eritrean troops 'to rescue Amhara forces'.[18] Following the announcement, Tigrayan troops made further retreats, including a withdrawal from Afar. Ethiopian sources confirmed that the Tigrayans had pulled back from Filakit and Gashena on the Weldiya–Woreta front; from Hayq on the Dessie front; from Sekota and its surrounding area on the Wag front; and from Zarima and Chew Ber on the North Gonder front.

There were unofficial reports of local insurgencies around Kobo and North Gonder emerging in rural areas that had been largely left unoccupied by the Tigrayans. These were causing problems for

Tigrayan supply lines, making further advances hard to sustain. In addition, there were unofficial reports from Tigrayan sources of significant Eritrean troop deployments in Gonder and Dessie to prevent these two important cities from falling into Tigrayan hands. This has not been independently verified.

By early October 2021 there were reports that Ethiopia was planning a massive offensive across the Amhara region. Abiy's government had just been formally inaugurated following his election victory and was apparently determined to assert its power with solid gains on the battlefield. An Amhara regional official spoke of an impending 'irreversible operation' to be carried out 'on all fronts'.[19]

On 8 October major air and ground offensives were launched by combined Ethiopian and Amharan forces around Geregera, Wegeltena, Wurgessa and Haro. The principal objective seemed to be the capture of Weldiya and Kobo, with a possible advance further north. From the Haro front, an Ethiopian detachment was mobilised from Arerit, probably attempting to enter Weldiya from the north-east. Similarly, a major offensive was launched at Geregera aiming to advance along the B22 highway all the way to Dilb and then descend on Weldiya. In the meantime, another Ethiopian and Amara detachment carried out a comprehensive offensive in Wegeltena, aiming to cut the Weldiya–Gashena road at Dilb by advancing across the rugged hills of the Ambassel range to the north-west. This would sever the Tigrayan supply lines to Gashena and isolate Tigray's forces at Geregera and Gashena. On the Wurgessa front, Ethiopian and Amhara forces attempted a major assault along the A2 highway to break through Tigrayan fortifications around Mersa and advance to Weldiya. Weldiya was clearly one major Ethiopian objective and was being approached from a variety of directions.

After several days of fierce fighting on all fronts, it became clear that the Ethiopian troops were not achieving their objectives. By 12 October, after four days of fighting, no appreciable progress had been made by the coalition, apart from a few gains around Arbit on the Gashena front. Around this time, Getachew Reda, spokesperson for the Tigray government, claimed that the ENDF had suffered 'staggering losses'. General Tsadkan, a member of Mekele's central command, predicted: 'I don't think this will be a protracted fight—a matter of days, most probably weeks. The ramifications will be military, political and diplomatic'.[20] It was apparent that the Tigrayans were confident that they had inflicted significant damage on their adversaries and that the Ethiopian offensives had all but failed.

On 12 October, after absorbing waves of Ethiopian attacks over several days, the Tigrayans launched counter-attacks. Emboldened by the 'staggering losses' the Ethiopian forces suffered, these counter-attacks were predictably ambitious in their objective of capturing the strategic cities of Dessie and Kombolcha. Brigadier General Haileselassie Girmay, one of the commanders of Tigray's forces on the southern front, revealed that his troops had executed an attack on Dessie from four directions.[21] One detachment moved from around Faji and Kul Bayine towards Tis Abalima and, by following the hills to the east of the A2 highway, took a turn to the right of Hayq Lake and advanced on Tita. Another detachment advanced from the Tigrayan stronghold around Mersa and went west of the A2 highway all the way to Marye heights before turning towards Kutaber. Another unit advanced between them, along the A2 highway. It sought to destroy Ethiopia's dense entrenchments at Sudan Sefer, Wuchale and Wurgessa and then to move onwards towards Borumeda. In the far west, yet another detachment, which had neutralised Ethiopia's forces around Wegeltena, advanced to the south-east and linked up with the Tigrayan forces from Marye. The two then coordinated their assault with the other divisions to mount an attack on the Ethiopian base at Borumeda. The Tigrayans then headed directly for Dessie.

At the same time another unit was making a steady advance into the Afar region through Habru and by 18 October was in the vicinity of Chifra. The Tigray military command claimed to have destroyed 27 of the 34 Ethiopian divisions that took part in their 'irreversible offensive'. This was an extraordinary claim, which cannot be verified, even though it is apparent that the Ethiopians had suffered major losses. The battles that decided the fate of Dessie took place near Borumeda and Tita and around Mount Tosa. The Tigrayans emerged victorious. Tigray was left in control of the strategically significant towns of Wegeltena, Wuchale and Chifra. Two days later, with the fall of Bistima, Hayq and the strategic heights of Marye, Dessie and Kombolcha were within artillery range. When it was evident that

Dessie and Kombolcha would be captured, the Ethiopians responded with a series of air raids on Tigray, starting on 18 October and continuing for the next ten days. Mekele was bombed more than five times, while other towns like Adwa, Agbe and Mai Tsebri also sustained significant damage during air raids.

Progress towards Dessie remained slow and the Tigrayans only reached its outskirts at the end of October. After sporadic fighting against Amhara forces, they slowly took control of several parts of the city, starting from Wollo University. However, after they had captured most of the city, a rapid Ethiopian counter-offensive on 30 October momentarily forced them to withdraw to the surrounding hills. In the meantime, another Tigrayan detachment captured Kombolcha, to the south of Dessie. By 3 November, despite widespread fears that Dessie would be the scene of prolonged urban fighting, Tigray was back in control of the city after minimal combat.

With the fall of Dessie and Kombolcha, the road to Shewa was suddenly wide open. The next defensible terrain was 177 kilometres further on. The federal government was becoming desperate. The prime minister called on all citizens to 'march with any weapon and resources they have to defend, repulse and bury the terrorist TPLF'.[22] The Amhara regional government said: 'All government institutions must suspend their regular activities and should direct their budget and all their resources to the survival campaign ... officials on every level should mobilise and lead ... to the front'.[23] The government announced a curfew of 8 pm and urged citizens to provide private vehicles to support the campaign. The Oromo, meanwhile, took Kemise town, cutting the A2 highway from Addis Ababa to Dessie.

The fall of the federal government appeared to be a real possibility and the shock waves spread through society. Many recalled that after the TPLF captured Dessie in 1991, President Mengistu Haile Mariam, who led the country during the Derg regime, fled the country.[24] Was history about to be repeated? The foreign community in Addis began to pack their bags and plan to leave.

By late November 2021 flights out of Addis were sold out and the departures had become an exodus.[25] The Americans called for their nationals to leave on 7 November, and soon other nations took similar decisions.[26] The large 'danger' symbol that appeared on the website of the French embassy in Ethiopia said it all: 'In light of the situation in Ethiopia, French nationals are formally called upon to leave the country without delay.' The UK made a similar appeal. 'I am urging all British Nationals—whatever their circumstance—to leave immediately, while commercial flights are readily available and Addis Ababa Bole International Airport remains open,' Britain's minister for Africa, Vicky Ford, said in a statement on 24 November. UN employees were also strongly advised to get out of Ethiopia as soon as possible.

Meanwhile, the Tigrayans and Oromo had launched a new alliance, bringing in other ethnic groups. On 5 November, the allies jointly announced the formation of a new coalition, the United Front of Ethiopian Federalist and Confederal Forces, to include seven other military organisations representing Afar, Gambella, Agaw, Sidama, Benishangul, Somali and Qemant nationalities.[27] The coalition was intended to take over federal power, once Addis had fallen. It would pave the way for a transitional government. In the event the alliance was more symbolic than effective, although the Tigrayan and Oromo relationship did pay dividends.

The fighting continued unabated, with several advances. After consolidating their control of Dessie and Kombolcha, the Tigrayans attacked in three directions along the B11, A2, and B21 highways. Their advance along the B11 was intended to capture the town of Mille and sever the Addis Ababa–Djibouti highway, the main economic artery of Ethiopia, linking the country to the sea. Two other offensives were intended to advance towards Addis Ababa, and unseat the Abiy government, just as the TPLF had done in 1991 with its Eritrean and Oromo allies.

While one Tigrayan advance was on the verge of capturing Shewa Robit, after a bitter fight against determined Ethiopian and Amhara resistance, another detachment moved south of the B21 highway into the rural area of South Wollo, capturing the towns in their path. Were Ilu and Degolo fell to Tigrayan forces. One advance then proceeded towards Merhabete, probably to cut the A3 highway at Fiche and move on the capital from this direction. Meanwhile other units made a sharp turn southwards from Degolo and penetrated into North Shewa, seizing Mahal Meda, Molale and Mezezo.

Just twenty days after the capture of Dessie, Tigrayan forces had advanced an astonishing 209 kilometres and were in the vicinity of Debre Sina. The town lies at an extraordinarily high altitude of 2,700 metres. Just beyond, the road rises to the Termaber Pass with its Italian-built tunnel. With its rough terrain, it was the most suitable spot for the Ethiopian army and their allies to make a last stand. There were fears that if Debre Sina fell, nothing was likely to prevent the Tigrayans from advancing to Addis Ababa. Yet just at this moment fortunes changed and the war was turned on its head.

Tigray defeated in Afar; Ethiopia rearms and retaliates

As early as mid-July 2021, Tigrayan forces had launched repeated attacks in an attempt to penetrate the Afar region and sever the Addis Ababa–Djibouti road. During earlier operations, an army-sized detachment of Tigrayan troops had taken control of Yalo, Golina and Ewa *weredas* and tried to advance to the Chifra–Mille road. However, successive offensives were repulsed by the determined resistance of the Afar special forces and the Ethiopian military, and this eventually forced the Tigrayans to conduct a complete withdrawal from Afar. After the failure of Ethiopia's October offensives, the drive into Afar was renewed. The Tigray military carried out a series of attacks, one of which managed to advance through the Habru *wereda* of Amhara region and capture Chifra. Nevertheless, despite Tigrayan claims of inflicting heavy losses on the Ethiopian units, attempts to make a further advance towards the strategic junction at Mille faced dogged resistance. The Tigrayans were unable to move very far beyond Chifra.

Following the fall of Kombolcha, Tigrayan forces, in alliance with their Oromo allies, made yet another attempt to capture Mille, this time through Bati. Again, after advancing as far as Eli Wuha in Afar, they encountered further fierce resistance, forcing them to retreat to Kasa Gita. It seems that in a last-ditch effort to break Ethiopian defensive lines and capture Mille, Tigrayan troops suffered heavy losses, far greater than on other fronts. The ability of Ethiopian and Afar troops to halt the advance was enhanced by the terrain, which was open and flat—ideal for artillery and aerial bombardments, which decimated the Tigrayan troops. Another factor was the use of drones, which played a critical part in changing the nature of the war.

Ethiopia was first reported to be using drones early in the war. In November 2020, it was said that Emirati drones stationed in Eritrea (probably fired from the UAE base in Assab) played an important role in destroying Tigrayan heavy weapons—and possibly their limited stock of missiles.[28] But these Emirati attacks ended in early 2021. The Tigrayans claimed drones had attacked their forces, but the response was scepticism. Bellingcat, which investigated the claims in November 2020, concluded: 'In sum, the claims made by the Tigray forces are not impossible, but so far they seem improbable'.[29] By August 2021 Bellingcat had changed its opinion and accepted that Chinese-made drones were being used, but was still unconvinced that Iranian drones were in the Ethiopian armoury: 'higher quality imagery would be needed to state anything conclusively'.[30]

It is now clear that drones from China, Turkey and Iran played an important—probably critical—role in turning fortunes in this war, both in November 2020 and again a year later after the UAE supplies were resumed. The Ethiopian use of drones for surveillance and attack appears to have played a significant role in reversing the spectacular gains made by the Tigrayan forces.

> 'The precision-guided munitions are sure to have wreaked havoc among Tigray Defence Forces' fire-support assets such as tanks and artillery,' says Stijn Mitzer, author of Oryx blog, a website investigating armed proliferation. 'Although these munitions are less effective against spread out groups of fighters, the psychological effect of drone strikes likely did much to weaken the morale of TDF fighters.'[31]

The drones that the Ethiopians flew themselves (rather than the early attacks by the UAE) were gradually acquired during 2021. In November 2021 an analyst calling himself Gerjon had tracked more than 100 flights carrying arms over the previous year.[32] It is not clear that all these flights involved drones.

Ethiopia paid for the weapons with hard-earned foreign exchange. In the first three months of 2021, Turkey's defence and aviation exports to Ethiopia rose to $51 million, up from $203,000 in the same period in 2020.[33] While Iran and China provided some of the weapons, it was the Turkish Bayraktar TB2 combat drones that really changed the conduct of the war. The relationship between Ethiopia and Turkey was cemented during a visit to Ankara by Abiy on 18 August 2021. He went to sign an important military cooperation agreement with Turkish president Recep Tayyip Erdoğan.[34] Very soon the direct transfer of drones got under way. According to African Intelligence, by mid-November 2021 the Ethiopian Air Force had received between six and ten Bayraktar TB2 drones.[35] These were stationed at the Harar Meda airbase at Bishoftu, southeast of Addis. They had were transferred on 20 and 25 August and again on 24 September.

The Turkish drones were supplemented by Chinese Wing Loong I drones, which were also detected at Harar Meda.[36] Iranian Qods Mohajer-6 drones were spotted at Semera, the capital of the Afar region.[37] They were deployed to halt the Tigrayan offensive into Afar. The front lines at Chifra and surrounding areas were much closer to Semera than the Harar Meda airbase. Drones, along with other aerial attacks and heavy artillery support, contributed significantly to arresting the advance on Mille.

The drones also allowed the Ethiopian military to track Tigrayan movements over remote, mountainous terrain. Their slow flight speed meant the drones could be deployed over an area for hours, focusing on details that reconnaissance jets would be hard pressed to identify. They could be quickly returned to base for refuelling and rearming, and be back over the battleground in a few hours. With the new equipment came the expertise required to use it. Al Jazeera noted: 'Turkish advisers and training staff bring a wealth of knowledge on how to successfully use these systems.'[38]

As the Ethiopian military became increasingly adept at deploying the new technology, the drones destroyed Tigrayan heavy weapons and trucks. 'Definitely the drones have been crucial,' concluded Alex de Waal.[39] 'They were primarily effective in disrupting the TDF logistics. There is a single tarmac road from Tigray south all the way to Shewa, and during December there were about a dozen drones at any one time patrolling that road and shooting at any trucks moving along the road, making it extremely difficult and hazardous for the TDF to supply its front lines.'

As the front lines moved towards Addis Ababa, drone attacks were stepped up against Tigrayan advances. The drones sparked hopes among the regime's supporters that all was not yet lost. It was a critical moment and the prime minister announced to the public that he would go to the battlefield to lead the army from the front, like an Ethiopian emperor of old.[40] Abiy's announcement whipped up patriotism and support for the government's war effort, even though it was not clear exactly where the Ethiopian leader went or what role he played at the front. Ethiopian television showed truckloads of men going to the battlefront armed with no more than hoes and machetes.

By late 2021 Tigrayan forces were advancing south on five fronts, like the fingers of a glove. Its troops were strung out along the A2 highway, which runs south to north, between Addis Ababa and Mekele, and on both sides of the road. They were highly vulnerable to an attack from either east or west. Abiy chose to launch an assault from the Afar region, using his most powerful remaining forces, to sever Tigrayan supply lines. Ethiopian and Afar troops quickly recaptured Chifra. It was a major victory and put an end to Mekele's ambitions of taking Mille and cutting Addis Ababa's links with Djibouti and the outside world.

On 1 December 2021 the government advanced on several fronts. In a single day Amhara and Ethiopian troops recaptured a string of towns which the Tigrayans had earlier taken at such a cost. Eyewitnesses reported that Tigrayans in Kombolcha, Dessie and Lalibela had started packing up and withdrawing 'without a single bullet fired'. In less than a week the Ethiopian led coalition recaptured Dessie, Kombolcha, the A2 highway to the south, and all of the B11 highway from Bati. Few actual battles took place during these operations, beyond some fierce exchanges of artillery fire. Several videos posted on social media showed the destruction of Tigrayan vehicles and heavy weapons. Drone strikes against supply lines had succeeded in disrupting the logistical and military capacity of the Tigrayan forces.

The Ethiopian government claimed to have inflicted heavy losses on the Tigrayan troops. Abiy went on state media to announce the recapture of Kasa Gita and Chifra. 'The enemy has been defeated. We scored an unthinkable victory with the eastern command in one day … Now in the west, we will repeat this victory.'[41] 'The youth of Tigray is perishing like leaves. Knowing they are defeated, it is being led by one who does not have a clear vision or plan,' Abiy told the Ethiopian public. 'They should surrender today.'

The Tigrayans, on the other hand, claimed they were withdrawing for strategic reasons and not because they had been defeated. Tigray's military command said: 'We are making territorial adjustments on our own terms and so as to pave the way for strategic offensives'.[42] In early December, with only a partial withdrawal in place, the Tigrayan leadership maintained that the 'pullback' was merely 'a limited territorial and strategic adjustment'.[43] This led to a belief among observers that the Tigrayans would not pull out of the Amhara region completely, but would try to retain strategic areas of northern Wollo, mainly territories beyond Weldiya, and mount their defence from there.

However, on 10 December 2021, an Ethiopian offensive advanced from Afar through Boren and cut the Mekele–Weldiya road north of Weldiya. This left the bulk of Tigray's forces to the south of Kobo in a precarious situation, facing imminent encirclement in hostile territory.

Two days later, the Tigrayan forces launched massive counter-attacks to the west and south-west, as a result of which they were able to recapture, after heavy fighting, the areas around Lalibela and Gashena. Tigrayan sources claimed that government forces suffered huge losses, but this was not independently verified. The objective of the offensives appears to have been to secure the Lalibela–Sekota road to allow the withdrawal of Tigrayan troops in and around Weldiya. The units around Gashena held off attacks from the B22 highway, while the bulk of Tigrayan forces undertook an orderly withdrawal into Tigray itself. Over the next week, Ethiopian forces rapidly advanced north up the A2 highway, recapturing Mersa, Weldiya, Gobiye, Hara Gebeya, Kobo Robit and Kobo.

Around the same time, drone attacks against Alamata were a prelude to a ground offensive which enabled the rapid recapture of

Alamata. An attempt to advance further and capture Korem, however, faced stiff resistance from Tigrayans in well-fortified positions.

The Ethiopian army's determined offensives and advances shook the Tigrayan leadership. They released a statement claiming that the Tigrayan withdrawal was undertaken in order to give 'priority for peace' and called on the international community to take firm measures to force the Ethiopian government to halt their assault.[44] 'I have ordered those units of the Tigray Army that are outside the borders of Tigray to withdraw to the borders of Tigray within immediate effect,' Tigray president Debretsion Gebremichael said in a letter to UN secretary general Antonio Guterres. On 24 December 2021, following repeated calls from international organisations for a ceasefire, the Ethiopian government announced that it had ordered its forces 'to maintain the areas it has controlled'. Plans to advance on Mekele were, at least temporarily, put on hold.

After thirteen months of continuous fighting, this was the first time both sides officially announced a ceasefire. Although there were sporadic outbreaks of fighting, neither side made serious attempts to advance. The war had witnessed an extraordinary see-saw. Both sides had attacked and retreated as their adversaries responded to offensives with counter-attacks involving thousands of combatants and a concomitant number of casualties.

By the first week of January 2022 the front lines in southern Tigray had stabilised. The Tigrayans were in firm control of most of the southern Tigray border of Raya. At the same time, Amhara militia and Ethiopian troops retained areas around Waja, while Afar forces controlled Chercher. The fighting on the south-western front, on the road to Gonder, however, remained fluid and relatively intense. There were unofficial reports that the Tigrayans had repulsed waves of attacks by Amhara forces and, after temporarily ceding control of the areas around Adi Arkay, eventually recaptured them. Attempts by the Amhara to retake Tselemti *wereda* and confine the Tigrayans beyond the Tekeze River had failed. Meanwhile, a new round of drone attacks was reported widely across Tigray, resulting in hundreds of civilian casualties. Among the targeted areas were Hiwane, Dedebit, Korem, Maichew and Samre, the attacks being aimed at civilian morale rather than military objectives.

As the other front lines quietened down, clashes began to be reported along the Afar–Tigray border. Both regional governments accused each other of instigating the fighting, while the federal government remained strangely quiet. Tigray's military command claimed sneak attacks by Eritrean and Afar forces had taken place in Edaga Hamus, Atsbi and Des'a, and appealed to Afar religious and community elders to put a stop to these provocations by the Afar administration. On January 26, Tigray launched attacks into the Afar region and, after brief battles, was able to take control of Ab'Ala and Magala as well as the strategic locations around them. Following the military setbacks, the Afar administration complained of not receiving support from the Ethiopian military and insisted that the aim of the Tigrayans was, once again, to cut the Djibouti–Addis Ababa road. The statement may have been an attempt to encourage the Ethiopian army to come to their aid, but the federal government resisted getting involved, treating the fighting as localised incidents.

By the end of January, Ethiopian and Amhara forces had withdrawn from the remaining parts of southern Tigray. At this point, with the exception of the large area of western Tigray and some areas along the border with Eritrea, most of the territory constitutionally part of Tigray remained in the hands of the Tigrayan forces. Moreover, Tigrayan forces had advanced well into Afar region and were holding large areas adjacent to the Afar–Tigray border as buffer zones.

The months of February and March saw intense efforts by international actors to bring the belligerents to the negotiating table. On 24 March, the Ethiopian government declared 'an indefinite humanitarian truce' that was to begin immediately.[45] The statement released by the government of Tigray the following day replicated the gesture, insisting that they were committed to 'the cessation of hostilities effective immediately'.[46] On 25 April the Tigrayan spokesman Getachew Reda claimed that 'our forces have left all of Afar', adding that he hoped it meant that desperately needed food aid could finally arrive in Tigray.[47] At the end of April 2022, despite indications of renewed military movements along the Amhara–Tigray border, and intermittent reports of clashes with the Eritreans, the truce appeared to be holding.

Conclusion

The Tigray war is among the most devastating conflicts in Ethiopia's modern history. Indeed, it was almost certainly the most brutal war the world saw in 2021. When it began, Abiy had been dismissive. He described it as a small-scale 'law enforcement operation' that he promised would be 'wrapped up soon'.[48] Instead, the conflict was transformed into a war without apparent end. The international media suggest that tens of thousands of civilians and combatants have been killed and wounded.[49] These figures appear far too low. Estimates by a team from the University of Ghent in Belgium, led by Professor Jan Nyssen, put the casualties at between 200,000 and 500,000. 'With the assistance of citizen scientist Tim van den Bempt, we made the assessment that so far there are between 150,000 and 200,000 starvation deaths, 50,000 to 100,000 victims of direct killings, and more than 100,000 additional deaths due to lack of health care'.[50]

Since no independent investigation has been permitted by the Eritrean or Ethiopian governments, this estimate cannot be verified, but the assessment is made by cautious academics and appears close to the truth. The cost of this conflict for civilians has certainly been immense. Women have been abused and brutally raped. 'In the first eight months of the war 2,200 cases [of sexual abuse] were reported in Tigray and 940 in Amhara,' a UN team of experts reported. But they admitted the figures were probably 'an underestimation of the true extent' of the violence.[51] Millions have been displaced, homes, schools and clinics destroyed, while six million people live without outside aid of any kind, and Addis Ababa and Asmara have cut all communications to the outside world. This is no accident. Mark Lowcock, then the UN's most senior humanitarian official, accused Eritrea of being responsible for the policy of starving the Tigrayans into submission. 'In an interview with Reuters on Thursday, Lowcock said Eritrean soldiers and local fighters are deliberately blocking supplies to the more than 1 million people in areas outside government control. "Food is definitely being used as a weapon of war."'[52]

The war transformed Tigray. The resistance became a truly popular movement. The Tigrayan military now has among its ranks fighters from all sections of Tigrayan society: opposition leaders, scholars, farmers, and urban dwellers. It enjoys strong support from the people in general. Vocal backers of the armed resistance include religious leaders, the elderly, human rights advocates and international personalities.

The federal government, for its part, has relentlessly worked at gaining the support of the non-Tigrayan population for its continuing operations against what it has labelled a 'terrorist organisation'. Its war propaganda has increasingly resorted to rhetoric that not only doesn't differentiate between the people of Tigray and the armed resistance of the Tigrayan military, but accuses the entire people of treason. Some of Abiy's closest advisers have called for genocidal revenge against the people of Tigray. Daniel Kibret, social affairs adviser to the prime minister, called for their extinction in a television broadcast in January 2022.[53] The mayor of Dire Dawa, an Islamic supporter of the prime minister, described Tigrayans on Ethiopian television as being 'worse than the devil himself and they should be exterminated, erased from the face of the earth'.[54] This kind of rhetoric whipped up a deeply ingrained hostility between Tigrayan and Amhara society, which threatens to have an enduring impact on the entire region.

Both sides of the conflict have shown remarkable efficiency in utilising their strengths to shift the tide of the war in their favour. Tigrayan forces drew upon Tigray's military tradition, the solidarity which characterises the society, and its experienced military leadership. This allowed it to chart a course that saw the Tigrayan resistance refashioned from an apparently defeated force, after its withdrawal from Mekele, into a conventional army. Its forces could not only wrest most of Tigray from the grip of two of the largest and most experienced armies of East Africa, but then rapidly advance towards the gates of Addis. The discipline of its forces also allowed a rapid, and extremely difficult, retreat at the end of 2021, when it seemed that they could be cut off and isolated.

The Ethiopian government, on the other hand, appears to have recognised from early on that its greatest strength lay in the huge human and material resources of the country. Consequently, it invested heavily in propaganda and in the purchase of advanced weapons. This enabled Abiy to survive, despite the near destruction of Ethiopia's national army. By the end of 2021 he had reversed the Tigrayan gains and driven the enemy from Shewa, all the way to Tigray's borders. Ethiopia was remarkably successful in mobilising hundreds of thousands of militia and barely trained civilians from all over the country, and delivering them to the battlefields, where they fought with bravery and determination. The Ethiopian government was also adept at making the best use of its geopolitical opportunities to acquire the drones and other advanced weaponry which played a decisive part in forcing the Tigrayans to retreat back to Tigray. Combining large-scale if poorly trained armies with sophisticated weaponry allowed the Ethiopian forces to turn the tide of this war in their favour. Their Eritrean allies have continued to support the war, despite suffering atrocious casualties. The absence of any kind of democracy in Eritrea prevented President Isaias from being challenged about his strategy, tactics or the sacrifices that have been involved.

In terms of military strategies, the Tigrayans appear to have recalibrated their engagements by choosing techniques and environments appropriate to its military capability. Acutely aware that they have a limited population from which to recruit, they generally avoided large-scale full-frontal battles across flat, open landscapes where superiority in manpower and artillery would be decisive. Even in conventional battles their forces performed manoeuvres that followed principles similar to those adopted in guerrilla warfare, without risking mass casualties. Only when geography forced them to, did the Tigrayans attack across open terrain, as during their attempts to sever the vital Addis–Djibouti road. If they had cut off Ethiopia's access to the sea, Tigray would have gained a strong bargaining chip in negotiating with Abiy. The federal government successfully countered the repeated offensives into Afar by securing the allegiance of locals, deploying the bulk of its forces on this front, and employing drones supported by heavy artillery.

With the assistance of Eritrea's president Isaias and ethnic militia, Abiy managed to foil one of Mekele's primary objective: liberating western Tigray. If successful, this would have given the Tigrayans a crucial supply line to Sudan. However, the corridor to Sudan remained sealed.

The cost of the war to Ethiopia has been enormous. It required the sacrifice of a large proportion of its professional army and drained the Ethiopian economy. Ultimately, Ethiopian diplomatic leverage, its popular mobilisation and its successful utilisation of combat drones reversed what appeared to be a near-certain Tigrayan victory. There is now a military stalemate. The Ethiopian–Eritrean coalition appears incapable of advancing further into Tigray without risking another military catastrophe. Tigrayan forces, on the other hand, are unlikely to attempt another offensive into Amhara or Afar, unless they can find an answer to the drones. Yet, Tigray remains under siege, with tragic consequences for its people. This was clearly expressed by Tigray's General Tsadkan when he said at the end of April 2022: 'We all know that our people are dying in large numbers due to disease and starvation. A siege is tough. The people of Tigray have perhaps faced what it has never faced before in its history.'[55] No government can allow this to continue indefinitely without finding a response. As long as Tigray remains under *de facto* siege, and its disputes with the neighbouring regions of Amhara and Afar are unresolved, the prospect of another round of even more brutal warfare remains a serious possibility if peace talks fail.

PART FIVE

IMPACT OF WAR

9

DESTROYING THE SOCIAL AND ECONOMIC FABRIC OF TIGRAY

Martin Plaut

Introduction

As discussed in an earlier chapter, Tigray was partially transformed, after the overthrow of the Derg in 1991, from being an economic backwater and brought into the mainstream of Ethiopian development. By contrast, the Eritrean economy has languished in the doldrums. Under the Italians it was the economic powerhouse of Horn; after independence in 1993 it stalled. President Isaias has little interest in the development of his country. This may seem odd, to say the least. It went against the promise made to the Eritrean people in the ruling party's National Charter. This established as an objective the 'gradual development of a strong national economy, based on appropriate agriculture, industrial, commercial and other services, which satisfies the needs of our people, develops our own resources, enables responsible utilization of the national environment and resources, and is oriented towards a free market.'[1] Despite having absolute control over Eritrea since coming to power in 1991, President Isaias has made no attempt to downplay the country's failure to thrive. In an interview on 17

February 2021, he was asked about the impact of Covid on the Eritrean economy, and replied:

> What economy? It is 'hand to mouth economy' subsistence. It is not a big economy with productive added value. We do not have big factories, farms that use new technology, industry etc. What we have now is a subsistence economy but we are working out plans that can help us move to a sustainable economy. This is why I say there has not been any business in Eritrea that has been interrupted or closed down because of COVID. Which ones? None: because they do not exist.[2]

Keeping the country impoverished, but strictly supervised by ruthless security services armed with the powers of indefinite imprisonment and torture, suits the president and his associates.[3] It is a development model similar to North Korea's. Most of the population is either trapped in subsistence agriculture or else in 'national service'—a form of indefinite conscription which the UN Human Rights Council declared was a form of slavery.

Was it any surprise, then, that Eritreans were delighted when their southern border with Tigray was opened in September 2018? No wonder that they flooded into Tigray to buy the goods Tigrayan factories were producing and Tigrayan traders were importing. What anger or frustration did President Isaias experience as his citizens imported goods from Tigray that they might have produced themselves? We cannot know, but the experiment was soon terminated. By December 2018 it was over: the border was once more sealed. But the awareness that Tigrayans were thriving just across the Mereb River was a lesson not lost on the president. Destroying the factories, health clinics and schools that the Tigrayans had successfully established was not just part of the costs of war; it was in all likelihood driven by Isaias's thirst for revenge, based on the resentments discussed in earlier chapters.

This chapter focuses on the situation in Tigray, but the war has had an impact on all of Ethiopia. While the Tigrayan economy has been badly damaged, the wider impact has been enormous. In addition to the physical damage inflicted on the Afar and Amhara regions, the Ethiopian economy—previously Africa's most rapidly growing—has itself been downgraded. Ethiopia's overall economic growth for 2021 was forecast to slow significantly from 6 per cent in 2020 to just 2 per cent in 2021—the lowest level in almost two decades, according to the IMF.[4] Just how severe the situation was, was revealed in October 2021,[5] when the IMF refused to release a growth forecast for Ethiopia for the next four years.[6] By early 2022 the IMF felt able to forecast Ethiopian growth but showed this had almost halved.[7] It was estimated that military expenditure would reach $502 million (£365 million) by the end of 2021, up from $460 million the previous year.[8] UN secretary general Antonio Guterres said the conflict had 'drained over a billion dollars from the country's coffers'.

By March 2022 the situation had deteriorated still further. Inflation rose to 37.7 per cent in May 2022. Ethiopia applied to the G20 group of wealthy countries for its debt to be restructured.[9] Abiy attempted to gain access to foreign exchange by creating a sovereign wealth fund, into which key assets like Ethiopian Airlines, Ethio Telecom and mines, industrial parks, hotels and land would be placed. These were said to be worth $150 billion, but far from being a sign of a wish to open up the economy it was interpreted as a desperate attempt to raise funds. By the end of December 2021, Ethiopia's Central Bank announced that it had only $1.6 billion left in its coffers, the equivalent of 1.3 months of imports.[10] 'When Abiy Ahmed started the war, he thought that the few billion dollars that the UAE gave him would not run out; that's why he dared to say to me, "there isn't a people you can't subdue using money and might,"' said Tigray's General Tsadkan. 'The dollars have now run out. He is facing a crisis. The economic situation Ethiopia is currently facing is very tough.'[11] The general's remarks were, of course, those of a hostile commentator, but they appeared to have the measure of the situation.

Looting and destruction

Tigray has been sealed off from the outside world since the war began. As a result, it is not possible to provide an authoritative account of the destruction of factories and shops; schools and health centres. The World Bank summarises the damage: 'The war has led to massive destruction of business enterprises, infrastructure, and disruptions of major public services (electricity, telephone, banking and transport services).'[12] In April 2022 a pro-Tigrayan website attempted to collate the information, listing nine factory sites that had been destroyed or damaged.[13] Photographs and video were shared on social media of the ruined sites looted by troops.[14]

These businesses had been developed mainly as a result of the investments of EFFORT—the Endowment Fund for the Rehabilitation of Tigray. They grew out of the work of the TPLF during the years when the movement fought the Derg and continued, after 1991, when the Tigrayans came to government. EFFORT had done what it could to bring investment and jobs to the region, which had been badly neglected. Together the firms provided work for approximately 47,000 people—a means of obtaining a better life.[15] However, as indicated earlier, the jobs were viewed by other Ethiopians (and even by Eritreans) as the result of the misappropriation of Ethiopian resources for Tigray. This may have been wide of the mark, but it helps explain the ferocity of the looting and attacks on these industries.

A World Peace Foundation report concluded that thousands of jobs had been lost. At the Almeda textile factory in Adwa, soldiers first dismantled all the sewing machines and then removed them, before destroying the heavy machinery and infrastructure. The factory had provided 8,000 jobs when at full capacity. The attack on the Almeda plant was followed by the destruction of the industrial area that contained a privately owned water bottling plant, a flour mill and a shoe factory.[16] 'They have destroyed Tigray, literally,' said Mulugeta Gebrehiwot. In the year since that assessment the situation has only deteriorated. The fighting has continued, drone attacks have targeted the region's manufacturing, while banking and communications remain severed. The industries of Tigray, which once supplied many products to the Ethiopian market, and which exported to the wider world, have been unable to obtain vital inputs or send their products beyond the region.

Worldwide, armies regularly attempt to deprive their enemies of key assets. These tactics were also adopted by the Tigrayans. The airport at Axum was deliberately sabotaged by Tigrayan forces, with trenches dug into the runway to prevent the arrival of Ethiopian troops, weapons and ammunition.[17] Similarly, the Ethiopians destroyed a key bridge across the Tekeze River to halt the Tigrayan advance, despite its being vital for aid supplies into Tigray.[18] Both actions—controversial as they were—could be defended as attempts to deprive the enemy of strategic assets. However, targeting the private property and businesses of enemy populations falls into a different category, and civilians are protected under international humanitarian law.[19] Eritrean soldiers were accused of systematically looting homes and businesses as they advanced into Tigray in late 2020.[20] An eyewitness saw the pillaging of shops in the town of Adwa by Eritreans, who broke down doors, before being followed by young women, brought from Eritrea for the purpose. They looted the goods, piling them into vehicles. 'On the streets, all you see is now looting, they break every store, every electronics store, every shop ... They break it, they get in, and they take everything in their bag, and they put it in trucks. And a couple of armed Eritrean soldiers would be waiting for them in the safety of the [vehicles]. And they take everything ... They were taking even the smallest thing.'[21]

A Belgian journalist, Stijn Vercruysse, was one of the few to manage to gain access to the region to report on the destruction.

> Even in places where the fighting seems to be over, people do not dare to return to their homes because they are afraid of Eritrean soldiers who loot houses and harass people. 'We have been able to establish that everything indicates that Eritrean soldiers have crossed the border wearing Ethiopian uniforms,' says Stijn Vercruysse. 'It appears that they participated in the fighting and that they are at least helping to secure the region. But instead of securing, they would loot the Tigre's homes.'[22]

Vercruysse filmed tanks laden with goods seized from Tigrayan homes. The footage showed trucks piled high with everything from bedsteads to doors and machinery being driven back to Eritrea.

The looting of Tigrayan homes, shops and factories was accompanied by systematic attempts to deprive the population of food by attacking farms and food stores. The World Peace Foundation cited video and satellite evidence of crops burned, orchards cut down and cattle and other animals killed.[23] Sometimes farmers were forced at gunpoint to cook their animals for the troops. At other times there was just wanton destruction. Oxfam quoted one farmer: 'Crops were burnt down in some places including mine. The total loss of my crop—an estimated 1.5 ton—could have fed my family of seven at least for ten months.'[24] Across Tigray, food stores were pillaged and scorched-earth tactics used by the Eritrean and Ethiopian forces.[25] Whole villages, warehouses, expanses of fields and crops, mango orchards and grain stores were destroyed.[26]

The refugee camps that housed nearly 100,000 Eritrean refugees were also attacked by Eritrean forces, their residents killed and raped and their homes looted, according to Human Rights Watch.[27] On some occasions Tigrayans are said to have joined in. "Eritrean refugees have been attacked both by the very forces they fled back home and by Tigrayan fighters,' said Laetitia Bader, Horn of Africa director at Human Rights Watch. 'The horrific killings, rapes, and looting against Eritrean refugees in Tigray are evident war crimes.'

Attacking Tigray's healthcare and educational services

From 1981 the TPLF gradually constructed healthcare based in local communities. In the first year 20 health stations were built in different districts.[28] The following year a further 21 were added, until they extended across the areas the TPLF controlled. When the war ended in 1991, there were 138 clinics in all, serviced by 76 doctors and around 1,000 community health workers.[29] As the Ethiopians, and particularly the Eritreans, advanced into Tigray in late 2020 they vandalised and destroyed public facilities across the region that had been built over many years. Images appeared on social media of health clinics with medical equipment broken and files and medicines scattered across the floor. The walls of the clinics were daubed with abusive messages. The health care system, which was savagely attacked, had been painstakingly developed.

One attack was graphically detailed by the Safeguarding Health in Conflict Coalition.

In the early hours of Sunday morning, May 16, 2021 Ethiopian soldiers armed with assault rifles and grenades stormed the University Teaching and Referral Hospital in Axum, Tigray region. This raid was in retaliation for the staff of the facility speaking to CNN about the health impacts of the Ethiopian government's blockade of medication into Tigray region. The soldiers threatened health care workers and contaminated the operating room, forcing all surgical procedures to stop. The next day the facility was raided again.[30]

The Safeguarding Health report made it clear that some attacks had also been carried out by Tigrayan forces, after the withdrawal of Ethiopian troops and their allies from Tigray in June 2021.[31] 'For example, in December TDF forces looted ventilators and anaesthesia equipment from Dessie Specialized Hospital in Dessie town, Tigray region, preventing all surgical operations from being performed.'

In March 2021 the medical charity Médecins Sans Frontières (MSF) published this detailed assessment:

Health facilities across Ethiopia's Tigray region have been looted, vandalised and destroyed in a deliberate and widespread attack on healthcare, according to teams from Médecins Sans Frontières (MSF). Of 106 health facilities visited by MSF teams between mid-December 2020 and early March 2021, nearly 70% had been looted, and more than 30% had been damaged; just 13% were functioning normally ...

In many health centres, such as in Debre Abay and May Kuhli in North-West Tigray, teams found destroyed equipment, smashed doors and windows, and medicine and patient files scattered across floors ...

Every fifth health facility visited by MSF teams was occupied by soldiers. In some instances, this was temporary; in others the armed occupation continues. In Mugulat in east Tigray, Eritrean soldiers are still using the health facility as their base. The hospital in Abiy Addi in central Tigray, which serves a population of half a million, was occupied by Ethiopian forces until early March.[32]

MSF emergency coordinator Kate Nolan explained what they found. 'The army used Abiy Addi hospital as a military base and to stabilise their injured soldiers. During that time, it was not accessible to the general population. They had to go to the town's health centre, which was not equipped to provide secondary medical care—they can't do blood transfusions, for example, or treat gunshot wounds,' said Nolan. MSF found that few health facilities in Tigray had ambulances any longer, since most had been seized by armed groups. Vehicles were being used by soldiers near the Eritrean border, to transport goods. As a result, patients had to travel long distances, sometimes walking for days, to reach health services.

Worse was to follow. On 24 June 2021 three MSF health workers were murdered.[33] 'Maria Hernandez, our emergency coordinator; Yohannes Halefom Reda, our assistant coordinator; and Tedros Gebremariam Gebremichael, our driver, were travelling yesterday afternoon when we lost contact with them. This morning, their vehicle was found empty and a few metres away, their lifeless bodies.' The following month the situation had deteriorated so badly that MSF decided—reluctantly—to suspend all operations in Tigray.[34] This was lifted in October 2021, but the situation was too precarious to restart medical programmes.[35] By November 2021, with a state of emergency across Ethiopia, MSF suspended its work in other parts of the country.

Most of Tigray's health care was not provided by charities like MSF, but by the region's own doctors, nurses and healthcare workers.[36] The war has had a terrible impact on their work. An article in the *BMJ Global Health* outlined the result.[37] It concluded: 'Six months into the war, only 30% of hospitals, 17% of health centres, 11.5% of ambulances and none of the 712 health posts were functional.' That was the situation in June 2021, and it has continued to deteriorate since then.

Healthcare workers, like everyone else in Tigray, have suffered terribly from the Ethiopian and Eritrean blockade. By February 2022 even nurses and doctors at the Ayder hospital in Mekele were reduced to begging for food.[38] A doctor told the BBC that it had become normal to see health staff queuing for food parcels. This was partly the result of food simply not being available and partly because of the banking system being closed, preventing salaries from being paid. The doctor explained that a lack of medical supplies had affected treatment. Instead of sterilised surgical gauze, essential for cleaning wounds during and after surgery, Ayder Hospital had been relying on donations of clothes and cloth, which were then cut up and sterilised. Video showed surgical gloves were being recycled, with the blood washed off them, as there were no replacements.[39]

In June 2022 the situation eased slightly. Convoys of trucks were allowed into Tigray. This was welcomed by US secretary of state Antony Blinken. 'In the past seven days, more than 1,100 trucks have reached Tigray to deliver life-saving food, malnutrition treatment and health supplies, and other essential relief items to those who are most vulnerable as a result of the hard work of all the humanitarians committed to saving lives,' Blinken said in a statement.[40] This was accompanied by an airlift which brought in approximately 11 tonnes of health (7.4 tonnes) and nutrition (3.6 tonnes) supplies in a week.[41] These are helpful but are no replacement for far larger, regular supplies to end the crisis.

The impact of the war on the health system is, unsurprisingly, replicated across Tigray's educational system. The teaching offered to young Tigrayans was a high point of the administration. Much of the infrastructure now lies in ruins, its classes scattered and its teachers dead or wounded. Human Rights Watch reported in May 2021 that government forces had taken control of schools in Mekele, transforming them into barracks.[42] 'After occupying the school for several weeks, they left; trucking away computers, plasma screens, and food. Interim authorities soon began to repair the damage so that classes could resume, but soldiers returned in February and occupied the school for another three months'. When the Ethiopian soldiers pulled out of Mekele for good, they left the school in ruins, with abuse scrawled over the walls. A resident described the graffiti: '"Tigray and snakes are the same"; "Tigray must be cleansed"; "Tigray must be cleansed for the development of the country"; insults about junta, "Tigray are junta". There were a lot of different things that were written about Tigray women that I cannot repeat. It is too painful'.

An initial assessment of how much has been lost was prepared by the head of Tigray's Education Bureau, Dr Shishay Amare.[43] Prior to the war nearly 1.5 million students were being taught by 46,598 teachers, in 2,221 primary and 271 senior schools. By the time the report was written many had lost their lives; and much of the infrastructure was lost or severely damaged. Over 96 per cent of buildings had been damaged, with 442 completely destroyed. This has left huge numbers of Tigrayan children without schooling. The UN reported in June 2022 that 'an estimated 1.4 million children in Tigray are entering their third year without access to education'.[44]

These are the bald facts. They do not explain the psychological impact of the war on the educational sector or the suffering caused by the loss of earnings, which has reduced teachers to a state of destitution. In some areas there is little that remains.

Rape and sexual violence

Mark Lowcock, then UN's head of humanitarian affairs and emergency relief coordinator, told the Security Council in April 2021 that it was his view that sexual violence was being used as a weapon of war in Tigray.[45] 'Nearly a quarter of reports received by one agency involve gang rape, with multiple men assaulting the victim; in some cases, women have been repeatedly raped over a period of days. Girls as young as eight are being targeted,' Lowcock said. It is not clear exactly how many such assaults have taken place. The UN Population Fund (UNFPA) provided an estimate in June 2021 that 26,000 people had suffered sexual violence.[46] The UNFPA has provided no update since then.

'During the period of November through June 2021, Tigrayan females were the primary targets of war-related sexual violence,' reported the World Peace Foundation.[47] 'From information we have collected, victims of rape included little girls as young as four years old and teenage girls. In addition, women of all ages, including pregnant and nursing women, grandmothers and great-grandmothers were sexually violated.'

According to a range of reports, the sexual abuse of Tigrayan women appears to have been more than 'just' for the sexual gratification of troops. A number took place in public or in front of families. Sometimes family members were forced to participate. The United States Agency for International Development found that 39 per cent of women and girls who were abused reported being raped inside their homes, and 33 per cent of the victims were gang-raped.[48] Of these, 44 per cent were raped by Ethiopian troops and a further 33 per cent by Eritreans; 6 per cent were raped by both Ethiopians and Eritreans. An 18-year-old woman lost her arm when she tried to fight off her attackers; her grandfather was shot in the leg for trying to protect her. He had attempted to argue with her attackers that rape was 'abnormal and against our religious beliefs.'[49] These public attacks were designed to break the morale of a family or an entire community.

The attacks on men, seldom reported, were apparently done for a similar reason. 'A few Tigrayan male survivors of sexual violence, boys and men, came forward seeking medical care because of traumatic injuries they had sustained due to anal rape. One reported he was held by the ENDF in their camp where he was repeatedly anally raped. It is extremely difficult for men and boys to come forward to report sexual violence against themselves, but we do know that the ENDF used rape against Tigrayan men and boys in this war.'[50]

Breaking the spirit of Tigrayans was one objective. The second was 'ethnic cleansing'—an apparent attempt to eliminate Tigrayans as a people; a form of genocide. Access to Tigray has been blocked by the Ethiopian and Eritrean authorities, but CNN sent a team to report from Sudan.

A CNN team in Hamdayet, a sleepy Sudanese town on the Ethiopian border where thousands of refugees from Tigray have gathered in recent months, spoke with several women who described being raped as they fled fighting. 'He pushed me and said, "You Tigrayans have no history, you have no culture. I can do what I want to you and no one cares,"' one woman said of her attacker. She told CNN she is now pregnant. Many say they were raped by Amhara forces who told them they were intent on ethnically cleansing Tigray, a doctor working at the sprawling refugee camp in Hamdayet told CNN. 'The women that have been raped say that the things that they say to them when they were raping them is that they need to change their identity—to either Amharize them or at least leave their Tigrinya status ... and that they've come there to cleanse them ... to cleanse the blood line,' Dr. Tedros Tefera said. 'Practically this has been a genocide,' he added.'[51]

A similar finding was reported by CBS News[52] and by Channel 4 News, which broadcast a harrowing 15-minute-long report.[53] It is also possible that the aim was sterility: to make the women infertile or incapable of bearing children any longer.

While the most systematic rape has been inflicted on the Tigrayans, Tigrayan troops have also been involved in sexual abuse. Amnesty International said that 16 women from the town of Nefas Mewcha in the Amhara region were raped by fighters from the Tigray People's Liberation Front during the group's attack on the town in mid-August 2021.[54] 'The testimonies we heard from survivors describe despicable acts by TPLF fighters that amount to war crimes, and potentially crimes against humanity. They defy morality or any iota of humanity,' said Agnès Callamard, Amnesty International's secretary general.

This was not an isolated incidence. Workeye Zenebe, a 21-year-old, left her home near the eastern Amhara town of Kobo soon after it was captured by Tigrayan forces.[55] Without a weapon she was sent to the front line after just a month of rudimentary training. Workeye says she enlisted to avenge the rapes and killings she had seen in her village. Her fury knew no bounds. 'The TPLF is the worst thing,' she said. 'They must be eliminated from the earth.' Tigray's leadership has promised to investigate such allegations and to cooperate with any international investigation that is launched. This is welcome but unlikely to proceed while the war is under way. These are extremely serious accusations, and such abuses are the responsibility of the troops and the officers involved. However, the scale and frequency of these attacks appear dwarfed by the atrocities inflicted by Eritrean and Ethiopian forces, although it isn't clear that we will ever know for certain.

A commission of inquiry was established by the Ethiopian government's Human Rights Commission and the United Nations Commissioner for Human Rights.[56] Filsan Abdi, then federal Ethiopian minister of women, children and youth, defended the government, saying that it 'had a zero-tolerance policy towards any form of sexual violence'.[57] Filsan was told to create a task force that would investigate widespread claims of rape and recruitment of child soldiers, which she duly did. 'We brought back the most painful stories, and every side was implicated', she recalls. 'But when I wanted to release our findings, I was told that I was crossing a line. "You can't do that", is what an official very high up in Abiy's office called and told me. And I said, "You asked me to find the truth, not to do a propaganda operation. I am not trying to bring down the government—there is a huge rape crisis for God's sake. Child soldiers are being recruited by both sides. I have the evidence on my desk in front of me"'.[58] Filsan attempted to reflect this in the report but was blocked. When her subordinates at the ministry wouldn't release the full report, she tweeted that 'rape has taken place conclusively and without a doubt' in Tigray.[59]

The joint Ethiopian government and UN report was published in November 2021. At 156 pages long, it was substantial but seriously compromised.[60] The joint investigation team was unable to visit most of the key areas and were regarded with suspicion by the Tigrayans, who saw the presence of government-sanctioned investigators as likely to lead to a biased and inadequate exercise.[61] The findings of the joint investigation—which reported that all sides had committed atrocities—were not widely accepted. In September 2021, Filsan resigned from her ministry and subsequently left the country. In December 2021, speaking to the *Washington Post*, she said she had been instructed to revise the report to say that only TPLF-aligned fighters had committed crimes.[62]

A further attempt to get at the truth was initiated by the UN in December 2021. Plans were made for a fresh UN independent investigation team to collect and assess the evidence. It was to be led by the highly respected former International Criminal Court prosecutor Fatou Bensouda. Plans for the investigation were approved by the UN, despite objections from the Ethiopian government, who were supported by China and Russia.[63] The Ethiopians immediately set about undermining the new investigation, and it is not clear how it will progress. Lucy Kassa reported that the security forces in the Amhara region attempted to burn critical evidence in western Tigray.[64] Kassa said that three days after the funding for the UN's independent investigation was approved, a campaign to destroy evidence of atrocities began. She quoted eyewitnesses who saw the exhumation of the bodies of 200 Tigrayans buried in two mass graves. 'On 4 April, the Amhara militias and the Fano [militia] youth group exhumed the remains. They gathered wood, sprayed something we never saw before and burned the remains they collected. The remains crumbled and turned into ash.'[65]

A UN Human Rights Commission team finally arrived in Addis Ababa in July 2022, for a six-day visit.[66] There was, however, little indication that the Ethiopian authorities were prepared to allow them the unfettered access to the war zones which their mission required. Ethiopian national security adviser Redwan Hussein and justice minister Gedion Timothewos met diplomats from the UN and EU, US special envoys, and ambassadors of the US, France, Italy, Germany and the UK to spell out the conditions for the UN investigators.[67] These included insisting that the investigators would only be allowed a 'round trip' to Mekele—giving them no chance to visit some of the remoter locations in which abuses had been committed. At the end of their visit to Addis, the commissioners reiterated their request for unhindered access to the relevant areas for their investigation, without receiving any assurance that this would be forthcoming.[68]

At the same time the commission publicised an appeal for the submission of information.[69] This had been made months earlier, but without publicity, and set a deadline of 31 July 2022—giving Tigrayans (most of whom had no internet or phone access) almost no time to respond. This resulted in pleas for the deadline to be extended.

As the war drags on, all that can be said with certainty is that the suffering has been appalling and the human and material costs have been immense. Rebuilding the physical infrastructure will be a huge task, requiring international assistance. Healing the social and psychological damage may take even longer.

10

SURROUNDED AND STARVING

HOW AID HAS BEEN CUT, CROPS DESTROYED AND THE POPULATION FACES A FAMINE

Martin Plaut and Felicity Mulford

Introduction

Perhaps nothing underlined the plight of the people of Tigray more than the simple, dignified statement by the president of Mekele University on 28 March 2022. Dr Fana Hagos told Tigrayan television viewers that three members of her staff had died.[1] None had been paid by the university since June 2021; one had succumbed because medication was not available, the other two because of shortages of basic supplies. '[The staff are] facing hardship because of the [high] cost of living. They experience anxieties from the daily challenge of getting food,' she explained. Every death is, of course, a tragedy, but this was not news of the fate of the old or the very young, who are often the first to die. Nor was this news from a remote corner of rural Tigray. These were university employees—middle-class Tigrayans— in the capital, Mekele. Life, even for this relatively privileged section of society, had become so hard, food was so scarce, that they were simply unable to survive. It is a story being replicated across the length and breadth of Tigray.

The lives of Tigray's people deteriorated sharply as soon as the war began in November 2020. Phones were cut, electricity disrupted, and flights halted. As the assault on Mekele and other cities and villages escalated, this situation intensified. When the Ethiopian and Eritrean forces captured the regional capital at the end of November, a new administration was put in place. They were Tigrayans hand-picked by Addis Ababa to suit the latter's needs, but were regarded by many as 'Abiy's stooges'. Nonetheless, the blockade was largely ended; flights and communications resumed along with convoys of food and other essentials. This lasted until June 2021 when the Tigrayan forces drove their enemies from most of Tigray. The government that Addis had imposed fled, while the retreating Ethiopian forces looted banks and shops. Only western Tigray and some areas along the border of Eritrea remained in enemy hands. The Ethiopian and Eritrean blockade was immediately reimposed and has remained in force ever since. It was, as Mark Lowcock, then UN's most senior aid coordinator put it, a deliberate strategy to defeat the Tigrayans by starving them out.[2] 'We are hearing of starvation-related deaths already', he said in June 2020.

After Lowcock made that statement, the situation deteriorated further. By March 2021, it was already regarded by the UN as 'extremely serious'. A year later it was considered desperate. 'The food distribution in Tigray has reached an all-time low,' the UN said.[3] Food stocks had been all but depleted, with only 68,000 people receiving any rations at all. This was a tiny fraction of those in need. 'An estimated 870,000 people need to be reached every week for the 5.2 million people targeted to receive food baskets every six weeks', said the UN Office for the Coordination of Humanitarian Affairs. 'About 454,000 children are estimated to be malnourished in Tigray in 2022. Out of this more than 115,000 are severely malnourished and about 120,000 pregnant and lactating women (PLW) are malnourished'.[4]

Behind these cold, hard facts lie tragic stories of personal hardship, suffering and loss. It is a tale of communities sharing their last supplies, of eking out every meal; of families sitting up all night as their children cry; first loudly, then quietly, then not at all, as they slip away; of old people leaving home, because they cannot face being a burden on their families anymore; of proud people begging in the streets, and deaths in hamlets and villages. This is the face of starvation.

A history of hardship and famine

Tigrayans are no strangers to dire hardship. The region has a lengthy history of famines, which have repeatedly devastated the community.[5] The Tigray region of northern Ethiopia is situated in the highlands among rugged terrain. Set within the Tekeze Basin, the region is characterised by steep escarpments interspersed with flat plains. Miles of cropland are interrupted by the occasional bush, shrub or patch of grassland, while forests are few and far between.[6] Three-quarters of all Tigrayans live in rural communities, relying on subsistence farming to provide their main source of food.[7] This has meant that, historically, harvest failures can be enough to plunge rural families into famine. The stony soils contribute to the low crop yields,[8] and many households rely on seasonal work to ensure that they can pay for additional food when needed, or else turn to food provided by international aid agencies. The World Bank estimated that in the first two months of the war, when the Eritrean and Ethiopian armies were fighting deep inside Tigray, wage related economic activity dropped by 20 per cent.[9]

Tigray has faced repeated droughts.[10] Although rains have failed throughout Ethiopian history, these are becoming more pronounced as a result of climate change.[11] Every two to five years, moderate to severe droughts have affected Tigray, limiting water availability and increasing the vulnerability of livestock to diseases.[12] The droughts can be explained by a combination of climatic and human factors.[13] The highlands are badly overcrowded—an issue which has become worse as the population has grown in recent decades. Land has been divided and subdivided as families grow. It is far from abnormal to see farmers ploughing slopes so steep that in other countries they would only be used for non-arable purposes. Yet ox-drawn wooden ploughs are still to be seen, on the most inhospitable terrain.

With topsoil eroded, land becoming sandier and fewer rains, the ability of Tigrayans to grow crops has diminished.[14] In 1990, it was estimated that 1,900 million tons of soil were being eroded annually due to human activities, with 76 per cent of the highlands significantly eroded, and 4 per cent unable to support food production at all.

The pressures of climate change and population were intensified by a series of poor policies implemented by successive regimes. Over 100,000 people died in Tigray in the famine of 1958.[15] Emperor Haile Selassie attempted to conceal the famine that hit Wollo in 1972–3; this was an important factor in his overthrow by the military in 1974.[16] As Alex de Waal puts it: 'Emperor Haile Selassie considered that the peasants and nomads of Wollo were shaming His reputation by starving, and resolved to ignore them. Reports of famine were consistently ignored or denied.'[17] Under the military regime that replaced the emperor, Tigray and Amhara regions were devastated by a drought and accompanying famine, exacerbated by war against the TPLF. At least 400,000 people are estimated to have died between 1983 and 1985.[18] This was a famine played out on television screens around the world. But the international community tended to concern itself with climatic and developmental issues: the politics and conflict that underlay the devastating famine were downplayed or even ignored.[19]

During the nearly three decades during which the TPLF played a leading role in Ethiopian politics—mostly under Meles Zenawi—the region's agriculture and ecology were central to the country's development programme. Tigray received attention and investment from Addis Ababa, and the results were tangible. The Tigray regional government created its own strategy based on conservation and rehabilitation of the natural landscape, with the aim of improving food security.[20] Help was given to farmers through subsidies for fertilisers and micro-finance mechanisms.[21] By obtaining access to new technologies and sharing knowledge of farming practices that were suitable for the land, small farmers were able to improve their output. Another successful policy supporting local families was the food-for-work programme, which improved food security and asset procurement in rural areas of Tigray.[22] A study which investigated the effectiveness of these programmes indicated an 8.6 per cent increase in food self-sufficiency in Tigray between 2000 and 2008.[23] According to the UN's Integrated Food

Security Phase Classification (IPC), an internationally recognised measure for the level of food security in specific geographic areas, prior to the conflict of 2020–2 Tigray was deemed food secure (IPC Phase 1).[24]

The impact of the war

Once the war began, however, the deterioration in the lives of Tigrayans was rapid and dramatic. By January 2021 aid workers were beginning to use the word 'famine' to describe their view of what was happening on the ground in north-west Tigray. Leaked minutes from a Tigray Emergency Coordination Centre meeting noted: 'People are dying because of starvation. In Adwa people are dying while they are sleeping.'[25] The number of people already in need of food aid in January ranged from 2.2[26] to 4 million.[27] In the north-western, central and eastern *weredas* of Tigray, up to 50 per cent of the inhabitants were already estimated to be in desperate need of humanitarian assistance.[28] In Adigrat, 'everybody is asking for food', said the Médecins Sans Frontières' emergency programme coordinator in an interview in January. 'Every time we reach a new area, we find food, water, health services depleted, and a lot of fear among the population.'[29]

In a joint statement in February, three Tigrayan opposition parties, the Tigray Independence Party, Salsay Weyane Tigray, and National Congress of Great Tigray, said that without immediate food aid and medical supplies to the region, a 'looming humanitarian disaster of biblical proportion' would become a 'gruesome reality in Tigray'.[30] However, restrictions on access implemented by the federal government greatly impeded the work of relief agencies, including the UN. The limited number of agencies which were allowed to operate in the region were met with hostility, and some became the target of attacks. The UN was repeatedly warned of the seriousness of the situation. In April 2021 approximately 6 million people were affected by the conflict, in every part of Tigray.[31] In a written statement on 15 April, Linda Thomas-Greenfield, the US ambassador to the UN, estimated that as many as 5.2 million people were food insecure and required assistance.[32]

In a closed-door meeting of the UN Security Council in April 2021, Mark Lowcock reiterated earlier claims that people were already starving to death.[33] 'We received the first report this week of four internally displaced people dying from hunger. I then received a report just this morning of 150 people dying from hunger in Ofla woreda—just south of Mekelle,' Lowcock told council members. 'It is a sign of what lies ahead if more action is not taken. Starvation as a weapon of war is a violation [of war conventions].'

Many conflict-affected communities have been left without food supplies, seeds for the next harvest, livestock or safe housing. They have lost their savings and supplementary incomes. When information does seep out from behind the communication blackout, it indicates that the conditions on the ground in Tigray are far worse than predicted. This situation was not the result of the fighting or of a natural disaster: it was a deliberate policy by the conquerors to strip the land bare, so as to deprive Tigrayan forces of sources of food.

Hunger denied, aid halted

Abiy Ahmed continued to reject reports of the deprivation the people of Tigray were enduring. As he went to cast his vote in the Ethiopian election on 21 June 2021, he told the BBC: 'There is no hunger in Tigray. There is a problem in Tigray and the government is fixing it.'[34] Few in the UN or the humanitarian community agreed. There is even concern that the current situation could be like the famine of 1983–5.[35] This prediction is based on two related problems.

First, the population of Tigray can no longer escape to safety in Sudan. Nor can the trucks that brought in so much food and medication from Sudan in the 1984–5 famine make their way into Tigray. This is because a vast slice of land that linked Tigray and Sudan was captured by the Ethiopian and Eritrean governments, supported by Amhara special forces, in one of the first offensives of the war. The aim was clear: to cut possible supply routes to Sudan, as well as meet the grievances of the Amhara community who claimed that western Tigray was part of their ancestral lands.[36] The attack on Humera (where the borders of Sudan, Ethiopia and Eritrea meet) began on 9 November.[37] Tigrayan forces were forced northwards and eastwards, only narrowly escaping encirclement and capture. There then followed the expulsion of Tigrayan civilians. By April 2021 the International Organization for Migration (IOM) reported that 'there are some 1,000,052 internally displaced persons (IDPs) in Tigray region'.[38] The largest number fled to the north-western Tigrayan town of Shire where, according to the IOM, '445,309 IDPs are residing in overcrowded collective shelters, including schools, within the host community and in open spaces. A majority of them are from Western and Northwestern Tigray'. By May 2021 Tigrayan websites were publishing documents that apparently showed Amhara farmers were being offered Tigrayan farms to settle on.[39]

While most Tigrayans fled deeper into their own region, some did manage to cross into Sudan. By mid-June 2021 the UN High Commissioner for Refugees (UNHCR) recorded that 63,212 had made this journey.[40] The numbers would have been higher had Ethiopian and Eritrean forces not been stationed to turn them back at the border.[41] The BBC carried this report from refugees in Sudan: 'The number of refugees fleeing the northern Tigray region of Ethiopia—where federal and regional forces are engaged in fighting—has reduced drastically after soldiers were deployed to the border with Sudan.' The BBC first spotted the soldiers at the Hamdayet border crossing point, and heard testimonies from refugees who said their relatives were being blocked from leaving Ethiopia.

> 'I arrived yesterday morning and I wanted to go back home to bring my family here', said one man who did not want to be identified. Speaking on the banks of River Sittet in Hamdayet, he told the BBC he had been unable to return to Tigray to get his relatives because 'there are soldiers on the border and those who had gone before me were asked not to return'.[42]

Denied access to Sudan, Tigrayans have been at the mercy of the Ethiopians and Eritreans, who control access to their region. As indicated earlier, there have been regular interruptions and disruptions to the aid flows, with large areas beyond the reach of humanitarian organisations.

The second reason why a humanitarian catastrophe is likely has to do with the ports of Eritrea, Assab and Massawa, which are the obvious routes to transport the vast quantities of grain and other essential supplies into government-held areas, just as they were in 1983–5. Then the main problem was a lack of transport in the initial phases, but this was later overcome.[43] Today the ports and roads of Eritrea are closed to the humanitarian agencies.[44] This could change, but at present there is no alternative to bringing in the aid via Djibouti, which may struggle to cope with the quantities required. Even if this can be done, the assistance will have to be delivered to Tigray from the east and the south, along roads which were (in June 2021) beset by fighting. As the evidence of the closure of the road into Tigray in 1985 suggests, President Isaias would feel no compunction about putting the lives of tens of thousands of Tigrayans at risk. Interviewed in June 2021, Paulos Tesfagiorgis, who was the head of the Eritrean Relief Association in Sudan during the 1984–5 famine, believes it is essential to find a way of accessing the Eritrean ports. He remarked: 'The needs are so huge … There is really no alternative. The international community must put pressure on Isaias to allow the use of the ports.'[45] At the time of writing in 2022, that prospect is further away than ever.

The only alternative would be to use air drops of food, as Britain's Royal Air Force did in 1985. The programme, authorised by Margaret Thatcher and named Operation Bushel, was useful, supplying 32,000 tonnes of aid.[46] But in the overall context of the humanitarian effort, it was little more than a drop in the ocean. Since there is little likelihood of authorising such an operation, it might be regarded as an act of aggression. Undertaking a similar programme in the current crisis would be helpful (particularly in providing medicines to remote locations), but it is not a realistic alternative to a full-scale land and sea aid operation.

Tightening the blockade

Following the retreat of the Tigrayan forces from the Amhara and Afar regions at the end of 2021, the blockade of Tigray intensified. This has occurred despite deliberately caused starvation being a crime in Ethiopian (and international) law. The Ethiopian Penal Code (2004), notably Article 270(i), 'War Crimes Against the

Civilian Population', declares enforced starvation a crime. It makes illegal 'the confiscation, destruction, removal, rendering useless or appropriation of property such as foodstuffs, agricultural areas for the production of foodstuffs, crops, livestock, drinking water installations and supplies and irrigation works, health centres, schools'.[47] Yet the joint investigation undertaken by the UN and the Ethiopian Human Rights Commission (EHRC) in 2021 made no reference to starvation crimes or the war crime of starvation. Interestingly, neither the UN's Michelle Bachelet nor Daniel Bekele, head of the EHRC, referred to starvation crimes or mentioned the inclusion of starvation crimes within the remit of the investigation during their addresses to the Human Rights Council. For those concerned with the deliberate destruction of food systems within Tigray, and accountability for the war crime of starvation, this is a major issue. Specialist commentators concluded that the report was 'neither impartial nor independent'.[48]

By September 2021 the restrictions on aid convoys were already severe. The UN aid coordination office said that since July less than a tenth of the trucks required to feed Tigray had managed to get through.[49] Bad as this was, once the Tigrayan troops retreated into Tigray in December 2021 even this flow diminished further and then all but stopped.[50] Flights by the UN's airline UNHAS were suspended in September 2021, following Ethiopia air raids.[51] These flights, despite having only small payloads, were important in rotating UN staff and bringing in vital medical supplies. They were resumed in 2022, but by April had only managed to bring in some 360 tonnes—roughly the equivalent of nine truckloads.[52] But with no fuel being allowed into Tigray, many UN trucks were stranded inside the region, only able to leave much later when fuel was delivered.

On top of this, the UN has faced the expulsion of its staff. In an interview with Reuters on 28 September, the UN's senior aid coordinator, Martin Griffiths, warned of impending famine should aid not get through the blockade, stating that Tigray would become a 'stain on our conscience'.[53] When asked what was needed, he replied, 'Get those trucks moving'. He continued, 'This is man-made, this can be remedied by the act of government'.[54] His words were clear: people were starving to death under the *de facto* government blockade of food, medical supplies and fuel.[55] In a similar interview with the Associated Press, Griffiths also mentioned the unacceptable allegations made against humanitarians, calling for the Ethiopian government to provide evidence of misconduct so that a proper investigation by the UN could occur. However, he noted that 'so far as I'm aware, we haven't had such cases put to us'.[56]

The Ethiopian government rejected his claims, stating that there was no blockade, and instead repeated its stance that the lack of trucks returning from Tigray was holding up the aid effort.[57] On 30 September Ethiopia retaliated. Seven high-level UN humanitarian officials were given 72 hours to leave the country.[58] Among those expelled were officials leading the humanitarian response and documenting ongoing human rights abuses. The Ethiopian government accused them of 'meddling in the internal affairs of the country' and claimed to have warned the UN previously of their misdemeanours.[59] These included diverting aid to the TPLF, violating security arrangements, and 'disinformation'.[60] It would seem that the expulsions were a reaction to Griffiths's remarks just days earlier.[61] This led to an emergency UN Security Council meeting on 1 October, but there was little visible response from Security Council members.

A 'truce'

The war and the accompanying hardship continued throughout 2021 and into 2022. In late November 2021 the Tigrayans and their allies halted their advance towards Addis Ababa and pulled their forces back to Tigray itself. There followed a period of intermittent fighting along the borders of the region, but little more. Although there were clashes in the Afar region, there were no major offensives in early 2022. At the same time, the blockade of Tigray by its enemies continued, with devastating consequences. This was acknowledged by General Tsadkan in a frank speech to the Tigrayan people. 'We all know that our people are dying in large numbers due to disease and starvation. A siege is tough. The people of Tigray have perhaps faced what it has never faced before in its history. We have to alleviate and solve this,' General Tsadkan admitted.[62]

With the situation deteriorating daily, on 24 March there was, apparently, some good news. The Ethiopian government announced a 'humanitarian truce'.[63] It said the ceasefire could 'pave the way for the resolution of the conflict in northern Ethiopia without further bloodshed', and analysts in the country expressed hopes that if it held, the deal might lead to a diplomatic resolution. The Tigray government immediately welcomed the announcement, saying that it wanted to see actions, and not just words.[64] 'We call on the Ethiopian authorities to go beyond empty promises and take concrete steps to facilitate unfettered humanitarian access to Tigray.' It would take almost two weeks for the first convoy to enter the region, through Afar. It was the first for more than a hundred days, bringing what the World Food Programme described as 500 tonnes of food and nutrition supplies 'for communities on the edge of starvation'.[65]

The aid was welcome but was nowhere near meeting the needs of the more than 2 million people in severe need of humanitarian aid, including at least 400,000 people facing famine conditions.[66] By May 2022 the World Food Programme said it was delivering food supplies to 461,542 people: less than a quarter of those in the most severe need, and far less than what was required.[67]

Tigrayans were sceptical of the very notion that a truce was in place. Meaza Gebremedhin, a member of the Tigrayan diaspora, speaking to Al Jazeera on 25 May 2022, said that the truce was meant to allow unrestricted aid deliveries, but less than 14 per cent of what was needed had been delivered.[68] In her view the Ethiopian government was continuing to use starvation as a tactic of war. No aid corridor had been established and Tigrayans were dying of hunger. 'There is no optimism,' she said. 'The international community prematurely celebrated the declaration of a humanitarian truce, but it has not been translated into meaningful action.'

By April 2022 the Famine Early Warning System issued this assessment: 'At a minimum, Emergency (IPC Phase 4) outcomes exist in Tigray, with households in Catastrophe (IPC Phase 5). It is possible outcomes are worse, but given access constraints, information is insufficient to confirm or deny this.'[69] In blunter language, famine had arrived.

INTERLUDE

FEVEN'S STORY[1]—A CLINICAL PSYCHOLOGIST IN MEKELE

Feven's walk from home to her workplace takes about an hour. It's not an easy walk—and not simply because Feven has had little to eat. Much harder is the suffering she witnesses of the people she passes on the way.

'Some women sit in the street, with almost nothing to wear. They have lost everything—they can just cover the essentials,' Feven explains. 'And there are the teenagers. Many are now hobbling with sticks—they have been wounded in the fighting. There are so many beggars, some just children of three or four years old. Always new faces, begging for food or money. They ask for a few cents, but what can we give them?

'I look at the faces of people on the streets. No one is laughing any more. Not a smile. Just anxiety and hunger. No emotion. It's exceptional when you see anyone laugh.'

Mekele, once a vibrant, noisy city, has been transformed. 'Now only the odd bread shop is open,' Feven says. 'There's no music or singing. No one in the cafés. Only a few taxis, which are exorbitantly expensive, and the occasional government car.'

Feven is a clinical psychologist at Tigray's main medical institution, the Ayder Referral Hospital. Although the hospital has been damaged in the fighting, it is still functioning. But the situation is critical: it has no food for its 240 patients; it has had no drugs for diabetes since June 2021; since early 2022 it has had almost no medicines at all.[2]

Before she leaves home, Feven has breakfast with her family. It is just *kicha*—a local flat bread, eaten with cooked onion and spices. 'My father is diabetic. He needs proper nutrition, but we don't have things like eggs. I can't get them.'

Many of the patients Feven sees are survivors of torture and sexual violence. Others have been traumatised by the violence they and their communities have endured.

'One 19-year-old woman came to see me. Her face was covered, something that's not in our culture. I told her she must fill in a form and get an appointment. She said: "I can't. You must see me now!"'

Feven agreed to make an exception. The young woman didn't want her name to be recorded anywhere in the hospital system. Her mother was ill and the teenager was now the only economic support for the family. In desperation, she had turned to prostitution.

'Now she has money to pay for her mother's medication. But she feels terrible. She hates her own body. In our society it is so hard even to lose your virginity—but to turn to prostitution! I felt her pain. I thought she would be my only patient with this problem, but two weeks later I had another young woman, a teenager, who was also doing this business. Many girls are now on the streets at night to bring in cash for their families.'

Feven was asked to visit a nearby town. The clinic there had no psychologist on their staff. In a day, she saw ten or more patients.

'Some told me that their close family members had committed suicide. They could not face their children or parents suffering for lack of food.' Of the people she saw, two had close family members who had taken their lives rather than witness their family starve.

'Many are strong Christians. "If it was not forbidden, I would kill myself," people told me. People are suffering so much.' Feven's voice was testimony to her personal anguish. 'As a clinical psychologist I should have a therapist I can turn to, but there is no one. I use various techniques to support myself and I just keep going.

'My parents are here and so are my aunts. I have friends of the same age. At night, I speak to them. I share my emotions. I cry if I need to. Connecting socially is very important.'

So, why do Tigrayans keep fighting?

Feven finds the question almost incomprehensible. 'The people of Tigray didn't fight because the government asked them to. I've been to rural areas and to urban areas. Clients tell me they went to fight because their child would lose everything if they didn't fight. There's no alternative.

'People have joined the Tigray Defence Forces not because they support the TPLF, but because of the brutal sexual atrocities they have suffered. People were raped in front of their families. Many never went home after they were raped. Many girls and women just left home and joined the TDF. They signed up directly after they were raped. Men saw their families tortured, killed and raped in front of them. If they survived, they just joined up.

'I have had 331 patients who were sexually abused. What I am telling you is from their experience. These are not just stories. They want to kill the Tigrayan people and destroy us as a people—to humiliate a whole community. We are losing so many people.'

11

DIPLOMACY AND PROTEST

Martin Plaut

Introduction

Even before the fighting in Tigray began, diplomatic efforts were made to try to head off the conflict. Once it started, there were attempts to contain and halt it. The war would rapidly involve all the facets of the international community: from the African Union (AU), based in Addis Ababa, to the European Union (EU) in Brussels and the United Nations (UN) in New York. There were also interventions from individual states. The scale of this involvement was justified, for the war put the whole of the Horn of Africa in jeopardy.

The intensity of the conflict (which appeared to threaten Addis Ababa itself in November 2021), combined with the growing famine, spurred these efforts on. This should have been a problem that the AU was ideally placed to tackle, for it happened on its doorstep. The case for African intervention also chimed with the oft-repeated slogan 'African solutions to African problems'.[1] Yet the AU floundered and—precisely because it was so close to the war—struggled to find an adequate response. The UN did little better, despite secretary general Antonio Guterres having 'offered his good offices' to end the conflict within days of the first clashes.[2] The West, led by the

US and the EU, has offered aid, sent delegations, appointed special representatives, cajoled, threatened and even imposed sanctions.

In response to the international pressure Abiy Ahmed and Isaias Afwerki sought alternative allies. The UAE has been a solid supporter of the axis forged by Ethiopia, Eritrea and Somalia in 2018, which planned this conflict. The Arabs have underpinned their support with substantial financial flows. As the war has unfolded, so too has the supply of armaments and munitions.[3] Ties with Turkey, Iran, China and Russia have been strengthened as the Ethiopian leader reached out to friends who would provide weaponry without asking awkward questions about human rights. China and Russia have also used the threat of their veto at the UN Security Council to prevent the world body from holding the actors in the Tigray conflict to account.

These events have taken place at a time when international attention lay elsewhere. The Tigray war has therefore had only limited attention from foreign ministries. Yet the war has had appalling consequences, well beyond the battlefield. The need for action was never more pressing, yet there was little sign of effective pressure or persuasion being applied to end the crisis. Even the most egregious of crimes have resulted in only muted responses. As Human Rights Watch observed on 8 December 2021:

> A full year has passed since Eritrean government forces massacred Tigrayan civilians in Ethiopia's historical town of Axum. But survivors of the massacre and of other atrocities in Tigray are still no closer to accessing justice and redress—an accountability shortfall that is fuelling further abuses as conflict spreads ... Concrete measures to pave the way for accountability—such as the establishment of a robust international investigative mechanism—are key. Yet international bodies still seem unwilling to take concrete measures to press warring parties to prevent further atrocities. The Security Councils of both the UN and the African Union—bodies mandated to ensure peace and security—have remained largely paralysed. Each body has made only one public statement condemning abuses and the UN Security Council has not formally included Ethiopia on its agenda.[4]

This has been a sorry saga—a display of how divided the international community can appear to be in the face of intransigence, no matter how urgent the crisis.

The African Union

Despite the wider Horn being threatened by the Tigray war, the interventions from the region and from Africa in general have been remarkably muted. The exceptions to this are Eritrea and Somalia, participants in the conflict. The AU's silence on the atrocities committed against Tigray was sharply criticised by Mulugeta Gebrehiwot, a former director of the Institute for Peace and Security Studies at Addis Ababa University.

> When Tigraians at the height of the war were being brutally murdered, raped, and cleansed from their places of origin by joint forces of the Ethiopian National Defense Forces, the Eritrean Defense Forces, and assorted special police forces and militias, the Chairperson of the Commission, Moussa Faki, was heard congratulating the Ethiopian government for its 'bold steps to preserve the unity, stability and respect for the constitutional order of the country; which is legitimate for all states ... The Chairperson of the AU and by extension his envoy are rightfully considered partial to its belligerent by the Tigraian coalition fighting for the survival of its people.'[5]

It should not be forgotten that South African president Cyril Ramaphosa, as chair of the AU, intervened swiftly in an attempt to find a negotiated solution when the war erupted in November 2021. He established a three-person mediation team consisting of former African presidents, with the support of Ethiopian president Sahle-Work Zewde. She was in South Africa in 'her capacity as Special Envoy of Prime Minister Abiy Ahmed'. A statement was released at the end of her visit.

> President Cyril Ramaphosa has appointed three African 'distinguished Statespersons': Joaquim Chissano, former President of the Republic of Mozambique; Ellen Johnson-Sirleaf,

former President of the Republic of Liberia; Kgalema Motlanthe, former President of the Republic of South Africa—as Special Envoys of the African Union to help to mediate between 'the parties to conflict' in Ethiopia, a statement released by the office of the AU Chairperson said.[6]

Teferi Melesse Desta, the Ethiopian ambassador to Britain, confirmed on the BBC that his country had accepted the appointment of the envoys to mediate in the crisis.[7] 'The government of Ethiopia has accepted the initiative of the African Union chairperson, the President of South Africa, to appoint three special envoys to find a solution to the current situation in Ethiopia,' said Teferi.

Unfortunately, it immediately became apparent that neither the president nor the ambassador spoke on behalf of their government. The peace initiative was rejected by Abiy.[8] The prime minister's office described news that the three envoys would travel to Ethiopia to mediate in the conflict as 'fake'. So ended the first, possibly the best, opportunity to nip the war in the bud. All three former presidents did indeed travel to Addis and were received by Abiy, but it was no more than a courtesy call. For the prime minister this was an internal conflict that would be settled within the country: it did not require outside intervention. This was a position that was never likely to hold since the conflict was, from the beginning, a regional war, with Somali and Eritrean troops involved in the fighting.[9]

Following this rejection, the AU searched for alternative mediators who would be acceptable to all concerned. In August 2021 the organisation turned to former Nigerian president Olusegun Obasanjo.[10] It was an unfortunate choice. Obasanjo had observed the 2021 Ethiopian election, held on 5 June. Most international observers had refused to participate, since the voting was manifestly unfair. A month earlier the EU's senior diplomat, Josep Borrell, announced that it would also not send monitors to the election. 'The EU regrets the refusal of the fulfilment of standard requirements for the deployment of any Electoral Observation Mission, namely the independence of the Mission and the import of mission communication systems,' Borrell said.[11] The decision was a blow to the credibility of the election, which nonetheless went ahead. The result was a 'landslide' for the prime minister, who won 410 of 436 contested seats.[12]

The war prevented the election from being held in Tigray. Several important parties (particularly from Oromia) withdrew from the vote, after their candidates were arrested and their offices vandalised. Despite this, the AU's election observer mission endorsed the election. 'Overall the election and election day processes were conducted in an orderly, peaceful and credible manner,' Obasanjo told a press conference in Addis on 23 June 2021.[13] The former Nigerian president's willingness to ignore the evidence of electoral fraud did nothing to persuade Tigrayans that he was an impartial arbiter who could work with all the warring parties. Former South African president Thabo Mbeki pointed out that Obasanjo's attempts to mediate had been a signal failure, and that the AU's key committees had failed to address the problem.[14] Despite the criticism, Obasanjo persevered with his mission, while the AU and Western powers looked to include other mediators, including the Kenyans.

Kenya steps in

As a neighbour, Kenya would inevitably have an interest in the Tigray war. Kenya was engaged from the start of the conflict, acting as host to international meetings. Nairobi also serves as an important base for the international media, since their work in Ethiopia has been so constrained by the government. Kenya has also played a significant role at the UN, where it became a non-permanent member of the Security Council in January 2021, representing the African bloc. In July 2021 Kenya's permanent representative to the UN, Martin Kimani, urged all parties to the Tigray war to lay down their arms.[15] On 26 August 2021 Kimani told the Security Council that what was needed was an 'Ethiopian-owned process to mediate the deep divides'.[16] While recommending that the Council urge Eritrea to withdraw its forces, he also called on Ethiopia's government to acknowledge the existence of legitimate grievances, while appealing to Tigray's armed forces to withdraw from neighbouring regions, and stressing the need for unfettered humanitarian access before famine returned.

The chief of the Kenyan Defence Forces explained the significance of the war for his country.[17] 'Ethiopia—with its population of more than one hundred million—is hugely strategic for us,' said General Robert Kibochi. As the Tigrayans and their Oromo allies advanced towards Addis Ababa in November 2021, Kenya recalled all its police to cope with any possible influx of weapons and refugees should the conflict spill over into northern Kenya.[18]

The Kenyan role was underlined by the meeting President Biden held with Kenya's president Uhuru Kenyatta in October 2021.[19] It was the American leader's first face-to-face meeting with an African leader. There followed contacts with US secretary of state Antony Blinken, who discussed the urgent need for a ceasefire with the Kenyan presidency, to allow negotiations to take place.[20] According to the State Department, 'President Kenyatta and Secretary Blinken agreed on the importance of unhindered humanitarian access for all communities affected by the conflict and reiterated their support for an inclusive political dialogue.'

Between the Kenyans, the AU and Obasanjo progress was gradually made. In November 2021 photographs appeared on social media of the former Nigerian president holding talks with Tigray's president Debretsion.[21] Obasanjo told the BBC that he had been received by the Tigrayan leader with respect, while insisting that all negotiations had to take place through his office.[22] The latter remark was an apparent reference to suggestions that others might take over the mediation. At the end of May 2022 Obasanjo again travelled to Mekele to consult with Debretsion. Again, no statement was made, but a photograph appeared of the two men in conversation.[23] Then, on 13 June, the Tigrayans published an open letter to the AU and the wider international community, outlining how they hoped negotiations would proceed.[24] Signed by Debretsion, the letter declined suggestions that Tanzania might host the talks. Instead, Debretsion said Tigray held firm to 'the agreement among the Parties to meet in Nairobi for negotiations hosted and facilitated by the President of Kenya'. Tigrayan scepticism about Obasanjo was also reiterated. Debretsion said the Nigerian had only been received in Mekele 'on the basis of the principle of African hospitality, respect for an elder, and respect for the institution of the African Union'.

The statement included this acid comment: 'However, the proximity of the High Representative to the Prime Minister of Ethiopia has not gone unnoticed by our people.' Clearly the Tigrayan government was not willing to forget or forgive Obasanjo's previous stand.

In June 2022 Debretsion addressed the Tigrayan public on television to explain the 'talks about talks'.[25] He acknowledged criticism that Tigrayans had been kept in the dark about what had been going on. The Tigray president made clear that negotiations had not yet begun: rather, the discussions were about a formal cessation of hostilities. At the same time, he laid out his administration's preconditions—the five 'red lines' that he said it was not prepared to cross. Debretsion called for a referendum on the future of Tigray, although he accepted that this did not have to take place immediately. Secondly, he insisted that the borders of Tigray had to remain where they had been prior to the conflict, including those of western Tigray—as recognised by the Ethiopian constitution. Thirdly, Debretsion insisted that Tigray would maintain its army since his people could not rely on the Ethiopian National Defence Force for their security. 'The army that massacred us cannot be our protector,' he argued. Fourthly, Eritreans had to withdraw from all of Tigray, including areas like Irob and Adiyabo, where the Eritrean government had begun issuing Eritrean identity documents. Finally, he called for an international investigation into the genocide that had been inflicted upon his people. Debretsion insisted that negotiations had to be transparent and public rather than held behind closed doors.

The Ethiopian government responded in mid-June 2022 by establishing a committee to oversee the planned negotiations. 'Negotiation needs a lot of work. A committee has been established and it will study how we will conduct talks,' Abiy told the Ethiopian parliament.[26] He said deputy prime minister Demeke Mekonnen would lead the committee, which was given ten to fifteen days to work on the finer details of what would be negotiated.

Somalia

The dramatic end to years of bitterness between Eritrea and Ethiopia obscured the fact that there was a third party in this relationship:

Somalia. In July 2018—in the same month as Abiy visited Asmara to seal the peace deal between Eritrea and Ethiopia—there was a three-day visit to Asmara by Somali president Mohamed Abdullahi Farmaajo, the first by a Somali leader for 15 years.[27] Prior to Eritrea's independence in 1993 Isaias and other Eritrean leaders had close links with Somalia and used Somali passports to travel on. The ties between the two countries were therefore considerable. There were further bilateral visits in August 2018 and April 2019.[28] This culminated in a summit in Asmara between the leaders of Eritrea, Ethiopia and Somalia on 27 January 2020, which resulted in a trilateral agreement on regional security.[29]

The immediate impact of the Tigray war on Somalia was the withdrawal of some of the Ethiopian troops who had been fighting al-Shabaab, to bolster the Ethiopian army's strength in Tigray. Then in January 2021 reports appeared that young Somalis had been sent to Eritrea to be trained and to fight in Tigray.[30] Their fate and the Somali role in the Tigray war have been explored in this book. Angry Somali parents repeatedly demonstrated in Mogadishu, demanding that their government disclose the whereabouts of their sons who were taken to Eritrea.[31]

On 15 May 2022 Somalia's long-delayed presidential elections saw Farmaajo lose power to Hassan Sheikh Mohamud.[32] At his swearing-in, President Mohamud promised to work with regional states and Somalia's international partners.[33] On 9 July the president travelled to Eritrea for a four-day working visit, apparently seeking the return of over 5,000 Somali soldiers. President Isaias was said to be demanding $50 million to allow their release. Mohamud reviewed the troops at the Sawa training base with Isaias.[34] The two men signed an agreement pledging cooperation in a range of fields, including security, but there was no mention of the Somali troops.[35] All President Mohamud could do was to reassure the worried parents that their sons would be home 'soon'.[36]

There were uncorroborated rumours that the Qataris had offered US$300 million three years previously for the training of the Somali conscripts, but then reneged on the deal. This is said to explain why Isaias effectively took the young men hostage. The UAE has reportedly attempted to resolve the issue, but its relations with Eritrea have deteriorated in recent months. Resolving the issue is critical for President Mohamud, who has a string of urgent issues to confront: one of the most serious droughts for years and an upsurge in support for the Islamist rebels of al-Shabaab. At least he has President Biden's renewed commitment to Somali security: Washington returned 500 of the American troops that President Trump had withdrawn.[37]

The United States

The US and Eritrea have had poor relations for over a decade, but Ethiopia is a different matter. US friendship and engagement with Ethiopia have been long-standing and enduring, despite Ethiopia turning to the Soviet Union under the Derg (1974–87). Ethiopia is seen as a loyal US ally and an anchor in the volatile Horn. It has been a partner in the fight against militant Islamists—who in 1998 attacked US embassies in Kenya and Tanzania, killing 240 people, including 12 Americans, and leaving more than 4,500 people wounded.[38] The bombings impressed on the Americans the need to fight militants across the world, years before the 11 September 2001 attacks on New York and Washington. Ethiopia is also proximate to important US markets and security interests in the Middle East, as well as the vital shipping channels of the Red Sea and Suez Canal.

However, in recent years clouds have appeared over this relationship. Increasingly, Ethiopia has become a theatre of Chinese economic and diplomatic competition. In addition, the US took the side of Egypt in its dispute with Ethiopia over the Grand Ethiopian Renaissance Dam on the Nile. On 23 October 2020—on the eve of the Tigray war—President Trump tweeted that Egypt might, and probably should, 'blow up' the dam. Ethiopia responded with understandable outrage.[39] The American response to the war in Tigray can be viewed from these perspectives. Washington has attempted to navigate a course between its own national needs and obtaining a secure and humane outcome in Tigray.

The US Congress was the first to publicly react to the outbreak of fighting. The day after the start of the war, Republican congressman Michael McCaul, the senior minority member of the Foreign Affairs

Committee of the House of Representatives, voiced his concerns.[40] The following day, six Democratic congressmen expressed theirs.[41] Bicameral and bipartisan statements gathered force, outraged at Ethiopian and Eritrean behaviour as the weeks wore on and as atrocity reports mounted. Such cross-party support for an issue was a rarity in America's badly divided political life.

What motivated the members of Congress? Initially there were no broad-based, grass-roots campaigns among American voters. Rather, they appeared to be responding to calls for action from their constituents of Tigrayan and Eritrean descent. Legislators felt duty-bound to serve constituent interests and their own re-election prospects. Politicians were also reflecting the post-war American view of the nation's role (however unevenly realised) in defending international human rights, reinforced by concerns that the Horn might fracture, thereby benefiting Islamist groups. A powerful statement was delivered by former senior American diplomats, a day after the conflict began.[42] Three former US assistant secretaries of state (Johnnie Carson, Chester Crocker, Jeffrey Feltman) joined former ambassadors in warning of the possible consequences:

> The fragmentation of Ethiopia would be the largest state collapse in modern history. Ethiopia is five times the size of pre-war Syria by population, and its breakdown would lead to mass interethnic and interreligious conflict; a dangerous vulnerability to exploitation by extremists; an acceleration of illicit trafficking, including of arms; and a humanitarian and security crisis at the crossroads of Africa and the Middle East on a scale that would overshadow any existing conflict in the region, including Yemen.

Congress was ahead of the Trump administration in sensing the gravity of the Tigray conflict. A senior official in the administration confirmed that the initial clashes took the US by surprise but went on to say that the war immediately became the top African priority for the State Department and the National Security Council.[43] It is hard to believe that the State Department had missed so many warnings, months before the war began. Professor Kjetil Tronvoll wrote on 25 October 2020—ten days before the fighting—that, having studied the Horn for 30 years, he had seldom seen 'a clearer case of a coming violent conflict'.[44] The following day, this author wrote an article entitled 'War Clouds Gather in Northern Ethiopia: Tensions between Tigray, Eritrea and Addis Ababa',[45] making a similar prediction. On 31 October 2020 the respected Horn analyst Rashid Abdi tweeted: 'Afewerki & Abiy actively considering military action to settle dispute with Tigrai. They are deaf to calls for dialogue, de-escalation. A war is coming. Eritrean troops making provocative manoeuvers on border. International community indulged Abiy. It bears full responsibility'.

Was the Trump administration really caught unawares? In an in-depth article based on interviews with 60 senior diplomats, military personnel and government ministers from the US, Europe and the Middle East, Harry Verhoeven and Michael Woldemariam concluded that American claims that they had no forewarning of the conflict, and only became aware of the massive involvement of Eritrean troops some weeks after the war broke out, are 'simply not credible' and were 'flatly contradicted' by their interviewees.[46] The authors quote a senior British diplomat whom they interviewed. 'Look: we could see the build-up of tensions and armaments for months. All the rhetoric, the militia parading, the muscle flexing in the Amhara region … Some high-ranking US officials clearly thought: sometimes you gotta do a clean-up job. Better have the Prime Minister do it quickly.'[47]

Within 24 hours of the onset of the fighting, the US spoke to Demeke Mekonnen, Ethiopia's deputy prime minister.[48] Washington attempted to find a way to halt the war, while stressing that it did not see an equivalence between two sides—since the government represented a sovereign nation while the Tigrayans were 'a region in rebellion'. It was probably no coincidence that the outbreak of the war came at the time of the US presidential election. President Trump was fully engaged in attempting to claim that it was a fraudulently conducted and 'stolen' election. Events in the Horn of Africa were of little concern to many of the most senior staff, including Trump's secretary of state Mike Pompeo. However, on 4 November, using Twitter, Pompeo condemned the Tigrayan attack on Ethiopia's Northern Command base.[49] On 15 November, the assistant secretary of state for African affairs also condemned Tigray's missile attack on Asmara.[50] On 17 November, Pompeo again blamed

315

the TPLF, and praised Eritrea for its forbearance in not retaliating against the Tigrayans.[51] For the Trump administration the Tigrayans were clearly the villains in the fray.

Blaming the Tigrayans for initiating the war was suspect at best: the people of Tigray were enduring the most intense suffering, with refugees flooding into Sudan.[52] On 13 November the UN High Commissioner for Human Rights warned of the danger of chaos, heavy casualties, mass displacement and war crimes.[53] A group of 17 senators wrote to Pompeo, expressing fears of a humanitarian catastrophe and urging him to speak directly to Ethiopian prime minister Abiy, to push for an immediate ceasefire and respect for international law.[54] On the same day, President-elect Biden's incoming secretary of state Antony Blinken tweeted about the conflict.[55] 'Deeply concerned about the humanitarian crisis in Ethiopia, reports of targeted ethnic violence, and the risk to regional peace and security.'

The role of the Eritreans in the war may have taken a few days to become clear. The US thought, at least initially, that the Ethiopian government had little ability to control the movement of Eritrean forces.[56] By 20 November 2020, reliable reports were emerging that Eritrean forces were participating in the war and that Eritrean refugee camps in Tigray housing close to 100,000 people were under attack.[57] Three days later, Chris Coons—a leading Democratic senator and a personal friend of Biden—telephoned Abiy, presumably at Biden's request.[58] Yet it was not until 30 November that Pompeo called Abiy to express his 'grave concern, at the turn of events'.[59] Pompeo said he had urged Abiy to end the fighting, start a dialogue and allow unhindered humanitarian access. At the end of December 2020 the State Department announced that it was providing new aid funding, calling for unhindered humanitarian access and condemning violations of international law, while urging the protection of Eritrean refugees in Tigray.[60]

Despite the attempt by President Trump to frustrate his successor's inauguration, the succession took place on 20 January 2021, and President Biden was sworn into office. The policy of his administration was very different from President Trump's, forcefully and repeatedly calling for an end to the war. Eritrea was also called upon to leave Tigray and allow human rights investigations to begin.[61] At his congressional confirmation hearing, Blinken expressed his dismay about events in Tigray and about the safety of Eritrean refugees trapped in the region. He argued that the US was now engaged, rather than 'being AWOL'—a pointed rebuke of the preceding administration.

On 26 January 2021 Blinken was confirmed as secretary of state, and, indicating the urgency of the situation and the priority it was being accorded, on 4 February he called Abiy, urging him to allow aid into Tigray.[62] When there was little movement, the US said that it would link further economic assistance to Ethiopia to that country's conduct in Tigray.[63] The *New York Times* reported (presumably by way of a deliberate leak) that the government had determined that Ethiopian troops and allied militia were conducting a systematic campaign of ethnic cleansing.[64] Biden's new ambassador to the UN, Linda Thomas-Greenfield, decried what she referred to as 'conflict-induced starvation'.[65] The following day Blinken called Abiy, pressing him to protect civilians and bring an immediate end to hostilities as well as secure the withdrawal of Amhara and Eritrean forces.[66] At the UN Security Council, Thomas-Greenfield called for a halt to the atrocities,[67] warning that the war in Tigray was leading to a 'man-made' hunger crisis.[68]

According to several accounts, under Biden the US diplomatic engagement with the war in Tigray became its highest African priority. Washington's aims were clear: an end to hostilities and human rights violations, the exit of Eritrean forces, and humanitarian aid for Tigray. However, there was little progress on any front. With few high-level staff yet to be confirmed at the State Department, Biden asked Senator Coons to visit Addis Ababa on 20 March.[69] The move seemed bold and hopeful. Coons claimed he made some progress: that Abiy had agreed to international dialogue and had condemned the ongoing human rights violations.[70] Within days Abiy publicly acknowledged the presence in Tigray of Eritrean forces[71]—a development seemingly predicated on agreeing to remove them from his country. Yet these initiatives failed. Coons expressed disappointment—there had been no ceasefire and no acknowledgment of ethnic cleansing.[72] Coons said Abiy had denied there had been forced relocation of Tigrayans from western Tigray, and had assured him there 'had been and would be no ethnic cleansing'.

A sense of deflation appeared to emanate from the US government, which responded by taking the issue to the UN. Thomas-Greenfield challenged the Security Council: 'Do African lives not matter as much as those experiencing conflict in other countries?'[73] On 22 April China and Russia allowed a Western-initiated Security Council resolution calling for 'a scaled up humanitarian response and unfettered humanitarian access' as well as 'a restoration of normalcy'. The resolution also expressed 'deep concern about allegations of human rights violations and abuses, including reports of sexual violence against women and girls'; and it urged 'investigations to find those responsible and bring them to justice'.[74] It was a start. Ireland had drafted the resolution, but Thomas-Greenfield, who did much of the heavy lifting, was plainly delighted.[75] 'Today, the UN Security Council spoke with one voice in expressing concern over the devastating humanitarian situation in Tigray', she declared.

In April 2021 Biden appointed Jeffrey Feltman (an experienced diplomat who had signed the original statement warning of the implications of the war for Ethiopia) as special envoy to the Horn of Africa. Blinken again called Abiy, once more demanding the withdrawal of Eritrean forces.[76] As part of a tour that included discussions about Ethiopia's Nile dam with Egypt and Sudan, Feltman met Isaias in Asmara, before going on to Addis for talks with Abiy. The Asmara event was the first high-level meeting between the US and Eritrea in years.[77]

Yet, as ethnic cleansing and other atrocities continued, the US (like Europe and the UN) appeared unable to influence the conflict. Chinese competition and other geo-strategic interests loomed darkly over the crisis, while Russia and China continued to block more direct action at the UN. The US did pause most of its non-humanitarian assistance to Ethiopia and linked a resumption of that assistance to progress on humanitarian matters.[78] In March 2021 Washington imposed a range of sanctions on Eritrea, but refrained from taking similar action against Ethiopia or Ethiopians—presumably to retain the diplomatic leverage it felt it held. The policy was regularly reviewed, with sanctions gradually being ratcheted up.

It is difficult to call into question President Biden's personal commitment to the situation in Ethiopia and Tigray. He expended time and political capital to try to halt the conflict, but with limited success. Blinken himself is the stepson of a Holocaust survivor—a circumstance that informs his world view. However, nations can seldom impose their ideas about human rights upon others. The Biden administration effected a change of direction and assumed a vigour that had been missing during the Trump era, but the primary direction of American policy did not alter dramatically.

Diplomacy reflects the interests of nations, not sentiment: nations have no permanent friends or allies, only permanent interests.[79] Ethiopia has long been America's primary partner in the Horn. The key objectives of US policy include maintaining the country's unity and territorial integrity. This predisposes Washington to regard the incumbent leader, Abiy, as a critical partner, despite the fact that Blinken had reservations about his character and his election in 2021 (which Blinken described as 'not free or fair').[80] Having said this, the US believed there was no military solution to the Tigray war, and negotiations were the only realistic option, with the AU the legitimate mediator. The Biden administration has worked hard at the UN and with the EU, and tried to work closely with the AU, Kenya and South Africa.[81]

The second strategy has revolved around aid. This had two purposes: both to influence the Abiy government and, reflecting a genuinely humanitarian motive, to meet the increasingly critical needs of the Tigray region (and, more recently, of neighbouring Amhara and Afar). For example, on 13 October 2021 Blinken announced additional aid to meet the needs of 6–7 million people in northern Ethiopia. This increase amounted to $26 million, bringing total US aid to $663 million since the crisis began, while at the same time the US called for a ceasefire to allow the aid to reach its intended destinations.[82] In April 2022 there was a further announcement of $114 million in additional humanitarian aid, to be shared across the Horn of Africa to meet the needs of people hit by drought.[83] However, the 'carrot' of aid appears to have had as little impact on the Ethiopian government as pressure or negotiations. Rather, Addis Ababa spurned the US's most senior aid representative, Samantha Power, in August 2021, as *Foreign Policy* reported.

> When Samantha Power, head of the U.S. Agency for International Development (USAID), visited Ethiopia last week to seek greater access for humanitarian aid workers in Tigray, she was asked in a press conference why she hadn't met with the Ethiopian prime minister. 'He was not in the capital today on my day here,' she said. Behind the scenes, multiple U.S. officials familiar with the matter said that Abiy's office did not respond to U.S. requests for a meeting with Power, effectively rebuffing the senior U.S. cabinet member and underscoring the increasingly strained relationship between Washington and Addis Ababa.[84]

Just in case President Biden missed this demonstration of defiance, Abiy also snubbed Feltman, who flew to the Ethiopian capital the following week.[85] It was not until November 2021 that Feltman finally met the prime minister.

With the Biden administration making little headway with the Ethiopians or the Eritreans, the US turned to a tougher approach. In May 2021 the US announced further sanctions: reducing aid and denying visas to some government and military officials of both countries.[86] This included 'Amhara regional and irregular forces and members of the Tigray People's Liberation Front (TPLF)—responsible for, or complicit in, undermining resolution of the crisis in Tigray'. These developments were followed by sanctions against the Eritrean Defence Forces chief of staff Filipos Woldeyohannes on 23 August 2021. In taking this step, the US cited his role as commander of the forces that were responsible for gross human rights abuses during their campaign inside Ethiopia.[87]

This ratcheting-up of limited sanctions had little obvious effect, and so, on 17 September, there followed an announcement of much wider sanctions against Eritrea and Ethiopia.[88] Again the actual sanctions were delayed, presumably pending negotiations. But on 12 November, under the new framework, specific sanctions were indeed imposed as before, against Eritrean leaders, with the suggestion that Ethiopians and Tigrayans would be targeted as well if they did not begin serious negotiations.[89] The sanctions were applied against key Eritrean officials involved in running the government, the sole political party—the PFDJ—and the Eritrean Defence Forces. Important institutions, including the Red Sea Trading Corporation and the Hidri Trust, had sanctions applied against them as well. So too were named individuals: Hagos Ghebrehiwet W. Kidan, the economic adviser to the PFDJ, and Abraha Kassa Nemariam, the head of the Eritrean National Security Office. Explaining the decision, Blinken said: 'Eritrea's destabilizing presence in Ethiopia is prolonging the conflict, posing a significant obstacle to a cessation of hostilities, and threatening the integrity of the Ethiopian state.'[90] The sanctions order expressly exempted humanitarian aid.

The response from the Eritrean government was predictably scathing. The Ministry of Information complained: 'That the primary aim of the illicit and immoral sanctions is to inculcate suffering and starvation on the population so as to induce political unrest and instability is patently clear. But adding insult to injury, its architects unabashedly maintain that "the sanctions are not aimed at harming the Eritrean people". No one can really be deceived by these crocodile tears'.[91] The Americans responded robustly. The US embassy in Asmara posted on its Facebook page a lengthy statement rebutting Eritrean government allegations and yet again calling for Eritrea to withdraw from Tigray.[92]

The American embassy continued to use social media to robustly criticise the Eritrean government. The chargé d'affaires, Steven C. Walker, frustrated by his inability to engage in a dialogue with the Eritrean government, took to posting strongly critical statements on the embassy's Facebook page.[93] On 12 June 2022 Walker took the war of words a step further, participating in a broadcast by the Eritrean opposition satellite broadcast, Erisat. He openly attacked the Eritrean government for its repression of freedom of speech.[94] It was something of a rarity: an official of the State Department appearing from an American embassy, with the US flag besides him, on an opposition television channel that the Eritrean government certainly regarded as hostile.

US relations with Eritrea had by now deteriorated from frosty to hostile. This was underlined by Eritrea's decision to vote against the motion condemning Russian aggression in Ukraine on 2 March 2022.[95]

Moscow was clearly delighted, and the Eritrean foreign minister was received in Russia with promises of (unspecified) rewards.

On 2 November 2021 Biden took a powerful fresh step against Ethiopia's economic interests. He announced that on 1 January 2022 the US would remove Ethiopia from the free trade pact known as the African Growth and Opportunity Act (AGOA) if Ethiopia had not mended its ways by then.[96] The looming threat of tariffs caused considerable distress within Ethiopia's textile and apparel manufacturing and export industries, which were significant sources of employment and foreign exchange. On 21 November, Power, in an address to the EU Foreign Affairs Council's development committee, mentioned the need for humanitarian access. She went on to call for international financial institutions to suspend debt restructuring and new loans for the Ethiopian government, saying that the IMF had already taken this step.[97]

Washington also turned to Kenya, in the hope that President Kenyatta could help curtail the war. Kenyatta visited Biden in the White House in October 2021—the first African leader to be received by the incumbent.[98] In the following month Kenyatta went to see the Ethiopian prime minister and is said to have been told that Abiy was willing to make compromises to halt the fighting.[99] On 5 November 2021, owing at least in part to American efforts, the Security Council finally called for a ceasefire.[100]

Feltman—perhaps attempting to maintain the momentum—was quoted as saying that 'nascent progress' was being made in talks to end the war, and that all that was lacking was an end to hostilities.[101] In particular, he said that the parties had at last come to identify the key issues and to contemplate the elements of a diplomatic process.[102] Yet at the time the war showed few signs of abatement, and Abiy continued to mobilise every resource at his disposal in an attempt to finally break the Tigrayan offensives.

The US ended 2021 by threatening to impose further sanctions against Ethiopia, but the role of Feltman, as special envoy, was drawing to an end. He made a final visit to the region in January 2022, to be replaced by David Satterfield, the outgoing US ambassador to Turkey.[103] President Biden continued to try to move the Ethiopia leader, speaking on the phone to Abiy again on 10 January.[104] This was followed, in late January, by the first visit to the region by the newly appointed Satterfield. He met President Kenyatta, but there was no public revelation of what—if anything—was achieved. Satterfield made a further visit to the Horn at the end of March 2022, but again little was revealed.[105]

However, economic pressure (rather than diplomacy) was beginning to tell. Ethiopia was already in real economic difficulties. In April 2022 Ethiopia sent a high-level delegation to Washington to negotiate with the US Treasury, State Department, USAID and the special envoy for the Horn of Africa, while also attending key meetings of the IMF and World Bank.[106] In response, the IMF sent its own team to Ethiopia in mid-June 2022. The *Addis Standard* reported that the IMF had briefed creditors on 19 July and hinted at sending a 'program negotiation mission' to Ethiopia between late September and mid-October, 'provided conditions are right', according to a document seen by the paper.[107] 'This will mean Ethiopia will see a new program by 2024, and that will give confidence to creditors to restructure [Ethiopia's] debt,' an economic analyst closely following the development told *Addis Standard*. This was badly needed. By August 2022 Ethiopian debt was trading at 3,489 points (3.5 per cent) above US Treasury yields (1,000 points is a widely accepted definition of debt distress).[108]

In the US itself, events continued to unfold. There was activity in Congress, which decided, in principle, to implement sanctions against Ethiopia. This took place despite intense campaigning by Ethiopian government-paid lobbyists (who were countered by Tigrayan lobbying).[109] At the end of March 2022 the Senate Foreign Relations Committee passed the Ethiopia Peace and Stabilization Act of 2022 (S. 3199) and sent it to the full Senate for consideration[110] That event matched the passage in February, by the House of Representatives' Foreign Affairs Committee, of the Ethiopia Stabilization, Peace, and Democracy Act (H.R. 6600), before it was considered by the full House. Passing the bills did not make them law; but they were greeted with dismay by the Ethiopian government.[111] They were described by Ethiopia's ambassador as containing 'extremely dangerous contents that would compromise the sovereignty of the country and bend political and economic choices to the will of external actors'.[112] The bills were unlikely to become law, but they indicated the way the wind was blowing in Congress, despite the fervent objections of many Ethiopian American activists. They signalled to the White House and State Department what Congress expected.

Satterfield made a final visit to the Horn at the end of April 2022, without obvious success.[113] Apparently fed up with in-fighting inside the State Department, Satterfield decided to resign. There have been suggestions that a lack of support from the top of the Biden administration, together with frustration at resistance from the Africa Bureau within the State Department, may have contributed to Satterfield's decision.[114] As *Foreign Policy* noted: 'Satterfield's departure comes just over three months after his initial appointment as special envoy, replacing Jeffrey Feltman, a former top U.S. and U.N. diplomat who served for less than a year on the job.' Mike Hammer, former ambassador to the Democratic Republic of Congo, was appointed to replace him.[115]

At the same time, it was reported that members of the US administration had visited Mekele for talks with the Tigrayan government.[116] General Tsadkan said the unnamed envoy had met President Debretsion. The general said the American explained the difficulties the Ethiopian economy was experiencing and how Abiy was selling off the country's assets, including Ethiopian Airlines, Ethio Telecom and the Ethiopian power authority to Turkish or Arab investors. The government was, he claimed, begging the IMF and World Bank for funds. This narrative was uncorroborated but hardly implausible.

The US position was summarised in a statement at the end of April 2022.[117] Blinken reiterated appeals for aid deliveries to be stepped up, while applauding Abiy's decision to lift the State of Emergency. He welcomed Tigray's decision to withdraw 'most' of its forces from Afar and its commitment to a peaceful resolution of the conflict. The secretary of state said: 'We now urge the parties, as my team and I have in recent days, to seize the opportunity to advance a negotiated ceasefire, including the necessary security arrangements, and call for the restoration of essential services in Tigray on an urgent basis.' The American statement said nothing about the Eritrean troops still stationed inside Ethiopia and did not threaten fresh sanctions measures if the appeal was ignored.

By mid-2022 there were indications that the US, working with the EU, had finally made some progress by increasing pressure on Addis Ababa. In May–June 2022 the first signs of movement were appearing, with terms for negotiations being openly discussed by both Addis Ababa and Mekele. Where once the Tigrayans had been regarded as 'terrorists' who had to be crushed in what Abiy regarded as a limited 'law enforcement' operation, they were now being considered as potential negotiating partners. Diplomatic and economic pressure was beginning to tell on Abiy and his government.

The European Union and Britain

The EU worked closely with the US in an attempt to halt the war. Brussels is, of course, in a more difficult position than Washington, since it must reach agreement between all 27 member states to act effectively. It is less agile than its American allies, but Europe is still an important player in the Horn. Working in unison was essential, and in June 2021 there was a concerted effort by both the Americans and Europeans to try to end the war. US ambassador to the UN Thomas-Greenfield pushed for the Security Council to meet publicly on Tigray. 'What are we afraid of? What are we trying to hide? The Security Council's failure is unacceptable,' Thomas-Greenfield told a US and EU virtual event on Tigray.[118]

The Europeans reacted to the crisis with expressions of concern and calls for a ceasefire as well as funding for refugees crossing into Sudan.[119] The European Parliament intervened on 26 November 2020 with an urgent resolution, supporting mediation efforts and diplomatic contacts.[120] Janez Lenarčič, European commissioner for crisis management, and Josep Borrell, high representative of the EU, gradually began using more forceful language to express their concerns. Their proposals have focused increasingly on access to Tigray for the aid agencies. In December 2020 the EU warned it would delay budget support to Ethiopia if the situation did not improve. On 15 January 2021, Borrell said that 'possible war crimes' had been committed in Tigray.[121] At the same time, Europe announced it had suspended budgetary aid to Ethiopia worth €88 million until Ethiopian aid reached the needy in Tigray.[122] Borrell said he told Ethiopia's foreign minister Demeke Mekonnen that 'in particular in the absence of full humanitarian access to all areas of the conflict, we have no alternative but to suspend' the funds. This tough stance has not been maintained. By mid-2022 the EU had earmarked US$1 billion to Ethiopia for the period 2021–7.[123] The only remaining reservation was that the money would be disbursed in small tranches, outside the EU's planned seven-year country programme, and not through direct funding to the government in Addis Ababa.

In February 2021 EU representatives openly acknowledged the presence of Eritrean troops in Tigray, but they called for Eritrea to withdraw its troops only after the US had done so.[124] Europe's next step was diplomatic: the appointment of the EU's special envoy, Finnish foreign minister Pekka Haavisto.[125] Haavisto was a good choice, with excellent experience of the region, and he travelled to the Horn in early February 2021.[126] Briefing EU ministers, Haavisto described the situation as 'out of control', complaining that the Ethiopian government had not provided him with a 'clear picture' during his visit.[127]

Despite Haavisto's powerful critique, ministers delivered a mixed message when they issued the European Council's conclusions on 11 March 2021. They acknowledged 'Ethiopia's important role as a strategic partner and a key multilateral actor', before going on to reiterate their 'great concern regarding the situation in the Tigray region and the wider region'.[128] The Council stated that it wished to pursue a constructive dialogue with the Ethiopian government to deal with these concerns. Analysts regarded the statement as weak—a failure to support their envoy. Instead, Haavisto was asked to make further visits to the region in early April 2021. These included the UAE, Saudi Arabia and Egypt, as well as a stop-off in the Tigrayan regional capital, Mekele. After the second visit, he warned the situation was dire. Despite this, EU vice president Josep Borrell merely indicated that Europe wanted to send an observer mission to monitor the Ethiopian elections, if the situation permitted.[129]

The 2021 Ethiopian election went ahead without EU monitors, having failed to meet Europe's minimum conditions. 'It is disappointing that the EU has not received the assurances necessary to extend to the Ethiopian people one of its most visible signs of support for their quest for democracy,' Josep Borrell said.[130] The decision was a blow to the credibility of the June election, which nonetheless went ahead. Predictably, the result produced a 'landslide' for the prime minister.[131] Despite their concerns, the Europeans continued to recognise Abiy and to engage with him and his administration.

In July 2021 Annette Weber replaced Alex Rondos as the EU special representative for the Horn of Africa.[132] She has been almost invisible, with almost no public profile, although she did discuss the situation in Ethiopia with other actors, such as Saudi Arabia in November 2021.[133] In February 2022, Weber said she was 'cautiously optimistic' about the ceasefire between Ethiopia and Tigray, but has otherwise refrained from public statements.[134] Europeans have suggested that the US and the AU need time and space to see if they can make progress. The EU explained that it continued to rely mostly on 'regional and African Union mediation efforts, led by Special Representative Obasanjo, trusting that these will deliver peace'.[135] In July 2022, after months of silence, Annette Weber appeared in Addis Ababa. She held talks with Ethiopia's deputy prime minister and minister of foreign affairs, Demeke Mekonnen, before travelling to Mekele with US special envoy Mike Hammer for discussions with Debretsion. According to an agreed statement, they backed the AU mediation efforts, while calling for the swift restoration of electricity, telecom, banking and other basic services to Tigray, and returned to Addis with a letter for Abiy, 'providing security guarantees for those who need to work to restore services'.[136]

Besides seeking to adopt coordinated measures, European states have taken individual measures in an attempt to put pressure on the Ethiopian authorities. In August 2021 France—which had promised to back plans for the rebirth of the Ethiopian navy in the Red Sea—withdrew its support for the project.[137] The agreement, reached between President Macron and Abiy in March 2019, would have seen $100 million come from Paris.[138] The re-establishment of the navy was probably one of the 'wins' Abiy would have hoped to see flowing from his alliance with President Isaias in 2018. The Ethiopian navy would have been based in the Eritrean ports of Assab or Massawa, as it was during the days of the Ethiopian Empire.[139] The independence of Eritrea put an end to the navy, even though some vessels continued operating from Yemen and, then, Djibouti.

Ireland became an important player at the UN Security Council in shaping policy towards Ethiopia after it gained a seat there in January 2021. It was one of the main supporters of a UN Security Council statement in November 2021 calling for an immediate ceasefire.[140] Following the adoption of the statement, Irish ambassador Byrne Nason complained that 'the Council's voice matters on this issue, and it has the power to deliver change. We remained silent for too long.' [141] Ethiopia reacted by expelling four of Ireland's six diplomats from Addis Ababa.[142]

Overall, however, the EU and its member states have contributed relatively little in practice to resolving or ending the war, beyond lending support to American and African initiatives. A former Dutch diplomat, familiar with the Horn of Africa, said he was unable to raise any interest in the subject from his government.[143] Speaking off the record in December 2021, an EU diplomat complained that while the situation was deteriorating rapidly, there was little sign of genuine European engagement: 'The EU has so far stayed silent.'[144] Human Rights Watch was scathing about the EU's inaction.

> [As the] EU's foreign policy is determined by unanimity, resistance from key member states risks undermining crucial efforts, including calling for a Human Rights Council special session that could establish an investigative mechanism. European and other countries initially said they wanted to first see the outcome of a joint UN Office of the High Commissioner for Human Rights (OHCHR) and Ethiopian Human Rights Commission (EHRC) investigation opened in March. The joint report is now out, and recommends an international investigative mechanism, but some EU member states still appear reluctant to heed that call.[145]

This assessment was supported by the EU's foreign policy chief Josep Borrell, who pointed to the inability of the bloc to take concerted action as the situation in Ethiopia deteriorated.[146] Borrell described this as 'one of my biggest frustrations ... because we were not able to react properly to the large-scale human rights violations, mass rapes using sexual violence as a war arm, killings and concentration camps based on ethnic belonging.' He added: 'We haven't been able to stop it, and neither to take coercive measures due to the lack of unanimity in the Council.' Borrell refrained from naming the member states that were blocking action.

The Europeans have attempted to rein in Eritrea and Ethiopia. The EU called, unsuccessfully, for a $300 million loan to Ethiopia from the World Bank to be postponed.[147] In April 2021, to underline its frustration with Eritrean intransigence, the EU withdrew most of its aid to Eritrea.[148] Yet, in June 2022, a European delegation was back in Asmara, holding talks with the Eritrean government. Apart from posting a delegation photograph, no details were provided of what had been achieved.[149]

The European position should, however, be contrasted with the unquestioning support for the Ethiopian and Eritrean war effort from its Arab allies as well as China, Russia and Turkey. Overall, the EU finds it difficult to take a firm stand on the war, since this would mean alienating its key regional partner, Ethiopia. As a result, it has sent confused messages and appeals from Brussels have largely fallen on deaf ears. In addition, although EU countries such as Ireland have been pushing for action in the UN Security Council, Europe does not—openly at least—make effective use of its strategic alliances to strengthen its calls for an end to the hostilities and human rights abuses. It has hardly been a convincing stand from one of the world's most powerful regional organisations.

Meanwhile, Britain's voice has been muted, at best, since leaving the EU. While continuing to have some influence through its seat on the UN Security Council, London has had diminished leverage in world affairs. Under Boris Johnson, the British concentrated on winning alternative markets for their exports and Africa has received little attention. Despite no major steps being taken by the British government, pressure exerted in Parliament secured some minor concessions. Sustained interest from MPs in the House of Commons, and by the House of Lords, has focused on securing small but meaningful shifts in government policy. British politicians highlighted the presence of Eritrean troops in Ethiopia and their alleged human rights abuses. This is one area in which the UK has taken a firm position, repeatedly calling for the Eritrean forces to withdraw.[150]

There was also considerable public alarm at the use of sexual violence and rape in the conflict. The UK projects itself as a global leader in preventing sexual violence in conflict, after its 2012 summit on the topic and launch of the Preventing Sexual Violence in Conflict Initiative. In June 2021 the UK deployed an expert to conduct an initial scoping mission in Ethiopia, but tangible outcomes are unclear.[151] The UK also cut direct bilateral aid to Ethiopia from £240.5 million to £107.6 million planned for 2021/22.[152] However, beyond these measures and statements in Parliament, the overarching policy of the British government appears to favour continuing engagement with the governments of Ethiopia and Eritrea, despite the absence of evidence that such contacts are having any meaningful impact on policy.

Gulf states, Iran and Turkey

The relationship between the Horn of Africa and the nations of the Arabian Peninsula and North Africa are ancient and deep. In more recent times, Cairo was home to Eritrean nationalists pressing for their country's freedom from the 1950s. Ethiopia came to suspect that Egypt was supporting Eritrean independence for duplicitous reasons. Ethiopians believed that Egypt was using Eritrean independence activists as a means of weakening the Ethiopian state so that it would be incapable of utilising the waters of the Blue Nile, upon which Egypt was so dependent. One element of the relationship with the Arab world was therefore distrust; another was reliance. The Eritrean independence movement depended on Arab states for support as they fought the Ethiopian state. Syria and Yemen gave Eritrean movements training, limited military equipment, and financial and diplomatic support. This assistance only increased Ethiopian concerns about the motivation of its Arab neighbours. It is possible to see both elements at play today.

President Isaias is nothing if not pragmatic about his foreign relations and is willing to drop friends and change direction if it suits his purposes. His ties with Iran illustrate the point. In 2007 the president began cultivating relations with Tehran, making positive statements about Iran's right to enrich uranium for peaceful purposes, at a meeting of the Non-Aligned Movement.[153] In May 2008, Isaias met Iranian president Mahmoud Ahmadinejad in Tehran to bolster cooperation between the two states. The Eritrean government granted Iran access to Assab port, providing Tehran with a base from which to conduct maritime operations in the Red Sea and Indian Ocean. There were even suggestions from Eritrean opposition sources that Iranian arms were being supplied to Houthi rebels in the Yemen.[154]

Isaias then ditched his Iranian allies, instead moving support to the Saudis and the UAE—on the opposite side of the Sunni–Shia divide. Since 2015 Isaias has been a regular visitor to Riyadh. In return, the UAE and the Saudis were allowed to build bases in the port of Assab and use Asmara airport for attacks on Yemeni forces.[155] In 2016, the UN Monitoring Group on Somalia and Eritrea reported on 'the rapid construction of what appears to be a military base with permanent structures' at Assab.[156] According to security analysts, the base included its own port, airbase, and a military training facility,[157] where the UAE trained elite Yemeni forces.[158] In return, the Eritreans are reported to have received aid from the UAE to upgrade their infrastructure.[159] The base was closed in February 2021, as the UAE pulled back from involvement in the civil war in Yemen.[160] It is not clear what sparked this change of direction, but this may have been a response to American pressure following the atrocities committed in the Tigray war.[161] There are rumours that President Isaias saw this as a betrayal, and that relations between Asmara and Abu Dhabi soured as a result.

As noted previously, many nations and initiatives were involved in ending the bitter 'no-peace, no-war' stalemate that followed the 1998–2000 Ethiopia–Eritrea border war. The US played an important role, but so too did Saudi Arabia and the UAE.[162] Substantial funding was provided to both nations by Dubai. It was reported that Ethiopia received no less than $3 billion in June 2018.[163] Eritrea would also have received promises of UAE largesse. There were even reports that the UAE was to fund a pipeline from the Eritrean ports to Addis Ababa, but little more of this plan was ever heard.[164] Exactly how much either Ethiopia or Eritrea actually received has not been made public.

When the Tigray war erupted in November 2020, the UAE was accused of supplying drones that destroyed much of the Tigrayan armour and military hardware.[165] Some questioned the veracity of this evidence.[166] But a year later more substantial evidence was provided, including photographs showing that the UAE had indeed armed the Ethiopians.[167] As one report put it: 'Although the exact drone type that forms the basis for the UCAV (unmanned combat aerial vehicles) design is as of yet unknown, they are identical in design to two UCAVs that were shot down by Houthi forces in Yemen.'[168] The drones—and other military equipment—were delivered in October 2021 by what was described as a UAE 'air bridge' to support Ethiopia's war effort in Tigray. Everything from guns and ammunition to 50 ambulances were flown into Ethiopia by the UAE.

In 53 days, at least 51 suspicious cargo flights reached Ethiopia, most of them landing at Harar Meda air base. A total of 45 of those cargo flights originated in the UAE while six came from Iran. In the latter case, it can be presumed that the Boeing 747 and Il-76 cargo aircraft used carried Mohajer-6 unmanned combat aerial vehicles (UCAVs) confirmed to have been delivered to Ethiopia onboard, although the delivery of other types of Iranian weaponry to the ENDF can't be ruled out either.[169]

A second source tracked no fewer than 45 flights from the UAE to Ethiopia.[170] Later this increased to two flights a day.[171] These drone deliveries were supplemented by Chinese-manufactured Wing Loong I.[172] Evidence for this has gradually mounted. Chinese media openly discussed the training of Ethiopian police in the use of drone technology.[173] Flights were also tracked between Chengdu in China (where the Wing Loong I is manufactured) to Harar Meda airbase in Ethiopia. After the drones' arrival at the airbase, they were reportedly 'hastily moved to a nearby hangar to avoid their detection by prying eyes, an effort which nonetheless evidently failed'.[174] Information about the airlift from China was corroborated by another source, tracking a flight from Chengdu and another from Dalian.[175] A Wing Loong 1 was spotted flying over Mekele, while satellite images showed the Chinese drones at Ethiopia's military airport of Harar Meda, south of Addis Ababa, in November 2021.[176]

China and Iran were useful sources of drones; however, they were not the main providers of these armaments; Turkey was. The relationship between Addis Ababa and Ankara had been developing for some time. This was part of a drive by Turkey's president Recep Tayyip Erdoğan to extend his country's influence in the Red Sea and the Horn of Africa in what has been described as a 'neo-Ottoman revival',[177] involving a base in Somalia and a planned base in Sudan.[178] Turkey's relationship with Ethiopia gradually gathered pace. In 2005, there were just three Turkish companies in Ethiopia; by early 2021 there were 200, ranging from wire and textiles to beverages. In January 2018 it was reported that the value of Turkish investments in Ethiopia had reached $2.5 billion.[179]

In August 2021 Abiy visited Ankara, meeting with President Erdoğan. A military deal and accompanying financial arrangements were negotiated.[180] Since then Turkish drones have been assembled in Ethiopia.[181] The weapons, for both surveillance and tactical use, were built at a training and intelligence centre of the Information Network Security Agency (INSA).[182] The director general of INSA, Temesgen Tiruneh, was in overall charge of the programme, and the prime minister is said to have frequently visited the site, ten kilometres from Addis. The drones played an important—perhaps a decisive role—in Abiy's war effort. Al Jazeera concluded in December 2021 that they had tipped the conflict towards the Ethiopian government.

> All these drones search the battlefield, guided by remote pilots back at base. Analysts, intelligence specialists, military planners and army commanders can see and share the high-resolution images being fed back giving a far clearer picture of the battlefield and the enemy's intentions. The Tigrayan forces have no such capability and would have armoured units, air defence systems, mobile radar sites and command and control posts destroyed at a far greater rate.[183]

Abiy has been able to rely on Turkey and the UAE, together with China and Iran, for support and for weapons. With Russia they have provided an alternative pole of international authority at a time when the EU and the US, upon whom Ethiopia has traditionally relied, have become increasingly critical of the prime minister's administration.

China

China has had an important but seldom acknowledged role in the conflict. With Russia, it repeatedly used its position on the UN Security Council to block discussion of the situation in Tigray and to resist attempts by Western powers to impose sanctions of any kind on the combatants, even when UN staff were expelled by the Ethiopian authorities.[184] The work of the Chinese and the Russian delegations in delaying and blocking serious consideration of the situation had severe consequences, according to the then head of UN emergency operations, Mark Lowcock. 'Effective diplomatic maneuvers in New York' by Russia and China meant 'the Ethiopians were quite successful in staving off open meetings in the Security Council for months and months and months', he said in an interview after retiring.[185] According to Lowcock, 'The Ethiopians basically wanted to starve the Tigrayans into submission or out of existence. That was objective one, but objective two was to do that without attracting the global opprobrium that is associated with deliberately causing a famine taking hundreds of thousands or millions of lives.'

China resisted further action at the UN on the grounds of national sovereignty. 'China firmly supports Ethiopia's efforts to safeguard national sovereignty and independence, believes that the Ethiopian government has the capacity and wisdom to properly handle its internal affairs ... China will adhere to its consistent position and oppose external forces interfering in Ethiopia's internal affairs under the pretext of human rights.'[186]

Opposing sanctions was just the tip of the iceberg of Chinese involvement in the region. China maintains a major base in Djibouti. It is not alone in this. Japan, the US, France, Italy, Spain, Germany and (prospectively) India use the Red Sea state as external bases from which to project their military influence.[187] Since 2017 Djibouti has also been central to China's 'Belt and Road Initiative' stretching from Beijing to the Red Sea and the Mediterranean. Ethiopia has been a major beneficiary of Chinese investment, which has brought everything from a renewed railway from Djibouti to Addis, to a mass transit system in the capital and factories producing a wide range of goods. Between 2000 and 2018, Chinese investment is said to have reached $13.7 billion.[188]

Chinese finances have strengthened the Ethiopian economy: it is now the largest foreign investor in the country, overtaking the US.[189] Chinese trade with Ethiopia quintupled in the last decade, with China being allowed to take a stake in the country's politically sensitive telecoms sector, which was closed to Western investors.[190] This spurred economic growth, underpinning the war effort.

China also has significant links with Eritrea. Relations between the two countries were reinforced with the visit of China's state councillor and foreign minister Wang Yi in January 2022. Isaias thanked China for its role in enhancing a 'balanced global order predicated on respect of international law'—code for China's refusal to allow the Tigray war to be dealt with by the Security Council.[191] There was agreement on the development of Eritrea's ports of Massawa and Assab, as well as on mining. These developments, together with the Chinese decision to appoint a 'special envoy' to deal with the Horn of Africa, underline Beijing's determination to enhance its status as a significant regional actor.[192]

China has been building its relationship with Eritrea for years, with investments in the mining sector showing substantial growth. China has taken a share of a number of mines. Among these is Danakali Ltd, a potash deposit straddling the Ethiopian border, which has enough of the mineral to continue production well into the next century.[193] Links were formalised and strengthened when Eritrea joined China's 'Belt and Road' Initiative in November 2021.[194] John Calabrese has suggested that Beijing was using the war in Tigray as a reason to move away from its reliance on Ethiopia in the Horn of Africa.[195] 'As things have unravelled in Ethiopia, Beijing might have decided to further diversify its relations in the Horn by cementing ties with Eritrea,' Calabrese argued. He may have a point, but the suggestion that China will ditch its ties with Ethiopia appears overstated.

Competing for public opinion

Diplomacy was accompanied by a fierce contest for support among diverse diasporic groups. A propaganda war was fought, aimed primarily at Western democracies, which are open to democratic pressure.[196] The battle for Western public attention has a long history in relation to Ethiopia. This was seen during the 1983–5 famine,[197] and can traced back much further, to the campaigns waged by Sylvia Pankhurst in support of Ethiopian resistance to the Italian invasion of 1935.[198] The Tigray war left many in the Ethiopian and Eritrean communities abroad saddened, angry and bereft of hope as they watched their families torn apart. Many had little or no information, while some felt guilt for being abroad and unable to contribute directly to resolving the crisis. It was a time of deep anxiety and stress. Communities that supported the governments of Ethiopia, Eritrea or Somalia could look to their governments for information and leadership. For those who opposed these regimes, the situation was far bleaker. As the conflict unfolded, people in the diaspora reached out to one another and created new networks. For Eritreans, some of whom have been excluded from their country's affairs since before independence, this was an exile they had long endured.[199]

After the events of 2001, when Isaias cracked down on critics inside his own party as well as crushed all independent journalism, many former supporters of the EPLF fled the country and joined the Eritrean Liberation Front (ELF) in exile.[200] Yet the bitter divisions of the Eritrean civil wars between the EPLF and ELF (1972–4 and 1980–1) continued to fester among Eritreans living abroad. The diaspora has been unable to form a united front against Isaias. However, gradually and painfully, these rifts are beginning to heal. A new, younger generation of Eritrean opposition activists came together in 2019 in the Yiakl (Enough!) movement.[201] On 18–20 November 2021, after months of difficult negotiations, the Eritrean United National Front was founded, supported by many civic societies and opposition groups.[202] The Front declared that it would 'embark on armed resistance' against the 'totalitarian regime of Isayas/PFDJ' with the aim of freeing Eritrea of repression, and guaranteeing the country's sovereignty. Importantly, the Front expressed its solidarity with the Tigrayan people. Yet by mid-2022 there were only limited signs of these words being turned into action.

For Tigrayans of all political persuasions, the war was a novel and, possibly even more so, a shocking experience. Their communities came under fierce attack from Ethiopian officials, who vilified them.[203] Broadcasts—including some by Daniel Kibret, Abiy's social affairs adviser—openly advocated genocide.[204] He compared the Tigrayans to the devil and said they should be 'the last of their kind'. The US described his speeches as 'hateful rhetoric' that was 'dangerous and unacceptable'.[205]

As the crisis unfolded, Tigrayans found new ways of uniting and expressing their anger and support. There were demonstrations across the world, from Australia to America. Sometimes they took novel forms, including a 24-hour global virtual link-up of the Tigrayan opposition, '24 Hours for Tigray'. Broadcast on 9 March 2021, one segment was linked to the next, as the broadcast went around the world.[206] Using pre-recorded messages and live events, the programme was hosted by Tigrayans, supported by Eritreans, who did a remarkably professional job of presenting a programme of such complexity. Others adopted novel forms of protest. Twitter was used to pressure Western supermarkets not to sell Ethiopian flowers on Valentine's Day 2021, whose sale provided revenues for the Ethiopian state. In October 2021 Tigrayans in Norway laid toys outside the Nobel Peace Prize offices and the Norwegian parliament, symbolising the children whose lives have been lost in the war.[207] These protests took place alongside traditional marches, petitions and calls to legislators.

The Ethiopian diaspora around the world—estimated to be 2.5 million strong—is as divided, as the Eritrean.[208] Some support their government and some do not. As the BBC reported: 'The conflict has deeply divided the Ethiopian community in Washington DC—the largest in the US. Ethiopians abroad watch with dismay.'[209] Both sides are eloquent, articulate and engaged. Merga Yonas Bula, a doctoral student who has been researching Ethiopia's diaspora in Germany, believes that the advent of social media was important in this mobilisation. 'Social media platforms became an alternative for them to voice their discontent. And beyond that, social media became a tool for resistance ... to mobilize resources and financing, and also to share their strategies.'[210]

Attempts to mobilise opinion have perhaps been most intense in the US, where the Biden administration has worked hard to try to end the war. The public protests were supplemented by professional, paid lobbying of Congress, and considerable sums were paid by both sides.[211] These ideological battles have been fierce, deeply dividing communities that were once united.

TRT World reported on the rifts that emerged.

> The violence is, however, no longer restricted to the Horn of Africa. It is slowly tearing apart the Ethiopian immigrant community and even families some 13,000 kilometres away in the US where more than 300,000 Ethiopia-born immigrants live, mostly in the capital Washington DC, and the neighbouring states of Maryland and Virginia. For months they have held protests, both for and against the TPLF. They are divided over Prime Minister Abiy Ahmed's leadership, the role of the UN, the US and its allies, and the Western media. The discord has crept into churches, social gatherings and even onto breakfast tables.[212]

The clashes on social media have been expressed in the most intemperate, sometimes abusive terms. These have begun to be studied by the Shorenstein Center's Technology and Social Change project at the Harvard Kennedy School.[213] They found that Tigrayans focused largely on raising awareness of the conflict, while supporters of Abiy sought to disprove their opponents' claims. Both made misleading or sometimes false claims, but the study found that official communications and pro-government users' posts often sought to discredit any content contradicting the federal government's narrative as 'disinformation'.

'It is a complex case that interacts with the geopolitics of the Horn of Africa, historical trauma, activism, hate speech, misinformation, platform manipulation, and propaganda, all in the midst of an ongoing civil conflict ... It became a war about the narrative,' *Addis Standard* founder and editor-in-chief Tsedale Lemma told Voice of America.[214] It is an ideological conflict that has been exacerbated by the restrictions on reporting on the Tigray war, which have allowed misinformation to flourish and rumour to replace fact. These divisions will be hard to overcome.

Diplomacy assessed

Following the return of the Tigrayan forces to within the borders of Tigray, the Ethiopian military announced that it would 'pause' in the positions it had captured. This was welcomed by UN secretary general Antonio Guterres.[215] He also welcomed the Tigrayan message that they had withdrawn from neighbouring Afar and Amhara regions and returned to Tigray.

However, 2021 ended without a resolution to the conflict or the blockade. As the UN reported on 30 December, the situation in Tigray continued to deteriorate.[216] These extracts from the report indicate just how serious it was. 'Fighting had held up convoys, as a result no trucks with humanitarian aid cargo entered Tigray since 14 December ... Overall, 1,338 trucks have entered the region since 12 July, which represents less than 12 per cent of the supplies required to meet the scale of humanitarian needs. In Tigray, the humanitarian situation remains dire with more than 5.2 million people or 90 per cent of the population in need of humanitarian assistance.'

The year also ended with many expressions of concern from the US and EU, together with limited sanctions. If anyone emerged from these diplomatic efforts with credit, it was President Biden. He has done all that could have been asked of an American president (short of going to war), to try to end the fighting. In June 2022 the European emergency response coordinator, Janez Lenarčič, went to Tigray, holding talks with Debretsion and visiting Mekele's main hospital, where conditions were shocking. Lenarčič described the situation as 'desperate' and called for fuel supplies and basic services to be restored. 'Tigrayans have suffered enough!' he declared.[217] His plea for lifting the blockade was backed by the EU.[218]

The AU has, as we have seen, struggled to deal with this grim crisis on its doorstep. Having lost the initial opportunity provided by South Africa's president Ramaphosa, it has struggled to engage with the combatants using Kenyatta and Obasanjo. The UN Security Council remained, as ever, hamstrung from taking decisive action by the threat of a Chinese or Russian veto, while the Americans, Europeans and Russians have been consumed by the conflict in Ukraine.

Behind the scenes some progress was made. Kenya's president Kenyatta and former Nigerian president Obasanjo remained engaged, and it gradually became clear that talks, which had previously seemed unlikely, might get under way. By August 2022 the Ethiopian and Tigrayan governments were preparing for negotiations, while the EU and US had sent senior diplomats to Addis and Mekele to see how they might encourage the process. The Tigrayans were laying out their terms for talks, although it was far from clear how some of their demands—including the return of western Tigray—would be accommodated.

Abiy was no longer labelling the Tigrayans 'terrorists' who had to be crushed in a law-and-order operation, but he was having difficulties with his Amhara allies. Alex de Waal summed up his dilemma: 'Abiy faces the trickiest path. When he built a coalition for war, he dismantled the constituency for peace. He now faces the ruins of both, but needs a credible peace process for his own survival.'[219] This assessment is probably accurate, but the Tigrayans have tensions of their own: there is no clarity about what their region's status might be in future while popular sentiment calls for full independence.

As has been frequently observed, it is easier to start a war than to end it.

CONCLUSION
PERSISTING OBSTACLES TO PEACE?

Martin Plaut and Sarah Vaughan

In 1988, towards the end of the Derg period, Basil Davidson, the most eminent of Britain's twentieth-century Africanists, observed: 'Once the Dergue had overthrown the emperor and his subordinate authorities, Ethiopian territorial integrity became possible only with an end to authoritarian centralism. Much has been said and written about this necessary condition for peace in Ethiopia. Nothing substantial has been done. To the contrary, the old centralism has been displaced by a new centralism.'[1]

Davidson was a passionate supporter of Eritrean independence but also a believer in Ethiopia's territorial integrity. Yet he knew, from his long years of experience in the Horn of Africa and across the continent, that this would require challenging the notion of a centralised state. A decentralised and democratised Ethiopia was the vision he cherished. After the recent years of war, that vision is as elusive today as it was three and a half decades ago. Since then, Eritrea has won its independence but not its freedom. Eritreans live under 'inherently toxic totalitarianism' in what one observer has described as 'a human rights house of horrors', deprived of every vestige of democracy.[2] Its people are trapped between grinding poverty, endless wars, and the perils of migration. Yet the Eritrean government has played a critical—probably seminal—role in the tragic war that this book has chronicled: it is as much 'Eritrea's war in Tigray' as Ethiopia's.

Meanwhile, since the millennium Ethiopia's political economy has become yet more complex as society has changed and levels of urbanisation, education and aspiration have grown with economic change and a youthful population. In the new century, arguably the most thoughtful of a new generation of Ethiopia's analysts observed: 'If the discourse of both civil society and ethnicity are equally part of how the anti-democratic tendencies within the African state are reproduced, then perhaps we should reframe the current reforms of the EPRDF as part of the constant pull of the African state between a supposedly culturally-based decentralised despotism and a top-down, urban-based authoritarian modernism.'[3]

The introduction to this volume identified land, power and empire as three unresolved issues on which Ethiopia's war in Tigray turned, and they remained central to a sustainable resolution of the war at the time of writing. The centralisation–decentralisation 'pull' was at the core of Ethiopia's visceral political divide over how to approach the legacies of its imperial past, and it remained the central political driver of the war in Tigray. The TPLF-led government of Tigray regional state favoured one side of the argument, and the Ethiopian federal government and its Eritrean and Ethiopian nationalist political allies the other. Yet, as this book has documented, these were not debating points of constitutional nicety, but matters which influenced the balance of power across the Horn. They dictated the extent to which neighbouring groups were threatened by, and could threaten, their neighbours. Ethiopia's power plays continued to be about the domination of power, not about how to share it.

Beneath the power politics, the control of key economic resources has been a central driver of the war. As one commentator has put it: 'In fact, the war on Tigray was not only a power struggle but a huge grab of land and assets. The internment of Tigrayans in Addis Ababa en masse late last year [2021] amounted to a massive shakedown, as their businesses have been confiscated and they are extorted to pay bribes to make phone calls, get medicine or—if they can afford it—buy their release.'[4]

Of these economic resources, in late 2022 it was competing claims over land that looked set to dog the success of any process of negotiation, even one premised on a return to the constitutional *status quo ante bellum.* It is arguably in relation to competition for land that the commonalities between the war in Tigray and the devastating dynamics of conflict elsewhere in Ethiopia emerge most clearly. As noted in Chapter 5, the Tigray war involved only one set of the powerful and complex threads of violence that have dogged Ethiopia. When it erupted in November 2020, the Ethiopian government had already been waging a counterinsurgency campaign against the Oromo Liberation Army in Oromia for almost two years. It is in respect of the rights of city dwellers and local Oromo farmers vis-à-vis Addis Ababa (or Finfinne) and the lucrative centres along the development corridors of the Rift Valley that the political projects of (centralised) 'urban authoritarianism' and (decentralised) 'rural despotism' rub up against each other most sharply. These are fault lines that will not be easily resolved, and the longer Ethiopia's multiple wars continue, the more difficult it will become to resolve them.

* * *

The Tigray war has been characterised by extremes of brutality against civilians. Key aspects of this are documented in Part Five of this book on the impact of war (Chapters 9 to 11). The abuses included multiple instances of extrajudicial executions, primarily of men and boys, indiscriminate aerial and artillery bombardment of civilian targets, and a campaign of rape and sexual torture against Tigrayan women and girls of all ages. In areas where land was claimed by neighbouring regions, Tigrayan populations were forcibly displaced. Civilians in Tigray were prevented from escaping the conflict when the government closed the border to Sudan within days of the outbreak of fighting. What was for a few days the fastest flow of refugees anywhere in the world was abruptly cut off. Meanwhile, civilians of Tigrayan origin in other parts of Ethiopia were prevented from leaving the country, and many were detained in terrible circumstances. Little is known of the fate of thousands of military personnel of Tigrayan origin who were interned when war broke out. Displaced persons and refugees have also been targeted, with reports that some Eritreans may have been subject to forcible rendition back to Eritrea or prevented from leaving the arena of conflict. Internally displaced persons and refugees were subjected to attack, both on the ground and from the air.

The chief burden of this abuse has been borne by Tigrayans, but populations across the Horn have also suffered. Eritreans were forcibly conscripted under the rubric of 'national service' and sent to die on the battlefields of Tigray. There were also Somalis, thousands of whom were sent to Eritrea under false pretences and thrown into the conflict. Then there were the Ethiopian militia and new recruits to the Ethiopian National Defence Force who were taken to the front lines armed with minimal training and inadequate equipment—in some cases only machetes and agricultural instruments (Chapter 8). Civilians in neighbouring regional states have also suffered the devastating effects of war, including abuses at the hands of Tigrayan forces, as the war swept into their home areas. All have paid a terrible price. Many will continue to do so for the rest of their lives.

But in Tigray itself, this has not been a war in the normal sense of the term. It has been a systematic campaign to eradicate Tigray as a social and political entity. As serious as the killings, detentions and rapes of Tigrayan civilians was the systematic campaign to destroy the social and economic fabric of Tigray. Ethiopian and Eritrean forces achieved this by means of wholesale looting and the deliberate destruction of items essential to the survival and livelihoods of Tigrayans during the period from November 2020 to June 2021; their effects were exacerbated when their two governments blocked assistance to the region. As explored in Chapter 9, this targeted looting and destruction went far beyond any military rationale and speaks of a determination to exterminate a population, with echoes of the Ethiopian wars of the 1980s.

'The Ethiopian government placed Tigray under siege, encircling it and cutting off essential services, commercial traffic, and humanitarian access. Given the scale of escalating deprivation, this was tantamount to a starvation siege …'[5] The result of this strategy was enforced starvation, as discussed in Chapter 10. For much of the period from the start of the war until mid- to late 2021, Tigray was kept in a state of siege under what even the UN called a *de facto* blockade to halt food, fuel and medicines, and a blackout affecting banking, telecommunications and electricity services. Although some relief food trickled into the region from the spring of 2022, by August 2022 it was barely 15 per cent of what UN agencies said was needed. At the time of writing, even this flow had again been blocked by the Ethiopian government. In mid-2022 it was known that the numbers of those dying slow and excruciating deaths from starvation were mounting in Tigray—initially infants and the elderly, and those whose health was complicated by medical conditions that could not be treated after Tigray's health systems had been looted, destroyed and deprived of drugs. The continuing block on media and reporting meant that at the time of writing it was impossible to know how many may have died or may have continued to face an awful and agonising death.

It is worth dwelling briefly on the historical parallels with Ethiopia's famine in the mid-1980s, which also affected Tigray (as well as large areas of North Wollo and Wag Himra in what is now north-east Amhara). Much of the contemporary coverage suggested natural causes—drought—as key, but close analysis suggests that this was not the primary driver of starvation deaths. Rather, as now, multiple evidence indicates that the deliberate military and political strategies of the Ethiopian government and its allies caused many of these deaths. In sum,

> it would not be correct to attribute the 1984–85 famine to an overall food shortage. There was a severe drought … but famine was not inevitable and the pattern of who starved when and where was the result of political decisions … One set of political causes of famine was misguided economic policies … another and more substantial set of causes was military … The famine as a whole can be considered a crime.[6]

There are other parallels—some military, others of international diplomacy or policy, and several have been referred to in Chapter 2. The Ethiopian government's aerial bombardment of market centres was a feature of the war in the 1980s. When at least 43 civilians were killed at a market in Togoga in Tigray on 22 June 2021, the UN expressed its concern, and Reuters reported that medical assistance to the wounded was blocked by military personnel closing the road to Mekele.[7] Less remarked upon was the fact that this strike took place on the well-known anniversary of a notorious bombardment of the market in the Tigrayan town of Hawzen by the Derg on 22 June 1988, in which several thousand market-goers are thought to have died.[8]

A second set of parallels relates to failures of the international community to act in a timely way to try to address a famine which—then as now—was 'out of sight and out of mind'. International bureaucrats in Ethiopia have for many decades been quick to declare that 'famine has been averted' even when the factors driving it remained in place. When in July 2022 the UN World Food Programme's head of operations for northern Ethiopia repeated precisely this claim about Tigray,[9] many heard the echo of earlier failures, which also persisted after the Derg period.[10] As seasoned observers have noted drily, 'Famines in Ethiopia are neither declared nor averted, but rather are declared to be averted.'[11]

* * *

There has been a tendency in the coverage of Ethiopia's Tigray war to assume two things. Firstly, that the humanitarian toll is an inherent and unavoidable consequence of any violent conflict as civilians are regrettably caught in the crossfire. This is not an adequate explanation of the situation in Tigray, where the available evidence suggests that the Ethiopian government and its allies employed a series of carefully calculated intentional strategies specifically designed to target civilians. The second assumption is that all sides are equally guilty of causing any unfortunate consequences of war. This assumption is also false.

As David Alton, Helen Clark and Michael Lapsley wrote in a letter to *The Guardian* newspaper in November 2021, 'no side to the conflict is angelic … but only one side has committed violations on a scale and nature that could credibly qualify as genocide—and that, we regret to say, is the coalition of the Ethiopian government, under the prime minister, Abiy Ahmed; the Amhara regional government; and the state of Eritrea'.[12] Other analysts agree:

> All parties bore a share of responsibility for the outbreak of the
> war, but overwhelming evidence available at the time of writing

indicates it was the coalition of Ethiopian Federal forces, Amhara regional forces, and Eritrean troops who committed starvation crimes on a large scale, thereby creating a famine of a scale and depth that is likely to surpass that of Somalia (2011) and Yemen (2015 to the present) ... The Ethiopian army, the Eritrean army, and the militia and special forces of the neighbouring Amhara region took control of the region and committed a wide range of atrocities including pillage, the war crime of starvation, and rape.[13]

The introduction to this book noted that throughout much of 2020, and even as far back as 2019, the war was both predictable and widely predicted. The veteran politician Siye Abraha (quoted at the beginning of this book) also correctly predicted the terrible consequences and scope of the war if political invective were to escalate into violence. But the conflict was not simply the result of Ethiopian tensions. The war was the result of plans and plots in Asmara as well as in Addis Ababa (see Chapter 6). The series of meetings between Eritrean president Isaias and Ethiopian prime minister Abiy that began after their reconciliation in July 2018 laid the foundations for what has unfolded. This culminated in the trilateral alliance between Eritrea, Ethiopia and Somalia in September of that year. Gradually all three leaders drew up plans that led to the Tigray war. As the analyst Goitom Gebreluel concluded:

the destabilisation of the Horn of Africa is primarily a function of the domestic politics of Ethiopia, Eritrea, and Somalia. Abiy, Afwerki, and Abdullahi forged the tripartite alliance in 2018 with the aim of moulding the regional order according to their domestic political ideals. The three leaders are opposed to federalism, the accommodation of ethnonational diversity, and institutionalised governance. Instead, they prefer a centralised state under the command of a strongman who rules by fiat.[14]

Ethiopia's and Eritrea's leaders visited each other's key military facilities in the months and weeks before the outbreak of the war. It was clear to most who knew the region what was about to unfold before the first shot was fired. Almost all of this took place away from the media. Reporters, national and international, have been excluded from the war zone. Eritrea—among the most secretive states in the world—allows no unrestricted reporting.[15] Ethiopia, under its new prime minister, has increasingly adopted these same tactics.

Meanwhile, Ewelina Ochab and David Alton have challenged the lazy assumptions that a block on reporting meant that we simply didn't know better or that civilian suffering in Tigray was an accidental side-effect of the war.

> What we do know is that gross human suffering has been caused by man-made events. What we do know is that much of it was planned and is systematic. What we do know is that in Eritrea people have been brutalised and taught to hate Tigrayans as their enemy. What we do know is that in this dirty war the greatest price is being paid by those who are defenceless—and the highest price of all is being paid by women, an estimated 10,000 of whom have been raped. No-one wielding the levers of power can plausibly say they didn't know. Let no-one say they weren't warned. Let no one say there were no predictors of genocidal crimes.[16]

Among the multiple predictors of genocidal crimes, one was hate speech. Years before the war began, the exceptional risk to civilians of their ethnic identity had already become clear. 'Five warning signs for mass, ethnically targeted violence [were] flashing red'—these included the demonising of Tigrayans as "cancer", "weeds", "rats" and "terrorists"'.[17] Remarkably, 'demonising' is precisely the right word here, as rhetoric deployed during the course of the war has regularly referred to the TPLF as 'satanic'. The words of an adviser to the Ethiopian prime minister in September 2021, comparing the Tigrayans to the 'devil' and saying they should be 'the last of their kind', are perhaps the most egregious instance of this phenomenon,[18] and they drew widespread condemnation. They are by no means an isolated incident.

* * *

It is worth dwelling briefly on the dynamics of political and ethnic antagonisms and (more recently) hate speech, which flicker like electric currents through the intricate historical resources recounted in this book. Chapter 1 looked at the status of the Axumite Empire, centred on Axum in what is now Tigray, as the cradle of the notion of 'ancient Ethiopia'. It noted how during the Era of Princes (later seen in nationalist consciousness as emblematic of the chaos and disorder of decentralisation) Gonderine cohesion disintegrated, and historical perspectives began to diverge between Gonder and Tigray. Finally the chapter considered how the late nineteenth-century Battle of Adwa, also located in Tigray, became the pre-eminent illustration of the notion of 'unconquered Ethiopia' while at the same time creating new tensions and resentments. The northern littoral (what is now Eritrea) remained with Italy, leaving the areas now making up Tigray increasingly peripheral as the Ethiopian empire state expanded south, west and east under a 'dangerously potent militarism'.[19]

Herein lies a first set of ironies. Tigray as a geographical arena and historical concept became central to the twentieth-century self-conception of Ethiopian nationalism as 'ancient and unconquered'. Meanwhile, for most of the twentieth century its people experienced what many increasingly came to regard as marginalisation and exclusion. Italian occupation created new precedents; Tigrayan elites lost land to their southern competitors; and at the end of the Second World War, revolt in eastern Tigray was brutally suppressed with British collaboration.

Chapter 2 explored how ethnic antagonisms had persisted in Ethiopian student politics of the 1960s, feeding interest in the idea of 'self-determination for Ethiopia's nations, nationalities and peoples', and bleeding into the bitter relationships between the militant post-imperial movements of the 1970s and 1980s. The willingness (or not) to countenance political mobilisation based on ethnicity became a central fault line dividing Ethiopia's politicians ever since. Vicious and condemnatory narratives that 'othered' political opponents were normalised in student discourse and tempered into hard steel in the violence of the Red Terror of the 1970s and the civil wars of the 1980s. In this context Tigrayan nationalism was fanned both by the Eritrean precedent of nationalist armed struggle to the north and by the brutal counterinsurgency strategies adopted by the Derg. It also drew on the TPLF's deep roots in Tigrayan society and its deployment of resonant historical resources and narratives.

Part Two of the book explored the emergence of the current constellation of political antagonists within the period of living memory. Chapter 3 looked at the three sets of opponents of the EPRDF and its system of multinational or 'ethnic' federalism during the post-1991 period: ethno-nationalist competitors, including the Oromo Liberation Front, who felt themselves excluded under federalism; the government of newly independent Eritrea; and the opposition pan-Ethiopianist bloc, which challenged the EPRDF government in elections in 2005. Each of these three opponents ethnicised their critique of federalism, focusing their venom not on the government or EPRDF per se, but on Tigrayan *'weyane'* or the TPLF.

The discussion in this book explored the growth and explosion of hostility between Eritrean and Tigrayan politicians and drew attention to the lingering political impact of the Ethio-Eritrean war of 1998–2000. The legacy of the Ethio-Eritrean war has had a powerful impact on regional relations, as well as on Ethiopia's domestic politics. Ironically, Ethiopia's military victories during the war did not have the effect of consolidating support for the TPLF-led EPRDF government. 'Non-Tigrayans generally perceived the EPRDF regime as a minority government, controlled by Tigrayans from within and without [i.e. from Eritrea]. The close link between the TPLF and the EPLF leaderships, at least as it was understood from the outside, led to the belief among the Ethiopian people, and particularly the Amhara, that they were ruled by outsiders.'[20]

The Ethio-Eritrean war had three further effects. Firstly, it soured relations between the EPLF and TPLF. The conflict, and especially the reverses inflicted on Eritrea, remained a driver for President Isaias, after the defeat his forces suffered in 2000. Secondly, in Ethiopia, support for the 2020 war also drew on retaliation, 'not only for the invasion of Badme, but for the previous eight years of humiliation and the loss of Eritrea itself'. As a result, popular Ethiopian nationalist support for the war also contributed to a sense of 'revenge' against the TPLF for having 'given away' Eritrea. 'Ethiopians from all walks of life wanted to take back the land which they felt was rightfully theirs, and to restore the dignity they felt was lost in 1993 when Eritrea gained independence. Simultaneously with crushing the

EPLF, they also felt that the TPLF was humiliated, since these had been comrades in arms'.[21]

Thirdly, the Ethio-Eritrean war created a first chink in the notion of the invincibility—and unity—of the EPRDF.

> The [1998–2000 Ethio-Eritrean] war did not boost the EPRDF's popularity as one might have expected, but quite the contrary: First, the origins of the war were generally understood as a Tigrinya affair, implicating the TPLF itself; thus the Ethiopian government was blamed for the outbreak of war. Secondly, the EPRDF call for war backfired, since they did not achieve the popular objective of the war: to regain lost territories … It was both a modern nation-building war fought over a piece of land and backed by arguments grounded in international law, and also a pre-modern war in its political rationale, conceived as feuding between different feudal princes within the imperial realm of Abyssinia.[22]

Chapter 3 traced the emergence of anti-TPLF and anti-Tigrayan hate speech in the Eritrean propaganda of the Ethio-Eritrean war (1998–2000) and in pan-Ethiopian nationalist activism associated with the contested elections of 2005. A decade later, these seeds of opposition fed into the Oromo and Amhara protests of 2014–18. Chapter 4 demonstrates how the temptation to resort to ethnic mobilisation against perceived 'Tigray dominance' migrated from Eritrean and opposition rhetoric into the ranks of the ruling party. This sentiment emerged more strongly within the EPRDF after the death of its chairman in 2012. Under weaker central leadership, the four fronts of the ruling party began to consolidate their regional state power bases and mobilise against one another. Ethnicised political mobilisation offered a tempting shortcut to legitimacy, at a time when the economy was faltering. Tensions and violence grew, and an anti-TPLF 'Oromara alliance' emerged within the EPRDF, to back a new Oromo prime minister in 2018.

Part Three of the book documented the path to war, while Part Four explored the series of dramatic turns which military events took in 2020 and 2021. By this time, the ethnic hate speech which had crackled as an undercurrent in Ethiopian politics was explicitly, overtly and actively mobilised to secure the loyalty of a constellation of Ethiopian and Eritrean actors against Tigray.

* * *

Former British foreign secretary David Miliband has recently written about the 'age of impunity' in which we are now living.

> The fight against impunity in war zones is a legal as well as a moral imperative, since the rights of civilians are delineated in UN charters, conventions, and laws. Yet those who violate these laws are supported and encouraged by systems that shield them from accountability: military rules of engagement that gloss over international humanitarian law, political coalitions that look the other way when members transgress, and appeals to national sovereignty that shield wrongdoing from investigators and observers.
>
> Today, countervailing power is needed in international relations to build up systems and cultures of accountability that can counteract those of impunity. Where impunity thrives on secrecy, countervailing power demands transparency. Where impunity dismisses calls for accountability as foreign meddling, countervailing power points to the UN Charter and demands [it] be honored. Those who take the lives of noncombatants in battle— shelling their homes, bombing their health centers, rounding up and killing them simply because of their ethnicities—must not be able to do so without consequence. Such crimes should be the focus of a drive against impunity, because they represent the tip of the iceberg: if civilian life cannot be protected in conflict zones, then what hope is there for harder cases, where there is no official conflict?[23]

The often-harrowing events described in this book deserve to be documented and understood in their own right. But viewed from the perspective articulated by Miliband, the events of Ethiopia's Tigray war also have a wider import. They offer wider lessons for the contemporary world and place urgent demands for the kind of countervailing power he describes. There is a weight of evidence that 'the men who made famine in Tigray in 2021 appear to have done so confident that they would enjoy impunity for their crimes'.[24]

Global events elsewhere—particularly since Russia's attack on Ukraine in February 2022—further distracted the international community, at a time when a more sophisticated understanding of Ethiopia's politics was urgently needed: one that looked beyond its perennial status as a 'drought-affected', 'impoverished' 'aid recipient' to analyse the political processes behind these stereotypes.

It is hard to see how Ethiopia and Tigray can emerge from the current round of bloodletting without such analysis and a public process of debate and reconciliation. Writing about Ethiopia's 1980s starvation crimes, which were not subsequently prosecuted, Alex de Waal remarked: 'For those who have emerged from this protracted and degrading ordeal, it is the intimate abuses and violations, suffered and perpetrated, within the family and among neighbours, that are the most vivid in the memory, and least spoken about.'[25]

As a generation's grim experiences have been repeated, Tigray is struggling to find a new place within the region. Tigrayans have repeatedly discussed whether to remain part of Ethiopia or seek an independent status within the Horn of Africa. This is, of course, a destiny that only they can decide. Ethiopians, as well as others within the region, will have a stake in their future, but peace will only be achieved if Tigrayans feel comfortable with their status. The Tigrayans' neighbours will remain their neighbours whatever the status of their polity vis-à-vis the rest of Ethiopia: one can only wonder how future coexistence can be secured.

There is nothing unique about this. Somaliland has striven for international recognition as an independent state for years. While it has failed to achieve the sovereign status of Eritrea or South Sudan, most would argue that it has been more successful than either. Other African nations and people have made similar claims, though the African Union has generally attempted to halt the disintegration of its members. Beyond Africa, other nations have joined, and left, wider unions. The Soviet Union collapsed; Yugoslavia dissolved into its constituent parts; the Czechs and Slovaks went their own ways; Britain joined—and then left—the European Union; and the union of the UK's constituent nations remains contested. The Chinese successfully regained Hong Kong and would dearly love to incorporate Taiwan. Do any of these changes actually improve the lives or the prospects of their respective peoples? Once the old flags have come down and new ones have been hoisted to much jubilation, lives must be shaped as before. Children are born and educated; adults work and fall in love; the elderly fade and die.

The conflict and suffering documented in this book are a blot on the conscience of all who have done little to halt them or even stoked the fires. Those who supplied drones to the Ethiopian military have much to answer for. But so, too, does the African Union, which has been singularly unable to rise to the challenge of dealing with a major crisis on its doorstep. The Chinese, Russians and others consistently blocked measures at the United Nations, thwarting the attempts to discuss the crisis. At the time of writing, the AU, UN, US, EU and China all had special envoys in the Horn, focused on the Tigray war. None had been able to support moves towards a credible process of negotiation.

This war, like so many others, has spilled beyond the original site of the conflict. To some degree all Ethiopians have been sucked into the whirlpool, either being directly affected by violence or seeing their economic prospects and those of their children undermined by the costs of military priorities and military destruction. A similar fate has befallen tens of thousands of Eritreans and Somalis. Basil Davidson's vision of an end to authoritarian centralism as a precondition for peace in Ethiopia continues to resonate and must surely inform a return to the construction of political solutions. Melding his vision with Centime Zeleke's focus on the need to curb the anti-democratic tendencies of the state could point to a more profound—even inclusive—reframing of Ethiopian political competition, transcending its central division. At the time of writing, that prospect seems distant. The real question is how to achieve that kind of more fundamental reframing.

AFTERWORD

Martin Plaut and Sarah Vaughan
9 November 2022

Two years on — a deal to end the war?

On Wednesday 2 November 2022, representatives of the Ethiopian government and of the TPLF surprised many of those following AU-led talks in Pretoria with an announcement that they had signed an 'Agreement for Lasting Peace through a Permanent Cessation of Hostilities',[1] designed 'permanently [to] silence the guns and end the two years of conflict in Northern Ethiopia.' A week later, on the day this afterword was written, the most senior military commanders of the two sides were meeting in Nairobi in a third day of discussions to try to agree the detailed implementation of the various provisions of the peace deal.

What had brought about this apparent sea-change? The answer is the utter horror of ten weeks of unprecedented carnage after intensive fighting erupted again on 24 August 2022. Fighting raged on as many as eighteen different fronts in and around Tigray; it involved multiple hundreds of thousands of ground troops,[2] with horrifying artillery and aerial assaults on Tigrayan towns and civilians; it may have caused the deaths of as many as 100,000 combatants in a matter of a few weeks.[3] The Tigray Chief of Staff claimed in mid-September that Ethiopian casualties were in excess of anything in the Ethiopian

Defence Force's history.[4] A number of Ethiopian media sources concurred.

The cost to civilians, on top of two years of suffering, was horrifying. The International Crisis Group reported the chilling testimony of a UN official quoting an Eritrean commander interviewed from Barentu: this affirmed an Eritrean strategy to drive Tigrayan civilians ahead of the fighting with a scorched earth policy of comprehensive destruction and looting: effectively attempting to kettle civilians into a shrinking Tigrayan-held area in the centre of the region, where they would perish without food.[5] By the end of October, the UN reported that more than 210,000 people in northwest Tigray alone had been newly displaced 'due to continued airstrikes and shelling on multiple fronts.'[6]

Press reports indicated that the extraordinary costs of the war were put before the parties during the Pretoria negotiations when they began in earnest in late October 2022.[7] Meanwhile the war had also taken a terrible economic toll on the Ethiopian economy, and this too seemed likely to have motivated negotiators. The country was reported to have less than a month's worth of foreign exchange in its reseres, after having lost investment and spent heavily on weaponry. The IMF, which had refused to consider new funding while the war raged,[8] soon indicated that technical talks were underway as the Fund 'weighed its next options'.[9]

Starvation as a 'method of warfare'

The pause in full-scale military confrontation from the end of 2021 was – as outlined in Chapter 8 – fragile and intermittent. Fighting took place on a number of fronts, particularly on the border with the Afar region in the early months of 2022. Otherwise, up to August, Tigrayan forces remained broadly within Tigray, and Ethiopian and Eritrean forces did not push further into Tigray other than the areas they already occupied in the west, northeast and southeast. Full-scale war had been halted for the best part of nine months.

From April 2022 some aid flowed into Tigray, but as discussed in Chapter 10, in wholly inadequate quantities. The day before fighting recommenced in August, the federal government again halted convoy permits: UN logistics cluster figures for the months of April to August indicated a total of 5,610 trucks entered Tigray, carrying less than a quarter of a million metric tonnes of cargo, and around two and a half million litres of fuel - a fraction of needs.[10] Otherwise, the Ethiopian government's blockade remained in force and in August the full siege resumed.

In September 2022 a UN Human Rights Council-mandated International Commission of Human Rights Experts on Ethiopia found reasonable grounds to believe that all sides had committed violations, but singled out Ethiopian forces for 'intentionally using starvation of civilians as a method of warfare'.[11] Ongoing refusal to allow communications, power, banking, travel, trade or the payments of government budgets and salaries - as well as adequate food and medicine – meant the strangulation of the Tigray region, and starvation of its population. The situation was intolerable and it was clear to all concerned that there were only two alternatives: successful negotiations or the resumption of war.

The war resumes

Both sides had used the lull to retrain and re-position their forces and on 24 August the dam burst. Intense fighting was, in a critical way, different from previous offensives: there were reports of large-scale transfers of Ethiopian forces into Eritrea.[12] It appeared that the strategy and tactics of the war were being increasingly driven by Asmara, rather than Addis Ababa. More than ten divisions of Eritrean forces and a supporting Ethiopian detachment, reportedly airlifted into Massawa, prepared to attack Tigray across the region's northern border. Heavy artillery kept up indiscriminate bombardment of Tigrayan towns on the Zalambessa, Tsorena, and Rama fronts in the north, with multiple drone attacks, and yet the Eritrean and Ethiopian forces made only limited progress southwards.

Federal allies launched a twin-pronged offensive into southern Tigray. Ethiopia's 6th and 8th commands, together with three divisions of Amhara Special Forces and thousands of Fano and Amhara militia, attempted to capture Maichew and destroy Tigrayan forces on the southern front. After days of intense fighting Tigrayan forces counterattacked. The scale of the fighting resembled the battles around Yechila, which had set the stage for Tigray's recapture of Mekele in June 2021.

In early September the Ethiopian government launched offensives on five fronts: through Weldiya, Abergele, Adi Arkay, Wolkait and Sheraro. Tens of thousands of Ethiopian troops, including elite commando and republican guard units, attacked on the Weldiya front, resulting in some of the fiercest and bloodiest battles in recent Ethiopian history. The Ethiopian offensive on Abergele aimed to threaten Mekele – the regional capital. Initial battlefield successes led some Ethiopian officials to predict the swift capture of Mekele but Tigrayan resistance reversed many of the Ethiopian gains. It was only by airlifting troops into Lalibela that the Ethiopians stabilised the southern front.

As the fighting unfolded Eritrean and Ethiopian commanders assessed their tactics. Ethiopia's Chief of Staff, Field Marshal Berhanu Jula, reportedly met Eritrean Chief of Staff, General Filipos Woldeyohannes, early in October in the Ethiopian border town of Humera to plan the next offensive.[13]

In the south-west, around Adi Arkay and in the northwest around Sheraro, the story was now very different. The Ethiopian forces pushed northwards from Adi Arkay, while a twin-pronged Ethiopian and Eritrean offensive from Badme overwhelmed Tigrayan defensive lines and captured large areas including Sheraro town. On 27 September the Tigrayan town of Adi Da'ero was flattened by airforce jets and a few days later on 5 October 2022 more than fifty people were reported to have been killed and seventy injured when a school known to be housing IDPs was targeted there.[14] A Red Cross ambulance driver, and an IRC staff member were killed in October, making a total of twenty-seven humanitarian workers killed since November 2020.[15] Tigrayan forces were pushed back after inflicting significant losses on the advancing coalition. The two federal allied offensives converged on the town of Shire, which was attacked by artillery and drones, and captured on 17 October.

Tigrayan forces fell back to the historic city of Adwa, site of the famous Ethiopian defeat of the Italians in 1896, before continuing to retreat southwards until they reached Abi Adi on 25 October.

The same day the Tigrayans ambushed the advancing Ethiopians near Adwa. There were days of heavy fighting, with the BBC reporting the use of tanks and heavy artillery, noting 'the outcome of the fighting near Adwa could determine who controls the two roads leading to Mekelle, the capital of Tigray'.[16] Some commentators termed the B30 road from Sheraro to Adwa 'the Highway to Hell,' suggesting that Eritreans were trapped and under siege.[17] The Tigrayan forces too paid a heavy price.

By deploying a mixture of conventional and guerrilla tactics, the Tigrayans managed either to stem the Ethiopian and Eritrean advance, or else to fall back and allow an advance, only then to encircle their opponents in ambush. The nature of the onslaught they faced had two consequences, already mentioned. Firstly, the advances into Tigray resulted in the flight of vast numbers of civilians. They left behind towns devastated by weeks of shelling and constant attack. The United States Holocaust Memorial Museum warned of a heightened risk of genocide: 'the situation has deteriorated exponentially as Ethiopian security forces, supported by Eritrean forces and Amhara special forces, have seized key towns and cities imperilling vulnerable Tigrayan civilians.'[18]

Secondly, the rate of attrition among troops was extraordinary, with tens of thousands killed and wounded. Excluding combatants, the best estimate of the mortality among civilians (from massacres, lack of health care and famine) had also risen rapidly. Professor Jan Nyssen and his team at Ghent University calculated civilian deaths at between 380,00 and just over 600,000 prior to the August-November offensives.

All parties mobilised their civilians, but Eritrea was swept bare of almost every man and woman capable of bearing arms.[19] There were verified reports of men as old as 70 called up to fight. Villagers who tried to hide their relatives had their homes searched and sealed, with families thrown onto the streets until their children came forward to serve. There were reports of hospitals in towns in southern Eritrea overflowing with casualties from the war front. Yet President Isaias and his closest associates, in the military and the ruling party, continued the drive into Tigray, regardless of the human cost.

The dynamics of the deal – back to the beginning?

The agreement signed on 2 November forbade 'all kinds of hostilities, direct and indirect, including proxy wars, hate speech, propaganda, airstrikes, landmines' and – arguably most significantly of all – collaboration with any 'foreign force' hostile to either of the parties: an implicit reference to Eritrea, which is nowhere named in the Agreement.[20] As it had been since 2018, Eritrea's role remained the 'elephant in the room' at the time of writing. On the day the agreement came into force, prime minister Abiy lauded a friendly state who had stood alongside the country 'like one region of Ethiopia'.[21] On Saturday 5 November 2022, Eritrean MiGs reportedly bombed Abi Adi in Tembien, in breach of the Cessation of Hostilities Agreement – to which, of course, Eritrea was not a signatory. Heavy fighting was reported to have continued after the deadline for cessation at Zalambessa and Adigrat (involving Eritrean forces) and Chercher (involving Amhara forces).[22] On Monday 7 November, Ethiopian Government negotiator Redwan Hussein spoke of a potential 'third party' spoiler – apparently referring to Eritrea. On the same day Eritrean state-affiliated media called for the Amhara regional government to accept the deal only subject to a specific consideration of its 'rights, interests, identity and boundaries'.[23] The response of the Eritrean government to the peace deal remained an open question, with ramifications across the region.

The Ethiopian prime minister claimed that 'Ethiopia's proposal had been accepted 100%'.[24] Meanwhile Getachew Reda of the TPLF noted that Tigray had made 'painful concessions' to achieve the Permanent Cessation of Hostilities Agreement. Amongst key concessions made by the Tigrayans, two were particularly 'painful' and – if incautiously implemented – were expected to heighten the sense of injustice in the region and undermine the prospects for a sustainable peace.

The first was political principle. The TPLF apparently accepted that their September 2020 election had been unconstitutional and agreed that it be repeated in the course of a transitional process supervised by the National Election Board of Ethiopia. This arguably conceded a central premise of resistance to the federal centre. As the government of Tigray, the TPLF and their allies had argued that they fought the war in self-defence – but also in order to achieve a return to Ethiopia's existing constitutional framework that they claimed had been breached by the federal government when it postponed elections. It was therefore a remarkable political coup for Addis Ababa that Tigray's leaders proved willing to renounce their status as its legitimately elected government, whilst recognising prime minister Abiy's federal government.

The second was disarmament: a practical concession of Tigray region's capacity to defend its right to self-determination, with immediate security implications. The concession of TPLF 'disarmament within 30 days' was expected to prove exceptionally complex. The important caveat – that TPLF combatants would disarm 'subject to the security situation' in Tigray – seemed likely to shape the events of subsequent weeks. In a strongly worded statement, meanwhile, on 5 November 2022 the Global Society of Tigrayan Scholars, whilst welcoming an agreement for peace in general terms, took exception to the disarmament clause as 'illogical,' with the potential to undermine the very ceasefire the agreement set out to secure.[25]

As was the case during the summer months of 2020 when Ethiopia slid into war, much hinged in November 2022 on interpretation of the constitutional order. Then, as earlier, it remained to be seen how much the parties would be able to agree on in practice. This book has set out the profundity of the divisions between Ethiopian politicians on constitutional matters. A week after the Agreement came into force, no food, medicines or fuel had moved to reach Tigray's desperate civilians. Many in the international community seemed to have accepted a horrifying situation in which binding principles of international humanitarian law had become grist to the mill of political negotiation and brinkmanship.[26]

Peace – with justice?

At the time of writing, several other issues were proving of great concern to observers of the peace deal. One was that of accountability and an independent and credible process of justice – transitional or otherwise. The Agreement seemed to place this under the Ethiopian government's purview, a situation unlikely to satisfy either the diverse victims of its actions or international principles of impartial investigation. Human Rights Watch expressed concern about the lack of detail on processes of accountability – and the failure to mention 'the situation for civilians in Western Tigray, the site of an ethnic cleansing campaign'.[27] Amnesty International similarly commented that 'further strides must be taken to address the accountability deficit' for 'crimes which cannot simply be washed away',[28] calling for unfettered access for international investigators.

Peace requires justice if it is to endure. As this book has discussed, peace with impunity, peace that excludes or buries the narratives of key constituencies, will not serve.

APPENDIX

LOGBOOK OF IRREGULAR FLIGHTS BY ETHIOPIAN AIRLINES TO ASMARA AND MASSAWA (ERITREA)

Date	Flight No.	Destination	AC	Tail	Arrival in Local Time	Departure in Local Time	Flight Type	Remarks
25/09/2020	ET8312	ADD-ASM-ADD	B73W	ETALK	12:29	13:23	Chartered	Irregular
20/10/2020	ET8312	ADD-ASMADD	B738	ETAQQ	02:17	13:53	Chartered	Irregular
03/11/2020	ET3102	ADD-MQX-ADO	B789	ETA UR		17:31	Cargo	
03/11/2020	ET310Q	ADD-MQX-ADO	A3 50	ETATY		21:05	Cargo	
06/11/2020	ET8312	ADD-ASM-ADD	B73W	ETALK	13:13	14:29	Chartered	irregular
7-9/11/2020	ET8124	ADD-GDQ-ASM-GDQ-ADD	DH8	ETASA	11/07/2021 10:16	11/09/2021 17:50	Chartered	irregular
8-9/11/2020	ET3312	ADD-MSW-BJR-ADD	B77X	ETA PS	11/08/2021 11:24	11/09/2021 07:02	Cargo	
12/11/2020	ET3312	ADD-ASM-ADD	B788	ETATJ	15:01	19:18	Cargo	
13/11/2020	ET2144	ADD-BJR-ASM-G DQ-ADD	B738	ETAOA	13:16	15:03	Chartered	Irregular
13/11/2020	ET2206	ADD'DIR' ASM' ADD	B763	ETALO	1300	15:30	Chartered	Irregular
13/11/2020	ET2142	ADD- BJR-ASM-ADD	B738	ETAQP	13:10	15:38	Chartered	irregular
13/11/2020	ET3314	ADD-ASM-ADD	B73F	ETAWC	19:53	21:48	Cargo	

Date	Flight No.	Destination	AC	Tail	Arrival in Local Time	Departure in Local Time	Flight Type	Remarks
16/11/2020	ET8312	ADD-ASM-J E D-AS M* ADD	B788	ETATK	11.55-18:29	13:48-19:39	Chartered	Irregular
19/11/2020	ET3312	ADD-ASM-ADD	B788	ETATL	11:19	12:40	Cargo	
22/11/2020	ET3314	ADD-ASM-ADD	B788	ETATI	13:33	15:10	Cargo	
24/11/2021	ET3312	ADD-ASMADD	B763	ETALP	13:40	16:23	Cargo	
26/11/2020	ET8312	ADD-ASM-ADD	B788	ETAOR	13:48	15:40	Chartered	Irregular
28/11/2020	ET3J12	ADD-ASM-ADD	B738	ETAPF	12:17	14:11	Cargo	
02/12/2020	ET3312	ADD-ASM-ADD	DH8	ETANJ	11:37	12:55	Cargo	
05/12/2020	ET8334	ADD-EBB-ASM-ADD	B788	ETAQV	18:05	19:27	Chartered	Irregular
18/12/2020	ET8312	ADD-ASM-ADD	B763	ETALO	12:27	13:55	Chartered	Irregular
20-21/12/2020	ET3706	ADD-ASM-ADD	B73F	ETAWC	12/20/21 5;48;00 PM	12/21/21 9;02;00 AM	Cargo	
29/01/2021	ET8312	ADD-ASM-ADD	B763	ETALO	11:42	13:05	Chartered	Irregular
05/02/2021	ET8312	ADD-ASM-ADD	DH8	ETARM	08:55	16:10	Chartered	irregular
IS/02/2021	ET8312	ADD-ASMADD	B788	ETAOU	12:53	14:24	Chartered	irregular
01-02/03/2021	ET8312	ADD-ASM-ADD	DH8	ETARM	03/01/2021 11:47	03/02/2021 10:00	Chartered	irregular

APPENDIX

Date	Flight No.	Destination	AC	Tail	Arrival in Local Time	Departure in Local Time	Flight Type	Remarks
12/03/2021	ET8312	ADD–ASM–ADD	B763	ETALP	12:26	13:58	Chartered	irregular
01/04/2021	ET8312	ADD–ASM–ADD	B788	ETATG	11:55	13:33	Chartered	irregular
16/04/2021	ET8312	ADD–ASM–ADD	B763	ETALP	12:04	13:48	Chartered	irregular

NOTES

INTRODUCTION

1. Siye Abraha interviewed by Rara Media, 18 February 2020, posted 8 May 2020, accessed July 2022, https://www.youtube.com/watch?v=3TjFIvS_6xw.
2. R. Reid, *Frontiers of Violence in North-East Africa*, Oxford: OUP, 2011.
3. R. Reid, *War in Pre-colonial Eastern Africa*, Oxford: James Currey, 2007, p. 8.
4. Reid, *War*, p. 8.
5. Abyssinia was used (historically and by outside powers) to refer to the Semitic (primarily Tigrigna- and Amharic-speaking) and predominantly Christian areas of the northern plateau, now in Eritrea and the Amhara and Tigray regions of northern Ethiopia.
6. J. Markakis, 'Ethnicity in Political Mobilisation, Conflict Resolution, and State Organisation in Ethiopia', report for the Netherlands Organisation for International Development Cooperation, The Hague, 2000, p. 8. See also Merera Gudina, *Ethnic Nationalism and Ethiopia's Quest for Democracy 1960–1997*, Düren: Shaker, 2003.
7. C. Tilly, *Coercion, Capital and European States*, Oxford: Blackwell, 1990; C. Clapham, *The Horn of Africa: State Formation and Decay*, London: Hurst, 2017, ch. 2.
8. P. Engelbert and R. Hummel, 'Let's Stick Together: Understanding Africa's Secessionist Deficit', *African Affairs*, 39 (1) 2005, pp. 399–667. See also L. de Vries, P. Engelbert and M. Schomerus (eds.), *Secessionism in African Politics*, Cham: Palgrave Macmillan, 2019.
9. 'What Now for Ethiopia's Multinational Federation?', Ethiopia Insight, 2 February 2020, accessed February 2020, https://www.ethiopia-insight.com/2020/02/02/what-now-for-ethiopias-multinational-federation/.
10. H. Slim, *Solferino 21: Warfare, Civilians and Humanitarians in the Twenty-First Century*, London: Hurst, 2022, p. xxxiii.
11. J. Butler, *Frames of War: When Is Life Grievable?*, London: Verso, 2016.

1.   THE LONG ARC OF HISTORY

1.   Abraha Gedamu, 'Review of Levine's *Wax and Gold*', *Ethiopia Observer*, 11 (3) 1967, pp. 226–43.

2.   J. Markakis, 'The Legacy of the Past on Ethiopia's Modern Political Life', *Review of African Political Economy*, 2020, https://roape.net/2020/03/12/the-legacy-of-the-past-on-ethiopias-modern-political-life/.

3.   K. Tronvoll, 'The Anatomy of Ethiopia's Civil War', *Current History*, 121 (835) 2022, pp. 163–9.

4.   D. Phillipson, *Foundations of an African Civilisation: Aksum and the Northern Horn, 1000 BC—AD 1300*, Oxford: James Currey, 2012.

5.   The story of the Queen of Sheba has much to do with the retrospective myth-making of a later imperial period, especially the *Kebra Negast* (Glory of Kings) chronicle of fourteenth-century Shewa. Were she contemporaneous with the conventional dates of King Solomon's reign in Jerusalem (970–931 BCE), her reign in Axum would have predated the Axumite empire by the best part of a thousand years. 'There is no evidence that any Aksumite ruler ever claimed Solomonic descent.' S. Kaplan, 'Solomonic Dynasty', in *Encyclopaedia Aethiopica*, vol. 4, Wiesbaden: Harrassowitz, 2010, p. 688.

6.   Phillipson, *Foundations*, pp. 75–8.

7.   Phillipson, *Foundations*, p. 99. See also A. Lawler, 'Church Unearthed in Ethiopia Rewrites the History of Christianity in Africa', *Smithsonian Magazine*, 10 December 2019, accessed July 2022, https://www.smithsonianmag.com/history/church-unearthed-ethiopia-rewrites-history-christianity-africa-180973740/.

8.   Phillipson, *Foundations*, ch. 15.

9.   Adhana Haile Adhana, 'Tigray: The Birth of a Nation within the Ethiopian Polity', in M.A. Mohammed Salih and J. Markakis (eds.), *Ethnicity and the State in Eastern Africa*, Uppsala: Nordiska Afrikainstitutet, 1998, p. 43.

10.   Phillipson, *Foundations*, ch. 16.

11.   Phillipson, *Foundations*, p. 210.

12.   How long the Zagwe kings ruled before their defeat in 1270 is debated. Phillipson gives a useful synopsis of the debates, in *Foundations*, p. 228.

13.   Kaplan, 'Solomonic Dynasty', p. 688. 'Later Ethiopian royal historiography depicts Yǝkunno Amlak as a descendant of … the last Aksumite king.' See also D. Nosnitsin and M.-L. Derat, 'Yǝkunno Amlak', in *Encyclopaedia Aethiopica*, vol. 5, Wiesbaden: Harrassowitz, 2014, pp. 43–6.

14.   The Oromo now constitute Ethiopia's largest language group. This period of historical migration saw significant patterns of mingling and assimilation, particularly between Oromo and Amhara groups in the areas of Shewa (broadly the areas of Amhara and Oromia regions around Addis Ababa) and further north in Wollo (in eastern Amhara region).

15.   M. Abir, *Ethiopia: The Era of the Princes: The Challenge of Islam and the Re-unification of the Christian Empire*, London: Longmans, 1968.

16.   For two thoughtful recent reflections on the juxtaposition of these historical episodes, see Mohammed Girma, 'Ethiopia Needs a New Rallying Point Instead of Recycling Its Painful Past', The Conversation, 12 August 2019, accessed July

2022, https://theconversation.com/ethiopia-needs-a-new-rallying-point-instead-of-recycling-its-painful-past-121531; Abel Tesfaye, 'Does Ethiopia Really Need Another Tewodros II?', Ethiopia Insight, 30 December 2019, accessed January 2021, https://www.ethiopia-insight.com/2019/12/30/does-ethiopia-really-need-another-tewodros-ii/.

17. J. Young, *Peasant Revolution in Ethiopia: The Tigray People's Liberation Front, 1975–1991*, Cambridge: CUP, 1997, p. 43, quoting R. Hess, *Ethiopia: The Modernisation of Autocracy*, Ithaca: Cornell University Press, 1970, p. 50.

18. Abel Tesfaye, 'Does Ethiopia Really Need Another Tewodros II?', notes the explicit parallel that has been drawn between Tigrayan *Ras* Mikhael Sehul's move on Gonder which ushered in the Era of Princes and the TPLF's move on Addis Ababa bringing federalism.

19. Adhana, 'Tigray', p. 44.

20. E.S. Pankhurst, *Ethiopia: A Cultural History*, London, 1955, quoted by R. Greenfield, *Ethiopia: A New Political History*, London: Pall Mall Press, 1965, p. 96.

21. Bahru Zewde, *A History of Modern Ethiopia, 1855–1974*, London: James Currey, 1991, p. 111.

22. See S. Rubenson, *The Survival of Ethiopian Independence*, London: Heinemann, 1976, p. 316, map 5, for the extent of Menelik's claims in 1891. Menelik's claims incorporated a strong element of what one might call 'performativity' (or wishful thinking), being widely published in a circular distributed to interested colonial powers. Additionally, 'to make Ethiopian claims effective, the wily ruler dispatched his soldiers ... to establish proof of control and pre-empt rights of possession'. J. Markakis, *Anatomy of a Traditional Polity*, Oxford: Clarendon, 1974, pp. 24–5.

23. With French Somaliland (Djibouti) in March 1897; with British Somaliland (June 1987); Italian Eritrea (1900); Anglo Sudan (1902); British East Africa (Kenya) (1907); and Italian Somaliland (1908). With the exception of changes in the status of the border with Eritrea between 1960 and 1991, these border agreements have broadly persisted.

24. There is a debate as to whether Tigrigna and Amharic are descended from Ge'ez, or whether all three share a common ancestor.

25. M.L. Bender, J.D. Bowen, R.L. Cooper and C.A. Ferguson (eds.), *Language in Ethiopia*, London: OUP, 1976, p. 13.

26. J.S. Trimingham, *Islam in Ethiopia*, London: Frank Cass, 1965, p. 15. Note that whether the historical Bete Israel are rightly regarded as part of Judaism has been disputed.

27. Bahru, *History of Modern Ethiopia*, p. 31.

28. Bahru, *History of Modern Ethiopia*, p. 60.

29. R. Caulk, 'Territorial Competition and the Battle of Embabo', *Journal of Ethiopian Studies*, 13 (1) 1975.

30. R. Caulk, 'The Occupation of Harar: January 1887', *Journal of Ethiopian Studies*, 9 (2) 1971.

31. D. Donham, 'Old Abyssinia and the New Ethiopian Empire: Themes in Social History', in D. Donald and W. James (eds.), *The Southern Marches of Imperial Ethiopia*, Cambridge: CUP, 1986, p. 23.

32. Bahru, *History of Modern Ethiopia*, p. 45.

33. H.G. Marcus, *A History of Ethiopia*, Berkeley: University of California Press, 1994, p. 65; Bahru, *History of Modern Ethiopia*, p. 61.

34. 'Paradoxically Adwa was both a negation and an affirmation of Wichale.' Gebru Tareke, *Ethiopia: Power and Protest; Peasant Revolts in the Twentieth Century*, Oxford: OUP, 1991, p. 41. Post-Adwa a new treaty was signed clarifying Italy's recognition of Ethiopian independence. For the debate between Rubenson and Giglio on the question of Italian intentions at Wuchale and discrepancies between the Amharic and Italian texts, see Rubenson, *Survival of Ethiopian Independence*, p. 385, n. 415.

35. Bahru Zewde singles out Gebre Egziabher Gila Mariam as particularly 'unsparing in his criticism of Menelik'. Bahru Zewde, *Pioneers of Change in Ethiopia*, Oxford: James Currey, 2002, pp. 66, 134.

36. Note the view of Richard Reid: 'certainly Menelik was nowhere near strong enough, either in economic or in purely military terms, to contemplate some kind of grand campaign to drive the Italians into the Red Sea'. R. Reid, *Frontiers of Violence in North-East Africa*, Oxford: OUP, 2011, p. 98.

37. Gebru, *Ethiopia: Power and Protest*, p. 232, n. 25; see also H.G. Marcus, *The Life and Times of Menelik II: Ethiopia 1844–1913*, Oxford: Clarendon, 1975, p. 176.

38. cf. Rubenson, *Survival of Ethiopian Independence*, p. 368.

39. H. Erlich, *Ras Alula and the Scramble for Africa: A Political Biography; Ethiopia and Eritrea 1875–1897*, Lawrenceville: Red Sea Press, 1996, p. xi.

40. Reid, *Frontiers of Violence*, pp. 89–90, quoting A.B. Wylde, *Modern Abyssinia*, 2nd edn, Westport: Negro Universities Press, 1970, pp. 174, 220–1.

41. C. Clapham, *Transformation and Continuity in Revolutionary Ethiopia*, Cambridge: CUP, 1988, pp. 205–6; also cited by Alemseged, *Identity Jilted*, pp. 21–2.

42. R. Pankhurst, 'The Great Ethiopian Famine of 1888–1892: A New Assessment', *Journal of the History of Medicines and Allies Sciences*, 21 (2–3) 1966.

43. Bahru, *History of Modern Ethiopia*, p. 71.

44. Author's interviews, Tigrayan farmers, Sheraro area, November 1988.

45. Adhana, 'Tigray'. Cf. Teshale Tibebu's contention that 'Amhara and [Oromo] were not ethnic terms. Amhara was a metaphor for power (and the person identified as such could as well be an Oromo from Shawa, a Gurage, a Tigrayan), and [Oromo] for the relative lack of it, (a shorthand for the conquered 'others'). For Muslims, Amhara meant a Christian with a gun.' Teshale Tibebu, *The Making of Modern Ethiopia, 1897–1974*, Lawrenceville: Red Sea Press, 1995, p. 45. Note that Teshale's original deploys an alternative derogatory term for Oromo that was in contemporary usage in the period under discussion.

46. Alemseged, *Identity Jilted*, p. 45.

47. Bahru, *Pioneers of Change in Ethiopia*, p. 133.

48. Thus, for instance, those who resent Afewerk's anti-Tigrayan sentiments are keen to stress his 'fulsome espousal of the Fascist cause'. Bahru, *Pioneers of Change in Ethiopia*, p. 57. The ranks of Tigrayan elites of the period provide numerous example of similar perfidy. Consciousness of such historical issues returned with a vengeance during the 1998–2000 Ethio-Eritrean war.

49. Yohannes IV had already tried 'to avoid becoming a parochial Tigrean monarch. Amharic, not Tigrigna, was made the official language at his court.' Erlich, *Ras Alula*, p. 2.

50. Bahru, *Pioneers of Change in Ethiopia*, p. 132.

51. Roughly 'peasant-governor'. There is an enormous literature on the operation of this system, its relation with traditional land tenure patterns in the north, and the extent to which both should be understood as a 'feudal arrangement'. See D. Crummey, *Land and Society in the Christian Kingdom of Ethiopia, from the Thirteenth to the Twentieth Century*, Oxford: James Currey, 2000; J.M. Cohen and D. Weintraub, *Land and Peasants in Imperial Ethiopia*, Assen: Van Gorcum, 1975; H. Hoben, *Land Tenure among the Amhara of Ethiopia*, Chicago: University of Chicago Press, 1973; J. McCann, *From Poverty to Famine in Northeast Ethiopia: A Rural History 1900–1935*, Philadelphia: University of Pennsylvania Press, 1987; and G. Ellis, 'The Feudal Paradigm as a Hindrance to Understanding Ethiopia', *Journal of Modern African Studies*, 14 (2) 1976, pp. 275–95. Dealing more explicitly with the period after the Second World War are S. Fullerton-Joireman, *Property Rights and Political Development in Ethiopia and Eritrea, 1941–74*, Oxford: James Currey, 2000; J. Markakis and Ayele Nega, *Class and Revolution in Ethiopia*, Nottingham: Spokesman, 1978; M. Stahl, *Ethiopia: Political Contradictions and Agricultural Development*, Stockholm: Liber Tryck, 1974. Bahru Zewde gives one of the most succinct and best summaries of the system which the Abyssinians exported and adapted to the south at the end of the nineteenth century; see Bahru, *History of Modern Ethiopia*, p. 87.

52. Bahru, *History of Modern Ethiopia*, p. 88.

53. Bahru, *History of Modern Ethiopia*, pp. 92–3.

54. These were often identified on the basis of phenotypic features. The Amharic term *shanqala*, commonly translated as 'slave', was long used to refer to the people of the periphery, distinguished by their black skin and height, features which regional cultures continue to be jarringly racially conscious of.

55. Gebru, *Ethiopia: Power and Protest*, pp. 40–1: 'By absorbing the traditional polities Menelik was able to construct a broader social base to the imperial state … A new dominant class that was trans-ethnic and transregional was definitely emerging parallel to the evolving state society … As subordinated ruling groups in the occupied territories accepted Christianity and became fully dependent on the imperial state for the conditions of their reproduction, they lost their organic ties to indigenous communities.'

56. There were exceptions: Sheikh Khojele at Assosa (now in Benishangul-Gumuz) and Aba Jiffar at Jimma (now western Oromia) retained the local trappings of their rule under a more indirect system.

57. J. Markakis, *National and Class Conflict in the Horn of Africa*, Cambridge: CUP, 1987, pp. 73–4.

58. Gebru, *Ethiopia: Power and Protest*, p. 41.

59. This included, for instance, the adoption of 'the lion of Judah … as part of the Imperial styles, [which] is of no great antiquity'. E. Ullendorff, *Ethiopia and the Bible*, Oxford: OUP, 1968, p. 11, drawing on S. Rubenson, 'The Lion of the Tribe of Judah: Christian Symbol and/or Imperial Title', *Journal of Ethiopian Studies*, 3 (2) 1965.

60. Reid, *Frontiers of Violence*, p. 91.

61. Asafa Jalata, *Oromo Nationalism and the Ethiopia Discourse*, Lawrenceville: Red Sea Press, 1993.

62. D. Levine, *Greater Ethiopia: The Evolution of a Multiethnic Society*, Chicago: University of Chicago Press, 1974, and *Wax and Gold: Tradition and Innovation in Ethiopian Culture*, Chicago: University of Chicago Press, 1965, and Marcus, *A History of Ethiopia*, have come in for particular criticism along these lines. Much of the ethno-nationalist literature associated with the Eritrean or Oromo causes is at least equally guilty of flat assertions of truth and 'true' political interpretation.

63. Levine, *Greater Ethiopia*, p. 21.

64. Levine, *Greater Ethiopia*, p. 69.

65. The term was coined by Ali Mazrui, *Soldiers and Kinsmen in Uganda: The Making of a Military Ethnocracy*, Beverly Hills: Sage, 1975. It has been used of Ethiopia by John Markakis. See K. Fukui and J. Markakis, 'Introduction', in Fukui and Markakis (eds.), *Ethnicity and Conflict in the Horn of Africa*, Oxford: James Currey, 1994, p. 8.

66. Bahru, *History of Modern Ethiopia*, p. 121.

67. A. Sbacchi, *Ethiopia under Mussolini: Fascism and the Colonial Experience*, London: Zed, 1985, p. 36; Greenfield, *Ethiopia*, p. 230.

68. Sbacchi, *Ethiopia under Mussolini*, p. 160.

69. Sbacchi, *Ethiopia under Mussolini*, p. 161.

70. M.F. Perham, *The Government of Ethiopia*, London: Faber & Faber, 1948, p. 124.

71. Sbacchi, *Ethiopia under Mussolini*, pp. 36, 162–4.

72. Bahru, *History of Modern Ethiopia*, pp. 175–6.

73. Sbacchi, *Ethiopia under Mussolini*, p. 85. The governorships were Amhara, Oromo-Sidama, Harar (including Arsi), Somali, and Eritrea (including Tigray and 'Danakil' in Afar).

74. Sbacchi, *Ethiopia under Mussolini*, p. 159.

75. Sbacchi, *Ethiopia under Mussolini*, p. 86.

76. Gebru, *Ethiopia: Power and Protest*, p. 48, who also draws on Sbacchi, is an exception.

77. See Greenfield, *Ethiopia*, p. 271, and Bahru, *History of Modern Ethiopia*, pp. 178–83, on the 'mutilated' nature of Ethiopian independence under the Anglo-Ethiopian agreements of 1942 and 1944.

78. 'British plans for both Eritrea and the Ogaden ... amounted to a perpetuation of the administrative divisions set up during the Italian Occupation.' Bahru, *History of Modern Ethiopia*, p. 181.

79. The 'Tigray–Tigrigne' project. See G.K.N. Trevaskis, *Eritrea: A Colony in Transition, 1941–52*, Oxford: OUP, 1960; H. Erlich, *Ethiopia and the Challenge of Independence*, Boulder: Lynne Rienner, 1986; and Tekeste Negash, *Ethiopia and Eritrea: The Federal Experience*, Uppsala: Nordiska Afrikainstitutet, 1997.

80. Trevaskis, *Eritrea*.

81. Greenfield, *Ethiopia*, ch. 15.

82. Clapham, 'Haile Selassie's Government', DPhil thesis, University of Oxford, 1966, p. 90, cited in P. Schwab, *Decision Making in Ethiopia*, London: Hurst, 1972.

83. Clapham, *Transformation and Continuity*, p. 27.

84. Bahru, *History of Modern Ethiopia*, p. 140.

85. Haile Sellassie, *The Autobiography of Emperor Haile Sellassie I*, translated by E. Ullendorff, Oxford: Clarendon, 1976, p. 57.

86. See for instance the commentary of Professor Ghelawdewos Araia, April 2022, accessed May 2022, https://www.youtube.com/watch?v=BmT6YEvxsCY.

87. Bahru, *History of Modern Ethiopia*, p. 140.

88. Bahru, *History of Modern Ethiopia*, p. 143.

89. Haile Selassie Gugsa, great-grandson of Emperor Yohannes IV, was a notable collaborator. Haile Sellassie, *The Autobiography*, p. 243.

90. C. Clapham, *Haile Selassie's Government*, London: Longman, 1969, pp. 67ff.

91. Clapham, *Haile Selassie's Government*, p. 71.

92. Mengesha Seyoum, great-grandson of Emperor Yohannes IV, interviewed by Dimtsi Weyane, posted 13 April 2021, accessed April 2021, https://twitter.com/EAfricanAffairs/status/1382097580721635329?s=20&t=Hty6iYHNeiskH_DyRnvb8A.

93. In the same interview Mengesha Seyoum indicates that the area up to Aloha Melash (close to Weldiya) was administered under Tigray. Posted 13 April 2021, accessed April 2021, https://twitter.com/EAfricanAffairs/status/1382097580721635329?s=20&t=Hty6iYHNeiskH_DyRnvb8A. At the time these administrative shifts arguably had more to do with elite political manoeuvring and the building of powerful alliances than with ethnicity per se.

94. Clapham, *Haile Selassie's Government*, p. 64.

95. Bahru, *History of Modern Ethiopia*, p. 109.

96. Bahru, *Pioneers of Change in Ethiopia*, pp. 210–11.

97. Bahru, *Pioneers of Change in Ethiopia*, p. 211.

98. Clapham, *Haile Selassie's Government*, p. 87.

99. Clapham, *Haile Selassie's Government*, pp. 88–9.

100. Schwab, *Decision Making in Ethiopia*, p. 138.

101. Clapham, *Haile Selassie's Government*, p. 91.

102. The Bale case perhaps comes closest.

103. Markakis, *Anatomy of a Traditional Polity*, p. 40.

104. C. Clapham, 'The Era of Haile Selassie', in G. Prunier and E. Ficquet (eds.), *Understanding Contemporary Ethiopia: Monarchy, Revolution and the Legacy of Meles Zenawi*, London: Hurst, 2015, p. 205.

2. CHALLENGING THE EMPIRE

1. R.R. Balsvik, *Haile Selassie's Students: The Intellectual and Social Background to Revolution, 1952–1977*, East Lansing: Michigan State University African Studies Centre, 1985, p. xiii.

2. Elleni Centime Zeleke demonstrates how 'historiography and political practice have been instrumentally connected since the 1970s in Ethiopia'. Centime Zeleke, *Ethiopia in Theory*, Leiden: Brill, 2020, p. 149.

3. The Ethiopian debate draws on the terminology and conceptualisations developed by Lenin and Stalin, as discussed later in the chapter.

4. For a critical and evocative reading of the continued resonance of this period in later politics, see Centime Zeleke, *Ethiopia in Theory*.

5. Centime Zeleke, *Ethiopia in Theory*, captures both the profound importance of the movement and this diaspora nostalgia particularly well.

6. Kiflu Tadesse, *The Generation: The History of the Ethiopian People's Revolutionary Party, Part I: From the Early Beginnings to 1975*, Silver Spring: Independent Publishers, 1993; Kiflu Tadesse, *The Generation, Part II: Ethiopia, Transformation and Conflict*, Lanham: University Press of America, 1998; Babile Tola, *To Kill a Generation: The Red Terror in Ethiopia*, Washington DC: Free Ethiopia Press, 1989.

7. The more realistic—albeit not always dispassionate—analyses of the student movement have come from survivors in this category. Gebru Mersha's unsentimental account is a good example: 'The Emergence of the Ethiopian "Left" in the Period 1960–1970 as an Aspect of the Formation of the "Organic Intellectuals"', paper submitted to a conference on the Ethiopian Revolution and Its Impact on the Horn of Africa, 29–30 May 1987. See also Bahru Zewde's (controversial) *Documenting the Ethiopian Student Movement: An Exercise in Oral History*, Addis Ababa: Forum of Social Studies, 2010.

8. See particularly Balsvik's remarkable outsider's work, *Haile Selassie's Students*. More recent assessments include Bahru Zewde *The Quest for Socialist Utopia: The Ethiopian Student Movement c. 1960–1974*, Oxford: James Currey, 2014; Centime Zeleke, *Ethiopia in Theory*; and the more hostile Messay Kebede, *Radicalism and Cultural Dislocation in Ethiopia, 1960–1974*, Rochester: University of Rochester Press, 2008.

9. Comment made by Tesfaye Habisso, July 1991, Charter comment (English translation of the ETV video soundtrack of the proceedings, Assefa Gezahegn, for the author, June–July 1994).

10. The text is reproduced at https://www.marxists.org/history/erol/ethiopia/nationalities.pdf. A conference marking fifty years since its publication was held in Addis Ababa in November 2019.

11. Balsvik, *Haile Selassie's Students*; Bahru Zewde, *A History of Modern Ethiopia, 1855–1974*, London: James Currey, 1991, pp. 220ff; Bahru, *Quest*.

12. J. Markakis, *Anatomy of a Traditional Polity*, Oxford: Clarendon, 1974, p. 358.

13. R.R. Balsvik, 'An Important Root of the Ethiopian Revolution', in Abebe Zegeye and S. Pausewang (eds.), *Ethiopia in Change: Peasantry, Nationalism and Democracy*, London: Academic Press, 1994, p. 86.

14. Balsvik, 'An Important Root', p. 87.

15. Balsvik, 'An Important Root', p. 91.

16. Andargachew Tiruneh, *The Ethiopian Revolution 1974–1987: A Transformation from an Aristocratic to a Totalitarian Autocracy*, Cambridge: CUP, 1993, pp. 135–6.

17. Balsvik, 'An Important Root', p. 89.

18. Markakis, *Anatomy of a Traditional Polity*, p. 360.

19. Bahru, *History of Modern Ethiopia*, p. 223.

20. Balsvik, *Haile Selassie's Students*, p. 244, reporting advice apparently given Haile Selassie I by Kassa Wolde Mariam, Haile Selassie I University (later Addis Ababa University) president, 1962–9.

21. Kiflu, *The Generation, Part I*, p. 52.

22. Balsvik, *Haile Selassie's Students*, p. 43.

23. Kiflu, *The Generation, Part I*, p. 52.

24. Balsvik, *Haile Selassie's Students*, p. 279.

25. O. Klineberg and M. Zavalloni, *Nationalism and Tribalism among African Students*, Paris and The Hague: Mouton, 1969, p. 241.

26. *News and Views*, 30 April 1966.

27. Balsvik, *Haile Selassie's Students*, p. 279.

28. Kiflu, *The Generation, Part I*, p. 53.

29. Balsvik, *Haile Selassie's Students*, p. 278.

30. Balsvik, *Haile Selassie's Students*, p. 279.

31. Balsvik, *Haile Selassie's Students*, pp. 279–80.

32. Balsvik, *Haile Selassie's Students*, p. 281; see also Kiflu, *The Generation, Part I*, p. 52.

33. Kiflu, *The Generation, Part I*, p. 52.

34. Author's interviews, former members of the student movement, Addis Ababa, November 1997, and Addis Ababa and Mekele, October–November 1998; cf. also Kiflu, *The Generation, Part I*, p. 52.

35. Mekonnen Bishaw, who died in 2007, was, with Mesfin Wolde Mariam, one of two representatives of AAU at the 1991 Charter Conference, which ushered in federalism. He was among those academics controversially dismissed by the incoming EPRDF-led government in 1992.

36. Walleligne Mekonen, 'On the Question of Nationalities in Ethiopia', *Struggle* (organ of the University Student Union of Addis Ababa), 5 (2) 17 November 1969, p. 4.

37. Walleligne, 'On the Question of Nationalities', p. 5.

38. Walleligne, 'On the Question of Nationalities', pp. 6–7.

39. D. Donham, *Marxist Modern: An Ethnographic History of the Ethiopian Revolution*, Berkeley: University of California Press, 1999. See the excellent discussion of Centime Zeleke, *Ethiopia in Theory*, pp. 102ff.

40. Markakis, *Anatomy of a Traditional Polity*, p. 188.

41. Balsvik, *Haile Selassie's Students*, p. 240.

42. Kiflu, *The Generation, Part I*, p. 46.

43. Balsvik, *Haile Selassie's Students*, p. 242.

44. Interview, former university Dean of External Affairs, Mekele, October 1998.

45. Balsvik, *Haile Selassie's Students*, p. 145.

46. Andargachew, *The Ethiopian Revolution*, pp. 29–30.

47. Gebru Mersha, 'The Emergence of the Ethiopian "Left"', p. 31.

48. Dawit Wolde Giorgis, *Red Tears*, Trenton: Red Sea Press, 1989, pp. 10–11. Major Dawit—himself an early enthusiast for Marxist ideology—was a senior member of the Derg regime before defecting to the US in the 1980s.

49. The union of states must take place voluntarily, 'on a truly democratic, truly internationalist basis, which is unthinkable without the freedom of separation' (G. Zinoviev and V.I. Lenin, 'Socialism and War', in Lenin, *Collected Works*, XVIII, 1930 [1915], p. 373); 'A socialist of a great nation or a nation possessing colonies who does not defend this right is a chauvinist' (V.I. Lenin, 'The Revolutionary Proletariat and the Rights of Nations to Self-determination', in Lenin, *Collected Works*, XVIII, 1930 [1915], p. 235). See H.B. Davis, *Nationalism and Socialism:*

Marxist and Labor Theories of Nationalism to 1917, New York: Monthly Review Press, 1967, p. 195.

50. Bahru, *History of Modern Ethiopia*, p. 222.

51. The papers, by Andreas Esheté, Hagos Gebre Yesus, Alem Habtu, and Melesse Ayalew, were published in ESUNA (Ethiopian Student Union in North America), *Challenge*, 10 (1) February 1970.

52. ESUNA, *Challenge*, 1970, p. 58.

53. The pseudonym was chosen to symbolise 'two generations of opposition to the Hayla-Sellase regime': the Black Lion Takele Welde-Hawaryat, who opposed the emperor from the moment he went into exile in 1936, and the student leader Tilahun Gizaw, who had been murdered in 1969. See Bahru Zewde, 'The Intellectual and the State in Twentieth Century Ethiopia', in H.G. Marcus (ed.), *New Trends in Ethiopian Studies: Papers of the 12th Conference of Ethiopian Studies*, Lawrenceville: Red Sea Press, 1994, pp. 483–96. The paper is assumed to have been written by the radical student group which set up in Algiers after their 1969 hijacking of an Ethiopian Airlines plane, led by Berhane Meskal Redda, who went on to lead the influential EPRP.

54. Bahru, 'The Intellectual and the State', pp. 483–4. More than another quarter-century after it was written, Bahru's comment remains truer than ever.

55. J. Markakis and Ayele Nega, *Class and Revolution in Ethiopia*, Nottingham: Spokesman, 1978, pp. 65–7.

56. Balsvik, *Haile Selassie's Students*, p. 278.

57. Ruth Iyob, *The Eritrean Struggle for Independence*, Cambridge: CUP, 1995, pp. 105–6.

58. Isaias Afwerki, for instance, had left AAU to fight with the nationalists in 1966, spending some time in China during the Cultural Revolution; other leaders who abandoned their studies in Addis Ababa were Haile Mariam Wolde Tensaie and Muse Tesfa Mikael. Amanuel Gebre Yesus attempted in 1969–70 to convince the other members of the Algiers group to fight in Eritrea, and his eventual departure to do so forced the others to engage with the issue.

59. Balsvik, *Haile Selassie's Students*, p. 282.

60. As for instance, in Tilahun Gizaw's defeat in the student union presidential elections of 1969, mentioned above. 'Tilahun Gizaw and his supporters … were accused of being agents for this or that secessionist organisation. According to *Struggle* and Tilahun Gizaw, "tribalism, ethnocentrism and localism" were exploited in the campaign and decided the election against Tilahun.' Balsvik, *Haile Selassie's Students*, p. 282.

61. Balsvik, *Haile Selassie's Students*, p. 283.

62. Markakis, *Anatomy of a Traditional Polity*, p. 391. Other academic authorities on the period dispute this, noting that many officers were members of the student body.

63. Veteran geographer Professor Mesfin Wolde Mariam was among those to write with outrage about these events and how they were covered up, both at the time and later. See his *Rural Vulnerability to Famine in Ethiopia, 1958–77*, Rugby: IT Publishing, 1986.

64. There are multiple accounts of this episode. One of the most interesting is Peter Gill, who interviewed several of the protagonists. P. Gill, *Famine and Foreigners: Ethiopia since Bandaid*, Oxford: OUP, 2010.

65. G. Prunier and E. Ficquet, 'Introduction', in G. Prunier and E. Ficquet (eds.), *Understanding Contemporary Ethiopia: Monarchy, Revolution and the Legacy of Meles Zenawi*, London: Hurst, 2015, p. 1.

66. See C. Clapham, *Transformation and Continuity in Revolutionary Ethiopia*, Cambridge: CUP, 1988; P. Gilkes, *The Dying Lion: Feudalism and Modernisation in Ethiopia*, London: Friedmann, 1982; Andargachew, *The Ethiopian Revolution*; F. Halliday and M. Molyneux, *The Ethiopian Revolution*, London: Verso, 1981.

67. J. Markakis, 'The Legacy of the Past on Ethiopia's Modern Political Life', *Review of African Political Economy*, 2020, p. 15. Other academic authorities on the period have questioned this assertion, suggesting that many of the officers had shared the university education of the students (personal communication).

68. Africa Watch, *Evil Days: Thirty Years of War and Famine in Ethiopia*, New York: Africa Watch, 1991, p. 102.

69. There is a large literature on the Derg's land reform. See, for instance, Desalegn Rahmato, *Agrarian Reform in Ethiopia*, Uppsala: Nordiska Afrikainstitutet, 1984. Also Clapham, *Transformation and Continuity in Revolutionary Ethiopia*, ch. 7.

70. Markakis, 'The Legacy of the Past', p. 16.

71. Clapham traces its origins in the candidates' use of recognised *iddirs*, during the imperial period, to organise electoral support. Clapham, *Transformation and Continuity in Revolutionary Ethiopia*, p. 131.

72. Africa Watch, *Evil Days*, p. 101 estimates that 'well in excess of 10,000' were killed during the Red Terror. 'The worst atrocities of the period' started in February 1977 when Mengistu 'labelled the EPRP [assassination] campaign the "white terror", and Atnafu Abate promised "for every revolutionary killed, a thousand counter-revolutionaries executed". The promised ratio was not to be much of an exaggeration'. Human Rights Watch, *Evil Days*, p. 102, quoting R. Lefort, *Ethiopia: An Heretical Revolution*, London: Zed, 1983, p. 99. By mid-1977 the EPRP had been effectively wiped out in the towns, and the Derg turned on its erstwhile ally Me'ison, with further rounds of slaughter in October and December 1977 and through much of 1978. See Kiflu, *The Generation, Part II*; also Babile, *To Kill a Generation*.

73. The dramatic reversal of superpower alignment in the Horn followed Mohammed Siad Barre's miscalculated attempt to reincorporate the Ogaden by force, sensing Ethiopian weakness in 1977. Moscow unceremoniously relocated its military advisers from Mogadishu to Addis Ababa.

74. Clapham, *Transformation and Continuity in Revolutionary Ethiopia*, p. 128.

75. Clapham, *Transformation and Continuity in Revolutionary Ethiopia*, p. 215. Among those commentators to have taken this view are, for instance, M. Ottaway and D., *Ethiopia: Empire in Revolution*, New York: Africana, 1978, p. 84.

76. The multi-language literacy campaign, which began in 1979, promoted nine languages.

77. Markakis, 'The Legacy of the Past', p. 16.

78. Provisional Military Advisory Committee, 'Ten Point Programme', late 1974.

79. General Aman, himself an Eritrean, was killed by the Derg on 22 November 1974, ending all possibility of conciliation in Eritrea.

80. In contrast to imperial shuffling of regional elites (in all areas except Tigray), in a relatively successful attempt to break the regional ties of loyalty which underpinned traditional fiefdoms.

81. Clapham, *Transformation and Continuity in Revolutionary Ethiopia*, p. 202.

82. Author's interview, ISEN member, Addis Ababa, November 1999.

83. Clapham, *Transformation and Continuity in Revolutionary Ethiopia*, p. 200.

84. ISEN, 'Report of Activities' [in Amharic], including note of an address by Mengistu Haile Mariam, April 1984, Addis Ababa.

85. Author's interview, ISEN member, Addis Ababa, 9 November 1999.

86. Clapham, *Transformation and Continuity in Revolutionary Ethiopia*, p. 204.

87. Abel Tesfaye, 'Does Ethiopia Really Need Another Tewodros II?', Ethiopia Insight, 30 December 2019, accessed January 2021, https://www.ethiopia-insight. com/2019/12/30/does-ethiopia-really-need-another-tewodros-ii/.

88. See also the astute commentary of Jacques Bureau, 'Introduction', in Guebrè-Heywèt Baykedagne, *L'Empereur Menelik et l'Ethiopie*, Addis Ababa: Maison des Etudes Ethiopiennes, 1993, pp. iii–iv.

89. Alemseged Abbay, *Identity Jilted or Re-imagining Identity?*, Lawrenceville: Red Sea Press, 1998, p. 332.

90. J. Markakis, *National and Class Conflict in the Horn of Africa*, Cambridge: CUP, 1987, p. 63.

91. Author's interview, TPLF founder member, Mekele, October 1998.

92. It is of course something which recent pro-government propaganda has gone to remarkable lengths explicitly to deny. See, for instance, Hermela Aregawi's interview with Kidane Afwerki, May 2022, https://www.youtube.com/watch?v=gAcIYoiEx9Y.

93. Markakis, *Anatomy of a Traditional Polity*, p. 48.

94. R. Greenfield, *Ethiopia: A New Political History*, London: Pall Mall Press, 1965; Adhana Haile Adhana, 'Tigray: The Birth of a Nation within the Ethiopian Polity', in M.A. Mohammed Salih and J. Markakis (eds.), *Ethnicity and the State in Eastern Africa*, Uppsala: Nordiska Afrikainstitutet, 1998. The circumspect treatment accorded the Tigrayan Orthodox Church by the Marxist TPLF is discussed at length by J. Young, *Peasant Revolution in Ethiopia: The Tigray People's Liberation Front, 1975–1991*, Cambridge: CUP, 1997, and was prominent among the factors behind its success.

95. Tadesse Tamrat, *Church and State in Ethiopia, 1270–1527*, Oxford: Clarendon, 1972, pp. 21ff.

96. Young, *Peasant Revolution in Ethiopia*, p. 31.

97. D. Crummey, *Land and Society in the Christian Kingdom of Ethiopia, from the Thirteenth to the Twentieth Century*, Oxford: James Currey, 2000, p. 221.

98. Adhana, 'Tigray', pp. 44–5.

99. W. Plowden, *Travels in Abyssinia and the Gala Country*, London, 1868, p. 39.

100. Adhana, 'Tigray', pp. 45–6.

101. H. Erlich, *Ethiopia and the Challenge of Independence*, Boulder: Lynne Rienner, 1986, p. 129.

102. J. Hammond cites British Foreign Office evidence that Menelik 'tried to impose his own governors on Tigray, but met massive resistance'. J. Hammond, *Sweeter than Honey*, Oxford: Third World First, 1989, p. 16.

103. Gebru Tareke, *Ethiopia: Power and Protest; Peasant Revolts in the Twentieth Century*, Oxford: OUP, 1991, p. 135.

104. Erlich, *Ethiopia*, p. 131.

105. Gebru, *Ethiopia*, p. 89.

106. Gebru, *Ethiopia*, pp.106–7.

107. Gebru, *Ethiopia*, p. 116.

108. Gilkes, 1975, p. 190.

109. Erlich, *Ethiopia*, p. 133.

110. Author's interview, TPLF member then researching the organisation's history, Addis Ababa, October 1998.

111. Gebru, *Ethiopia*.

112. Gebru, *Ethiopia*, p. 122.

113. Gebru, *Ethiopia*, p. 121. Tigray continued to be ruled by its factional traditional elite and Gebru points to a key difference with the south of the country: 'In the south the gentry … would not dare incite the peasantry because they themselves would have become the principal target. In the north the disenfranchised nobles could have challenged the state only by inciting the peasants.' Gebru, *Ethiopia*, p. 83.

114. Gebru, *Ethiopia*, p. 121.

115. Gebru, *Ethiopia*, p. 122.

116. Author's interview, TPLF founder member, Mekele, 7 October 1998.

117. British planes bombed Mekele on market day, inflicting 'considerable casualties', a precedent which undoubtedly resonated during the TPLF campaign against the Derg, which saw similar bombings of Tigray's market centres, and which was remarked upon when a British ambassador visited Mekele in the early 1990s.

118. Alemseged, *Identity Jilted*, p. 333.

119. For more extensive histories of the TPLF in English, see Young, *Peasant Revolution in Ethiopia*; also two accounts written by former TPLF leaders: Aregawi Berhe, in *A Political History of the Tigray People's Liberation Front (1975–1991)*, Los Angeles: Tsehai, 2009; and Mulugeta Gebrehiwot Berhe, *Laying the Past to Rest: The EPRDF and the Challenges of Ethiopian State Building*, London: Hurst, 2020.

120. Interview, TPLF founder member, Mekele, October 1998.

121. Alemseged, *Identity Jilted*, pp. 100–2.

122. Alemseged, *Identity Jilted*, pp. 99–100.

123. Author's interview, Tigrayan former academic, Mekele, October 1998.

124. A pseudonym. See Hammond, *Sweeter than Honey*, pp. 27–9; M. Woldemariam, *Insurgent Fragmentation in the Horn: Rebellion and Its Discontents*, Cambridge: CUP, 2018, pp. 187–90.

125. Author's interviews, TPLF veterans, Mekele and Addis Ababa, October–November 1998.

126. Author's interview, former academic, Mekele, October 1998.

127. See Young, *Peasant Revolution in Ethiopia*, ch. 4; also Woldemariam, *Insurgent Fragmentation*, pp. 189ff.

128. See Alemseged, *Identity Jilted*, pp. 118ff; Hammond, *Sweeter than Honey*.

129. Author's interview, TPLF founder member, Mekele, 8 October 1998.

130. Also described as 'public relations officers'; author's interview, TPLF historian, Addis Ababa, January 1999.

131. TPLF fighter quoted by Hammond, *Sweeter than Honey*, p. 20.

132. Alemseged, *Identity Jilted*, p. 119.

133. Africa Watch, *Evil Days*, p. 4. There is an extensive literature on the Ethiopian famine of the mid-1980s, much of the best work written by Alex de Waal (including Africa Watch, *Evil Days*; *Famine Crimes: Politics and the Disaster Relief Industry in Africa*, Oxford: James Currey, 1997, ch. 6; *Mass Starvation: The History and Future of Famine*, Cambridge: Polity, 2018, pp. 78–9, and ch. 8). Also among the most useful and readable are also P. Gill, *A Year in the Death of Africa*, London: Paladin, 1986, and *Famine and Foreigners*. See also Dawit Wolde, *Red Tears*, written by the Derg's relief and rehabilitation commissioner through the period, who later fled to the US.

134. De Waal/Africa Watch for instance suggests that across northern Ethiopia (Tigray and Wollo) 'the famine of 1983–5 is estimated to have killed a minimum of 400,000 people, not including those killed by resettlement'. Africa Watch, *Evil Days*, p. 5.

135. Africa Watch, *Evil Days*, p. 14. The book goes on to add: 'The government attempted to conceal this fact, and in doing so was abetted by the United Nations, which in August 1985 produced a mendacious report endorsing the government's claim that it was feeding most of the famine victims in Tigray, at a time when it was in fact feeding very few indeed'. When in 1985 the UN recommended a reduction in the appeal for food aid for Ethiopia, its own most senior official in Addis Ababa 'described the UN's response to the emergency as "an exercise in cynicism"'. Gill, *Famine and Foreigners*, p. 38.

136. Africa Watch, *Evil Days*, p. 30.

137. Suzanne Franks gives a detailed discussion of the impact of Michael Buerk and Mohammed Amin's famous report from Korem, Tigray, broadcast by the BBC in October 1984. Franks, *Reporting Disasters: Famine, Aid, Politics and the Media*, London: Hurst, 2013.

138. Gill, *Famine and Foreigners*, p. 41. The anecdote is also retold by De Waal in an article for the *London Review of Books*, 'Steal, Burn, Rape, Kill: Famine in Tigray', 17 June 2021.

139. Gill, *Famine and Foreigners*, p. 46, citing doctoral work conducted by Alula Pankhurst, *Resettlement and Famine in Ethiopia*, Manchester: Manchester University Press, 1992.

140. Gebru Tareke, *The Ethiopian Revolution: War in the Horn of Africa*, New Haven: Yale University Press, 2009, p. 149. For detailed discussion of resettlement, see A. Pankhurst and F. Piguet, *Moving People in Ethiopia*, Oxford: James Currey, 2009. For a trenchant assessment of the Derg's twin resettlement and villagisation programmes as 'authoritarian social engineering', see J.C. Scott, *Seeing Like a State*, New Haven: Yale University Press, 1998.

141. Dawit, *Red Tears*. This expression has returned in rhetoric advocating the starvation of Tigray since the war erupted in November 2020.

142. Gill, *Famine and Foreigners*, p. 61, citing the account given by a US diplomat, D. Korn, *Ethiopia, the US and the Soviet Union*, London: Croom Helm, 1986.

143. Markakis, *National and Class Conflict*, p. 254.

144. E. Gellner, *Thought and Change*, London: Weidenfeld and Nicolson, 1964, p. 160.

145. M. Duffield and M. Prendergast, *Without Troops and Tanks*, Trenton: Red Sea Press, 1994.

146. Author's notes, Addis Ababa and Mekele, 1991.

147. On the establishment of the EPDM and TPLF facilitation of this process, see S. Vaughan, 'The Addis Ababa Transitional Conference of July 1991: Its Origins, History and Significance', occasional paper 51, University of Edinburgh, Centre of African Studies, 1994, p. 6.

148. It was, famously, an EPDM cadre who, when interviewed by the BBC after perestroika later in the decade, expressed enthusiasm for Albania's political direction and dubbed Gorbachev a 'bourgeois revisionist'.

149. Young, *Peasant Revolution in Ethiopia*, pp. 117–18.

150. Tekeste Melake, 'The Battle of Shire (February 1989): A Turning Point in the Protracted War in Ethiopia', in Marcus, *New Trends in Ethiopian Studies*, pp. 963–80. For an overall account of the Ethiopian civil wars of the 1970s and 1980s, see Gebru, *The Ethiopian Revolution*.

151. Young, *Peasant Revolution in Ethiopia*, p. 117.

152. Elderly peasant farmer, TPLF *baito* congress, near Sheraro, December 1988, author's notes.

153. On the formation of the OPDO from among Oromo POWs of the TPLF and EPLF, see Vaughan, 'The Addis Ababa Transitional Conference', pp. 6–7.

154. This small body of Derg officers captured by TPLF, notably at Shire in February 1989, soon joined other EPRDF organisations.

155. EPRDF sources report that the official establishment of the Front had been put off for some years in the hope that it might include other parties. Author's interview, EPRDF politburo member, Addis Ababa, July 1994.

156. Alemseged, *Identity Jilted*, pp. 170–1.

3.   REWORKING THE EMPIRE

1.   S. Vaughan, 'The Addis Ababa Transitional Conference of July 1991: Its Origins, History and Significance', occasional paper, 51, University of Edinburgh, Centre of African Studies, 1994.

2.   See also S. Vaughan, 'Federalism, Revolutionary Democracy and the Developmental State, 1991–2012', in G. Prunier and E. Ficquet (eds.), *Understanding Contemporary Ethiopia: Monarchy, Revolution and the Legacy of Meles Zenawi*, London: Hurst, 2015, pp. 283–311, on which this discussion draws.

3.   As already noted in Chapter 2, this language, which was also used by students in the imperial period, originates with Stalinist and Soviet thinking on self-determination. In practice, little or no differentiation according to the three categories was made in contemporary Ethiopia.

4.   The Southern regional state was subdivided in the period after 2018 and, at the time of writing in early 2022, was made up of three recognised federated

entities: the Southern Peoples, South-West Peoples and Sidama regional states, with further states likely.

5. But since subdivided; see previous note.

6. C. van der Beken, *Unity in Diversity: Federalism as a Mechanism to Accommodate Ethnic Diversity; The Case of Ethiopia*, Zurich and Berlin: LIT, 2012.

7. In early 1991, neighbouring Somalia had descended into full collapse.

8. Author's interview, then president of the Transitional Government of Ethiopia, Addis Ababa, August 1994.

9. D. Horowitz, *A Democratic South Africa? Constitutional Engineering in a Divided Society*, Berkeley: University of California Press, 1991, p. 29. Thus the argument is not only that an ethnic classification will in itself reinforce ethnic division; but, in addition, the fact of a lack of consensus on the desirability of an ethnic classification is likely (in itself) to exacerbate the conflict in which it can be expected to result: what Horowitz calls a 'meta-conflict'.

10. Walle Engedayehu, 'Ethiopia: Democracy and the Politics of Ethnicity', *Africa Today*, 40, 1993, pp. 29–52; also 'Ethiopia: The Pitfalls of Ethnic Federalism', *Africa Quarterly*, 32 (2) 1994, pp. 149–92.

11. Aaron Tesfaye, 'Is Federalism Viable in Ethiopia?', in H.G. Marcus (ed.), *New Trends in Ethiopian Studies: Papers of the 12th Conference of Ethiopian Studies*, Lawrenceville: Red Sea Press, 1994; and, more sympathetically, P. Henze, 'The Economic Dimension of Federalism in the Horn of Africa', in P. Woodward and M. Forsyth (eds.), *Conflict and Peace in the Horn of Africa: Federalism and Its Alternatives*, Aldershot: Dartmouth, 1994, pp. 124–30.

12. Vaughan, 'The Addis Ababa Transitional Conference'.

13. Cf. Andreas Esheté, 'Taking the Charter Seriously', *Imbylta*, 2 (2) 1992, pp. 3–13.

14. Author's interview, TGE Boundary Commission member, Addis Ababa, 9 November 1999.

15. Thus, for instance, the 1991 conference explicitly avoided historical discussion of the Eritrean issue as likely to become mired in multiple competing narratives. See Vaughan, 'The Addis Ababa Transitional Conference', p. 52; also J. Sorensen, *Imagining Ethiopia: Struggles for History and Identity in the Horn of Africa*, New Brunswick: Rutgers University Press, 1993, pp. 38ff.

16. Author's interview, then prospective EPRDF member of the TGE Boundary Commission, Addis Ababa, August 1991.

17. Author's interview, former ISEN researcher and Transitional Boundary Commission member, Addis Ababa, 9 November 1999. As a result, in the 1980s it was concluded that 'language was not a good criterion on which to base an administrative division'. See Chapter 2.

18. Vaughan, 'The Addis Ababa Transitional Conference'; S. Vaughan, 'Responses to Ethnic Federalism in Ethiopia's Southern Region', in D. Turton (ed.), *Ethnic Federalism: The Ethiopian Experience in Comparative Perspective*, Oxford: James Currey, 2006, pp. 181–207.

19. Vaughan, 'Responses to Ethnic Federalism'.

20. Human Rights Watch, 'Political Competition in Oromia', May 2005, accessed September 2006, https://www.hrw.org/reports/2005/ethiopia0505/8.htm.

21. T. Hagmann, *Talking Peace in the Ogaden*, London and Nairobi: Rift Valley Institute, 2014; S. Vaughan, 'Ethiopia, Somalia and the Ogaden', in L. de Vries, P. Engelbert and M. Schomerus (eds.), *Secessionism in African Politics*, Cham: Palgrave Macmillan, 2019, pp. 91–123.

22. Vaughan, 'The Addis Ababa Transitional Conference'.

23. Eshetu Chole, 'Opening Pandora's Box: Preliminary Notes on Fiscal Decentralisation in Ethiopia', *Northeast African Studies*, (NS) 1 (1) 1994, pp. 7–30.

24. G. Prunier, 'The Eritrean Question', in G. Prunier and E. Ficquet (eds.), *Understanding Contemporary Ethiopia: Monarchy, Revolution and the Legacy of Meles Zenawi*, London: Hurst, 2015, p. 233.

25. *The Economist*, 11 June 1998, accessed September 2021, https://www. economist.com/international/1998/06/11/why-are-they-fighting.

26. K. Tronvoll and Tekeste Negash, for instance, entitled their book *Brothers at War: Making Sense of the Ethio-Eritrean War*, Oxford: James Currey, 2000.

27. Ruth Iyob, *The Eritrean Struggle for Independence*, Cambridge: CUP, 1995, p. 143.

28. Prunier, 'Eritrean Question', p. 235.

29. Mulugeta Gebrehiwot Berhe, *Laying the Past to Rest: The EPRDF and the Challenges of Ethiopian State Building*, London: Hurst, 2020, p. 56.

30. Mulugeta, *Laying the Past to Rest*, p. 56.

31. Mulugeta, *Laying the Past to Rest*, takes the first view; Aregawi Berhe, in *A Political History of the Tigray People's Liberation Front (1975–1991)*, Los Angeles: Tsehai, 2009, takes the second.

32. J. Young, *Peasant Revolution in Ethiopia: The Tigray People's Liberation Front, 1975–1991*, Cambridge: CUP, 1997, p. 93. He also comments that a TPLF source suggested that 'it is not particularly likely that they [the EPLF] even knew about it at the time: half of the TPLF itself didn't know about the famous manifesto, after all'. This changed later, of course, after Eritrean and Derg propaganda about the 'secessionist manifesto'.

33. G.K.N. Trevaskis, *Eritrea: A Colony in Transition, 1941–52*, Oxford: OUP, 1960, p. 109.

34. Tekeste Negash, *Ethiopia and Eritrea: The Federal Experience*, Uppsala: Nordiska Afrikainstitutet, 1997.

35. As Gilkes and Plaut note, 'the [highlanders] were slow to support the independence struggle … The major factor in the end was the failure of the Ethiopian government to produce an acceptable administration.' P. Gilkes and M. Plaut, *War in the Horn: The Conflict between Eritrea and Ethiopia*, London: Royal Institute of International Affairs, 1999, p. 6, n. 3.

36. TPLF sources also suggested that one of the reasons for maintaining its troops in Eritrea during the famous Red Star campaign was to try to bolster EPLF resolve to fight on for independence, given that clandestine negotiations with the Derg over confederation were known to be taking place. Author's interviews, Addis Ababa, 2000.

37. J. Markakis, *National and Class Conflict in the Horn of Africa*, Cambridge: CUP, 1987, p. 246. Although Pateman suggests that some form of land reform had been carried out in a third of Eritrean villages by 1987, Tronvoll notes that this 'did not change the social status of the people' between lineages. K. Tronvoll,

Mai Weini: The Story of a Highland Village in Eritrea, Trenton: Red Sea Press, 1998, p. 208; R. Pateman, *Even the Stones Are Burning*, Trenton: Red Sea Press, 1990.

38. Tronvoll, *Mai Weini*, p. 261.

39. Young, *Peasant Revolution in Ethiopia*.

40. TPLF 'on our differences with the EPLF', *People's Voice*, Special issue, 1986, p. 6.

41. TPLF 'a great leap forward', *People's Voice*, 1986, p. 6.

42. EPLF, *Adulis*, May 1985, p. 5.

43. Young, *Peasant Revolution in Ethiopia*, p. 141.

44. This was not only a theoretical possibility: from the 1980s, the TPLF did have a relationship with the ELF splinter Democratic Movement for the Liberation of Eritrea (DMLE). Young, *Peasant Revolution in Ethiopia*, p. 157.

45. Gebru Tareke, *The Ethiopian Revolution: War in the Horn of Africa*, New Haven: Yale, 2009, pp. 247ff, 262ff.

46. *Eritrea Profile*, 2 (27) September 1995, cited in Tronvoll, *Mai Weini*.

47. Prunier, 'Eritrean Question', p. 248.

48. J.R. Campbell, *Nationalism, Law and Statelessness: Grand Illusions in the Horn of Africa*, London: Routledge, 2014, pp. 26–7.

49. For a discussion of this and other economic issues, see Worku Aberra, 'Asymmetric Benefits: The Ethio-Eritrea Common Market (1991–1998)', *International Journal of African Development*, 4 (1) 2016, https://scholarworks. wmich.edu/cgi/viewcontent.cgi?article=1097&context=ijad.

50. T. Killion, *Historical Dictionary of Eritrea*, Lanham: Scarecrow, 1998, p. 399, cited by Prunier, 'Eritrean Question', p. 249.

51. Prunier, 'Eritrean Question', p. 250.

52. This perspective is developed in R.M. Trivelli, 'Divided Histories, Opportunistic Alliances: Background Notes on the Ethiopian-Eritrean War', *Africa Spectrum*, 33 (3) 1998, pp. 257–89. The unsubstantiated view was actively promoted and much repeated in diplomatic circles in Asmara that 'this was the plan: that a trap was laid, and the Eritrean government walked into it, enabling the Ethiopian government to claim that it was the victim of armed aggression'. R. Reid, 'Elite Bargains and Political Deals Project: Ethiopia–Eritrea Case Study', UK Government Stabilisation Unit, February 2018, p. 8, accessed February 2021, https://assets.publishing.service.gov.uk/government/uploads/system/uploads/attachment_data/file/766022/Ethiopia_Eritrea_case_study.pdf.

53. Network of Eritrean Professionals in Europe, *A War Without Cause*, n.d., pp. 10–11, cited among others by Gilkes and Plaut, *War in the Horn*, p. 23.

54. C. Clapham, *The Horn of Africa: State Formation and Decay*, London: Hurst, 2017, p. 122: 'it seems clear that on neither side did the national leadership intend or expect a war … although the speed with which Eritrean forces occupied the contested area indicated a level of preparedness entirely lacking on the Ethiopian side'.

55. The British also saw this as a way potentially to remove western Eritrea to Sudan.

56. Trevaskis, *Eritrea*, p. 65.

57. One other exception may be the small early Tigray Liberation Front (TLF) under the influence of its patron, the ELF.

58. M. Plaut, 'Background to War: From Friends to Foes', in D. Jacquin-Berdal and M. Plaut (eds.), *Unfinished Business: Ethiopia and Eritrea at War*, Trenton: Red Sea Press, 2004, pp. 1–22.

59. Clapham, *The Horn of Africa*, p. 123; Reid, 'Elite Bargains and Political Deals Project'.

60. Reid, 'Elite Bargains and Political Deals Project', p. 3.

61. Reid, 'Elite Bargains and Political Deals Project', p. 3.

62. 'Christopher Clapham has drawn attention to the striking flaw at heart of the Boundary Commission ruling, namely that it flew in the face of the result of the fighting—literally requiring Ethiopia to snatch defeat from the jaws of victory.' S. Healy and M. Plaut, 'Ethiopia and Eritrea: Allergic to Persuasion', Chatham House briefing paper, January 2007, accessed March 2007, https://www.chathamhouse.org/sites/default/files/public/Research/Africa/bpethiopiaeritrea.pdf. They cite C. Clapham, 'Notes on the Ethio-Eritrea Boundary Demarcation', unpublished MS, 16 October 2003. See also Clapham, *The Horn of Africa*, pp. 124–8. The 'positive law' argument is controversial, and has also been used to maintain (for instance) that the TPLF should have fallen into line with PM Abiy in 2018–20.

63. Reid, 'Elite Bargains and Political Deals Project', p. 3.

64. Clapham, *The Horn of Africa*, p. 130.

65. *The Economist*, 14 August 2018, accessed September 2018, https://www.economist.com/the-economist-explains/2018/08/14/why-eritrea-is-called-africas-north-korea. See also N. Hirt, 'Thirty Years of Autocratic Rule: Eritrea's President Isaias Afewerki, between Innovation and Destruction', in J.-N. Bach (ed.), *Routledge Handbook of the Horn of Africa*, London: Routledge, 2022, pp. 317–26; M. Plaut, *Understanding Eritrea: Inside Africa's Most Repressive State*, London: Hurst, 2016.

66. Xan Rice, *The Guardian*, 28 July 2011, accessed May 2022, https://www.theguardian.com/world/2011/jul/28/eritrea-planned-ethopia-bomb-attack.

67. Reid, 'Elite Bargains and Political Deals Project', p. 4.

68. See for instance, R. Reid, *Shallow Graves: A Memoir of the Ethio-Eritrean War*, London: Hurst, 2020, pp. 164ff.

69. Reid, *Shallow Graves*, p. 143. The memoir gives a candid account of the author's reappraisal of the EPLF but is arguably less sensitive to the propagandist elements of some of what it documents about the TPLF. It offers an illuminating window on Eritrean prejudice.

70. Faisal Ali and Mohamed Kheir Omar, 11 April 2022, accessed May 2022, http://democracyinafrica.org/a-portrait-isaias-afworki-the-man-the-dictator/#.

71. Assefa Fiseha, *Federalism and the Accommodation of Diversity in Ethiopia: A Comparative Study*, Nijmegen: Wolf, 2010.

72. Solomon Nigussie, *Fiscal Federalism in the Ethiopian Ethnic-Based System*, Addis Ababa: AAUP, 2008.

73. K. Tronvoll, *War and the Politics of Identity in Ethiopia*, Oxford: James Currey, 2009.

74. Medhane Taddesse and J. Young, 'TPLF: Reform or Decline?', *Review of African Political Economy*, 2003, pp. 389–403; Paulos Milkias, 'Ethiopia, the TPLF, and

the Roots of the 2001 Political Tremor', *Northeast African Studies*, 10 (2) 2003, pp. 13–66.

75.   S. Vaughan and K. Tronvoll, *The Culture of Power in Contemporary Ethiopian Political Life*, Stockholm: Sida, 2003, pp. 136ff.

76.   R. Lefort, 'Powers—Mengist—and Peasants in Rural Ethiopia: The May 2005 Election', *Journal of Modern Ethiopian Studies*, 45 (2) 2007, pp. 253–73.

77.   S. Vaughan, 'Ethnic and Civic Nationalist Narratives in Ethiopia', in T. Harrison and S. Drakulic (eds.), *Beyond Orthodoxy: New Directions in the Study of Nationalism*, Vancouver: University of British Columbia Press, 2011, pp. 154–82.

78.   P. Gilkes, 'Elections and Politics in Ethiopia, 2005–2010', in G. Prunier and E. Ficquet (eds.), *Understanding Contemporary Ethiopia: Monarchy, Revolution and the Legacy of Meles Zenawi*, London: Hurst, 2015, pp. 313–31; L. Aalen and K. Tronvoll, 'The End of Democracy? Curtailing Political and Civil Rights in Ethiopia', *Review of African Political Economy*, 26 (120) 2009, pp. 193–207.

79.   The name Genbot 7, sometimes also G7 or PG7, refers to 15 May, the date of the 2005 election.

80.   L. Aalen, *The Politics of Ethnicity in Ethiopia*, Leiden: Brill, 2009, p. 52.

81.   Reuters, 7 May 2005, accessed July 2022, https://www.arabnews.com/node/266513.

82.   Aalen, *The Politics of Ethnicity in Ethiopia*, p. 52.

83.   Cf. also Aalen and Tronvoll, 'The End of Democracy?', p. 195. 'Ruling party officials consistently claimed that opposition parties were sowing seeds of ethnic hatred by questioning the rights of nationalities to self-determination. In retrospect, this attack on the opposition was a way of preparing the ground for the government's massive clampdown that was to come after the elections'. In retrospect, from the time of writing, this arguably cynical reading perhaps needs to be re-evaluated. Some of the most trenchant criticism of the EPRDF during the 2005 period, however, came from other commentators who have become advocates of the war in Tigray from 2020.

84.   Lyons, *The Puzzle of Ethiopian Politics*, Boulder: Lynne Rienner, 2019, ch. 6.

85.   Aalen and Tronvoll, 'The End of Democracy?'

86.   Meles Zenawi, 'States and Markets: Neoliberal Limitations and the Case for the Developmental State', in A. Noman, K. Botchwey, H. Stein and J. Stiglitz (eds.), *Good Growth and Governance in Africa: Rethinking Development Strategies*, Oxford: OUP, 2012, pp. 140–74.

87.   D. Rodrik, 'Political Economy and Development Policy', *European Economic Review*, 36 (2–3) 1991, cited in Meles, 'States and Markets'.

88.   Vaughan and Tronvoll, *The Culture of Power*; S. Vaughan, 'Revolutionary Democratic State Building: Party, State and People in EPRDF's Ethiopia', *Journal of Eastern African Studies*, 5 (4) 2012, pp. 619–40.

4.   THINGS FALL APART

1.   Author's interview, Addis Ababa, September 2012.

2.   R. Lefort, 'The Ethiopian Economy: The Developmental State versus the Free Market', in G. Prunier and E. Ficquet (eds.), *Understanding Contemporary*

Ethiopia: Monarchy, Revolution and the Legacy of Meles Zenawi, London: Hurst, 2015, p. 391.

3. World Bank, 'Ethiopia's Great Run: The Growth Acceleration and How to Pace It', Washington DC: World Bank, 12 November 2015, accessed January 2016, https://openknowledge.worldbank.org/handle/10986/23333.

4. E. Ficquet, 'The Ethiopian Muslims: Historical Processes and Ongoing Controversies', in Prunier and Ficquet, *Understanding Contemporary Ethiopia*, pp. 110ff. Also E. Ficquet, 'The Civil Rights Movement of Ethiopian Muslims in 2012: Historical Grounds and Driving Forces', in J.-N. Bach (ed.), *Routledge Handbook of the Horn of Africa*, London: Routledge, 2022, pp. 472–80.

5. Abdurahmnan Omar, 'The Ethiopian Muslims Protest in an Era of Social Media', Master's thesis, Uppsala University, 2020, https://uu.diva-portal.org/smash/get/diva2:1467630/FULLTEXT01.pdf.

6. New Humanitarian, 15 November 2021, accessed January 2022, https://www.thenewhumanitarian.org/fr/node/252801.

7. D. Shinn, 'Ethiopia: Muslim–Christian Relations', paper presented 16 January 2014, accessed January 2021, https://www.scribd.com/document/200405076/Ethiopia-Muslim-Christian-Relations.

8. There is much more to be written about the relationship between the Muslim protests of 2011–13 and the Oromo protests from 2014. It is interesting to note that the architects of federalism in 1991 saw the link between Oromo nationalism and religious mobilisation. They were keen to preserve the integrity of Oromia for several related reasons: one was because of the way in which Oromo nationalism had emerged, with roots across the multi-religious Oromo area; a second was to ensure that the broad, diverse region of Oromia operated as a 'large secular bulwark' against radicalisation.

9. World Bank, 'Great Run', p. 4.

10. World Bank, 'Great Run', p. 4.

11. Cepheus Capital, 'Ethiopia's Recent Trade Performance: A Data Pack and Some Observations', 25 September 2020, accessed November 2020, https://cepheuscapital.com/wp-content/uploads/2020/09/Ethiopia-Trade-Review-FY-2019-20.pdf.

12. Lefort, 'Ethiopian Economy'.

13. For more detailed discussion of these dynamics, see, for instance, A. Pankhurst, P. Bevan, C. Dom, A. Tiumelissan and S. Vaughan (eds.), *Changing Rural Ethiopia: Community Transformations*, Los Angeles: Tsehai, 2018.

14. The balance of male and female members varied very significantly between the EPRDF member fronts: well over 40 per cent were women within the TPLF (where separate structures for men and women boosted the participation of women, including rural women), but less than 20 per cent of ANDM members, and only 12 per cent among Amhara farmer members. Rural Oromo and Southern political networks had relatively more women members than in Amhara, arguably reflecting different gender norms in different parts of the country, as well as different political histories and cultures of power. These differentials also influenced the social integration (or lack of it) of each of the regional state fronts which made up the ruling party.

15. Daniel Mulugeta gives an excellent account of the limitations of the state–society relationship at the micro-level in Gojjam, for instance. See Daniel Mulugeta, *The Everyday State in Africa: Governance Practices and State Ideas in Ethiopia*, London: Routledge, 2020.

16. Conclusions in this section draw on the author's research in the four EPRDF regions, during 2012, 2013 and 2014.

17. R. Lefort, 'Unrest in Ethiopia: The Ultimate Warning Shot?', Open Democracy, 2 February 2016, accessed March 2016, https://www.opendemocracy.net/en/unrest-in-ethiopia-ultimate-warning-shot/.

18. Author's notes, Bahir Dar, March 2015.

19. J. Mosley, 'Ethiopia's Elections Are Just an Exercise in Controlled Political Participation', *The Guardian*, 22 May 2015, accessed May 2022, https://www.theguardian.com/global-development/2015/may/22/ethiopia-elections-controlled-political-participation.

20. R. Lefort, 'Ethiopia after Its Electoral Drama: Second "Renewal" Imminent?', Open Democracy, 7 July 2015, accessed August 2015, https://www.opendemocracy.net/en/ethiopia-after-its-electoral-drama-second-renewal-imminent/, citing Sebhat Nega, interviewed June 2015.

21. Mukhtar Kedir and Aster Mamo.

22. K. Tronvoll, 'Falling from Grace: The Collapse of Ethiopia's Ruling Coalition', *Northeast African Studies*, 21 (2) 2022, p. 14, citing J.E. Owens, 'Cohesion: Explaining Party Cohesion and Discipline in Democratic Legislatures: Purposiveness and Contexts', *Journal of Legislative Studies*, 9 (4) 2006, p. 24.

23. Lefort, 'Second Renewal Imminent'.

24. Norwegian Refugee Council, November 2017, accessed December 2017, https://www.nrc.no/news/2018/november/700000-people-flee-conflict-to-seek-safety-in-somali-region-of-ethiopia/.

25. *Addis Standard*, 25 December 2017, accessed December 2017, https://addisstandard.com/breaking-news-abadula-gemeda-resigns-as-speaker-of-the-federal-parliament/.

26. Abdu Rahman Alfa Shaban, 'Ethiopia Govt Finally Accepts Shock Resignation of Speaker Abadula', Africanews, 25 December 2017, accessed December 2017, https://www.africanews.com/2017/12/25/ethiopia-govt-finally-accepts-shock-resignation-of-speaker-abadula/.

27. He had previously, from 2008, been regional head of administration and security, and effectively led the set-up of the Ethiopian Somali state special police. It was estimated to number between 30,000 and 40,000, even as high as 42,000.

28. In February 2016, the Gambella special police fought among themselves and against the army. Later the same year, Amhara special forces were involved in bloody clashes between Amhara and Qemant communities in North Gonder (Chapter 4). The Somali and Oromia special police forces were also heavily involved in the border clashes between the two regions between 2016 and 2018. Nearly a million people were displaced as a result.

29. Borkena, 7 December 2020, accessed January 2021, https://borkena.com/2020/12/07/regional-special-forces-unconstitutional-says-minister-for-peace/. See also A. Fitz-Gerald, 'Ethiopia's Security Dilemmas', 18 July 2019,

Royal United Service Institute (RUSI), accessed August 2019, https://rusi.org/explore-our-research/publications/commentary/ethiopias-security-dilemmas.

30. *Addis Zemen*, November 2020, accessed March 2021 (the contents of the page have since been concealed from public access), https://www.press.et/Ama/?p=13437.

31. See, for instance, UK Home Office, 'Country Policy and Information Note, Ethiopia: Actors of Protection' (*sic*), September 2020, accessed October 2021, https://assets.publishing.service.gov.uk/government/uploads/system/uploads/attachment_data/file/920200/ETH_-_CPIN_-_BN_AoP_-_V1.0e.pdf.

32. It was argued in the 1970s that the Derg's land reform gave it 'Oromo' credentials. In 1991, EPRDF had a tendency to contrast itself with the OLF as a 'moderate' force.

33. J. Zahorik, 'Understanding the Oromo Movements: From the Macha Tulama Association to the "Oromo Protests"', in J.-N. Bach (ed.), *Routledge Handbook of the Horn of Africa*, London: Routledge, 2022, pp. 11–20.

34. Author's research among student party members in 2012–13 indicated relatively high levels of tensions associated with ethno-nationalist sentiment on a number of university campuses

35. The monument memorialised the severing of breasts of Oromo women during Ethiopia's nineteenth-century imperial expansion.

36. Hassen Hussein, 'EPRDF's Master Marksman, Abay Tsehaye, Misfires Again', OPride, 18 January 2016, accessed February 2016 https://www.opride.com/2016/01/18/eprdf-s-master-marksman-abay-tsehaye-misfires-again/.

37. '"Such a Brutal Crackdown": Killings and Arrests in Response to Ethiopia's Oromo Protests', Human Rights Watch, 15 June 2016, accessed June 2019, https://www.hrw.org/report/2016/06/15/such-brutal-crackdown/killings-and-arrests-response-ethiopias-oromo-protests.

38. Getachew Reda, in a February 2016 press conference, alleged that the Eritrean government was behind the Oromo protests: 'they want to use OLF leftovers in Asmara and Genbot 7 to infiltrate agitators into Ethiopia'.

39. 'Recent Events and Deaths at the Irreecha Festival in Ethiopia', Human Rights Watch, 8 October 2016, accessed June 2019, https://www.hrw.org/news/2016/10/08/qa-recent-events-and-deaths-irreecha-festival-ethiopia.

40. *Qeerroo* is an Afaan Oromo term meaning 'bachelor', used initially to describe the youth movement of the Oromo protests in 2014–18.

41. T. Østebø, 'The Role of the Qeerroo in Future Oromo Politics', *Addis Standard*, 26 May 2020, accessed May 2020, https://addisstandard.com/analysis-the-role-of-the-qeerroo-in-future-oromo-politics/.

42. In fact the old Tsegedé *wereda* was divided into two (Tsegedé and Dansha) in the reorganisation by the government of Tigray in 2020.

43. A reported 3,000 ENDF personnel were killed by the TPLF in June 1988. Later in the year it was reported that Derg forces had come very close to capturing a convoy carrying both Meles Zenawi and Sebhat Nega in this area. See Aregawi Berhe, *A Political History of the Tigray People's Liberation Front (1975–1991)*, Los Angeles: Tsehai, 2009; Human Rights Watch, *Evil Days: Thirty Years of War and Famine in Ethiopia*, New York: Human Rights Watch, 1991, p. 261.

44. Of whom more than three-quarters were recorded as Tigrayan, with 23 per cent of the population Amhara, according to the census published in 1997.

45. Ethiopian Human Rights Commission (EHRC), unpublished report, 2016 (unofficial English translation), p. 91.

46. EHRC, unpublished report, 2016, pp. 71–1.

47. M. Labzaé, 'The War in Tigray (2020–2021): Dictated Truths, Irredentism and *Déjà-vu*', in J.-N. Bach (ed.), *Routledge Handbook of the Horn of Africa*, London: Routledge, 2022, p. 248.

48. M. Labzaé, 'Amhara Backlash: Nationalist Mobilizations, Irredentism and the "Wolqayt Question" in the Ethiopian Political Crisis and Civil War (c.2015–2021)', forthcoming, 2022.

49. ANDM convened a conference in Bahir Dar in the wake of the 2005 elections to discuss 'Who Are the Amhara?' Papers were delivered by John Markakis and Genenew Assefa among others.

50. See N. Nyssen, 'Database: Western Tigray in 96 Historical and Ten Ethno-linguistic Maps', Zenodo, 2022, for a compilation of historical and language maps of the area: https://zenodo.org/record/6554938#.YoNFJS8w2X2.

51. The history of administration of the Welkaiyt areas is a much-debated issue, and one on which history provides abundant resources to all sides in the controversy. The area was closely associated with a series of different rulers over the centuries: Wolde Selassie during the Era of Princes; Emperor Tewodros thereafter; back to the Tigrayan Emperor Yohannes IV after that; with Begemdir under Menelik, and closer to Gonder under Haile Selassie.

52. National census, 1994 (published 1997).

53. The same census also indicated that Amharic-speakers had jumped to 12 per cent of the population—clearly some who counted themselves as ethnic Tigrayans spoke Amharic, a finding also borne out in other detailed research on the area. See L. Hammond, *This Place Will Become Home: Refugee Repatriation to Ethiopia*, Ithaca: Cornell University Press, 2004. The fuzziness of mother tongue as an identifier of ethnic identity is an indication of the under-determination of social institutions, where the construction of category boundaries varies as a matter of empirical fact.

54. Raya is a second area of land in the south-east of Tigray, populated by Tigrigna-speakers.

55. A parallel process in Raya involved a relatively senior TPLF member who, during a year of study in the UK in 2018 as the TPLF's political star waned, seems to have decided to take the opportunity to reinvent himself (and presumably his political career) as an Amhara, shifting from TPLF to ANDM and, later, to the Prosperity Party.

56. Author's interviews, Addis Ababa and Mekele, 2016. See also Labzaé, 'Amhara Backlash'. After Tigray's investment law was changed, anyone wanting to be given an investment licence needed to have a minimum of 10 hectares of land. Where prospective investors had only seven or eight hectares, their holdings were in some cases reduced to five hectares, and they were treated as 'farmers', not 'investors.' Whether this applied to Colonel Demeke Zewdu himself, is, of course, disputed, but the policy seems to have been an important trigger of discontent that drove the Welkaiyt Committee's establishment.

57. It is perhaps noteworthy that another was Jimma: both had formed an eponymous capital of imperial administrative units, but they became mere zone towns, with limited administrative status, under federalism.

58. The events of June–July 2016 in Gonder triggered one of the first broadcast calls for action against Tigray and Tigrayans. In early August 2016 the diaspora-based ESAT TV station broadcast a 'call for solidarity from the people of Gonder' which stated that the violence in Gonder was 'a struggle between a minority tribe who want to exterminate us and get the upper hand to rule over us and we, the people, who suffering has never come to an end … This plan of havoc is prepared by 5 million people against the 95 million people … Do we wait until they exterminate us one by one? There is only one choice … taking measures by force … one way of removing the dead fish from the sea water is by drying the sea.' The broadcast also called on Ethiopians in Amhara and Afar to block roads into Tigray. https://www.youtube.com/watch?v=CXFXaWehyo4, accessed April 2022. The relation between ESAT and Genbot 7, formally revealed after 2018, is discussed in the next chapter. Both received Eritrean support.

59. William Davison, 'Ethnic Tensions in Gondar Reflect the Toxic Nature of Ethiopian Politics', *The Guardian*, 22 December 2016, accessed January 2017, https://www.theguardian.com/global-development/2016/dec/22/gondar-ethiopia-ethnic-tensions-toxic-politics.

60. Labzaé, 'War in Tigray', p. 246.

61. See R. Pankhurst, 'Fanno' in *Encyclopaedia Aethiopica*, vol. 2, Wiesbaden: Harrassowitz, 2005, p. 490; Tsehaye Berhane Selassie, *Ethiopian Warriorhood*, Oxford: James Currey, 2018; Labzaé, 'Amhara Backlash' on the reappropriation of the term.

62. Author's notes of conversations, 2020, 2021, 2022. The parallels with anti-Semitism are striking.

63. A notorious tweet of January 2016 read, 'Hagos is wetting his pants as his daylight robbery is about to end fast', Jawar Mohammed, posted 30 January 2015, https://twitter.com/Jawar_Mohammed/status/693243848961630208?s=20&t=H-9zmRqDEXsDRL5Rxy2ZEQ.

64. Horn Affairs, 23 August 2017, accessed June 2022, https://hornaffairs.com/2017/08/23/esat-radio-television-voice-genocide/.

65. Lemma Megersa, unofficial translation of speech, 7 November 2017, accessed April 2022, https://www.youtube.com/watch?v=aim-D4EKMlI.

66. See, for instance, the March 2022 interview of veteran OLF politician Lencho Latta for a recent elaboration of this position: 'Ethiopianiawinet has different meanings. I don't accept a kind of Ethiopiawinet that fully conforms with one ethnic identity and ignores the identity of other nations and nationalities. If Ethiopiawinet reflects Oromonet, Somalinet, Sidamanet, Amharanet and Tigraynet I accept that Ethiopiawinet. If they tell me to abandon my Oromonet and accept Ethiopiawinet, I don't accept that. I keep my Oromonet and want to add Ethiopiawinet as well. I accept this kind of Ethiopiawinet.' https://www.youtube.com/watch?v=LAFJak-905c, accessed April 2022.

67. Debretsion Gebremichael, interview, December 2017, accessed May 2022, https://www.youtube.com/watch?v=cU48Q6pMVrM.

68. Author's interviews, Addis Ababa, March–April 2018. The notion of Dr Abiy as 'the new Meles' had begun to be circulated in Oromo political circles for some weeks.

69. Author's notes, conversation with Ethiopian academic and intellectual, Addis Ababa, September 2012.

70. Leake Mekonen Tesfay, 'Towards a Comprehensive Prosecution Service in Ethiopia', *ESMP Academic Journal*, 19 January 2019, accessed January 2020, http://www.mpce.mp.br/wp-content/uploads/2018/05/13-Towards-a-Comprehensive-Prosecution-Service-in-Ethiopia-Noting-the-New-Developments.pdf.

71. See 'Why a Photo of Mengistu Has Proved So Controversial', BBC, 2 August 2018, https://www.bbc.co.uk/news/world-africa-45043811.

72. S. Vaughan and K. Tronvoll, *The Culture of Power in Contemporary Ethiopian Political Life*, Stockholm: Sida, 2003, p. 154.

5. THE REVIVAL OF IMPERIAL POLITICS AND THE PATH TO WAR

1. 'Move Fast and Break Things', Ethiopia Insight, 30 April 2019, accessed May 2019, https://www.ethiopia-insight.com/2019/04/30/move-fast-and-break-things/. The original coinage is attributed to Facebook founder Mark Zuckerberg and is the title of Mark Taplin's 2017 book on Facebook.

2. G. Prunier and E. Ficquet (eds.), *Understanding Contemporary Ethiopia: Monarchy, Revolution and the Legacy of Meles Zenawi*, London: Hurst, 2015, p. 2.

3. The phrase, with its religious overtones (even stronger in the Amharic '*ye chelema zemen*'), was quickly taken up by the prime minister's entourage and a willing media. See David Pilling, *Financial Times*, 18 November 2020, accessed December 2020, https://www.ft.com/content/b888c23a-45ed-4937-9154-3117cc23e202.

4. The original reference, taken up both by Marcus Garvey and by Rastafarianism, is from Psalm 68:31.

5. There is a wide literature on this nativist tradition, much of it shading from philosophy into theology. On the negative influence of alien secularism on the Ethiopian ideational system more broadly, see Yirga Gelaw Woldeyes, *Native Colonialism: Education and the Economy of Violence against Traditions in Ethiopia*, Trenton: Africa World Press, 2017, and Messay Kebede, *Radicalism and Cultural Dislocation in Ethiopia, 1960–1974*, Rochester: University of Rochester Press, 2008. A key figure in this reformulation and move to 'indigenisation' of Ethiopian philosophy and pedagogy was the prime minister's controversial adviser, Deacon Daniel Kibret.

6. Labzaé, 'War in Tigray', p. 249. See also Labzaé, 'Amhara Backlash' on the role of prophecy in mobilisation, particularly in Amhara.

7. A. DeCort, 'Christian Nationalism Is Tearing Ethiopia Apart', *Foreign Policy*, 22 June 2022, accessed June 2022, https://foreignpolicy.com/2022/06/18/ethiopia-pentecostal-evangelical-abiy-ahmed-christian-nationalism/.

8. Daniel Behailu, 'Medemer in a Land of Extremes', Ethiopia Insight, 15 February 2020, accessed February 2020, https://www.ethiopia-insight.com/2020/02/16/medemer-in-a-land-of-extremes/.

9. The prime minister claimed that he had released 60,000 prisoners, a great increase on the 6,000 released by his predecessor, Hailemariam. *Financial Times*, 24 January 2019, https://www.ft.com/content/433dfa88-36d0-11e9-bb0c-42459962a812.

10. R. Lefort, 'Ethiopia: Climbing Mount Uncertainty', Open Democracy, 21 October 2018, accessed November 2018, https://www.opendemocracy.net/en/ethiopia-climbing-mount-uncertainty/.

11. H. Verhoeven and M. Woldemariam, 'Who Lost Ethiopia? The Unmaking of an African Anchor State and US Foreign Policy', *Contemporary Security Policy*, 21 June 2022, pp. 7, 18.

12. Verhoeven and Woldemariam, 'Who Lost Ethiopia?', p. 4.

13. A. Shaw, 'Ethiopia at War', in *The Tigray War and Regional Implications*, vol. 1, Eritrea Focus Oslo Analytica, July 2021, p. 27. Anthony Shaw is the pseudonym of a long-standing observer of the politics of Ethiopia and the Horn.

14. Verhoeven and Woldemariam, 'Who Lost Ethiopia?', p. 4. In a departure from the past, Abiy's new team of economic advisers included a number of people seconded from the World Bank. A number of others were retained on salaries paid by UNDP.

15. Verhoeven and Woldemariam, 'Who Lost Ethiopia?', p. 13.

16. Verhoeven and Woldemariam, 'Who Lost Ethiopia?', p. 14.

17. Kana TV was established in April 2016, by the Moby Group in Dubai, in collaboration with Ethiopian production company BeMedia, owned by filmmaker Zeresenay Berhane Mehari, 251 Communications entrepreneur and Kazana Group chair Addis Alemayehou, and strategic head Nazrawi Ghebreselasie. It began by transmitting international dramas dubbed into Amharic, gradually introducing more locally produced content. After barely a year, *African Business* magazine, 8 May 2017, documented 'Ethiopia's addiction to Kana TV', which it indicated had grabbed 40–50 per cent of the prime-time market share. https://african.business/2017/05/economy/ethiopias-addiction-kana-tv/.

18. Labzaé, 'Amhara Backlash', p. 240.

19. Tom Gardner, 'Abiy Ahmed Is Not a Populist', *Foreign Policy*, 5 December 2018, accessed January 2019, https://foreignpolicy.com/2018/12/05/abiy-ahmed-is-not-a-populist-ethiopia-eprdf-tplf-modi-erdogan-populism/.

20. Shaw, 'Ethiopia at War', p. 27.

21. Addis Getachew and Seleshi Tessema, 'Ethiopia: New PM Receives Rapturous Welcome in Tigray', Anadolu Agency, 18 April 2018, accessed April 2018, https://www.aa.com.tr/en/africa/ethiopia-new-pm-receives-rapturous-welcome-in-tigray/1117346.

22. *Addis Standard*, 16 April 2018, accessed April 2018, https://addisstandard.com/news-pm-abiy-ahmeds-welqait-remark-in-mekelle-draws-criticism/. See also https://www.facebook.com/watch/?v=1889987277699806, accessed June 2022.

23. Author's interviews, Addis Ababa, May 2018.

24. The remarkably widely respected EPRDF national security chief Kinfe Gebremedhin was assassinated in 2001, in the wake of the Ethio-Eritrea war and the TPLF split, in murky circumstances which have not since become clear.

25. Verhoeven and Woldemariam, 'Who Lost Ethiopia?', p. 19.

26. The September 2018 investigation's verdict of suicide satisfied no one.

27. Gebrekirstos Gebremeskal, 'The War on Tigray', Ethiopia Insight, 18 December 2020, accessed June 2022, https://www.ethiopia-insight.com/2020/12/18/the-war-on-tigray-a-multi-pronged-assault-driven-by-genocidal-undercurrents/. Videos of the proceedings are at https://www.youtube.com/watch?v=9ehVfkoIf6M (Washington DC, 28 July 2018), https://www.youtube.com/watch?v=c5cygal4adE (Minnesota, 31 July 2018), and https://www.youtube.com/watch?v=feujpLmY2jQ (Los Angeles, 30 July 2018), all accessed June 2022.

28. BBC Amharic Service, August 2018, https://www.bbc.com/amharic/news-45019063. They were released three weeks later.

29. Zecharias Zelalem, 'Analyzing the Jijiga Stalemate', OPride, 11 August 2018, accessed September 2018, https://www.opride.com/2018/08/11/analyzing-the-jijiga-stalemate-exactly-what-was-at-stake-in-ethiopia-last-weekend/.

30. Verhoeven and Woldemariam, 'Who Lost Ethiopia?', p. 19; video of the event, showing the PM doing press-ups with the soldiers at the palace, accessed December 2018, is available at https://www.facebook.com/habtamugedebie/videos/1895424097178675/.

31. See, for instance, Alemayehu Weldemariam, 'Analysis', Ethiopia Insight, 15 November 2018, accessed February 2019, https://www.ethiopia-insight.com/2018/11/15/abiy-attacks-impunity-as-metec-and-niss-officials-held-for-graft-and-torture/.

32. See Felix Horne, 'Ethiopia's Torture Problem and the Court of Public Opinion', Human Rights Watch, https://www.hrw.org/news/2018/12/13/ethiopias-torture-problem-and-court-public-opinion.

33. Shaw, 'Ethiopia at War', p. 51.

34. David Pilling, 'Ethiopia's Ethnic Rivalries Threaten Abiy Ahmed's Reform Agenda', Financial Times, 27 March 2019, accessed July 2022, https://www.ft.com/content/1cbaac04-457f-11e9-a965-23d669740bfb on the swift change of mood.

35. Shaw, 'Ethiopia at War', p. 54.

36. A Tigrayan farmer quoted by Maggie Fick, Reuters, 16 December 2018, accessed January 2019, https://www.reuters.com/article/us-ethiopia-politics-tigray-idUSKBN1OF05F; such views were borne out in author's interviews, Mekele, October 2018.

37. Chatham House's Ahmed Soliman, quoted in the New Humanitarian, 14 February 2019, https://www.thenewhumanitarian.org/analysis/2019/02/14/Ethiopia-ethnic-displacement-power-shift-raises-tensions.

38. In a further supremely ironic twist, the appointment was made citing FDRE Article 62.9, which allows 'federal intervention if any State, in violation of the constitution, endangers the constitutional order'.

39. The Reporter Ethiopia, 19 October 2019, accessed October 2019, https://www.thereporterethiopia.com/article/eprdf-denouncestplfs-stance-over-unified-party.

40. Cited by Shaw, 'Ethiopia at War', p. 39.

41. 'Prosperity Party Is "Illegitimate"—TPLF', Addis Insight, 6 January 2020, accessed January 2020, https://addisinsight.net/prosperity-party-is-illegitimate-tplf/.
42. Author's interview, February 2021.
43. Verhoeven and Woldemariam, 'Who Lost Ethiopia?', note that this 'raised problems of moral hazard'.
44. Nobel Prize Committee citation, 11 October 2020, accessed October 2020, https://www.reuters.com/article/us-nobel-prize-peace-fulltext-idUSKBN1WQ15N.
45. Shaw, 'Ethiopia at War', p. 31.
46. Verhoeven and Woldemariam, 'Who Lost Ethiopia?', p. 20.
47. Shaw, 'Ethiopia at War', p. 31.
48. R. Lefort, 'Preaching Unity but Flying Solo, Abiy's Ambition May Stall Ethiopia's Transition', Ethiopia Insight, 25 February 2020, accessed February 2020, https://www.ethiopia-insight.com/2020/02/25/preaching-unity-but-flying-solo-abiys-ambition-may-stall-ethiopias-transition/.
49. Interview with Bekele Gerba, 8 August 2019, accessed September 2020, https://www.youtube.com/watch?v=Sts4I9_MMAQ.
50. Shaw, 'Ethiopia at War', p. 29.
51. Shaw, 'Ethiopia at War', p. 29.
52. Abiy Ahmed speech to parliament, 30 November 2020, translated by Negash Haile, posted 22 December 2020, accessed December 2020, https://www.ethiopia-insight.com/2020/12/22/the-causes-and-course-of-the-tigray-conflict-according-to-abiy-ahmed/.
53. Shaw, 'Ethiopia at War', pp. 29, 36.
54. Interview with Zeinab Badawi, BBC Hardtalk, June 2018. Andargachew also claimed that Abiy had threatened to resign if EPRDF didn't allow his release from jail.
55. Clip posted to Twitter on 16 July 2019, accessed June 2022, https://twitter.com/Haphtom/status/1150932607233925121. Some Facebook commentators went so far as to suggest that there had been a secret agreement to dismantle EPRDF and unite the ruling party with Ezema.
56. They included the Blue or Semayawi Party, the New Generation Party, the Gambella Regional Movement, Unity for Democracy and Justice, and the Ethiopia Vision party, which joined a month later.
57. To the chagrin of a sympathetic Election Board chairperson. Addis Standard, 3 June 2021, accessed June 2021, https://addisstandard.com/news-nebe-to-register-jailed-members-of-the-opposition-balderas-for-candidacy/.
58. Addis Standard, 23 February 2017, https://addisstandard.com/news-ethiopia-prosecutors-bring-multiple-criminal-charges-against-opposition-leader-dr-merera-gudina-two-others/.
59. Kassaye Chemeda comments broadcast on Walta TV, video posted 8 July 2020, accessed July 2022, https://twitter.com/yaredinho_r9/status/128134097-3470162944?s=20&t=7pEFzdbcORGSpVeUL2ldsw. Brigadier General Kassaye, who had fought at AfAbet, remained a controversial figure, stating in a January 2019 interview that 'weyane' had not defeated the Derg, and that Eritrea was rightfully part of Ethiopia.

60. In 2014, Alehubel defected from the ADFM in Eritrea to Sweden, and was accused of having stolen ADFM funds.

61. Despite government claims that all was resolved, it was reported that the ADP threatened an unspecified number of members of the ADFM executive committee with pre-existing criminal records—prior to their defections to Eritrea—to entice them into the merger.

62. Author's interviews, August 2019.

63. Author's interviews, August 2019.

64. Labzaé, 'Amhara Backlash'.

65. Author's interviews, 2020 and 2021.

66. The term *neftegna* has a precise historical reference in the context of nineteenth-century Ethiopian state formation. During the period of heightened Oromo nationalism post-2014, however, it acquired a new and particular toxicity, perceived by some Amhara nationalists or 'pan-Ethiopianist' nationalists and others as an (ethnicised) 'dog-whistle' slur against non-Oromo 'immigrants' in Oromia, and (they allege) deployed with the intent to incite violence against them. For others, the facts of *neftegna* involvement in the imperial administration of Oromia are a matter of historical record.

67. D. Levine, *Greater Ethiopia: The Evolution of a Multiethnic Society*, Chicago: University of Chicago Press, 1974, and *Wax and Gold: Tradition and Innovation in Ethiopian Culture*, Chicago: University of Chicago Press, 1965. See Chapter 1.

68. 'Ethiopia: Justice Needed for Deadly October Violence', Human Rights Watch, 1 April 2020, accessed April 2020, https://www.hrw.org/news/2020/04/01/ethiopia-justice-needed-deadly-october-violence.

69. In July 2022, a senior member of the Oromo Prosperity Party seemed to admit government complicity, in a series of opaque remarks.

70. Ermias Tasfaye, 'Chaos in the Rift', Ethiopia Insight, 5 January 2021, accessed January 2021, https://www.ethiopia-insight.com/2021/01/05/chaos-in-the-rift-a-microcosm-of-ethiopias-brutal-polarization/, and https://www.theafricareport.com/57957/ethiopia-understanding-oromias-mayhem-after-hachalus-murder/.

71. EHRC, investigation report, n.d., accessed July 2022, https://drive.google.com/file/d/1oGkx-fFhTX_9AHoIzjj8KwIeWpyPZu5O/view.

72. Ermias Tasfaye, 'Chaos in the Rift'. See Melkessa Gemechu, 'How Abiy Ahmed Betrayed Oromia and Endangered Ethiopia', *Foreign Policy*, 25 January 2022, for a non-government insider's perspective on these events, accessed May 2022, https://foreignpolicy.com/2022/01/25/abiy-ahmed-ethiopia-qeerroo-oromia-betrayed/.

73. Personal communication.

74. In Oromia, meanwhile, the moves also allowed the ruling party to consolidate its mobilisation ahead of elections, which finally took place (in most but not all constituencies) in mid-2021. With limited opposition, and the ruling party standing uncontested in a majority of the seats in Oromia, the Prosperity Party won a landslide. Al Jazeera, 10 July 2021, accessed June 2021, https://www.aljazeera.com/news/2021/7/10/ethiopias-ruling-party-wins-national-election-in-landslide. Elections were not held in eight constituencies in Oromia.

Africanews, 21 September 2021, accessed October 2021, https://www.
africanews.com/2021/09/21/ethiopia-announces-partial-second-round-
vote-that-includes-amhara-oromia-regions//. Although charges against OFC
leaders were dropped and they were finally released from jail in January 2022,
OLF leaders remained in detention, and in February 2022 it was reported that
a number were critically ill after a period of hunger strike. *Addis Standard*, 11
February 2022, accessed March 2022, https://addisstandard.com/news-olf-
leaders-on-hunger-strike-rushed-to-hospital-in-capital/.

75. Gebrekirstos, 'The War on Tigray'.
76. Eritrean Press, 2 July 2020, accessed July 2022, https://www.facebook.com/
     watch/?v=766856624054785.
77. Sisay Agena, speaking on ESAT, *Eletawi* programme, 1 July 2020, accessed July
     2022, https://www.youtube.com/watch?v=feujpLmY2jQ.
78. The directive establishing the Guard is dated 18 June 2022. The grenade attack,
     which killed two and injured several others, occurred on 23 June 2018.
79. The killings triggered an immediate late-night TV statement by a prime minister
     wearing military fatigues, and a ten-day internet blackout. Two years later
     General Se'are's bodyguard was sentenced to life imprisonment for the Addis
     Ababa deaths, after an investigation and (non-military) trial during which relevant
     witness testimony was not heard. *The Citizen*, 28 June 2021, accessed July 2021,
     https://www.thecitizen.co.tz/tanzania/news/africa/killer-of-ethiopia-army-
     chief-seare-mekonen-sentenced-to-life-in-prison-3453934.
80. See, for example, Borkena, 10 March 2020, accessed May 2020, https://
     borkena.com/2020/03/10/oromo-regional-state-added-thousands-of-special-
     forces-to-its-security-apparatus/.
81. On Kemal Gelchu's complex background see *Oromo Affairs* (blog), 7 January
     2012 [Ethiopian calendar], accessed March 2021, http://oromoaffairs.blogspot.
     com/2012/01/kemal-gelchu-co-olf-trojan-horse-part-i.html.
82. Video posted by Shewa Media, 7 June 2020, accessed January 2021, https://
     www.youtube.com/watch?v=0VxXkill7ug.
83. 'Clashes over Ethiopia's Tigray Region', International Crisis Group, 5 November
     2020, accessed November 2020, https://www.crisisgroup.org/africa/horn-
     africa/ethiopia/ethiopias-clash-tigray-getting-ceasefire-and-national-dialogue.
     See the citation by Reuters, 13 November 2020, accessed December 2020,
     https://www.reuters.com/article/us-ethiopia-conflict-military-factbox/
     factbox-the-forces-fighting-in-ethiopias-tigray-conflict-idUSKBN27T14J. Also
     the more nuanced discussion in Deutsche Welle Fact-Check, 7 December 2020,
     accessed December 2020, https://www.dw.com/en/dw-fact-check-tigray-
     conflict-is-also-a-battle-for-the-truth/a-55843907.
84. More detail about events between September 2018 and July 2020 is available
     at https://assets.publishing.service.gov.uk/government/uploads/system/
     uploads/attachment_data/file/900975/CPIN_-_Ethiopia_-_Opposition_to_
     the_government.pdf.
85. Shanee means 'group of five'; although widely used by the government (including
     occasionally to refer to the OLF itself), OLF Shanee is not a name used by any
     armed group to identify itself. On the government claim, see Ermias Tesfaye,

'Amid Blackout, Western Oromia Plunges Deeper into Chaos and Confusion', Ethiopia Insight, 14 February 2020, accessed February 2020, https://www. ethiopia-insight.com/2020/02/14/amid-blackout-western-oromia-plunges-deeper-into-chaos-and-confusion/.

86. Ermias Tasfaye, 'Amid Blackout'.
87. Africanews, 13 January 2019, accessed February 2019, https://www. africanews.com/2019/01/13/ethiopia-army-executing-airstrikes-against-olf-in-western-oromia/. EAF was reported to have used helicopter gunships during its crackdown in the Somali region in 2007–8: http://news.bbc.co.uk/1/hi/world/africa/7101598.stm; otherwise this was the first documented instance of aerial bombardment within Ethiopian territory since the heavy use of aerial bombing during the Derg-period civil war.
88. Ermias Tesfaye, 'Amid Blackout'.
89. 'Ethiopia: Communications Shutdown Takes Heavy Toll', Human Rights Watch, 9 March 2020, https://www.hrw.org/node/339303/printable/print.
90. Ermias Tesfaye, 'Amid Blackout'.
91. 'A Hidden War Threatens Ethiopia's Transition to Democracy', The Economist, 21 March 2020, accessed April 2020, https://www.economist.com/middle-east-and-africa/2020/03/19/a-hidden-war-threatens-ethiopias-transition-to-democracy.
92. BBC, 3 November 2020, accessed November 2020, https://www.bbc.co.uk/news/world-africa-54787034; and Amnesty International, 2 November 2020, accessed November 2020, https://www.amnesty.org/en/latest/news/2020/11/ethiopia-over-50-ethnic-amhara-killed-in-attack-on-village-by-armed-group/.
93. See for instance on Twitter, December 2020, https://twitter.com/DilNaodA/status/1338471602225356802?s=20&t=8ozJx3mk5F9s6IJcvYvl6A.
94. Addis Standard, 9 March 2021, accessed March 2021, https://addisstandard. com/news-gunmen-who-storm-a-local-church-kill-29-in-horoguduru-western-oromia/.
95. Associated Press, 19 June 2022, accessed July 2021, https://www.theguardian. com/world/2022/jun/19/ethiopia-more-than-200-amhara-people-killed-in-attack-blamed-on-rebels.
96. Addis Standard, 10 March 2021, accessed March 2021, https://addisstandard. com/letter-our-forces-are-absolutely-not-responsible-for-recent-killing-in-horo-guduru-ola-spokesperson/.
97. Lefort, 'Preaching Unity but Flying Solo'.
98. 'Bridging the Divide in Ethiopia's North', International Crisis Group, 11 June 2020, accessed July 2020, https://www.crisisgroup.org/africa/horn-africa/ethiopia/b156-bridging-divide-ethiopias-north.
99. Lefort, 'Preaching Unity but Flying Solo'.
100. New Humanitarian, 1 April 2020, accessed May 2020, https://www. thenewhumanitarian.org/news/2020/04/01/ethiopia-election-coronavirus.
101. Meaza Ashenafi, video posted to Twitter, 6 August 2019, accessed June 2022, https://twitter.com/ashenafi_meaza/status/1158763066487660545?s=20&t=7pEFzdbcORGSpVeUL2ldsw.

102. BBC Tigrigna-language reporter, Desta Gebremedhin, 5 September 2020, accessed September 2020, https://www.bbc.co.uk/news/world-africa-53807187.

103. Reuters, 5 September 2020, accessed October 2020, https://www.reuters.com/article/us-ethiopia-politics-idUSKBN25W0SA.

104. Al Jazeera, 11 September 2020, accessed September 2020, https://www.aljazeera.com/news/2020/9/11/governing-party-in-ethiopias-tigray-sweeps-regional-polls.

105. *Addis Standard*, 7 October 2020, quoting parliamentary House Speaker Aden Farah, accessed February 2022, https://www.facebook.com/permalink.php?story_fbid=3363529580361680&id=177352718979398.

106. Tweet, 8 October 2020, https://twitter.com/CohenOnAfrica/status/131431 9776374829057?s=20&t=7pEFzdbcORGSpVeUL2ldsw.

107. Daniel Berhanu, posted on Twitter, 11 October 2020, accessed June 2022, https://twitter.com/daniel_berhane/status/1315353771720011776?s= 20&t=7pEFzdbcORGSpVeUL2ldsw.

108. Mehari Maru, tweet and screenshot, 22 October 2020, accessed July 2022, https://twitter.com/DrMehari/status/1319341911451275265?s= 20&t=7pEFzdbcORGSpVeUL2ldsw. The delivery of supplies to combat locusts was also disrupted. See Tom Gardener, 'How War Threatens Ethiopia's Struggle against Worst Locust Swarm in 25 Years', *The Guardian*, 16 November 2020, accessed December 2020, https://www.theguardian.com/global-development/2020/nov/16/war-ethiopia-locust-swarm.

109. Tweet with screenshot, posted to Twitter 31 October 2020, accessed July 2022, https://twitter.com/Sanyiikoo_Oromo/status/1322360491990228992?s= 20&t=7pEFzdbcORGSpVeUL2ldsw.

110. Henok Gabisa, tweet with screenshot, posted to Twitter 30 October 2020, accessed July 2022, https://twitter.com/henokgabisa/status/1322302811-066011648?s=20&t=7pEFzdbcORGSpVeUL2ldsw.

111. See the clip at https://twitter.com/StalinTeklu/status/14941288270727-57765?s=20&t=N90IUlrZnJwD14rPsxFr_A.

112. R. Reid, *War in Pre-colonial Eastern Africa*, Oxford: James Currey, 2007, p. 71. See also R. Reid, 'Atrocity in Ethiopian History', *Journal of Genocide Research*, 24 (1) 2022, pp. 97–108.

113. G. Prunier, 'The Ethiopian Revolution and the Dergue Regime', in Prunier and Ficquet, *Understanding Contemporary Ethiopia*, p. 229.

6.   ERITREA, THE HORN AND THE PATH TO WAR

1. Reporters Without Borders, *World Press Freedom Index 2022*, accessed 23 May 2022, https://rsf.org/en/index.

2. 'Ethiopia, Eritrea Officially End War', Deutsche Welle, 9 July 2018, accessed 23 May 2022, https://www.dw.com/en/ethiopia-eritrea-officially-end-war/a-44585296.

3. 'Ethiopia and Eritrea Say War Over, U.N. Hails "Wind of Hope" in Africa', Reuters, 9 July 2018, accessed 23 May 2022, https://www.reuters.com/article/ethiopia-eritrea-idINKBN1JZ0LY.

4. 'Eritrea President Arrives at Addis Ababa Airport, First Visit in 22 Years', Al Arabia, 14 July 2018, accessed 23 May 2022, https://english.alarabiya.net/News/world/2018/07/14/Eritrea-president-arrives-at-Addis-Ababa-airport-first-visit-in-22-years.

5. The 1998–2000 border war and its consequences are explored in several publications, including Dominique Jacquin-Berdal and Martin Plaut (eds.), *Unfinished Business: Ethiopia and Eritrea at War*, Trenton: Red Sea Press, 2004; Tekeste Negash and Kjetil Tronvol, *Brothers at War: Making Sense of the Eritrean–Ethiopian War*, Oxford: James Currey, 2000; and Richard Reid, *Shallow Graves: A Memoir of the Ethiopia–Eritrea War*, London: Hurst, 2020.

6. Eritrea–Ethiopia Boundary Commission, Permanent Court of Arbitration, 30 November 2007, accessed 24 March 2022, https://pca-cpa.org/ar/cases/99/.

7. 'Eritrean Orthodox Tewahdo Church Hosts WCC Delegation', World Council of Churches, 3 October 2017, accessed 23 May 2022, https://www.oikoumene.org/news/eritrean-orthodox-tewahdo-church-hosts-wcc-delegation.

8. 'What Will Eritrea Get Out of Donald Yamamoto's Visit?', *Martin Plaut* (blog), 25 April 2018, accessed 23 May 2022, https://martinplaut.com/2018/04/25/what-will-eritrea-get-out-of-donald-yamamotos-visit/; 'Principal Deputy Assistant Secretary Yamamoto Travels to East Africa', US State Department, 21 April 2018, accessed 23 May 2013, https://2017-2021.state.gov/principal-deputy-assistant-secretary-yamamoto-travel-to-east-africa/index.html.

9. 'Group Conversation with PM Abiy', Aiga Forum, 22 May 2018, accessed 23 May 2022, http://www.aigaforum.com/news2018/conversation-with-pm-abiy.htm.

10. 'President Isaias on Official Visit to Saudi Arabia', Eritrea Ministry of Information, 23 July 2018, accessed 23 May 2022, https://shabait.com/2018/07/23/president-isaias-on-official-visit-to-saudi-arabia/.

11. 'UN Chief to Meet Ethiopia's PM on Monday after Peace Breakthrough with Eritrea', Reuters, 9 July 2018, accessed 23 May 2022, https://news.yahoo.com/un-chief-meet-ethiopias-pm-monday-peace-breakthrough-072304333--business.html.

12. 'U.N. Chief Says Sanctions on Eritrea Likely to Become Obsolete', Reuters, 9 July 2018, accessed 23 May 2022, https://www.reuters.com/article/us-ethiopia-eritrea-un-sanctions/u-n-chief-says-sanctions-on-eritrea-likely-to-become-obsolete-idUSKBN1JZ1UG.

13. 'The Nobel Peace Prize That Paved the Way for War', *New York Times*, 15 December 2021, accessed 23 May 2022, https://www.nytimes.com/2021/12/15/world/africa/ethiopia-abiy-ahmed-nobel-war.html.

14. 'UAE Hails Ethiopia, Eritrea Leaders after Rapprochement', Reuters, 24 July 2018, accessed 23 May 2022, https://www.reuters.com/article/us-ethiopia-eritrea-emirates-idUSKBN1KE1VY.

15. 'Leaders of Ethiopia, Eritrea Sign Accord in Saudi Arabia', Associated Press, 16 September 2018, accessed 23 May 2022, https://apnews.com/article/5d7733c32f2443af8fb91fea5edbde98.

16. 'The Nobel Peace Prize That Paved the Way for War', *New York Times*, 15 December 2021.

17. 'Ethiopia–Eritrea Border Reopens after 20 Years', BBC, 11 September 2018, accessed 23 May 2022, https://www.bbc.co.uk/news/world-africa-45475876.

18. 'Ethiopia–Eritrea Border Reopens after 20 Years', BBC, 11 September 2018.

19. 'Eritrea Closes Border Crossing to Ethiopians, Official and Residents Say', Reuters, 28 December 2018, accessed 23 May 2022, https://www.reuters.com/article/us-ethiopia-eritrea-idUSKCN1OR189.

20. 'Update on Renewed Influx from Eritrea—24 September 2018', Reliefweb, 24 September 2018, accessed 23 May 2022, https://reliefweb.int/report/ethiopia/update-renewed-influx-eritrea-24-september-2018.

21. 'Eritrea–Ethiopia Peace Leads to a Refugee Surge', New Humanitarian, 15 November 2018, accessed 23 May 2022, https://www.thenewhumanitarian.org/news-feature/2018/11/15/eritrea-ethiopia-peace-leads-refugee-surge.

22. UNHCR, 'Ethiopia Operation, Tigray Emergency, Eritrean Refugee Population Profile—Tigray Region', 4 November 2020, accessed 23 May 2022, https://reporting.unhcr.org/sites/default/files/UNHCR%20Ethiopia%20Eritrean%20refugees%20in%20Tigray%20dashboard%204%20November%202020.pdf.

23. 'Ethiopia, Eritrea Re-open Humera–Omhajer Border', New Business Ethiopia, 8 January 2018, accessed 23 May 2022, https://newbusinessethiopia.com/politics/ethiopia-eritrea-re-opens-humera-omhajer-border/.

24. A complete English translation of Isaias Afwerki's Eritrean TV interview, 17 February 2021, Eritrea Hub, 28 February 2021, accessed 23 May 2022, https://eritreahub.org/a-complete-english-translation-of-isaias-afwerkis-eritrean-tv-interview-17-february-2021.

25. Martin Plaut, 'Eritrea and Yemen: Control of the Shipping Lanes', *Review of African Political Economy*, 23 (67) March 1996, pp. 106–9.

26. Alex de Waal, *Islamism and Its Enemies in the Horn of Africa*, Bloomington: Indiana University Press, 2004, p. 208; Linda do Hoyos, 'Congo's Dictator Laurent Kabila Is Sitting on a Time-Bomb', *Executive Intelligence Review*, 24 (40) 3 October 1997, accessed 23 May 2022, https://larouchepub.com/eiw/public/1997/eirv24n40-19971003/eirv24n40-19971003_049-congos_dictator_laurent_kabila_i.pdf.

27. Ahmed Hassan, 'The Rise and Fall of the Sudan Alliance Forces (1) and (2)', African Arguments, October 2009, accessed 23 May 2022, https://africanarguments.org/2009/10/the-rise-and-fall-of-the-sudan-alliance-forces-1/; https://africanarguments.org/2009/10/the-rise-and-fall-of-the-sudan-alliance-forces-2/.

28. Cedric Barnes and Harun Hassan, 'The Rise and Fall of Mogadishu's Islamic Courts', *Journal of Eastern African Studies*, 1 (2) 2007, pp. 151–60.

29. UN Security Council, 'Report of the Monitoring Group on Somalia and Eritrea Pursuant to Security Council Resolution 1916 (2010)', S/2011/433, 18 July 2011, p. 13, accessed 23 May 2022, https://documents-dds-ny.un.org/doc/UNDOC/GEN/N11/380/08/PDF/N1138008.pdf?OpenElement.

30. 'Djiboutian–Eritrean Border Conflict', Wikipedia, accessed 23 May 2022, https://en.wikipedia.org/wiki/Djiboutian%E2%80%93Eritrean_border_conflict.

31. Nizar Manek and Mohamed Kheir Omer, 'Sudan Will Decide the Outcome of the Ethiopian Civil War', *Foreign Policy*, 14 November 2020, accessed 23 May 2022, https://foreignpolicy.com/2020/11/14/sudan-will-decide-outcome-ethiopian-civil-war-abiy-tigray/.

32. 'Eritrea and Somalia Agree to Restore Diplomatic Relations', Al Jazeera, 30 July 2018, accessed 31 July 2022, https://www.aljazeera.com/news/2018/7/30/eritrea-and-somalia-agree-to-restore-diplomatic-relations.

33. https://africa.cgtn.com/2020/01/27/somalia-ethiopia-and-eritrea-pledge-joint-anti-terror-war/.

34. https://villasomalia.gov.so/en/heads-of-state-and-government-meeting-between-eritrea-ethiopia-and-somalia-joint-communique/.

35. http://www.eritreaembassy-japan.org/data/Peace_and_Security_in_the_Horn_of_Africa_Eritrea's_View.pdf.

36. Ingo Henneberg and Sören Stapel, 'Cooperation and Conflict at the Horn of Africa: A New Regional Bloc between Ethiopia, Eritrea, and Somalia and Its Consequences for Eastern Africa', *Africa Spectrum*, 55 (3) 2020, https://journals.sagepub.com/doi/full/10.1177/0002039720936689.

37. H. Verhoeven and M. Woldemariam, 'Who Lost Ethiopia? The Unmaking of an African Anchor State and US Foreign Policy', *Contemporary Security Policy*, 21 June 2022, p. 21, https://www.tandfonline.com/doi/full/10.1080/13523260.2022.2091580.

38. 'Eritrean President to Visit Amhara Region', Addis Insight, 7 November 2018, https://addisinsight.net/eritrean-president-isaias-afeworki-to-visit-amhara-region/.

39. 'Prime Minister Abiy Holds Talks with President Isaias in Asmara', Ethiopia Monitor, 19 July 2020, accessed 23 May 2022, https://ethiopianmonitor.com/2020/07/19/prime-minister-abiy-holds-talks-with-president-isaias-in-asmara/.

40. 'Sawa at 33', Eritrea Ministry of Information, 15 August 2020, accessed 28 July 2022, https://shabait.com/2020/08/15/sawa-at-33/.

41. 'President Isaias Returns Home Concluding Working Visit to Ethiopia', Eritrea Ministry of Information, 15 October 2020, accessed 23 May 2022, https://shabait.com/2020/10/15/president-isaias-returns-home-concluding-working-visit-to-ethiopia/.

42. Private correspondence between author and Eritrean analyst, October 2020.

43. Naty Berhane Yifru, 'With Abiy in His Corner, Isaias Eyes TPLF Knockout', Ethiopia Insight, 26 March 2020, accessed 23 May 2022, https://www.ethiopia-insight.com/2020/03/26/with-abiy-in-his-corner-isaias-eyes-tplf-knockout/.

44. Naty Berhane Yifru, 'With Abiy in His Corner, Isaias Eyes TPLF Knockout'.

45. M. Labzaé, 'The War in Tigray (2020–2021)', in J.-N. Bach (ed.), *Routledge Handbook of the Horn of Africa*, London: Routledge, 2022, p. 241.

46. 'Eritrea Agrees to Withdraw Troops from Border Area, Ethiopia's PM Says', Reuters, 26 March 2021, accessed 23 May 2022, https://www.reuters.com/world/ethiopias-pm-says-eritrea-agreed-withdraw-troops-border-area-2021-03-26/.

47. Claire Wilmot, Ellen Tveteraas and Alexi Drew, 'Duelling Information Campaigns: The War over the Narrative in Tigray', Media Manipulation,

20 August 2021, accessed 23 May 2022, https://mediamanipulation.org/case-studies/dueling-information-campaigns-war-over-narrative-tigray.

48. Thomas Gardner, 'How Abiy's Effort to Redefine Ethiopia Led to War in Tigray', *World Politics Review*, 8 December 2020, accessed 23 May 2022, https://www.worldpoliticsreview.com/articles/29272/behind-the-tigray-ethnic-conflict-ethiopia-politics-of-federalism-and-a-fight-for-identity.

49. 'Ethiopia Appoints New Chief of Staff for Powerful Military', Bloomberg, 7 June 2020, accessed 23 May 2022, https://www.bloombergquint.com/politics/ethiopia-appoints-new-chief-of-staff-for-powerful-military.

50. '"Nobody Will Kneel": Tigrayans Defiant as Ethiopian Leader Cracks Down', Reuters, 16 December 2018, accessed 23 May 2022, https://www.reuters.com/article/us-ethiopia-politics-tigray-idUSKBN1OF05F.

51. 'Ethiopia Moving Troops from Eritrean Border amid New Peace', Associated Press, 14 December 2018, accessed 29 July 2022, https://apnews.com/article/d55c7b9fdab64f269b24ce7f441a1d98.

52. Martin Plaut, 'Tigray Protest Halts Army's Attempt to Move Heavy Weapons to Oromia', Harnnet, 1 January 2019, accessed 23 May 2022, http://www.harnnet.org/index.php/articles-corner/english-articles/item/5244-tigray-protest-halts-army-s-attempt-to-move-heavy-weapons-to-oromia; https://ecadforum.com/2019/01/09/military-trucks-blocked-in-tigray-region/.

53. Martin Plaut, 'Tigray Protest'.

54. 'Abiy Purged His Military High Command to Prepare for His War against the TPLF', Africa Intelligence, 22 February 2021, accessed 29 July 2022, https://www.africaintelligence.com/eastern-africa-and-the-horn/2021/02/22/abiy-purged-his-military-high-command-to-prepare-for-his-war-against-the-tplf,109645145-ge0.

55. 'Ethiopia Airlines Accused of Ethnic Profiling over Civil War with Tigray', *Daily Telegraph*, 4 December 2020, accessed 23 May 2022, https://www.telegraph.co.uk/news/2020/12/04/ethiopia-airlines-accused-ethnic-profiling-civil-war-tigray/.

56. 'As War Goes On in Ethiopia, Ethnic Harassment Is on the Rise', *New York Times*, 12 December 2020, accessed 23 May 2022, https://www.nytimes.com/2020/12/12/world/africa/Ethiopia-Tigray-ethnic.html.

57. 'Ethiopian Airlines Denies Ethnic Profiling Its Tigrayan Staff', Eritrea Hub, 11 February 2021, https://eritreahub.org/ethiopian-airlines-denies-ethnic-profiling-its-tigrayan-staff.

58. 'Ethiopian Airlines CEO Resigns over Health Issues', Reuters, 23 March 2022, accessed 23 May 2022, https://www.reuters.com/business/aerospace-defense/ethiopian-airlines-ceo-resigns-over-health-issues-2022-03-23/.

59. 'She Was in Abiy Ahmed's Cabinet as War Broke Out. Now She Wants to Set the Record Straight', *Washington Post*, 30 December 2021, accessed 23 May 2022, https://www.washingtonpost.com/world/2021/12/30/ethiopia-abiy-tigray-war/.

60. 'Ethiopia: Ethnic Tigrayans Forcibly Disappeared', Human Rights Watch, 18 August 2021, accessed 23 May 2022, https://www.hrw.org/news/2021/08/18/ethiopia-ethnic-tigrayans-forcibly-disappeared.

61. 'Ethiopian Troops Transported to the Tigray Frontline through Asmara—Reports', Eritrea Hub, 17 November 2020, accessed 23 May 2022, https://eritreahub.org/ethiopian-troops-transported-to-the-tigray-frontline-through-asmara-reports.

62. It was not until May 2022, at the inauguration of Somalia's next president, that President Farmaajo finally admitted that some 5,000 Somali troops had been sent to Eritrea, arguing that their return had been delayed by Somalia's sensitive elections, which concluded in May 2022. Harun Maruf, tweet, 23 May 2022, accessed 23 May 2022, https://twitter.com/HarunMaruf/status/1528659953778667520?s=20&t=LWUTGy_v2klylJyNWx6oqQ.

63. 'Report: "Hundreds of Somali Troops Used as Cannon-Fodder in Ethiopia's Tigray War"', Eritrea Hub, 17 January 2021, accessed 23 May 2022, https://eritreahub.org/report-hundreds-of-somali-troops-used-as-cannon-fodder-in-ethiopias-tigray-war.

64. 'Somali Men "Forced into Eritrean Army" under Impression They Were Signing Up for Security Jobs in Qatar', *Daily Telegraph*, 29 January 2021, accessed 21 April 2022, https://www.telegraph.co.uk/news/2021/01/29/somali-men-forced-eritrean-army-impression-signing-security/.

65. 'Anger in Somalia as Sons Secretly Sent to Serve in Eritrea Military Force', Reuters, 28 January 2021, accessed 21 April 2022, https://www.reuters.com/article/us-somalia-eritrea-security/anger-in-somalia-as-sons-secretly-sent-to-serve-in-eritrea-military-force-idUSKBN29X1F5.

66. 'Clandestine Training of Somali Forces in Eritrea Stirs Families' Concern', Voice of America, 19 February 2021, accessed 23 May 2022, https://www.voanews.com/a/africa_clandestine-training-somali-forces-eritrea-stirs-families-concern/6202295.html.

67. Lucy Kassa, 'Somali Troops Committed Atrocities in Tigray as New Alliance Emerged, Survivors Say', *Globe and Mail*, 20 January 2022, https://www.theglobeandmail.com/world/article-somali-troops-committed-atrocities-in-tigray-as-new-alliance-emerged/.

68. BBC *Focus on Africa* interview, 21 January 2022, https://www.bbc.co.uk/sounds/play/w172xwpcp26dhr4.

69. 'In Somalia, Mothers Fear Sons Were Sent to Ethiopia Conflict', Associated Press, 22 January 2021, accessed 23 May 2022, https://abcnews.go.com/International/wireStory/somalia-mothers-fear-sons-ethiopia-conflict-75421149.

70. 'Young Recruit Killed near Somalia's Capital after Escaping Training Camp in Eritrea', Somali Guardian, 13 July 2021, accessed 23 May 2022, https://somaliguardian.com/news/young-recruit-killed-near-somalias-capital-after-escaping-training-camp-in-eritrea/.

71. https://www.cia.gov/the-world-factbook/countries/ethiopia/#military-and-security.

72. International Institute for Strategic Studies, *The Military Balance 2021*, London: IISS, 2021.

73. https://www.cia.gov/the-world-factbook/countries/eritrea/#military-and-security.

74. CIA, *The World Factbook*, 2022, accessed 23 May 2022, https://www.cia.gov/the-world-factbook/countries/ethiopia/#military-and-security.

75. Crisis Group, 5 November 2020, accessed November 2020, https://www.crisisgroup.org/africa/horn-africa/ethiopia/ethiopias-clash-tigray-getting-ceasefire-and-national-dialogue. See the citation by Reuters, 13 November 2020, accessed December 2020, https://www.reuters.com/article/us-ethiopia-conflict-military-factbox/factbox-the-forces-fighting-in-ethiopias-tigray-conflict-idUSKBN27T14J. Also the more nuanced discussion in Deutsche Welle Fact-Check, 7 December 2020, accessed December 2020, https://www.dw.com/en/dw-fact-check-tigray-conflict-is-also-a-battle-for-the-truth/a-55843907.

76. International Institute for Strategic Studies, *Strategic Survey 2021: The Annual Assessment of Geopolitics*, London: IISS, 2021, pp. 326–7.

77. 'In-Depth Analysis: Towards Tigray Statehood?', *Addis Standard*, 14 May 2020, accessed 23 May 2022, https://addisstandard.com/in-depth-analysis-towards-tigray-statehood/.

78. 'Is Isaias Looking for a Final Confrontation with His Tigrayan Enemies?', Eritrea Hub, 21 July 2020, accessed 23 May 2022, https://eritreahub.org/is-isaias-looking-for-a-final-confrontation-with-his-tigrayan-enemies.

79 Kjetil Tronvoll, Facebook, 25 October 2020, accessed 23 May 2020, https://m.facebook.com/story.php?story_fbid=10218250164946237&id=1253796686%C2%ACif_t=nf_status_story%C2%ACif_id=1603676278109841&ref=m_notif.

80. 'The Tigray War', *Review of African Political Economy*, 8 December 2020, accessed 23 May 2022, https://roape.net/2020/12/08/the-tigray-war/.

81. Africa Intelligence, 5 November 2020, https://www.africaintelligence.com/.

82. 'Dr Debretsion Writes to 70 Countries in the World', BBC Tigrinya Service, 27 October 2020, accessed 23 May 2022, https://www.bbc.com/tigrinya/news-54641468.

83. 'Ethiopia: Statement by the High Representative/Vice-President Josep Borrell on the Latest Developments', European Union External Action, 2 November 2020, accessed 23 May 2022, https://eeas.europa.eu/headquarters/headquarters-homepage/87959/ethiopia-statement-high-representativevice-president-josep-borrell-latest-developments_en.

84. 'Tigray President Calls on His People to Prepare for War', Eritrea Hub, 3 November 2020, accessed 23 May 2022, https://eritreahub.org/tigray-president-calls-on-his-people-to-prepare-for-war.

85. 'Operations to Restore Law and Order in Ethiopia's Tigray Region', Walta, 24 December 2020, accessed 23 May 2022, https://waltainfo.com/operations-to-restore-law-and-order-in-ethiopias-tigray-region/.

86. 'Who Started the War on Tigray?', Tghat, 31 March 2021, accessed 23 May 2022, https://www.tghat.com/2021/03/31/who-started-the-war-on-tigray/.

87. UN OCHA, 'Ethiopia: Tigray Region Humanitarian Update', Situation Report no. 1, 7 November 2020, accessed 23 May 2022, https://reliefweb.int/sites/reliefweb.int/files/resources/ethiopia_situation_report_no.1_tigray_humanitarian_update_7_november_2020.pdf.

88. Mirjam van Reisen, Klara Smits and Kibrom Berhe, 'Who Triggered the Tigray War on 3 November 2020?', *Martin Plaut* (blog), 3 November 2020, accessed

23 May 2022, http://martinplaut.com/2021/11/03/who-triggered-the-tigray-war-on-3-november-2020/.

89. Van Reisen, Smits and Kibrom, 'Who Triggered the Tigray War?'

90. 'Ethiopia's Tigray Crisis: How a Soldier Survived an 11-Hour Gun Battle', BBC, 10 December 2020, accessed 23 May 2022, https://www.bbc.co.uk/news/world-africa-55215431.

91. 'Ethiopia's Tigray Crisis', BBC, 10 December 2020.

92. 'Ethiopia's Tigray Crisis', BBC, 10 December 2020.

93. 'The Midnight Confrontation That Helped Unleash Ethiopia's Conflict', Agence France-Presse, 27 November 2020, accessed 23 May 2022, https://www.france24.com/en/live-news/20201127-the-midnight-confrontation-that-helped-unleash-ethiopia-s-conflict.

94. 'Inside a Military Base in Ethiopia's Tigray: Soldiers Decry Betrayal by Former Comrades', Reuters, 17 December 2020, accessed 23 May 2022, https://www.reuters.com/article/us-ethiopia-conflict-attack-idUSKBN28R1IE.

95. 'In Ethiopia War, New Abuse Charges Turn Spotlight on Tigrayan Former Rulers', Reuters, 28 December 2021, accessed 23 May 2022, https://www.reuters.com/investigates/special-report/ethiopia-conflict-tplf/.

96. A complete English translation of Isaias Afwerki's Eritrean TV interview, 17 February 2021, Eritrea Hub, 28 February 2021, accessed 23 May 2022, https://eritreahub.org/a-complete-english-translation-of-isaias-afwerkis-eritrean-tv-interview-17-february-2021.

97. 'Is Ethiopia Headed for Civil War?', *Foreign Policy*, 5 November 2020, accessed 23 May 2022, https://foreignpolicy.com/2020/11/05/is-ethiopia-headed-for-civil-war/.

INTERLUDE

1. Nayna is a pseudonym.

7. TIGRAY FROM DEFEAT TO RECOVERY

1. Ermias Teka is the pseudonym of an Ethiopian journalist.

2. Armed Conflict Location and Event Data Project (ACLED), reporting period 1 January 2021—31 December 2021, accessed 21 April 2022, https://acleddata.com/dashboard/#/dashboard.

3. 'The Information Age Retreats from the Battlefield', Slate, 9 March 2021, accessed 21 April 2022, https://slate.com/news-and-politics/2021/03/ethiopia-tigray-violence-media-blackout.html.

4. UN OCHA, 'Ethiopia: Tigray Region Humanitarian Update', Situation Report no. 1, 7 November 2020, accessed 23 May 2022, https://reliefweb.int/sites/reliefweb.int/files/resources/ethiopia_situation_report_no.1_tigray_humanitarian_update_7_november_2020.pdf.

5. H. Verhoeven and M. Woldemariam, 'Who Lost Ethiopia? The Unmaking of an African Anchor State and US Foreign Policy', *Contemporary Security Policy*,

21 June 2022, p. 21, https://www.tandfonline.com/doi/full/10.1080/13523
260.2022.2091580.

6. 'Ethiopia Tigray Crisis: Abiy Issues "Ultimatum" as Civilians Flee Fighting', BBC,
18 November 2020, accessed 23 May 2022, https://www.bbc.co.uk/news/
world-africa-54960150.

7. 'From Shelled Ethiopian City, Doctors Tally Deaths and Plead for Help', *New
York Times*, 3 December 2020, accessed 23 May 2022, https://www.nytimes.
com/2020/12/03/world/africa/ethiopia-tigray-civilian-casualties.html.

8. 'Ethiopia's Tigray Crisis: PM Claims Capture of Regional Capital Mekele', BBC,
29 November 2020, accessed 23 May 2022, https://www.bbc.co.uk/news/
world-africa-55111061.

9. 'From Shelled Ethiopian City', *New York Times*, 3 December 2020.

10. 'Ethiopia "Will Be Digging Up Mass Graves for a Decade": Inside Tigray's Dirty
War', *Financial Times*, 26 March 2021, accessed 21 April 2022, https://www.
ft.com/content/23021d09-5dac-4ff5-b2a9-6b040ffdc6db.

11. 'Special Report: Health Official Alleges "Sexual Slavery" in Tigray; Women
Blame Soldiers', Reuters, 15 April 2021, accessed 21 April 2022, https://
www.reuters.com/www.reuters.com/article/us-ethiopia-conflict-rape-
specialreport/special-report-health-official-alleges-sexual-slavery-in-tigray-
women-blame-soldiers-idUSKBN2C20P0.

12. 'Ethiopia: Tigray Forces Summarily Execute Civilians', Human Rights
Watch, 9 December 2021, accessed 21 April 2022, https://www.hrw.org/
news/2021/12/10/ethiopia-tigray-forces-summarily-execute-civilians.

13. Martin Plaut, in Dominique Jacquin-Berdal and Martin Plaut, *Unfinished Business:
Ethiopia and Eritrea at War*, Trenton: Red Sea Press, 2004, p. 12.

14. 'Resistance in Exile: Eritrean Freedom Fighter Mesfin Hagos', Deutsche Welle,
5 May 2013, accessed 8 April 2022, https://www.dw.com/en/resistance-in-
exile-eritrean-freedom-fighter-mesfin-hagos/a-17205104.

15. 'Mesfin Hagos's Appeal to the People of Eritrea', Eritrea Hub, 20 November
2020, accessed 8 April 2022, https://eritreahub.org/mesfin-hagoss-appeal-to-
the-people-of-eritrea-catholic-church-prays-for-peace.

16. 'Mesfin Hagos's Appeal'.

17. https://youtu.be/z_J5lkRF5kA.

18. 'Fact-Check: Are Other Nations Involved in the War in Tigray?', Deutsche Welle,
19 February 2021, accessed 20 April 2022, https://www.dw.com/en/fact-
check-are-other-nations-involved-in-the-war-in-tigray/a-56891431.

19. 'Abiy Ahmed Finally Came Clean about Eritrean Troops: What Next?', Al
Jazeera, 2 April 2021, accessed 8 April 2022, https://www.aljazeera.com/
news/2021/4/2/abiy-ahmed-finally-came-clean-about-eritrean-troops-what-
next.

20. 'Abiy Ahmed Finally Came Clean'.

21. 'Exclusive: U.S. Says Reports of Eritrean Troops in Ethiopia's Tigray Are
"Credible"', Reuters, 11 December 2020, accessed 23 May 2022, https://www.
reuters.com/article/ethiopia-conflict-eritrea-usa-exclusive-idUSKBN28L06R.

22. 'Mesfin Hagos: Eritrea's Role in Ethiopia's Conflict and the Fate of Eritrean
Refugees', Eritrea Hub, 3 December 2020, accessed 8 April 2022, https://

eritreahub.org/mesfin-hagos-eritreas-role-in-ethiopias-conflict-and-the-fate-of-eritrean-refugees.

23. 'Ethiopia's PM Says Eritrea Will Withdraw Troops from Tigray', *The Guardian*, 26 March 2021, accessed 8 April 2022, https://www.theguardian.com/world/2021/mar/26/ethiopia-pm-eritrea-withdraw-troops-tigray-abiy-ahmed.

24. https://www.bloomberg.com/news/articles/2020-11-13/ethiopia-withdraws-thousands-of-troops-from-neighboring-somalia.

25. 'Exclusive: Ethiopia Says Disarms Tigrayan Peacekeepers in Somalia over Security', Reuters, 18 November 2021, accessed 21 April 2022, https://www.reuters.com/article/us-ethiopia-conflict-somalia-exclusive/exclusive-tigrayan-peacekeepers-in-somalia-disarmed-by-ethiopian-colleagues-sources-say-idUSKBN27Y1HC.

26. 'Exclusive: Ethiopia Says Disarms Tigrayan Peacekeepers'.

27. 'In Somalia, Mothers Fear Sons Were Sent to Ethiopia Conflict', Associated Press, 22 January 2021, accessed 21 April 2022, https://abcnews.go.com/International/wireStory/somalia-mothers-fear-sons-ethiopia-conflict-75421149.

28. Report of the Special Rapporteur on the Situation of Human Rights in Eritrea, Mohamed Abdelsalam Babiker, 'Situation of Human Rights in Eritrea', 12 May 2021, A/HRC/47/21, para. 20.

29. 'Somali Troops Committed Atrocities in Tigray as New Alliance Emerged, Survivors Say', *Globe and Mail*, 20 January 2022, accessed 7 April 2022, https://www.theglobeandmail.com/world/article-somali-troops-committed-atrocities-in-tigray-as-new-alliance-emerged/.

30. 'Hassan Sheikh's Dilemma over Somali Soldiers Training in Eritrea', Garowe Online, 25 May 2022, accessed 1 July 2022, https://www.garoweonline.com/en/news/somalia/hassan-sheikh-s-dilemma-over-somali-soldiers-training-in-eritrea.

31. 'Stranded Somali Soldiers Raise Questions about Horn Alliances', Council on Foreign Relations, blog by Michelle Gavin, 20 July 2022, https://www.cfr.org/blog/stranded-somali-soldiers-raise-questions-about-horn-alliances.

32. Gebru Tarkeke, *The Ethiopian Revolution: War in the Horn of Africa*, New Haven: Yale University Press, 2009, p. 98.

33. Gebru Tarkeke, *The Ethiopian Revolution*, p. 87.

34. Gebru Tarkeke, *The Ethiopian Revolution*, p. 92.

35. 'Gen. Tsadkan Gebretensae: Ethiopia's Tigray Rebel Mastermind', BBC, 1 July 2021, accessed 20 April 2022, https://www.bbc.co.uk/news/world-africa-57583208.

36. 'Gen. Tsadkan Gebretensae', BBC, 1 July 2021.

37. 'Gen. Tsadkan Gebretensae', BBC, 1 July 2021.

38. 'Ethiopian Conflict: Tigray Admits Firing Missiles at Eritrea', Sky News, 15 November 2020, accessed 20 April 2022, https://news.sky.com/story/ethiopian-conflict-tigray-admits-firing-missiles-at-eritrea-12133031.

39. 'NPR "Journalist" Utterly Failed to Provide Balanced Reporting by Confining Herself to Sheer Paraphrasing a One-sided Wild Allegation against Eritrea',

Eritrean Embassy, Washington, 1 April 2022, accessed 20 April 2022, https://shabait.com/2022/04/02/npr-journalist-utterly-failed-to-provide-balanced-reporting-by-confining-herself-to-sheer-paraphrasing-a-one-sided-wild-allegations-against-eritrea/.

40. 'Ethiopia's Tigray Leader Confirms Firing Missiles at Eritrea', Associated Press, 15 November 2020, accessed 20 April 2022, https://apnews.com/article/international-news-eritrea-ethiopia-asmara-kenya-33b9aea59b4c984562eaa86d8547c6dd.

41. 'Conflict in Ethiopia's Tigray Region Widens as Missiles Are Fired at Airports', *New York Times*, 14 November 2022, accessed 20 April 2022, https://www.nytimes.com/2020/11/14/world/africa/ethiopia-tigray-missiles-airport.html.

42. Martin Plaut, 'Tigray: One Hundred Days of War', African Arguments, 12 February 2021, accessed 20 April 2022, https://africanarguments.org/2021/02/tigray-one-hundred-days-of-war/.

43. UNHCR, 'Sudan Country Refugee Response Plan: January–December 2022', p. 16, https://reporting.unhcr.org/document/1765; 'Ethiopian Forces Said to Block Refugees from Entering Sudan', Associated Press, 3 December 2020, accessed 20 April 2022, https://apnews.com/article/sudan-ethiopia-bab9935d0f82ff394c435b3d9d9553fe.

44. '"They Have Destroyed Tigray, Literally": Mulugeta Gebrehiwot Speaks from the Mountains of Tigray', World Peace Foundation, 29 January 2021, accessed 20 April 2022, https://sites.tufts.edu/reinventingpeace/2021/01/29/they-have-destroyed-tigray-literally-mulugeta-gebrehiwot-speaks-from-the-mountains-of-tigray/.

45. Tigray TV, 25 November 2020, accessed 20 April 2022, https://youtu.be/7gu7sFCCpv4.

46. '"They Have Destroyed Tigray, Literally."'

47. 'Young Men Take Up Arms in Northern Ethiopia as Atrocities Fuel Insurgency', *The Guardian*, 21 March 2021, accessed 22 April 2022, https://www.theguardian.com/world/2021/mar/08/atrocities-insurgency-ethiopia-tigray.

48. 'Ethiopia: Investigation Reveals Evidence That Scores of Civilians Were Killed in Massacre in Tigray State', Amnesty International, 20 November 2020, accessed 6 April 2022, https://www.amnesty.org/en/latest/news/2020/11/ethiopia-investigation-reveals-evidence-that-scores-of-civilians-were-killed-in-massacre-in-tigray-state/.

49. The *fano*, or *fanos*, are an Amhara youth group, established in the 2010s as central power declined. It has been accused of involvement in several atrocities.

50. Laetitia Bader, 'Interview: Uncovering Crimes Committed in Ethiopia's Tigray Region', Human Rights Watch, 23 December 2020, accessed 6 April 2022, https://www.hrw.org/news/2020/12/23/interview-uncovering-crimes-committed-ethiopias-tigray-region.

51. 'Witnesses to Slaughter: The Conflict in Ethiopia', Reuters, 7 June 2021, accessed 6 April 2022, https://www.reuters.com/article/us-ethiopia-conflict-expulsions-graphic-idUSKCN2DJ114.

52. 'Witnesses to Slaughter'.

53. Nic Cheeseman and Yohannes Woldemariam, 'Ethiopia's Perilous Propaganda War', *Foreign Affairs*, 8 April 2021, accessed 6 April 2022, https://www. foreignaffairs.com/articles/africa/2021-04-08/ethiopias-perilous-propaganda-war.

54. 'Tigray: Ethiopian Army Kills Ex-Foreign Minister Seyoum Mesfin', Al Jazeera, 13 January 2021, accessed 6 April 2022, https://www.aljazeera.com/ news/2021/1/13/ethiopia-says-former-foreign-minister-killed-by-military.

55. Martin Plaut, 'Why the Axum Massacre Took Place', Eritrea Focus, 20 February 2021, accessed 22 April 2022, https://eritreahub.org/why-the-axum-massacre-took-place.

56. 'Ethiopia: Eritrean Troops' Massacre of Hundreds of Axum Civilians May Amount to Crime against Humanity', Human Rights Watch, 5 March 2021, accessed 6 April 2022, https://www.hrw.org/news/2021/03/05/ethiopia-eritrean-forces-massacre-tigray-civilians.

57. 'Ethiopia: The Massacre in Axum', Amnesty International, 26 February 2021, accessed 6 April 2022, https://www.amnesty.org/en/documents/ afr25/3730/2021/en/.

58. Getu Mak, 'Unholy Deeds in Tigray's Holy City', Ethiopia Insight, 26 March 2021, accessed 22 April 2022, https://www.ethiopia-insight.com/2021/03/26/ unholy-deeds-in-tigrays-holy-city/.

59. '"Horrible": Witnesses Recall Massacre in Ethiopian Holy City', Associated Press, 18 February 2021, accessed 22 April 2022, https://apnews.com/article/ witnesses-recall-massacre-axum-ethiopia-fa1b531fea069aed6768409bd1d20bfa?u tm_campaign=SocialFlow&utm_source=Twitter&utm_medium=AP_Africa.

60. 'Tigray Conflict: Joint Statement by HR/VP Borrell and Commissioner Lenarčič on Massacres in Axum', EU press release, 26 February 2021, accessed 22 April 2022, https://eeas.europa.eu/headquarters/headquarters-homepage_ en/93875/Tigray%20conflict:%20Joint%20Statement%20by%20HR/VP%20 Borrell%20and%20Commissioner%20Lenar%C4%8Di%C4%8D%20on%20 massacres%20in%20Axum; Hansard, vol. 697, 14 June 2021, accessed 22 April 2022, https://hansard.parliament.uk/Commons/2021-06-14/debates/ FFC5AFA0-DFA9-467C-8434-1EC96B35AD9E/Ethiopia.

61. In August 2021 a Tigrayan website produced information about 3,000 civilians killed during the fighting. 'The War on Tigray in Numbers: Initial Analysis of Civilian Massacres', Tghat, 11 August 2021, accessed 22 April 2022, https:// www.tghat.com/2021/08/11/the-war-on-tigray-in-numbers-initial-analysis-of-the-massacred-civilians/.

62. 'Tigray: Atlas of the Humanitarian Situation', Ghent University, 27 December 2021, accessed 7 April 2022, https://www.researchgate.net/ publication/349824181_Tigray_Atlas_of_the_humanitarian_situation. Email correspondence with the author, 25 May 2022.

63. Abiy Ahmed, official tweet, 9 November 2020.

64. 'Ethiopia's PM Abiy Ahmed Says Army Fighting "on Eight Fronts", Including Tigray', Al Arabiya, 4 April 2021, accessed 22 April 2022, https://english. alarabiya.net/News/world/2021/04/04/Ethiopia-s-PM-Abiy-Ahmed-says-army-fighting-on-eight-fronts-including-Tigray.

65. Tigray Media House, 22 December 2020, accessed 22 April 2022, https://www.facebook.com/261522124370013/posts/1020767315112153/?app=fb.

66. Tigray Media House, n.d., accessed 22 April 2022, https://youtu.be/dUwUmD_A260.

67. Dimtsi Weyane, Facebook, 14 January 2021, accessed 22 April 2022, https://www.facebook.com/watch/?v=400214517874452.

68. Dimtsi Weyane, Facebook, 11 February 2021, accessed 22 April 2022, https://www.facebook.com/dimtsiweyane/videos/902161903930979/?app=fb.

69. Dimtsi Weyane, Facebook, 12 February 2021, accessed 22 April 2022, https://youtu.be/DITmA2gHg3M.

70. Dimtsi Weyane, Facebook, 15 February 2021, accessed 22 April 2022, https://www.facebook.com/dimtsiweyane/videos/1372380593106357/?app=fbl.

71. Dimtsi Weyane, Facebook, 19 February 2021, accessed 22 April 2022, https://www.facebook.com/282348198530030/posts/3663465353751614/?app=fbl.

72. Martin Plaut, 'Situation Report EEPA Horn no. 85—16 February 2021', 16 February 2021, accessed 22 April 2022, https://martinplaut.com/2021/02/16/situation-report-eepa-horn-no-85-16-february-2021/.

73. Ethiopia map, 12 March 2021, accessed 22 April 2022, https://nitter.fdn.fr/MapEthiopia/status/1370442748185038853#m; https://www.facebook.com/dimtsiweyane/videos/445785693505490/?app=fbl.

74. Tigray Media House, n.d., accessed 20 March 2022, https://www.facebook.com/tmhtv/videos/171079998066137/?app=fbl; https://www.bbc.com/amharic/news-56481575.amp#click=https://t.co/b2BJkcieb8.

75. 'Abiy Ahmed: Eritrea "Will Withdraw" Troops from Ethiopia in Tigray Conflict', BBC, 26 March 2021, accessed 20 March 2022, https://www.bbc.co.uk/news/world-africa-56536360.

76. 'Eritrea Agrees to Withdraw Troops from Border Area, Ethiopia's PM Says', Reuters, 26 March 2021, accessed 20 March 2022, https://www.reuters.com/world/ethiopias-pm-says-eritrea-agreed-withdraw-troops-border-area-2021-03-26/.

77. 'Diplomats Back Claims Eritrean Troops Have Joined Ethiopia Conflict', The Guardian, 8 December 2020, accessed 20 March 2022, https://www.theguardian.com/world/2020/dec/08/diplomats-back-claims-eritrean-troops-have-joined-ethiopia-conflict.

78. Tigray Media House, 3 March 2021, accessed 20 March 2022, https://www.facebook.com/tmhtv/videos/3650642208317718/?app=fbl.

79. Dimtsi Weyane, Facebook, n.d., accessed 22 April 2022, https://www.facebook.com/dimtsiweyane/videos/464956238039523/?app=fbl.

80. Facebook, 26 April 2021, accessed 20 March 2022, https://www.youtube.com/watch?v=cgrGcIkj6BQ; https://www.youtube.com/watch?v=mo60DcgRPSc.

81. 'Tigray War: Independent Report of the Battle for Nirak', Eritrea Hub, 27 April 2021, accessed 22 April 2022, https://eritreahub.org/tigray-war-independent-report-of-the-battle-for-nirak.

82. Dedebit Media, 10 May 2021, accessed 22 April 2022, https://www.youtube.com/watch?v=V7eAgtd3Iq4.

83. Facebook, 14 February 2021, accessed 22 April 2022, https://youtu.be/ ZzpH5owidXY; https://www.facebook.com/VoT2025/videos/3851636794- 893463/?app=fbl.

84. Fidel Media, 6 April 2021, accessed 22 April 2022, https://youtu.be/8rzX 4RaFbK0.

85. 'Conflict in Ethiopia Draws Tigray Diaspora into Activism', Columbia News Service, Columbia Journalism School, 16 December 2020, https:// columbianewsservice.com/2020/12/16/conflict-in-ethiopia-draws-tigray- diaspora-into-activism/.

86. 'Ethiopia Is Fighting "Difficult and Tiresome" Guerrilla War in Tigray, Says PM', *The Guardian*, 4 April 2021, accessed 22 April 2022, https://www.theguardian. com/world/2021/apr/04/ethiopias-pm-says-military-fighting-difficult-and- tiresome-guerilla-war.

87. René Lefort, 'Ethiopia's Vicious Deadlock', Ethiopia Insight, 27 April 2021, accessed 22 April 2022, https://www.ethiopia-insight.com/2021/04/27/ ethiopias-vicious-deadlock/.

88. 'Benishangul: At Least 60 Civilians Mostly Women, Children Killed', Borkena, 12 January 2021, accessed 22 April 2022, https://borkena.com/2021/01/12/ benishangul-at-least-60-civilians-mostly-women-children-killed/.

89. Tigrai Media House, Facebook, accessed 22 April 2022, https://youtu.be/ zwz5EIqRcag.

90. 'Eritrean Troops Disguised as Ethiopian Military Are Blocking Critical Aid in Tigray', CNN, 1 May 2021, accessed 22 April 2022, https://edition.cnn. com/2021/05/12/africa/tigray-axum-aid-blockade-cmd-intl/index.html.

91. 'Eritrean Troops Disguised as Ethiopian Military'.

92. The offensive was named after *Ras* Alula, who played a critical part in defeating the Italians at the Battle of Adwa on 1 March 1896; https://www.africanidea. org/Abanega.pdf.

93. General Tadesse Worede, Dimtsi Weyane TV, 28 June 2022, accessed 6 August 2022, https://www.youtube.com/watch?v=n2hHVrmje-w.

94. It is worth noting that the Ethiopian government had announced that Eritrean forces were withdrawing from Tigray as early as 3 June 2021. This was inaccurate. https://www.youtube.com/watch?v=ZeggSODFSLw.

95. 'Tigray's Former Rulers Back in Mekele, Ethiopian Government Declares Ceasefire', Reuters, 29 June 2021, accessed 24 April 2022, https://www. reuters.com/world/africa/mekelle-under-our-control-spokesperson-tigrays- former-rulers-says-2021-06-28/.

96. 'Ethiopia's Tigray Conflict: Celebrations as Rebels Capture Territory', BBC, 29 June 2021, accessed 22 April 2022, https://www.bbc.co.uk/news/av/world- africa-57649011.

97. https://www.fanabc.com/english/ethiopian-governments-decision-in- response-to-proposal-of-tigray-interim-administration/.

98. World Bank Policy Research Paper 10004, World Bank, April 2022, accessed 25 July 24, 2022, https://documents1.worldbank.org/curated/ en/099237104142234870/pdf/IDU0852cd3970e8df04e170b3430d96d0e- 0c6179.pdf.

8.   THE PENDULUM OF WAR SWINGS – AND SWINGS AGAIN

1.   International Institute for Strategic Studies, *The Military Balance 2021*, London, 2021

2.   UN OCHA, 'Statement by Acting Humanitarian Coordinator for Ethiopia', 2 September 2021, accessed 24 April 2022, https://reliefweb.int/report/ethiopia/statement-acting-humanitarian-coordinator-ethiopia-grant-leaity-operational.

3.   'As Ethiopian Troops Exit Tigray, Time to Focus on Relief', International Crisis Group, 9 July 2021, accessed 23 May 2022, https://www.crisisgroup.org/africa/horn-africa/ethiopia/ethiopian-troops-exit-tigray-time-to-focus-relief.

4.   Office of the Prime Minister, YouTube, 30 June 2021, accessed 24 April 2022, https://www.youtube.com/watch?v=2xvv-YSRy3Y.

5.   'Message from Prime Minister Abiy Ahmed on the Current Situation in Tigray', Ethiopian Embassy, UK, 14 July 2021, accessed 22 March 2022, https://www.ethioembassy.org.uk/message-from-prime-minister-abiy-ahmed-on-the-current-situation-in-tigray/.

6.   'Tigray Defence Forces Commander Says Addis Ababa within Reach', *Daily News Egypt*, 25 July 2021, accessed 23 March 2022, https://dailynewsegypt.com/2021/07/25/tigray-Defense-forces-commander-says-addis-ababa-within-reach/.

7.   Getachew Reda, tweet, 23 July 2021, accessed 23 March 2022, https://twitter.com/reda_getachew/status/1418563919241793539?s=20&t=8sq1zmdeSkFw-PFg1j7-NA.

8.   Tigray TV, Facebook, 26 July 2021, accessed 23 March 2022, https://www.facebook.com/375713289640371/posts/970805050131189/?app=fbl.

9.   Tigray Media House, Facebook, n.d., accessed 23 March 2022, https://www.facebook.com/watch/live/?ref=watch_permalink&v=275316064360786.

10. Amhara Media Corporation, Facebook, 25 July 2021, accessed 23 March 2022, https://m.facebook.com/story.php?story_fbid=1594513697390285&id=1186971749719525&i.

11. 'News Analysis: Amhara Regional Gov't Cautions Community against "Infiltrators"; Woldia City Residents Call On Fed Gov't for Immediate Action', *Addis Standard*, 9 August 2021, accessed 24 March 2022, https://addisstandard.com/news-analysis-amhara-regional-govt-cautions-community-against-infiltrators-woldia-city-residents-call-on-fed-govt-for-immediate-action/.

12. 'Ethiopia Armed Group Says It Has Alliance with Tigray Forces', Voice of America, 11 August 2021, accessed 24 March 2022, https://www.voanews.com/a/africa_ethiopia-armed-group-says-it-has-alliance-tigray-forces/6209428.html.

13. The Agaw people, numbering around 900,000, live across Ethiopia and Eritrea. The population around the Eritrean town of Keren are known as Bilen. https://en.wikipedia.org/wiki/Agaw_people, accessed 24 March 2022.

14. 'Stench of Death: Villagers Flee Site of Ethiopia Mass Killings', Agence France-Presse, 15 September 2021, accessed 24 March 2022, https://www.france24.com/en/live-news/20210915-stench-of-death-villagers-flee-site-of-ethiopia-mass-killings.

15. 'Ethiopia: Tigray Forces Summarily Execute Civilians', Human Rights Watch, 9 December 2021, accessed 24 March 2022, https://www.hrw.org/news/2021/12/10/ethiopia-tigray-forces-summarily-execute-civilians.

16. Ermias Teka, 'Ethiopia's Competing Alliances: Can the Centre Hold?', Eritrea Hub, 5 September 2021, accessed 24 March 2022, https://eritreahub.org/ethiopias-competing-alliances-can-the-centre-hold.

17. Dimtsi Weyene, Facebook, 9 September 2021, accessed 24 March 2022, https://www.facebook.com/dimtsiweyane/posts/4246453625452781.

18. Dimtsi Weyene, Facebook, 9 September 2021.

19. Gizachew Muluneh, tweet, 7 October 2021, accessed 24 March 2022, https://twitter.com/GizachewMulune2/status/1446119558482305027.

20. 'Ethiopia Launches New Offensive on Tigray Rebels as Famine Looms', *New York Times*, 3 November 2021, https://www.nytimes.com/2021/10/12/world/africa/ethiopia-tigray-offensive.html.

21. Axumawian Media Network, YouTube, 28 November 2021, accessed 24 March 2022, https://www.youtube.com/watch?v=Lb_HtkFil74&t=1190s.

22. 'Tigrayan and Oromo Forces Say They Have Seized Towns on Ethiopian Highway', Reuters, 1 November 2021, accessed 25 March 2022, https://www.reuters.com/world/africa/tigrayan-forces-say-they-have-seized-another-town-ethiopias-amhara-region-2021-10-31/.

23. 'Tigrayan and Oromo Forces Say They Have Seized Towns'.

24. The TPLF and their allies entered Addis on 28 May 2021, but Mengistu had flown out of Ethiopia on 21 May. 'Mengistu Leaves Ethiopia in Shambles', *Washington Post*, 22 May 2021, accessed 23 May 2022, https://www.washingtonpost.com/archive/politics/1991/05/22/mengistu-leaves-ethiopia-in-shambles/77631652-4cfb-469a-8af0-d292f1ecc5ec/.

25. '"We Feel Helpless": Foreign Nationals Rush to Leave Ethiopia as War Intensifies', Agence France-Presse, 26 November 2021, accessed 25 March 2022, https://www.france24.com/en/africa/20211126-we-feel-helpless-foreign-nationals-rush-to-leave-ethiopia-as-war-intensifies.

26. 'United States Calls on Nationals to Leave Warring Ethiopia "Immediately"', Agence France-Presse, 7 November 2021, accessed 25 March 2022, https://genesisblocknews.com/international/united-states-calls-on-nationals-to-leave-warring-ethiopia-immediately/.

27. 'Nine Anti-Gov't Groups Team Up as Ethiopia Recalls Ex-soldiers', Al Jazeera, 5 November 2021, accessed 25 March 2022, https://www.aljazeera.com/news/2021/11/5/nine-anti-abiy-groups-team-up-as-ethiopia-recalls-ex-soldiers; 'Ethiopia's Tigray Forces Seek New Military Alliance', Reuters, 11 August 2021, accessed 25 March 2022, https://www.reuters.com/world/ethiopias-tigray-forces-seek-new-military-alliance-2021-08-11/.

28. Fred Harter, 'Ethiopia's Drone Wars: Iran, China and Turkey Deliver the Air Power behind Abiy's Resurgence', *Africa Report*, 25 January 2022, accessed 27 March 2022, https://www.theafricareport.com/169947/ethiopias-drone-wars-iran-china-and-turkey-deliver-the-air-power-behind-abiys-resurgence/.

29. Wim Zwijnenburg, 'Are Emirati Armed Drones Supporting Ethiopia from an Eritrean Air Base?', Bellingcat, 19 November 2020, accessed 27 March 2022,

https://www.bellingcat.com/news/rest-of-world/2020/11/19/are-emirati-armed-drones-supporting-ethiopia-from-an-eritrean-air-base/.

30. Wim Zwijnenburg, 'Is Ethiopia Flying Iranian-Made Armed Drones?', Bellingcat, 17 August 2021, accessed 27 March 2022, https://www.bellingcat.com/news/rest-of-world/2021/08/17/is-ethiopia-flying-iranian-made-armed-drones/. Bellingcat has attempted to track the drone suppliers, but some of the best work has been undertaken by two Dutch conflict analysts, Stijn Mitzer and Joost Oliemans, who established the Oryxspioenkop website after writing for defence specialists Jane's and Bellingcat. Oryxspionkop, accessed 27 March 2022, https://www.oryxspioenkop.com/. The other useful source has been the Twitter activist and blogger who calls himself Gerjon, who has tracked flights into Ethiopia and Eritrea: https://gerjon.substack.com/, accessed 27 March 2022.

31. James Jeffrey, 'Drones over Ethiopia', Quillette, 15 January 2022, accessed 27 March 2022, https://quillette.com/2022/01/15/drones-over-ethiopia/.

32. 'Ethiopian Cargo: Suspicious Flights from Turkey, the UAE and China', Gerjon's Aircraft Finds, 20 November 2021, accessed 26 March 2022, https://gerjon.substack.com/p/ethiopian-cargo-suspicious-flights?s=r.

33. 'Turkey Expands Armed Drone Sales to Ethiopia and Morocco—Sources', Reuters, 14 October 2021, accessed 27 March 2022, https://www.reuters.com/world/middle-east/turkey-expands-armed-drone-sales-ethiopia-morocco-sources-2021-10-14/.

34. 'Ethiopian Prime Minister Arrives in Ankara for Working Visit', Walta, 18 August 2021, accessed 27 March 2022, https://waltainfo.com/ethiopian-prime-minister-arrives-in-ankara-for-working-visit/.

35. 'Addis Set to Deploy Turkish Combat Drones against Tigray Rebels' Offensive', Africa Intelligence, 15 November 2021, accessed 20 November 2021, https://www.africaintelligence.com/eastern-and-southern-africa_diplomacy/2021/11/15/addis-set-to-deploy-turkish-combat-drones-against-tigray-rebels--offensive,109704605-art. 'The first flight from Corlu airport in Turkey, home to Baykar Makina's factories, was by an Ethiopian Airlines Boeing 777. The second and third deliveries were handled by the same carrier's Boeing 737s.'

36. 'Satellite Images Show Ethiopia's Expanding Drone Buildup', Oryxspioenkop, 17 November 2021, accessed 21 March 2022, https://www.oryxspioenkop.com/2021/11/satellite-images-show-ethiopias.html.

37. 'Iranian Mohajer-6 Drones Spotted in Ethiopia', Oryxspioenkop, 11 August 2021, accessed 21 March 2022, https://www.oryxspioenkop.com/2021/08/iranian-mohajer-6-drones-spotted-in.html.

38. 'How Armed Drones May Have Helped Turn the Tide in Ethiopia's War', Al Jazeera, 10 December 2021, accessed 27 March 2022, https://www.aljazeera.com/features/2021/12/10/how-armed-drones-may-have-helped-turn-tide-in-ethiopia-conflict.

39. Jeffrey, 'Drones over Ethiopia', Quillette, 15 January 2022.

40. Abiy Ahmed, tweet, 22 November 2021, accessed 27 March 2022, https://twitter.com/AbiyAhmedAli/status/1462858774633332736.

41. 'Ethiopia PM Claims War Gains, Urges Rebels to "Surrender"', Agence France-Presse, 30 November 2021, accessed 27 March 2022, https://www.france24.com/en/live-news/20211130-ethiopia-pm-claims-war-gains-urges-rebels-to-surrender.

42. Dimtsi Weyane, Facebook, 1 December 2021, accessed 27 March 2022, https://www.facebook.com/dimtsiweyane/posts/4509582432473231.

43. Dimtsi Weyane, Facebook, 1 December 2021.

44. 'Ethiopia Gov't Says Army Will Not Go Deeper into Tigray, for Now', Al Jazeera, 24 December 2021, accessed 27 March 2022, https://www.aljazeera.com/news/2021/12/24/ethiopia-govt-says-army-will-not-go-deeper-into-tigray-for-now.

45. 'Declaration of a Humanitarian Truce by the Government of Ethiopia', Facebook, FDRE Government Communications Service, 24 March 2022, accessed 27 March 2022, https://www.facebook.com/FDRECommunicationService/posts/137573522116463.

46. 'Statement by the Government of #Tigray on Cessation of Hostilities', Twitter, 24 March 2022, accessed 27 March 2022.

47. 'Tigray Rebels Leave Ethiopia's Afar Region: TPLF Spokesperson', Al Jazeera, 25 April 2022, accessed 10 May 2022, https://www.aljazeera.com/news/2022/4/25/tigray-rebels-leave-ethiopias-afar-region-officials.

48. Abiy Ahmed, tweet, 9 November 2020, accessed 27 March 2022, https://twitter.com/AbiyAhmedAli/status/1325724786547445760?s=20&t=yz9IsCBoCFeR1XlNCumydA.

49. 'Ethiopia's Tigray Conflict: Thousands Reported Killed in Clashes', BBC, 5 September 2021, accessed 27 March 2022, https://www.bbc.com/news/world-africa-58450223.

50. Professor Jan Nyssen, Ghent University, 'Tigray Mortality: Has War and Hunger Cost 500,000 Lives?', Eritrea Focus, 13 March 2020, accessed 28 March 2022, https://eritreahub.org/tigray-mortality-has-war-and-hunger-cost-500000-lives-professor-jan-nyssen-ghent-university.

51. 'Ethiopia's Civil War: The Women Who Paid the Price', BBC, 26 March 2022, accessed 28 March 2022, https://www.bbc.co.uk/news/world-africa-60648163.

52. 'Exclusive: UN Official Accuses Eritrean Forces of Deliberately Starving Tigray', Reuters, 14 June 2021, accessed 28 March 2022, https://www.reuters.com/world/africa/exclusive-un-official-accuses-eritrean-forces-deliberately-starving-tigray-2021-06-11/.

53. Twitter, 24 January 2022, accessed 28 March 2022, https://twitter.com/Brhane36/status/1485469001409044485?s=20. 'Weyane [Tigray] is not something we can understand. We can only erase it. For instance, Australia … there is an island called Tasmania which is found in southern Australia. They have destroyed Tasmanian tribes until only one person remained. There was only one person left for [continuity of] the race. Only one person! They have completely wiped them out. It is only by wiping it out. As I had said before, it is only by wiping out [of existence] the disease called Weyaneness … Firstly, so that it may not exist physically … Secondly, the [very] idea. The idea of Weyaneness

must never exist. Even in the form of an idea … When people say "Weyane" one ought to say "in the name of the father"! [a common Ethiopian orthodox reaction uttered against wickedness while crossing oneself]. Everyone [should say that]! [applause]. Never!'

54. 'Islamic Supporter of Abiy Ahmed Calls for Genocide in Blasphemy to His Faith', *Professor Tony Magana* (blog), 22 December 2021, accessed 28 March 2022, https://blog.ethiopianeurosurgery.com/islamic-supporter-of-abiy-ahmed-calls-for-genocide-in-blasphemy-to-his-faith.

55. 'General Tsadkan: What Is the Situation Like; It Enlightens Many Things', Lbona TV, 22 April 2022, accessed 29 April 2022, https://www.youtube.com/watch?v=WsV_YrX8qeE.

9.   DESTROYING THE SOCIAL AND ECONOMIC FABRIC OF TIGRAY

1. PFDJ National Charter, adopted by the 3rd Congress of the EPLF–PFDJ, Naqfa, 10–16 February 1994.

2. https://asenatv.com/a-complete-english-translation-of-isaias-afwerkis-eritrean-tv-interview-17-february-2021/.

3. US State Department, '2020 Country Reports on Human Rights Practices: Eritrea', 30 March 2021, accessed 19 April 2022, https://www.state.gov/reports/2020-country-reports-on-human-rights-practices/eritrea/. As the UN Human Rights Council report on Eritrea, published in 9 May 2016, concluded: 'The commission has reasonable grounds to believe that crimes against humanity, namely, enslavement, imprisonment, enforced disappearance, torture, other inhumane acts, persecution, rape and murder, have been committed in Eritrea since 1991.' UN Human Rights Council, 'Report of the Commission of Inquiry on Human Rights in Eritrea', A/HRC/32/47, 9 May 2016, accessed 29 April 2022, https://documents-dds-ny.un.org/doc/UNDOC/GEN/G16/093/42/PDF/G1609342.pdf?OpenElement.

4. 'Ethiopia's Economy Battered by Tigray War', BBC, 30 August 2021, accessed 29 April 2022, https://www.bbc.co.uk/news/world-africa-58319977.

5. 'Ethiopia Tries to Open Up Its Economy despite Tigray War', *Le Monde*, 13 April 2022, accessed 29 April 2022, https://www.lemonde.fr/en/international/article/2022/04/13/ethiopia-tries-to-open-up-its-economy-despite-tigray-war_5980428_4.html.

6. '"Bad Sign" as IMF Withholds Ethiopia Growth Forecast', *African Business*, 14 October 2021, accessed 29 April 2022, https://african.business/2021/10/trade-investment/bad-sign-as-imf-withholds-ethiopia-growth-forecast/.

7. IMF, 'Regional Economic Outlook, Sub-Saharan Africa', April 2022, p. 5.

8. 'Ethiopia's Economy Battered', BBC, 30 August 2021.

9. 'IMF Calls for Restructuring Chad's Debt', Agence France-Presse, 30 March 2022, accessed 29 April 2022, https://www.barrons.com/news/imf-calls-for-restructuring-chad-s-debt-01648679108.

10. 'IMF Calls for Restructuring Chad's Debt'.

11. 'The Secret Speech Given by General Tsadkan', Lbona TV, 22 April 2022, accessed 29 April 2022, https://www.youtube.com/watch?v=WsV_YrX8qeE.

12. Kibrom A. Aby et al., 'Near-Real-Time Welfare and Livelihood Impacts of an Active Civil War: Evidence from Ethiopia', Policy Research Working Paper 10004, April 2022, World Bank Group, p. 32, accessed 19 April 2022, https://openknowledge.worldbank.org/bitstream/handle/10986/37309/IDU0852cd3970e8df04e170b3430d96d0e0c6179.pdf.

13. Hayet Alem, 'Tigray Interim Official Says 100 Billion Birr Needed to Repair Destroyed EFFORT Companies in Eastern and Central Tigray', interview with EFFORT official, Tghat, 7 March 2021, accessed 18 April 2022, http://bit.ly/3bLGjrZ.

14. Desta Haileselassie Hagos, tweet, 26 December 2020, accessed 29 April 2022, https://twitter.com/DestaHHagos/status/1342717653102817280?s=20; @beberekett, tweet, 26 December 2020, accessed 29 April 2022, https://twitter.com/SEARE1120/status/1342779801493532673; https://twitter.com/GeradoShebeshe/status/1471299822519037955?s=20&t=2xItIwActGOf80hV1VJKEQ.

15. 'Starving Tigray: How Armed Conflict and Mass Atrocities Have Destroyed an Ethiopian Region's Economy and Food System and Are Threatening Famine', World Peace Foundation, 6 April 2021, p. 21, https://sites.tufts.edu/wpf/starving-tigray.

16. 'Starving Tigray', p. 44.

17. 'Tigray Crisis: How the Ethiopian Army and TPLF Clashed over an Airport', BBC, 26 November 2020, accessed 29 April 2022, https://www.bbc.co.uk/news/world-africa-55058212.

18. 'Bridge on Tekeze River in Ethiopia's Tigray Destroyed—Aid Group', Reuters, 1 July 2021, accessed 29 April 2022, https://www.reuters.com/world/africa/bridge-tekeze-river-ethiopias-tigray-destroyed-aid-group-2021-07-01/.

19. International Committee of the Red Cross, 'Civilians Protected under International Humanitarian Law', 29 October 2010, accessed 29 April 2022, https://www.icrc.org/en/doc/war-and-law/protected-persons/civilians/overview-civilians-protected.htm.

20. 'VRT NWS First in North of Tigray in Ethiopia: "This Is a Developing Humanitarian Disaster"', Eritrea Hub, 22 December 2020, accessed 29 April 2022, https://eritreahub.org/videos-in-belgian-report-translated-into-english.

21. 'Starving Tigray', pp. 27–8.

22. Stijn Vercruysse, VRT NWS, accessed 29 April 2022, https://www.vrt.be/vrtnws/nl/experten/stijn-vercruysse/.

23. 'Starving Tigray', pp. 31–4.

24. 'Conflict Compounded by Covid-19 and Climate Change Pushes Millions in Tigray to the Brink', Oxfam press release, 22 January 2021, https://heca.oxfam.org/latest/press-release/conflict-compounded-covid-19-and-climate-change-pushes-millions-tigray-brink.

25. S. Annys, T. vanden Bempt, E. Negash, L. de Sloover and J. Nyssen, 'Tigray: Atlas of the Humanitarian Situation', Journal of Maps, 2021, https://www.researchgate.net/publication/349824181_tigray_atlas_of_the_humanitarian_situation.

26. 'FIRIS Fire Alert', Twitter post, 15 January 2021, https://twitter.com/firis_firealert/status/1350302487199158274?s=20; 'Hundreds of Buildings Burned around Tigray Town, Research Group Says', Reuters, 25 February 2021; 'Ethiopia: "Hundreds Executed" in Tigray', Sky News, YouTube, 16 March 2021; Alex de Waal, 'The Mango Orchards of Zamra, Tigray', World Peace Foundation, 3 March 2021, https://sites.tufts.edu/reinventingpeace/2021/03/03/the-mango-orchards-of-zamra-tigray/.

27. 'Ethiopia: Eritrean Refugees Targeted in Tigray', Human Rights Watch, 16 September 2021, accessed 29 April 2022, https://www.hrw.org/news/2021/09/16/ethiopia-eritrean-refugees-targeted-tigray.

28. Gebre Ab Barnabas and Anthony Zwi, 'Health Policy Development in Wartime: Establishing the Baito Health System in Tigray, Ethiopia', *Health Policy and Planning*, 12 (1) March 1997, pp. 38–49, 42.

29. Gebre and Zwi, 'Health Policy Development in Wartime'.

30. 'Ethiopia: Violence against Health Care in Conflict, 2021', Safeguarding Health in Conflict Coalition, 11 July 2022, accessed 12 July 2022, https://insecurityinsight.org/wp-content/uploads/2022/05/2021-Ethiopia-SHCC-Factsheet.pdf.

31. 'Ethiopia: Violence against Health Care in Conflict, 2021'.

32. 'People Left with Few Healthcare Options in Tigray as Facilities Looted, Destroyed', MSF, 15 March 2021, accessed 29 April 2022, https://www.msf.org/health-facilities-targeted-tigray-region-ethiopia.

33. 'MSF Mourns Three Colleagues Brutally Murdered in Ethiopia', MSF, 25 June 2021, accessed 29 April 2022, https://www.msf.org/msf-mourns-three-colleagues-brutally-murdered-ethiopia.

34. 'MSF Calls for Tigray Murders Investigation and Safety for Humanitarian Workers', MSF, 7 July 2021, accessed 29 April 2022, https://www.msf.org/msf-calls-tigray-murders-investigation-and-respect-aid-workers.

35. https://www.msf.org/six-months-still-no-accountability-colleagues-killed-ethiopia.

36. 'Data Shows Siege and Destruction of Health System Are Causing Preventable Deaths in Tigray', Ethiopia Insight, 26 January 2022, accessed 29 April 2022, https://www.ethiopia-insight.com/2022/01/26/data-shows-siege-and-destruction-of-health-system-are-causing-preventable-deaths-in-tigray/.

37. H. Gesesew, K. Berhane, E.S. Siraj et al., 'The Impact of War on the Health System of the Tigray Region in Ethiopia: An Assessment', *BMJ Global Health*, 1 March 2022, accessed 29 April 2022, https://gh.bmj.com/content/6/11/e007328.

38. 'Ethiopia Civil War: Doctors among Those Begging for Food in Tigray', BBC, 28 January 2022, accessed 19 April 2022, https://www.bbc.co.uk/news/world-africa-60169326?at_medium=RSS&at_campaign=KARANGA.

39. 'Ayder: Health Professionals Wash and Reuse Gloves as Medical Aid Has Been Blocked from Reaching Tigray', YouTube, 18 January 2022, accessed 19 April 2022, https://www.youtube.com/watch?v=HZ8tQECiG8w.

40. State Department press statement, 7 June 2022, US Embassy Ethiopia, 7 June 2022, accessed 13 June 2022, https://et.usembassy.gov/humanitarian-assistance-to-communities-in-northern-ethiopia/.

41. UN OCHA, 'Northern Ethiopia Humanitarian Update, Situation Report, 11 June 2022', accessed 13 June 2022, https://reports.unocha.org/en/country/ethiopia.

42. 'Ethiopia: Tigray Schools Occupied, Looted', Human Rights Watch, 28 May 2021, accessed 23 May 2022, https://www.hrw.org/news/2021/05/28/ethiopia-tigray-schools-occupied-looted.

43. 'Summary Report of the Human and Material Damage on Tigray's Education', Tigray Education Bureau, December 2021.

44. UN OCHA, 'Northern Ethiopia Humanitarian Update, Situation Report, 11 June 2022'.

45. 'Sexual Violence Being Used as Weapon of War in Ethiopia's Tigray, U.N. Says', Reuters, 15 April 2021, accessed 23 May 2022, https://www.reuters.com/world/africa/sexual-violence-being-used-weapon-war-ethiopias-tigray-un-says-2021-04-15/.

46. UNFPA, 'Ethiopia Response to the Tigray Crisis, Situation Report, 15 to 30 June 2021', accessed 23 May 2022, https://reliefweb.int/report/ethiopia/unfpa-ethiopia-response-tigray-crisis-situation-report-15-30-june-2021.

47. 'What "Rape as a Weapon of War" in Tigray Really Means', World Peace Foundation, 10 August 2021, accessed 23 May 2022, https://sites.tufts.edu/reinventingpeace/2021/08/10/what-rape-as-a-weapon-of-war-in-tigray-really-means/.

48. 'Sexual Violence in Ethiopia's Tigray Region', Insecurity Insight, 30 March 2021, accessed 19 April 2022, http://insecurityinsight.org/wp-content/uploads/2021/03/Sexual-Violence-in-Ethiopia-Tigray-Region-30-March-2021.pdf.

49. '"They Told Us Not to Resist": Sexual Violence Pervades Ethiopia's War', *New York Times*, 1 April 2021, accessed 29 April 2022, https://www.nytimes.com/2021/04/01/world/africa/ethiopia-tigray-sexual-assault.html.

50. 'What "Rape as a Weapon of War" in Tigray Really Means'.

51. 'Practically This Has Been a Genocide', CNN, 22 March 2021, accessed 23 May 2022, https://edition.cnn.com/2021/03/19/africa/ethiopia-tigray-rape-investigation-cmd-intl/index.html.

52. 'Reports of Executions and Mass-Rape Emerge from the Obscured War in Ethiopia's Tigray Region', CBS, 25 March 2021, accessed 23 May 2022, https://www.cbsnews.com/news/ethiopia-tigray-news-executions-rape-war-atrocities-genocide/.

53. 'Tigray Conflict: The Testimonies of Alleged War Crimes', Channel 4 News, 23 March 2021, accessed 23 May 2022, https://www.channel4.com/news/tigray-conflict-the-testimonies-of-alleged-war-crimes.

54. 'Ethiopia: Survivors of TPLF Attack in Amhara Describe Gang Rape, Looting and Physical Assaults', Amnesty International, 9 November 2021, accessed 29 April 2022, https://www.amnesty.org/en/latest/news/2021/11/ethiopia-survivors-of-tplf-attack-in-amhara-describe-gang-rape-looting-and-physical-assaults/.

55. '"We Have to Prepare": Tigray's Neighbours on War Footing as Peace Remains Elusive', *The Guardian*, 2 February 2022, accessed 29 April 2022, https://www.

theguardian.com/global-development/2022/feb/02/tigray-neighbours-on-war-footing-as-ethiopia-peace-remains-elusive?CMP=Share_iOSApp_Other.

56. Ethiopian Human Rights Commission and United Nations High Commissioner for Human Rights, 'Report of the Ethiopian Human Rights Commission (EHRC) and Office of the United Nations High Commissioner for Human Rights (OHCHR): Joint Investigation into Alleged Violations of International Human Rights, Humanitarian and Refugee Law Committed by All Parties to the Conflict in the Tigray Region of the Federal Democratic Republic of Ethiopia', 3 November 2021, accessed 29 April 2022, https://reliefweb.int/report/ethiopia/report-ethiopian-human-rights-commission-ehrcoffice-united-nations-high-commissioner.

57. 'Removed Leader of Ethiopia's Tigray Promises "Resistance": Audio', Al Jazeera, 31 January 2021, accessed 3 May 2022, https://www.aljazeera.com/news/2021/1/31/ex-leader-of-ethiopias-tigray-region-vows-extended-resistance.

58. 'Setting the Record Straight: One of Ethiopia's Ex-Ministers Speaks Out on the War', *The Independent*, 4 January 2022, accessed 23 May 2022, https://www.independent.co.uk/news/world/africa/ethiopia-civil-war-abiy-ahmed-b1984968.html.

59. Filsan Ahmed, tweet, accessed 23 May 2022, https://twitter.com/1_filsan/status/1359945231765032973?s=20&t=v80kgIkH-LzbnJhbjD4fwA.

60. Ethiopian Human Rights Commission and United Nations High Commissioner for Human Rights, 'Joint Investigation into Alleged Violations of International Human Rights, Humanitarian and Refugee Law Committed by All Parties', 3 November, 2021, accessed 3 May 2022, https://www.ohchr.org/Documents/Countries/ET/OHCHR-EHRC-Tigray-Report.pdf; also available at https://reliefweb.int/report/ethiopia/report-ethiopian-human-rights-commission-ehrcoffice-united-nations-high-commissioner.

61. The shortcomings were acknowledged in the report. On pages 10 and 11 of the report, under the heading 'Challenges and Constraints', the authors said: 'The JIT faced several security, operational and administrative challenges in carrying out its investigation, in particular with respect to arrangement of planned visits to parts of Tigray. Key challenges included the harassment and intimidation of JIT members by Regional security forces, especially in Western and Southern Tigray; Government imposed restrictions on carrying communications equipment both by air and road; perceptions of mistrust of the UN in Western Tigray and Amhara administered areas; as well as of perceptions of bias against the EHRC in some parts of Tigray where some potential interviewees declined to be interviewed by the JIT because of the presence of EHRC personnel. Operational constraints included the closure of telecommunications, internet and banking services in the Tigray Region; the failure to date by the Government to release JIT satellite phones procured for the investigation which rendered safety and communications less certain; difficulty in obtaining necessary security clearances for travel owing to the dynamic security situation on the ground; insufficient vehicles for field visits; and, in one incident, restriction on the amount of cash (ETB10,000) that could be carried into Tigray'.

62. 'She Was in Abiy Ahmed's Cabinet as War Broke Out. Now She Wants to Set the Record Straight', *Washington Post*, 30 December 2021, accessed 23 May 2022, https://www.washingtonpost.com/world/2021/12/30/ethiopia-abiy-tigray-war/.

63. 'Ensure Funding for UN Investigation in Ethiopia', Human Rights Watch, 30 March 2022, accessed 10 May 2022, https://www.hrw.org/news/2022/03/30/ensure-funding-un-investigation-ethiopia.

64. Lucy Kassa, 'Ethiopia War: Evidence of Mass Killing Being Burned—Witnesses', BBC, 7 May 2022, accessed 10 May 2022, https://www.bbc.co.uk/news/world-africa-61335530.

65. Kassa, 'Ethiopia War'.

66. 'Ethiopia War: UN Investigative Human Rights Commission Debuts 6-Day Visit', Africanews, 26 July 2022, https://www.africanews.com/2022/07/26/ethiopia-war-un-investigative-human-rights-commission-debuts-6-day-visit/.

67. 'Ethiopia to Narrow Gaps with UN Commission of Human Rights: Ambassador Redwan', FanaBC, 28 July 2022, https://www.fanabc.com/english/ethiopia-to-narrow-gaps-with-un-commission-of-human-rights-ambassador-redwan/.

68. 'UN Rights Experts Hope for Unhindered Access without Delay to Relevant Areas for Investigation', *Addis Standard*, 2 August 2022, https://addisstandard.com/news-un-rights-experts-hope-for-unhindered-access-without-delay-to-relevant-areas-for-investigation/.

69. UN Human Rights Council, Call for submissions, n.d., accessed 30 July 2022, https://www.ohchr.org/en/hr-bodies/hrc/ichre-ethiopa/call-for-submissions.

10. SURROUNDED AND STARVING

1. Dr Fana Hagos, tweet, 28 March 2022, https://twitter.com/FitwiDesta/status/1508495391075053576?s=20&t=seBEy5JAdtA4WKaKlneK2A.

2. 'Starvation "Used as Weapon of War" in Ethiopia', *Daily Telegraph*, 4 June 2021, https://www.telegraph.co.uk/news/2021/06/04/world-must-wake-ethiopia-crisis-spectre-mass-starvation-returns/.

3. UN OCHA, 'Northern Ethiopia: Humanitarian Update. Situation Report', last updated 25 March 2022, accessed 29 March 2022, https://reports.unocha.org/en/country/ethiopia/.

4. UN OCHA, 'Northern Ethiopia: Humanitarian Update'.

5. This chapter draws on the work of Felicity Mulford in two reports. Felicity Mulford, 'The Humanitarian Situation: Aid, Food Security and Famine', in Habte Hagos and Martin Plaut (eds.), *Tigray War and Regional Implications*, 2 vols., Eritrea Focus and Oslo Analytica, June 2021 and March 2022, https://www.academia.edu/49552576/The_Tigray_War_and_Regional_Implications_Volume_1; https://www.academia.edu/71581951/The_Tigray_War_and_Regional_Implications_Volume_2_Final.

6. J. Nyssen, M. Jacob and A. Frankl, *Geo-trekking in Ethiopia's Tropical Mountains*, Cham: Springer, 2019, pp. 373–86; S. Deckers, J. Nyssen and S. Lanckriet, 'Ethiopia's Tigray Region Has Seen Famine Before: Why It Could Happen Again',

The Conversation, 2020, https://theconversation.com/ethiopias-tigray-region-has-seenfamine-before-why-it-could-happen-again-150181.

7. UNICEF, 'Situation Analysis of Children and Women: Tigray Region', https://www.unicef.org/ethiopia/media/2351/file/tigray%20region%20.pdf.

8. 'Starving Tigray: How Armed Conflict and Mass Atrocities Have Destroyed an Ethiopian Region's Economy and Food System and Are Threatening Famine', World Peace Foundation, 2021, https://sites.tufts.edu/wpf/files/2021/04/starving-tigray-report-final.pdf.

9. Kibrom A. Aby et. al., 'Near-Real-Time Welfare and Livelihood Impacts of an Active Civil War: Evidence from Ethiopia', Policy Research Working Paper 10004, World Bank Group, April 2022, p. 32, accessed 19 April 2022, https://openknowledge.worldbank.org/bitstream/handle/10986/37309/IDU0852cd3970e8df04e170b3430d96d0e0c6179.pdf.

10. Anne van der Veen and Tagel Gebrehiwot, 'Effect of Policy Interventions on Food Security in Tigray, Northern Ethiopia', *Ecology and Society* 16 (1) 2011, p. 18, http://www.ecologyandsociety.org/vol16/iss1/art18/.

11. G. Hadgu, K. Tesfaye and G. Mamo, 'Analysis of Climate Change in Northern Ethiopia: Implications for Agricultural Production', *Theoretical and Applied Climatology*, 121, 2015, pp. 733–47; A.B. Araya, 'Coping with Drought for Food Security in Tigray, Ethiopia', Ph.D. thesis, University of Wageningen, 2011; A. Berhane, G. Hadgu, W. Worku et al., 'Trends in Extreme Temperature and Rainfall Indices in the Semi-arid Areas of Western Tigray, Ethiopia', *Environmental Systems Research*, 9 (3) 2020, https://doi.org/10.1186/s40068-020-00165-6.

12. 'Ethiopia: The Pre-crisis Situation in Tigray', ACAPS, 2021, https://reliefweb.int/sites/reliefweb.int/files/resources/20210223_acaps_secondary_data_review_ethiopia_pre-crisis_situation_in_tigray.pdf.

13. Sharon Nicholson 'Climate, Drought, and Famine in Africa', in Art Hansen and Della E. McMillan (eds.), *Food in Sub-Saharan Africa*, Boulder: Lynne Rienner Publishers, 1986, pp. 107–28; J.G. Charney, 'Dynamics of Deserts and Drought in the Sahel', *Quarterly Journal of the Royal Meteorological Society*, 101, 1975, pp. 193–202; J. Otterman, 'Baring High-Albedo Soils by Overgrazing', *Science*, 186, 1974, pp. 531–3; M.H. Glantz, *Desertification: Environmental Degradation in and around Arid Lands*, Boulder: Westview Press, 1977.

14. Alemneh Dejene, *Environment Famine and Politics in Ethiopia: A View from the Village*, Boulder: Lynne Rienner Publishers, 1990.

15. Bahru Zewde, *A History of Modern Ethiopia: 1855–1974*, London: James Currey, 1991, p. 196.

16. Human Rights Watch, *Evil Days: Thirty Years of War and Famine in Ethiopia*, New York: Human Rights Watch, 1991, p. 57, accessed 1 April 2022, https://www.hrw.org/sites/default/files/reports/Ethiopia919.pdf.

17. Human Rights Watch, *Evil Days*, p. 60.

18. Human Rights Watch, *Evil Days*, p. 5.

19. Van der Veen and Tagel, 'Effect of Policy Interventions', p. 18.

20. Federal Democratic Republic of Ethiopia, *An Economic Development Strategy for Ethiopia*, Addis Ababa, 1994.

21. 'Starving Tigray', World Peace Foundation.

22. D.O. Gilligan and J. Hoddinott. 'Is There Persistence in the Impact of Emergency Food Aid? Evidence on Consumption, Food Security, and Assets in Rural Ethiopia', *American Journal of Agricultural Economics*, 89, 2007, pp. 225–42; Van der Veen and Tagel, 'Effect of Policy Interventions', p. 18.

23. Van der Veen and Tagel, 'Effect of Policy Interventions', p. 18.

24. 'Tigray Is Edging Closer to Famine', *The Economist*, 22 April 2021, https://www.economist.com/graphic-detail/2021/04/22/tigray-is-edging-closer-to-famine.

25. 'Ethiopia Tigray Crisis: Fear of Mass Starvation', BBC, 18 January 2021, https://www.bbc.co.uk/news/world-africa-55695123.

26. J. Nyssen, 'The Situation in Tigray at the Beginning of 2021', 2021, https://www.researchgate.net/publication/348296742_The_situation_in_Tigray_at_the_beginning_of_2021; Inter-Cluster Coordination Group and UNICEF Ethiopia, 'Updated Humanitarian Response Plan for Northern Ethiopia', 2020, https://reliefweb.int/sites/reliefweb.int/files/resources/northern_ethiopia_updated_humanitairan_response_plan_second_iteration_web.pdf.

27. UN OCHA, 'Ethiopia: Access Snapshot; Tigray Region', 2021, https://reliefweb.int/sites/reliefweb.int/files/resources/ocha_access_210120_snapshot_tigray02.pdf.

28. S. Annys, T. vanden Bempt, E. Negash, L. de Sloover and J. Nyssen, 'Tigray: Atlas of the Humanitarian Situation', *Journal of Maps*, 2021, https://www.researchgate.net/publication/349824181_tigray_atlas_of_the_humanitarian_situation.

29. 'Ethiopians Dying, Hungry and Fearful in War-Hit Tigray: Agencies', Reuters, 20 January 2021, https://www.reuters.com/article/us-ethiopia-conflict-iduskbn29p0x1.

30. 'Tigray Crisis: Ethiopia Region at Risk of Huge "Humanitarian Disaster"', BBC, 2 February 2021, https://www.bbc.co.uk/news/world-africa-55905108.

31. UN OCHA, 'Ethiopia: Tigray Region, Humanitarian Update Situation Report', April 2021, https://reports.unocha.org/en/country/ethiopia/#cf-1tz6tiwhuhbhu38j9bjewi; Annys et al., 'Tigray: Atlas of the Humanitarian Situation'.

32. 'Statement by US Ambassador to the United Nations Linda Thomas-Greenfield on the Situation in Ethiopia's Tigray Region', United States Mission to the United Nations, 2021, https://usun.usmission.gov/statement-by-ambassador-linda-thomas-greenfield-on-the-situation-in-ethiopias-tigray-region/.

33. 'UN: Hunger, Rape Rising in Ethiopia's Tigray', Voice of America, 15 April 2021, accessed 19 April 2022, https://www.voanews.com/a/ethiopia-tigray_un-hunger-rape-rising-ethiopias-tigray/6204632.html.

34. 'Ethiopia's Tigray Crisis: Abiy Ahmed Denies Reports of Hunger', BBC News, 21 June 2021.

35. Getachew Arage et al., 'Consequences of Early Life Exposure to the 1983–1985 Ethiopian Great Famine on Cognitive Function in Adults: A Historical Cohort Study', *BMJ Open*, 10 (9) 2020, pp. 1–8. Estimates of the number of deaths vary from 400,000 to 1 million.

36. Kjetil Tronvoll, 'Ethiopia's Tigray War Is Fueling Amhara Expansionism', *Foreign Policy*, 28 April 2021.

37. 'Ethiopia: Unlawful Shelling of Tigrayan Urban Areas', Human Rights Watch, 11 February 2021, accessed 6 September 2021, https://www.hrw.org/news/2021/02/11/ethiopia-unlawful-shelling-tigray-urban-areas.

38. 'Over 1 Million People Displaced Due to Conflict in Northern Ethiopia: IOM DTM', IOM news release, 23 April 2021, accessed 6 September 2021, https://www.iom.int/news/over-1-million-people-displaced-due-conflict-northern-ethiopia-iom-dtm.

39. 'After Ethnic Cleansing of Tigrayans from Western Tigray, Amhara State Proceeds to Lease and Distribute Their Farmlands to Amhara Investors', Tghat, 18 May 2021, accessed 6 September 2021, https://www.tghat.com/2021/05/18/after-ethnic-cleansing-of-tigrayans-from-western-tigray-amhara-state-proceeds-to-sale-and-distribute-their-farmlands-to-amhara-investors/.

40. UNHCR, 'Sudan: Eastern Border, Ethiopia Situation—Daily New Arrivals Update', 22 June 2021, accessed 6 September 2021, https://data2.unhcr.org/en/dataviz/144.

41. Anne Soy, 'Tigray Crisis: Ethiopian Soldiers Accused of Blocking Border with Sudan', BBC News, 28 November 2020.

42. Soy, 'Tigray Crisis'.

43. Theodore M. Vestal, 'Famine in Ethiopia: Crisis of Many Dimensions', *Africa Today*, 32 (4) 1985, p. 15.

44. Author's confidential communication with international humanitarian agency by phone, 16 July 2021.

45. Author's interview with Paulos Tesfagiorgis, by phone, 18 June 2021.

46. 'RAF Carried Out Vital Food Drops to Tackle Famine in Ethiopia', RAF, 25 April 2015, accessed 6 September 2021, https://www.rafbf.org/news-and-blogs/raf-carried-out-vital-food-drops-tackle-famine-ethiopia.

47. C. Odinkalu, P. Tesfagiorgis, A. de Waal and D. Burns, 'Neither Impartial nor Independent: The Joint UN–EHRC Human Rights Investigation in Tigray', World Peace Foundation, 11 October 2021, https://sites.tufts.edu/reinventingpeace/2021/10/11/neither-impartial-nor-independent-the-joint-un-ehrc-human-rights-investigation-in-tigray/.

48. Odinkalu et al., 'Neither Impartial nor Independent'; Ahmed Aboudouh, 'Fears for Humanitarian Crisis Engulfing Tigray as Abiy Ahmed Launches Make or Break War', *The Independent*, 15 October 2021, https://www.independent.co.uk/news/world/africa/ethiopia-tigray-war-humanitarian-population-b1938975.html

49. UN OCHA, 'Tigray Aid Situation Worsening by the Day, Warn UN Humanitarians', 2 September 2021, accessed 4 April 2022, https://news.un.org/en/story/2021/09/1099022.

50. 'First Aid Convoy in Three Months Reaches Ethiopia's Tigray: UN', Agence France-Presse, 1 April 2022, accessed 2 April 2022, https://uk.style.yahoo.com/first-aid-convoy-three-months-133014778.html.

51. 'UN Suspends All Flights to Tigray amid Ethiopian Air Raids', Al Jazeera, 22 October 2021, accessed 2 April 2022, https://www.aljazeera.com/news/2021/10/22/ethiopia-hits-tigray-in-fourth-day-of-air-strikes/.

52. 'First Food Aid for 100 Days Enters Tigray under "Humanitarian Truce"', *The Guardian*, 1 April 2022, accessed 2 April 2022, https://www.theguardian.com/

global-development/2022/apr/01/first-food-aid-for-100-days-enters-tigray-under-humanitarian-truce.

53. 'U.N. Aid Chief to Ethiopia on Famine in Tigray: "Get Those Trucks Moving"', Reuters, 29 September 2021, https://www.reuters.com/world/africa/un-aid-chief-ethiopia-famine-tigray-get-those-trucks-moving-2021-09-28/.

54. 'U.N. Aid Chief to Ethiopia on Famine in Tigray'.

55. C. Anna and E.M. Lederer, 'The AP Interview: Ethiopia Crisis "Stain on Our Conscience"', AP News, 29 September 2021, https://apnews.com/article/africa-health-united-nations-only-on-ap-famine-a2b1639797c2a31973ce12985d82b865.

56. Anna and Lederer, 'The AP Interview'.

57. UN Security Council Report, 'Ethiopia (Tigray): Meeting under "Any Other Business"', 1 October 2021, https://www.securitycouncilreport.org/whatsinblue/2021/10/ethiopia-tigray-meeting-under-any-other-business-3.php.

58. Ethiopian Embassy in the UK, 'Ministry of Foreign Affairs Press Release on the Expulsion of UN Officials', 1 October 2021, https://www.ethioembassy.org.uk/ministry-of-foreign-affairs-press-release-on-the-expulsion-of-un-officials-ethiopia/.

59. UN Security Council Report, 'Ethiopia (Tigray): Meeting under "Any Other Business"'.

60. Ethiopian Embassy in the UK, 'Ministry of Foreign Affairs Press Release'.

61. Gebrehiwot Berhe, 'Not Impartial, Not Principled, Non-Starter: African Union Mediation in Ethiopia', Globe News Net, 1 October 2021, https://globenewsnet.com/opinion/not-impartial-not-principled-non-starter-african-union-mediation-in-ethiopia/; A. Kumar, 'Millions at Risk as Ethiopia Expels UN Officials', Human Rights Watch, 1 October 2021, https://www.hrw.org/news/2021/10/01/millions-risk-ethiopia-expels-un-officials; UN Security Council Report, 'Ethiopia (Tigray): Meeting under "Any Other Business"'.

62. 'The Secret Speech Given by General Tsadkan: What Is the Situation Like; It Enlightens Many Things', Lbona TV, 22 April 2022, accessed 25 April 2022, https://www.youtube.com/watch?v=WsV_YrX8qeE.

63. 'Ethiopian Government Declares Tigray Truce to Let Aid In', The Guardian, 24 March 2022, accessed 3 April 2022, https://www.theguardian.com/world/2022/mar/24/ethiopian-government-declares-tigray-truce-to-let-aid-in.

64. 'Statement by the Government of Tigray on Cessation of Hostilities', Tghat, 24 March 2022, accessed 3 April 2022, https://tghat.com/2022/03/24/statement-by-the-government-of-tigray-on-cessation-of-hostilities/.

65. 'First Food Aid for 100 Days Enters Tigray under "Humanitarian Truce"'.

66. 'Food Aid Convoy Enters Tigray for the First Time in Months, World Food Program Says', CNN, 1 April 2022, accessed 3 April 2022, https://www.msn.com/en-us/news/world/food-aid-convoy-enters-tigray-for-the-first-time-in-months-world-food-program-says/ar-AAVKWgy.

67. WFP, 'Ethiopia Country Brief', May 2022, accessed 6 July 2022, https://docs.wfp.org/api/documents/WFP-0000140825/download/.

68. Al Jazeera, *The Stream*, 25 May 2022, accessed 29 May 2022, https://www. aljazeera.com/program/the-stream/2022/5/25/can-ethiopia-build-on-a-truce-to-end-war-in-tigray.

69. 'Ethiopia Food Security Outlook, April 2022', Famine Early Warning System, accessed 6 July 2022, https://fews.net/east-africa/ethiopia.

INTERLUDE

1. Feven Teklehaimanot is a clinical psychologist at Mekele's Ayder Referral Hospital. The interview took place online on 23 April 2022.

2. 'Tigray: The Deliberate Destruction of a Health System', Devex, 18 January 2022, accessed 22 April 2022, https://www.devex.com/news/tigray-the-deliberate-destruction-of-a-health-system-102252.

11. DIPLOMACY AND PROTEST

1. The author of the phrase, Professor George Ayittey, claims it has been misused and misunderstood. See George Ayittey, 'African Solutions for African Problems: The Real Meaning', Pan African Visions, n.d., accessed 15 June 2022, https:// panafricanvisions.com/2014/01/african-solutions-african-problems-real-meaning/.

2. 'Ethiopian PM Replaces Top Officials as Conflict in Tigray Region Escalates', Reuters, 8 November 2020, accessed 11 July 2022, https://www.reuters.com/ article/us-ethiopia-conflict-idUSKBN27O088.

3. 'The UAE–Ethiopia Airlift: The Investigation Techniques', Gerjon's Aircraft Finds, 10 October 2021, accessed 20 April 2022, https://gerjon.substack. com/p/the-uae-ethiopia-airlift-the-investigation;https://www.oryxspioenkop. com/2021/10/uae-air-bridge-supports-ethiopian.html.

4. Laetitia Bader, 'How International Bodies Can Help Prevent More Ethiopia Massacres', Human Rights Watch, 8 December 2021, accessed 20 April 2022, https://www.hrw.org/news/2021/12/08/how-international-bodies-can-help-prevent-more-ethiopia-massacres.

5. Mulugeta Gebrehiwot, 'Not Impartial, Not Principled, Non-Starter: African Union Mediation in Ethiopia', Global News Net, 1 October 2021, accessed 20 April 2022, https://sites.tufts.edu/reinventingpeace/2021/10/01/not-impartial-not-principled-non-starter-african-union-mediation-in-ethiopia/.

6. 'AU Chair Appoints Three Special Envoys to Help Mediate Ongoing Conflict in Ethiopia, Create Conditions for Inclusive Dialogue', *Addis Standard*, 21 November 2020, accessed 6 April 2022, https://addisstandard.com/news-alert-au-chair-appoints-three-special-envoys-to-help-mediate-ongoing-conflict-in-ethiopia-create-conditions-for-inclusive-dialogue/.

7. BBC Radio 4, *World Tonight*, 20 November 2020, accessed 6 April 2022, https:// www.bbc.co.uk/sounds/play/m000phyd.

8. 'Ethiopia Dismisses Mediation Talk from African Union Envoy Visit', Bloomberg, 21 November 2021, accessed 6 April 2022, https://www.bloomberg.com/

news/articles/2020-11-21/african-union-to-send-envoys-to-mediate-ethiopian-conflict.

9. 'Eritrea and Somalia Agree to Restore Diplomatic Relations', Al Jazeera, 30 July 2018, accessed 6 April 2022, https://www.aljazeera.com/news/2018/7/30/eritrea-and-somalia-agree-to-restore-diplomatic-relations.

10. 'The Chairperson of the AU Commission Appoints Former President H.E. Olusegun Obasanjo of Nigeria as High Representative for the Horn of Africa', African Union, 26 August 2021, accessed 6 April 2022, https://au.int/en/pressreleases/20210826/appointment-president-obasanjo-high-representative-horn-africa.

11. 'EU Scraps Plan to Observe Ethiopia Election', Reuters, 4 May 2021, accessed 20 April 2022, https://www.reuters.com/world/africa/eu-scraps-plan-observe-ethiopia-election-2021-05-04/.

12. 'Ethiopia: Abiy's Prosperity Party Wins Landslide Election Victory', Al Jazeera, 10 July 2021, accessed 20 April 2022, https://www.aljazeera.com/news/2021/7/10/ethiopias-ruling-party-wins-national-election-in-landslide.

13. 'Ethiopia Conducted Election in a "Credible" Manner, AU Observers Say', Reuters, 23 July 2021, accessed 20 April 2022, https://www.reuters.com/article/us-ethiopia-election-idAFKCN2DZ1F4.

14. Thabo Mbeki, Chief Luthuli Memorial Lecture, 10 December 2021, accessed 20 April 2022, https://s3.documentcloud.org/documents/21152083/former-president-thabo-mbeki-delivers-the-chief-luthuli-memorial-lecture.pdf.

15. 'Kenya: Tigray Crisis; Kenya Speaks as Ethiopia Counts Losses', *Daily Nation*, 3 July 2021, accessed 20 April 2022, https://allafrica.com/stories/202107030146.html.

16. UN Security Council, 'Peace and Security in Africa', 26 August 2021, accessed 20 April 2022, https://media.un.org/en/asset/k1d/k1ddd3misu.

17. 'East Africa: Gen Kibochi; Why Kenya Is Tense over Ethiopia War', *Daily Nation*, 29 July 2021, accessed 20 April 2022, https://allafrica.com/stories/202107290821.html.

18. 'Police Officers Recalled to Curb Spillover of Ethiopia War', Nation (Kenya), 13 November 2021, accessed 20 April 2022, https://nation.africa/kenya/news/police-officers-recalled-to-curb-spillover-of-ethiopia-war-3617660.

19. 'Biden to Meet Kenya President as War Roils Nearby Ethiopia', Associated Press, 12 October 2021, accessed 20 April 2022, https://apnews.com/article/joe-biden-abiy-ahmed-uhuru-kenyatta-ethiopia-africa-5c9fb5cd1e183b7a7ac065c23c169586.

20. 'Secretary Blinken's Call with Kenyan President Kenyatta', US State Department, 26 November 2021, accessed 20 April 2022, https://www.state.gov/secretary-blinkens-call-with-kenyan-president-kenyatta-2/.

21. Tsedale Lemma, tweet, 7 November 2021, accessed 15 June 2022, https://twitter.com/TsedaleLemma/status/1457392854570049548?s=20&t=Fjusz36mw5hQmdjA1XQ9Lw.

22. Rashid Abdi, tweet, 8 November 2021, accessed 15 July 2022, https://twitter.com/RAbdiAnalyst/status/1457731162336546821?s=20&t=Fjusz36mw5hQmdjA1XQ9Lw.

23. 'AU Horn Envoy Meets Tigray's Leader', *Addis Standard*, 31 May 2022, accessed 15 June 2022, https://allafrica.com/stories/202206010141.html.

24. Tigray External Affairs Office, tweet, 14 June 2022, accessed 15 June 2022, https://twitter.com/TigrayEAO/status/1536740440069885954?s=20&t=Fjusz36mw5hQmdjA1XQ9Lw.

25. Debretsion press conference, Tigray TV, 15 June 2022, accessed 16 June 2022, https://youtu.be/IKlUCxCK6-k.

26. 'Ethiopia's Abiy Says Body Formed to Negotiate with Tigray Rebels', Al Jazeera, 14 June 2022, accessed 16 June 2022, https://www.aljazeera.com/news/2022/6/14/ethiopias-abiy-says-body-formed-to-negotiate-with-tigray-rebels.

27. 'Somali President Begins Three-Day Visit in Eritrea as Diplomatic Relations Thaw', Deutsche Welle, 28 July 2018, accessed 20 April 2022, https://www.dw.com/en/somali-president-begins-three-day-visit-in-eritrea-as-diplomatic-relations-thaw/a-44865801.

28. Martin Plaut, 'Timeline: How the President Isaias—Prime Minister Abiy Relationship Developed', Eritrea Hub, 9 November 2020, accessed 20 April 2022, https://eritreahub.org/timeline-how-the-president-isaias-prime-minister-abiy-relationship-developed.

29. 'Ethiopia, Eritrea, Somalia Leaders Hold 3rd Tripartite Summit in Asmara', Africanews, 27 January 2020, accessed 20 April 2022, https://www.africanews.com/2020/01/27/ethiopia-eritrea-somalia-leaders-hold-3rd-tripartite-summit-in-asmara/; Heads of State and Government Meeting between Eritrea, Ethiopia and Somalia Joint Communiqué, Office of the President, Federal Republic of Somalia, 27 January 2020, accessed 20 April 2022, https://villasomalia.gov.so/en/heads-of-state-and-government-meeting-between-eritrea-ethiopia-and-somalia-joint-communique/.

30. 'In Somalia, Mothers Fear Sons Were Sent to Ethiopia Conflict', Associated Press, 22 January 2021, accessed 20 April 2022, https://abcnews.go.com/International/wireStory/somalia-mothers-fear-sons-ethiopia-conflict-75421149.

31. 'Somalia to Investigate Missing SNA in Tigray', Horn Observer, 13 June 2021, accessed 20 April 2022, https://hornobserver.com/articles/1057/Somalia-to-investigate-missing-SNA-in-Tigray.

32. 'Hassan Sheikh Mohamud: Who Is Somalia's New Leader?', BBC, 16 May 2022, accessed 23 April 2022, https://www.bbc.co.uk/news/world-africa-19556383?pinned_post_locator=urn:bbc:cps:curie:asset:9d1068a6-41c4-0e41-9b0f-273978d56af2&pinned_post_asset_id=19556383&pinned_post_type=share.

33. 'Hassan Sheikh Mohamud'.

34. Bashir Hashi Yusuf, tweet, 10 July 2022, https://twitter.com/BashirHashiysf/status/1546017870202540032?s=20&t=ul5G07WWCI3Jj70ynMmZkA; National ER Interest, tweet, 10 July 2022, https://twitter.com/NationalEr_Int/status/1546174210908852224?s=20&t=o5ZxUQT0gDxBntoIgjTlyw.

35. 'Eritrea–Somalia Joint Statement on the Visit of H.E. Hassan Sheikh Mohamud to Eritrea', Ministry of Information, Eritrea, 12 July 2022, https://shabait.

com/2022/07/12/memorandum-of-understanding-between-the-state-of-eritrea-and-the-federal-republic-of-somalia/.

36. Tweet, Dalsan TV, 14 July 2022, https://twitter.com/DalsanTv/status/1547470326786936834.

37. 'President Biden's Return to Somalia', *Wall Street Journal*, 17 May 2022, accessed 23 May 2022, https://www.wsj.com/articles/president-bidens-return-to-somalia-troops-al-shabaab-terrorism-africa-11652819075.

38. FBI, 'East African Embassy Bombings', accessed 9 April 2022, https://www.fbi.gov/history/famous-cases/east-african-embassy-bombings.

39. 'Ethiopia Blasts Trump Remark That Egypt Will "Blow Up" Dam', Associated Press, 24 October 2020, accessed 10 April 2022, https://abcnews.go.com/International/wireStory/ethiopia-blasts-trump-remark-egypt-blow-dam-73801774.

40. US House of Representatives, Foreign Affairs Committee, 'McCaul on Escalating Violence in Ethiopia', press release, 5 November 2020, accessed 10 April 2022, https://gop-foreignaffairs.house.gov/press-release/mccaul-on-escalating-violence-in-ethiopia/.

41. US House of Representatives, 'Members of Congress Weigh In Regarding Political Instability in Ethiopia', press release, 6 November 2020, accessed 10 April 2022, https://bass.house.gov/media-center/press-releases/members-congress-weigh-regarding-political-instability-ethiopia.

42. 'Statement on Ethiopia by the Senior Study Group on Peace and Security in the Red Sea Arena', US Institute of Peace, 5 November 2020, accessed 11 April 2022, https://www.usip.org/press/2020/11/statement-ethiopia-senior-study-group-peace-and-security-red-sea-arena.

43. Correspondence with a senior official in the Trump administration, April 2022.

44. Kjetil Tronvoll, Facebook, 25 October 2020, accessed 23 April 2022, https://m.facebook.com/story.php?story_fbid=10218250164946237&id=1253796686%C2%ACif_t=nf_status_story%C2%ACif_id=1603676278109841&ref=m_notif.

45. Martin Plaut, 'War Clouds Gather in Northern Ethiopia: Tensions between Tigray, Eritrea and Addis Ababa', Eritrea Hub, 26 October 2020, accessed 23 April 2022, https://wordpress.com/posts/eritreahub.org.

46. H. Verhoeven and M. Woldemariam, 'Who Lost Ethiopia? The Unmaking of an African Anchor State and US Foreign Policy', *Contemporary Security Policy*, 21 June 2022, p. 21, https://www.tandfonline.com/doi/full/10.1080/13523260.2022.2091580.

47. Verhoeven and Woldemariam, 'Who Lost Ethiopia?', p. 21.

48. Correspondence with a senior official in the Trump administration, April 2022.

49. Mike Pompeo, tweet, 4 November 2020, accessed 23 April 2022, https://twitter.com/secpompeo/status/1324121664108580875?lang=en.

50. https://twitter.com/AsstSecStateAF/status/1328015362999414786.

51. 'Pompeo Blasts Tigray Forces, Praises Eritrea over Ethiopia Fighting', Agence France-Presse, 17 November 2020, accessed 23 April 2022, https://www.barrons.com/news/pompeo-blasts-tigray-forces-praises-eritrea-over-ethiopia-fighting-01605631507.

52. 'As Fighting Rages in Ethiopia, Aid Groups Plead for Access to Refugees', *New York Times*, 17 November 2020, accessed 23 April 2022, https://www.nytimes. com/2020/11/17/world/africa/ethiopia-tigray-refugees.html.

53. 'UN's Bachelet Warns Tigray Attack May Amount to War Crimes', Africa Times, 13 November 2020, accessed 23 April 2022, https://africatimes.com/2020/11/13/ uns-bachelet-warns-tigray-attack-may-amount-to-war-crimes/.

54. Statement by US Senators, 19 November 2020, accessed 23 April 2022, https://www.vanhollen.senate.gov/imo/media/doc/2020%2011%2019%20 SecState%20re%20Ethiopia%20Tigray%20Conflict.pdf.

55. 'Stop Ethiopia War and Help Civilians, Biden Team Urges', Reuters, 19 November 2020, accessed 11 April 2022, https://www.reuters.com/article/ ethiopia-conflict/stop-ethiopia-war-and-help-civilians-biden-team-urges- idINKBN27Z18O.

56. Correspondence with a senior official in the Trump administration, April 2022.

57. 'Eritrea Interferes in Civil War in Tigray Region of Ethiopia', Human Rights Concern Eritrea, 20 November 2020, accessed 11 April 2022, https://hrc- eritrea.org/eritrea-interferes-in-civil-war-in-tigray-region-of-ethiopia/; https://www.eepa.be//wp-content/uploads/2020/11/Situation-Report- EEPA-Horn_18-November-2020.pdf.

58. 'Senator Coons Speaks with Ethiopian Prime Minister amidst Escalating Conflict', press release, 23 November 2020, accessed 11 April 2022, https:// www.coons.senate.gov/news/press-releases/senator-coons-speaks-with- ethiopian-prime-minister-amidst-escalating-conflict.

59. 'Pompeo Voices "Grave Concern" about Ongoing Tigray Hostilities', Reuters, 30 November 2020, accessed 11 April 2022, https://www.reuters.com/article/ ethiopia-conflict-usa/pompeo-voices-grave-concern-about-ongoing-tigray- hostilities-idUSKBN28A2HA.

60. 'The United States' Humanitarian Assistance Response to Conflict in Ethiopia's Tigray Region', Reliefweb, 23 December 2020, accessed 11 April 2022, https:// reliefweb.int/report/ethiopia/united-states-humanitarian-assistance-response- conflict-ethiopia-s-tigray-region.

61. 'US Says Eritrean Forces Should Leave Tigray Immediately', Associated Press, 27 January 2021, accessed 11 April 2022, https://apnews.com/article/eritrea- coronavirus-pandemic-africa-ethiopia-kenya-83b90a145d271eb39d664726 bd5acbe5; https://apnews.com/article/donald-trump-egypt-humanitarian- assistance- zethiopia-kenya-e3f47fc14084da52daea64fe078deaa6.

62. 'Secretary Blinken's Call with Ethiopian Prime Minister Abiy', State Department, 4 February 2021, accessed 26 April 2022, https://www.state.gov/secretary- blinkens-call-with-ethiopian-prime-minister-abiy-2/.

63. 'US: Aid Pause to Ethiopia No Longer Linked to Dam Dispute', Associated Press, 19 February 2021, accessed 26 April 2022, https://apnews.com/article/ donald-trump-egypt-humanitarian-assistance-ethiopia-kenya-e3f47fc14084da5 2daea64fe078deaa6.

64. 'Ethiopia's War Leads to Ethnic Cleansing in Tigray Region, U.S. Report Says', *New York Times*, 26 February 2021, accessed 26 April 2022, https://www.nytimes. com/2021/02/26/world/middleeast/ethiopia-tigray-ethnic-cleansing.html.

65. Ambassador Thomas-Greenfield, tweet, 1 March 2021, accessed 26 April 2022, https://twitter.com/USAmbUN/status/1366521830098534409.

66. 'Secretary Blinken's Call with Ethiopian Prime Minister Abiy', State Department, 2 March 2021, accessed 26 April 2022, https://www.state.gov/secretary-blinkens-call-with-ethiopian-prime-minister-abiy/.

67. 'UN Alleges War Crimes in Ethiopia's Tigray, Urges Eritrea Pullout', Agence France-Presse, 4 March 2020, accessed 26 April 2022, https://www.france24.com/en/live-news/20210304-un-alleges-war-crimes-in-ethiopia-s-tigray-urges-eritrea-pullout; https://usun.usmission.gov/remarks-by-ambassador-linda-thomas-greenfield-at-the-un-security-council-virtual-stakeout-following-security-council-discussions-on-ethiopia/.

68. 'Remarks by Ambassador Linda Thomas-Greenfield, US Mission to the UN', 11 March 2021, accessed 26 April 2022, https://usun.usmission.gov/remarks-by-ambassador-linda-thomas-greenfield-at-a-un-security-council-high-level-open-debate-on-conflict-driven-hunger/.

69. 'US Delegation, Top Ethiopian Officials Discuss Tigray Conflict', Voice of America, 22 March 2021, accessed 26 April 2022, https://www.voanews.com/africa/us-delegation-top-ethiopian-officials-discuss-tigray-conflict.

70. 'Department Press Briefing—March 23, 2021', State Department, 23 March 2021, accessed 26 April 2022, https://www.state.gov/briefings/department-press-briefing-march-23-2021/#post-228243-ETHIOPIA.

71. 'Ethiopia PM Ahmed Abiy Admits Eritrea Forces in Tigray', BBC, 23 March 2021, accessed 26 April 2022, https://www.bbc.com/news/world-africa-56497168.

72. 'Ethiopia Rejected U.S. Call for Unilateral Ceasefire during Talks, U.S. Says', Reuters, 25 March 2021, accessed 26 April 2022, https://news.yahoo.com/ethiopia-rejected-u-call-unilateral-225629610.html; https://www.voanews.com/africa/us-appeals-cease-fire-ethiopias-tigray-rejected.

73. 'Sexual Violence Being Used as Weapon of War in Ethiopia's Tigray, U.N. Says', Reuters, 15 April 2021, accessed 26 April 2022, https://www.reuters.com/world/africa/sexual-violence-being-used-weapon-war-ethiopias-tigray-un-says-2021-04-15/.

74. 'Security Council Press Statement on Ethiopia', UN press release, 22 April 2021, accessed 26 April 2022, https://www.un.org/press/en/2021/sc14501.doc.htm.

75. Ambassador Thomas-Greenfield, tweet, 22 April 2021, accessed 26 April 2022, https://twitter.com/USAmbUN/status/1385322141772652551.

76. 'Blinken Presses Ethiopia's Abiy on Withdrawal of Eritreans from Tigray', Reuters, 26 April 2021, accessed 26 April 2022, https://www.reuters.com/world/africa/blinken-presses-ethiopias-abiy-ensure-full-withdrawal-eritrean-troops-tigray-2021-04-26/.

77. 'US Envoy Heads to Horn of Africa', Voice of America, 3 May 2021, accessed 26 April 2022, https://www.voanews.com/africa/us-envoy-heads-horn-africa.

78. 'U.S. Will Not Resume Assistance to Ethiopia for Most Security Programs', Reuters, 13 March 2021, accessed 26 April 2022, https://www.reuters.com/article/us-ethiopia-conflict-usa-assistance/u-s-will-not-resume-assistance-to-ethiopia-for-most-security-programs-idUSKBN2B5070.

79. The quote is from Lord Palmerston, British prime minister, who observed: 'We have no eternal allies, and we have no perpetual enemies. Our interests are eternal and perpetual, and those interests it is our duty to follow.' Hansard, House of Commons, 1 March 1848, https://api.parliament.uk/historic-hansard/commons/1848/mar/01/treaty-of-adrianople-charges-against.

80. US State Department, 'Building a Stronger Democracy in Ethiopia', 25 June 2021, accessed 26 April 2022, https://www.state.gov/building-a-stronger-democracy-in-ethiopia/.

81. https://www.state.gov/visit-of-special-envoy-for-the-horn-of-africa-jeffrey-feltman-to-sudan/; https://www.state.gov/briefings/department-press-briefing-october-12-2021-2/#post-283304-ETHIOPIA2; https://www.state.gov/secretary-blinkens-meeting-with-south-african-foreign-minister-pandor-2/.

82. https://www.state.gov/united-states-announces-additional-humanitarian-assistance-for-the-northern-ethiopia-crisis/.

83. USAID, press release, 6 April 2022, accessed 26 April 2002, https://www.usaid.gov/news-information/press-releases/apr-6-2022-united-states-providing-114-million-humanitarian-assistance-respond-drought#:~:text=The%20United%20States%20is%20the,beginning%20of%20Fiscal%20Year%202022.

84. 'Why Did Ethiopia's Prime Minister Rebuff Samantha Power?', *Foreign Policy*, 11 August 2021, accessed 26 April 2002, https://foreignpolicy.com/2021/08/11/ethiopia-abiy-ahmed-samantha-power-usaid-biden-tigray-conflict-humanitarian-crisis/.

85. 'U.S. Envoy to Visit Ethiopia to Try to Halt Fighting', Reuters, 13 August 2021, accessed 26 April 2022, https://www.reuters.com/world/africa/us-envoy-visit-ethiopia-try-halt-fighting-2021-08-13/.

86. Antony Blinken, 'United States' Actions to Press for the Resolution of the Crisis in the Tigray Region of Ethiopia', press statement, 23 May 2021, accessed 26 April 2022, https://www.state.gov/united-states-actions-to-press-for-the-resolution-of-the-crisis-in-the-tigray-region-of-ethiopia/. 'Today, I am announcing a visa restriction policy under Section 212(a)(3)(C) of the Immigration and Nationality Act on the issuance of visas for any current or former Ethiopian or Eritrean government officials, members of the security forces, or other individuals—to include Amhara regional and irregular forces and members of the Tigray People's Liberation Front (TPLF)—responsible for, or complicit in, undermining resolution of the crisis in Tigray. This includes those who have conducted wrongful violence or other abuses against people in the Tigray region of Ethiopia, as well as those who have hindered access of humanitarian assistance to those in the region. Immediate family members of such persons may also be subject to these restrictions'.

87. US Treasury Department, 'Treasury Sanctions Eritrean Military Leader in Connection with Serious Human Rights Abuse in Tigray', 23 August 2021, accessed 26 April 2022, https://home.treasury.gov/news/press-releases/jy0329.

88. 'Executive Order on Imposing Sanctions on Certain Persons with Respect to the Humanitarian and Human Rights Crisis in Ethiopia', White House

press statement, 17 September 2021, accessed 26 April 2022, https://
www.whitehouse.gov/briefing-room/presidential-actions/2021/09/17/
executive-order-on-imposing-sanctions-on-certain-persons-with-respect-
to-the-humanitarian-and-human-rights-crisis-in-ethiopia/?fbclid=IwAR0R_
EcOxdMZ8hlvoO0MLUPwvx5i4YK2wh4bitp4bkXusfVAFhR2ouseobQ.

89. US Treasury Department, 'Treasury Sanctions Four Entities and Two Individuals
in Connection with the Crisis in Ethiopia', 12 November 2021, accessed 26
April 2022, https://home.treasury.gov/news/press-releases/jy0478.

90. 'Biden Sanctions Eritrean Forces over Ethiopia', The Hill, 11 November 2021,
accessed 26 April 2022, https://thehill.com/policy/international/581299-
biden-sanctions-eritrean-forces-over-ethiopia.

91. 'Eritrea Deplores Illicit and Immoral US Sanctions', Eritrea Ministry of
Information, 13 November 2021, accessed 26 April 2022, https://shabait.
com/2021/11/13/eritrea-deplores-illicit-and-immoral-us-sanctions/.

92. US Embassy Asmara, Facebook, 8 November 2021, accessed 26 April 2022,
https://www.facebook.com/usembassyasmara/photos/pcb.10159714399930
120/10159714404645120; https://www.facebook.com/usembassyasmara/.

93. US Embassy Asmara, Facebook, accessed 16 June 2022, https://www.facebook.
com/usembassyasmara/.

94. Chargé d'Affairs Steven C. Walker speech on Erisat, 12 June 2022, accessed 16
June 2022, https://www.youtube.com/watch?v=Dmafa2bQa9A.

95. 'Why Is Eritrea Backing Russian Aggression in Ukraine?', The Economist, 8 March
2022, accessed 29 May 2022, https://www.economist.com/the-economist-
explains/2022/03/08/why-is-eritrea-backing-russian-aggression-in-ukraine.

96. 'US Gives Ethiopia Ultimatum', Addis Standard, 2 November 2021, accessed 26
April 2022, https://addisstandard.com/breaking-us-gives-ethiopia-ultimatum-
to-access-agoa-privileges/.

97. USAID, 'Statement at the EU Foreign Affairs Council', 21 November 2021,
accessed 26 April 2022, https://www.usaid.gov/news-information/speeches/
nov-21-2021-administrator-power-eu-foreign-affairs-council-development.

98. 'Biden Welcomes Kenya's Kenyatta to the White House', Foreign Policy, 14 October
2021, accessed 26 April 2022, https://foreignpolicy.com/2021/10/14/uhuru-
kenyatta-kenya-white-house-biden/.

99. 'China's Influence Looms over Blinken's Africa Visit', New York Times, 19 November
2021, accessed 26 April 2022, https://www.nytimes.com/2021/11/19/
world/asia/blinken-africa-china-invest.html.

100. 'UN Security Council Calls for End to Fighting in Ethiopia', Voice of America,
5 November 2021, accessed 26 April 2022, https://www.voanews.com/a/un-
security-council-calls-for-end-to-fighting-in-ethiopia/6302401.html.

101. 'Military Moves in Ethiopia Risk Undermining Progress toward Peace Talks—
U.S. Envoy', Reuters, 24 November 2021, accessed 26 April 2022, https://
www.reuters.com/world/military-escalation-ethiopia-risks-undermining-
progress-toward-peace-talks-us-2021-11-23/.

102. https://www.state.gov/briefing-with-u-s-special-envoy-for-the-horn-of-
africa-ambassador-jeffrey-feltman-on-the-ongoing-situation-in-ethiopia/.

103. 'Exclusive: U.S. Special Envoy for Horn of Africa to Leave Post', Reuters, 5 January 2021, accessed 26 April 2022, https://www.reuters.com/world/africa/exclusive-us-special-envoy-horn-africa-feltman-leave-post-2022-01-05/.

104. 'Readout of President Biden's Call with Prime Minister Abiy Ahmed of Ethiopia', White House briefing, 10 January 2022, accessed 12 April 2022, https://www.whitehouse.gov/briefing-room/statements-releases/2022/01/10/readout-of-president-bidens-call-with-prime-minister-abiy-ahmed-of-ethiopia/.

105. 'Special Envoy for the Horn of Africa Satterfield Travel to Ethiopia', State Department, 21 March 2022, accessed 10 April 2022, https://www.state.gov/special-envoy-for-the-horn-of-africa-satterfield-travel-to-ethiopia/.

106. 'Ethiopian Delegation Conducts Extensive Deliberation with Key US Gov't Agencies', Ethiopia News Agency, 25 April 2022, accessed 26 April 2022, https://www.msn.com/en-xl/africa/other/ethiopian-delegation-conducts-extensive-deliberation-with-key-us-gov-t-agencies/ar-AAWAyvi.

107. 'IMF Hints Sending Program Negotiation Team to Ethiopia Come Fall "Provided Conditions Are Right"', *Addis Standard*, 23 July 2020, https://addisstandard.com/news-imf-hints-sending-program-negotiation-team-to-ethiopia-come-fall-provided-conditions-are-right/.

108. 'Gates-Backed Think Tank Seeks $50 Billion for Africa Debt', Bloomberg, 2 August 2022, https://uk.news.yahoo.com/gates-backed-thinktank-seeks-50-040001914.html.

109. Claire Wilmot, Ellen Tveteraas and Alexi Drew, 'Duelling Information Campaigns: The War over the Narrative in Tigray', Media Manipulation Casebook, 20 August 2021, accessed 10 April 2022, https://mediamanipulation.org/case-studies/dueling-information-campaigns-war-over-narrative-tigray.

110. 'US Senate Passes the Ethiopia Peace and Stabilization Act', Today (Nigeria), 31 March 2022, accessed 10 April 2022, https://www.today.ng/news/world/senate-passes-ethiopia-peace-stabilisation-416340.

111. 'Ethiopia Expresses Concern on US Bill HR6600, S.3199', New Business Ethiopia, 24 March 2022, accessed 10 April 2022, https://newbusinessethiopia.com/investment/ethiopia-expresses-concern-on-us-bill-hr6600-s-3199/.

112. 'H.R. 6600, S. 3199 Contain Extremely Dangerous Contents: Ambassadors', FanaBC, 29 March 2022, accessed 10 April 2022, https://www.fanabc.com/english/h-r-6600-s-3199-contain-extremely-dangerous-contents-ambassadors/.

113. 'Special Envoy for the Horn of Africa Satterfield Travel to Ethiopia', State Department, 21 March 2022.

114. 'How to Fix the Broken Position of the U.S. Special Envoy for the Horn', Just Security, 20 April 2022, accessed 26 April 2022, https://www.justsecurity.org/81178/how-to-fix-the-broken-position-of-u-s-special-envoy-for-the-horn-of-africa/.

115. 'Special Envoy for the Horn of Africa', US State Department, 1 June 2022, accessed 16 June 2022, https://www.state.gov/special-envoy-for-the-horn-of-africa-2/.

116. 'The Secret Speech Given by General Tsadkan', Lbona TV, 22 April 2022.

117. 'Building on Steps to End the Conflict in Ethiopia', State Department, 29 April 2022, accessed 3 May 2022, https://www.state.gov/building-on-steps-to-end-the-conflict-in-ethiopia/.

118. 'U.S. Pushes U.N. Security Council to Publicly Address Ethiopia's Tigray', Reuters, 10 June 2021, accessed 26 April 2022, https://www.usnews.com/news/world/articles/2021-06-10/us-pushes-un-security-council-to-publicly-address-ethiopias-tigray.

119. 'Tigray Conflict: EU Humanitarian Support to Ethiopian Refugees Reaching Sudan', European Sting, 26 April 2022, https://europeansting.com/2020/11/19/tigray-conflict-eu-humanitarian-support-to-ethiopian-refugees-reaching-sudan-2/.

120. 'European Parliament Resolution of 26 November 2020 on the Situation in Ethiopia', press release, 26 November 2020, accessed 26 April 2022, https://www.europarl.europa.eu/doceo/document/TA-9-2020-0330_EN.html.

121. 'EU's Borrell Says "Possible War Crimes" in Ethiopia's Tigray', Agence France-Presse, 15 January 2021, accessed 26 April 2022, https://news.yahoo.com/eus-borrell-says-possible-war-164629285.html.

122. 'EU Suspends Ethiopian Budget Support over Tigray Crisis', Reuters, 15 January 2021, accessed 26 April 2022, https://www.reuters.com/article/us-ethiopia-conflict-eu-idUSKBN29K1SS.

123. 'EU Planning €1B for Ethiopia to 2027', Devex, 11 July 2022, https://www.devex.com/news/eu-planning-1b-for-ethiopia-to-2027-103618.

124. 'EU Accuses Eritrea Forces of Fuelling Conflict', Bloomberg, 9 February 2021, accessed 26 April 2022, https://www.bloomberg.com/news/articles/2021-02-09/eu-accuses-eritrea-forces-of-fueling-conflict-in-ethiopia-region.

125. 'EU to Dispatch Humanitarian Negotiator to Ethiopia after Aid Suspension', Devex, 19 January 2021, accessed 26 April 2022, https://www.devex.com/news/eu-to-dispatch-humanitarian-negotiator-to-ethiopia-after-aid-suspension-98934.

126. 'Pekka Haavisto on Ethiopian Crisis: Conflict Will Not End Soon', EEPA, 25 February 2021, accessed 26 April 2022, https://www.eepa.be/?p=4801.

127. 'EU Envoy Warns Ethiopia Tigray Crisis "Out of Control"', Euractiv, 23 February 2021, accessed 26 April 2022, https://www.euractiv.com/section/global-europe/news/eu-envoy-warns-ethiopia-tigray-crisis-out-of-control/.

128. 'EU–Ethiopia Relations', press release, 11 March 2021, accessed 26 April 2022, https://www.consilium.europa.eu/en/press/press-releases/2021/03/11/eu-ethiopia-relations-eu-council-conclusions-stress-the-strategic-partnership-and-eu-s-deep-concerns-about-the-situation-in-the-tigray-region/.

129. '"Dire" Suffering Continues in Ethiopia War, EU Envoy Says', EUobserver, 21 April 2021, accessed 26 April 2022, https://euobserver.com/world/151617.

130. 'EU Scraps Plan to Observe Ethiopia Election', Reuters, 4 May 2021, accessed 26 April 2022, https://www.reuters.com/world/africa/eu-scraps-plan-observe-ethiopia-election-2021-05-04/.

131. 'Ethiopia: Abiy's Prosperity Party Wins Landslide Election Victory', Al Jazeera, 10 July 2021.

132. 'Council Appoints Three New EU Special Representatives for the Sahel, Central Asia and the Horn of Africa', Consilium, 21 June 2021, accessed 26 April 2022,

https://www.consilium.europa.eu/en/press/press-releases/2021/06/21/council-appoints-three-new-eu-special-representatives-for-the-sahel-central-asia-and-the-horn-of-africa/.

133. 'EU, Saudi Arabia "Share Same Concerns, Agree on Way Forward" in Horn of Africa, Bloc's Special Envoy Tells *Arab News*', *Arab News*, 24 November 2021, accessed 26 April 2022, https://www.arabnews.com/node/1974066/saudi-arabia.

134. 'EU Envoy "Cautiously Optimistic" about Ethiopia Ceasefire', Africanews, 2 November 2021, accessed 26 April 2022, https://www.africanews.com/2022/02/11/eu-envoy-says-cautiously-optimistic-about-ethiopia-ceasefire/.

135. 'Declaration by the High Representative on Behalf of the EU on the Situation in Ethiopia', Consilium, 4 November 2021, accessed 26 April 2022, https://www.consilium.europa.eu/en/press/press-releases/2021/11/04/declaration-by-the-high-representative-on-behalf-of-the-eu-on-the-situation-in-ethiopia/.

136. 'With Letter of Assurance, "There Should Be No Obstacle" for Services to Begin in Tigray: EU and US Special Envoys', *Addis Standard*, 2 August 2022, https://addisstandard.com/news-with-letter-of-assurance-there-should-be-no-obstacle-for-services-to-begin-in-tigray-eu-and-us-special-envoys/.

137. 'France Suspends Military Cooperation with Ethiopia', Agence France-Presse, 13 November 2021, accessed 26 April 2022, https://www.barrons.com/news/france-suspends-military-cooperation-with-ethiopia-01628854508?refsec=afp-news.

138. 'Ethiopia, France Sign Military, Navy Deal, Turn "New Page" in Ties', Reuters, 12 March 2019, accessed 26 April 2022, https://www.reuters.com/article/us-ethiopia-france-idUSKBN1QT2W3.

139. Ethiopia Navy, Wikipedia, accessed 26 April 2022, https://en.wikipedia.org/wiki/Ethiopian_Navy.

140. 'Security Council Press Statement on Ethiopia', UN, 5 November 2021, accessed 26 April 2022, https://www.un.org/press/en/2021/sc14691.doc.htm.

141. 'Statement by Ambassador Byrne Nason at the UNSC Briefing on Ethiopia', Irish Mission to the UN press statement, 8 November 2021, accessed 26 April 2022, https://www.dfa.ie/pmun/newyork/news-and-speeches/securitycouncil-statements/statementsarchive/statement-by-ambassador-byrne-nason-at-the-unsc-briefing-on-ethiopia.html.

142. 'Ethiopia Expels Irish Diplomats as EU, UK Citizens Urged to Flee Civil War', Politico, 24 November 2021, accessed 26 April 2022, https://www.politico.eu/article/ethiopia-expels-irish-diplomats-as-eu-uk-citizens-urged-to-flee-civil-war/.

143. Personal communication with the author.

144. 'EU Officials Fear Ethiopian Collapse amid "Dramatic Situation"', Euractiv, 26 November 2021, accessed 26 April 2022, https://www.euractiv.com/section/africa/news/eu-officials-fear-ethiopian-collapse-amid-dramatic-situation/.

145. 'How International Bodies Can Help Prevent More Ethiopia Massacres', Human Rights Watch, 8 December 2021, accessed 26 April 2022, https://www.thenewhumanitarian.org/opinion/2021/12/8/how-international-bodies-can-help-prevent-more-Ethiopia-massacres.

146. 'EU's Borrell Criticizes Countries over Reaction to Ethiopia Conflict', Politico, 13 December 2021, accessed 26 April 2022, https://www.politico.eu/article/josep-borrell-criticizes-eu-for-reaction-to-ethiopia-killings/.

147. 'Could $300 Million Derail Peace in Ethiopia?', Devex, 14 April 2022, accessed 15 April 2022, https://www.devex.com/news/devex-newswire-could-300-million-derail-peace-in-ethiopia-103045.

148. 'EU Pulls Eritrea Funding, Citing Tigray Conflict, "Lack of Interest"', Devex, 23 April 2021, accessed 27 April 2022, https://www.devex.com/news/eu-pulls-eritrea-funding-citing-tigray-conflict-lack-of-interest-99743.

149. 'EU Deputy Special Representative for the Horn in Asmara for Consultation June 6–8, 2022', EU press statement, 14 June 2022, accessed 15 June 2022, https://www.eeas.europa.eu/delegations/eritrea/eu-deputy-special-representative-horn-asmara-consultation-june-6-8-2022_en?s=97.

150. 'Tigray: Armed Conflict', Hansard, 22 July 2021, accessed 27 April 2022, https://questions-statements.parliament.uk/written-questions/detail/2021-07-22/38277.

151. 'Tigray: Armed Conflict', Hansard, 19 October 2021, accessed 27 April 2022, https://questions-statements.parliament.uk/written-questions/detail/2021-10-19/58899.

152. 'Aid Cuts for "Priority" African Region "Outrageous and Hypocritical"', Hansard, 23 September 2021, accessed 27 April 2022, https://committees.parliament.uk/committee/98/international-development-committee/news/157733/aid-cuts-for-priority-african-region-outrageous-and-hypocritical/.

153. 'Eritrea–Iran Foreign Relations', Critical Threats, 17 January 2009, accessed 27 April 2022, https://www.criticalthreats.org/analysis/eritrea-iran-foreign-relations#_ftn1.

154. 'Houthis Receive Arms from Iran via Eritrea', Yemen Post, 10 April 2010, accessed 27 April 2022, http://www.yemenpost.net/Detail123456789.aspx?ID=3&SubID=1548.

155. Eritrea maintained the base in Assab until early 2021, when it was dismantled, as the UAE pulled back from the war in Yemen. https://apnews.com/article/eritrea-dubai-only-on-ap-united-arab-emirates-east-africa-088f41c7d54d6a397398b2a825f5e45a.

156. 'Letter dated 7 October 2016 from the Chair of the Security Council Committee pursuant to Resolutions 751 (1992) and 1907 (2009) concerning Somalia and Eritrea addressed to the President of the Security Council', S/2016/920, UN, 31 October 2016, accessed 27 April 2022, https://undocs.org/S/2016/920.

157. 'West of Suez for the UAE', War on the Rocks, 2 September 2016, accessed 27 April 2022, https://warontherocks.com/2016/09/west-of-suez-for-the-united-arab-emirates/.

158. 'Yemen Counter-terrorism Mission Shows UAE Military Ambition', Reuters, 28 June 2016, accessed 27 April 2022, https://www.reuters.com/article/us-yemen-security-emirates-idUSKCN0ZE1EA.

159. 'Djibouti–UAE Diplomatic Crisis Brings Gulf States Closer to Eritrea', Madote, n.d., accessed 27 April 2022, http://www.madote.com/2015/05/djibouti-uae-diplomatic-crisis-brings.html.

160. 'UAE Dismantles Eritrea Base as It Pulls Back after Yemen War', Voice of America, 18 February 2021, accessed 27 April 2022, https://www.voanews.com/a/africa_uae-dismantles-eritrea-base-it-pulls-back-after-yemen-war/6202212.html.

161. Verhoeven and Woldemariam, 'Who Lost Ethiopia?', p. 22.

162. https://agsiw.org/ethiopia-eritrea-reconciliation-offers-glimpse-into-growing-uae-regional-influence/; https://wam.ae/en/details/1395302697325.

163. 'United Arab Emirates Gives Ethiopia $1 Billion Lifeline to Ease Foreign Exchange Crisis', CNBC, 18 June 2018, accessed 27 April 2022, https://www.cnbc.com/2018/06/18/united-arab-emirates-gives-ethiopia-1-billion-lifeline-to-ease-foreign-exchange-crisis.html.

164. 'UAE to Fund Oil Pipeline from Ethiopia to Eritrea', EastAfrican, 18 August 2018, accessed 27 April 2022, https://www.theeastafrican.co.ke/tea/business/uae-to-fund-oil-pipeline-from-ethiopia-to-eritrea-1400106,

165. 'Tigray: UAE Drones Support Ethiopia', African Military (blog), 16 November 2020, accessed 27 April 2022, https://www.africanmilitaryblog.com/2020/11/tigray-uae-drones-supports-ethiopia.

166. 'Are Emirati Armed Drones Supporting Ethiopia from an Eritrean Air Base?', Bellingcat, 19 November 2020, accessed 27 April 2022, https://www.bellingcat.com/news/rest-of-world/2020/11/19/are-emirati-armed-drones-supporting-ethiopia-from-an-eritrean-air-base/.

167. 'UAE Combat Drones Break Cover in Ethiopia', Oryxspioenkop, 5 October 2021, accessed 27 April 2022, https://www.oryxspioenkop.com/2021/10/uae-combat-drones-break-cover-in.html.

168. 'UAE Combat Drones Break Cover in Ethiopia'.

169. 'The Cargo Cleared for Print: UAE Wartime Deliveries to Ethiopia', Oryxspioenkop, 31 October 2021, accessed 27 April 2022, https://www.oryxspioenkop.com/2021/10/the-cargo-cleared-for-print-uae-wartime.html.

170. 'The UAE–Ethiopia Airlift: The Investigation Techniques', Oryxspioenkop, 10 October 2021, accessed 27 April 2022, https://gerjon.substack.com/p/the-uae-ethiopia-airlift-the-investigation; 'The UAE–Ethiopia Airlift: Fly Sky Airlines', Gerjon, 9 October 2021, accessed 27 April 2022, https://gerjon.substack.com/p/the-uae-ethiopia-airlift-fly-sky.

171. Gerjon, tweet, 9 November 2021, accessed 27 April 2022, https://twitter.com/Gerjon_/status/1458323299843313668?s=20.

172. 'Wing Loong Is Over Ethiopia: Chinese UCAVs Join the Battle for Tigray', Oryxspioenkop, 11 October 2021, accessed 27 April 2022, https://www.oryxspioenkop.com/2021/10/wing-loong-is-over-ethiopia-chinese.html.

173. http://www.xinhuanet.com/english/2018-11/14/c_137606105_3.htm.

174. http://www.xinhuanet.com/english/2018-11/14/c_137606105_3.htm.

175. 'The Weapons Airlift That Is Fuelling Ethiopia's Tigray War', Martin Plaut (blog), 15 November 2021, accessed 27 April 2022, http://martinplaut.com/2021/11/15/the-weapons-airlift-that-is-fuelling-ethiopias-tigray-war/.

176. 'Ethiopia Now Confirmed to Fly Chinese Armed Drones', PAX, 18 November 2021, accessed 27 April 2022, https://paxforpeace.nl/news/blogs/ethiopia-now-confirmed-to-fly-chinese-armed-drones.

177. 'Turkey and the New Scramble for Africa: Ottoman Designs or Unfounded Fears?', Brookings Institution, 19 May 2019, accessed 27 April 2022, https://www.brookings.edu/research/turkey-and-the-new-scramble-for-africa-ottoman-designs-or-unfounded-fears/.

178. 'Red Sea Rivalries: The Gulf, the Horn, and the New Geopolitics of the Red Sea', Brookings Institution, August 2019, accessed 27 April 2022, https://www.brookings.edu/wp-content/uploads/2019/06/Red-Sea-Rivalries-The-Gulf-The-Horn-and-the-New-Geopolitics-of-the-Red-Sea-1.pdf.

179. 'Africa: Ethiopia Tops Turkish Investment Destinations of Africa—EIC', Ethiopian Herald, 31 January 2018, accessed 27 April 2022, https://allafrica.com/stories/201801310663.html.

180. 'Erdoğan Backs Peaceful Resolution to Ethiopia's Tigray Conflict', Al Jazeera, 19 August 2021, accessed 27 April 2022, https://www.aljazeera.com/news/2021/8/18/erdogan-offers-to-mediate-end-to-ethiopias-tigray-conflict.

181. 'Missed Opportunities: Ethiopia's MALE UAV Programme', Oryxspioenkop, 20 August 2021, accessed 27 April 2022, https://www.oryxspioenkop.com/2021/08/missed-opportunities-ethiopias-male-uav.html.

182. 'Turkish Drones Reportedly Being Constructed in Addis', Eritrea Hub, 14 July 2021, accessed 27 April 2022, https://eritreahub.org/breaking-turkish-drones-reportedly-being-constructed-in-addis.

183. 'How Armed Drones May Have Helped Turn the Tide in Ethiopia's War', Al Jazeera, 10 December 2021, accessed 27 April 2022, https://www.aljazeera.com/features/2021/12/10/how-armed-drones-may-have-helped-turn-tide-in-ethiopia-conflict.

184. https://www.securitycouncilreport.org/whatsinblue/2021/10/ethiopia-tigray-meeting-under-any-other-business-3.php.

185. 'Exclusive: Russia, China Foiled UN Meetings on Tigray Famine, Says Lowcock', Devex, 21 June 2022, accessed 21 June 2022, https://www.devex.com/news/exclusive-russia-china-foiled-un-meetings-on-tigray-famine-says-lowcock-103473.

186. http://t.m.china.org.cn/convert/c_3ihwwm00.html.

187. See Elizabeth Cobbett and Ra Mason, 'Djiboutian Sovereignty: Worlding Global Security Networks', International Affairs, 97 (6) 2021, pp. 1767–84.

188. https://eusaleiden.com/2021/01/05/chinese-investment-in-ethiopia/.

189. Riccardo Crescenzi and Nicola Limodio, 'Chinese Investment and New Growth Patterns in Africa', LSE blog, 26 January 2021, accessed 29 May 2022, https://blogs.lse.ac.uk/gild/2021/01/26/how-chinese-investment-shape-new-growth-patterns-in-africa/.

190. Verhoeven and Woldemariam, 'Who Lost Ethiopia?', p. 12.

191. 'Eritrea and China Agree to Strengthen Strategic Partnership', Ministry of Information, Eritrea, 5 January 2022, accessed 27 April 2022, https://shabait.com/2022/01/05/eritrea-and-china-agree-to-strengthen-strategic-partnership/.

192. 'China Plans Peace Envoy for Conflict-Riven Horn of Africa', Reuters, 6 January 2021, accessed 27 April 2022, https://www.reuters.com/world/china/china-appoint-special-envoy-horn-africa-2022-01-06/.

193. The scale of the Chinese investments is outlined in the publication by Eritrea Focus for the UK All-Party Parliamentary Group on Eritrea: *Mining and Repression in Eritrea: Corporate Complicity in Human Rights Abuses*, June 2018, https://eritrea-focus.org/wp-content/uploads/2018/06/Mining-Repression-Eritrea-V1.pdf.

194. https://www.scmp.com/news/china/diplomacy/article/3157654/china-expands-african-reach-eritrea-guinea-bissau-join-belt.

195. https://www.scmp.com/news/china/diplomacy/article/3157654/china-expands-african-reach-eritrea-guinea-bissau-join-belt.

196. Nic Cheeseman and Yohannes Woldemariam, 'Ethiopia's Perilous Propaganda War', *Foreign Affairs*, 8 April 2021, accessed 18 April 2022, https://www.foreignaffairs.com/articles/africa/2021-04-08/ethiopias-perilous-propaganda-war.

197. Edward Kissi, 'Beneath International Famine Relief in Ethiopia: The United States, Ethiopia, and the Debate over Relief Aid, Development Assistance, and Human Rights', *African Studies Review*, 48 (2) 2005, pp. 111–32.

198. Neelam Srivastava, 'The Intellectual as Partisan: Sylvia Pankhurst and the Italian Invasion of Ethiopia', *Postcolonial Studies*, 24 (4) 2001, pp. 448–63.

199. Dan Connell and Tom Killion, *Historical Directory of Eritrea*, 2nd edn, Lanham: Scarecrow Press, 2011, pp. 150–2.

200. https://www.hrw.org/news/2001/09/20/escalating-crackdown-eritrea.

201. http://awate.com/eritreas-enoughyiakil-movement-way-forward/.

202. 'Eritrean United National Front Political Resolution of the Founding Conference', Eritrea Hub, 20 November 2021, accessed 27 April 2022, https://eritreahub.org/eritrean-united-national-front-political-resolution-of-the-founding-conference.

203. Meron Gebreananaye, Saba Mah'Derom and Kisanet Haile Molla, 'Four Ways the Ethiopian Government Manipulates the Media', Martin Plaut Wordpress, 1 January 2022, accessed 18 April 2022, http://martinplaut.com/2022/04/01/four-ways-the-ethiopian-government-manipulates-the-media-2/.

204. 'Ethiopian Prime Minister Abiy Ahmed's Social Affairs Adviser in Public Call for Genocide', Martin Plaut Wordpress, 24 January 2022, accessed 18 April 2022, http://martinplaut.com/2022/01/24/ethiopian-prime-minister-abiy-ahmeds-social-affairs-adviser-in-public-call-for-genocide/.

205. 'US Blasts "Dangerous" Rhetoric by Ally of Ethiopia PM', Agence France-Presse, 20 September 2021, accessed 18 April 2022, https://www.barrons.com/news/us-blasts-dangerous-rhetoric-by-ally-of-ethiopia-pm-01632159008.

206. https://www.facebook.com/24HoursforTigray/videos/466971417668773; https://www.youtube.com/watch?v=UtRWI8uAZyA.

207. 'A Story in Pictures: How Tigrayans Brought the Story of Their People's Suffering to Norway', Eritrea Hub, 8 October 2021, accessed 27 April 2022, https://eritreahub.org/a-story-in-pictures-how-tigrayans-brought-the-story-of-their-peoples-suffering-to-norway.

208. 'Ethiopia's Influential Diaspora Split on Abiy', Deutche Welle, 17 July 2020, accessed 27 April 2022, https://www.dw.com/en/ethiopias-influential-diaspora-split-on-abiy/a-54209290.

209. 'Ethiopian Civil War Divides Diaspora in the US', BBC, 18 December 2021, accessed 27 April 2022, https://www.bbc.co.uk/news/av/world-us-canada-59702496.

210. 'Ethiopian Civil War Divides Diaspora in the US'.

211. 'As US Congress Debates Tigray War, Rival Lobbying Intensifies', *Martin Plaut* (blog), 10 June 2021, accessed 27 April 2022, http://martinplaut.com/2021/06/10/as-us-congress-debates-tigray-war-rival-lobbying-intensifies/.

212. 'How Ethiopia War Is Sowing Discord 13,000-km Away among US Immigrants', TRT World, 25 December 2021, accessed 27 April 2022, https://www.trtworld.com/magazine/how-ethiopia-war-is-sowing-discord-13-000-km-away-among-us-immigrants-52986.

213. 'Duelling Information Campaigns', Media Manipulation Casebook, 20 August 2021, accessed 27 April 2022, https://mediamanipulation.org/case-studies/dueling-information-campaigns-war-over-narrative-tigray.

214. 'How Social Media Became a Battleground in the Tigray Conflict', Voice of America, 17 October 2021, accessed 27 April 2022, https://www.voanews.com/a/how-social-media-became-a-battleground-in-the-tigray-conflict-/6272834.html.

215. '"Grasp This Opportunity", Guterres Says, Following Announcements by Ethiopia and Tigray Forces', UN News, 24 December 2021, accessed 27 April 2022, https://news.un.org/en/story/2021/12/1108742.

216. UN OCHA, 'Ethiopia: Northern Ethiopia, Humanitarian Update, Situation Report', last updated 30 December 2021, accessed 27 April 2022, https://reports.unocha.org/en/country/ethiopia/.

217. Janez Lenarčič, tweet, 21 June 2022, accessed 23 June 2022, https://twitter.com/JanezLenarcic/status/1539308664489512960?s=20&t=Gy7Ji0w_9V2R2zny4Ai6Yw.

218. 'EU Urges Ethiopia to Lift Fuel Restrictions to Tigray', Agence France-Presse, 21 June 2022, accessed 23 June 2022, https://www.msn.com/en-us/news/world/eu-urges-ethiopia-to-lift-fuel-restrictions-to-tigray/ar-AAYIawG.

219. Alex de Waal, 'A Peace Process Is Possible in Ethiopia, but Obstacles Remain', Responsible Statecraft, 22 June 2022, https://responsiblestatecraft.org/2022/06/22/a-peace-process-is-possible-in-ethiopia-but-obstacles-remain/.

CONCLUSION

1. Lionel Cliffe and Basil Davidson, *The Long Struggle for Eritrea for Independence and Constructive Peace*, London: Spokesman, 1988, p. 195.

2. S. Walker, 'Totalitarianism Is Still with Us and Still Evil', *The Atlantic*, September 2022, accessed September 2022, https://www.theatlantic.com/international/archive/2022/09/eritrea-totalitarian-state-diplomatic-relations/671306/.

3. Elleni Centime Zeleke, *Ethiopia in Theory: Revolution and Knowledge Production, 1964–2019*, Leiden: Brill, 2008, p. 181.

4. A. de Waal, 'Ethiopia Needs More than Peace Talks', Responsible Statecraft, 19 January 2022, accessed February 2022, https://responsiblestatecraft.org/2022/01/19/ethiopia-needs-more-than-peace-talks/.

5. B. Conley, A. de Waal, C. Murdoch and W. Jordash, 'Introduction: Rendering Starvation Unthinkable—Preventing and Punishing Starvation Crimes', in B. Conley, A. de Waal, C. Murdoch and W. Jordash (eds.), *Accountability for Mass Starvation: Testing the Limits of the Law*, Oxford: OUP, 2022, p. 22.

6. B. Conley, R. DeFalco, Senai Abraha and A. de Waal, 'An Unprosecuted Crime', in Conley et al., *Accountability for Mass Starvation*, pp. 82–3.

7. K. Houreld, 'Medical Official: Air Strike Kills at Least 43 in Ethiopia's Tigray', Reuters, 23 June 2021, accessed July 2022, https://www.reuters.com/world/africa/witness-airstrike-kills-dozens-ethiopias-tigray-region-2021-06-23/.

8. Africa Watch, *Evil Days: Thirty Years of War and Famine in Ethiopia*, New York: Africa Watch, 1991, pp. 258ff. This source estimates 1,800 market-goers were killed.

9. Adrian van der Knaap, WFP, to BBC *Africa Today*, 15 July 2022: 'yes, famine has been averted' but 'we need much more to avert a much worse situation'. BBC *Africa Today* podcast, 16 July 2022, accessed July 2022, https://www.youtube.com/watch?v=SiN7EuaSFek.

10. See Sue Lautze and Daniel Maxwell on the early 2000s: 'The juxtaposition of remarks by the head of WFP claiming that famine had been averted with epidemiological evidence pointing to the contrary caused a flurry of debate in Addis Ababa. Two years after its publication, tempers in Ethiopia were still running high about the article'. S. Lautze and D. Maxwell, 'Ethiopia: 1999–2003', in S. Devereaux (eds.), *The New Famines*, London: Routledge, 2009, pp. 238–9.

11. Lautze, Sue, and Angela Raven-Roberts, 'Famine (Again) in Ethiopia?' in *Humanitarian Exchange*, no. 27, 2004, pp. 16-18, cited in Lautze, Sue, and Daniel Maxwell, 'Why Do Famines Persist in the Horn of Africa? Ethiopia 1999–2003' in Devereux, Stephen (ed.), *The New Famines* (London: Routledge, 2009), p. 239.

12. D. Alton, H. Clark and M. Lapsley, 'The Warning Signs Are There for Genocide in Ethiopia', letter to *The Guardian*, 26 November 2021, accessed July 2022, https://www.theguardian.com/commentisfree/2021/nov/26/ethiopia-genocide-warning-signs-abiy-ahmed.

13. Conley et al., 'Introduction', pp. 19–20.

14. Goitom Gebreluel, 'The Tripartite Alliance Destabilising the Horn of Africa', *Al Jazeera*, 10 May 2021, https://www.aljazeera.com/opinions/2021/5/10/the-tripatriate-alliance-that-is-destabilisng-the-horn-of-africa.

15. 'Eritrea: 20 Years of Dictatorship, Two Decades with No Independent Media', Reporters Without Borders, 18 September 2021, https://rsf.org/en/eritrea-20-years-dictatorship-two-decades-no-independent-media.

16. E.U. Ochab and D. Alton, *State Responses to Crimes of Genocide*, Cham: Springer Nature, 2022, p. 257. David Alton is a member of the British House of Lords, Helen Clark is a former prime minister of New Zealand, Michael Lapsley is president of Healing Memories.

17. Ochab and Alton, *State Responses to Crimes of Genocide*, p. 250, citing Alton, Clark and Lapsley, letter to *The Guardian*, 26 November 2021.

18. 'US Blasts Rhetoric by Ally of Ethiopia PM', Agence France-Presse, 20 September 2021, accessed September 2021, https://english.alarabiya.net/

News/world/2021/09/20/US-blasts-rhetoric-by-ally-of-Ethiopia-PM-who-compared-Tigrayans-to-the-devil.

19. R. Reid, *Frontiers of Violence in North-East Africa*, Oxford: OUP, 2011, p. 91.
20. K. Tronvoll, *War and the Politics of Identity in Ethiopia: The Making of Enemies and Allies in the Horn of Africa*, Oxford: James Currey, 2009, p. 202.
21. Tronvoll, *War and the Politics of Identity*, pp. 202–3.
22. Tronvoll, *War and the Politics of Identity*, p. 203.
23. D. Miliband, 'The Age of Impunity and How to Fight It', *Foreign Affairs*, 13 May 2021, accessed July 2022, https://www.foreignaffairs.com/articles/united-states/2021-05-13/age-impunity.
23. Conley et al., 'Introduction', p. 23.
24. A. de Waal, 'Truth, Memory and Starvation', in Conley et al., *Accountability for Mass Starvation*, p. 380.

AFTERWORD

1. The text of the agreement is available at *Addis Standard*, accessed November 2022, https://addisstandard.com/wp-content/uploads/2022/11/AU-led-Ethiopia-Peace-Agreement.pdf
2. Tigrayan General Tsadkan Gebretensaie suggested a total of 1 million combatants in a discussion hosted by the Heritage Foundation 29 September 2022, video posted 5 October 2022, accessed October 2022 https://www.heritage.org/africa; *Africa Confidential,* Vol. 63 No 22, 3 November 2022, suggested combined Ethiopian and Eritrea forces of half a million. A total figure in the region of at least 700,000 seems likely.
3. Kjetil Tronvoll on Twitter 15 October 2022, https://twitter.com/KjetilTronvoll/status/1581297399351631882?s=20&t=e8j176tLiaNcGgK8T-nfyw; *Africa Confidential*, Vol. 63, No.22, 3 November 2022, gave a figure of 90,000.
4. General Tadesse Werede press briefing, 13 September 2022, Tigray TV, accessed September 2022, https://www.youtube.com/watch?v=7ubGDQqFK8o&t=936s
5. Crisis Group, 20 October 2022, accessed October 2022, https://www.crisisgroup.org/africa/horn-africa/call-action-averting-atrocities-ethiopias-tigray-war; the testimony was confirmed in personal correspondence.
6. *Addis Standard*, 31 October 2022, accessed November 2022, https://addisstandard.com/news-over-half-a-million-people-newly-displaced-in-tigray-afar-and-amhara-since-militarized-conflict-resumed-in-august-unicef/ citing a UNICEF report dated 29 October 2022, accessed November 2022, https://reliefweb.int/report/ethiopia/unicef-ethiopia-humanitarian-situation-report-no-9-september-2022
7. *The East African*, 6 November 2022, accessed November 2022, https://www.theeastafrican.co.ke/tea/rest-of-africa/brinkmanship-cited-for-break-in-ethiopia-peace-deal-4009206
8. Reuters, 15 October 2022, accessed November 2022, https://www.reuters.com/world/africa/exclusive-ethiopia-debt-relief-delay-partly-due-civil-war-state-finmin-2022-10-15/

9. Reuters, 4 November 2022, accessed November 2022, https://news.yahoo.com/1-imf-says-talks-ethiopia-143355045.html; Bloomberg, 4 November 2022, accessed November   https://www.bloomberg.com/news/articles/2022-11-04/imf-welcomes-ethiopia-truce-amid-talks-on-economic-reform-plans?lead Source=uverify%20wall

10. Figures are compiled from UN logistics cluster updates from April through to September, accessed October 2022 https://logcluster.org/document/ethiopia-monthly-overview-august-2022

11. Report of the International Commission of Human Rights Experts on Ethiopia, A/HRC/51/46 published 19 September 2022, accessed October 2022, https://reliefweb.int/report/ethiopia/report-international-commission-human-rights-experts-ethiopia-ahrc5146-advance-unedited-version

12. *Daily Telegraph*, Tigray accuses Eritrea of launching 'full scale offensive' on the border, 21 September 2022, https://www.telegraph.co.uk/global-health/terror-and-security/tigray-accuses-eritrea-launching-full-scale-offensive-border/

13. *Africa Confidential,* Vol. 63 No 22, 3 November 2022

14. Declan Walsh, 10 October 2022, accessed October 2022, https://www.nytimes.com/2022/10/08/world/africa/ethiopia-tigray-war-talks-us.html, Simon Markson Twitter, 5 October 2022, accessed October 2022 https://twitter.com/MarksSimon/status/1577588725906870272?s=20&t=V4jP5U5mVlY6APjuMUx1ig

15. UN Ethiopia Situation Report, 15 October 2022, accessed November 2022, https://reliefweb.int/report/ethiopia/ethiopia-situation-report-15-oct-2022

16. https://twitter.com/willintune/status/1585302434385399808?s=20&t=IQb9O0F8Ko4DwPUFy_IPyg

17. Military and Foreign Affairs Network, Eritrean Army Highway to Hell OLA liberates towns, 31 October 2022, https://www.youtube.com/watch?v=FHE7wC1k300

18. US Holocaust Memorial Museum Press Release, 25 October 2022, accessed November 2022, https://www.ushmm.org/information/press/press-releases/museum-warns-of-heightened-risk-of-genocide-mass-atrocities-in-ethiopia

19. BBC, Eritreans hunted down as military call-up intensifies over Ethiopia's Tigray war, 12 October 2022, https://www.bbc.co.uk/news/world-africa-63208353

20. op.cit.,   https://addisstandard.com/wp-content/uploads/2022/11/AU-led-Ethiopia-Peace-Agreement.pdf

21. Abiy Ahmed, speech delivered in Arba Minch, 3 November 2022, accessed November 2022, https://youtu.be/RiLi8uU-Wsc

22. see Mirjam van Reisen on twitter, 5 November 2022, accessed November 2022 https://twitter.com/mvreisen/status/1588899389699133440?s=20&t=Yz-Z6850_D7pinfi1xKUjw

23. Eritrean Press Agency, 7 November 2022, accessed November 2022 https://www.facebook.com/eripressagency/posts/pfbid0iK7eyR4dbN1JDLc3pzS8nYdLWv8A7h3ewgzfWk3FQ9ZGgc7UTKDCf2BzG4LUwjNXl

24. Cara Anna, 3 November 2022, accessed November 2022 https://abcnews.go.com/International/wireStory/ethiopia-peace-deal-silence-terms-tigray-92618266

25. GSTS on twitter, 5 November 2022, accessed November 2022 https://
    twitter.com/GlobalGsts/status/1588827690626609154?s=20&t=Jgo
    YsONSI4Xb8vBZPT8fcA
26. See for instance Roland Kobia on twitter, 7 November 2022, accessed November
    2022 https://twitter.com/RolandKobia/status/1589621708478353409?s=20
    &t=e8j176tLiaNcGgK8T-nfyw
27. Human Rights Watch, 4 November 2022, accessed November 2022 https://
    www.hrw.org/news/2022/11/04/ethiopia-truce-needs-robust-rights-
    monitoring
28. Amnesty International, 3 November 2022, accessed November 2022 https://
    www.amnesty.org/en/latest/news/2022/11/ethiopia-peace-agreement/

INDEX

Note: Page numbers followed by '*n*' refer to notes and '*t*' refer to tables

447